MILTON

A Bibliography

For the Years 1624 – 1700

medieval & renaissance texts & studies

VOLUME 30

MILTON

A Bibliography

For the Years 1624 – 1700

Compiled by

John T. Shawcross

medieval & renaissance texts & studies

BINGHAMTON, NEW YORK

1984

Center for Medieval & Early Renaissance Studies
State University of New York at Binghamton
Binghamton, New York

Library of Congress Cataloging in Publication Data

Shawcross, John T.
    Milton : a bibliography for the years 1624–1700.

    (Medieval & renaissance texts & studies ; v. 30)
    Includes indexes.

    1. Milton, John, 1608–1674 — Bibliography.   I. Title.   II. Series.

Z8578.S52   1984   016.821′4   84–653
[PR3581]
ISBN 0–86698–064–4

Printed in the United States of America

For

William Riley Parker

who had light and direction, and sinews equall

Contents

Preface

The need for a bibliography of works by and about John Milton during the seventeenth century has been sorely felt by anyone attempting to assess his early reputation. Twentieth-century scholars have shown that Milton's works were more widely known and available in the seventeenth and eighteenth centuries than earlier commentators had thought. Yet no full and detailed assessment has been possible. The five books that have laid the most extensive groundwork for this compilation are John W. Good's *Studies in the Milton Tradition* (Urbana: University of Illinois, 1915; rptd., New York: Johnson Reprint Co., 1967); J. Milton French's *Life Records of John Milton* (New Brunswick: Rutgers University Press, 1949–57; rptd., Stapleton, New York: Gordian Press, 1966), five volumes; George Sensabaugh's *That Grand Whig, Milton* (Stanford: Stanford University Press, 1952; rptd., New York: Benjamin Blom, 1968); Sensabaugh's *Milton in Early America* (Princeton: Princeton University Press, 1964); and William Riley Parker's *Milton: A Biography* (Oxford: Clarendon Press, 1968), two volumes.

The present bibliography tries to bring together all manuscripts and editions of the works and all studies and critical statements concerning Milton's life and works, all allusions and quotations, and all significant imitations during the years 1624–1700. It is, thus, both bibliography and a kind of allusion book, and a source for a detailed examination of Milton's reputation in the seventeenth century. Undoubtedly there are books and manuscript materials which have not yet been associated with Milton, and in future years the present listing will be augmented. I do not include manuscript letters to Milton or manuscript materials such as annotations or Order Book entries; for such items see French's *Life Records*. A second compilation, in preparation, will carry the bibliography through the years 1701–1799.

There are two parts to this bibliography. Entries of primary works are arranged chronologically by year and alphabetically within years (with a few logical exceptions); to be noted, therefore, is that *Animadversions Upon the Remonstrants Defense*, for example, will appear under 1641 before *Of Reformation* although the former appeared in July and the latter in March. Included here is John Phillips's *Responsio* since Milton apparently aided in its production and since it has usually been printed in collections of his prose works. Entries generally follow standard bibliographic description. I have not, however, reported such matters as running heads, catchwords, etc., important though they are for bibliographic study, because I aim at providing a clear and immediately usable listing. Significant variants and states of text are recorded; others are only noted. Long "s" is altered to regular "s," except when it is significant (as often in entries from Shakespeare's *Works*).

The entries are numbered in roman type (1, 2, 3, etc.). Entries of "secondary" materials, that is, all items of the types listed above which are not versions of Milton's works, are arranged chronologically by year and alphabetically by title or manuscript source within years. Only John Dryden's *The State of Innocence*, since it is so significant in its relationship to *Paradise Lost*, is entered in fuller standard bibliographic description. Most dates are given in arabic numerals regardless of the original type. These entries are numbered in italics (*1, 2, 3*, etc.). Letters with references and similar manuscript allusions or criticism written before 1701 but unpublished or published after that date are listed under the date of composition. Manuscript materials are listed under the earliest suggested date of composition when not definitely known or are grouped together with all other undated items at the end as *Before 1701*. Generally New Style dating is given; however, where pertinent, I give dates in Old Style with New Style in parentheses.

Original spelling and punctuation are retained in the titles of secondary materials, but capitalization is revised to library form. Printing legends also follow library form, resulting in the omission of some information and the possible revision of punctuation. The location of the specific volume being reported is noted in each instance. As far as possible, all editions and reappearances of individual items are recorded. Citations in a later edition or issue which are not specified as to page are the same as the referral entry for that work. Brief annotations are included when the title does not indicate the subject or treatment; allusions and imitations are so designated.

Important bibliographic and textual matter is cited in the notes. State papers are referred to the Columbia Edition (usually Vol. 13) or to the Yale Prose, Vol. 5, Part 2 (edited by J. Max Patrick), when they do not appear in the Columbia Edition. For convenience, numbers are given following the catalogue designation when a work is listed in one of the three following bibliographic catalogues: STC, *A Short-Title Catalogue of Books Printed in England, Scotland, & Ireland And of English Books Printed Abroad 1475–1640, Compiled by A. W. Pollard & G. R. Redgrave* (London: Bibliographic Society, 1926), as well as the second edition (in progress) in two volumes (1976, Vol. 2 only), revised and enlarged by W. A. Jackson and F. S. Ferguson and completed by Katharine F. Pantzer (cited when different from the first edition); Wing, *Short-Title Catalogue of Books Printed in England, Scotland, Ireland, Wales, and British America and of English Books Printed in Other Countries 1641–1700, Compiled by Donald Wing* (New York: Columbia University Press, 1945), three vols. (the second edition of Wing, in progress, Vol. 1 only, is also cited when different from the first); Evans, *American Bibliography by Charles Evans, A Chronological Dictionary of All Books, Pamphlets and Periodical Publication Printed in the United States of America from the Genesis of Printing in 1639 Down to and Including the Year 1820* (Chicago: Blakely Press, 1903; rptd., New York: Peter Smith, 1941), twelve vols., and Vols. 13–14 (Worcester, Massachusetts: American Antiquarian Society, 1955; rptd., 1962).

Numerous problems in compiling this bibliography are to be noted: at times only one or few copies of a volume have been reported; at times information reported — dates, printer or publisher, library holdings — has been misleading or wrong (frequently a result, I fear, of a library's inadequate bibliographic procedures); often different editions of a work or works of a similar nature have been entered under differing headings in Wing; and commentators have implied allusions or alleged imitations where there are none. I have attempted to track down all works previously cited as referentially important to this Milton bibliography, but some show no relationship and are thus omitted (e. g., *The Devil's Cabinet-Council Discover'd*, 1660, in the Thomason collection). I have attempted to include all reported editions or issues of pertinent works, but various errors in such reportage remove an otherwise expected entry from this listing (e. g., a Wing entry for Robert Greville, Lord Brooke's *A Discourse Opening the Nature of that Episcopacie* gives the date 1681, but the edition is 1661; a Wing entry for John Dancer's translation of Corneille's *Nicomede* reports a unique copy of a second edition in the British Library, but apparently no such volume exists). A few unlocated items are entered here and a few annotations supply information concerning fugitive items. "Not in Wing" means 1) the item has not been discovered in Wing under any expected listing; or 2) the item is an edition or issue not distinguished in Wing. In some cases "See Wing" and a number will indicate lack of distinction among issues in Wing or inadequate information to determine the exact corresponding entry.

It is clear that a compiler of such a bibliography as this should examine virtually every item published in the seventeenth century and every manuscript collection, and it is manifestly clear that that is impossible. The most obvious case in point concerns catalogues of book sales. A great many catalogues with Miltonic listings are recorded here, and a great many others, which do not list a volume written by Milton or one citing him in an entry, have been examined. But I have not attempted to examine all surviving catalogues of the period, some of which appear to be unique. Examination not only of these catalogues but of other printed and manuscript materials from the seventeenth century, particularly from continental presses, will undoubtedly yield what could have been additional entries in this bibliography. I have been informed by Leo Miller that numerous additional copies of the Oldenburg Safeguard (Columbia No. 152) exist; Miller will be detailing this information in a forthcoming study.

The question of the state papers with which Milton had some connection is thorny and not settled. Robert T. Fallon, Miller, and I have each recently discovered new copies of papers accepted into the canon. While it certainly must be correct that a great many documents were produced for Cromwell and the Council of State that Milton had nothing to do with, the basis for rejecting an ascription of a state paper to Milton has been a faulty one. It has been assumed that the 1676 *Literae* (No. 321) was derived from Milton's manuscripts; typical is Patrick's comment, p. 816, concerning the 1676 version of a letter "which Milton kept in his papers." The assignment of the 1676 *Literae* as "Milton's papers" comes largely from Daniel Skinner's attempt to have the papers published. With a few additions the state papers in the 1676 *Literae* have been accepted as the canon. But Skinner's text (No. 319) is so different from the 1676 *Literae* in various ways that it is quite clear that it did not serve as a copy text or ancestor of a copy text. The Skinner MS, the Columbia MS (No. 271), the texts given by Gregorio Leti (No. 361), and the texts given in John Christian Lünig's *Literae Procerum Europae* (1712) provide overwhelming data that there were at least five collections of these Miltonic state papers, each with its own evidence to claim validity as a direct descendent from official copies. Further, to assume that Milton retained all the state papers he wrote or translated or revised from differing versions is not cogent. At this time the only conclusion to be drawn is that neither the canon nor the text of Milton's state papers is settled. Two examples which I have included as No. 244 suggest that these state papers should be examined as potentially having a connection with Milton because of their subject matter, its treatment, and the dates involved. Six other examples are cited as No. 269 (and see further Nos. 119 and 331). I have omitted, however, numerous other possibilities such as four letters in the Dutch archives from 1658, one of which must have been a companion to Columbia Nos. 124–125, and such as a letter from Oliver Cromwell to Zeeland, dated 16 June 1654, "Conventu vestro prouinciali iam," in British Library Additional MS 20,921, f. 120–120v, and in the Algemeen Rijksarchief, The Hague, Staten Generaal, Box 5901, and printed, among other places, as *Brief Vande Heere Protector Cromvvel Geschreven aende Heeren Staten van Zeelandt* (n. p. 1654), copy owned by the British Library. Unfortunately, I have not examined at first hand all of the state papers here reported, but in some cases have relied upon information previously printed.

A copy of Columbia No. 4 reported by Patrick, p. 509, in the Berkshire Record Office, Reading, does not exist; cf. French, II, 296–297, and V, 420. For this and other information on the state papers I am indebted to Leo Miller. The reputed copy of Columbia No. 44, once owned by the Reverend Pastor D. Ramsauer, Oldenburg, was a transcription from Leti (therefore dated after 1692) as Miller will evidence in a forthcomng article. I have included printings of the Dutch Manifesto (1652), the Spanish Manifesto (1655), and the Swedish Treaty (1656), even when they are translations of the English versions. Milton's connection is, of course, unresolved.

A specific problem is posed by the Articles of Peace between England and Holland (Columbia Nos. 167C, 167D, 167E, 167F). Milton's work has not been determined; he seems to have translated into Latin the English reaction to and suggested revisions of the Articles proposed by the Dutch. But which documents in this series of items have direct association with Milton is uncertain; cf. Nos. 119 and 331. Since I have listed the versions of the Dutch Manifesto, it is logical that I list editions and versions of the Articles of Peace, but these materials are not necessarily Miltonic.

Ascriptions such as *Hobson's Epitaph* and the foregoing state papers are all included here. Omitted are the numerous attributions made over the years which have been discounted as Milton's. For specific items, see the entry *Attributions* in *A Milton Encyclopedia*, ed. William B. Hunter (Lewisburg, Pa.: Bucknell University Press, 1978), I, 111–14. A recent argument renews the candidacy of *A Plot*

Discovered and Counterplotted (London, n. d.), copies at Yale University, General Theological Seminary, British Library (among others), dated 1641?. A variant issue will be found in the British Library under the title *Great Brittans Ruine Plotted*. But the evidence is most unconvincing. Undoubtedly there will be those who believe that such ascriptions and non-Miltonic texts as I have included should have been totally omitted, and others who would have preferred having them in a separate listing rather than chronologically inserted among items accepted into the canon. Similarly criticism will be raised against entering editions and issues as separate items rather than as subdivisions or annotations to a main entry (perhaps with subdivision enumeration). Since my aim is to make this a usable bibliography, complete as possible, and to allow for a sense of chronological development and reaction, I have chosen to divide only primary from secondary material and to provide indices to aid in finding entries.

Eight indices have been prepared: the first lists Milton's works and subjects related to Milton (e. g., "allusions," "versification and rhyme") with reference to entries; the second, devoted to state papers, lists all occurrences in cited materials, summarizes them by Columbia number, and alphabetizes them by initial phrases; the third gives all non-Miltonic titles (in brief form); the fourth lists all other authors (or names) cited (for example, Gregorio Leti, whose biography of Cromwell includes state papers, or Samuel Barrow, whose poem on *Paradise Lost* appears in many of the editions), including translators; the fifth notes designers and engravers; the sixth records printers and publishers; the seventh acknowledges the owners of printed copies cited; and the eighth reports manuscript holdings.

A number of libraries and individuals have been instrumental in my completing this compilation. I thank the following for having allowed me to check their resources: All Souls College Library (Oxford), the Arents Collection (New York Public Library), Balliol College Library (Oxford), Bayerisches Hauptstaatsarchiv (München), the Berg Collection (New York Public Library), the Bibliothèque Nationale, the Bodleian Library (Oxford University), the British Library, the Brotherton Collection (Leeds University), John Carter Brown Library (Brown University), Cambridge University Library, University of Chicago Regenstein Library, Christ Church College Library (Oxford), Christ's College Library (Cambridge), Columbia University Library, the William Andrews Clark Library, Drew University Library, Edinburgh University Library, Ehemalige Universitätsbibliothek (Helmstedt), Emmanuel College Library (Cambridge), Folger Shakespeare Library, Fordham University Library, Harvard University Libraries, Herzog-August Bibliothek (Wolfenbüttel), William B. Hunter, Jr. (University of Houston), Henry E. Huntington Library, University of Illinois Library, University of Kentucky Library, Lambeth Palace Library, the Library of Congress, the Lilly Library (Indiana University), Magdalen College Library (Oxford), the J. Pierpont Morgan Library, National Library of Scotland, New College Library (Edinburgh), New York Public Library, Newberry Library, Niedersächsische Landesbibliothek (Hannover), the James H. Osborn Collection (Yale University Library), Ted-Larry Pebworth (University of Michigan—Dearborn), Carl H.

Pforzheimer Library, Princeton Theological Seminary Library, Princeton University Library, the Public Record Office (London), the Rosenbach Collection (Philadelphia), Eric Rothstein (University of Wisconsin), Rutgers University Library, John Rylands Library, St. John's College Library (Cambridge), St. Paul's Cathedral Library (London), University of Southern California Library, G. William Stuart (Yuma, Arizona), Claude J. Summers (University of Michigan—Dearborn), Robert H. Taylor (Princeton, New Jersey), the University of Toronto Libraries, Trinity College Library (Cambridge), Trinity College Library (Dublin), Alexander Turnbull Library, Union Theological Seminary Library, University College Library (London), Victoria and Albert Museum, the National Library of Wales, University of Western Ontario Library, Dr. Williams's Library (London), University of Wisconsin Library, Joseph A. Wittreich, Jr. (Philadelphia), Worcester College Library (Oxford), Yale University Libraries, and York Minster Library.

Advice and information about specific matters have been graciously given by Frank Atkinson, C. B. L. Barr, Peter Beal, Günter Berghaus, Jeanie Brink, A. Barry Cameron, Kathleen A. Coleridge, Jackson I. Cope, Stuart A. Curran, Robert T. Fallon, Roy C. Flannagan, Harris H. Fletcher, Roland Mushat Frye, John F. Huntley, Richard Ide, David Jenkins, Kevin Kiernan, Nancy Lee-Riffe, Michael Lieb, Mary Mahl, Leo Miller, William Riley Parker, J. Max Patrick, C. A. Patrides, Annabel Patterson, Betty Rizzo, Eric Rothstein, Manuel Schonhorn, Marion Schulman, G. William Stuart, William P. Williams, and Joseph A. Wittreich, Jr. Additionally, Miss Coleridge's important compilation, *A Descriptive Catalogue of the Milton Collection in the Alexander Turnbull Library, Wellington, New Zealand* (Oxford: Oxford University Press, 1980), has been most helpful. Special thanks are due and sincerely given to Leo Miller and Günter Berghaus. For funding by the National Endowment for the Humanities and released time from the University of Kentucky, needed to bring this project to completion, I am most sincerely grateful.

Note

As this book was going to press, I came across another copy of an attributed Milton poem:

16A   Oxford. Bodleian Library. English Poetical MS f.27.

"Hobson's epitaph" (attributed), pp. 181–82. Scribal hand. Date of MS: 1638 (?).

Primary Bibliography

Primary Bibliography

1624

1   Longtown, Cumberland. Netherby Hall. Holograph MS.

Prolusion, "Mane citus lectum fuge" (in Latin); "Carmina Elegiaca": "Surge, age surge" (in Latin) and "Ignavus satrapam dedecet" (in Latin).

Date uncertain: 1624–25. Discovered with Commonplace Book in 1874; printed by Alfred Horwood in *A Common-Place Book of John Milton*. Westminster: Camden Society Publications, New Series, Vol. XVI (1876), pp. 61–62, 62–63, and 63 respectively. Autotype reproduction of MS in Public Record Office, listed as Autotypes | Milton &c. | Fac. 6 | Library | Shelf 156a. Photographs of PRO autotype in British Library, Additional MS 41,063 I, ff. 84–85.

1631

2   Cambridge. St. John's College Library. MS S.32.

"Hobson's epitaph" (attributed), f. 18v; "Another on the same" [Hobson], ff. 18v–19. The latter is assigned to "Jo: Milton." Scribal hand. Date of MS uncertain.

3   Cambridge, Massachusetts. Houghton Library (Harvard University). English MS 686.

"Hobson's epitaph" (attributed), f. 79. Scribal hand. Date of MS uncertain.

4   Dorchester. Dorset Record Office. MS D51/5.

"Hobson's epitaph" (attributed), p. 214. Scribal hand. Date of MS uncertain.

5   New Haven, Connecticut. James Osborn Collection, Yale University Library. Poetical Miscellany. Shelf mark: b 200.

"Hobson's epitaph" (attributed), p. 225. Scribal hand. Date of MS perhaps ca. 1640.

6   London. British Library. Additional MS 5808.

"Hobson's epitaph" (attributed), f. 2v. Scribal hand. Date of MS uncertain.

7   London. British Library. Additional MS 15,227.

     "Hobson's epitaph" (attributed), f. 74. Scribal hand. Date of MS uncertain.

8   London. British Library. Additional MS 30,982.

     "Hobson's epitaph" (attributed), f. 65–65v. Scribal hand. Date of MS uncertain.

9   London. British Library. Harleian MS 791.

     "Hobson's epitaph" (attributed), f. 45. Scribal hand. Date of MS uncertain.

10   London. British Library. Harleian MS 6057.

     "Hobson's epitaph" (attributed), ll.1–2, f. 15. Scribal hand. Date of MS uncertain.

11   London. British Library. Harleian MS 6931.

     "Hobson's epitaph" (attributed), f. 24v. Scribal hand. Date of MS uncertain.

12   London. British Library. Sloane MS 542.

     "Hobson's epitaph" (attributed), f. 52. Scribal hand. Date of MS uncertain.

13   London. British Library. Sloane MS 1446.

     "An Epitaph on the Marchioness of Winchester," ff. 37v–38v. Assigned to "Jo Milton of Chr: Coll Cambr." and dated "Ap: 15. 1631" (dated 1633 and corrected). Variations from printed text; apparently earlier version. Scribal hand. Date of MS uncertain but possibly after 1633.

14   Manchester. John Rylands Library. English MS 410.

     "Hobson's epitaph" (attributed), ff. 31v–32. Scribal hand. Date of MS uncertain.

15   Oxford. Bodleian Library. Corpus Christi College MS E.309.

     "Another on the same" [Hobson], f. 48; "Hobson's epitaph" (attributed), f. 48v. Scribal hand. Date of MS uncertain.

16   Oxford. Bodleian Library. English Poetical MS f.10.

     "Hobson's epitaph" (attributed), f. 101v. Scribal hand. Date of MS uncertain.

17   Oxford. Bodleian Library. Malone MS 21.

     "Another on the same" [Hobson], f. 69v. Scribal hand. Date of MS uncertain.

18   Oxford. Bodleian Library. Rawlinson Poetical MS 26.

"Hobson's epitaph" (attributed), f. 64–64v. Scribal hand. Date of MS uncertain.

19 Oxford. Bodleian Library. Rawlinson Poetical MS 117.

"Hobson's epitaph" (attributed), ff. 105v–106. Scribal hand. Date of MS uncertain.

20 Oxford. Bodleian Library. Tanner MS 465.

"Hobson's epitaph" (attributed), pp. 235–236. Scribal hand. Date of MS uncertain.

21 Philadelphia. Rosenbach Collection. MS 239/27.

"Hobson's epitaph" (attributed), pp. 359–360. Scribal hand. Date of MS uncertain.

22 San Marino, California. Henry E. Huntington Library. MS H.M. 116.

"Another on the same" [Hobson], pp. 100–101; "Hobson's epitaph" (attributed), p. 103. Scribal hand. Date of MS uncertain.

23 Washington, D. C. Folger Shakespeare Library. MS E.a.6.

"Hobson's epitaph" (attributed), f. 4–4v. Scribal hand. Date of MS uncertain.

24 Washington, D. C. Folger Shakespeare Library. MS V.a.96 (formerly MS 1.21).

"On the University Carrier," ff. 79v–80. Scribal hand. Date of MS uncertain.

25 Washington, D. C. Folger Shakespeare Library. MS V.a.97 (formerly MS 1.27).

"Hobson's epitaph" (attributed), p. 68. Scribal hand. Date of MS uncertain.

26 Washington, D. C. Folger Shakespeare Library. MS V.a.160 (formerly MS 452.1).

"Hobson's epitaph" (attributed), p. 50. Scribal hand. Date of MS uncertain.

1632

27 MR. WILLIAM | SHAKESPEARES | COMEDIES, | HISTORIES, and | TRAGEDIES. | Published according to the true Originall Copies. | *The second Impression.* | [portrait] | *LONDON,* | Printed by *Tho. Cotes*, for *Robert Allot*, and are to be fold at his shop at the signe | of the Blacke Beare in Pauls Church-yard. 1632. |

First issue, imprint A, first variant. Folio in sixes. A^6 $*^4$ A–Z Aa–Bb^6 Cc^2 a–y aa–zz aaa–ccc^6 ddd^4. First signature: A3 signed A2; A4 correctly signed. Copy misbound: A1–2 A6 A2[3] A4–5 *1–4. Variant state of text. Note "fold" for "sold."

"On Shakespear," called "An Epitaph on the admirable Dramaticke Poet, W. Shakespeare," appears on A5. Text of poem appears in three states; see Nos. 50 and 52 for Effigies A and B. Copy gives Effigies C: Poet, [title]; VV. [title]; SHAKESPEARE. [title]; *honour'd* [1]; *Vnder* [4]; *ſtarre-ypointing* [4]; Fame, [5]; *whil'st* [9]; *ſlow-endevouring* [9]; *Art* [9]; *Impreſsion* [12]; *tooke* [12]; *lie* [15]. Variant text from that published by Milton. STC 22274. Copy owned by New York Public Library.

28   M^R· WILLIAM | SHAKESPEARES | COMEDIES, | HISTORIES, and | TRAGEDIES. | Published according to the true Originall Copies. | *The second Impression.* | [portrait] | *LONDON,* | Printed by *Tho. Cotes,* for *Robert Allot,* and are to be fold at the signe | of the Blacke Beare in Pauls Church-yard. 1632. |

Different issue of No. 27. First issue, imprint A, second variant. "On Shakespear," A5; Effigies C. STC 22274a. Copy owned by New York Public Library.

29   M^R· WILLIAM | SHAKESPEARES | COMEDIES, | HISTORIES, and | TRAGEDIES. | Published according to the true Originall Copies. | *The second Impression.* | [portrait] | *LONDON,* | Printed by *Tho. Cotes,* for *William Aspley,* and are to be sold at the signe | of the Parrat in Pauls Church-yard. 1632. |

Different issue of No. 27. First issue, imprint A, third variant. Copy misbound: A1–2 A5 A2[3] A4 A6 *1–4. "On Shakespear," A5; Effigies C. STC 22274b. Copy owned by New York Public Library.

30   M^R· WILLIAM | SHAKESPEARES | COMEDIES, | HISTORIES, and | TRAGEDIES. | Published according to the true Originall Copies. | *The second Impression.* | [portrait] | *LONDON,* | Printed by *Tho. Cotes,* for *Richard Meighen,* and are to be sold at the middle | Temple Gate in Fleetstreet. 1632. |

Different issue of No. 27. First issue, imprint A, fourth variant. "On Shakespear," A5; Effigies C. STC 22274d. Copy owned by Folger Shakespeare Library, Folio 2, No. 2.

31   M^R· WILLIAM | SHAKESPEARES | COMEDIES, | HISTORIES, and | TRAGEDIES. | Published according to the true Originall Copies. | *The second Impression.* | [portrait] | *LONDON,* | Printed by *Tho. Cotes,* for Iohn *Smethwick,* and are to be sold at his shop | in Saint *Dunstans* Church-yard. 1632. |

Different issue of No. 27. First issue, imprint B, fifth variant. Copy misbound: A1 [a2 laid in] A2[3] A4 *2–3 A6 A5 *4 *1. "On Shakespear," A5; Effigies C. STC 22274e. Copy owned by New York Public Library.

32 M^R· WILLIAM | SHAKESPEARES | COMEDIES, | HISTORIES, and | TRAGEDIES. | Published according to the true Originall Copies. | *The second Impression.* | [portrait] | *LONDON,* | Printed by *Tho. Cotes,* for *Richard Hawkins,* and are to be sold at his shop | Chancery Lane, neere Serjeants Inne. 1632. |

Different issue of No. 27. First issue, imprint B, sixth variant. "On Shakespear," A5; Effigies C. See STC 22274c. Copy owned by Folger Shakespeare Library, Folio 2, No. 11.

33 M^R· WILLIAM | SHAKESPEARES | COMEDIES, | HISTORIES, and | TRAGEDIES. | Published according to the true Originall Copies. | *The second Impression.* | [portrait] | *LONDON,* | Printed by *Tho. Cotes,* for *Richard Hawkins,* and are to be sold at his shop | in Chancery Lane, neere Serjeants Inne. 1632. |

Different issue of No. 27. First issue, imprint B, seventh variant. Variant of No. 32. STC 22274c. Copy owned by New York Public Library.

1633

34 Oxford. Bodleian Library. Ashmole MS 36, 37.

"On Time," f. 22v. Variations from printed text; earlier text. Date of MS uncertain. Scribal hand.

1634

35 Cambridge. Trinity College Library. MS R.3.4.

Also known as the Cambridge MS. Holograph and scribal hands; unidentified scribes cited as X and Y. Original folio quire (twenty-five leaves; 50 pages) to which have been added a half-sheet (the so-called "pasted leaf" of *Comus*) and two extant leaves (four pages) of a quarto gathering. A folio leaf has been added as a cover. Workbook with corrections and deletions.

Contents:
p. 1: "Arcades," with false start, ll. 1–45, holograph.
p. 2: "Arcades," ll. 46–95, holograph.
p. 3: "Arcades," ll. 96–109, holograph.
p. 4: "At a Solemn Music," draft one, ll. 1–28; draft two, ll. 1–16, holograph.

p. 5: "At a Solemn Music," draft two, ll. 17–28; draft three, ll. 17–28; draft four, ll. 1–28, holograph.

p. 6: Letter to an Unknown Friend, draft one, with copy of Sonnet 7, holograph.

p. 7: Letter to an Unknown Friend, draft two, holograph.

p. 8: "On Time," holograph; "Upon the Circumcision," holograph.

p. 9: Sonnet 8, scribal hand (John Phillips?) with holograph title replacing original title; Sonnet 9, holograph; Sonnet 10, holograph.

p. 10: blank.

p. 11: blank.

p. 12: blank.

p. 13: "Comus," ll. 1–48, holograph.

p. 14: "Comus," ll. 49–108, holograph.

p. 15: "Comus," ll. 109–172, holograph with one correction by unidentified scribe (X).

p. 16: "Comus," ll. 173–235, holograph with two scribal corrections (X).

p. 17: "Comus," ll. 236–304, holograph.

p. 18: "Comus," ll. 305–356, 366–372, holograph with two scribal corrections (X).

p. 19: "Comus," ll. 373–431, with remnant of left margin of pasted leaf giving lines 350–365, holograph.

p. 20: "Comus," ll. 432–493, holograph.

p. 21: "Comus," ll. 494–560, holograph.

p. 22: "Comus," ll. 561–624, holograph.

p. [A]: "Comus," ll. 672–706, holograph; recto of pasted leaf.

p. [B]: blank; verso of pasted leaf.

p. 23: "Comus," ll. 625–727, holograph.

p. 24: "Comus," ll. 728–755, 673–696, 702–703, 756–769, holograph.

p. 25: "Comus," ll. 770–779, 806–858, holograph.

p. 26: "Comus," ll. 859–923, holograph.

p. 27: "Comus," ll. 924–973, holograph.

p. 28: "Comus," ll. 974–979, 1014–1015, 980–983, 988–999, 1012–1023, holograph.

p. 29: "Comus," ll. 976–1023, holograph.

p. 30: "Lycidas," ll. 1–14, 142–151 (draft one), 142–151 (draft two), 58–63, holograph.

p. 31: "Lycidas," ll. 1–63, holograph.

p. 32: "Lycidas," ll. 64–122, holograph.

p. 33: "Lycidas," ll. 123–141, 151–166, holograph.

p. 34: "Lycidas," ll. 165–193, holograph.

p. 35: Plans and subjects (three character outlines for *Paradise Lost,* other subjects), holograph.

p. 36: Plans and subjects (subjects from the Bible, some with brief prose outlines, one with a character outline), holograph.

p. 37: Plans and subjects (on British history), holograph.

p. 38: Plans and subjects (on British history, with section continued from p. 39), holograph.

p. 39: Plans and subjects (prose outlines for *Abram from Morea, Baptistes*, and *Sodom*), holograph.

p. 40: Plans and subjects (prose outlines for *Sodom*, continued, and *Adams Banishment*, with a few additional subjects from the New Testament), holograph.

p. 41: Plans and subjects (on Scotch history; two sections continued from p. 40; two prose outlines on *Moabitides or Phineas* and *Christus patiens*), holograph.

p. 42: blank.

p. 43: Sonnet 13 (two drafts), holograph with title added to second draft by unidentified scribe [Y]); Sonnet 11, holograph. Y is the scribe of the Bradshaw letter (see No. 161).

p. 44: Sonnet 14 (two drafts), holograph.

p. [2]: Sonnet 13, scribe Y; Sonnet 14, scribe Y. Page 2 of quarto gathering, misbound.

p. [1]: Sonnet 11, scribe Y; Sonnet 12, scribe Y; heading and note by Jeremy Picard. Page 1 of quarto gathering, misbound.

p. 45: Sonnet 12, holograph with correction by scribe Y; Sonnet 15, holograph (with possible alteration by another hand); Sonnet 16, by John Phillips with corrections by scribe Y; holograph note followed by note by John Phillips.

p. 46: Sonnet 17, by John Phillips; "On the Forcers of Conscience," by John Phillips with corrections by scribe Y.

p. [7]: Sonnet 21, ll. 5–14, by Cyriack Skinner; Sonnet 22, by Cyriack Skinner. Page 7 of quarto gathering.

p. [8]: Sonnet 23, by Jeremy Picard. Page 8 of quarto gathering.

p. 47: blank.

p. 48: blank.

p. 49: blank.

p. 50: blank.

Missing quarto sheets, pp. [3–6], presumably gave Sonnets 15, 16, 17, 18, 19, 20, 21 (ll. 1–4), and "On the Forcers of Conscience." Dating of manuscript is uncertain: 1634? or 1637? through 1658?.

Published by William Aldis Wright as *Facsimile of the Manuscript of Milton's Minor Poems*. Cambridge: Cambridge University Press, 1899. Also published as *John Milton Poems. Reproduced in Facsimile from the Manuscript in Trinity College, Cambridge. With a Transcript* (Menston, England: Scolar Press, 1972) with revisions of Wright's transcript and corrections of 1970 printing.

36   London. Bridgewater House. The Bridgewater MS. (On deposit in the British Library.)

A Maske | Represented before the right | ho:^ble the Earle of Bridgewater

| Lord president of Wales and the | right ho.ᵇˡᵉ the Countesse of -- |
Bridgewater. | At Ludlow Castle the | 29th of September 1634 | The chiefe
persons in the repʳsentacoñ were: | *The Lord Brackley* || *The Lady Alice* | Mr
Thomas [bracket] Egerton || Author Jo: Milton. |

Dated: 1634? 1637? Scribal hand.

Published in facsimile by Harris F. Fletcher in *John Milton's Complete Poetical
Works*. Urbana: University of Illinois Press, 1943-48. I (1943) 301-339.

37   London. British Library. Additional MS 11,518.

"Five songs set for a Mask presented at Ludlo Castle, before the Earl of
Bridgewater Lord President of the Marches. October 1634," ff. 1-2v. Dated:
1634?-1637?. Scribal hand. Words and music.

Published in facsimile by Harris F. Fletcher in *John Milton's Complete Poetical
Works*. Urbana: University of Illinois Press, 1943-48. I (1943) 341-344.

38   London. British Library. Additional MS 52,723.

Henry Lawes's MS, owned by the Misses Church of Beaconfield, on per-
manent loan to British Library. "The 5 songs following were sett for A Maske
presented at Ludlo Castle before yᵉ Earle of Bridgewater Lord president,
of yᵉ Marches. October. 1634," Nos. 74-78. Dated: 1634?-1637?. In Lawes's
hand. Words and music.

Published in facsimile by Pamela J. Willetts as *The Henry Lawes Manuscript*.
London: British Museum, 1969.

1635

39   London. British Library. Additional MS 36,354.

Commonplace Book. Holograph and scribal hands. Dating is uncertain:
1635? or 1637? through 1665?. In English, Latin, Greek, Italian, and French.

Attached is a letter to Milton from Henry Lawes (written ca. April 1638),
on the back of which are two holograph lines of poetry ascribed to Milton:
"Fixe heere yee overdaled sphears | that wing the restlesse foote of time."
MS published in facsimile by Alfred Horwood as *A Common-Place Book of
John Milton*. Westminster: Camden Society, 1876. The letter was printed
by Horwood in the printed version of the Commonplace Book in the Camden
Society Publications, New Series, Vol. XVI (1876), p. xvi.

1637

40   A MASKE | PRESENTED | At Ludlow Castle, | 1634: | *On Michaelmas night, before the* | RIGHT HONORABLE, | IOHN *Earle of Bridgewater, Vicount* BRACKLY, | *Lord Præsident* of WALES, And one of | His MAIESTIES most honorable | Privie Counsell. | ——— | *Eheu quid volui misero mihi! floribus austrum* | *Perditus* --- | ——— | *LONDON,* | Printed for *HVMPHREY ROBINSON,* | at the signe of the *Three Pidgeons* in | *Pauls Church-yard.* 1637. |

Date: probably early 1638. Printer: Augustine Mathewes (?). Quarto. A^2 B–E^4 F^2; iv + 36 pp. [i], title page; [ii], blank; [iii-iv], letter; 1–35, work; [36], blank. With a letter from Henry Lawes to John Egerton. British Library copy, C.34.d.46, contains misprinted proof-sheet, D4r. Carl H. Pforzheimer Library copy has nine autograph corrections. STC 17937. Copy owned by New York Public Library.

1638

41   JUSTA | EDOVARDO KING | naufrago, | ab Amicis mœrentibus, | amoris & | μνείας χάριν. | ════ | *Si rectè calculum ponas, ubique naufragium est.* | Pet. Arb. | ════ | *CANTABRIGIÆ:* | Apud *Thomam Buck,* & *Rogerum Daniel,* celeberrimæ | Academiæ typographos. 1638. |

Quarto. A–D^4 E^4(+ E^2) F–H^4 I^2; viii + 36, ii + 26 pp. Pp. 31–34, signed E4 and presumably [E5], are an inserted half-sheet. The "original" [E4] signature follows with "original" pp. 31–32 altered in ink to 35–36. Copy owned by Berg Collection, New York Public Library, does not make page corrections.

"Lycidas," pp. 20–25 of part two, which has separate title page and pagination:

[triple black border] | Obsequies to | the memorie | of | *Mr* EDWARD KING, | *Anno Dom.* | 1638. | - - - - | [ornament] | - - - - | Printed by *Th. Buck,* and *R. Daniel,* | printers to the *Universitie* of | *Cambridge:* 1638. |

Two states: see British Library copy, 1077.d.51. Autograph corrections in Cambridge University Library copy and British Library copy, C.21.c.42. A scrap of proof for p. 21 exists inside the back cover of Cambridge University Library copy of *De Literis & Lingua Getarum* [etc.]. Editore Bon. Vulcanio Burgensi, C. Plantin, 1597. Copies exist of the English poems alone. Printer of English section seems to have been Thomas Buck. STC 14964. Copy owned by New York Public Library.

1639

42   Vatican. Library. Barb. Lat. 2182.

Holograph letter to Lucas Holstenius (Holste), dated 29 March 1639, ff. 57–58v. Printed as Letter No. 7 in *Epistolarum Familiarium Liber Unus* (No. 317), dated 30 March. Facsimile given by Joseph M. Bottkol in *PMLA*, 68 (1953) 617–627. In Latin.

1640

43   [double-ruled border] | A | BANQVET | OF JESTS. | *OR* | A COLLEC-TION OF || *Court.* | *Camp.* | *Colledge.* | *Citie.* | *Country.* [right-hand bracket] | [left-hand bracket] IESTS. || ———— | In two *BOOKES.* | ———— | The sixth *Edition*, much enlarged | for the delight of the Reader. | ———— | LON-DON, | Printed for *Richard Royston*, and | are to be sold at his Shoppe | in *Ivie-Lane* at the signe | *of the Angell*   1640. |

Sometimes assigned to Archie Armstrong. Duodecimo. A–O^{12}. "Another on the same" [Hobson], pp. 129–131, entitled, "*Vpon old* Hobson *the Carrier of* Cambridge." "Hobson's Epitaph" (attributed), pp. 131–132. STC 1371. Copy owned by Cambridge University Library.

44   [ornament] | EPITAPHIVM | DAMONIS. | ARGVMENTVM. | [head-note] |

No title page; unpaged. Place given, p. [8]: "Londini." Printer: Augustine Mathewes (?). Dated: 1640 (?). Quarto. A^4; 8 pp. [1–8], work. STC 6218. Unique copy in British Library, C.57.d.48.

45   POEMS: | VVRITTEN | BY | VVIL. SHAKE-SPEARE. | Gent. | ———— | [ornament] | ———— | Printed at *London* by *Tho. Cotes*, and are to be sold by *Iohn Benson*, dwelling in | S^t. *Dunstans* Church-yard. 1640. |

Octavo. *^{4} A–L^8 M^4. "On Shakespear," [K8–K8v]. Variant title and text. STC 22344. Copy owned by New York Public Library.

46   [illustrated title page, various scenes and characters] | WITTS | RECREA-TIONS | Selected from | the finest Fancies | of Moderne Muses. | ———— | WITH | *A Thousand* | *out Landish Proverbs.* | London. *Printed for Humph. Blunden at ye Castle in Corn-hill* | 1640. |

Selected by G[eorge] H[erbert] and printed by R. H[odgkinson], according to the Stationers' Register; entered 15 October 1639. Octavo. A^4[–A1] B–L^8 M^4[–M4] Aa–Cc^8; A–D^8 E^4; unpaged. Many errors in signatures. "Hobson's epitaph" (attributed), No. 96 of Epitaphs, Cc1, entitled, "*On Hobson the Carrier.*" STC 25870. Copy owned by University of Illinois.

1641

47 ANIMADVERSIONS | UPON | The Remonstrants | Defence, |
AGAINST | SMECTYMNVVS. | —— | [device] | —— | LONDON,
| Printed for *Thomas Underhill*, and are | to be sold at the Signe of the *Bible*
in | *Woodstreet*, 1641. |

Printers: Richard Oulton and Gregory Dexter. Quarto. [A]^1 B–F^4 G^2 H–I^4
K^4(–K3); ii + 66 pp. Apparently what is now [A]^1 was printed as K3, making K4 now appear as K3. [A1] sometimes has deckle edge with stub between B and C (see copy in University of Kentucky Library). Cancel, G3–4,
pp. 45–48, yielding text of 64 pp. C1–3 given as B1–3; variant has C1 B2
C3 (see copy in University of Kentucky Library). Various states of text,
including nonprinting of comma after "Defence" on title page (see copy in
University of Kentucky Library). [i], title page; [ii], blank; 1–4, preface;
4–68, work; [65–66], blank. [65–66] sometimes missing. Dated: July. Wing,
M2089. Copy owned by New York Public Library.

48 AN ANSWER | TO A BOOK ENTITVLED, | AN HUMBLE | REMON-
STRANCE. | *In which,* || The Originall of [bracket] LITURGY |
EPISCOPACY [bracket] is discussed. || *And Quæres propounded Concerning*
both. | The PARITY of Bishops and Presbyters in Scrip- | ture Demonstrated.
| The occasion of their IMPARITIE in Antiquitie | discovered. | The DIS-
PARITIE of the Ancient and our Mo- | derne Bishops manifested. | The
ANTIQVITIE of Ruling Elders in the | Church vindicated. | The PRE-
LATICALL Church Bownded. | IEREMY 6. 16. | *Thus saith the Lord, stand*
in the waies and Behold, and aske | for the old way, which is the good way, and walke
therein. | Turtull. de præscr. adu. hæres. | *Id Dominicum et verum, quod prius*
traditum: id autem ex- | traneum et falsum quod sit posterius. | Written by SMEC-
TYMNVVS. | —— | Printed in the yeare 1641. |

Quarto. A–G ^{4}(–G4) gg^4 ggg^2 H–L^4(–L1) M^4 N^1; ii + 104 pp. [i], title
page; [ii], blank; 1–83, work; [84], blank; 85–94, "A Postscript" (attributed).
Pagination: 1–52 53–54 53–54 53–54 53–54 53–54 53–54 55–94. Dated:
March. Authors comprising the joint author Smectymnuus were: Stephen
Marshall, Edmund Calamy, Thomas Young, Matthew Newcomen, and
William Spurstow.

"A Postscript" given on M–N, pp. 85–94. Wing, M748A. Copy owned by
University of Kentucky Library.

49 [ornamented border] | AN ANSWER | TO A BOOKE ENTITVLED, |
AN HVMBLE | REMONSTRANCE. | *In which,* || The Originall of
[bracket] LITURGY | EPISCOPACY [bracket] is discussed. || *And Quæres*
propounded concerning both. | The PARITY of Bishops and Presbyters in Scrip-
| ture Demonstrated. | The occasion of their IMPARITY in Antiquity |
discovered. | The DISPARITY of the Ancient and our Moderne | Bishops

manifested. | The ANTIQUITY of Ruling Elders in the Church | vindicated. | The PRELATICALL Church Bownded. | IEREMY 6. 16 | *Thus saith the Lord, stand in the wayes, and Behold, and aske for* | *the Old Way, which is the Way, and walke therein.* | Tertul. de præscr. adv. hæres. | *Id Dominicum & verum, quod prius traditum: id autem extraneum* | *& falsum quod sit posterius.* | ——— | Written by SMECTYMNVVS. | ——— | *LONDON,* | Printed for *I. Rothwell,* and are to be sold by *T. N.* at the | Bible in Popes-Head-Alley. 1641. |

Different edition of No. 48. Quarto. A–N^4 O^1; ii + 104 pp. [i], title page; [ii], blank; 1–93, work; [94], blank; 95–104, "A Postscript" (attributed). Errors in pagination: p. 79 given as 89; pp. 95–104 (N–O) given as 85 96 97 88 89 100 101 92 103 104. Wing, M748. Copy owned by University of Kentucky Library.

50 M^R· WILLIAM | SHAKESPEARES | COMEDIES, | HISTORIES, and | TRAGEDIES. | Published according to the true Originall Coppies. | *The second Impression.* | [portrait] | *LONDON,* | Printed by *Tho. Cotes,* for *Robert Allot,* and are to be sold at his shop at the signe | of the blacke Beare in Pauls Church-yard. 1632. |

Reprint of No. 27 in 1641 (?). Second issue. Portrait printed over "*LON-DON*".

"On Shakespear," A5; Effigies A: Poet [title]; W. SHAKESPEARE. [title]; *honour'd* [1]; *Under* [4]; *ſtarre-ypointed* [4]; *Fame,* [5]; *whil'st,* [9]; *ſlow-endevouring* [9]; *Art,* [9]; *Impreſsion* [12]; *tooke:* [12]; *lie,* [15]. Not in Wing; noted inaccurately under STC (1) 22274; cited in STC (2) as 22274e.3. Copy owned by New York Public Library.

51 M^R· WILLIAM | SHAKESPEARES | COMEDIES, | HISTORIES and | TRAGEDIES. | Published accodring to the true Originall Copies. | *The second Impression.* | [portrait] | *LONDON,* | Printed by *Tho Cotes,* for *Robert Allot,* and are to be sold at his shop at the signe | of the blacke Beare in *Pauls* Church yard, 1632. |

Reprint of No. 27 in 1641 (?). Third issue, first variant. Second title page; nonswash italic "I." Added to copy of STC 22274 (No. 27), with title page laid in.

"On Shakespear," A5; Effigies C. Not in Wing, not in STC (1), cited in STC (2) as 22274e.5. Copy owned by New York Public Library.

52 M^R· V^{V}ILLIAM | SHAKESPEARES | COMEDIES, | HISTORIES and | TRAGEDIES. | Published according to the true Originall Copies. | *The second Impression.* | [portrait] | *LONDON,* | Printed by *Tho Cotes,* for *Robert Allot,* and are to be sold at his shop at the signe | of the blacke Beare in *Pauls* Church yard, 1632. |

Reprint of No. 27 in 1641 (?). Third issue, second variant. Not noted by William Todd in *Studies in Bibliography*, 5 (1952) 81–108. Nonswash italic "I."

"On Shakespear," A5; Effigies B: Poet, [title]; W. *Shakeſpeare*. [title]; honor'd [1]; *Vnder* [4]; *ſtarre-ypointing* [4]; Fame, [5]; *whil'ſt* [9]; *ſlow-endeavouring* [9]; *Art* [9]; *impreſsion* [12]; *tooke* [12]; *lie* [15]. Not in Wing; not in STC. Copy owned by Folger Shakespeare Library, Folio 2, No. 15.

53 M^R· V^{V}ILLIAM | SHAKESPEARES | COMEDIES, | HISTORIES and | TRAGEDIES. | Published according to the true Originall Copies. | *The second Impression.* | [portrait] | *LONDON,* | Printed by *Tho Cotes,* for *Robert Allot,* and are to be sold at his shop at the signe | of the blacke Beare in *Pauls* Church yard, 1632. |

Reprint of No. 27 in 1641 (?). Third issue, third variant. Variant of No. 52. Nonswash italic "I."

"On Shakespear," A5; Effigies B. Not in Wing; not in STC. Copy owned by Columbia University Library.

54 OF | PRELATICAL | EPISCOPACY, | AND | VVhether it may be deduc'd from | the Apostolical times by vertue of those Test- | monies which are alledg'd to that purpose | in some late Treatises: | One whereof goes under the Name of | IAMES' | ARCH-BISHOP | OF | ARMAGH · | [or-naments] | London, Printed by *R. O. & G. D.* for *Thomas* | *Underhill,* and are to be sold at the signe of the | *Bible,* in *Wood-Street,* 1641. |

Printers: Richard Oulton and Gregory Dexter. Quarto. π^2 A–C^4; iv + 24 pp. [i–ii], blank; [iii], title page; [iv], blank; [1]–24, work. [i–ii] sometimes missing; [1–8], unpaged. Variant states: "Whither" on title page (see British Library copy T.993.(4)); "Ttm," margin, p. [2], changed to "Tim"; other accidentals. Dated: June–July. Wing, M2133. Copy owned by New York Public Library.

55 OF | PRELATICAL | EPISCOPACY, | AND | VVhether it may be deduc'd from | the Apostolical times by vertue of those Testi- | monies which are alledg'd to that purpose | in some late Treatises: | One whereof goes under the Name of | IAMES' | ARCH-BISHOP | OF | ARMAGH · | [or-naments] | London, Printed by *R. O. & G. D.* for *Thomas* | *Underhill,* and are to be sold at the signe of the | *Bible,* in *Wood-Street,* 1641. |

Different issue of No. 54; note "Testi-" on title page. Cancel stub of π^2 seen between A4v and B1. Not in Wing. Copy owned by Berg Collection, New York Public Library.

56 OF | REFORMATION | Touching | CHVRCH-DISCIPLINE | IN | ENGLAND: | And the CAVSES that hither- | to have hindred it. | ———

| TWO BOOKES, | *Written to a FREIND.* | ——— | [device] | ——— |
Printed, for *Thomas Underhill*   1641. |

Printed in London, probably by Richard Oulton alone. Quarto. A^2 B–M^4
N^2; iv + 92 pp. [i], title page; [ii], blank; [iii], errata; [iv], blank; 1–90,
work; [91–92], blank. [91–92] sometimes missing. Variant states: A sig. unsigned and signed; two lines reset on p. 6 through deletion of "the" before
"*lost Truth*"; and inclusion of "Lib. I" in heads on pp. 2, 3, 6, 7; other accidentals in B, D, and E. Bodleian copy 4° F.56.Th. has manuscript
(autograph?) corrections. Dated: May. Wing, M2134. Copy owned by New
York Public Library.

57   [illustrated title page] | WITT'*s* | RECREATIONS | *Augmented,* | *with* | In-
genious | CONCEITES | *for the wittie,* | And | Merrie Medecines | *for the*
| Melancholie. | ——— | *See the next Page.* | London. *Printed for Humph: Blunden*
at ye Castle in Corn-hill | [1641 given above within illustration] |

Title page:
WITS | Recreations. | *CONTAINING,* | 630. Epigrams. | 160: Epitaphs,
| Variety of [bracket] || Fancies | *and* | Fantasticks, || Good for melancholly
humours. | ——— | Mart. *Non cuique datur habere nasum.* | ——— | *LON-*
DON, | Printed by *Thomas Cotes,* for *Humphry* | *Blunden* at the Castle in |
Corn-Hill. 1641. |

Compiler: Sir John Mennes (?). Octavo. π^1 [A]^2 B–Y^8(–Y8) Z^4(–Z4); unpaged. "Hobson's epitaph" (attributed), No. 124 of Epitaphs, R1v–R2, entitled, "Another." Wing, M1720. Copy owned by Henry E. Huntington
Library.

1642

58   AN | APOLOGY | Against a Pamphlet | CALL'D | A Modest Confutation
| of the Animadversions upon | the Remonstrant against | SMECTYM-
NUUS. | ——— | [device] | ——— | LONDON, | Printed by *E. G.* for
Iohn Rothwell, and are | to be sold at the signe of the Sunne | in *Pauls* Church-
yard. 1642. |

Printer: Edward Griffin. Quarto. π^2 A–G^4 H^2; iv + 60 pp. [i–ii], blank;
[iii], title page; [iv], blank; 1–59, work; [60], blank. [i–ii] sometimes missing. One erratum on p. 59. Variant states. Dated: April. Wing, M2090.
Copy owned by University of Kentucky Library.

59   THE | REASON | OF | Church-governement | Urg'd against | PRELA-
TY | By Mr. *John Milton.* | In two Books. | [ornaments] | [device] | [or-

naments] | LONDON | Printed by *E. G.* for *Iohn Rothwell*, and are to be sold | at the Sunne in *Pauls* Church-yard. 1641. |

Printer: Edward Griffin. Quarto. π^1 A–H^4 χ^1; ii + 66 pp. π2 apparently used for χ1. [i], title page; [ii], blank; 1–3, preface; 3–65, work; [66], errata. Some page variants. Dated: January 1642. Wing, M2175. Copy owned by University of Kentucky Library.

1643

60   [border of ornaments] | THE | DOCTRINE | AND DISCIPLINE | *OF* | DIVORCE: | RESTOR'D TO THE GOOD | OF BOTH SEXES, | From the bondage of Canon Law, | and other mistakes, to Christian freedom, | guided by the Rule of Charity. | Wherein also many places of Scripture, have | recover'd their long-lost meaning. | Seasonable to be now thought on in the | Reformation intended. | ——— | MATTH. 13. 52. | *Every Scribe instructed to the Kingdome of Heav'n, is like the Maister* | *of a house which bringeth out of his treasurie things old and new.* | ——— | *LONDON,* | Printed by *T. P.* and *M. S.* In Goldsmiths | Alley. 1643. |

Printers: Thomas Payne and Matthew Simmons. Edition 1. Quarto. [A]^1 B–G^4 H^1; ii + 50 pp. [A]2 used for H1; H1 sometimes bound immediately after [A]1. [i], title page; [ii], blank; 1–48, work; [49–50], errata. Dated: late July or August. Wing, M2108. Copy owned by University of Kentucky Library.

1644

61   [double-ruled border] | *AREOPAGITICA*; | A | SPEECH | OF | Mr. *JOHN MILTON* | For the Liberty of VNLICENC'D | PRINTING, | To the PARLAMENT of *ENGLAND.* | ——— | [four-line epigraph from Euripides in Greek] | ——— | [five-line translation] | ——— | *LONDON,* | Printed in the Yeare, 1644. |

Printer unknown; may have been Augustine Mathewes. Quarto. A–E^4 F^2; ii + 42 pp. [i], title page; [ii], blank; 1–40, work; [41–42], blank. [41–42] sometimes missing. Variant states. Some copies have MS correction on p. 12 of "wayfaring" to "warfaring". Dated: November. Wing, M2092. Copy owned by University of Kentucky Library.

62   [double-ruled border] | THE | Doctrine & Discipline | OF | DIVORCE: | Restor'd to the good of both SEXES, | From the bondage of CANON

LAW, and | other mistakes, to the true meaning of Scrip- | ture in the Law and Gospel compar'd. | Wherin also are set down the bad consequences of | abolishing or condemning of Sin, that which the | Law of God allowes, and Christ abolisht not. | Now the second time revis'd and much augmented, | In Two BOOKS: | To the Parlament of *England* with the Assembly. | ———— | The Author *J. M.* | ———— | MATTH. 13. 52. | *Every Scribe instructed to the Kingdome of Heav'n, is like the | Maister of a house which bringeth out of his treasury things | new and old.* | Prov. 18. 13. | *He that answereth a matter before he heareth it, it is folly and | shame unto him.* | ———— | *LONDON,* | Imprinted in the yeare 1644. |

Printer(s): Thomas Payne (?) and Matthew Simmons. Edition 2 of No. 60. Quarto. A–G^4(± G2) H–L^4 M^1; viii + 82 pp. K4 sometimes cancelled and reset. [i], title page; [ii], blank; [iii–viii], preface; 1–82, work. Errata, p. 82. With cancel, G2, occasionally with stub showing either horizontally (with correct pagination) or vertically. Various signatures in various states, copies being composite of corrected and uncorrected states. Various MS corrections (by printing house scribe) in many copies. Wing, M2109. Copy owned by New York Public Library.

63   [double border of ornaments] | THE | IVDGEMENT | OF | MARTIN BUCER, | CONCERNING | DIVORCE. | Writt'n to *Edward* the sixt, in his se- | cond Book of the Kingdom of Christ. And now Englisht. | Wherin a late Book restoring the | *Doctrine and Discipline of Divorce,* | is heer confirm'd and justify'd by the | authoritie of MARTIN BUCER. | *To the Parlament of England.* | ———— | JOHN 3. 10. | *Art thou a teacher of Israel, and know'st not these things?* | ———— | Publisht by Authoritie. | ———— | *LONDON,* | Printed by *Matthew Simmons,* 1644. |

Quarto. A–E^4 F^1; xvi + 26 pp. [i], title page; [ii], blank; [iii–viii], testimonies; [ix–xvi], preface; 1–24, work; [25–26], "A Postscript." Dated: July. Wing, B5270. Copy owned by New York Public Library.

64   [row of ornaments] | Of Education. To Master *Samuel Hartlib.* |

No title page. Printed for Thomas Johnson, London. Edition 1. Quarto. A^4; 8 pp. 1–8, work. Dated: June. Wing, M2132. Copy owned by New York Public Library.

1645

65   Cambridge. Emmanuel College Library. Peter Sterry MSS. MS 289.

Holograph. "At a Solemn Music," ll. 1–7, drawn from *Poems* (No. 70), p. 182. Dating uncertain: after 1645.

66   *COLASTERION:* | A REPLY TO | A | NAMELES ANSVVER |
AGAINST | *The Doctrine and Discipline of Divorce.* | WHERIN | The trivial
Author of that Answer is disco- | ver'd, the Licencer conferr'd with, and
the | Opinion which they traduce defended. | ——— | By the former Author,
J. M. | ——— | Prov. 26. 5. | *Answer a Fool according to his folly, lest hee bee*
wise in his | *own conceit.* | ——— | Printed in the Year, 1645. |

Printed in London by Matthew Simmons; dated 4 March. Quarto. [A]^2
B-D^4 E^2; iv + 28 pp. [i-ii], blank; [iii], title page; [iv], blank; 1-27, work;
[28], blank. [i-ii] sometimes missing. Wing, M2099. Copy owned by New
York Public Library.

67   [double-ruled border] | THE | Doctrine & Discipline | OF | DIVORCE:
| Restor'd to the good of both SEXES, | From the bondage of CANON
LAW, and | other mistakes, to the true meaning of Scrip- | ture in the Law
and Gospel compar'd. | Wherin also are set down the bad consequences of
| abolishing or condemning of Sin, that which the | Law of God allowes,
and Christ abolisht not. | Now the second time revis'd and much augmented,
| In Two BOOKS: | To the Parlament of *England* with the Assembly. |
——— | The Author *I. M.* | ——— | Matth. 13. 52. | *Every Scribe instructed*
to the Kingdome of Heav'n, is like the | *Maister of a house which bringeth out of his*
treasury things | *new and old.* | Prov. 18. 13. | *He that answereth a matter before*
he heareth it, it is folly and | *shame unto him.* | ——— | *LONDON:* | Imprinted
in the yeare 1645. |

Edition 3 of No. 60, derived from corrected and uncorrected sheets of Edition 2 (No. 62). Quarto. A-L^4 M^2; viii + 84 pp. [i], title page; [ii], blank;
[iii-viii], To the Parlament; 1-82, work; 82, errata; [83-84], blank. Two
states. Printers were apparently Thomas Payne (?) and Matthew Simmons.
Wing, M2110. Copy owned by University of Kentucky Library.

68   [no border] | THE | Doctrine and Discipline | OF | DIVORCE; | Restor'd
to the good of both SEXES, | From the Bondage of CANON LAW, and
| other mistakes, to the true meaning of Scripture in | the LAW and
GOSPEL compar'd. | Wherein also are set down the bad consequences of
a- | bolishing or condemning of Sin, that which the Law | of God allows,
and Christ abolisht not. | Now the second time Revis'd, and much
Augmented, | In Two BOOKS: | To the Parliament of *England,* with the
Assembly. | - - - - | The Author *J. M.* | - - - - | Matth. 13. 52. | *Every*
Scribe instructed to the Kingdom of Heav'n, is like the | *Master of a House which*
bringeth out of his Treasury things | *new and old.* | Prov. 18. 13. | *He that answereth*
a matter before he heareth it, it is folly | *and shame unto him.* | - - - - | *LONDON*:
| Imprinted In the Year 1645. |

Pirated edition of No. 67. Quarto. A-L^4 M^2; viii + 84 pp. [i], title page;

[ii], blank; [iii–viii], To the Parlament; 1–[82], work; [83–84], blank. Pp. 42–47 incorrectly numbered; pp. 69–72 repeated in pagination, making last page 78. No errata, but not all corrections were made in text. Two minor variants. Wing, M2111. Copy owned by University of Kentucky Library.

69   Oxford. Bodleian Library. Tanner MS 466.

William Sancroft's transcription of Psalm 136, pp. 34–35 (ff. 20v–21) and "On the Morning of Christ's Nativity," pp. 60–66 (ff. 33v–36v), from *Poems* (No. 70). Dated: after 1645.

70   POEMS | OF | Mr. *John Milton*, | BOTH | ENGLISH and LATIN, | Compos'd at several times. | ———— | *Printed by his true Copies.* | ———— | The SONGS were set in Musick by | Mr. HENRY LAWES Gentleman of | the KINGS Chappel, and one | of His MAIESTIES | Private Musick. | — *Baccare frontem* | *Cingite, ne vati noceat mala lingua futuro,* | Virgil, Eclog. 7. | ———— | *Printed and publish'd according to* | *ORDER.* | ———— | *LONDON,* | Printed by *Ruth Raworth* for *Humphrey Moseley,* | and are to be sold at the signe of the Princes | Arms in *Pauls* Church-yard. 1645. |

Octavo. a^4 π^1 A–G^8 H^4 A–E^8 F^4; x + 120, 88 pp. [i–ii], blank; [πr], blank; [πv], portrait; [v], title page; [vi], blank; [vii–x], preface; 1–120, text of English poems; [1], title page; [2], blank; 3–10, testimonies; 11–87, text of Latin poems; [88], blank.

Three states of text: see "Elegia prima," l. 13. Autograph corrections in Bodleian copy, 8° M168 Art (kept as Arch G.f.17): see "At a Solemn Music," "On the University Carrier," "Il Penseroso," prefatory note to testimonies, and "Elegia septima." Portrait and/or first leaf sometimes missing.

Title page for Latin poems:
Joannis Miltoni | *LONDINENSIS* | POEMATA. | Quorum pleraque intra | Annum ætatis Vigesimum | Conscripsit. | *Nunc primum Edita.* | [device] | *LONDINI,* | Typis *R. R.* Prostant ad Insignia Principis, | in Cœmeterio D. *Pauli,* apud *Humphredum* | *Moseley.* 1645. |

Contents:
Humphrey Moseley, "The Stationer to the Reader," pp. [a3–a4]
"On the Morning of Christ's Nativity," pp. 1–12
Psalm 114 (English), pp. 12–13
Psalm 136, pp. 13–16
"The Passion," pp. 16–19
"On Time," pp. 19–20
"Upon the Circumcision," pp. 20–22
"At a Solemn Music," pp. 22–23
"An Epitaph on the Marchioness of Winchester," pp. 23–26

"Song: On May Morning," pp. 26-27
"On Shakespear," p. 27
"On the University Carrier," p. 28
"Another on the same" [Hobson], pp. 29-30
"L'Allegro," pp. 30-36
"Il Penseroso," pp. 37-44
Sonnet 1, pp. 44-45
Sonnet 2, p. 45
Sonnet 3, pp. 45-46
Canzone, pp. 46-47
Sonnet 4, p. 47
Sonnet 5, pp. 47-48
Sonnet 6, p. 48
Sonnet 7, p. 49
Sonnet 8, pp. 49-50
Sonnet 9, p. 50
Sonnet 10, p. 51
"Arcades," pp. 51-56
"Lycidas," pp. 57-65
"Comus," pp. [67]-120; includes Henry Lawes's letter to Lord Bracley, pp. 69-70, and Sir Henry Wotton's letter to Milton, pp. 71-73
Testimonies, pp. 3-10; includes poems by Gianbattista Manso, p. 4; Giovanni Salsilli, p. 4; Selvaggi, p. 4; Antonio Francini, pp. 5-9; and prose commendation by Carlo Dati, p. 10
Elegia prima, pp. 11-15
Elegia secunda, pp. 15-16
Elegia tertia, pp. 16-19
Elegia quarta, pp. 19-24
Elegia quinta, pp. 25-30
Elegia sexta, pp. 31-35
Elegia septima, pp. 35-39
"In Proditionem Bombardicam," p. 40
"In Eandem" (Gunpowder Plot: "Siccine ... "), p. 40
"In Eandem" (Gunpowder Plot: "Purgatorem ... "), p. 41
"In Eandem" (Gunpowder Plot: "Quem modo ... "), p. 41
"In Inventorem Bombardae," pp. 41-42
"Ad Leonorem Romae Canentem," p. 42
"Ad Eandem" (Leonora Baroni: "Altera ... "), pp. 42-43
"Ad Eandem" (Leonora Baroni: "Credula ... "), p. 43
"In Obitum Procancellarii Medici," pp. 44-46
"In Quintum Novembris," pp. 46-55
"In Obitum Praesulis Eliensis," pp. 56-58
"Naturam Non Pati Senium," pp. 59-61
"De Idea Platonica," pp. 62-63

"Ad Patrem," pp. 63–68
Psalm 114 (Greek), p. 69
"Philosophus ad Regem," p. 70
"Ad Salsillum," pp. 70–72
"Mansus," pp. 72–76
"Epitaphium Damonis," pp. 77–89

Dated: later 1645; date of 2 January 1646 is purchase date by George
Thomason. Portrait by William Marshall; "In Effigei Ejus Sculptorem" given
beneath. Wing, M2160. Copy owned by University of Kentucky Library.
Separate copies of the Latin poems exist. Latin poems are listed separately
by Wing as M2159.

71   POEMS | OF | Mr. *John Milton*, | BOTH | ENGLISH and LATIN, | Com-
      pos'd at several times. | ———— | *Printed by his true Copies.* | ———— | The
      SONGS were set in Musick by | Mr. HENRY LAWES Gentleman of |
      the KINGS Chappel, and one | of His MAIESTIES | Private Musick. |
      —*Baccare frontem* | *Cingite, ne vati noceat mala lingua futuro,* | Virgil, Eclog. 7.
      | ———— | *Printed and publish'd according to* | *ORDER.* | ———— | *LONDON,*
      | Printed by *Ruth Raworth* for *Humphrey Moseley,* | and are to be sold at the
      signe of the Princes | Arms in S. *Pauls* Church-yard. 1645. |

      Another issue of No. 70. Not in Wing. Copy owned by University of Western
      Ontario Library.

72   [double-ruled border] | Tetrachordon: | EXPOSITIONS | UPON | The
      foure chief places in Scripture, | which treat of Mariage, or nullities in
      Mariage. || On [bracket of four lines, the first and third turned over to the
      line below] | Gen. 1. 27. 28. compar'd and explain'd by Gen. 2. 18.2.24.
      | Deut. 24. 1. 2. | Matth. 5. 31. 32. with Matt. 19. from the 3^d. v. to the
      11th. | 1 Cor. 7. from the 10th to the 16th. || Wherin the Doctrine and
      Discipline of Divorce, as was | lately publish'd, is confirm'd by explanation
      of Scrip- | ture, by Testimony of ancient Fathers, of civill lawes | in the
      Primitive Church, of famousest | Reformed Divines, | And lastly, by an
      intended Act of the Parlament and | Church of England in the last yeare
      of | EDVVARD the sixth. | ———— | By the former Author *J. M.* | ————
      | [four-line epigraph from Euripides in Greek] | ———— | *LONDON:* | Printed
      in the yeare 1645. |

      Printers: Thomas Payne and Matthew Simmons. Quarto. A–O^4; viii +
      104 pp. [i], title page; [ii], blank; [iii–viii], preface; 1–102, work; [103–104],
      blank. Errata, p. 102 ("98"). G1-2 mispaged 37–40 rather than 41–44 (er-
      ror is continued). State 1: second p. 39 given as 36; State 2: corrected. Dated:
      4 March. Wing, M2184. Copy owned by University of Kentucky Library.

73   [illustrated title page] | WITT'S RECREATIONS | refined | & *Augmented,*

| *with* | Ingenious | CONCEITES | *for the wittie,* | *And* | Merrie Medicines | *for the* | Melancholie. | ——— | *See the next Page.* | London. *Printed for* H. B. *at the Castle in Corn-hill.* 1645 |

Title page:
[border of ornaments] | RECREATION | FOR | *Ingenious Head-peeces.* | OR, | A Pleasant Grove for their Wits | to walke in, | Of [bracket] || *Epigrams,* --630. | *Epitaphs,* --180. | *Fancies,* a number. | *Fantasticks,* abundance. || ——— | Good for Melancholy Humors. | ——— | *Mart. Non cuique datur habere nasum.* | ——— | *LONDON,* | Printed by *R. Cotes* for *H. B.* at the Castle | in Cornehill, 1645. |

Compiler: Sir John Mennes (?). Octavo. A^4(-A^1) B–Z^8 Aa^4; unpaged. A5–8 probably used for Aa. "Old Hobsons Epitaph" (attributed), No. 13 (*recte* 137, but next poem is numbered 133 and the error is continued), on P8v–Q1. Wing, M1712. Copy owned by Folger Shakespeare Library.

1647

74 New York City. New York Public Library. Manuscript Room. Holograph MS.

Letter to Carlo Dati, dated 20 April 1647. Printed in *Epistolarum Familiarium Liber Unus* (No. 317) as Letter No. 10, dated 21 April. In Latin.

75 Oxford. Bodleian Library. MS, Latin Miscellany d.77*, attached to Milton's *Poems* (1645), catalogued 8° M168 Art, but kept as Arch G.f.17.

"Ad Joannem Rousium." In Latin. Hand of John Phillips with one-word autograph correction. Dated: 23 January 1647.

MS published in facsimile by Harris F. Fletcher in *John Milton's Complete Poetical Works*. Urbana: University of Illinois Press, 1943–48. I (1943) 459–462.

1648

76 CHOICE PSALMES | PUT INTO | MUSICK, | For Three Voices. | The most of which may properly enough be sung | by any three, with a Thorough Base. | COMPOS'D by || *Henry* | and *William* [bracket] | *Lawes,* Brothers; and Servants to | His Majestie. || With divers Elegies, set in Musick by sev'rall Friends, upon the | death of WILLIAM LAWES. | And at the end of the Thorough Base are added nine Canons of | Three and Foure Voices,

made by *William Lawes.* | ———— | *LONDON,* | Printed by *James Young,* for *Humphrey Moseley,* at the Prince's Armes Church in Corn-hill. 1648. |

Quarto. A^4 a^2 M-X^4; unpaged. Sonnet 13, a1v. Wing, L640. Copy owned by Folger Shakespeare Library.

1649

77   [ornamented border] | ARTICLES | OF PEACE, | MADE AND CON- | CLUDED | with the *Irish* Rebels, and Papists, | by JAMES Earle of OR- | MOND, | For and in behalfe of the late King, | and by vertue of his Autoritie. | Also a Letter sent by *Ormond* to | Col. JONES, Governour of *DUBLIN,* | with his Answer thereunto. | *And* | A Representation of the *Scotch* Presbytery | at *Belfast* in *Ireland.* | Upon all which are added Observations. | ———— | *Publisht by Autority.* | ———— | *LONDON;* | Printed by *Matthew Simmons* in *Aldersgate-streete.* | 1649. |

Quarto. π^1 A-H^4 χ^1; ii + 66 pp. [i], title page; [ii], blank; 1–2, letter; 2–34, Articles of Peace; 34–40, letters; 41–45, A Necessary Representation; 45–65, Observations; [66], blank.

Title of section written by Milton:
OBSERVATIONS UPON | the Articles of Peace with the *Irish* Rebels, on the Letter of *Ormond* | to Col. *Jones,* and the Representation | *of the* Presbytery *at* Belfast. |

Wing, A863. Copy owned by Folger Shakespeare Library.

78   [rubricated] | ΕΙΚΟΝΟΚΛΑ'ΣΤΗΣ | IN | Answer | *To a Book Intitl'd* | Ε'ΙΚΩ'Ν ΒΑΣΙΛΙΚΗ̄, | THE | PORTRATURE of his Sacred Majesty | in his *Solitudes* and *Sufferings.* | ———— | The Author *I. M.* | ———— | PROV. 28. 15, 16, 17. | 15. *As a roaring Lyon, and a ranging Beare, so is a wicked Ru-* | *ler over the poor people.* | 16. *The Prince that wanteth understanding, is also a great op-* | *pressor; but he that hateth covetousnesse shall prolong his dayes.* | 17. *A man that doth violence to the blood of any person, shall fly* | *to the pit, let no man stay him.* | Salust. Conjurat. Catilin. | Regium imperíum, quod initio, conservandæ libertatis, atque augendæ rei- | pub. causâ fuerat, in super- | biam, dominationem que se convertit. | Regibus boni, quam mali, suspec- | tiores sunt; semperque his aliena virtus for- | midolosa est. | Quid libet im- | punè facere, hoc scilicet regium est. | - - - - | Published by Authority. | - - - - | *London,* Printed by *Matthew Simmons,* next dore to the gilded | Lyon in Aldersgate street. 1649. |

Edition 1. Quarto. [A]^2 B-Z Aa-Ii^4 Kk^2; xiv + 242 pp. [i–ii], blank; [iii], title page; [iv], blank; [v–xiv], preface; 1–242, work. [i–ii] sometimes missing. Two states. Dated: October or November. Wing, M2112. Copy owned by University of Kentucky Library.

79   Leeds. Leeds University Library. Brotherton Collection. Marten-Loder MSS, Third Series, Vol. XI.

State paper, Columbia No. 151, dated 2 April 1649, draft in Latin with autograph corrections by Milton, f. 1. Erroneously alleged to be in hand of Henry Marten.

State paper, Yale No. 2, dated 2 April 1649, draft in Latin with autograph corrections by Milton, f. 2. Erroneously alleged to be in hand of Henry Marten.

80   London. British Library. Stowe MS 305.

Anonymous transcription of extracts from *Eikonoklastes*, Edition 1 (No. 78), ff. 89v–137v. Dated: after 1649.

81   London. Public Record Office. MS SP 18/1.

Translation of letter from Princess Sophie to Prince Maurice, Columbia No. 165, dated 13 April 1649, in hand of John Phillips with autograph corrections and additions, No. 55, f. 142. German original appears as No. 54, f. 140–140v.

Translation of letter from Princess Sophie to Prince Rupert, dated 13 April 1649, in hand of John Phillips, No. 56, f. 143. Printed in Columbia Edition, XVIII, 653; see Yale No. 3. French original appears as No. 53, f. 138–138v.

82   London. Public Record Office. MS SP 25/94.

State paper, Columbia No. 1, dated 10 August 1649, copy in English, pp. 369–373.

83   London. Public Record Office. MS SP 82/7.

State paper, Columbia No. 151, dated 2 April 1649, copy in English, ff. 122–123.

State paper, Columbia No. 1, dated 10 August 1649, copy in English, ff. 138–141.

84   [ornamented border] | THE TENURE OF | KINGS | AND | MAGIS-TRATES: | PROVING, | That it is Lawfull, and hath been | held so through all Ages, for any, | who have the Power, to call to account a | Tyrant, or wicked KING, and after | due conviction, to depose, and put | him to

death; if the ordinary MA- | GISTRATE have neglected, or | deny'd to doe it. | And that they, who of late, so much blame | Deposing, are the Men that did it themselves. | ——— | *The Author*, J. M. | ——— | *LON-DON*, Printed by *Matthew Simmons*, at the Gilded | Lyon in Aldersgate Street, 1649. |

Edition 1. Quarto. A–E^4 F^2; ii + 42 pp. [i], title page; [ii], blank; 1–42, work. Two states. Wing, M2181. Copy owned by Yale University Library. Reported variant copy owned by Emmanuel College Library, Cambridge, reads as above; the "ed" of "Gilded" printed weakly but distinctly.

85   [ornamented border within a double rule] | THE TENURE OF | KINGS | AND | MAGISTRATES: | PROVING, | That it is Lawfull, and hath been | held so through all Ages, for any, who | have the POWER, to call to account a Tyrant, or | wicked KING, and after due conviction, to | depose, and put him to death; if the ordina- | ry MAGISTRATE have neglected, or de- | ny'd to doe it. | And that they, who of late so much blame | Depos-ing, are the Men that did it themselves. | ——— | *Published now the second time with some additions, and* | *many Testimomies also added out of the best & learnedest a-* | *mong Protestant Divines asserting the position of this book.* | ——— | *The Author*, J. M. | ——— | *LONDON*, | Printed by *Matthew Simmons*, at the Gilded Ly- | on in Aldersgate Street, 1649. |

Edition 2, Issue 1, of No. 84. Note "*Testimomies*". Date: often considered to be early 1650, but more likely ca. October 1649. Quarto. A–H^4; ii + 62 pp. [i], title page; [ii], blank; [1]–60, work; [61–62], blank. [61–62] sometimes missing. State one of text. See Wing, M2182. Copy owned by New York Public Library.

86   [ornamented border within double rule] | THE TENURE OF | KINGS | AND | MAGISTRATES: | PROVING, | That it is Lawfull, and hath been | held so through all Ages, for any, who | have the POWER, to call to account a Tyrant, or | wicked KING, and after due conviction, to | depose, and put him to death; if the ordina- | ry MAGISTRATE have neglected, or de- | ny'd to doe it. | And that they, who of late so much blame | Depos-ing, are the Men that did it themselves. | ——— | *Published now the second time with some additions, and* | *many Testimonies also added out of the best & learnedest a-* | *mong Protestant Divines asserting the position of this book.* | ——— | *The Author*, J. M. | ——— | *LONDON*, | Printed by *Matthew Simmons*, at the Gilded Ly- | on in Aldersgate Street, 1649.

Edition 2, Issue 2, of No. 84. Note "*Testimonies*"; cf. No. 85. State two of text. See Wing, M2182. Copy owned by Harvard University Library. University of Illinois Library copy x821 | M64 | N9 | 1649^2 has both states of text, and may be a variant issue in that the "n" of "been" (1. 6) is out of line.

1650

87 [rubricated] | 'ΕΙΚΟΝΟΚΛΑ'ΣΤΗΣ. | *IN* | ANSWER | To a book Intitl'd | 'ΕΙΚΩ'Ν ΒΑΣΙΑΙΚΗ̄, | THE | Portrature of his sacred Majesty | in his *Solitudes* and *Sufferings*. | ———— | The AUTHOR *J. M.* | ———— | PROV. 28. 15, 16, 17. | 15. *As a roaring Lyon, and a ranging Beare, so is a wicked Ru-* | *ler over the poor people.* | 16. *The Prince that wanteth understanding, is also a great* *op-* | *pressor; but he that hateth covetousness shall prolong his dayes.* | 17. *A man* *that doth violence to the blood of any person, shall fly* | *to the pit, let no man stay* *him.* | Salust. Conjurat. Catilin. | Regium imperíum, quod initio, conser- vandæ libertatis, atque augendæ reipub. causâ | fuerat, in superbiam, dominationemque se convertit. | Regibus boni, quam mali, suspectiores sunt; semperq; his aliena virtus formidolosa est. | Impunè quælibet facere, id est regem esse. Idem Bell. Jugurth. | ———— | Publish'd now the second time, and much enlarg'd. | ———— | *London*, Printed by *T. N.* and are to be sold by *Tho. Brewster* | and *G. Moule* at the three Bibles in *Pauls* Church-Yard | near the West-end, 1650. |

Edition 2 of No. 78. Quarto. π^2 A-Z Aa-Gg^4 Hh^2; xviii + 230 pp. [i-iv], blank; [v], title page; [vi], blank; [vii-xviii], preface; 1-230, work. [i-iv] sometimes missing. Printer: Thomas Newcomb. Wing, M2113. Copy owned by New York Public Library.

88 [rubricated] | 'ΕΙΚΟΝΟΚΛΑ'ΣΤΗΣ. | *IN* | ANSWER | *To a Book Intitl'd* | 'ΕΙΚΩ'Ν ΒΑΣΙΛΙΚΗ̄, | THE | Portrature of his sacred Majesty | in his *Solitudes* and *Sufferings*. | ———— | The AUTHOR *J. M.* | ———— | PROV. 28. 15, 16, 17. | 15. *As a roaring Lyon, and a ranging Beare, so is a wicked Ru-* | *ler over the poor people.* | 16. *The Prince that wanteth understanding, is also a great* *op-* | *pressor; but he that hateth covetousness shall prolong his dayes.* | 17. *A man* *that doth violence to the blood of any person, shall fly* | *to the pit, let no man stay* *him.* | Salust. Conjurat. Catilin. | Regium imperíum, quod initio, conser- vandæ libertatis, atque augendæ reipub. causâ | fuerat, in superbiam, dominationemque se convertit. | Regibus boni, quam mali, suspectiores sunt; semperq; his aliena virtus formidolosa est. | Impunè quælibet facere, id est regem esse. Idem Bell. Jugurth. | ———— | Publish'd now the second time, and much enlarg'd. | ———— | *London*, Printed by *Thomas Newcomb* in Thamestreet over | against *Baynards-Castle*   M DC L. |

Another issue of No. 87. Quarto. A-Z Aa-Gg^4 Hh^2; xiv + 230 pp. [i], title page; [ii], blank; [iii-xiv], preface; 1-230, work. Wing, M2114. Copy owned by Folger Shakespeare Library.

89 ['Εικονοκλαστης. Caput primum de Parliamento a rege postremum indicto. London: 1650.]

Latin translation of No. 87. Translator: Lewis Du Moulin. No copy is known, but it is cited by Anthony Wood, from White Kennet, in *Athenae Oxonienses*, ed. Philip Bliss (1820), IV, 126, and by Gui Patin in No. *163*, who assigned the translation to Lewis's brother Peter (Milton's antagonist).

90   London. Public Record Office. MS SP 18/1.

See Letter 89, f. 183, for rough draft of a non-Miltonic translation of the original state paper, Columbia No. 157, dated after 28 November 1650.

91   [ornamented border] | THE TENURE OF | KINGS | AND | MAGIS-TRATES: | PROVING, | That it is Lawfull, and hath been | held so through all Ages, for any, who | have the POWER, to call to account a Tyrant, or | wicked KING, and after due conviction, to | depose, and put him to death; if the ordina- | ry MAGISTRATE have neglected, or de- | ny'd to doe it. | And that they, who of late so much blame | Deposing, are the Men that did it themselves. | ———— | *Published now the second time with some additions, and* | *many Testimonies also added out of the best & learnedest a-* | *mong Protestant Divines asserting the position of this book.* | ———— | *The Author,* J. M. | ———— | *LONDON,* | Printed by *Matthew Simmons*,nextdoore to the Gil- | Lyon in Aldersgate Street, 1649. |

Edition 2, Issue 3, of No. 84. Date: uncertain; between October 1649 (?) and 15 February 1650 (?). State two of text. Not in Wing. Copy owned by Union Theological Seminary Library (McAlpin Collection).

92   [ornamented border] | THE TENURE OF | KINGS | AND | MAGIS-TRATES: | PROVING, | That it is Lawfull, and hath been | held so through all Ages, for any, who | have the POWER, to call to account a Tyrant, or | wicked KING, and after due conviction, to | depose, and put him to death; if the ordina- | ry MAGISTRATE have neglected, or de- | ny'd to doe it. | And that they, who of late so much blame | Deposing, are the Men that did it themselves. | ———— | *Published now the second time with some additions, and* | *many Testimonies also added out of the best & learnedest a-* | *mong Protestant Divines asserting the position of this book.* | ———— | *The Author,* J. M. | ———— | *LONDON,* | Printed by *Matthew Simmons*,nextdoore to the Gil- | Lyon in Aldersgate Street, 1650. |

Edition 2, Issue 4, of No. 84. Perhaps dated around 15 February 1650. State two of text. Wing, M2183. Copy owned by New York Public Library.

93   [illustrated title page] | WITT'S | RECREATIONS | refined | *Augmented,* | *with* | Ingenious | CONCEITES | *for the wittie,* | *And* | Merrie Medicines | *for the* | Melancholie. | ———— | *See the next Page.* | Printed by M. S. sould by I. Hancock in Popes head Alley 1630. |

Reissue of illustrated title page of former edition, not containing "Hobson's epitaph" (attributed). To this is added a new title page and new edition:

[border of ornaments] | RECREATION | FOR | *Ingenious Head-peeces.* | OR, | A Pleasant Grove for their Wits | to walke in, | Of [bracket] || *Epigrams*, 700. | *Epitaphs*, 200. | *Fancies*, a number. | *Fantasticks*, abundance. || ———— | With their Addition, Multiplica- | tion, and Division. | ———— | Mart. *Non cuique datur habere nasum.* | *LONDON*, Printed by *M. Simmons*, and are to be | sold by *John Hancock* in *Popes-head* Alley. | 1650. |

Compiler: Sir John Mennes (?). Octavo. A–Z Aa–Bb^8; unpaged. A1 (il-lustrated title page) frequently missing. "Old Hobsons Epitaph" (attributed), No. 148, on N6v. Wing, M1713. Copy owned by Newberry Library.

1651

94   Cambridge. Cambridge University Library. Baker MS XXXV. Shelf mark: Mm.1.46.

State paper, Columbia No. 7, dated 21 January 1651, copy in Latin, pp. 149–150. Patrick, p. 539, calls this Baker MS XVIII and locates the letter on p. 148. (Baker MSS I–XXIII have been in the British Library since the mid-nineteenth century.) Date of MS: late seventeenth century.

95   CLAUDII | SALMASII | DEFENSIO REGIA | *PRO* | CAROLO I. | *ET* | JOANNIS MILTONI | DEFENSIO POPULARIS, | *PRO* | POPULO ANGLICANO, | Contrà CLAVDII Anonimi, aliàs SALMASII | DEFEN-SIONEM REGIAM. | *Accesserunt huic editioni* INDICES *locupletissimi* | [arms] | *PARISIIS,* | Apud viduam MATHVRINI DV PVIS, | Viâ Iacobæâ, sub signo Coronæ, M. DC. L. | ———— | *CVM PERM* ⊢ *SSIONE* |

First issue of combined reissue of Salmasius's *Defensio Regia* and *Defensio prima* (No. 103), with inaccurate date. The first "I" of "Permissione" is printed as shown; the phrase appears to be in italics. Quarto. * ã ẽ A–Z Aa–Pp^4(-Pp4) A–P^4; 8 + xvi + 302 + x + 110 pp. Pp. 151–160 repeated; other pagination errors. Last page given as 282, an error for 292, but 302 *recte.* Cancel stubs between Pp3 and A1. [1–2], blank; [3], title page; [4], blank; [5–8], index to *Defensio Regia*; [i], title page for *Defensio Regia*; [ii], blank; [iii–xvi], preface; 1–282 [292], text of *Defensio Regia*; [293–294], cancelled; [i], title page for *Defensio prima*; [ii], blank; [iii–x], preface; 1–104, text of *Defensio prima*; [105–110], index. Copy owned by Christ's College Library, Cambridge.

96   CLAUDII SALMASII | DEFENSIO REGIA, | *PRO* | CAROLO I. Rege Angliæ &c. | *ET* | JOANNIS MILTONI | DEFENSIO, | *PRO* | POPULO

ANGLICANO, | *Contrà* CLAVDII *Anonymi*, aliàs SALMASII | DEFEN-
SIONEM REGIAM. | *Accesserunt huic editioni* INDICES *locupletissimi.* | [arms]
| *PARISIIS,* | Apud viduam MATHVRINI DV PVIS, | Viâ Iacobæâ, sub
signo Coronæ, M. DC. LI. | ——— | *CVM PERMISSIONE.* |

Another issue of No. 95 with new title page and correct date. Copy owned
by University of Kentucky Library.

97   [Gdaǹsk, Poland. Wojewódzkie Archiwum Pánstwowe. Formerly Staatsar-
      chiv der Freien Stadt Danzig.]

      State paper, Columbia No. 15, dated 6 February 1651, copy in Latin. Loca-
      tion of state paper uncertain.

98   JOANNIS MILTONI | Angli | PRO POPULO ANGLICANO | DEFEN-
      SIO | Contra *Claudii Anonymi,* aliàs *Salmasii,* | Defensionem REGIAM. |
      [Commonwealth arms within circular border] | *LONDINI,* | Typis *Du-*
      Gardianis. Anno Domini   1651. |

      Edition 1, Issue 1. Quarto. [A]^2 B-Z Aa-Ff^4; xxii + 206 pp. [i-ii], blank;
      [iii], title page; [iv], blank; [v-xxi], preface; [xxii], blank; 1-205, work; [206],
      blank. Whether this issue had an A1 leaf is uncertain. Issue 1 of Madan
      No. 1; thus No. 1a. Wing, M2166. Copy owned by Harvard University
      Library.

99   JOANNIS MILTONI | Angli | PRO POPULO ANGLICANO | DEFEN-
      SIO | Contra *Claudii Anonymi,* aliàs *Salmasii,* | Defensionem REGIAM. |
      [Commonwealth arms within an ornamental square form] | *LONDINI,* |
      Typis *Du-Gardianis.* Anno Domini   1651. |

      Edition 1, Issue 2, of No. 98. Quarto. A^2 B-Z Aa-Ff^4; xxii + 206 pp. [i-ii],
      blank; [iii], title page; [iv], blank; [v-xxi], preface; [xxii], blank; 1-205,
      work; [206], blank. Issue 2 of Madan No. 1; thus No. 1b. Not in Wing.
      Copy owned by Cambridge University Library (shelf mark: SSS.44.32).

100   JOANNIS MILTONI | Angli | PRO POPULO ANGLICANO | DEFEN-
      SIO | Contra *Claudii Anonymi,* aliàs *Salmasii,* | Defensionem REGIAM. |
      [Commonwealth arms within an ornamental square form] | *LONDINI,* |
      Typis *Du-Gardianis.* Anno Domini   1651. |

      Edition 1, Issue 3, of No. 98. Quarto. A^2 B-Z Aa-Ff^4; xxii + 206 pp. [i],
      title page; [ii], blank; [iii], errata; [iv], blank; [v-xxi], preface; [xxii], blank;
      1-205, work; [206], blank. Reverses A1 and A2 of Issue 2 and prints errata
      on A2. Hyphen in *"Du-Gardianis"* does not always print, as in second copy
      in New York Public Library. Issue 3 of Madan No. 1; thus No. 1c. Not
      in Wing. Copy owned by University of Kentucky Library.

Variant state: N (pp. 71–78) reset; regular A in "An", catchword, p. 72, and "Anglicano," p. 78, but swash A in "Anglicano," p. 76. Copy owned by Harvard University Library (shelf mark: 14496.13.4*).

101 JOANNIS MILTONI Angli | PRO | POPULO ANGLICANO | DEFEN-SIO | Contra *Claudii Anonymi*, aliàs *Salmasii*, | Defensionem REGIAM. | ———— | *Editio emendatior.* | ———— | [arms] | *LONDINI*, | Typis *Du-Gardianis*. Anno Domini 1651. |

Edition 2 of No. 98. Folio in fours. A–Z Aa–Mm^4; viii + 272 pp. [i–iv], blank; [v], title page; [vi–vii], blank; [viii], errata; 1–20, preface; 21–263, work; [264–268], blank; [269–272], blank and cropped. A1–2 intact. Large paper copy. Madan No. 2. Wing, M2167. Copy owned by Morgan Library.

A4, with errata, missing and not in evidence in copy owned by Columbia University Library, Copy 2. A1–2 and Mm1–4 missing. Copy owned by University of Kentucky Library reverses A4: [v], title page; [vi], blank; [vii], errata; [viii], blank. A1–2 and Mm1–4 missing. Copy owned by New York Public Library reverses A3 and A4: [v], blank; [vi], errata; [vii], title page; [viii], blank. A1–2 and Mm1–4 missing. Regular paper copy. Copy owned by Durham University Library does not have a variant title page as has been reported.

102 JOANNIS MILTONI | Angli | DEFENSIO | PRO POPULO ANGLI-CANO: | Contra *Claudii Anonimi*, aliàs *Salmasii*, | DEFENSIONEM RE-GIAM. | [arms] | *LONDINI*, | Typis *Du Gardianis*. Anno Domini 1651. |

Another edition of No. 98, probably at Gouda, perhaps by G. de Hoeve. Note position of "DEFENSIO." Quarto. A–P^4; x + 110 pp. [i], title page; [ii], blank; [iii–x], preface; 1–104, work; [105–110], Index. Madan No. 3. Wing, M2168 (also, in error, M2106). Copy owned by New York Public Library.

103 IOANNIS MILTONI | Angli | PRO POPVLO ANGLICANO | DEFEN-SIO, | *Contra* | CLAVDII ANONYMI, aliàs SALMASII, |DEFEN-SIONEM | REGIAM | [arms] | *LONDINI*, | Typis DV GARDIANIS, | Anno Domini 1651. |

Another edition of No. 98, at Utrecht, by Theodorus ab Ackersdijck and Gisbertus à Zijll. Issue 1. Title page is not a cancel. Duodecimo. A–L^{12}; xx + 244 pp. [i], title page; [ii], blank; [iii–xx], preface; 1–244, work. Madan No. 4; should be No. 4a. Various states. Wing, M2165 (?). Copy owned by New York Public Library.

The description of a copy reported in the Grolier Club's *Catalogue of Original and Early Editions of Some of the Poetical and Prose Works of English Writers from*

Wither to Prior (New York: Grolier Club, 1905), three vols., No. 583 (II, 182), seems to be filled with errors: spelling, line divisions, lack of accent, italics, and supposedly a triangular ornament rather than the Commonwealth arms. Its collation suggests it is a variant of Madan No. 4, and Madan in his revised bibliography reported this, indicating that he had not seen this copy, which would be unique. But it apparently does not exist, its variations being simply errors of reportage.

104   IOANNIS MILTONI | Angli | PRO POPVLO ANGLICANO | DEFEN-SIO, | *Contra* | CLAVDII ANONYMI, aliàs SALMASII, | DEFEN-SIONEM | REGIAM | [arms] | *LONDINI,* | Typis DV GARDIANIS, | Anno Domini 1650. |

Issue 2 of No. 103. Cancel title page. "0" of date partially erased or due to defect in "1"; probably printed shortly before 15 March 1651. Copy in Columbia University Library shows stubs of A1 cancel between A1 and A2, and A12 and B1. Should be Madan No. 4b. Wing, M2165 (?). Copy owned by University of Kentucky Library.

105   IOANNIS MILTONI | Angli | PRO POPVLO ANGLICANO | DEFEN-SIO, | *Contra* | CLAVDII ANONYMI, aliàs SALMASII, | DEFEN-SIONEM | REGIAM | [arms] | *LONDINI,* | Typis DV GARDIANIS, | Anno Domini   1651. |

Issue 3 of No. 103. Cancel, with stubs visible, for A1 (title page). Should be Madan No. 4c. Not in Wing. Copy owned by Berg Collection, New York Public Library; catalogued as reading "1650," erased, but this is in error.

106   JOANNIS MILTONI | Angli | PRO POPULO ANGLICANO | DEFEN-SIO | *Contra* | CLAUDII ANONYMI, aliàs SALMASII, | DEFENSIO-NEM | REGIAM. | [variant arms] | *LONDINI,* | Typis DU-GARDIANIS, | ANNO DOMINI   1651. |

Another edition of No. 98. Duodecimo. A–L^{12}; xx + 244 pp. [i], title page; [ii], blank; [iii–xx], preface; 1–244, work. Madan No. 5. Wing, M2168A. Copy owned by William B. Hunter, Jr., University of Houston.

107   IOANNIS MILTONI | Angli | PRO POPVLO ANGLICANO | DEFEN-SIO, | *Contra* | CLAVDII ANONYMI, aliàs SALMASII, | DEFEN-SIONEM | REGIAM. | *Cum Indice.* | [arms] | *LONDINI,* | Typis DV GAR-DIANIS, | Anno Domini   1651. |

Another edition of No. 98, by Ludovic Elzevier at Leyden. Duodecimo. A–L^{12} M^4; 272 pp. [1], title page; [2], blank; 3–22, preface; 23–260, work; [261–272], Index. Madan No. 6. Wing, M2168B. Copy owned by University of Kentucky Library.

108 IOANNIS MILTONI | Angli | PRO POPVLO ANGLICANO | DEFEN-
SIO, | *Contra* | CLAVDII ANONYMI, aliàs SALMASII, | DEFEN-
SIONEM | REGIAM. | [arms] | *LONDINI,* | Typis DV GARDIANIS,
| Anno Domini 1651. |

Another edition of No. 98, by Ludovic Elzevier at Leyden. Duodecimo.
A-M^{12}; 288 pp. [1], title page; [2], blank; 3–24, preface; 25–283, work;
[284–288], blank. Perhaps earlier than No. 107 since no Index is included.
Madan No. 7. Wing, M2168C. Copy owned by University of Kentucky
Library.

109 [IOANNIS MILTONI | Angli | PRO POPULO ANGLICANO | DEFEN-
SIO, | *Contra* | CLAUDII ANONYMI, aliàs SALMASII, | DEFEN-
SIONEM | REGIAM. | [arms] | *LONDINI,* | Typis DU GARDIANIS,
| Anno Domini 1651. |]

Alleged edition of No. 98, reported as sixteenmo in 285 pp. by Alphonse
Willems in *Les Elzevier* (Bruxelles, 1880). Madan No. 8, but apparently does
not exist. Madan speculates that Willems was reporting a copy of No. 108
erroneously.

110 JOANNIS MILTONI | Angli | PRO POPULO ANGLICANO | DEFEN-
SIO | *Contra* | CLAUDII ANONYMI, aliàs SALMASII, | *Defensionem* |
REGIAM. | [arms] | *LONDINI,* | Typis DU GARDIANIS. | Anno Domini
1651. |

Another edition of No. 98, by Jean Jansson at Amsterdam. Duodecimo.
π^2 A-O^{12} P^{10} Q^6; [2] + xl + 330 pp. P6–7 perhaps used for π1–2; P8
is signed P6. [1–2], blank and missing; [i], title page; [ii], blank; [iii–xl],
preface; 1–330, work. Various states. Madan No. 9. Wing, M2168D. Copy
owned by John T. Shawcross, University of Kentucky.

111 JOANNIS MILTONI | Angli | PRO POPULO ANGLICANO | DEFEN-
SIO | *Contra* | CLAUDII ANONYMI, aliàs | SALMASII, | *Defensionem* |
REGIAM. | [different device] | *LONDINI,* | Typis DU GARDIANIS. |
Anno Domini   1651. |

Another edition of No. 98. Duodecimo. A-S^{12} T^6; xxxiv + 410 pp. [i],
title page; [ii], blank; [iii–xxxiv], preface; 1–389, work; [390–410], Index.
Madan No. 10. Wing, M2168E. Copy owned by New York Public Library.

112 JOANNIS MILTONS | Engelsmans | VERDEDIGINGH | des gemeene
Volcks van | Engelandt, | *Tegens* | CLAUDIUS *sonder Naem,* | alias |
Salmasius | Konincklijcke Verdedigingh. | [arms] | *Wt het Latijn overgeset,*
| Na de Copy gedruckt tot Londen, | by DU GARDIANIS. 1651. |

Dutch translation of No. 98, printed by G. de Hoeve at Gouda. Duodecimo.

A–O^{12} P^6; xxvi + 322 pp. [i], title page; [ii], blank; [iii–xxvi], preface; 1–319, work; [320–322], blank. Madan No. 11. Copy owned by William Andrews Clark Library.

113   London. Public Record Office. SP 25/96.

State paper, Columbia No. 21, dated 14 July 1651, copy in English, p. 29.

English draft of state paper translated into Latin by Milton (not discovered), p. 201. See Columbia Edition XIII, 637–638; Yale No. 27.

114   Oldenburg. Niedersächsische Staatsarchiv. Best. 20, Tit. 38, No. 73, fasc. 5.

Letter to Hermann Mylius, dated 7 November 1651, copy in Latin, scribal hand, No. 2; Columbia No. 50.

Letter to Hermann Mylius, dated 7 November 1651, original in Latin, scribal hand, No. 3; Columbia No. 50.

Letter to Hermann Mylius, dated 31 December 1651, original in Latin, scribal hand, No. 4; Columbia No. 52a. Date altered to 2 January 1652. Printed as Letter 11 in *Epistolarum Familiarium Liber Unus* (No. 317), in earlier version (?).

115   Oxford. Bodleian Library. Rawlinson MS A.2.

State paper, Columbia No. 23, To the Spanish Ambassador, dated 27 March 1651, draft in English, pp. 156–158.

Possible state paper, not given in Columbia, but referred to by Patrick, p. 553, as "a letter which the Council ordered Milton to send to the ambassador on March 27, 1651," citing *CSPD, 1651*, p. 134. Printed in English in *A Collection of the State Papers of John Thurloe, Esq*; London: Printed for the Executors of the Late Mr. Fletcher Gyles, Thomas Woodward, and Charles Davis, 1742. Ed. Thomas Birch. I, 175–176. Copy owned by New York Public Library.

116   Oxford. Bodleian Library. Rawlinson MS D.230.

Text and index of *Defensio prima*, plus quotations from Salmasius's *Defensio Regia*, Part 3, ff. 1–129. Date of MS: after 1651.

117   Simancas, Spain. Archivo General. Legajo 2528.

State paper (attributed). Columbia No. 170A, dated 21 January 1651, original and copy in Latin.

1652

118   Marquis of Bath. MS. Vol. XII of his MS Collection.

Letter to Bulstrode Whitelocke, dated 12 February 1651 (i. e., 1652), f. 41. Scribal hand.

119   Copenhagen. Rigsarkivet. T. K. U. A., A.II.16. Akter og dokumenter vedrørende det politiske forhold til England 1649-59.

Documents concerning the Danish-English peace negotations, including Latin and English originals, dated from 13 April 1652 through 2 October 1652; e. g., various versions of the Articles of Peace in Latin and English, and "The Answere of the Councell of State to the fourteen Articles," dated 8 July 1652, in English and in Latin ("Responsum Concilij Status ad quatuordecim Articulos").

120   Copenhagen. Rigsarkivet.

State paper, Columbia No. 24, original in Latin.

State paper, Columbia No. 29 (twice), original in English on which original in Latin is based.

State paper, Columbia No. 30 (twice), original in English on which original in Latin is based.

State paper, Columbia No. 35, original in Latin.

121   DECLARITIE | Van het | PARLAMENT | Van de Republijck | VAN | ENGELANT: | Verhalende de affairen ende het | procederen tusschen dese Repu- | blijcke, ende de Staten Generael | vande Vereenichde Provintien | van Nederlant, ende de tegen- | woordighe verschillen veroor- | saeckt aen de zijde van de Staten. | Getranslateert uyt het Engels. | [device] | TOT AMTSERDAM. | Gedruckt by Lieve de Lange, in 't jaer 1652. |

Dutch translation of No. 126. Quarto. A-B⁴; 16 pp. [1], title page; [2], blank; [3]-13, work (pp. 3-8 unpaged); 13, Tot den Leser; [14-16], blank. B (pp. 9-13) in reduced type. Copy owned by New York Public Library.

122   DECLARITIE | van't | Parlement van Enghelandt, | RAECKENDE | De Affairen ende Proceduren tusschen | de Republijcke en de Staten Generael van | de Vereenighde Nederlanden, | SAMPT | De Geschillen veroorsaeckt vander Staten zijde. | [device] | ———— | Na de Copye tot Londen, door last van 't Parlement, gedruckt | by Iohn Fielt, haren Ordinaris Drucker, 1652. |

Another Dutch translation of No. 126. Quarto. A⁴; 8 pp. [1], title page; [2], blank; [3-8], work. Copy owned by New York Public Library.

123 DECLARITIE | Van't | *PARLEMENT van Engelandt,* | *Raeckende* | De Affairen ende Proceduren tusschen dese Republijcke | en de Staten Generael vande Ver-eenighde | Nederlanden, | *Sampt* | De Geschillen ver-oorsaeckt van der | Staten zijde. | [device] | ———— | Nade Copye tot Londen, door last van't Parlement ghedruckt | by Iohn Fielt, haren ordinaris Drucker, 1652. |

Another edition of No. 122. Quarto. $A^4 B^2$; 12 pp. [1], title page; [2], blank; [3–11], work; [12], blank. Copy owned by New York Public Library.

124 DECLARITIE | Van't | Parlement van Engelandt, | RAKENDE | De Affairen ende Proceduren tusschen dese | Republijcke, en de Staten Generael van de Ver- | eenighde Nederlanden, | SAMPT | De Geschillen veroorsaeckt van der | Staten zijde. | [device] | Na de Copye tot Londen, | ———— | Door last van 't Parlement gedruckt, by John Fielt, | haren ordinaris Drucker, Anno 1652. |

Another edition of No. 122. Comma after "Engelandt" represented by a virgule. Quarto. A^4; 8 pp. [1], title page; [2], blank; [3–8], work. Copy owned by British Library.

125 LA | DECLARATION | DU | Parlement de la Republique | D'ANGLETERRE, | Sur les Affaires & Procedures entre cette | Republique, & les Estats Generaux des Provinces | Unies des Pays Bas; Et les Differens sur- | venus, dont les Estats ont donné le | sujet de leur part. | Et la Response du Parlement sur les trois | Memoires presentés par les Ambassadeurs Ex- | traordinaires des Estats Generaux, sur l'occa- | sion du Combat, qui s'est derniere- | ment donné entre les deux Flotes. | Avec la Relation de ce qui s'est passé au dit Combat entre la | Flote d'Angleterre & celle d'Hollande. | COMME AUSSI, | Un Récueil des Procedures du Traité commencé entre le | Parlement de la République d'Angleterre, & le Sr Pauw | Ambassadeur Extraordinaire des Estats Generaux | des Provinces Unies. | ———— | *Traduits fidelement de l'Anglois & imprimés par* | *Ordre du Conseil d'Estat.* | ———— | [ornamental device] | *A LONDRES;* | Par *Guil. Du Gard* Imprimeur dudit Conseil. 1652. |

French translation of No. 126. Quarto. A–K^4; ii + 78 pp. [i], title page; [ii], Au Lecteur; 1–15, Declaration; 16–76, various related documents including letters; [77–78], blank. Copy owned by Folger Shakespeare Library.

126 [decorated border] | A | DECLARATION | OF THE | Parliament of the Commonwealth | OF | ENGLAND, | Relating to the Affairs and Proceedings between this | *Commonwealth* and the States General of the United | Provinces of the *Low-Countreys,* and the present Differ- | ences occasioned on the STATES part. | And the ANSWER of the *Parliament* to Three

PAPERS | from the Ambassadors Extraordinary of the *States General,* | upon occasion of the late Fight between the *Fleets.* | With a NARRATIVE of the late Engagement betvveen | the English and Holland FLEET. | As also | A *Collection* of the Proceedings in the Treaty between the | Lord PAUW, Ambassador Extraordinary from the *States* | *General* of the United Provinces, and the Parliament | of the Commonwealth of ENGLAND. | ———— | Friday the Ninth of *Iuly,* 1652. | ORdered by the Parliament, *That no person whatsoever, with-* | *out particular License from the Parliament, do presume to* | *Print the Declaration (Entituled,* A Declaration of the Parlia- | ment of the Commonwealth of *England,* Relating to the Affairs | and Proceedings between this Commonvvealth and the States | General, *&c.) Nor any the Papers therewith printed, other then* | *the Printer to the Parliament.* | Hen: Scobell, Cleric. Parliamenti. | ———— | *London,* Printed by *Iohn Field,* Printer to the Parliament of *England,* 1652.

English version of work translated into Latin, which translation is ascribed to Milton, No. 157. See Columbia Edition XVIII, 10ff., and Columbia No. 167E.

Quarto. A-I^4; 72 pp. [1], title page; [2], blank; [3-14], text of Declaration; 15-16, Answer to Three Papers; 17-19, Narrative of the late Engagement; 20-70, Collection of the Proceedings; [71-72], blank and missing. Wing, E1511. Copy owned by New York Public Library.

127   [decorated border] | A | DECLARATION | OF THE | Parliament of the Commonwealth | OF | ENGLAND, | Relating to the Affairs and Proceedings between this | *Commonwealth* and the States General of the United | Provinces of the *Low-Countreys,* and the present Differ- | ences occasioned on the STATES part. | And the ANSWER of the *Parliament* to Three PAPERS | from the Ambassadors Extraordinary of the *States General,* | upon occasion of the late Fight between the *Fleets,* | With a NARRATIVE of the late Engagement betvveen | the English and Holland FLEET. | As also | A *Collection* of the Proceedings in the Treaty between the | Lord PAUW, Ambassador Extraordinary from the *States* | *General* of the United Provinces, and the Parliament | of the Commonwealth of ENGLAND. | ———— | Friday the Ninth of *Iuly,* 1652. | ORdered by the Parliament, *That no person whatsoever, with-* | *out particular License from the Parliament, do presume to* | *Print the Declaration (Entituled,* A Declaration of the Parlia- | ment of the Commonwealth of *England,* Relating to the Affairs | and Proceedings between this Commonvvealth and the States | General, *&c.) Nor any the Papers therewith printed, other then* | *the Printer to the Parliament.* | Hen: Scobell, Cleric. Parliamenti. | ———— | *London,* Printed by *Iohn Field,* Printer to the Parliament of *England,* 1652. |

Another issue of No. 126. See pp. 3, 6, 7, 15, etc. Pp. [71-72], blank and present. Issue not in Wing. Copy owned by New York Public Library.

128   [decorated border] | A | DECLARATION | OF THE | Parliament of the
Commonwealth | OF | ENGLAND, | Relating to the Affairs and Pro-
ceedings between this | *Commonwealth* and the States General of the United
| Provinces of the *Low-Countreys*, and the present Differ- | ences occasioned
on the STATES part. | And the ANSWER of the *Parliament* to Three
PAPERS | from the Ambassadors Extraordinary of the *States General*, | upon
occasion of the late Fight between the *Fleets*. | With a NARRATIVE of the
late Engagement betvveen | the English and Holland FLEET. | As also |
A *Collection* of the Proceedings in the Treaty between the | Lord PAUW,
Ambassador Extraordinary from the *States* | General of the United Provinces,
and the Parliament | of the Commonwealth of ENGLAND. | —––—— | Fri-
day the Ninth of *Iuly*, 1652. | ORdered by the Parliament, *That no person
whatsoever, with-* | *out particular License from the Parliament, do presume to* | *Print
the Declaration (Entituled,* A Declaration of the Parlia- | ment of the Com-
monwealth of *England*, Relating to the Affairs | and Proceedings between
this Commonvvealth and the States | General, *&c.*) *Nor any the Papers therewith
printed, other then* | *the Printer to the Parliament.* | Hen: Scobell, Cleric. Parliamen-
ti. | —––—— | *London*, Printed by *Iohn Field*, Printer to the Parliament of
England, 1652. |

Another issue of No. 126. See pp. 3, 6, 7, 19, 25, 27, 31, 40 (reset sigs.
A, C, D, E). Issue not in Wing. Copy owned by New York Public Library.

129   A | DECLARATION | OF THE | PARLIAMENT of the COMMON-
WEALTH | OF | ENGLAND, | Relating to the Affairs and Proceedings
be- | tween this *Common-wealth*, and the States Generall of the | United Prov-
inces of the *Low-Countreys*, and the pre- | sent Differences occasioned on the
STATES part. | And the ANSWER of the *Parliament* to Three PAPERS
from the Am- | bassadors Extraordinary of the *States Generall*, upon occa-
sion | of the late Fight between the *Fleets*. | With a NARRATIVE of the
late Engagement between the | *English* and *Holland* FLEET. | *As also* | A
Collection of the Proceedings in the Treaty between the Lord *Pauw*, | Am-
bassador Extraordinary from the *States Generall* of | the United Provinces,
and the Parliament of | the *Commonwealth* of ENGLAND. | —––—— | [device]
| —––—— | *Printed at* Leith *by* Evan Tyler, 1652. |

Another edition of No. 126. Quarto. A–E^4; 40 pp. [1], title page; [2], blank;
3–9, text of Declaration; 10–11, Answer of Parliament to Three Papers;
11–12, Narrative; 13–38, Collection of the Proceedings. Pp. 35–36 repeated
and error is continued. Not in Wing (1); Wing (2), E1511A. Copy owned
by New York Public Library.

130   DICHIARAZIONE | DEL PARLAMENTO DELLA | REPUBLICA
D'INGHILTERRA | Interno à gli affari, e maniere tennte tra questa
Republica | e gli Stati Generali delle Prouuincie Vnite de' Paesi | bessi; E

le differenze sopragiusta à che gli Sta- | ti hanno dato occasione dal canto loro. | *E la risposta del Parlamento alle tre memorie presentate* | *da gli Ambasciatori straordinari de gli Stati Gene-* | *rali in occasione della Battaglia, ch'è seguita* | *ultimamente tra le due Armati.* | Con en Relazione di quanto è passato in essa Battaglia tra l'Armata | d'Inghilterra, e quella d'Olanda, | COME ANCO | *Vna raccolta de i progressi del Trattato principiati fra il Parlamento della* | *Republica d'Inghilterra, e'l Sig. Pauu Ambasciatore straordinario* | *de gli Stati Generali delle Prouincie unite.* | [device] | IN FIRENZE | Nella Stamperia di S. A. S. MDCLII. | ———— | *Con licenza de' Superiori.* |

Italian translation of No. 126. Quarto. A–H A–B^4 χ^1; 64 + 18 pp. [1], title page; [2], blank; 3–64, discussion of the Anglo-Dutch negotiations; 1–18, Declaration. Copy owned by British Library.

131   'ΕΙΚΟΝΟΚΛΑ'ΣΤΗΣ, | OU | Réponse au Livre intitulé | 'ΕΙΚΩ'Ν ΒΑΣΙΛΙΚΗ̄: | OU | Le Pourtrait de sa Sacrée Majesté | durant sa Solitude & ses | Souffrances. | ———— | Par le Sr JEAN MILTON. | ———— | Traduite de l'Anglois sur la séconde | & plus ample Edition; & revûë | par l'Auteur. | A laquelle sont ajoûtées diverses Pièces, | mentionnées en ladite Réponse, | pour la plus grande com- | modité du Lecteur. | ———— | A *LONDRES* | Par *Guill. Du-Gard*, Imprimeur du | Conseil d'Etat, l'an 1652. Et se vend | par *Nicolas Bourne*, à la porte Mé- | ridionale de la vieille Bourse. |

French translation of No. 87. Translator: John Dury. Octavo. A^4 B–Z Aa–Ii^8 Kk^4; xxxii + 480 pp. [i], half title; [ii], quotations; [iii], title page; [iv], blank; [v–vii], Au Lecteur; [viii], errata; [ix–xxxi], preface; [xxxii], blank; 1–451, work; [452–456], Pamela's prayer; [457–477], other documents; [478–479], Contents; [480], blank. Two states: first state, C2 given as G2; p. 441 printed as p. 414; catchword "Préface" given on A4v and catchword on Kk2v given as "une"; second state corrects, omits catchword on A4v, and corrects catchword on Kk2v to "un' ". Wing, M2116. Copies owned by Yale University Library (first state) and Folger Shakespeare Library (second state).

132   Den Engelske Repub: | MANIFEST, | Hvor udi Parliamentet foregifver alle de | tvistige Stridigheder, som nu imellen | dennem oc de Høymectige | Herrer STATER | Aff de forenede Nederlandske | Provincier ere: | Først Tryckt tie Londen aff den Odinairis Bogtry- | cker, efster det Engelske Parliamentis eller Regierings | Befalning den 28. Julij, Anno 1652 | Menige Mand til villie aff det Engelske Sprog | paa Danske offversœt. | ———— | Prentet 1 Aar | ic. |

Danish translation of No. 126. Some commas represented by virgules. Quarto. A^4 B^2; 12 pp. [1], title page; [2], blank; [3–12], work. Copy owned by British Library.

133 Gazette (Paris). No. 132. 8 November 1652. Pp. 1045–56.

DECLARATION | DV PARLEMENT DE LA REPV- | blique d'Angleterre, sur les diffé- | rans d'entr'elle & les Estats Gé- | néraux des Provinces-vnies des Païs bas. |

Colophon: "A Paris, du Bureau d'Adresse, aux Galleries du Louvre, devant la rue S. Thomas, le 8 Novembre 1652." Discussion in French with citations from No. 126 in French translation. Folio. I12–L12. Copy owned by Yale University Library.

134 The Hague. Algemeen Rijksarchief. Staten Generaal 1329.

State paper, Columbia No. 167E and Yale No. 38, dated 15 March 1652, copy in Latin.

135 The Hague. Algemeen Rijksarchief. Staten Generaal 6915.

State paper, Columbia No. 167C, dated 30 January 1652, original in Latin.

State paper, Columbia No. 167D, dated 30 January 1652, original in Latin.

136 IOANNIS MILTONI | Angli | PRO POPULO ANGLICANO | DEFEN-SIO, | *Contra* | CLAUDII ANONYMI, aliàs SALMASII, | DEFEN-SIONEM | REGIAM. | [arms] | *LONDINI*, | Typis Du GARDIANIS, | Anno Domini   1652. |

Another edition of No. 98 from Gouda or Antwerp (?). Final "I" of "MILTONI" is only slightly larger than the rest of the type and is printed on a slant; it has been recorded as the same size as the rest of the type. Duodecimo. A–H^{12}; 192 pp. [1], title page; [2], blank; 3–16, preface; 17–192, work. Madan No. 12. Wing, M2169. Copy owned by University of Kentucky Library.

Copy owned by Columbia University Library has arms in color.

137 [JOANNIS MILTONI | Angli | PRO POPULO ANGLICANO | DEFEN-SIO, | *Contra* | CLAUDII ANONYMI, aliàs SALMASII, | DEFEN-SIONEM | REGIAM. | *LONDINI*, | Typis Du GARDIANIS, | Anno Domini   1652.]

Alleged reprint of No. 98 from Leipzig, printed by Hans Bauer and published by Tobias Riese; see Nos. *254–260*. No copy located. Probably a close reprint of a London or Dutch reprint. Not in Madan.

138 JOANNIS MILTONI | Angli | PRO POPULO ANGLICANO | DEFEN-SIO, | *Contra* | CLAUDII ANONYMI, aliàs SALMASII, | DEFEN-SIONEM | REGIAM. | *Cum Indice.* | [arms] | *LONDINI*, | Typis DU GAR-DIANIS, | Anno Domini   1652. |

Another edition of No. 98, by Theodorus ab Ackersdijck et Gisbertus à Zijll, at Utrecht. Duodecimo. A–M^{12}; 288 pp. [1], title page; [2], blank; 3–22, preface; 23–276, work; [277–288], Index. Comma after "SALMASII" is battered and looks like a period. Madan No. 13. Wing, M2169A. Copy owned by John T. Shawcross, University of Kentucky.

Variant states: see, for example, copy owned by University of Kentucky Library, which could lead to reportage of the number of pages in error. Page numbers 254, 273, 276 (last page of text) given as 274, 275, 278 respectively; device on p. 278 (*recte* 276) did not completely print; index title on p. [277] reads "RE'RUM".

139 Joannis Philippi | ANGLI | RESPONSIO | Ad | Apologiam *Anonymi* cu- | jusdam tenebrionis pro | *Rege* & *Populo Angli-* | *cano* infantissimam. | ———— | [ornaments] | ———— | *LONDINI,* | Typis *Du-gardianis.* An. Dom. | M. DC. LII. |

Author: John Phillips, but Milton apparently aided his nephew in writing this tract. Printed by William Dugard in London. Edition 1, perhaps printed in December 1651. Octavo. [A]^2 B–R^8 S^2; iv + 260 pp. S3–4 used for A1–2; note deckled S2 and errata leaf. [i], blank; [ii], errata; [iii], title page; [iv], blank; 1–39, introduction; [40], blank; 41–258, work; [259–260], blank and missing. Wing, P2098. Copy owned by Folger Shakespeare Library.

Copy in Union Theological Seminary Library (McAlpin Collection) is bound: [i], title page; [ii], blank; [iii], blank; [iv], errata.

140 JOANNIS PHILIPPI | ANGLI | RESPONSIO | AD | Apologiam *Anonymi* cujus- | dam tenebrionis pro Rege | & *Populo Anglicano* | infantissimam. | [arms] | *LONDINI.* | Typis DV·GARDIANIS. | *An. Dom.* M. DC. LII. |

Counterfeit reprint of No. 139. Printer seems to have been Jean Jansson, in Amsterdam. Hyphen in "DV-GARDIANIS" appears as if a period, and period after "DC." of date is hardly noticeable in copy reported; both are clear in Huntington Library copy. Duodecimo. A–D^{12} E^8; 112 pp. [1], title page; [2], blank; 3–19, introduction; [20], blank; 21–112, work. Copy owned by Princeton University Library.

141 JOANNIS PHILIPPI | ANGLI | RESPONSIO | AD | Apologiam *Anonymi* cujusdam | tenebrionis pro *Rege* &c | *Populo Anglicano* in- | fantissimam. | [arms] | *LONDINI,* | ———— | Typis DU-GARDIANIS. | An. Dom. M. DC. LII. |

Another edition of No. 139. Printer was Jean Jansson, in Amsterdam. Duodecimo. A–C^{12}; 72 pp. [1], title page; [2], blank; 3–13, introduction; [14], blank; 15–69, work; [70–72], blank. Copy owned by University of Kentucky Library.

142   IOANNIS PHILIPPI | ANGLI | RESPONSIO | AD | Apologiam *Anonymi*
       cujus- | dam tenebrionis pro *Rege* | & *Populo Anglicano* | infantissimam. |
       [device] | *LONDINI,* | Typis DV-GARDIANIS. | An. Dom. M. DC. LII. |

       Another edition of No. 139. Printer was Ludovic Elzevier in Leyden.
       Duodecimo. A–D^{12} E^8; 112 pp. [1], title page; [2], blank; 3-19, introduc-
       tion; [20], blank; 21-112, work. Copy owned by Henry E. Huntington
       Library.

143   London. Public Record Office. SP 25/66.

       State paper, Columbia No. 152 (Oldenburg Safeguard), copy in English,
       No. 16, pp. 324-326.

144   London. Public Record Office. SP 82/8.

       State paper, Columbia No. 18, dated March 1651 [1652], two copies in
       English, pp. 128-129, 130.

       State paper, Columbia No. 25, dated [13] April 1652, copy in English, p.
       132; copy in Latin, p. 134.

       State paper, Columbia No. 16, dated [13] April 1652, copy in English, p.
       136; copy in Latin, p. 138.

145   London. Public Record Office. SP 103/3.

       Safeguard for the Duke of Holstein, 1652, revised from Oldenburg Safeguard
       (Columbia No. 152), copy in Latin, pp. 52-53.

       State paper, Columbia No. 29, copy in English, pp. 265-266.

       State paper, Columbia No. 30, copy in English, pp. 266-268.

146   London. Public Record Office. SP 103/24.

       State paper, Columbia No. 152 (Oldenburg Safeguard), copy in English,
       pp. 54-55; two copies in Latin, pp. 170b-c and 216-217.

       Copy of 1652 Holstein Safeguard (see No. 145), in Latin, pp. 221-222.

147   MANIFEST | Der Repub: von | Engelandt, | Worin das Parliament alle
       die Streitig- | keiten enweisen, welche zwischen ihnen und den | Ho. Mo.
       Herren | STATEN | Der vereinigten Niederländischen | Provintzien sein.
       | Gedruckt zu Londen bey dem *ordinarien* Buchdrucker | auff Befehl des
       Parliaments von Engelandt | den 28. Julij 1652. | Aus dem Englischen ins
       Teutsche übergesetzet. | —— | Gedruckt im Jahr *M. DC. LII.* |

       German translation of No. 126. Commas represented by virgules. Quarto.

$A^4 B^2$; 12 pp. [1], title page; [2], blank; [3-12], work. Copy owned by British Library.

148   Das | MANIFEST, | Oder | Endtliche Crklärung von | Republicq von Engelandt. | Darinnen erzehlet werden | Die Reden, Ursachen, vnd Motiva, so selbige | Regierung vermeinet zu haben, vmb Rechtmässig den Krieg | den Hoch. vnnd mogenden Herren Staten General der Vereinigten Niederlanden | von Hollande, ic. anzuthun, in 13. Artickeln meist bestehend. | Auss der Engelländischen sprachen ins Teutsch v- | bersetzet durch ein Liebhaber der Warheit, vnd dess | Vatterlands. | Nach der zu Londen bey John Fielt, vnd zu Amsterdamb für | Crispin de Pas in beyden Sprachen gedruckten Copeyen nachgedruckt | [device] | Zu Cöllen, | Bey Caspar Erffens, in der S. Mariengartengass, | bey der Burchmawren. | Im Jahr der Geburt Christi 1652. |

Another German translation of No. 126 with thirteen Articles of Peace (see Columbia No. 167E). Most commas represented by virgules. Place: Cologne. Quarto. $[A]^4$; 8 pp. [1], title page; [2-4], Articles of Peace; [5-8], Manifesto. Copy owned by British Library.

149   Het Manifest | VAN | ENGELANDT, | Waer in verhaelt worden de reden en Moti- | ven die sy sustineren to hebben, om ons recht vaer- | diglijck den Oorlog aen to doen, bestaende | in 13. voorname Artijckelen. | *Vyt Engelsch ghetrowelijk overgeset in onse Ne- | derduytse Tale, door een Liefhebber des Vaderlandts.* | [device] | Naer de Copye, | In's Gravenhage, by Iacob Iansz. |

Dated: 1652. Does not publish the Declaration (No. 126); gives thirteen Articles of Peace (see Columbia No. 167E). Quarto. $[A]^2$; 4 pp. [1], title page; [2], foreword; [3-4], Articles of Peace. Partially in reduced type. Copy owned by British Library.

150   *Mercurius Politicus.* No. 91, 26 February-4 March 1652.

Sentence perhaps written by Milton according to French (III, 205-206), p. 1443: "First for *Kings*, give me leave to shew (what I once published upon another occasion) that tis no new thing for Kings to be deprived, or punish't with death for their crimes in government." Attribution denied by Elmer A. Beller in *Huntington Library Quarterly*, 5 (1942) 479-487. Copy owned by Morgan Library.

151   Oldenburg. Niedersächsische Staatsarchiv. Aa Grafschaft Oldenburg, Best. 20, Tit. 38, No. 73a, Litt. H.

Copies of state paper, Columbia No. 152 (Oldenburg Safeguard), Nos. 1 in Latin and 2 in English.

State paper, Columbia No. 39, dated 17 February 1652, original in English, No. 4.

State paper, Columbia No. 39, dated 17 February 1652, original in Latin, No. 5. With Milton's autograph signature.

152   Oldenburg. Niedersächsische Staatsarchiv. Best. 20, Tit. 38, No. 73, fasc. 5.

Letter to Hermann Mylius, dated 8 January 1652, original in Latin, No. 5 (scribal hand); Columbia No. 55.

Letter to Hermann Mylius, dated 20 January 1652, original in Latin, No. 6 (scribal hand); Columbia No. 57.

Letter to Hermann Mylius, dated 10 February 1652, original in Latin, No. 7 (scribal hand); Columbia No. 59.

Letter to Hermann Mylius, dated 13 February 1652, original in Latin, No. 8 (Edward Phillips's hand); Columbia No. 63.

Letter to Hermann Mylius, dated 21 February 1652, original in Latin, No. 9 (scribal hand); Columbia No. 65.

153   Oxford. Bodleian Library. Tanner MS 53.

State paper, Columbia No. 24, copy in English, f. 8.

State paper, Columbia No. 31, copy in English, f. 12.

State paper, Columbia No. 27, copy in English, f. 100.

State paper, Columbia No. 19, copy in English, f. 219.

154   Oxford. Bodleian Library. Tanner MS 55.

State paper, Columbia No. 39, dated 17 February 1652, copy in English, f. 137. Identified by Leo Miller as being in the hand of Gualter Frost, who thus may be credited with its composition.

155   Het Rechte | Manifest van | de Republijcke van | ENGELANDT, | Waer in het Parlament alle de verschillen | vertoont die tusschen haer en de Ho. Mo. Heeren | STATEN | Der Vereenichde Nederlanden sijn. | *Gedruckt tot Londen by d'Ordinaris Drucker, door last van het | Parlament van Engelandt den 28 Iulij 1652.* | [device] | Uyt het Engels in onse Nederduytsche Tale getrouwelijck overgeset. | Tot Rotterdam, Gedruckt by *Ian Gerritsz* aen de Marct, 1652. |

Dutch translation of No. 126. Quarto. A^4; 8 pp. [1], title page; [2-8], work. Copy owned by British Library.

156   HET RECHTE | MANIFEST | Van de Republijcke van | ENGELANDT,

| Waer het parelement alle de verschillen vertoont | die tusschen haer en de Ho. Mo. Heeren | STATEN | Der Vereenichde Nederlanden sijn. | *Gedruckt tot Londen by d'Ordinaris Drucker, door last van het* | *Parlement van Engelandt den 28 Julii* 1652. | [device] | Uyt het Engels in onse Nederduytsche Tale getrouwelijck overgeset. | ———— | Tot Rotterdam, Gedruckt by *Ian Gerritsz.* woonende | by het Marcktvelt inden Rommeyn. Anno 1652. |

Another edition of No. 155. Quarto. A^4; 8 pp. [1], title page; [2–8], work. Copy owned by British Library.

157   SCRIPTUM | Parlamenti Reipublicæ | ANGLIÆ | De iis quæ ab has Repub. cum Pote- | statibus Fœderatarum Belgii Provinciarum Ge- | neralibus, & quibus progressibus acta sunt; | déque controversiis in præsentia exortis, | quibus prædictæ Potestates occâsio- | nem præbuere. | Adjicitur & Responsum Parlamenti ad ternas chartu- | las à D^{nis} Legatis Potestatum generalium Ex- | traordinariis, ex occasione pugnæ nvalis inter | Anglorum & Belgarum classes consertæ. | Unà cum illius pugnæ, sicuti commissa est, narratione. | Postremò scripta illa in unum collata, quæ inter Parla- | mentum Reipub. Angliæ & D^{num} Adrianum Pauw, | Legatum Fœderatarum Belgiis Provinciarum Extraor- | dinarium, cum de pace agerent, ultro | citró- que reddita sunt. | ———— | [ornament] | ———— | *LONDINI,* | Typis *Du-Gardianis,* Anno Domini   1652. |

Attribution. Latin translation of No. 126. Quarto. A-K^4; ii + 78 pp. [i], title page; [ii], blank; 1–14, Scriptum; 15–74, numerous other relevant documents; [75], errata; [76–78], blank. See Columbia Edition XIII, 641, and XVIII, 8–79. Wing, E2285. Copy owned by British Library.

158   Simancas, Spain. Archivo General. Legajo 2528.

State paper, Columbia No. 8, dated 30 January 1652, copy in Latin.

State paper, Columbia No. 32, dated 11 November 1652, copy in Latin.

159   Stockholm. Riksarkivet.

State paper, Columbia No. 19, dated 11 March 1652, original in Latin.

1653

160   Kiel. Schleswig-Holsteinisches Landesarchiv. Abteilung 7.

File Nr. 499: Safeguard for the Duke of Holstein, dated 1 December 1653, original in Latin. See No. 145 in this bibliography.

File Nr. 1431: Copy of Safeguard for Oldenburg (Columbia No. 152), in Latin, altered into Safeguard for the Duke of Holstein.

File Nr. 1431: Printed text of Safeguard for the Duke of Holstein (1653), in Latin.

161   London. Public Record Office. SP 18/33.

State paper, Letter to John Bradshaw, dated 21 February 1653, p. 75. Scribal hand (Y).

162   Oxford. Bodleian Library. Rawlinson MS A.5.

State paper. Safeguard for the Duke of Holstein, Denmark, pp. 192–194. Undated. Copy in Latin.

Derived from the Safeguard for Count Oldenburg (Columbia No. 152) except for alterations of names. Not included in Columbia or Yale. Printed in *A Collection of the State Papers of John Thurloe, Esq;* London: Printed for the Executors of the Late Mr. Fletcher Gyles, Thomas Woodward, and Charles Davis, 1742. Ed. Thomas Birch. I, 385–386, where it is given as a copy of the Oldenburg Safeguard, which it is not, as pointed out by Robert T. Fallon. Copy owned by New York Public Library.

163   Oxford. Bodleian Library. Tanner MS 53.

State paper, Columbia No. 36, copy in English, ff. 188–189.

State paper, Columbia No. 37, copy in English, f. 199.

164   Venice. Archivio dello Stato. Senato, Secreta Dispacci, Francisco. Under date of 24 January 1653.

State paper, Columbia No. 36, original in Latin, dated 8 January 1653.

165   Zürich. Staatsarchiv.

State paper, Columbia No. 40, original in Latin, dated 18 November 1653.

1654

166   [ornamented border] | AN | APOLOGY | FOR | SMECTYMNUUS. | WITH THE | REASON | OF | CHURCH-GOVERNMENT. | ——— | BY | JOHN MELTOM, Gent. | ——— | [device] | ——— | *LONDON,* | Printed for *John Rothwell,* at the Fountain and Beare | in *Cheapside,* 1654. |

Reissue of Nos. 58 and 59, with new title page for volume (i. e., for *Apology*) but same title page for *Reason.* Quarto. π^1 A-G^4 H^2, π^1 A-H^4 χ^1; ii + 60, ii + 66 pp. [i], title page; [ii], blank; 1–59, text of *Apology*; 59, erratum; [60], blank; [i], title page for *Reason*; [ii], blank; 1–3, preface; 3–65, text of *Reason*; [66], errata. Wing, M2091. Copy owned by New York Public Library, with *Reason* bound separately.

167 [ornamented border] | AN | APOLOGY | FOR | SMECTYMNUUS˙ | WITH THE | REASON | OF | CHURCH-GOVERNMENT. | ——— | BY | JOHN MILTON, Gent. | ——— | [device] | ——— | *LONDON*, | Printed for *John Rothwell*, at the Fountain and Beare | in *Cheapside*, |

Variant issue of No. 166; reissue of Nos. 58 and 59, with new title page for volume. Note corrected spelling of name, lack of date, and position of period after "SMECTYMNUUS". Not in Wing. Copy owned by Christ's College Library, Cambridge, with *Reason* bound separately.

168 Artickel | Dess zwischen dem Durchleuchtigen Herrn, Herrn | Olivier Cromwel, Protectorn der Republic von Engel: Schott: | vnd Irland, rc. einer: vnd den Hochmögenden Herren General Staden | der Vereinigten Nieder- ländischen Provincien, anderseits, | zu Westmünster geschlossenen | ewigen | Friedens, Verein vnd | Verbündnuss. | [device] | Getruckt im Jahr M DC LIV. | ——— | Franckfurt, bey Wilhelm Serlin. |

Commas represented by virgules. German translation of the Dutch Articles of Peace. Quarto. A–B^4 C^2; 20 pp. [1], title page; [2], blank; 3–17, 33 Ar- ticles; 18–19, Cromwell's proclamation; 19–20, Dutch statement. Copy owned by British Library.

169 Articles de Paix, d'Union & | de Confederation, durable a perpetuité, con- clus entre, | le Serenissimae & tres-Haut Seigneur OLIVIER. | Seigneur Protecteur de la Republique d'Angleterre, | d'Escosse, & d'Irlande, &c. d'vne part: Et les Hauts & | Puissans Seigneurs les Estats Generaux des Provinces Vnies des Pays-bas d'autre. | [device] | A LA HAYE, | Chez la Veufue, & Heritiers de Hillebrand Jacobssz de Wouw, | Imprimeurs Ordinaires des Hauts & Puissants Seigneurs, Mes- | seigneurs les Estats Generaux des Pro- vinces Unies | du Pays-bas. A^o 1654. *Avec Privilege.* |

French translation of the Dutch Articles of Peace. Quarto. A–C^4; 24 pp. [1], title page; [2], blank; [3–18], 33 Articles; [18–19], Cromwell's proclama- tion; [19–21], Dutch statement; [22], English ratification; [22–23], Dutch ratification; [23–24], Dutch announcement. Copy owned by British Library.

170 [double-ruled border] | ARTICLES | OF | Peace, Union and Confedera- tion, | Concluded and Agreed | between his Highness | *OLIVER* Lord PRO- TECTOR | Of the Common-wealth of | ENGLAND, SCOTLAND & IRELAND, | and the Dominions thereto belonging. | And the Lords the STATES GENERAL | of the United Provinces of the | NETHERLANDS. | In a Treaty at *Westminster* bearing date the fift of *April* | Old Style, in the

year of our Lord God 1654. | ===== | *London*, Printed by *William du-Gard* and *Henry Hills*, | Printers to His Highness the Lord Protector, 1654. |

Official English text of the Articles of Peace. Folio. Eeee-Kkkk^2; 24 pp. [289], title page; [290], blank; 291-312, 33 Articles. Part of continuously (but erratically) signed and paged collection of state papers: *A Collection of All the Proclamations Passed* [etc.], 1654; Wing, C7046. *Articles* separately listed as Wing, C7040. Copy owned by British Library.

Copy in Trinity College Library, Dublin, is separated from collection but is the same edition. Edition listed as Wing, C7040D, the Folger Shakespeare Library, is also a copy of this printing.

171   THE | ARTICLES | Of the Perpetual | PEACE, | Concluded | Between His Highnesse | *OLIVER*, Lord PROTECTOR | of the Common-wealth of | *ENGLAND, SCOTLAND, & IRELAND*, &c. | on the one Part, | AND | The High and Mighty Lords, the | STATES-GENERAL | Of the United Netherlandish Provinces, | on the other Part. | ——— | Faithfully Translated out of the Dutch Copie, | Printed there, and now Reprinted at *London* | *May 2*, 1654. |

Another edition of the Articles of Peace. Quarto. A-B^4 C^2; ii + 18 pp. [i], title page; [ii], blank; 1-16, 33 Articles; 17, Dutch announcement; [18], blank. Wing, A3873. Copy owned by British Library.

Copy in Bodleian Library is a quarto (this edition), not a folio as reported under Wing, A3861.

172   ARTICOLI DI PACE. | Vnione, e Confederazione, conclusi, & accordati fra | S. A. Oliuiero Lord Protettore della Republica d'In | Ghilterra, Scorzia, & Hibernia, con li Dominij à | quelli appartenenti, & li Lords li Stati Gene- | rali delle Prouincie vnite delli Paesi Bassi. | *In vn Trattato tenuto à Westminster sotto dato di 5. Aprile Stilo vechionell'Anno del N. S. 1654.* |

Italian translation of the Articles of Peace. No title page. Included in Italian report of news (1653-56) with separate pagination. A^6; 12 pp. [1-8], 33 Articles; [8-9], Cromwell's proclamation; [9-10], Dutch statement; [10-11], English ratification; [11-12], Dutch ratification. Copy owned by British Library.

173   ARTICVLEN | Van den | VREDE, | Vereeniging, ende altijt- | duerendt Verbondt, | *Tusschen den Alder-doorluchtighsten ende Hooghsten Heer* | OLIVIER, | Heer Protecteur der Republijck van Engelandt, | Schotlandt en Yerlandt, &c. | ENDE | *De Hooghe en Moghende HEEREN* | STATEN GENERAEL | der Vereenichde Nederlantsche Provintien | ter ander zijde ghesloten. | [device] | Gedruckt na de originele Copye besloten tot Londen. 1654. |

Dutch translation of the Articles of Peace. Octavo. A^8; 16 pp. [1], title page; [2], blank; [3], poem on the peace; [4], blank; [5-16], 33 Articles, with marginal comments. Copy owned by British Library.

174 ARTICULEN | *VAN* | VREDE ende CONFEDE- | RATIE. | *Tusschen de* | REPUBLIQUE van ENGELANDT. | *Ende de* | STATEN GENERAEL, | van de Vereenighde Nederlantische Provintien. | [device] | *In Sehtaven Haege* | by de Weduwe ende Erfgenaem van Salomon van Wouteren. 1654. |

Dutch translation of an earlier version of the Articles of Peace. Quarto. A^4 B^2; 12 pp. [1], title page; [2-12], 29 Articles, with comments. Copy owned by British Library.

175 ARTICULEN | *VAN* | VREDE ende CONFEDE- | RATIE | *Tusschen de* | REPUBLIQUE van ENGELANDT, | *Ende de* | STATEN GEN ERAEL | van de Vereenighde Nederlantsche Provintien. | [device] | *Tot Harderwijck*, | Voor *RYCKAERT* de VREDE, in 't Iaer ons Heeren 1654. |

Dutch translation of an earlier version of the Articles of Peace; see No. 174. Quarto. A-B^4; 16 pp. [1], title page; [2], blank; [3-15], 29 Articles, with marginal comments; [16], blank. Copy owned by British Library.

176 ARTICULI | PACIS, | Unionis, & Confœderationis, | Inter | Serenissimum & Celsissimum Dominum, | OLIVARIUM, | Dominum PROTEC-TOREM | Reipub. *Angliæ, Scotiæ, & Hiberniæ*, ab unâ; | ET | Celsos, Potentésque Dominos, | ORDINES GENERALES | Fœderatarum Belgii Provinciarum | ab altera parte conclusæ. | ———— | *Ex originali transcriptum.* | ———— | *Excusam* | *Londini*, Typis *Guil. Du-Gard* & *Henr. Hills*, M̄. D̄C. L̄. I̅V̅. |

Official Latin text of the Articles of Peace. Quarto. A-D^4; ii + 30 pp. [i], title page; [ii], blank; 1-30, 33 Articles. Wing, C7043. Copy owned by British Library.

177 Articuli Pacis, Unionis, & | Confœderationis perpetuò duraturæ, inter Serenissi- | mum & Celsissimum Dominum OLIVARIVM, | Dominum Protectorem Reipublicæ Angliæ, Scotiæ & | Hiberniæ, &c. ab una; Et Celsos, Potentesque Domi- | nos Ordines Generales Fœderatarum Belgii Provincia- | rum ab altera parte, conclusæ. | [device] | *HAGÆ-COMITIS*, Typis Viduæ ac Hæredum Hillebrandi Jacobi á Wouw, Celso- | rum & Præ potentum Dominorum ordinum Generalium | Ordinarii Typographi. An- | no 1654. | *Cum Privilegio.* |

Dutch reprint of No. 176. Quarto. A-C^4; 24 pp. [1], title page; [2], blank; [3-16], 33 Articles; [17-18], state paper to the States General, dated 14

March 1654; [18-20], Dutch statement; [21-22], state paper to the States General, dated 19 April 1654; [22-23], Dutch ratification; [24], Dutch announcement. Copy owned by British Library.

178 ARTYKELEN | *VAN* | VREDE ende CONFEDE- | RATIE | *Tusschen de* | REPUBLYCK van ENGELANDT, | *Ende de* | STATEN GENERAEL | van de Vereenighde Nederlantsche Provintien. | [ornaments] | *Tot Wtrecht*, Voor *R*YCKAERT de VREDE, | in 't Iaer ons Heeren 1654. |

Reissue (?) of No. 175. Copy owned by British Library.

179 Basel. Staatsarchiv.

Parallel state paper, Columbia No. 170B, dated 17 March 1654, original in Latin.

180 Bremen. Staatsarchiv. W.9.b.1.

State paper, Columbia No. 48, dated 27 October 1654, copy in Latin.

State paper, Columbia No. 49, dated 27 October 1654, original in Latin.

181 Ewige | Friedens Artickeln | Welche getroffen | Zwischen Herrn Oliuarium Protectoren | der Republic | Engel- Scott-und Irlandt an einer, | Und | General Staten der Vereinigten Prouintzen | in Hollandt, anderer seyten: | Auss der in Latein getruckten Copey zu Londen Anno 1654. in die | Teutsche Sprach von einem vnpartheischen Patrioten vbergesezt mit | müglichem fleiss, ohne einiger Partheyen bewusten oder | vermeinten præjudiss. | [illustration] | Gedruckt zu Cölln, Bey Henrich Krafft an der Würffelpfort in der Sonn. |

Commas represented by virgules. Place: Cologne. Dated: 1654 (?). German translation of the Articles of Peace. Quarto. A-B^4; 16 pp. [1], title page; [2-14], 33 Articles; [14-15], Cromwell's proclamation; [15-16], Dutch statement. Copy owned by British Library.

182 EXTRACT | *Van de* | ARTICULEN | BERAEMT | *Tusschen de Republijcken van* | ENGELANT | *Ende de* | VEREENIGDE | NEDERLANDEN. | [device] | TOT AMSTERDAM, | *Voor Frans Claessen, op de Nieuwendijck.* | ANNO 1654. |

Version of No. 174. Quarto. A^4; 8 pp. [1], title page; [2], blank; [3-8], brief statements of 29 Articles. Copy owned by British Library.

183 Geneva. Archives d'État. Pièces Historiques, No. 3272.

State paper, Columbia No. 170B, dated 27 March 1654, original in Latin.

184 The Hague. Algemeen Rijksarchief. Box 5900.

Copy of *Articles of Peace, Union, and Confederation* in Latin, dated 28 April 1654. Copies of two versions of Cromwell's proclamation, in Dutch, dated 26 April 1654 and 28 April 1654.

185   *Joannis MiltonI* | ANGLI | PRO | POPULO ANGLICANO | DEFENSIO | SECUNDA. | Contra infamem libellum anonymum | cui titulus, | *Regii sanguinis clamor ad* | *cælum adversus parri-* | *cidas Anglicanos.* | ———— | LONDINI, | Typis Neucomianis, 1654. |

Edition 1. Octavo. π^1 A–L^{8}(–L8); ii + 174 pp. Probably L8 used for π1. At times stub of folded π appears between first and second gatherings; at times stub of blank L8 appears. [i], title page; [ii], blank; 1–173, work; [174], errata. Date: May. Wing, M2171. Copy owned by John T. Shawcross, University of Kentucky.

186   JOANNIS MILTONI | ANGLI | DEFENSIO | SECUNDA | *PRO* | POPULO ANGLICANO: | Contra infamem libellum | anonymum cui titulus, | *Regii sanguinis clamor ad coelum* | *adversus parricidas Anglicanos* | [device] | *LONDINI,* | Typis NEUCOMIANIS, 1654. |

Another edition of No. 185. False imprint from Adrian Vlacq, The Hague. Vlacq "I." "*PRO*" and "*LONDINI*" appear to be italics. Duodecimo. π^1 A–E^{12} F^{6}(–F3); ii + 130 pp. F3 used for π1. F1–6 (–F3) set in larger type (pp. 121–130). [i], title page; [ii], blank; 1–130, work. Copy owned by Christ's College Library, Cambridge; shelf mark: FF.5.6.

187   JOANNIS MILTONI | ANGLI | DEFENSIO | SECUNDA | *PRO* | POPULO | ANGLICANO: | Contra infamem libellum | anonymum cui titulus, | *Regii sanguinis clamor ad cælum* | *adversus parricidas Anglicanos.* | Editio secunda auctior & emendatior. | [ornaments] | *HAGÆ-COMITVM,* | Ex Typographia ADRIANI VLACQ. | ———— | M. DC. LIV. |

Another edition of No. 185. Duodecimo. π^8 A–E^{12} F^4; xvi + 128 pp. Apparently F5–12 used as π8. A–E^{12} reprinted from Vlacq "I" (No. 186); F^4 reset in same type as rest of volume. Vlacq "A" ("II"). [i–ii], blank; [iii], title page; [iv], blank; [v–xvi], Præfatio ad Lectorem; 1–128, work. Preface by Vlacq. Date: uncertain. Copy owned by Union Theological Seminary Library (McAlpin Collection).

188   JOANNIS MILTONI | DEFENSIO | SECUNDA | Pro Populo Anglicano: | Contra infamem Libellum anonymum, | cujus Titulus, *Regii sanguinis clamor* | *adversus parricidas Anglicanos.* | Accessit | ALEXANDRI MORI | Ecclesiastæ, Sacrarumque litterarum | Professoris | FIDES PUBLICA, | Contra calumnias IOANNIS MILTONI | Scurræ. | [ornament] | *HAGÆ-COMITVM,* | Ex Typographia ADRIANI VLACQ. | ———— | M. DC. LIV.

Reprint of No. 185 and reissue of No. *319*. Reissue of Vlacq "A" ("II"), No. 187, with π^8 reset and outer forme of F^4 reset to accommodate addition of More's tract. Vlacq "B" ("III"). Duodecimo. π^8 A–E^{12} F^4, A–E^{12} F^6; xvi + 128, 132 pp. [i], title page; [ii–iv], To the Reader, by Georgius Crant-zius; [v–xvi], Typographus Pro Se-Ipso, by Vlacq; 1–128, text of *Defensio secunda*; [1], title page for *Fides Publica*; [2], blank; 3–129, text of *Fides Publica*; [130–131], Typographus Lectori, by Vlacq; [132], blank.

Title page for *Fides Publica*:
ALEXANDRI | MORI | Ecclesiastæ & Sacrarum | Litterarum Professoris | FIDES PUBLICA, | *Contra Calumnias* | *IOANNIS MILTONI* | [ornament] | *HAGÆ-COMITVM,* | Ex Typographia ADRIANI VLACQ. | ———— | M. DC. LIV. |

Date: October 1654 or later. Copy owned by New York Public Library.

189   Laeste vast-ghestelde | ARTICULEN, | *Van* | VREDE ende CON-FOEDERATIE, | *Tusschen* | De Republijcke van ENGELLANDT, | Ende | De STATEN GENERAEL van de | Ver-eenighde Nederlandtsche | Pro-vincien. | Besloten ende verteyckent, tot West-Munster, door de | weder-zijdts Ghecommitteerden ende Ambassadeurs. | op den vijfden Aprilis, 1654 | [device] | *Ghedruckt tot Leeuvvarden,* | ———— | By CLAUDE FONTEYNE, Ordinaris Boeck-Drucker | der Edele Moghende Heeren Staten van Frieslandt. | [cropped] |

Another Dutch edition of the Articles of Peace. Incomplete copy. Dated: 1654 (?). A–C^4 [D^2 (?), missing]; 28 (?) pp. [1], title page; [2–22], 33 Ar-ticles; [23–24], Cromwell's proclamation; [25–28], missing. Copy owned by British Library.

190   LEONIS AB AITZEMA | HISTORIA | PACIS, | A | FOEDERATIS BELGIS. | AB | Anno cIɔ Iɔc xxi. ad hoc usque tempus | TRACTACTÆ. | [device] | LUGDUNI BATAVORUM, | Ex Officinâ JOANNIS & DANIELIS ELSEVIER, | Academiæ Typographorum. | — | cIɔ Iɔc LIV. | [rubricated] |

Quarto. *^{2} A–Z Aa–Zz Aaa–Zzz Aaaa–Zzzz Aaaaa–Rrrrr^4 Sssss^2; iv + 872 + 6 pp. Sssss3–4 used for *1–2. *Scriptum Parlamenti Reipub. Angliae*, pp. 803–810, with other pertinent documents, pp. 811–837. *Articuli Pacis, Vnionis, & Confoederationis*, pp. 853–862, thirty-three articles, with other documents generally printed with the *Articles of Peace* (Cromwell's declaration, Dutch answer, British ratification, Dutch ratification, Dutch statement), pp. 862–868. Copy owned by University of Chicago Library.

191   London. British Library. Additional MS 4156.

State paper, Columbia No. 49, dated 27 October 1654, copy in Latin, f. 95.

State paper, Columbia No. 46, dated July 1654, preliminary draft (?) in English, ff. 121–124. See Patrick, p. 675.

192 Oldenburg. Niedersächsische Staatsarchiv. Aa Grafschaft Oldenburg, Best. 20, Tit. 38, No. 83, fasc. 3.

State paper, Columbia No. 44, original in Latin, No. 47 (also 97).

State paper, Columbia No. 45, copy in Latin, dated 29 June 1654, No. 48 (also 98).

193 Over-gheset uyt de Latijn- | sche Tale. | Articulen van Vrede, Unie, | ende eeuwich Verbondt, besloten tusschen Syn Doorluch- | tighste Hoogheyt, den Heere OLIVIER, Heere Protector | vande Republijcque van Engelandt, Schotlandt ende Yr- | landt, etc. ter eenre: Ende de Hooge ende Mogende Heeren | Staten Generael der Vereenighde Nederlandtsche Provin- | tien, ter andere zyde. | [device] | IN 'sGRAVEN-HAGE, | By de Weduwe, eñ Erfgenamen van wylen Hillebrandt Iacobsz | van Wouw, Ordinaris Druckers vande Hoogh Mogende | Heeren Staten Generael. | Anno 1654. | *Met Privilegie.* |

Another Dutch translation of the Articles of Peace. Quarto. A–B^4 C^2; 20 pp. [1], title page; [2], blank; [3–13], 33 Articles; [14–15], Cromwell's proclamation; [15–16], Dutch statement; [16–17], English ratification; [17–18], Dutch ratification; [18–20], Dutch announcement. Copy owned by British Library.

194 Over-geset uyt de Latijn- | sche Tale. | Articulen van Vrede, Unie, | ende eenwigh Verbondt, besloten tusschen Sijne Doorluch- | tighste Hoogheyt, den Heere OLIVIER, Heere Protector | van de Republijcque van Engelandt, Schotlandt ende Yr- | landt, &c. ter eenre: Ende de Hooge ende Mogende Heeren | Staten Generael der Vereenighde Nederlandtsche Provin- | tien, ter andere zijde. | [device] | IN 'sGRAVEN-HAGE, | By de Weduwe, ende Erfgenamen van wylen Hillebrandt Jacobsz | van Wouw, Ordinaris Druckers van de Hoogh Mogende | Heeren Staten Generael. Anno 1654. | Mer Privilegie. |

Commas represented by virgules. A different issue of No. 193. Copy owned by University of Western Ontario Library.

195 [Over-gheset uyt de Latijnsche Tale. Articulen van Vrede ... besloten tusschen ... Olivier, Heere Protector vande Republicque van Engelandt, Schotlandt ende Yrlant ... Ende de ... Staten Generael der Vereenighde Nederlandtsche Provintien. R. de Vrede. 'sGravenhage, 1654.]

An alleged quarto edition listed in the British Library Catalogue, but destroyed. No other copy has been located.

196   Paris. Archives du Ministère des Affaires Étrangères. Corr. Pol. Angleterre.
       LXIII.

       State paper (attributed), copy in Latin, dated 29 June 1654, f. 475. See
       French III, 402–403.

197   Sidste, Sandferdige, oc Stand- | hafftige Forligte | Ereds oc Eorbunds | AR-
       TICULER, | Oc | CONFOEDERATION | Imellem Den Republic. af
       Engelland; oc de Stater | Generael aff de forene de Nederlandtske | Provin-
       cier. | Til West-Munster aff begge Parters com- | mitterende Ambassadeurs
       den 5. Aprilis | ANNO 1654. | Aff Originalen (først tryckt til Lecuvarden,)
       | oc nu paa Dantske udsat. | [device] | I Kiøben haffn, Aar 1654. |

       Danish translation of Articles of Peace. Most commas represented by
       virgules. Part German type. Quarto. A–B^4; 16 pp. [1], title page; [2–16],
       33 Articles. Copy owned by British Library.

198   [ornamented border] | SMECTYMNUUS REDIVIVUS. | BEING | An
       Answer to a Book, entituled, | AN HUMBLE | REMONSTRANCE. |
       In which, || The Originall of [bracket] LITURGY | EPISCOPACY [bracket]
       is discussed. || *And Quæres propounded concerning both.* | The PARITY of Bishops
       and Presbyters in Scrip- | ture Demonstrated. | The occasion of their IM-
       PARITY in Antiquity | discovered. | The DISPARITY of the Ancient and
       our Mo- | derne Bishops manifested. | The ANTIQUITY of ruling Elders
       in the Church | vindicated. | The PRELATICALL Church Bounded. |
       JEREMY 6.16. | *Thus saith the Lord, stand in the wayes, and behold, and aske
       for | the Old way, which is the way, and walk therein.* | Terrul. de præscr. adv.
       hæres. | *Id Dominicum & verum, quod prius traditum: id autem extraneum | & falsum
       quod sit posterius.* | ———— | LONDON, | Printed by *T. C.* for *John Rothwell,*
       at the Fountaine | and Beare in *Goldsmiths-row* in *Cheapside.* 1654. |

       Reprint of No. 48. Edited by Thomas Manton. Quarto. [A]^1 a^2 A^4(–A1)
       B–K^4; vi + 78 pp. a1–2 inserted between A1 and A2. [i], title page; [ii],
       blank; [iii–vi], To the Reader, by Manton; 1–71, work; 71–78, "A Postscript"
       (attributed). "A Postscript" is given on K. Wing, M784. Copy owned by
       Union Theological Seminary Library (McAlpin Collection). The Universi-
       ty of Kentucky copy of Joseph Hall's *A Humble Remonstrance* has Manton's
       preface transcribed by a seventeenth-century hand on a preceding leaf (rec-
       to and verso).

199   Stockholm. Riksarkivet.

       State paper, Columbia No. 46, dated 29 August 1654, original in Latin.

       State paper, Columbia No. 48, dated 27 October 1654, original in Latin.

200   [illustrated title page] | WITT'S | RECREATIONS | refined | & *Augmented,*

| *with* | Ingenious | CONCEITES | *for the wittie,* | *And* | Merrie Medicines | *for the* | Melancholie. | ———— | *See the next Page.* | Printed by M. S. sould by Edw: Archer in Little-Brittain. 1654. |

Title page:
[row of ornaments, top and bottom; rules on sides] | RECREATION | *FOR* | Ingenious Head-peeces. | OR, A | Pleasant Grove. | *FOR THEIR* | WITS TO WALK IN. | *Of* [bracket] || *Epigrams,* 700. | *Epitaphs,* 200. | *Fancies,* a number. | *Fantasticks,* abundance. || ———— | With their Addition, Multiplication, | and Division. | ———— | Mart. *Non cuique datur habere natum.* | ———— | *LONDON,* Printed by *M: Simmons,* in | *Aldersgate-*Street. 1654. |

Compiler: Sir John Mennes (?). Octavo. A–Z Aa–Bb^8; unpaged. "Old Hobsons Epitaph" (attributed), No. 148, on N6v. Wing, M1714. Copy owned by Library of Congress. Illustrated title page missing in copy owned by Princeton University Library.

1655

201   ARTICULI | PACIS UNIONIS, | *ET* | Confœderationis perpe- | tuò duraturæ, | *INTER* | *Serenissimum & Celsissimum,* | D. OLIVARIUM, D. Protecto- | rem Reipublicæ Angliæ, Scotiæ & | Hiberniæ, &c. ab una; & Celsos, | Potentesque Dominos Ordines Ge- | nerales Fœderatarum Belgii Pro- | vinciarum ab altera parte | conclusæ. | *Unâ eam Iconibus Præcipuorum Maris* | *Præfectorum.* | [device] | *AMSTELODAMI,* | Apud JACOBUM MEURSIAM, | Prostant apud JOANNEM JANSSONIUM Ju- | niorem, An. cIↃ Iↄ c LV. |

Another edition of the Dutch Articles of Peace. Duodecimo. A–B^{12}; 48 pp. [1], title page; [2], blank; [3]–22, 33 Articles; 22–24, Cromwell's proclamation; 25–27, Dutch statement; 27–29, English ratification; 29–32, Dutch ratification; 32–35, Dutch announcement; 35–38, state paper to Zeeland, dated 16 June 1654; 38–41, discussion; 41–42, further statement from Commission; 43–48, blank. Portraits tipped in. Copy owned by British Library.

202   [double-ruled border] | A | DECLARATION | OF | HIS | HIGHNES, | By the Advice of | HIS COUNCIL; | Setting forth, | On the Behalf of this *Commonwealth,* the | Justice of their Cause against | SPAIN. | ———— | [decorated arms in circle] | ———— | Friday the 26th of *October,* 1655. | *ORdered by His Highness the Lord Protector, and the Council,* | *That this Declaration be forthwith printed and published.* | Hen: Scobell, Clerk of the Council. | ———— | *LONDON,* | Printed by HENRY HILLS and JOHN FIELD, | Printers to His Highness, MDCLV. |

First edition from a series of such documents with continuous signatures and pages; cf. No. 170 in this bibliography. English version of work translated into Latin, which translation is ascribed to Milton; see No. 221. Columbia No. 169.

Folio. Hh–Pp^2; 32 pp. [113], title page; [114], blank; 115–142, work; [143–144], blank. Text in black letter. Wing, C7081. Copy owned by Columbia University Library.

203 A | DECLARATION | OF | HIS HIGHNES, | By the Advice of | HIS COUNCIL; | Setting forth, | On the behalf of this *Commonwealth*, the | Justice of their Cause Against | SPAIN: | ———— | [ornaments] | ———— | Friday the 26. of *October*, 1655. | *ORdered by His Highness the Lord Protector, and the Council,* | *That this Declaration be forthwith Printed and Published.* | Hen: Scobel, Clerk of the Council. | ———— | EDINBURGH, Re-printed by *Christopher Higgins*, in *Harts-* | Close, over against the Trone-Church. MDCLV. |

Reprint of No. 202. Quarto. A–B^4 C^2; 20 pp. [1], title page; [2], blank; 3–20, work. Not in Wing. Copy owned by Henry E. Huntington Library.

204 DECLARITIE | ofte | MANIFEST | Van | SYNHOOCHEYT | Door Advijs van | SYNEN RAEDT, | Thoonenede uyt de naem van dese *Republijck*, de Recht- | veerdicheyt van haer Sake tegens | *SPAENGIEN.* | Getranslateert uyt het Engels volgens de Copie ghedruckt by | *Henry Hills* ende *Iohn Field*, Druckers van *Sijn Hoocheyt.* | [device] | ANNO M. DC. LV. |

Dutch translation of No. 202. Quarto. A–B^4 C^2; 20 pp. [1], title page; 2–18, work; [19–20], blank. Copy owned by New York Public Library.

205 Gazette (Paris). No. 172. 22 December 1655. Pp. 1441–52.

SVITE DV | MANIFESTE | DE MYLORD PRO- | tecteur d'Angleterre, contre | l'Espagne. |

Paraphrase of Spanish treaty (No. 202); in French. Copy owned by New York Public Library.

206 Geneva. Archives d'État. Pièces Historiques. No. 3290.

State paper, Columbia No. 51, dated 25 May 1655, copy in Latin.

State paper, Columbia No. 59, dated 7 June 1655, original in Latin.

Possible state paper, Columbia No. 170B, dated 27 March 1655, original in Latin.

Possible state paper, Columbia No. 170C, dated 7 June 1655, original in Latin.

207   The Hague. Algemeen Rijksarchief. Box 5901, No. 2105. Formerly Staten Generaal 6915.

State paper, Columbia No. 54, dated 25 May 1655, original in Latin.

208   HISTORIARUM | NOSTRI | TEMPORIS. | *Authore* | ADOLPHO BRACHELIO. | *Pars Posterior* | In ANNUM 1652. Continuata, | *Cujus summarium Lector post secundum* | *folium reperiet,* | Adjecti in Fine Articuli Pacis inter Anglos & Ba- | tavos cum Iconibus Illustrium in navali | prælio virorum. | [emblem] | *AMSTELODAMI,* | Apud JACOBUM van MEURS | (alcographum. | Prostant Apud JOH. JANSSONIUM Junior. | Anno Dom. 1655. |

To this is added a copy of No. 201. B11–12 missing. Portraits tipped into Brachelius's work and after copy of *Articuli.* Copy owned by University of Illinois Library.

209   *Joannis Milton*I | ANGLI | PRO SE | DEFENSIO | CONTRA | *Alexandrum Morum* | ECCLESIASTEN, | Libelli famosi, cui titulus, | *Regii sanguinis clamor ad* | *cœlum adversùs Parricidas* | *Anglicanos,* authorem rectè | dictum. | ——— | [ornaments] | ——— | *LONDINI,* | Typis Neucomianis. 1655. |

Octavo. [A]^2 B–N^8 O^6; iv + 204 pp. O7–8 used for [A]^2. [i–ii], blank; [iii], title page; [iv], blank; 1–204, work. Variant states. Date: August. Wing, M2172. Copy owned by Christ's College Library, Cambridge.

210   IOANNIS MILTONI | ANGLI | *PRO SE* | DEFENSIO | *CONTRA* | ALEXANDRUM MORUM | ECCLESIASTEN, | Libelli famosi, cui titulus, *Regii* | *sanguinis clamor ad cœlum adversùs* | *Parricidas Anglicanos*, authorem | rectè dictum. | [device] | *HAGÆ-COMITVM,* | Ex Typographia ADRIANI VLACQ. | ——— | M. DC. LV. |

Reprint of No. 209. Duodecimo. π^4 A–H^{12} I^8; viii + 208 pp. I9–12 used for π^4. [i], title page; [ii], blank; [iii–viii], Typographus Lectori, by Vlacq; 1–144 and 149–211, work; [212], blank. Page numbers 145–148 omitted. Copy owned by Columbia University Library.

211   JOANNIS MILTONI | DEFENSIO | SECUNDA | Pro Populo Anglicano: |Contra infamem Libellum anonymum, | cujus Titulus, *Regii sanguinis clamor* | *adversus parricidas Anglicanos.* | Accessit | ALEXANDRI MORI | Ecclesiastæ Sacrarumque litterarum | Professoris | FIDES PUBLICA, | Contra calumnias IOANNIS MILTONI | Scurræ. | [ornament] | *HAGÆ-COMITVM,* | Ex Typographia ADRIANI VLACQ. | ——— | M. DC. LIV. |

Reprints of Nos. 185 and *319.* Reissue of Vlacq "B" ("III"), No. 188 (*Defensio secunda* and *Fides Publica*) combined with No. *349* (*Fides Publica* and *Sup-*

plementum). First part of No. 188: reissued unchanged; A–E^{12} of No. *349* was reset and F^6 G–K^{12} L^6 were reissued. Numerous differences in text. Vlacq "C" ("IV"). Date was not altered to 1655. Copy owned by Henry E. Huntington Library.

212 London. British Library. Harleian MS 6665.

Early draft of state paper, Columbia No. 54, in Latin, but addressed to Swiss Cantons, pp. 339–341.

213 London. Public Record Office. SP 31/3/98 (Transcripts from the French Archives). See No. 220.

State paper, Columbia No. 139, copy in Latin, pp. 15–16.

State paper, Columbia No. 112, copy in Latin, pp. 17–18.

State paper, Columbia No. 56, copy in Latin, pp. 82–84.

State paper, similar to Columbia No. 57, apparently a revision, in Latin, dated 31 July 1655, p. 85. See Columbia Edition XVIII, 650.

214 London. Public Record Office. SP 9/61.

De doctrina christiana. In hand of Daniel Skinner, Jeremy Picard, and others. Dating is uncertain: 1655?–1674?. First printed by Charles R. Sumner as *Joannis Miltoni Angli De Doctrina Christiana Libri Duo Posthumi, Quos Ex Schedis Manuscriptis Deprompsit*. Cantabrigiæ: Typis Academicis Excudit Joannes Smith, 1825.

215 London. Public Record Office. SP 92/24.

State paper, Columbia No. 54, copy in Latin, pp. 210–211.

State paper, Columbia No. 53, copy in Latin, pp. 212–213.

State paper, Columbia No. 139, copy in Latin, pp. 214–215.

State paper, Columbia No. 55, copy in Latin, pp. 216–217.

State paper, Columbia No. 51, copy in Latin, pp. 218–219.

All are close to versions printed in Samuel Morland's *History of the Evangelical Churches* (1658), No. 258; they may have been copied for him.

216 London. Public Record Office. SP 96/6.

State paper, Columbia No. 59, copy in Latin, p. 121.

217 MANIFEST | Oder | Erklärung, vorgebracht bey seiner Hochheit, | dem Protector | OLIVIER CROMWEL, | von seinen Räthen, | In dem Nahmen

der Republic, die Gerechtigkeit | derselben gegen Spanien betreffend. | Auss
der Engelländischen, in die Hochdeutsche Spraach übersetzt. | Im Jahr,
M. DC. LV. |

Most commas represented by virgules. German translation of No. 202.
Quarto. A–B^4; 16 pp. [1], title page; [2], blank; 3–16, work. Partially in
roman type, partially in German font. Copy owned by University of Kentucky Library.

218   EEN | MANIFEST | *Ofte* | Een Declaritie, gedaen by sijne | Hoogheydt,
den Protector *Olivier* | *Cromwel*, door advijs van sijne Raedt. | *Vertoonende
in den name van dese Republijcque,* | *de gerechtigheyt van hare saeck tegen* SPANGIEN.
| Vertaelt uyt de authentijcke Copye tot London, ge- | druckt by *Hendrick
Hills* en *Ian Field*, Druckers van | sijne HOOGHEYT, Anno 1655. | [device]
| t'AMSTELREDAM, | Voor *Ian Hendricks* en *Ian Rieuwertsz.*
Boeckverkoopers, 1655. |

Dutch translation of No. 202. Quarto. A–B^4; 16 pp. [1], title page; [2],
blank; [3–16], work. Copy owned by University of Kentucky Library.

219   MANIFIESTO | DEL | PROTECTOR | DE | INGLATERRA, | Hecho
con accuerdo de su Consejo, declarando à | fabor desta Republica, la Iustiçia
de su | Causa contra | ESPAÑA. | *Traduçido del Inglès en Español.* | [device]
| Viernes à 26. de Ottubre 1655. estilo viejo. | *Se ha ordenado por su Alteça
el Señor Protector y Consejo que esta Declaraçion* | *se estampe y publique luego. Fir-
mado.* Henrrique Escobel, *Secretario del* | *Consejo.* | ——— | LONDRES, |
Impreso por Henrrique Hills y Juan Field, Estampadores de su | Alteça.
1655. |

Spanish translation of No. 202. Quarto. A–C^4 D^2; 28 pp. [1], title page;
[2], blank; 3–27, work; [28], blank. Copy owned by Newberry Library.

220   Paris. Archives du Ministère des Affaires Étrangères. Corr. Pol., Angleterre.
LXVI.

State paper, Columbia No. 112, dated 25 May 1655, original in Latin, f. 60.

State paper, Columbia No. 139, dated 25 May 1655, copy in Latin, f. 61.

State paper, similar to Columbia No. 57, apparently a revision, dated 31
July 1655, original in Latin, f. 96. See Columbia Edition XVIII, 650.

State paper, Columbia No. 56, dated 31 July 1655, copy in Latin, f. 98.

221   [ruled border] | SCRIPTUM | DOM. PROTECTORIS | *Reipublicæ Angliæ,
Scotiæ, Hi-* | *berniæ,* &c. | Ex consensu atque sententiâ | CONCILII SUI
| EDITUM; | In quo hujus Reipublicæ Causa contra | HISPANOS | justa

esse demonstratur. | ———— | [device] | ———— | *LONDINI:* | Excudebant *Henricus Hills* & *Iohannes Field*, | Impressores Dom. Protectori. 1655. |

Attribution. Latin translation of No. 202. Quarto. A–F^4; iv + 44 pp. [i–ii], blank; [iii], title page; [iv], blank; 1–42, work; [43–44], blank. State paper, Columbia No. 169. Wing, C7165. Copy owned by University of Kentucky Library.

222   Turin. Archivio dello stato.

State paper, Columbia No. 51, dated 25 May 1655, copy in Latin.

State paper, Columbia No. 59, dated 7 June 1655, copy in Latin.

223   Zürich. Staatsarchiv.

State paper, Columbia No. 55, dated 25 May 1655, original in Latin.

1656

224   Amsterdam. Gemeentelijke Archiefdienst. MS 15-1, No. 15.

Original state paper to the City of Amsterdam, dated 13 June 1656, beginning "Tametsi potentes." In Latin. Variant of Columbia No. 142.

225   APOGRAPHUM | LITERARUM | *Serenissimi Protectoris* | OLIVERII GROMWELLI, | *Quas scripsit ad Excelsos & Præpotentes* | D. D. ORDINES GENERALES | FŒDERATI BELGII | *Die* $\frac{21}{31}$ *Augsti,* 1656. | Unà cum. |

RESPONSO eorundem ORDINUM | *AD* | D. PROTECTOREM | *Dato 22. Septembris* 1656. | [ornament] | ANNO M,DC.LVI. |

Place and publisher unknown. Quarto. [A]^2; 4 pp. [1], title page; [2–3], work; [4], Dutch response. State paper, Columbia No. 75, in Latin, dated 21 August 1656. Copy owned by British Library.

226   Brandenburg. Staatsarchiv.

State paper, Columbia No. 142, dated 13 June 1656, copy in Latin.

227   Copenhagen. Rigsarkivet.

State paper, Columbia No. 87, original in Latin.

228   The Hague. Algemeen Rijksarchief. Staten General, Box 5901.

Copy of Swedish treaty in Latin, Columbia No. 170. Usually dated ca. 22

April 1656; dated 22 September 1656 by later hand. Variations in introduction, articles 2 and 3 omitted, endorsements omitted.

Two copies of Swedish treaty, in Dutch, Columbia No. 170.

State paper, Columbia No. 75, original in Latin, dated 21 August 1656.

State paper, Columbia No. 70, dated 30 May 1656, original in Latin.

State paper, Columbia No. 69, dated 31 May 1656, original in Latin.

Variant state paper, Columbia No. 142, to United Provinces, dated 13 June 1656, original in Latin. Variations are due to changed recipient.

Copy of passport for Romswinckel, Columbia No. 141, dated 13 June 1656, in Latin.

State paper, Columbia No. 80, dated 10 September 1656, original in Latin.

229   LITERÆ | *AB* | OLIVARIO | PROTECTORE | ANGLIÆ &c. | *AD* | Sacram Regiam Majestatem | Sueciæ. | *Datæ 7. Februarij ANNO M,DC.LVI.* |

Place and publisher unknown. Quarto. [A]^2; 4 pp. [1], title page; [2], Address from Cromwell to Gustavus of Sweden; 3, work; 4, non-Miltonic letter to Ferdinand III of Germany. Work is state paper, Columbia No. 63, dated 7 February 1656. In Latin. Copy owned by University of Kentucky Library.

230   London. Public Record Office. SP 31/3/99 (Transcription from French Archives). See No. 238.

State paper, Columbia No. 146, copy in Latin, p. 8.

231   London. Public Record Office. SP 31/3/100 (Transcription from French Archives). See No. 238.

State paper, Columbia No. 74, copy in Latin, pp. 57–58.

232   London. Public Record Office. SP 103/69.

Swedish Treaty, Columbia No. 170, dated 17 July 1656, official copy in Latin, ff. 122–131 (but disbound).

233   MEMORIAEL | Ofte | SCHRIFT | Van | DON STEPHANO DE GAMARRA | Ambassadeur vanden CONINGH VAN SPANGIEN | Residerende in s' Graven-Hage, | overgegeren aende Heeren | STATEN GENERAEL | der Vereenichde Provintien den $\frac{21}{31}$ Iulij 1656. | Mitsgaders een | BRIEF | Van de Heere PROTECTOR CROMWEL | Aen | De

Heeren STATEN GENERAEL gedateert | den 21. Augusti 1656. | Ende
een | AMTWOORT Van de Heeren STATEN GENERAEL op de |
voorschreve brief, ghedateert den 22. September 1656. | ANNO M. DC.
LVI. |

Place: The Hague (?). Quarto.)(^{4} B^2; 12 pp. Printing of text is confused.
Order of signatures:)(1)(3)(4)(2 B1 B2; order of pages of text: 6, 7,
4, 5, 3, 8, 9, 10, 11.)(1r, p. [1], is the title page;)(1v, p. [2], gives text
of p. 6;)(2r, p. [7], is blank;)(2v, p. [8], gives text of p. 8;)(3r, p. [3],
gives text of p. 7;)(3v, p. [4], gives text of p. 4;)(4r, p. [5], gives text
of p. 5;)(4v, p. [6], gives text of p. 3; B1r, p. [9], gives text of p. 9; B1v,
p. [10], gives text of p. 10; B2r, p. [11], gives text of p. 11; B2v, p. [12],
is blank. State letter, Columbia, No. 75, in Dutch, appears on pp. 7-9,
i. e.,)(3r,)(2v, B1r, printed as pp. [3], [8], [9]. Copy owned by British
Library.

234 Oxford. Bodleian Library. Rawlinson MS A.14.

State paper. Letter to Hamet Basha, variant of Columbia No. 161, p. 402,
copy in English.

Printed in *A Collection of the State Papers of John Thurloe, Esq*; London: Printed
for the Executors of the Late Mr. Fletcher Gyles, Thomas Woodward, and
Charles Davis, 1742. Ed. Thomas Birch. I, 745. Copy owned by New York
Public Library.

235 Oxford. Bodleian Library. Rawlinson MS A.34.

State paper. Columbia No. 140, pp. 205-208, copy in English.

Printed in *A Collection of the State Papers of John Thurloe, Esq*; London: Printed
for the Executors of the Late Mr. Fletcher Gyles, Thomas Woodward, and
Charles Davis, 1742. Ed. Thomas Birch. IV, 415. Copy owned by New
York Public Library.

236 Oxford. Bodleian Library. Rawlinson MS A.42.

State paper, Columbia No. 75, copy in Latin, ff. 319-320.

Printed in *A Collection of the State Papers of John Thurloe, Esq*; London: Printed
for the Executors of the Late Mr. Fletcher Gyles, Thomas Woodward, and
Charles Davis, 1742. Ed. Thomas Birch. V, 330. Copy owned by New York
Public Library.

237 Oxford. Bodleian Library. Rawlinson MS A.58.

State paper. Preliminary draft of Swedish Treaty, Columbia No. 170, f.
188-188v, with notes of particulars, f. 190, copy in English.

Printed in *A Collection of the State Papers of John Thurloe, Esq*; London: Printed for the Executors of the Late Mr. Fletcher Gyles, Thomas Woodward, and Charles Davis, 1742. Ed. Thomas Birch. IV, 486–487. Copy owned by New York Public Library.

238   Paris. Archives du Ministère des Affaires Étrangères, Corr. Pol., Angleterre. LXVI.

State paper, Columbia No. 146, dated 14 April 1656, original in Latin.

State paper, Columbia No. 74, dated 25 September 1656, original in Latin.

239   Stockholm. Riksarkivet.

State paper, Columbia No. 63, dated 7 February 1656, original in Latin.

State paper, Columbia No. 67, dated 19 April 1656, original in Latin.

State paper, Columbia No. 72, dated 30 July 1656, original in Latin.

State paper, Columbia No. 75, dated August 1656, copy in Latin.

State paper, Columbia No. 83, dated 22 October 1656, original in Latin.

240   VERAX | PRODROMUS | IN | DELIRUM. |

Dated: 1656 (?). Place: Amsterdam (?). Quarto. A–B^4 C^2; 20 pp. [1], title page; [2], blank; 3–15, Verax Prodromus in Delirum; 16–18, state paper, Columbia No. 75; 19, answer from United Provinces; [20], blank. Copy owned by British Library.

1657

241   A | BANQUET | OF | JESTS | New and old. | *OR* | Change of Cheare | BEING | A COLLECTION | OF || [left-hand bracket] Modern *Jests* | Witty *Jeeres* | Pleasant *Taunts* | Merrie *Tales*. || ———— | The last *Edition*, much enlarged. | ———— | LONDON, | Printed for *R. Royston*, at the Angell | in Ivy Lane. 1657. |

Sometimes assigned to Archie Armstrong. Duodecimo. A–I^{12} K^4. "Another on the same" [Hobson], pp. 82–83. "Hobson's epitaph" (attributed), pp. 83–84. Wing, A3705. Copy owned by the Arents Collection, New York Public Library.

242   A | BOOK | OF THE | Continuation *of* Forreign Passages. | *That is,* | Of the Peace made between this Common-wealth, | & that of the united Prov-

inces of the Netherlands, | with all the Articles of that Peace. *Apr.* 5. 1654. | *And the* | Articles of Peace, Friendship and Entercourse agreed | between *England* and *Sweden*, in a Treaty at *Upsall.* | *May* 9. 1654. | *As also* | The substance of the Articles of the Treaty of Peace | betwixt *England* and *France.* Given at White Hall | the 20 of *Novemb*: 1655. | *From Generall* Blakes *Fleet,* | The Turks in *Argier* do consent to deliver up all the | English slaves, and desire a firme Peace for ever: | And in *Tunnis* Road we battered their Castle of | *Porta-ferina,* and set on fire their fleet in the Har- | bour. *Apr.* 9. 1655. | *MOREOVER,* | *An attempt on the Island of* Jamaica, *and taking the Town of St.* Jago de la viga, | *beating the Enemy from their Forts and Ordnance, being a body of* 3000 *men, and* | *so took possession of the Island,* May 10 1655. *With a full Description thereof.* | With a true Narrative of the late Successe which it hath pleased God to give | to some part of the Fleet of this Common-wealth, the Speaker, the Bridg- | water, the Plimouth Frigots, against the King of *Spains* West India Fleet: | the value of what is taken and possessed by the calculation of the Spaniards | about nine millions of pieces of eight, and 350 prisoners, and all this with- | out the losse of one vessell of the English, 1656. | *He hath shewed his people the power of his works, that he may give them* | *the heritage of the Heathen,* Psal. III. 6. | ———— | *LONDON:* Printed by *M. S.* for *Thomas Jenner* at the South-entrance | of the Royall Exchange. 1657. |

Printer: Matthew Simmons. Quarto. A–H⁴; ii + 62 pp. *"Articles of Peace, Friendship and Entercourse concluded and agreed between* England *and* Sweden. *May 9. 1654.",* pp. 10–20. In English. Swedish Treaty, made on 11 April 1654 and confirmed ca. May 1656 (according to Bulstrode Whitelocke). Latin version, "Foedus Anglicum," attributed to Milton, is dated 17 July 1656; Columbia No. 170. Wing, B3716. Copy owned by New York Public Library.

243 Bremen. Staatsarchiv. W.9.b.1.

Possible state paper, in Latin, dated 16 January 1657. See French IV, 132.

Possible state paper, in Latin, dated 30 June 1657. See French IV, 157–158.

244 Copenhagen. Rigsarkivet. T. K. U. A., A.II.16. Akter og dokumenter vedrørende det politiske forhold til England 1649–59.

Possible state paper to Frederick III (on Philip Meadows's credentials), "Cùm quod uterq Princeps Nobis Amicitiae foedere," dated 20 August 1657, signed by Cromwell, original in Latin. See Patrick, p. 800, and cf. Columbia No. 98 on Meadows.

Possible state paper to Frederick III (on William Jephson), "Ejus Celsitudo exortus hosce inter Regiam Majtem Sveciae, et Regem Daniae, belli motús perceperit," dated 19 October 1657, signed by Cromwell, original in Latin. Cf. other state papers on Jephson: Columbia Nos. 92, 94, 95, 96, 97, 99, 101.

245   [Gdańsk. Wojewódzkie Archiwum Pánstwowe. Formerly Staatsarchiv der Freien Stadt Danzig.]

State paper, Columbia No. 90, dated 10 April 1657, original in Latin. Location uncertain.

246   The Hague. Algemeen Rijksarchief. Box 5902^{I}.

State paper, Columbia No. 104, dated 12 November 1657, copy in Latin.

State paper, Columbia No. 104, dated 12 November 1657, original in Latin.

State paper, Columbia No. 105, dated 17 December 1657, two copies, one in Latin, one in Dutch and Latin.

247   The Hague. Algemeen Rijksarchief. Box 5902^{II}.

State paper, Columbia No. 105, dated 17 December 1657, original in Latin.

248   Kiel. Schleswig-Holsteinisches Landesarchiv. Abteilung 7.

File Nr. 1432: State paper, Columbia No. 99, dated 20 August 1657, original in Latin.

249   London. British Library. Additional MS 4157.

State paper, Columbia No. 103, dated October 1657, f. 176, copy in Latin.

250   Lubeck. Archiv der Hansestadt Lubeck.

State paper, Columbia No. 97, dated 20 August 1657, original in Latin.

251   Moscow. Archives.

State paper, Columbia No. 91, dated 10 April 1657, copy in Latin.

252   Oxford. Bodleian Library. Rawlinson MS A.46.

State paper. Columbia No. 92, copy in English, pp. 43-44.

Printed in *A Collection of the State Papers of John Thurloe, Esq;* London: Printed for the Executors of the Late Mr. Fletcher Gyles, Thomas Woodward, and Charles Davis, 1742. Ed. Thomas Birch. VI, 479. Copy owned by New York Public Library.

253   Oxford. Bodleian Library. Rawlinson MS A.53.

State paper. Instructions to Richard Bradshaw, variant of Columbia No. 164, copy in English, pp. 104-105v.

Printed in *A Collection of the State Papers of John Thurloe, Esq*; London: Printed for the Executors of the Late Mr. Fletcher Gyles, Thomas Woodward, and Charles Davis, 1742. Ed. Thomas Birch. VI, 278–279. Copy owned by New York Public Library.

254 Stockholm. Riksarkivet.

State paper, Columbia No. 92, dated 20 August 1657, original in Latin.

255 Venice. Collegio Secreta. Lettere Principi. Under 1 November 1657.

State paper, Columbia No. 103, original in Latin, dated 22 October 1657.

1658

256 [double-ruled border] | *The Cabinet-Council*: | Containing the Cheif ARTS | OF | EMPIRE, | And MYSTERIES of | STATE; | DISCABINETED | In *Political* and *Polemical Aphorisms*, | grounded on *Authority*, and *Experience*; | And illustrated with the choicest | Examples and Historical | Observations. | ———— | By the Ever-renowned Knight, | Sir WALTER RALEIGH, | Published | By JOHN MILTON, ESQ; | ———— | *Quis Martem tunicâ tectum Adamantinâ dignè scripserit?* | ———— | *London*, Printed by *Tho. Newcomb* for *Tho. John-* | *son* at the sign of the Key in St. *Pauls* Churchyard, | near the West-end. 1658. |

Erroneously attributed to Ralegh; by "T. B." Milton served as editor. Dated: May (?). Octavo. A^4 B–N^8 O^4; viii + 200 pp. [i], title page; [ii], blank; [iii–iv], To the Reader (signed: "John Milton."); [v–viii], Contents; 1–199, work; [200], blank. Variant states in sig. D. Wing, R156. Copy owned by University of Kentucky Library.

257 Florence. Archivo di Stato.

State paper, Columbia No. 117, dated 14 May 1658, original in Latin.

258 [double-ruled border] | THE | HISTORY | OF | The Evangelical Churches | Of the Valleys of | PIEMONT. | CONTAINING | A most exact *Geographical* Description of the Place, and | a faithfull Account of the Doctrine, Life, and Persecutions of | the Ancient Inhabitants. | TOGETHER, | With a most naked and punctual Relation of the late | BLOUDY MASSACRE, 1655. And a Narrative of | all the following Transactions, to the Year of Our LORD, | 1658. | All which are justified, partly by divers Ancient *Manuscripts* | written many hundred Years before CALVIN or LUTHER, and | partly by other most Authentick Attestations: The true | *Originals* of the greatest part whereof, are to be seen in their proper

Languages | by all the curious, in the Public *Library* of the famous Univer-
sity | of CAMBRIDGE | ———— | Collected and compiled with much pains
and industry, By *SAMUEL MORLAND*, Esq; | During his abode in *Geneva*,
in quality of HIS | HIGHNESS *Commissioner Extraordinary* for the Affairs
| of the said VALLEYS, and particularly for the | *Distribution* of the *Collected*
Moneys, among the remnant of | those poor distressed People. | ———— |
REVEL. 6.9. | And when he had opened the fifth Seal, I saw under the
Altar the souls of them that were slain for the word of God, | and for the
testimony which they held; And they cried with a loud voice saying, How
long O Lord, holy and | true, dost thou not judge and avenge our bloud
on them that dwell on the earth? [quotation in black letter] | ———— | *LON-*
DON. | Printed by *Henry Hills*, one of His Highness's Printers, for *Adoniram*
Byfield, and are to be sold at the three Bibles in *Cornhill*, next to *Popes-head* | Alley,
1658 | [rubricated] |

Red printing is often out of line; "CAMBRIDGE" overprints. Folio in fours.
A^6 a-e g-h B-Z Aa-Zz Aaa-Mmm ^{4}(-Mmm4) Nnn-Zzz Aaaa-Xxxx^4;
lxviii + 710 pp. Leaf Mmm4 missing; text and paging continuous. Printing of state papers in Latin and in English: Columbia No. 53, pp. 554–555;
Columbia No. 58, pp. 556–557; Columbia No. 54, pp. 558–560; Columbia
No. 55, pp. 561–562; Columbia No. 139, pp. 564–565; Columbia No. 51,
pp. 572–574; Columbia No. 56, pp. 609–611; Columbia No. 110, pp.
700–703; Columbia No. 111, pp. 703–705. Wing, M2779. Copy owned by
New York Public Library.

259   *Joannis MiltonI* | ANGLI | PRO |Populo Anglicano | DEFENSIO | Contra
Claudii Anonymi, aliàs | SALMASII | DEFENSIONEM REGIAM. | ————
| *Editio correctior & auctior, ab Autore* | *denue recognita.* | ———— | [ornaments]
| ———— | *LONDINI,* | Typis *Neucombianis*, Anno Dom. 1658. |

Revised edition of No. 98, with postscript (pp. 170–171). Duodecimo.
A-H^{12}; xvi + 176 pp. [i], title page; [ii], blank; [iii-xv], preface; [xvi],
blank; 1–171, work; [172], errata; [173–176], blank. Madan No. 14,Wing,
M2170. Copy owned by Columbia University Library.

260   London. Public Record Office. SP 31/3/102 (Transcription from French
Archives). See No. 262.

State paper, Yale No. 150, copy in Latin, p. 201.

261   New Haven, Connecticut. James Osborn Collection, Yale University. Commonplace Book. Shelf mark: b63.

Copy of "A Mask," dated 1658, drawn from 1645 *Poems* (No. 70), with title
page and dramatis personae. Separately paged; 42 pp. Commonplace Book
dated: 1600–1708.

262 Paris. Archives du Ministère des Affaires Étrangères, Corr. Pol., Angleterre. LXVI.

State paper, Yale No. 150, dated 20 May 1658, original in Latin.

263 Paris. Archives du Ministère des Affaires Étrangères, Corr. Pol., Angleterre. LXIX.

State paper, Columbia No. 118, dated 19 June 1658, copy in Latin.

State paper, Columbia No. 144, dated 1 July 1658, original in Latin.

State paper, Columbia No. 125, dated 6 September 1658, copy in Latin.

264 Stockholm, Riksarkivet.

State paper, Columbia No. 108, dated 2 April 1658, original in Latin.

State paper, Columbia No. 120, dated 4 June 1658, original in Latin.

State paper, Columbia No. 127, dated 13 November 1658, original in Latin.

265 WIT | RESTOR'D | In severall Select | POEMS | Not formerly publish't. | ——— | [device] | ——— | *LONDON,* | Printed for *R. Pollard, N. Brooks,* and | *T. Dring,* and are to be sold at the Old | *Exchange,* and in *Fleetstreet.* 1658. |

Compiler: Sir John Mennes (?). Octavo. [A]^1 B-O^8(-O8); ii + 190 pp. O8 used as [A]1. "Hobson's Epitaph" (attributed), pp. 83-84; "On the University Carrier," pp. 84-85; "Another on the same" [Hobson], pp. 85-86. Wing, M1719. Copy owned by Folger Shakespeare Library.

266 Zürich. Staatsarchiv.

State paper, Columbia No. 111, dated 26 May 1658, original in Latin.

1659

267 COMMENTARIOLUS | *DE* | STATU CONFOE- | DERATARUM PRO- | VINCIARUM BELGII. | *Editio quinta auctior & emendatior.* | AC-CESSIT | De eadam materia | PAULI MERULÆ | DIATRIBA. | Nec Non | *Decretum Ordd. Holl. & West-Frisiæ,* | *De Antiquo Iure Reip. Batavicæ,* | [ornaments] | HAGÆ-COMITUM, | ——— | Ex Typogr. ADRIANI VLACQ. | cIɔIɔ c LIX. |

Duodecimo(₊*₊)^6 A-H^{12} I^6; xii + 204 pp. Includes edition of the Latin Articles of Peace on H4-I5, pp. 175-202. [175], title page for Articles; [176], blank; 177–202, 33 Articles with abbreviated proclamation dated 28 April 1654.

Title page for Articles:
ARTICULI | PACIS. | UNIONIS, | ET | CONFOEDERATIONIS | Perpetuò duraturæ, inter Se- | renissimum & Celsissimum Domi- | num OLIVARIUM, Domi- | num Protectorem Reipubl. An- | gliæ, Scotiæ, & Hiberniæ, &c. ab | una: Et Celsos Potentesque Domi- | nas ORDINES GENERALES | Fœderatarum Belgii Provinciarum | ab altera parte conclusæ. |

Copy owned by British Library.

268 [ruled border] | Considerations | TOUCHING | The likeliest means to remove | HIRELINGS | out of the church. | Wherein is also discourc'd | Of || [left bracket] *Tithes,* | *Church-fees,* | *Church-revenues*; || And whether any maintenance of ministers can be settl'd | by law. | ———— | The author *J. M.* | ———— | *LONDON:* Printed by *T. N.* for *L. Chap-* | *man* at the Crown in Popes- | head Alley. 1659. |

Printer was Thomas Newcomb. Duodecimo. A–G^{12} H^6; xxiv + 156 pp. A12 missing. [i–ii], blank; [iii], title page; [iv], blank; [v–xxii], preface; [xxiii–xxiv], blank; 1–153, work; [154–156], blank. Dated: August. Wing, M2101. Copy owned by New York Public Library.

269 Copenhagen. Rigsarkivet. T. K. U. A., A.II.16. Akter og dokumenter vedrørende det politiske forhold til England 1649–59.

Four possible state papers, each dated 30 June 1659, and each beginning, "Cùm voluntate ac mutu." See French V, 454, citing only one. Originals in Latin. The letters introduce envoys Edward Montagu, Algernon Sidney, Sir Robert Honywood, and Thomas Boone, and the numerous copies (with slight variations) may indicate that a letter was delivered by each of the envoys.

Possible state paper to Frederick III, "Praedilectum Nobis et perquàm fidelem Edvardum Mountagu . . . Cujus ergo profectionem Majestate Vestra," dated 17 March 1659, signed by Richard Cromwell (twice), original and copy in Latin.

Possible state paper to Frederick III, "Sincerè Nobis dilectum et fidelem Philippem Meadowe Equitum," dated 30 June 1659, signed William Lenthall (twice), original and copy in Latin.

270 HISTORIARUM | NOSTRI | TEMPORIS. | *Authore* | ADOLPHO BRACHELIO. | *Pars Posterior* | In ANNUM 1652. Continuata, | *Cujus summarium Lector post secundum* | *folium reperiet,* | Adjecti in Fine Articuli Pacis

inter Anglos & Ba- | tavos cum Iconibus Illustrium in navali | prælio virorum. | [emblem] | *AMSTELODAMI,* | Apud JACOBUM van MEURS | (alcographum. | Prostant Apud JOH. JANSSONIUM Junior. | Anno Dom. 1659. |

Reissue of No. 208. Copy owned by Yale University Library.

271   New York City. Columbia University Library. Columbia MS. MS X823 M64 / S52.

Dated: after 1659. Two scribal hands. Contents: commonplace book entries (authorship uncertain), "Proposalls of certaine expedients for the preventing of a civill war now feard, & the settling of a firme government" (attributed), pp. 19–21; *A Letter to a Friend Occasioned by the Ruptures in the Commonwealth,* pp. 21–23; state papers, pp. 23–79. "Proposals" and some state papers first published in Columbia Edition XVIII, 221–226, 509–510, and XIII, 491–506.

State papers are those published in *Literae,* No. 321, except for two omissions, Columbia Nos. 20 and 43a; those in the Skinner MS (Columbia Nos. 137–150) except for Columbia Nos. 139–142; and ten additions, not authenticated as connected with Milton with certainty: Columbia Nos. 155–164. Columbia No. 49 (and No. 154) appears twice as Nos. 59 and 85, the latter being crossed out.

272   Stockholm. Riksarkivet.

State paper to Sweden (attributed), Columbia No. 135 bis, original and copy in Latin, dated 30 June 1659.

State paper, Columbia No. 129, dated 28 January 1659, original in Latin.

State paper, Columbia No. 150, dated 25 April 1659, original in Latin.

273   [ruled border] | A | TREATISE | OF | Civil Power | IN | Ecclesiastical causes: | *SHEWING* | That it is not lawfull for any | power on earth to compell | in matters of | Religion. | ——— | *The author* J. M. | ——— | *London,* Printed by *Tho. Newcomb,* | *Anno* 1659. |

Duodecimo. A–D^{12}; xii + 84 pp. [i], title page; [ii], blank; [iii–xii], preface; 1–83, work; [84], blank. Dated: February. Two states of text: State 1, "powr", p. 13; "*Feed*", p. 13; State 2 corrects. Wing, M2185. Copies owned by Yale University Library (State 1) and New York Public Library (State 2).

1660

274 BRIEF | NOTES | Upon a late | SERMON, | TITL'D, | *The Fear of God and the King*; | Preachd, and since Publishd, By | *MATTHEW GRIFFITH*, D. D. | And Chaplain to the late KING. | Wherin many Notorious Wrestings of Scripture, | and other Falsities are observd by *J. M.* | ——— | [emblem] | ——— | *LONDON*, | Printed in the Year   1660. |

Quarto. A–B⁴; ii + 14 pp. [i], title page; [ii], blank; 1–13, work; [14], blank. Two states of page numbers for 1 and 5: State 1, numbers reversed; State 2, corrected. Dated: April. Wing, M2097. Copies owned by Morgan Library (State 1) and New York Public Library (State 2).

275 THE | READIE & EASIE | WAY | TO | ESTABLISH | A | Free Commonwealth, | AND | The EXCELLENCE therof | Compar'd with | The inconveniences and dangers of | readmitting kingship in this nation. | ——— | *The author* J. M. | ——— | [ornaments] | ——— | *LONDON*, | Printed by *T. N.* and are to be sold by *Livewell Chapman* | at the Crown in Popes-Head Alley. 1660. |

Edition 1. Printer was Thomas Newcomb. Quarto. A–B⁴ C²; ii + 18 pp. [i], title page; [ii], blank; 1–18, work. Dated: March. See No. *487* for errata. Wing, M2173. Copy owned by New York Public Library.

276 [ruled border] | The readie and easie way | to establish a | free Commonwealth; | *and the excellence therof com* | *par'd with the inconveniencies* | *and dangers of readmit-* | *ting Kingship in* | *this Nation.* | ——— | The second edition revis'd and | augmented. | ——— | The author J. M. | ——— | [long dash] *et nos* | *consilium dedimus* Syllæ, *demus populo nunc.* | ——— | *LONDON*, | Printed for the Author, 1660. |

Edition 2 of No. 275. Duodecimo. A–D¹² E⁶; 108 pp. [1], title page; [2], blank; 3–108, work. Dated: early April. Wing, M2174. Copy owned by Harvard University Library.

277 [ornamented border] | SMECTYMNUUS REDIVIVUS. | BEING | An Answer to a Book, entituled, | AN HUMBLE | REMONSTRANCE. | *In which*, || The Original of [bracket] LITURGY | EPISCOPACY [bracket] is discussed. || *And Quæries propounded concerning both.* | The PARITY of Bishops and Presbyters in Scri- | pture demonstrated. | The occasion of the IMPARITY in Antiquity | discovered | The DISPARITY of the Ancient and our Mo- | dern Bishops manifested. | The ANTIQUITY of ruling Elders in the Church vindicated. | The PRELATICALL Church Bounded. | *Com-posed by five Learned and Orthodox Divines.* | ——— | JER. 6.16. | *Thus saith the Lord, stand in the wayes, and behold, and ask for the Old way, which* | *is the*

way, and walk therein. | Terrul. de præscr. adv. hæres. | *Id Dominicum & verum, quod prius traditum: id autem extraneum & falsum* | *quod sit posterius.* | ——— | *LONDON,* | Printed for *John Rothwell,* at the *Fountain* in *Goldsmiths-* | *Row* in *Cheapside.* And now republished, 1660. |

Reissue of No. 198 with new title page. See Wing, M785. Copy owned by Union Theological Seminary Library (McAlpin Collection). Wing, M786 and M788 are in error.

278   [double-ruled border] | Smectymnuus | Redivivus | Being an Answer to a Book, entitled | *AN HUMBLE* | REMONSTRANCE. | *In which,* | The original of || [bracket] LITURGY | EPISCOPACY [bracket] || is discussed. | *And Quæries propounded concerning both.* | The PARITY of Bishops and Presbyters in Scri- | pture demonstrated. | The occasion of the IMPARI-TY in Antiquity | discovered | The DISPARITY of the Ancient and our Mo- | dern Bishops manifested. | The ANTIQUITY of ruling Elders in the Church | vindicated. The PRELATICALL Church Bounded. | *Composed by five Learned and Orthodox Divines.* | ——— | JER. 6.16. | *Thus saith the Lord, stand in the wayes, and behold, and ask for the Old way, which* | *is the Way, and walk therein.* | Tertul. de præscr. adv. hæres. | *Id Dominicum & verum, quod prius traditum: id autem extranem & falsum* | *quod sit posterius.* | ——— | *LONDON,* | Printed for *John Rothwell,* at the *Fountain* in *Goldsmiths-* | *Row* in *Cheapside.* And now republished, 1660. |

Different reissue of No. 198 with new title page; see No. 277. See Wing, M785. Copy owned by Princeton Theological Seminary Library.

1661

279   APHORISMS | OF | STATE, | GROUNDED | On Authority and Experi- | ence, and illustrated with the choycest Examples and Hi- | storical Obser- vations. | ——— | By Sr. WALTER RALEIGH Kt. | ——— | [device] | *LONDON,* | Printed for *Tho. Johnson,* at the Golden | Key in St. *Paul's* Church-yard, 1661. |

Reissue of No. 256. Octavo. A^4(± A1, –A2) B–N^8 O^4; vi + 200 pp. A1-2 cancelled; stub present between replacement A1 and A3. [i], title page; [ii], blank; [iii–vi], Contents; 1–199, work; [200], blank. Cancelled A2, former pp. [iii–iv], would have printed Milton's "To the Reader." Running title: "The Cabinet-Council". Wing, R153. Copy owned by Balliol College Library, Oxford.

280   [double-ruled border] | Smectymnuus | REDIVIVUS. | Being an Answer to a Book, intituled | *AN HUMBLE* | REMONSTRANCE | *In which* ||

The Original of [bracket] LITURGY | EPISCOPACY [bracket] is discussed || *And Queries propounded concerning both.* | The PARITY of Bishops and Presbyters in Scripture de- | monstrated. | The occasion of the IMPARI-TY in Antiquity disco- | vered. | The *Disparity* of the Ancient and our Modern Bishops ma- | nifested | The ANTIQUITY of Ruling Elders in the Church | vindicated. | The PRELATICAL Church Bounded. | *Composed by five Learned and Orthodox Divines.* | ———— | THE Fifth EDITION. | ———— | JER. 6. 16. | *Thus saith the Lord, stand in the ways, and behold, and aske for the Old way, which* | *is the way, and walk therein.* | Ter. de Præs. adv. hæres. | *Id Dominicum & verum, quod prius traditum: id autem extraneum & falsum quod* | *sit posterius.* | ———— | *LONDON,* | Printed for *John Rothwell,* at the *Fountain* in *Goldsmiths-Row* in | *Cheapside,* 1661. |

Another edition of No. 198. Quarto. A^2 A-I^4 K^2; vi + 74 pp. K3-4 used for A^2. [i], title page; [ii], blank; [iii-vi], Thomas Manton's To the Reader; 1-68, work; 68-73, Postscript (attributed); [74], blank. Last paragraph of p. 73 in reduced type. Wing, M787. Copy owned by John Carter Brown Library, Brown University.

1662

281   [double-ruled border] | THE | LIFE | AND | DEATH | OF | Sir Henry Vane, K$^{t.}$ | OR, | A short *Narrative* of the main *Passages* of his | Earthly Pilgrimage; Together with a true Account | of his purely Christian, Peaceable, Spiritual, GOS- | PEL-PRINCIPLES, DOCTRINE, LIFE, and | WAY of WORSHIPPING GOD, for which he | Suffered Contradiction and Reproach from all sorts | of Sinners, and at last, a violent Death, *June* 14. | *Anno,* 1662. | To which is added, His last EXHORTATION to | his Children, the day before his Death. | ———— | Printed in the Year, 1662. |

Author: George Sikes. Place: London. Quarto. A-V^4 X^2; 164 pp. Sonnet 17 given on pp. 93-94, with allusion. Wing, S3780. Copy owned by University of Kentucky Library.

1663

282   M$^{R.}$ WILLIAM | SHAKESPEARES | Comedies, Histories, and Tragedies. | Published according to the true Original Copies. | *The Third Impression.* | [portrait] | *LONDON,* | Printed for *Philip Chetwinde,* 1663. |

Edition 3, Issue 1, of No. 27. Contains seven additional plays. Folio in sixes. Preliminary leaves, a^4 b^6, with a3 marked A2. "An Epitaph on the admirable

Dramatick Poet, W. Shakespeare," b5, in variant text, including "starre-ypointing" (as in Effigies C). Wing, S2913. Copy owned by Berg Collection, New York Public Library.

283   MR. WILLIAM | SHAKESPEARES | Comedies, Histories, and Tragedies. | Published according to the true Original Copies. | *The Third Impression.* | *LONDON,* | Printed for *Philip Chetwinde,* 1663. |

Reissue of No. 282. Title page, without portrait, laid in. Apparently transitional title page between Issue 1 and Issue 2 (No. 287). Not in Wing. Copy owned by New York Public Library.

284   [illustrated title page] | WITT'S | RECREATIONS | refined | & *Augmented,* | *with* | Ingenious | CONCEITES | *for the wittie,* | *And* | Merrie Medicines | *for the* | Melancholie. | ——— | *See the next Page.* | Printed by M: Symmons and S: Symmons 1663. |

Reissue of No. 200 with 1654 title page intact. See Wing, W3222. Copy owned by Princeton University Library.

285   [illustrated title page] | WITT'S | RECREATIONS | refined | & *Augmented,* | *with* | Ingenious | CONCEITES | *for the wittie,* | *And* | Merrie Medicines | *for the* | Melancholie. | ——— | *See the next Page.* | Printed by M: Symmons and S: Symmons   1663. |

Title page:
[ruled border] | RECREATION | *FOR* | Ingenious Head-peeces. | OR, A | Pleasant Grove. | *FOR THEIR* | WITS TO WALK IN. | *Of* [bracket] || *Epigrams,* 700. | *Epitaphs,* 200. | *Fancies,* a number. | *Fantasticks,* abundance. || ——— | With their new Addition, Multipli- | cation, and Division. | ——— | Mart. *Non cuique datur habere nasum.* | ——— | LONDON, *Printed by* S. Simmons, *in* | Aldersgate-*Street.* 1663. |

Reissue of No. 200 with 1663 illustrated title page (No. 284) and a new title page for 1663. See Wing, W3222. Copy owned by Library of Congress. Copy owned by Bodleian Library does not have illustrated title page.

286   [illustrated title page] | WITT'S | RECREATIONS | refined | & *Augmented,* | *with* | Ingenious | CONCEITES | *for the wittie,* | *And* | Merrie Medicines | *for the* | Melancholie. | ——— | *See the next Page.* | Printed by M: Symmons and S: Symmons   1663. |

Title page:
[ruled border] | RECREATION | *FOR* | Ingenious Head-Peeces: | OR A | Pleasant Grove | *FOR THEIR* | WITS TO WALK IN. | *Of* [bracket] || *Epigrams,* 700. | *Epitaphs,* 200. | *Fancies,* a number. | *Fantasticks,* abundance. || ——— | With their new Addition, Multipli- | cation and Division. |

——— | Mart. *Non cuique datur habere nasum.* | ——— | *LONDON*, Printed for *John Stafford*, living in | *George*-Yard near *Fleet-Bride.* |

Reissue of No. 200 with 1663 illustrated title page (No. 284) and a new title page. Dated: 1663; see p. [432]. Apparently Wing, M1715. Copy owned by Henry E. Huntington Library.

1664

287 M^R· WILLIAM | SHAKESPEAR'S | Comedies, Histories, and Tragedies. | Published according to the true Original Copies. | *The third Impression.* | And unto this Impression is added seven Playes, never | before Printed in Folio. | *viz.* | *Pericles* Prince of *Tyre.* | The *London Prodigall.* | The History of *Thomas* L^d· *Cromwell.* | Sir *John Oldcastle* Lord *Cobham.* | The *Puritan Widow.* | A *York-shire* Tragedy. | The Tragedy of *Locrine.* | [device] | *LONDON*, Printed for *P. C.* 1664. |

Edition 3, Issue 2 (see Nos. 282 and 283), of No. 27. Printed for Philip Chetwinde. Folio in sixes. Preliminary leaves, a^4 b^6, with a3 marked A2. "An Epitaph on the admirable Dramatick Poet, W. Shakespeare," b5, in variant text, including "starre-ypointing" (as in Effigies C). Wing, S2914. Copy owned by New York Public Library.

1665

288 New York City. J. Pierpont Morgan Library. MS of *Paradise Lost*, Book I.

Dated: ca. 1665. Scribal hand, with various scribal correctors, including Edward Phillips. Copy text for Edition 1, 1667 (No. 291). First published in facsimile by Helen Darbishire, ed. *The Manuscript of Milton's Paradise Lost Book I.* Oxford: Clarendon Press, 1931.

289 [illustrated title page] | WITT'S | RECREATIONS | refined | & *Augmented*, | *with* | Ingenious CONCEITES | *for the wittie,* | *And* | Merrie Medicines | *for the* | Melancholie. | ——— | *See the next Page.* | Printed by M: Symmons and, S: Symmons 1663. |

Title page:
[ruled border] | RECREATION | *FOR* | Ingenious Head-Peeces: | OR A | Pleasant Grove | *FOR THEIR* | WITS TO WALK IN. || Of [bracket] *Epigrams*, 700. | *Epitaphs*, 200. | *Fancies*, a number. | *Fantasticks*, abundance.

|| ——— | With their new Addition, Multipli- | cation and Division. | ——— | Mart. *Non cuique datur habere nasum.* | ——— | *LONDON*, Printed for John Stafford, living in | *George-*Yard near *Fleet-Bridge.* 1665. |

Reissue of No. 200 with 1663 illustrated title page slightly redrawn (No. 284) and a new title page (cf. No. 286). Not in Wing. Copy owned by the Arents Collection, New York Public Library.

1667

290 Kassel. Murhardsche Bibliothek der Stadt Kassel. Poet. MS 4° 2.

"Das Verlustigte Paradeiss auss und nach dem Englishchen I. M. durch T. H. zu übersetzen angefangen—voluisse sat": German verse translation of *Paradise Lost* I–III and beginning of IV, by Theodore Haak. Dating uncertain: ca. 1667–ca. 1680.

Holograph. Quarto. 56 pp. Printed in Pamela R. Barnett. *Theodore Haak, F. R. S. (1605–1690). The First German Translator of* Paradise Lost. 'S-Gravenhage: Mouton and Co., 1962. Appendix 3, pp. 189–260.

291 [double-ruled border] | Paradise lost. | A | POEM | Written in | TEN BOOKS | By *JOHN MILTON.* | ——— | Licensed and Entred according | to Order. | ——— | *LONDON* | Printed, and are to be sold by *Peter Parker* | under *Creed* Church neer *Aldgate*; And by | *Robert Boulter* at the *Turks Head* in *Bishopsgate-street*; | And *Matthias Walker*, under St. *Dunstons* Church | in *Fleet-street*, 1667. |

Edition 1, Issue 1. Printer: Samuel Simmons. Quarto. π^2 A–Z Aa–Tt^4 Vv^2; iv + 340 pp. [i–ii], blank; [iii], title page; [iv], blank; [1–340], work. Vv3–4 were used to print π^2. Two and three states of text. Dated: August. Wing, M2136. Copy owned by New York Public Library.

292 [double-ruled border] | Paradise lost. | A | POEM | Written in | TEN BOOKS | By *JOHN MILTON.* | ——— | Licensed and Entred according | to Order. | ——— | *LONDON* | Printed, and are to be sold by *Peter Parker* | under *Creed* Church neer *Aldgate*; And by | *Robert Boulter* at the *Turks Head* in *Bishopsgate-street*; | And *Matthias Walker*, under St. *Dunstons* Church | in *Fleet-street*, 1667. |

Edition 1, Issue 2, of No. 291. Title page has typographical differences and appears with slight variations; most notable is reduction of size of type for "By *JOHN MILTON.*" Wing, M2137. Copy owned by New York Public Library.

293 [illustrated title page] | WITT'S | RECREATIONS | refined | & *Augmented*, | *with* | Ingenious CONCEITES | *for the wittie*, | *And* | Merrie Medicines | *for the* | Melancholie. | ———— | *See the next Page.* | Printed by M: Symmons and, S: Symmons   1663. |

Title page:
[double-ruled border] | Recreation, | FOR | Ingenious Head-Pieces: | OR, A | Pleasant Grove | FOR THEIR WITS TO WALK IN, | Of [bracket] || *Epigrams*, 700. | *Epitaphs*, 200. | *Fancies*, a Number. | *Fantasticks*, Abundance. || ———— | With their Addition, Multiplication | and Division. | ———— | Mart. *Non cuique datur habere nasum.* | ———— | *LONDON*, Printed by *S. Simmons* in | *Aldersgate*-Street, 1667. |

Reissue of No. 200 with variant 1663 illustrated title page (cf. No. 284) and new title page. Wing, M1716. Copy owned by British Library.

294 [illustrated title page] | WITT'S | RECREATIONS | refined | & *Augmented*, | *with* | Ingenious CONCEITES | *for the wittie*, | *And* | Merrie Medicines | *for the* | Melancholie. | ———— | *See the next Page.* | Printed by M: Symmons and, S: Symmons   1663. |

Title page:
[ruled border] | Recreation, | FOR | Ingenious Head-Pieces: | OR, A | Pleasant Grove | FOR THEIR | WITS TO WALK IN, || Of [bracket] *Epigrams*, 700. | *Epitaphs*, 200. | *Fancies*, a Number. | *Fantasticks*, Abundance. || ———— | With their Addition, Multiplication | and Division. | ———— | Mart. *Non cuique datur habere nasum.* | ———— | *LONDON*, Printed by *S. Simmons*, and | are to be sold by *Thomas Helder*, at the *Angel* in | *Little Britain*, 1667. |

Reissue of No. 200 with 1663 illustrated title page (cf. No. 284) and new title page. See Wing, M1717. Copy owned by Arents Collection, New York Public Library. Copy in Henry E. Huntington Library has date 1663 on illustrated title page altered in ink to 1667.

295 [illustrated title page] | WITT'S | RECREATIONS | refined | & *Augmented*, | *with* | Ingenious | CONCEITES | *for the wittie*, | *And* | Merrie Medicines | *for the* | Melancholie. | ———— | *See the next Page.* | Printed by M: Symmons and S: Symmons   1667. |

Title page:
[ruled border] | Recreation, | FOR | Ingenious Head-Pieces: | OR, A | Pleasant Grove | FOR THEIR | WITS TO WALK IN, || Of [bracket] *Epigrams*, 700. | *Epitaphs*, 200. | *Fancies*, a Number. | *Fantasticks*, Abundance. || ———— | With their Addition, Multiplication | and Division. | ———— | Mart. *Non cuique datur habere nasum.* | ———— | *LONDON*, Printed by *S.*

Simmons, and | are to be sold by *Thomas Helder*, at the *Angel* in | *Little Britain*, 1667. |

Reissue of No. 200 with new illustrated title page and 1667 title page (No. 294). See Wing, M1717. Copy owned by Folger Shakespeare Library.

1668

296 COMMENTARIOLUS | DE | STATU CONFOE- | DERATARUM PRO- | VINCIARUM BELGII. | *Editio sexta auctior & emendatior.* | AC-CESSIT | De eadem materia | PAULI MERULÆ | DIATRIBA. | Nec non | *Decretum Ordd. Holl. & West-* | *Frisiæ, De Antiquo Jure Reip. Batavicæ.* | [device] | Ex Typogr. ADRIANI VLACQ. | *Sumptibus JOHANNI VLACQ.* | cIɔIɔc LXVIII. |

Reissue of No. 267. Copy owned by National Library of Scotland.

297 [double-ruled border] | Paradise lost. | A | POEM | IN | TEN BOOKS | The Author *J. M.* | ——— | Licensed and Entred according | to Order. | ——— | *LONDON* | Printed, and are to be sold by *Peter Parker* | under *Creed* Church near *Aldgate*; And by | *Robert Boulter* at the *Turks Head* in *Bishopsgate-street*; | And *Matthias Walker*, under St. *Dunstons* Church | in *Fleet-street*, 1668. |

Edition 1, Issue 3A, of No. 291 (note change to "The Author *J. M.*" as well as date). First issue of first edition (cf. No. 291) according to Hugh Amory (*The Book Collector*, 32 [1983] 41–66), largely because of initials here and change of legend in No. 299, despite date. Wing, M2138. Copy owned by New York Public Library.

298 [double-ruled border] | Paradise lost. | A | POEM | IN | TEN BOOKS. | The Author *J. M.* | ——— | Licensed and Entred according | to Order. | ——— | *LONDON* | Printed, and are to be sold by *Peter Parker* | under *Creed* Church near *Aldgate*; And by | *Robert Boulter* at the *Turks Head* in *Bishopsgate-street*; | And *Matthias Walker*, under St. *Dunstons* Church | in *Fleet-street*, 1668. |

Edition 1, Issue 3B, of No. 291 (see No. 297). Period has been added after "BOOKS." Not in Wing. Copy owned by Morgan Library.

299 [double-ruled border] | Paradise lost. | A | POEM | IN | TEN BOOKS. | ——— | The Author | *JOHN MILTON.* | ——— | [device] | ——— | *LONDON,* | Printed by *S. Simmons*, and to be sold by *S. Thomson* at | the *Bishops-Head* in *Duck-lane*, *H. Mortlack* at the | *White Hart* in *Westminster* Hall,

M. Walker under | St. *Dunstans* Church in *Fleet-street*, and *R. Boulter* at | the *Turks-Head* in *Bishopsgate* Street, 1668. |

Edition 1, Issue 4, of No. 291. Reissue with different title page, and addition of errata, discussion of verse, and arguments, as prefatory material. Two states of "The Printer to the Reader" in preliminary material. Quarto. *A* a A–Z Aa–Tt⁴ Vv²; xvi + 340 pp. [i], title page; [ii], blank; [iii], Printer to the Reader; [iii–xiii], Arguments; [xiv–xv], The Verse; [xvi], errata; [1–130], work. Wing, M2139. Copies owned by New York Public Library (six-line "Printer to the Reader") and by the Berg Collection, New York Public Library (four-line "Printer to the Reader").

1669

300 [ruled border] | ACCEDENCE | Commenc't | GRAMMAR, | Supply'd with sufficient RULES, | For the use of such as, | Younger or Elder, are desi- | rous, without more trouble | then needs, to attain the *Latin* | *Tongue*; the elder sort especi- | ally, with little teaching, and | their own industry. | —— | *J. M.* | *LONDON,* | Printed by *S. Simmons*, next door to | the *Golden Lion* in *Aldersgate-street*, 1669. |

Edition 1, Issue 1. Duodecimo. A–C¹²; iv + 68 pp. [i], title page; [ii], blank; [iii–iv], To the Reader; 1–65, work; 65, errata; [66–68], blank. Pp. [67–68] missing. Dated: June. Wing, M2088A. Copy owned by Columbia University Library.

301 [ruled border] | ACCEDENCE | Commenc't | GRAMMAR, | Supply'd with sufficient | RULES, | For the use of such (Younger | or Elder) as are desirous, with- | out more trouble than | needs to attain the | *LATIN TONGUE*; | The Elder sort especially, with | little Teaching, and their | own Industry. | —— | *By* JOHN MILTON. | —— | *LONDON,* Printed for *S. S.* and are | to be sold by *John Starkey* at the Miter in *Fleet-* | *street*, near *Temple-bar.* 1669. |

Edition 1, Issue 2, of No. 300. Title page cancelled. Printer: Samuel Simmons. Pp. [67–68] intact. Wing, M2088. Copy owned by New York Public Library.

302 [double-ruled border] | Paradise lost. | A | POEM | IN | TEN BOOKS. | —— | The Author | *JOHN MILTON.* | —— | *LONDON,* | Printed by *S. Simmons*, and are to be sold by | *T. Helder* at the Angel in *Little Brittain.* | 1669. |

Edition 1, Issue 5, of No. 291. Reissue with different title page and with preliminary material; see No. 299. Title page is sometimes tipped in. Wing erroneously lists four separate issues or editions, M2140–2143 for the two 1669 issues (see No. 303). Copies owned by New York Public Library (copy 7, No. 1, four-line "Printer to the Reader"; copy 7, No. 2, six-line "Printer to the Reader").

303   [double-ruled border] | Paradise lost. | A | POEM | IN | TEN BOOKS. | ——— | The Author | *JOHN MILTON.* | ——— | *LONDON,* | Printed by *S. Simmons*, and are to be sold by | *T. Helder*, at the *Angel* in *Little Brittain*, | 1669. |

Edition 1, Issue 6, of No. 291. Reissue with different title page and with preliminary material; see No. 299. "The Printer to the Reader" is omitted. Preliminary material (sigs. *A* a) and Z and Vv were reset. There are two states of the discussion of the verse in this second printing, and three states of Vv. See No. 302 for Wing listing. Copy owned by Berg Collection, New York Public Library.

304   [rubricated] | SAKEN van STAET | EN | OORLOGH, | In, ende om-treut de | VEREENIGDE NEDERLANDEN, | Beginnende met het Jaer 1645, ende eyndi- | gende met het Jaer 1656. | *Door* d'HEER | LIEUWE van AITZEMA, | DERDE DEEL. | [device] | In 'sGRAVEN-HAGHE, | ——— | By JOHAN VEELY, JOHAN TONGERLOO, ende JASPER DOLL, | Boeck-verkoopers, ANNO 1669. |

Articles of Peace with the Dutch (Columbia No. 167E), under date of 1652: III, 694–698. In Dutch. Manifest from Parliament (see No. 126), under date of 1652: III, 722–724. In Dutch. Swedish Treaty (Columbia No. 170), under date of 11 April 1654: III, 1086–91. In Dutch. Spanish Treaty (see No. 202), under date of 1655: III, 1018 [1158]–1164. In Dutch. Copy owned by New York Public Library.

1670

305   Cambridge, Massachusetts. Houghton Library (Harvard University). English MS 14496.34.

"The Digression | To com in Lib. 3. page 110. after these words. | [from one misery to another.]" |

Scribal hand. 12 pp. Variant form of No. 328, with additions. Dated: 1670 or after. Brackets and virgules given in MS. A different and later hand has added after "Digression": "in Miltons History of England. | ".

306 THE | HISTORY | OF | BRITAIN, | *That part especially now call'd* |
ENGLAND. | *From the first Traditional Beginning, continu'd to the* | *NORMAN*
CONQUEST. | *Collected out of the antientest and best Authours* | *thereof by* | ———
| *JOHN MILTON.* | ═════ | *LONDON,* | Printed by *J. M.* for *James Allestry,*
at the *Rose* | and *Crown* in St. *Paul's Church-Yard,* | M DC LXX. |

Edition 1, Issue 1. Quarto. [A]^2 B–Z Aa–Zz^4 Aaa^2; iv + 364 pp. [i], blank;
[ii], portrait; [iii], title page; [iv], blank; 1–308, work; [309–361], Index
(Table); [362], blank; [363], errata; [364], blank. Variant states of text.
Printer was John Macock. Portrait by William Faithorne. Dated: November.
Wing, M2119. Copy owned by New York Public Library.

1671

307 THE | HISTORY | OF | BRITAIN, | That part especially now called |
ENGLAND. | FROM | The first Traditional Beginning, | Continued to
the | *NORMAN CONQUEST.* | Collected out of the Antientest and best
AUTHORS | thereof: | ——— | by *JOHN MILTON.* | ——— | *LONDON,*
| Printed by *J. M.* for *Spencer Hickman,* at the *Rose* in | St. *Paul's Church-Yard,*
MDCLXXI. |

Edition 1, Issue 2, of No. 306. [A]$^{2(\pm A2)}$ B–Z Aa–Zz^4 Aaa^2; iv + 364
pp. [i], blank; [ii], portrait; [iii], title page; [iv], blank; 1–308, work;
[309–361], Index (Table); [362], blank; [363], errata; [364], blank. Variant
states of text. Wing, M2120. Copy owned by Princeton University Library.

A1, the portrait leaf, is often missing. See copy owned by Columbia University Library.

308 OLDENBURGISCHE | FRJEDENS- | und der benachbarten Oerter |
KRIEGS- | HANDLUNGEN. | [etc.] | von Johann-Just Winkelmann |
HochFürstl: Hessischen | auch vermaligen Hoch Gräfl: Oldenburgischen
| Rath und Historigrapho. | [device] |

Published in Oldenburg in 1671. Sixmo. π A–Z Aa–Zz Aaa–Ggg^6 Hhh^4.
Bound: π1–5 A1 π6 A2 [etc.]. Safeguard for Count Oldenburg, in Latin,
pp. 390–391, dated 17 February 1652, with Milton's attesting signature.
State paper, Columbia No. 152. Discussion in German, pp. 390–391. Copy
owned by New York Public Library.

309 PARADISE | REGAIN'D. | A | POEM. | In IV *BOOKS.* | To which is
added | *SAMSON AGONISTES.* | ——— | The Author | *JOHN MILTON.*
| ═════ | *LONDON,* | Printed by *J. M.* for *John Starkey* at the | *Mitre* in
Fleetstreet, near *Temple-Bar.* | MDCLXXI. |

Edition 1. Octavo. [A]^2 B–O^8 P^4; iv + 112, 104 pp. [i], blank; [ii], license; [iii], title page; [iv], blank; 1–111, text of *Paradise Regain'd*; [112], blank; [1], title page for *Samson Agonistes*; [2], blank; 3–5, Of a Dramatic Poem; 6, Argument; 7, Dramatis Personae; [8], blank; 9–101, text of *Samson Agonistes*; [102], omissa; [103], errata; [104], blank.

Title page for *Samson Agonistes*:
SAMSON | AGONISTES, | A | DRAMATIC POEM. | ———— | The Author | *John Milton.* | ———— | *Aristot. Poet. cap. 6.* | [one-line Greek quotation] | [two-line Latin quotation] | ===== | *LONDON*, | Printed by *J. M.* for *John Starkey* at the | *Mitre* in *Fleetstreet*, near *Temple-Bar.* | MDCLXXI. |

Printer may have been John Macock. Press variations of texts and in errata. University of Kentucky Library, for example, has copies of both states; see p. 67, *PR* III, 241 ("loah", State 1; "loth", State 2). Wing, M2152. Copy owned by New York Public Library.

Copy owned by University of Western Ontario Library has cancelling leaf replacing N3, with p. 70 of *Samson Agonistes* misnumbered 79. Copies of both poems alone exist. No copy with a date of 1670 is known although this date is given by some early biographers and library catalogues; it was also advertised in a catalogue for Starkey dated, in part, in May 1670. It was licensed on 2 July 1670, and entered in the Term Catalogues for Michaelmas Term 1670 (see No. *616*).

1672

310   [ruled border] | *JOANNIS MILTONI* | Angli, | Artis Logicæ | Plenior Institutio, | AD | *PETRI RAMI* | Methodum concinnata, | ===== | Adjecta est Praxis Annalytica & *Petri* | *Rami* vita. Libris duobus. | ===== | *LONDINI*, | Impensis *Spencer Hickman*, So- | cietatis Regalis Typographi, ad | insigne *Rosæ* in *Cæmeterio*, | *D. Pauli.* 1672. |

Duodecimo. A–B^{12}(–B1, B2) C–K^{12} L^6; xx + 228 pp. A11 signed B1; A12 unsigned and used as B2. Stubs are visible; at times two or three letters of text are visible. Frequent errors in pagination. [i–iii], blank; [iv], portrait; [v], title page; [vi], blank; [vii–xvii], preface; [xviii], blank; [xix], errata; [xx], blank; 1–219, work; 220–223 [*recte* 228], Life. Portrait is William Dolle's engraving of the Faithorne painting. Wing, M2093. Copy owned by New York Pubic Library.

Copy owned by William B. Hunter, Jr., University of Houston, lacks [i–iv], including portrait; [v–xx] are bound as: [v–viii], [xi–xii], [ix–x], [xv–xvi], [xiii–xiv], [xvii–xx].

1673

311 [ruled border] | *JOANNIS MILTONI* | Angli, | Artis Logicæ | Plenior In-
stitutio, | AD | *PETRI RAMI* | Methodum concinnata. | ——— | Adjecta
est Praxis Annalytica & | *Petri Rami* vita; Libris duobus. | ——— | *LON-
DINI,* | Impensis *S. H.* Prostant pro *R. Boulter* | ad Insigne Capitis *Turcæ*
exadversum | Mercatorio Regali in Vico vulgò | Cornhill [black letter] dic-
to, 1673. |

Edition 2 (basically a reissue) of No. 310. A^{12}(± A3) B^{12}(-B1, B2) C-K^{12}
L^6; xx + 228 pp. Cancel stubs between A3 and A4, and A10 and B1. A11
signed B1; A12 unsigned and used as B2. [i–iii], blank and missing; [iv],
portrait missing; [v], title page; [vi], blank; [vii–xvii], preface; [xviii], blank;
[xix], errata; [xx], blank; 1–219, work; 220–223 [*recte* 228], Life. Wing,
M2094. Copy owned by William Andrews Clark Library.

312 OF | True Religion, | HÆRESIE, | SCHISM, | TOLERATION, | And
what best means may be | us'd against the growth of | POPERY | ———
| The Author *J. M.* | ——— | *LONDON* | Printed in the Year, 1673. |

Quarto. B-C^4; 16 pp. [1], title page; [2], blank; 3–16, work. Variant states;
e. g., see p. 12, mispaged 13, and p. 13, mispaged 12. Dated: May. Wing,
M2135. Copy owned by University of Kentucky Library.

313 [double-ruled border] | POEMS, &c. | UPON | Several Occasions. | ———
| BY | Mr. *JOHN MILTON:* | ——— | Both ENGLISH and LATIN, &c.
| Composed at several times. | ——— | With a small Tractate of | EDUCA-
TION | *To Mr.* HARTLIB. | ===== | *LONDON,* | Printed for *Tho. Dring*
at the *White Lion* | next *Chancery Lane* End, in | *Fleet-street.* 1673. |

Edition 2 of shorter poems (see No. 70) with additions; Edition 2 of *Of Education* (No. 64). Issue 1. Octavo. *A*^{4} A-S^8; viii + 166, 122 pp. [i], title page;
[ii], blank; [iii–vii], Contents; [viii], errata; 1–165, English poems; [166],
blank; [1], title page for Latin poems; [2], blank; 3–10, Testimonies; 11–94,
Latin (and Greek) poems; 95–117, *Of Education*; [118–122], Advertisements.

Title page for Latin poems:
Joannis Miltoni | *LONDINENSIS* | POEMATA. | Quorum pleraque intra
Annum | ætatis Vigesimum Conscripsit. | *Nunc primum Edita.* | ——— |
[device] | ——— | *LONDINI,* | Excudebat *W. R.* Anno 1673. |

Contents:
"On the Morning of Christ's Nativity," pp. 1–12
"A Paraphrase on Psalm 114," p. 13
"Psalm 136," pp. 14–17
"On the Death of a fair Infant dying of a Cough," pp. 17–21

Testimony by Dati, p. 10
Elegia prima, pp. 11–15
Elegia secunda, pp. 15–16
Elegia tertia, pp. 16–19
Elegia quarta, pp. 19–24
Elegia quinta, pp. 25–30
Elegia sexta, pp. 31–35
Elegia septima, pp. 35–39
"In Proditionem Bombardicam," p. 40
"In eandem," p. 40
"In eandem," p. 41
"In eandem," p. 41
"In inventorem Bombardæ," p. 42
"Ad Leonoram Romæ canentem," p. 42
"Ad eandem," pp. 42–43
"Ad eandem," p. 43
"Apologus de Rustico et Hero," p. 44
"In Obitum Procancellarii Medici," pp. 45–47
"In Quintum Novembris," pp. 47–56
"In Obitum Præsulis Eliensis," pp. 57–59
"Naturam non pati senium," pp. 60–62
"De Idea Platonica," pp. 63–64
"Ad Patrem," pp. 64–69
"Psalm CXIV," p. 70 (in Greek)
"Philosophus ad regem," p. 71 (in Latin and Greek)
"In Effigei Ejus Sculptorem," p. 71 (in Greek)
"Ad Salsillum," pp. 71–73
"Mansus," pp. 74–78
"Epitaphium Damonis," pp. 79–89
"Ad Joannem Rousium," pp. 90–94
"Of Education," pp. 95–117

Dated: November. Printer may have been William Rawlins. Second leaf of this issue signed *A*2. Wing, M2161. Copy owned by New York Public Library.

314 [double-ruled border] | POEMS, &c. | UPON | Several occasions. | ———
| BY | Mr. *JOHN MILTON:* | ——— | Both ENGLISH and LATIN, &c.
| Composed at several times. | ——— | With a small Tractate of | EDUCA-
TION | *To Mr.* HARTLIB. | ====== | *LONDON*, | Printed for *Tho. Dring*
at the *Blew Anchor* | next *Mitre Court* over against *Fetter* | *Lane* in *Fleet-street.*
1673. |

Edition 2, Issue 2 of No. 313. Second leaf of this issue signed *A*2. Not in Wing. Copy owned by University of Kentucky Library.

315 [double-ruled border] | POEMS, &c. | UPON | Several Occasions. | ———
| BY | Mr. *JOHN MILTON:* | ——— | Both ENGLISH and LATIN, &c.
| Composed at several times. | ——— | With a small Tractate of | EDUCA-
TION | *To Mr.* HARTLIB. | ══════ | *LONDON,* | Printed for *Tho. Dring*
at the *Blew Anchor* | next *Mitre Court* over against *Fetter* | *Lane* in *Fleet-street.*
1673. |

Edition 2, Issue 3 of No. 313. Second leaf is not signed. Not in Wing. Copy
owned by New York Public Library.

1674

316 [ruled-border] | A | DECLARATION, | OR | Letters Patents of the Elec-
tion | of this present | King of POLAND | *John the Third,* | Elected on the
22d of *May* last past, | *Anno Dom.* 1674. | Containing the Reasons of this
Election, the | great Vertues and Merits of the said Se- | rene Elect, | His
eminent Services in War, e- | specially in his last great Victory against the
| Turks [black letter] and Tartars, [black letter] whereof many Parti- | culars
are here related, not published before. | *Now faithfully translated from the Latin
Copy.* | ——— | *LONDON,* | Printed for *Brabazon Aylmer,* at the Three
Pigeons in *Cornhil,* 1674. |

Quarto. A–B⁴; ii + 14 pp. [i–ii], blank and missing; [1], title page; [2],
blank; 3–12, work; [13–14], blank. Dated: July. Wing, D779. Copy owned
by British Library.

317 [ruled border] | *Joannis Miltonii* Angli, | EPISTOLARUM FAMILIARIUM
| *LIBER UNUS*: | *QUIBUS* | Accesserunt, Ejusdem, jam olim in Col- | legio
Adolescentis, | PROLUSIONES | Quædam | ORATORIAE. | ══════ |
LONDINI, | Impensis *Brabazoni Aylmeri* sub Signo | *Trium Columbarum* Via
vulgo | Cornhill [black letter] dicta, *An. Dom.* 1674. |

Octavo. A–K⁸; 160 pp. [1–2], blank; [3], title page; [4], blank; [5–6], To
the Reader, by Aylmer; 7–66, letters; 67–155, prolusions; [156], errata;
[157–158], Advertisements; [159–160], blank and missing. Dated: May. Letters numbered 1–31 in Columbia Edition, Vol. 12; prolusions numbered
1–7. Wing, M2117. Copy owned by University of Kentucky Library.

318 [double-ruled border] | Paradise Lost. | A | POEM | IN | TWELVE
BOOKS. | ——— | The Author | *JOHN MILTON.* | ——— | The Second
Edition [black letter] | Revised and Augmented by the | same Author. |
——— | *LONDON,* | Printed by *S. Simmons* next door to the | *Golden Lion*
in *Aldersgate-street,* 1674. |

Edition 2 of No. 291 (299) revised. Octavo. π^1 A^4 B-Y^8; 2 + viii + 336 pp. [1], blank; [2], portrait; [i], title page; [ii], blank; [iii–iv], Barrow's poem; [v–vi], Marvell's poem; [vii–viii], The Verse; 1–333, work; [334–336], blank. With commendatory poems by S. B. (Samuel Barrow?) in Latin and by Andrew Marvell in English. Portrait is William Dolle's engraving of the Faithorne painting. Arguments are dispersed among books. Two states of A–D; some alteration of page numbers in later sigs. plus a one-word change in Argument to Book X. Dated: July. Wing, M2144. Copy owned by University of Kentucky Library.

1675

319 London. Public Record Office. SP 9/194.

Daniel Skinner MS of transcription of state papers. Dated: ca. 1675. Omits thirteen papers given in *Literæ* (No. 321): Columbia No. 18–20, 22–24, 26, 28–30, 32, 43a, 97. Adds fourteen letters not given in *Literæ*: Columbia Nos. 137–150.

320 [double-ruled border] | Paradise Lost. | A | POEM | IN | TWELVE BOOKS. | ———— | The Author | *JOHN MILTON.* | ———— | The Second Edition [black letter] | Revised and Augmented by the | same Author. | ———— | *LONDON,* | Printed by *S. Simmons*, and are to be sold by *T. Helder*, | at the sign of the *Angel* in *Little Britain*, 1675. |

Reissue of No. 318. State 2 of text except for recto of B signature, which is State 1. Not in Wing. Copy owned by University of Illinois Library.

1676

321 LITERÆ | *Pseudo-Senatûs Anglicani*, | CROMWELLII, | Reliquorumque Perduellium | nomine ac jussu con- | scriptæ | A | JOANNE MILTONO. | [basket of fruit] | Impressæ Anno   1676. |

Edition 1. Printed in Amsterdam by Peter and John Blaeu. Duodecimo. π^2 A-K^{12}; iv + 240 pp. [i], title page; [ii], blank; [iii–iv], Ad Lectorem; 1–234, text of state papers; [235–240], blank. [237–240] missing. Two states. Contents: Columbia Nos. 1–136. Wing, M2128. Copy owned by John T. Shawcross, University of Kentucky.

322 LITERÆ | *Pseudo-Senatûs Anglicani*, | CROMWELLII, | Reliquorumque Perduellium | nomine ac jussu con- | scriptæ | A | JOANNE MILTONO. | [face] | Impressæ Anno   1676. |

Another edition of No. 321. Printed in Brussels by E. Fricx. Differences throughout due to reprinting. Duodecimo. π^2 A-I^{12} K^{10}; iv + 236 pp. π^2 printed as part of sheet K. [i], title page; [ii], blank; [iii–iv], Ad Lectorem; 1–234, text of state papers; [235–236], blank. Not in Wing. Copy owned by University of Kentucky Library.

1677

323   [double-ruled border] | THE | HISTORY | OF | BRITAIN, | That Part especially now call'd | ENGLAND. | From the first Traditional Beginning, | Continu'd to the | NORMAN CONQUEST. | Collected out of the Antientest and | Best Authours thereof by | ——— | *JOHN MILTON.* | ═══ | *LONDON*, | Printed by *J. M.* for *John Martyn* at the | Sign of the *Bell* in St *Paul's Church-Yard*, | MDCLXXVII. |

Edition 2, Issue 1, of No. 306. Octavo. A-Z Aa-Cc^8; 416 pp. [1–2], blank; [3], title page; [4], blank; 5–357, work; [358], blank; [359–416], Index. Printer was John Macock. Wing, M2121. Copy owned by University of Kentucky Library.

1678

324   [double-ruled border] | THE | HISTORY | OF | BRITAIN, | That Part especially now call'd | ENGLAND. | From the first Traditional Beginning, | Continu'd to the | NORMAN CONQUEST. | Collected out of the Antientest and | Best Authours thereof by | ——— | *JOHN MILTON.* | ——— | The second Edition. [black letter] | ═══ | *LONDON*, | Printed by *J. M.* for *Mark Pardoe* and are to be sold | at the *Black Raven* over against *Bedford-House*, in the | *Strand*. 1678. |

Edition 2, Issue 2, of No. 306; see No. 323. A2 cancelled. Wing, M2122. Copy owned by University of Kentucky Library.

325   [double-ruled border] | Paradise Lost. | A | POEM | IN | TWELVE BOOKS. | ——— | The Author | *John Milton.* | ——— | The Third Edition. [black letter] | Revised and Augmented by the | same Author. | ——— | *LONDON*, | Printed by *S. Simmons* next door to the | *Golden Lion* in *Aldersgate-street*, 1678. |

Edition 3; see No. 318. Octavo. A^4 B-Y^8; viii + 336 pp. [i], title page; [ii], blank; [iii–iv], Barrow's poem; [v–vi], Marvell's poem; [vii–viii], The

Verse; 1–331, work; [332–336], blank. [333–336] missing. Wing, M2145. Copy owned by New York Public Library.

Frequently the engraved portrait by William Dolle is tipped in, as it is in the copy owned by Joseph A. Wittreich, Jr., Philadelphia. In the James Osborn Collection, Yale University Library, shelf mark: pb9, is Francis Atterbury's copy with numerous notes; e. g., pertinent sentences from *Reason of Church-Government* and the "Printer to the Reader" from the 1668/1669 issues.

1680

326   PARADISE | REGAIN'D. | A | POEM. | In IV *BOOKS.* | To which is added | *SAMSON AGONISTES.* | ———— | The Author | *JOHN MILTON.* | ═══ | *LONDON,* | Printed for *John Starkey* at the *Mitre* | in *Fleet-street,* near *Temple-Bar.* | MDCLXXX. |

Edition 2 of No. 309. Octavo. A–H^8 I^4; 136 pp. [1], blank; [2], license; [3], title page; [4], blank; 5–70, text of *Paradise Regain'd*; [71], title page for *Samson Agonistes*; [72], blank; 73–75, Of a Dramatic Poem; 76, Argument; 77, Dramatis Personae; [78], blank; 79–132, text of *Samson Agonistes*; [133–136], Advertisements. Wing, M2153. Copy owned by University of Kentucky Library.

Title page for *Samson Agonistes*:
SAMSON | AGONISTES, | A | DRAMATIC POEM. | ———— | The Author | *John Milton.* | ———— | *Aristot. Poet. cap. 6.* | [one-line Greek quotation] | [two-line Latin quotation] | ═══ | *LONDON,* | Printed for *John Starkey* at the *Mitre* | in *Fleet-street,* near *Temple-Bar.* | MDCLXXX. |

327   A | SUPPLEMENT | TO | D$^R.$ DU MOULIN, | TREATING | Of the likeliest Means to Remove [black letter] | HIRELINGS | OUT OF THE | CHURCH | OF | ENGLAND. | With a brief VINDICATION of | MR RICH. BAXTER. | ———— | By *J.* M. | ———— | *LONDON,* | Printed in the Year *M DC LXXX.* |

An edition of No. 268. Folio. [A] B–G^2; 28 pp. [1], title page; [2], blank; 3–27, work; [28], blank. Wing, M2180. Copy owned by Morgan Library.

1681

328 M[r] John Miltons | CHARACTER | OF THE | Long Parliament [black letter] | AND | ASSEMBLY of DIVINES. | In MDCXLI. | ——— | Omitted in his other Works, and never before Printed, | And very seasonable for these times. | ——— | [device] | ——— | *LONDON:* | Printed for *Henry Brome*, at the *Gun* at the West- | end of St. *Pauls*. 1681. |

Quarto. A-B⁴; iv + 12 pp. [i], title page; [ii], blank; [iii–iv], To the Reader; 1–11, work; [12], blank. Dated: April. Wing, M2098 (erroneously also T3590, assigned to Sir James Tyrrell). Copy owned by University of Kentucky Library.

329 Oxford. Bodleian Library. MS Dep. c. 162.

State paper, Columbia No. 26, copy in Latin, No. 85.

State paper, Columbia No. 157, copy of Spanish original, No. 5a.

Patrick includes No. 6a as part of state paper No. 26, Anglo-Portuguese Negotiations. MS is Nalson Papers, Vol. X. Date: before 1682.

330 Oxford. Bodleian Library. MS Dep. c. 170.

State paper, Columbia No. 7, copies in Latin and English, No. 39a, ff. 81–82.

State paper, Columbia No. 16, copy in English, No. 41, ff. 86–87.

State paper, Columbia No. 155, copy in English, No. 48, f. 100, and copy in English, No. 51, f. 106; both in Gualter Frost's hand.

State paper, Columbia No. 156, copy in English, No. 49, ff. 102–103, and copy in English, No. 50, ff. 104–105; both in Gualter Frost's hand.

State paper, Columbia No. 157, copy in English, No. 53, ff. 110–111.

State paper, Columbia No. 21, copy in Latin, No. 66, ff. 136–137.

Copies of the Spanish originals of Columbia Nos. 155 and 156 are included as No. 106, f. 251, and No. 99, ff. 233–234, respectively.

Two anonymous English translations of the original of Columbia No. 157 appear as Nos. 46 and 47 on ff. 96–97 and 98–99.

State paper, Columbia No. 170A (attributed), is found in English three times (ff. 77–78, 134–135, 192) and in Latin twice (ff. 84v, 118–119).

Patrick cites Nos. 123–160 as state paper No. 26, Anglo-Portuguese Negotiations. MS is Nalson Papers, Vol. XVII. Date: before 1682.

331 Oxford. Bodleian Library. MS Dep. c. 171.

State paper, Columbia No. 24, copy in Latin, No. 6.

State paper, Columbia No. 19, copy in Latin, No. 34.

State paper, Columbia No. 27, copy in Latin, No. 144.

State paper, Columbia No. 31, copy in Latin, No. 145.

State paper, Columbia No. 26, copy in English, No. 149.

State paper, Columbia No. 36, copy in Latin, No. 156.

State paper, Columbia No. 25, copy in English, No. 160; copy in Latin, No. 161.

State paper, Columbia No. 40, copy in Latin, No. 162; copy in English, No. 164.

State paper, Columbia No. 152, copy in Latin, No. 168; copy in English, No. 169.

Copy of the Holstein Safeguard (issued December 1653) is found as No. 172 in Latin. Basically same as that in SP 103/3, with some language changed; see No. 145 in this bibliography.

Negotiations with the States-General are given as Nos. 83 (2), 87, 88, 89, and dated 15 (25) April, 17 (27) April, 9 (19) May, 10 (20) May, 17 (27) May 1651. These were read before the Council on 2 July 1651 (see Nos. 7, 9, 11, 12, 13). Thurloe (*A Collection of the State Papers of John Thurloe* [1742], ed. Thomas Birch) includes copies of four of these items in English: see I, 179 (2), 181–182, 182–183. Patrick does not mention, as he does the Anglo-Portuguese Negotiations (No. 26). Milton's connection with either of these sets of papers is undetermined. The original Thurloe papers will be found in the Bodleian Library, Rawlinson MS A.2, on pp. 175–177, 178, 189, and 192–195 respectively. This manuscript is currently disbound and Articles 1–5 of the last item, published in 1742, are now missing; they should have appeared on pp. 190–191.

Copy of *The Declaration of Parliament against the States-General* (see Nos. 126 and 157 in this bibliography) is found as No. 139 and dated 7 July 1652.

MS is Nalson Papers, Vol. XVIII. Date: before 1682.

1682

332   [double-ruled border] | A Brief | HISTORY | OF | MOSCOVIA: | AND | Of other less-known Coun- | tries lying eastward of *Russia* as | far as *Cathay*. | Gather'd from the Writings of se- | veral Eye-Witnesses. | ——— | By

JOHN MILTON. | ———— | *LONDON,* | Printed by *M. Flesher,* for *Brabazon Ayl-* | *mer* at the *Three Pigeons* against the | *Royal Exchange.* 1682. |

Octavo. A^4 B–H^8; viii + 112 pp. [i], title page; [ii], blank; [iii–vii], preface; [viii], advertisement; 1–107, work; 108–109, bibliography; [110–112], blank. Dated: February. Wing, M2096. Copy owned by University of Kentucky Library.

333 MILTONS | REPUBLICAN-LETTERS | *OR* | A Collection of such as were | written by Comand | *of the* | *LATE COMMONWEALTH* | OF | ENGLAND; | *from the Year* 1648. *to the Year* 1659. | Originally writ by the learned | JOHN MILTON, | Secretary to those times, and now trans- | lated into English, by a Wel-wisher | of *Englands* honour. | ———— | Printed in the Year 1682. |

Quarto. π^1 *^{1} A–R^4; iv + 136 pp. [i], title page; [ii], blank; [iii–iv], Courteous Reader; 1–136, work. Imprecise rendering of state papers, Columbia Nos. 1–136, from *Literæ* (No. 321). Not in Wing. Copy owned by British Library.

334 Das | Verlustigte | [row of ornaments] | Paradeis, | Auss | JOHANN MILTONS | Zeit seiner Blindheit | In Englischer Sprache abgefassten | unvergleichlichen Gedicht | In | Unser gemein Teutsch | übergetragen und verleget | Durch E. G. V. B. | [device] | In Zerbst | Bey Johann Ernst Bezeln. | ———— | ANNO M DC LXXXII. |

Comma represented by virgule. Translation of No. 318 into German verse by Ernst Gottlieb von Berge. Octavo. π^1)o($^{8(-}$)o(^{8}) A–Z^8; xvi + 368 pp.)o(8 used for frontispiece, redrawn from the Faithorne engraving. [i], blank; [ii], portrait; [iii], title page; [iv], Dedication; [v–vi], preface; [vii–viii], To the Reader; [ix–xi], The Verse; [xii–xiii], Barrow's poem in Latin; [xiv–xvi], Marvell's poem; 1–367, work; [368], blank. Includes arguments. Copy owned by New York Public Library.

1683

See also No. *954* in Part II.

335 Oxford. Bodleian Library. Aubrey MS 10.

John Aubrey, "Ideas of Education of Young Gentlemen." Dated: 1683/4 ff. Noted on f. 6 as Chapter XXXIII (an appendix, actually) is "An Extract of Mr J. Miltons letter to Mr S. H."; Chapter XXXIII is found on ff. 147–151 (all rectos, versos blank). Also cited on f. 119; and possible general influence from *Of Education* passim.

336 [illustrated title page] | WITT'S | RECREATIONS | refined | & *Augmented*, | *with* | Ingenious | CONCEITES | *for the wittie,* | *And* | Merrie Medicines | *for the* | Melancholie. | ———— | *See the next Page.* | London   Printed for John Hancock 1683 |

Title page:
[double-ruled border] | Recreation | For Ingenious Head-Pieces: | OR, | A Pleasant GROVE | FOR THEIR | WITS to Walk in. | OF | *Epigrams* 700. | *Epitaphs* 200. | *Fancies* a Number. | *Fantasticks* Abundance. | With their Addition, Multiplication, | and Division. | ALSO | Variety of New Songs Alamode, | AND | LETTERS upon several Occasions, | both Serious and Jocose. | *Now newly added to this Impression.* | - - - - | *London*, Printed for *John Hancock*, at the *Three Bibles* | over against the *Royal EXCHANGE* in *Cornhill*, 1683 |

Compiler: Sir John Mennes (?). Duodecimo. A–N^{12} O^6. No. 148 of Epitaphs, "Old Hobsons Epitaph" (attributed), p. 134. Wing, M1718. Copy owned by Harvard University Library.

1684

337 [Enchiridion Linguæ Latinæ: or, A Compendious Latin Dictionary. London, 1684.]

Unknown, but reported by Edward Phillips in his "Life of Milton" (No. 367), and by Anthony Wood in *Athenæ Oxoniensis* (1721), Vol. II, Col. 1118. Copy owned by John T. Shawcross, University of Kentucky. Compare Nos. *772* and *1363*. See also remarks in No. *1141*.

338 [Speculum Linguæ Latinæ: or, A Succinct and New Method. London, 1684.]

Unknown, but reported by Edward Phillips in his "Life of Milton" (No. 367), and by Anthony Wood in *Athenæ Oxoniensis* (1721), Vol. II, Col. 1118. Copy owned by John T. Shawcross, University of Kentucky. Compare Nos. *772* and *1363*. See also remarks in No. *1141*.

1685

339 [double-ruled border] | M$^{R.}$ William Shakespear's | COMEDIES, | HISTORIES, | AND | TRAGEDIES. | Published according to the true Original Copies. | Unto which is added, SEVEN | PLAYS, | Never before

Printed in Folio: | *VIZ.* || *Pericles* Prince of *Tyre.* | The *London Prodigal.* | The History of *Thomas* Lord | *Cromwel.* [left-hand bracket] | Sir *John Oldcastle* Lord *Cobham.* | The *Puritan Widow.* | A *Yorkshire* Tragedy. | The Tragedy of *Locrine.* [right-hand bracket] || ——— | *The Fourth Edition.* | ——— | [device] | ——— | *LONDON,* | Printed for *H. Herringman, E. Brewster,* and *R. Bentley,* at the *Anchor* in the | *New Exchange,* the *Crane* in St. *Pauls* Church-Yard, and in | *Russel*-Street *Covent-Garden.* 1685. |

Edition 4 of No. 27. Printed by Robert Roberts and others. Folio in sixes. Variant issues have reprinted sheets. Preliminary sheets are π^6, with $\pi3$ marked A. "AN | EPITAPH | On the admirable Dramatick Poet, *WILLIAM SHAKESPEAR.* |" printed on $\pi5v$ or p. [x]. Text as given in other editions of Shakespeare, including "Starry-pointing", line 4 (Effigies C). List of Works given on $\pi6$. Copy in Berg Collection, New York Public Library, gives List of Works on $\pi4$ and "Epitaph" on $\pi6v$ or p. [xii]. Wing, S2915. Copy owned by New York Public Library, Copy 1.

340 [double-ruled border] | M$^{R.}$ William Shakespear's | COMEDIES, | HISTORIES, | AND | TRAGEDIES. | Published according to the true Original Copies. | Unto which is added, SEVEN | PLAYS, | Never before Printed in Folio: | *VIZ.* || *Pericles* Prince of *Tyre.* | The *London Prodigal.* | The History of *Thomas* Lord | *Cromwel.* [left-hand bracket] | Sir *John Oldcastle* Lord *Cobham.* | The *Puritan Widow.* | A *Yorkshire* Tragedy. | The Tragedy of *Locrine.* [right-hand bracket] || ——— | *The Fourth Edition.* | ——— | [device] | ——— | *LONDON,* | Printed for *H. Herringman, E. Brewster, R. Chiswell,* and *R. Bentley,* at the *Anchor* | in the *New Exchange*; and at the *Crane,* and *Rose* and *Crown* in St. *Pauls* | Church-Yard, and in *Russel*-Street *Covent-Garden.* 1685. |

Different issue of No. 339. "Epitaph" given on $\pi5v$; List of Works, on $\pi6$. Wing, S2916. Copy owned by Folger Shakespeare Library, Folio 4, No. 8.

341 [double-ruled border] | MR William Shakespear's | COMEDIES, | HISTORIES, | AND | TRAGEDIES. | Published according to the true Original Copies. | Unto which is added, SEVEN | PLAYS, | Never before Printed in Folio. | *VIZ.* || *Pericles* Prince of *Tyre.* | The *London Prodigal.* | The History of *Thomas* Lord | *Cromwel.* [left-hand bracket] | Sir *John Oldcastle* Lord *Cobham.* | The *Puritan Widow.* | A *Yorkshire* Tragedy. | The Tragedy of *Locrine.* [right-hand bracket] || ——— | *The Fourth Edition.* | ——— | [device] | ——— | *LONDON,* | Printed for *H. Herringman,* and are to be sold by *Joseph Knight* | and *Francis Saunders,* at the *Anchor* in the Lower Walk | of the *New Exchange.* 1685. |

Different issue of No. 339. Title page is reset, with many typographical changes, a different device, and a different printing legend. "Epitaph" given on π5v; List of Works, on π6. Includes some reprinted sheets. Wing, S2917. Copy owned by New York Public Library, Copy 2.

1686

342 Paradisus Amissa, | POEMA HEROICUM, | Quod à | *JOANNE MILTONO* Anglo | Anglicè scriptum in | Decem Libros digestum est: | Nunc autem à | *Viris quibusdam Natione eadem oriundis* | IN | LINGUAM ROMANAM | Transfertur. | ——— | LIBER PRIMUS. | ——— | Imprim. *Nov.* 18. 1685. *R. L'Estrange.* | ——— | *LONDINI:* | Impensis *Thomæ Dring,* ad Insigne *Occæ* | in Vico Fleetstreet [black letter] dicto. | cIɔ Iɔ C LXXXVI. |

Latin verse translation of Book I of *Paradise Lost.* Dedication signed J. C. Quarto. A-E⁴; viii + 32 pp. [i], title page; [ii], blank; [iii–v], dedication; [vi], To the Reader and Errata; [vii–viii], advertisements; 1–32, work. Wing, M2155. Copy owned by New York Public Library.

1687

343 [double-ruled border] | THE | HISTORY | OF THE | CITY and STATE | OF | GENEVA, | From its First Foundation to this present Time. | ——— | Faithfully Collected from several MANUSCRIPTS of | *Jacobus Gothofredus,* Monsieur *Chorier,* and Others. | ——— | By | *ISAAC SPON,* Doctor of Physick, and one of | the Fellows of the Colledge of *LYONS.* | ——— | LICENSED, *Dec.* 14. 1685. | *RO. L'ESTRANGE.* | ——— | LONDON, | Printed for *Bernard White.* MDCLXXXVII. |

Editor: Jacob Spon. Quarto. π A² B-Z Aa-Kk⁴; viii + 256 pp. [i], blank; [ii], frontispiece; [iii], title page; [iv], blank; [v–vii], preface; [viii], license; 1–250, work; [251–256], Index. Summary of state paper to Geneva (Columbia No. 59), dated 7 June 1655, with some quotation, p. 180. Wing, S5017. Copy owned by Folger Shakespeare Library.

344 New Haven, Connecticut. James Osborn Collection, Yale University. Commonplace Book. Shelf mark: b52/1.

Two volumes. Vol. I: state paper, Columbia No. 57, entitled, "A true Coppy of the Protectors Letter to Cardinall Mazzarini, dated 26 December 1656," pp. 88–89. In English. Date of MS: uncertain.

1688

345   [double-ruled border] | Paradise Lost. | A | POEM | In Twelve Books. |
——— | The AUTHOUR | *JOHN MILTON.* | ——— | The Fourth Edi-
tion, Adorn'd with Sculptures. [black letter] | ——— | *LONDON,* | Printed
by *Miles Flesher,* for *Richard Bently,* at the | Post-Office in *Russell-street,* and
Jacob Tonson at the | Judge's-Head in *Chancery-lane* near *Fleet-street.* | M DC
LXXXVIII. |

Edition 4. Folio in fours. [A]-B^2 C-Z Aa-Xx^4 Yy-Zz Aa^2; iv + 352 pp.
Pp. 219-220 repeated. Pagination: 1-219 [220] 219-250 151-197 [298]-343
[344-350]. Stubs between pp. 202-203, 226-227, 152-153, 196-197. [i],
title page; [ii], blank; [iii], The Verse; [iv], blank; 1-343, work; [344], blank;
[345-350], Subscribers. Z2 given for Zz. Sometimes attached are *Paradise
Regain'd* and *Samson Agonistes* (No. 348).

Frontispiece is Robert White's engraved portrait with Dryden's epigram,
tipped in. Illustrations tipped in for each book: those for Books III, V, VI,
VII, VIII, IX, X, XI by John Baptista de Medina, engraved by M.
Burghers; Book IV, by Bernard Lens, engraved by P. P. Bouche; Book XII,
by Henry Aldrich, engraved by Burghers; and Books I, II, uncertain but
engraved by Burghers. See also No. 346. Designs are owned by Victoria
and Albert Museum (Dyce Collection). The edition was planned and executed by various people connected with Christ Church College, Oxford,
such as Aldrich. Publication was supported by John, Lord Somers, and thus
often associated with him. Wing, M2146. Copy owned by Columbia University Library.

346   [double-ruled border] | Paradise Lost. | A | POEM | In Twelve Books. |
——— | The AUTHOUR | *JOHN MILTON.* | ——— | The Fourth Edi-
tion, Adorn'd with Sculptures. [black letter] | ——— | *LONDON,* | Printed
by *Miles Flesher,* for *Richard Bently,* | at the Post-Office in *Russell-street.* | M
DC LXXXVIII. |

Different issue of No. 345. Pagination: 1-219 [220] 219-250 151-196
297-343 [344-350]. No stubs. Wing, M2148. Copy owned by University
of Kentucky Library.

New York Public Library copy has note on blank leaf preceding frontispiece
by Horace Walpole, stating that "Mr. [Walter] Harte" told him that the illustration for Book XII was designed by "Dr. [Henry] Aldrich." Walpole
says that the original designs had been owned by "Dr. [Theophilus] Met-
calf." A similar note appears in the copy owned by the Victoria and Albert
Museum (Dyce Collection).

347   [double-ruled border] | Paradise Lost. | A | POEM | In Twelve Books. |

———— | The AUTHOUR | *JOHN MILTON.* | ———— | The Fourth Edition, Adorn'd with Sculptures. [black letter] | ———— | *LONDON,* | Printed by *Miles Flesher,* for *Jacob Tonson,* at the | Judge's-Head in *Chancery-lane* near *Fleet-street.* | M DC LXXXVIII. |

Different issue of No. 345. Pagination as in No. 346. No stubs. Wing, M2147. Copy owned by Berg Collection, New York Public Library.

348 [double-ruled border] | Paradise Regain'd. | A | POEM. | ———— | In IV BOOKS. | To which is added | Samson Agonistes. | ———— | The Author | *JOHN MILTON.* | ===== | *LONDON,* | Printed by *R. E.* and are to be sold by | *Randal Taylor* near *Stationers-Hall.* | M DC LXXXVIII. |

Edition 3 of No. 309. Folio. A–R^2 A–H^4; ii + 66, vi + 58 pp. [i], title page; [ii], blank; 1–66, text of *Paradise Regain'd*; [i], title page for *Samson Agonistes*; [ii], blank; [iii–iv], Of a Dramatic Poem; [v], Argument; [vi], Dramatis Personae; 1–57, text of *Samson Agonistes*; [58], blank. Printer may have been Richard Everingham. The separate and quarto gathering for *Samson Agonistes* suggests a second printer. It appears as a separate volume in some libraries.

Title page for *Samson Agonistes*:
[double-ruled border] | Samson Agonistes, | A | DRAMATICK | POEM. | ———— | The AUTHOUR | *JOHN MILTON.* | ———— | [quotation from Aristotle in Greek and Latin] | ———— | *LONDON,* | Printed, and are to be Sold by *Randal Taylor* | near Stationers-Hall, M DC LXXXVIII. |

Wing, M2154 and M2177. Copy owned by University of Wisconsin, bound with *Paradise Lost,* 1692 (No. 362).

1689

349 *Pro Populo Adversus Tyrannos:* | ———— | OR THE | Sovereign Right [black letter] | AND | POWER | OF THE | PEOPLE | OVER | TYRANTS, | Clearly Stated, and plainly Proved. | With some Reflections on the late po- | sture of Affairs. | ———— | *By a true Protestant English-man, and Well-wisher to* | *Posterity.* | ———— | *London,* Printed in the Year, 1689. |

Altered version of *Tenure of Kings and Magistrates,* Edition 1 (No. 84). Perhaps by Sir James Tyrrell. Quarto. A–C^4 D^2; 28 pp. [1], title page; [2], blank; 3–27, work; [28], blank. Publisher was Randal Taylor. Wing, M2164. Copy owned by New York Public Library.

1690

350 ΕΙΚΟΝΟΚΛΑ'ΣΤΗΣ | IN | ANSWER | To a Book Intitul'd | E'IKΩ'N
BAΣIΛIKH̃, | THE | *Portracture* of his Sacred MAJESTY | *King CHARLES*
the *First* | in his *Solitudes* and *Sufferings.* | ——— | By *John Milton.* | ———
| Prov. 28. 15, 16, 17. | 15. *As a roaring Lyon, and a ranging Bear, so is a wicked*
Ruler | *over the poor People.* | 16. *The Prince that wanteth Understanding, is also*
a great Oppressor, | *but he that hated Covetousness shall prolong his Days.* | 17. *A*
Man that doth violence to the Blood of any Person, shall fly | *to the Pit, let no Man*
stay him. | *Salust. Conjurat. Catilin.* | Regium imperium, quod initio, conser-
vandæ libertatis, atque | augendæ reipub. causâ fuerat, in superbiam,
dominati- | onemque se convertit. | Regibus boni, quam mali, suspectiores
sunt; semperque hi[s] | aliena virtus formidolosa est. | Quidlibet impunè
facere, hoc scilicet regium est. | ——— | *Amsterdam,* Printed in the Year,
1690. |

Reprint of Edition 1 (No. 78). Printed in London. Octavo. A–O^8; xvi +
208 pp. [i–ii], blank and missing; [iii], title page; [iv], blank; [v–xvi], preface;
1–207, work; [208], Contents. Cancel, A8. Preface discusses controversy
over *Eikon Basilike.* Wing, M2115. Copy owned by New York Public Library,
Copy 2.

New York Public Library, Copy 1, has unsigned leaf preceding title page,
"An Advertisement" and the Earl of Anglesey's "Memorandum," concern-
ing the authorship of *Eikon Basilike.* A1 missing. Columbia University
Library, Copy B823 M64 / Q1 / 1690b, has reset preceding leaf containing
"An Advertisement" and the "Memorandum." F. F. Madan ("A New
Bibliography of the *Eikon Basilike*," Oxford Bibliographical Society, Publica-
tions, N. S. 3 [1949], p. 139) reports that the "Advertisement/Memoran-
dum" sheet is sometimes bound at the end; no copy examined confirms this.

351 LITERÆ | nomine | *SENATUS ANGLICANI,* | CROMVVELLII |
RICHARDIQUE | Ad diversos in Europa Principes | & Respublicas exaratæ
| *a* | JOANNE MILTONO, | quas nunc primum | *in Germania recudi fecit*
| M. JO. GEORG. PRITIUS. | [device] | *LIPSIÆ & FRANCOFURTI,*
| Sumptibus JO. CASPARI MAYERI. | Typis CHRISTIANI BANCK-
MANNI. | ANNO M DC XC. |

Reprint of No. 321 (or 322). Duodecimo.):(^{8} A–M^{12} M^2; xvi + 292 pp.
[i], title page; [ii], blank; [iii–viii], Dedication; [ix–xvi], Pritius's preface;
1–292, work. State papers, Columbia Nos. 1–136. Copy owned by University of Kentucky Library.

352 [double-ruled border] | PARAPHRASIS | POETICA | IN TRIA | *JOHAN-*
NIS MILTONI, | Viri Clarissimi, | POEMATA, | *VIZ.* | PARADISUM
AMISSUM, | PARADISUM RECUPERATUM, | ET | SAMSONEM

AGONISTEN. | ———— | AUTORE | *GULIELMO HOGÆO.* | ═══ |
LONDINI, | Typis Johannis Darby, Anno Domini, | MDCXC. |
[rubricated] |

Latin verse translations of *Paradise Lost, Paradise Regain'd* and *Samson Agonistes*
by William Hog. *Paradise Lost* given in ten-book version of Edition 1.
Arguments printed together preceding poem; see No. 299.

Octavo. A a^8 b^2 B–Z Aa Kk^8; xxxvi + 512 pp. [i–ii], blank; [iii], title page;
[iv], blank; v–xviii, Dedication; xix–xxi, prefatory poem; xxii–xxiii, To the
Reader; [xxiv], To the Readers; [xxv], title page for *Paradise Lost*; [xxvi],
blank; [xxvii–xxxvi], Arguments; 1–362, text of *Paradise Lost*; [363], title
page for *Paradise Regain'd*; [364], blank; 365–437, text of *Paradise Regain'd*;
[438], blank; [439], title page for *Samson Agonistes*; [440], blank; [441], Persons; [442], Argument; 443–510, text of *Samson Agonistes*; [511–512], blank.

Title page for *Paradise Lost*:
PARAPHRASIS | POETICA | IN | *JOANNIS MILTONI* | Paradisum
Amissum. | POEMA | Decem Libris comprehensum. | ———— | AUTORE
| GULIELMO HOGÆO. | ———— | Ovid. *de arte amandi,* Lib. 3. | *Est Deus
in nobis, sunt & commercia Cæli,* | *Sedibus ætheris spiritus ille venit.* | ———— |
LONDINI, | Anno Domini MDCXC. |

Title page for *Paradise Regain'd*:
PARAPHRASIS | POETICA | IN | *JOANNIS MILTONI* | Paradisum
Recuperatum. | POEMA | Quatuor Libris comprehensum. | ———— | [or-
nament] | ———— | *LONDINI,* | Anno Domini MDCXC. |

Title page for *Samson Agonistes*:
PARAPHRASIS | POETICA | IN | *JOANNIS MILTONI* | Samsonem
Agonisten. | POEMA Dramaticum. | ———— | Autore eodem |
GULIELMO HOGÆO. | ———— | [ornament] | ———— | *LONDINI,* An-
no Domini MDCXC. |

Wing, M2158. Copy owned by University of Kentucky Library.

1691

353 HISTOIRE | D'OLIVIER | CROMWEL. | [ornament] | A PARIS, | Chez
CLAUDE BARBIN, au Palais, sur le second | Perron de la sainte Chapelle.
| ———— | M. DC. XCI. | *AVEC PRIVILEGE DU ROY.* |

Author: François Raguenet. Quarto. a e^4 i^4(–i4) A–Z Aa–Zz Aaa–Lll^4; xxii
+ 456 pp. Frontispiece is a portrait of Cromwell.

"Manifeste des Anglois, au sujet de la même Guerre dont il est parlé dans le même Livre," French translation of Dutch *Declaration*, No. 126, given on pp. 371–380, and "Articles du Traite' de Paix d'entre l'Angleterre & la Hollande, dont il est parlé dans le Livre" (Columbia No. 167E), given on pp. 380–393. Copy owned by New York Public Library.

354   HISTOIRE | D'OLIVIER | CROMWEL. | [device] | *Suivant la Copie imprimée* | A PARIS, | Chez CLAUDE BARBIN. | ———— | M DC XCI. |

Perhaps from Cologne (?). Different edition of No. 353. Duodecimo. π A–R^{12}; xxiv + 408 pp. "Manifeste," pp. 333–342; "Articles," pp. 342–355.

Six references in advertisement on pp. π6 (*Defensio prima*), π6v (French *Eikonoklastes*, Du Moulin, Morisot, Ziegler, and Schaller).

Copy owned by University of Kentucky Library.

355   HISTOIRE | D'OLIVIER | CROMWEL. | *TOME PREMIER.* | [device] | A UTRECHT, | Chez PIERRE ELZEVIER. | ———— | M. DC. XCI. |

Another edition of No. 353. Two volumes. Vol. 1: six references in advertisement on a6v and a7. Vol. 2: title page, same as for Vol. 1 except "*SECOND.*" for "*PREMIER.*". Duodecimo. π^2 A–N^{12} O^8; iv + 328 pp. "Manifeste," pp. 183–199; "Articles," pp. 199–222.

Copy owned by Columbia University Library.

356   Johannis Miltoni | PARADISI AMISSI | Liber Primus | EX | ANGLICANA LINGUA | IN | LATINAM CONVERSUS. | ———— | [device] | ———— | *CANTABRIGIÆ*, | Ex Officina *Jo. Hayes*, Celeberrimæ Academiæ Typogra- | phi; Impensis *Sam. Simpson*, Bibliopol. *Cantab.* 1691. |

Translation of Book I of *Paradise Lost* into Latin verse, by Thomas Power. Quarto. A–D^4; viii + 24 pp. [i], blank; [ii], Imprimatur; [iii], title page; [iv], blank; [v–vi], Dedication; [vii–viii], preface; 1–22, work; [23–24], blank and missing. Wing, M2156. Copy owned by Columbia University Library.

357   [double-ruled border] | Paradise Lost. | A | POEM | In Twelve Books. | ———— | The AUTHOUR | *JOHN MILTON.* | ———— | The Fifth Edition, Adorn'd with Sculptures. [black letter] | ———— | *LONDON,* | Printed for *Richard Bently* in *Covent-garden*, | and *Jacob Tonson* in *Chancery-lane* near | *Fleetstreet.* MDCXCI. |

Edition 5, Issue 1. Folio in fours. π^1 [A]–B^2 C–Z Aa–Uu^4 Xx^2; 2 + iv + 336 pp. [1], blank; [2], portrait; [i], title page; [ii], blank; [iii], The Verse; [iv], blank; 1–336, work. Illustrations including portrait from Edition 4 (1688), No. 345, tipped in. Wing, M2149. Copy owned by University of Kentucky Library.

1692

358 [double-ruled border] | THE | Arts of Empire, [black letter] | AND | Mysteries of State | Discabineted. | IN | Political and Polemical Aphorisms, | grounded on Authority and Ex- | perience. | AND | Illustrated with the Choicest Examples | and Historical Observations. | ———— | By the Ever-renowned Knight | Sir WALTER RALEIGH, | Published | By JOHN MILTON Esq; | ———— | *Quis Martem tunica tectum, Adamantina digné scripserit?* | ———— | *LONDON*, | Printed by *G. Croom*, for *Joseph Watts* at the | *Angel* in St. *Paul*'s Church-yard, 1692. |

Another edition of No. 256. Octavo. π^1 A^4 B-Q^8; 2 + viii + 240 pp. [1], blank; [2], portrait; [i], title page; [ii], blank; [iii–iv], Milton's "To the Reader"; [v–viii], Contents; [viii], Advertisement; 1-238, work; [239–240], books for sale. Portrait tipped in. Wing, R155. Copy owned by University of Kentucky Library.

359 A | DEFENCE | OF THE | People of *ENGLAND*, | *BY* | *JOHN MILTON*: | In *ANSWER* to | *Salmasius*'s Defence of the King. | ═══ | Printed in the Year 1692. |

English translation of No. 98 by Joseph Washington. Apparently published in London, perhaps by Nathaniel Rolls. Octavo. A a B-Q^8 R^4; 8 + xxiv + 248 pp. [1–2], blank; [3], title page; [4], blank; [5–8], preface; i–xxii, Milton's preface; [xxiii–xxiv], blank; 1-246, work; [247], Advertisement; [248], blank. Advertisement lists books in the controversy over the author-ship of *Eikon Basilike* and notes that "The Learned Answer to this Book of Mr. *Milton*, being published in *Latin*, is very well worth Translating, for the benefit of *English* Readers." Wing, M2104. Copy owned by University of Kentucky Library.

360 HISTOIRE | D'OLIVIER | CROMVVEL | *TOME PREMIER.* | [device] | A UTRECHT. | Chez PIERRE ELZEVIER. | ———— | M. DC. XCII. |

Another edition of No. 353. Two volumes. Vol. 1: listings as in No. 351; first five items on ã5v, last item on ã6r. Vol. 2: title page differs: CROM-VVEL. | *TOME SECOND.* | Duodecimo. A^{12}($\pm$A^1) B-K^{12} L^6; 252 pp. Cancel title page, although the edition is not a reissue of No. 352. "Mani-feste," pp. 141-153; "Articles," pp. 153-171. Copy owned by Bodleian Library.

361 HISTORIA, | E Memorie recondite sopra alla | VITA DI | OLIVIERO CROMVELE, | Dette il | TIRANNO SENZA VIZI, | Il | PRINCIPE SENZA VIRTU. | *Scritta da* | GREGORIO LETI. | PARTE PRIMA. | *Divisa in sette Libri, & arricchita di molte* | *Figure.* | [device] | AMSTERDAMO,

| Appresso PIETRO, E GIOVANNI BLAEV, | cIɔ Iɔ C XCII. |

Two vols. Vol. 2: same title page as Vol. 1 except "PARTE SECONDA." and "*otto Libri*,". Octavo. A–Z Aa–Pp⁸; 608 pp. [1], title page; [2], blank; 3–592, work; [593–608], Index. In Italian. Copy owned by Folger Shakespeare Library.

State papers in Latin with reference to Milton as translator (in Italian) on p. 569:
Columbia No. 5, pp. 64–65
Columbia No. 3, pp. 66–67
Columbia No. 4, pp. 67–68
Columbia No. 6, pp. 69–70
Columbia No. 9, pp. 70–72
Columbia No. 1, pp. 78–80
Columbia No. 11, pp. 103–104
Columbia No. 14, pp. 104–105
Columbia No. 15, pp. 105–106
Columbia No. 10, pp. 186–188
Columbia No. 13, pp. 189–190
Columbia No. 17 (and No. 20), pp. 266–267
Columbia No. 22, pp. 273–275
Columbia No. 23, pp. 275–277
Columbia No. 40, pp. 333–336
Columbia No. 167E, pp. 349–351 (in part)
Columbia No. 46, pp. 361–363
Columbia No. 47, pp. 370–371
Columbia No. 44, pp. 374–375
Columbia No. 50, pp. 375–376
Columbia No. 52, pp. 405–408
Columbia No. 56, pp. 408–410
Columbia No. 58, pp. 411–412
Columbia No. 51, pp. 413–416
Columbia No. 59, pp. 423–425
Columbia No. 62, pp. 425–427
Columbia No. 64, pp. 428–430
Columbia No. 63, pp. 430–431
Columbia No. 60, pp. 431–432
Columbia No. 57, p. 454
Columbia No. 91, pp. 461–462
Columbia No. 116, pp. 490–491
Columbia No. 115, pp. 491–492
Columbia No. 118, pp. 498–499
Columbia No. 119, pp. 499–500
Columbia No. 110, pp. 504–507

Columbia No. 112, pp. 507–509
Columbia No. 109, pp. 511–512
Columbia No. 120, pp. 518–519
Columbia No. 124, p. 561
Columbia No. 125, pp. 561–562
Columbia No. 126, pp. 562–563
Columbia No. 128, pp. 563–564
Columbia No. 130, pp. 564–565
Columbia No. 131, pp. 565–566
Columbia No. 132, pp. 566–567
Columbia No. 133, pp. 567–568
Columbia No. 134, pp. 569–570
Columbia No. 135, pp. 579–580
Columbia No. 136, pp. 580–581

Despite some apparent errors of date and slight differences in texts, these versions supply or correct dates, signatories, and closes missing or in error in other known versions.

362 [double-ruled border] | Paradise Lost. | A | POEM | In Twelve Books. | ———— | The AUTHOUR | *JOHN MILTON.* | ———— | The Fifth Edition, Adorn'd with Sculptures. [black letter] | ———— | *LONDON,* | Printed for *Jacob Tonson* at the *Judge's-* | Head in *Chancery-lane* near *Fleet-* | street. M DC XCII. |

Issue 2 of No. 357. Title page is not a cancel. Wing, M2150. Copy owned by University of Wisconsin.

1693

363 [double-ruled border] | Paradise Lost | A | POEM | In Twelve Books. | ———— | The AUTHOUR | *JOHN MILTON.* | ———— | The Fourth Edition, Adorn'd with Sculptures. [black letter] | ===== | *LONDON*: | Printed by *R. E.* for *Jacob Tonson,* at the *Judge's* | Head, near the *Inner Temple Gate* in *Fleetstreet.* | M DC XCIII. |

Another issue of No. 357 (and see No. 362). Title page is not a cancel. Printer may have been Richard Everingham. Not in Wing. Copy owned by the University of Illinois Library.

1694

364   [double-ruled border] | THE | Gentleman's Journal: | OR THE MONTH-
LY | MISCELLANY. | In a Letter to a Gentleman in the Country. | Con-
sisting of *News, History, Philosophy*, | *Poetry, Musick, Translations*, &c. | ———
| MAY, 1694. | ——— | To be continued Monthly. | ——— | Vol. [device]
III. | ——— | *LONDON*, Printed for *Henry Rhodes*, at the *Star*, the Corner
| of *Bride-lane*, in *Fleet-street*, 1694. | Where are to be had compleat Sets for
the two last years, or sin | gle ones for every month. |

Editor: Peter Motteux. Thomas Power's Latin verse translation of *Paradise
Lost* III, 1–55, pp. 129–131, entitled, "*Authoris cæcitas ab ipso deplorata. E Libro
3º Miltoni.*" Listed in Contents, p. [110]. Copy owned by New York Public
Library.

365   [double-ruled border] | THE | Gentleman's Journal: | OR THE MONTH-
LY | MISCELLANY. | In a Letter to a Gentleman in the Country. | Con-
sisting of *News, History, Philosophy*, | *Poetry, Musick, Translations*, &c. | ———
| JUNE, 1694. | ——— | To be continued Monthly. | ——— | Vol. [device]
III. | ——— | *LONDON*, Printed for *Henry Rhodes*, at the *Star*, the Corner
| of *Bride-lane*, in *Fleet-street*, 1694. | Where are to be had compleat Sets for
the two last years, or sin- | gle ones for every month. |

Editor: Peter Motteux. Thomas Power's Latin verse translation of *Paradise
Lost* IV, 440–491, pp. 172–174 [166–168], entitled, "*E. Libro 4º Evæ responsum.*" Listed in Contents, p. [146]. Copy owned by New York Public Library.

366   [double-ruled border] | THE | Gentleman's Journal: | OR THE MONTH-
LY | MISCELLANY. | In a Letter to a Gentleman in the Country. | Con-
sisting of *News, History, Philosophy*, | *Poetry, Musick, Translations*, &c. | ———
| JULY, 1694. | ——— | To be continued Monthly. | ——— | Vol. [device]
III. | ——— | *LONDON*, Printed for *Henry Rhodes*, at the *Star*, the Corner
| of *Bride-lane*, in *Fleet-street*, 1694. | Where are to be had compleat Sets for
the two last years, or sin | gle ones for every month. |

Editor: Peter Motteux. Thomas Power's Latin verse translation of *Paradise
Lost* V, 153–208, pp. 201–202, entitled, "*Hymnus Matutinus, è Libro quinta.*"
Listed in Contents, p. [182]. Copy owned by New York Public Library.

367   [double-ruled border] | LETTERS | OF | STATE, | Written by | Mr. John
Milton, | To most of the Sovereign | Princes and Republicks of | *EUROPE*.
| From the Year 1649. Till | the Year 1659. | ——— | To which is added,
An Account of his | Life. Together with several of his | Poems; And a
Catalogue of his | Works, never before Printed. | ——— | *LONDON:* |
Printed in the Year, 1694. |

Edward Phillips's translation of *Literæ* (No. 321), with some differences, together with "The Life of Mr. John Milton," garbled versions of Sonnets 15, 16, 17, and 22, and a catalogue of the works. First publication of Sonnets 15, 16, and 22.

Duodecimo. A a^{12} b^6 B–P^{12}; 6 + liv + 336 pp. [1], title page; [2], blank; [3-6], To the Reader; i–xliv, Life; xlv, Sonnet 16; xlvi, Sonnet 15; xlvii, Sonnet 17; xlviii, Sonnet 22; [xlix–liv], Catalogue; 1–336, work. Issue 1: "Six Verses", p. xxxv, 1. 6. Three omissions from *Literæ*: Columbia Nos. 20, 93, 123. See Wing, M2126. Copy owned by University of Kentucky Library.

368 [double-ruled border] | LETTERS | OF | STATE, | Written by | Mr. John Milton, | To most of the Sovereign | Princes and Republicks of | *EUROPE.* | From the Year 1649. Till | the Year 1659. | ———— | To which is added, An Account of his | Life. Together with several of his | Poems; And a Catalogue of his | Works, never before Printed. | ———— | *LONDON:* | Printed in the Year, 1694. |

Issue 2 of No. 367. "Ten Verses", p. xxxv, 1. 6. See Wing, M2126. Copy owned by University of Kentucky Library.

369 LUSUS AMATORIUS: | SIVE, | Musæi Poema | DE | HERONE & LEANDRO, | E Græcâ in Latinam Linguam Translatum. | CUI | Aliæ (tres scilicèt) accedunt Nugæ Poëticæ. | ———— | *Authore* C. B. *è Coll. Di. Jo. Bapt. soc.* | ———— | [two lines from Ovid] | ———— | Imprimatur, *Sept.* 18 1693. | EDWARD COOKE. | ———— | LONDINI, | Prostant venales apud Thomam Speed, [name in black letter] ad Insigne | *Trium Coronarum* in vico vulgò vocato *Cornhill*, 1694. |

Author: Charles Blake. Quarto. A–D^4; iv + 28 pp. [i], title page; [ii], blank; [iii], dedication; [iv], blank; 1-27, poems; [28], advertisement. Latin verse translation of Eve's dream, *PL* V, 28–93, entitled, "Fragmentum Libri Quinti Poëmatis verè Divini, quod *Paradisus Amissa* inscribitur, à *Johanne Miltono* Anglicè conscripti, Latino Carmine donatum," pp. 15–20. An argument for the passage is also given. Wing, M3133. Copy owned by William Andrews Clark Library.

370 PARAPHRASIS LATINA, | IN | Duo Poemata, | (Quorum alterum a Miltono, alterum | a Clievelando Anglice scriptum fuit) | Quibus deploratur Mors juvenis præclari & eru- | diti, D. Edvardi King, qui Nave, qua vecta- | batur, Saxo illisa, | in Oceano Hybernico sub- | mersus est. | Autore Gulielmo Hogæo. | ———— | TWO POEMS. | (The one whereof was Penn'd by | *Milton*, and the other by *Clieveland*) | Upon the Death of a worthy and learned young | Gentleman, Mr. *Edward King*, who was | drown'd in the

Irish Seas: to which is added | a *Latin* Paraphrase on both, which was penn'd | by *W. H.* | ———— | *LONDON*, Printed for the Author, 1694. |

Author: William Hog. Said to be published for Hugh Newman in the Term Catalogues. Quarto. [A]^2 B–C^4 D^2; v + 19 pp. [i], title page; [ii], poem on Cambridge in Latin; [iii], dedication; [iv], blank; [v], To the Reader; 1–14, *Lycidas* in English and Latin facing texts; 15–19, Cleveland's poem on King in English and Latin facing texts. Odd numbered pages are on versos; even numbered pages, on rectos. Wing, M2157. Copy owned by British Library.

371   LA VIE | D'OLIVIER CROMWEL. | PREMIERE PARTIE. | [device] | A AMSTERDAM, | Chez ANTOINE SCHELTE, Marchand | Libraire, près la Bourse. | M DC XCIV. |

Author: Gregorio Leti. French edition and translation of No. 361. Translator: Jean Le Pelletier. Two volumes. Vol. 2: same title page as Vol. 1 except "SECONDE". Duodecimo. π^2 A–Z^{12} Aa^8 Bb^6; iv + 555 + 25 pp. Bb7–8 used for π^2. [i–ii], blank; [iii], title page; [iv], blank; 1–555, work; [556–578], Index; [579], errata; [580], blank. Illustrations tipped in. Copy owned by Columbia University Library.

State papers in Latin or in Latin and French translation or in French translation sometimes with Latin head. Some omissions from original edition. Some letters are abbreviated; some translations are partially paraphrase. Reference to Milton as translator (in French) on p. 526:
Columbia No. 5 (French), pp. 54–55
Columbia No. 6 (French), pp. 57
Columbia No. 9 (French), pp. 58–59
Columbia No. 1 (French), pp. 64–66
Columbia No. 11 (Latin), pp. 90–91, and (French), p. 91
Columbia No. 10 (French), pp. 158–159
Columbia No. 13 (French), pp. 161–162
Columbia No. 17 (French), pp. 233–234 (and No. 20)
Columbia No. 22 (Latin), pp. 241–242
Columbia No. 40 (Latin), pp. 301–304
Columbia No. 46 (French), pp. 329
Columbia No. 47 (French), p. 337
Columbia No. 44 (Latin head only), p. 339
Columbia No. 50 (Latin), pp. 340–341, and (French), p. 341
Columbia No. 52 (Latin), pp. 369–371, and (French), pp. 371–373
Columbia No. 56 (Latin), pp. 373–375, and (French), pp. 375–376
Columbia No. 58 (Latin), pp. 377–378, and (French), pp. 378–379
Columbia No. 51 (Latin), pp. 380–382, and (French), pp. 382–385
Columbia No. 59 (Latin), pp. 391–392, and (French), pp. 392–393

Columbia No. 62 (Latin), pp. 393–395
Columbia No. 64 (Latin), pp. 396–398
Columbia No. 63 (Latin), pp. 398–399
Columbia No. 60 (Latin), pp. 399–400
Columbia No. 57 (Latin), p. 419, and (French), p. 420
Columbia No. 91 (French), p. 426
Columbia No. 116 (French), pp. 451–452
Columbia No. 115 (French), p. 452
Columbia No. 118 (French), pp. 457–458
Columbia No. 119 (French), p. 458
Columbia No. 110 (Latin), pp. 462–465, and (French), pp. 465–468
Columbia No. 112 (Latin), pp. 468–469, and (French), pp. 469–470
Columbia No. 109 (French), p. 472
Columbia No. 120 (French), pp. 478–479
Columbia No. 124 (French), pp. 516–517
Columbia No. 125 (French), pp. 517–518
Columbia No. 126 (French), pp. 518–519
Columbia No. 128 (French), pp. 519–520
Columbia No. 130 (French), p. 521
Columbia No. 131 (French), p. 522
Columbia No. 132 (French), p. 524
Columbia No. 133 (French), pp. 524–525
Columbia No. 134 (French), p. 527
Columbia No. 135 (French), pp. 539–540
Columbia No. 136 (French), pp. 540–541

1695

372 A | DEFENCE | OF THE | PEOPLE | OF | ENGLAND. | ——— | By
JOHN MILTON. | ——— | In Answer to *Salmasius*'s De- | fence of the King.
| ——— | [device] | ===== | Printed in the Year 1695. |

Another issue of No. 359. Cancel title page. $A^8(\pm A2)$ a B-Q^8 R^4. Wing,
M2104A. Copy owned by British Library.

373 A | DEFENCE | OF THE | PEOPLE | OF | ENGLAND. | ——— | By
JOHN MILTON. | ——— | In Answer to *Salmasius*'s De- | fence of the King.
| ——— | [ornamental device] | ——— | *LONDON;* | Printed for *Nathaniel
Rolls*, at his Auction-house | in *Petty-Canons Hall*, near the North-side of |
St. *Paul*'s Church. 1695. |

Another issue of No. 359. Cancel title page. $A^8(\pm A2)$ a B-Q^8 R^4. Wing,
M2105. Copy owned by Yale University Library.

374   [double-ruled border] | THE | HISTORY | OF | BRITAIN, | That Part
        especially now call'd | ENGLAND. | From the first Traditional Beginning,
        | Continu'd to the | NORMAN CONQUEST. | Collected out of the An-
        cientest and | Best Authors thereof, by | ———— | *JOHN MILTON.* | ════
        | *LONDON*, | Printed by *R. E.* for *R. Scot, R. Chiswell,* | *R. Bently, G.
        Sawbridge*; and are to be Sold | by *A. Swall,* and *T. Child,* in St. *Paul's* |
        Church-yard. 1695. |

        Edition 3, Issue 1 (?), of No. 306. Printer may have been Richard Ever-
        ingham. Octavo. A–Z Aa–Cc^8; 416 pp. [1–2], blank and missing; [3], title
        page; [4], blank; 5–357, work; [358], blank; [359–416], Index. A1 present
        and blank in copy owned by Alexander Turnbull Library. Wing, M2124.
        Copy owned by University of Kentucky.

375   [double-ruled border] | THE | HISTORY | OF | BRITAIN, | That Part
        especially now call'd | ENGLAND. | From the first Traditional Beginning,
        | Continu'd to the | NORMAN CONQUEST. | Collected out of the An-
        cientest and | Best Authors thereof, by | ———— | *JOHN MILTON.* | ════
        | *LONDON*, | Printed for *Ri. Chiswell.* Sold by *Nath. Roles,* | at his Auction-
        House in *Petty-Cannons-* | Hall, near the North side of St. *Paul's-* | Church.
        M DC XCV. |

        Edition 3, Issue 2 (?), of No. 306. Reissue of No. 374. A2 is a cancel. A1v
        has White's engraved portrait with Dryden's epigram beneath pasted on in
        copy reported. Wing, M2123. Copy owned by New York Public Library.

376   [double-ruled border] | Paradise Lost. | A | POEM | In Twelve Books. |
        ———— | The AUTHOUR | *JOHN MILTON.* | ———— | *The Sixth Edition,
        with Sculptures.* | ———— | To which is added, | Explanatory NOTES upon
        each Book, and a TABLE | to the POEM, never before Printed. | ————
        | *LONDON*, | Printed by *Tho. Hodgkin,* for *Jacob Tonson,* at the | Judge's-
        Head near the *Inner-Temple Gate,* in *Fleet-street.* | M DC XC V. |

        Edition 6. Separate copy of *Paradise Lost*; see No. 382. Folio in fours. A–B^2
        C–Z Aa–Yy^4; iv + 348 pp. Pp. 219–[220] repeated. [i], title page; [ii], blank;
        [iii], The Verse; [iv], blank; 1–343, work; [344–346], Table. Portrait by
        White, with Dryden's epigram, and the 1688 illustrations tipped in. Ex-
        planatory Notes are missing in each separate copy of the poem examined.
        Verse numbers are given for the poem. Second printing and issue of this
        edition of *Paradise Lost*; compare No. 381.

        Heading for *Table*:
        ════ | A | TABLE | Of the most remarkable Parts of | MILTON's *Paradise
        Lost,* | Under the Three Heads of | *Descriptions, Similies,* and *Speeches.* | [etc.] |

        Second printing of *Table*; compare No. 381. *Table* printed frequently in the
        eighteenth century as the Index.

Wing, M2151. Copy owned by Folger Shakespeare Library.

377   [double-ruled border] | Paradise Lost. | A | POEM | In Twelve Books. |
────── | The AUTHOUR | *JOHN MILTON.* | ────── | *The Sixth Edition,*
with Sculptures. | ────── | To which is added, | Explanatory NOTES upon
each BOOK, and a TABLE | to the POEM, never before Printed. | ──────
| *LONDON,* | Printed by *Tho. Hodgkin,* for *Jacob Tonson,* at the | Judge's-
Head near the *Inner-Temple Gate,* in *Fleet-street.* | M DC XC V. |

Same as No. 376, but with this is bound (contemporary) the 1688 *Paradise*
Regain'd and *Samson Agonistes* (No. 348), reissued. Volume was created by
adding unsold copies of the 1688 *Paradise Regain'd* and *Samson Agonistes* to
the 1695 *Paradise Lost,* separated from the 1695 *Poetical Works,* second printing and second issue. A new edition of *Paradise Regain'd* and *Samson Agonistes*
(No. 379) was also required; see No. 378.

Wing, M2151, M2154, M2177. Copy formerly owned by G. William Stuart,
Jr., Yuma, Arizona; now in Alexander Turnbull Library.

378   [double-ruled border] | *Paradise Lost.* | A | POEM | In Twelve Books. |
────── | The AUTHOUR | *JOHN MILTON.* | ────── | *The Sixth Edition,*
with Sculptures. | ────── | To which is added, | Explanatory NOTES upon
each BOOK, and a TABLE | to the POEM, never before Printed. | ──────
| *LONDON,* | Printed by *Tho. Hodgkin,* for *Jacob Tonson,* at the | Judge's-
Head near the *Inner-Temple Gate,* in *Fleet-street.* | M DC XC V. |

Another reissue of No. 376, but with this is bound (contemporary) the 1695
Paradise Regain'd and *Samson Agonistes* (No. 379), reissued. Compare No. 377.

Wing, M2151 and/or Wing, M2163. Copy owned by University of Kentucky Library.

379   [double-ruled border] | Paradise Regain'd. | A | POEM. | ────── | In IV.
BOOKS. | ────── | To which is added | Samson Agonistes. | ────── | The
Author | *JOHN MILTON.* | ═════ | *LONDON:* | Printed by *R. E.* and
are to be sold by | *John Whitlock* near *Stationers-Hall.* | MDCCXV. |

Note error in date. Folio in fours. A–H^4 I^2 A–H^4; ii + 66, vi + 58 pp.
[i], title page; [ii], blank; 1–66, text of *Paradise Regain'd*; [i], title page for
Samson Agonistes; [ii], blank; [iii–iv], Of a Dramatic Poem; [v], Argument;
[vi], Dramatis Personae; 1–57, text of *Samson Agonistes*; [58], blank. Printer
may have been Richard Everingham. Same page distribution as in the 1688
edition, but the works have been reset and errors corrected; e. g., "ends,"
p. [v] of *Samson Agonistes,* to "ends."

Title page for *Samson Agonistes*:
[double-ruled border] | Samson Agonistes, | A | DRAMATICK | POEM.

| ——— | The AUTHOR | *JOHN MILTON.* | ——— | *Aristot.* Poet. Cap.
6. | [quotation in Greek] | [quotation in Latin] | ——— | *LONDON:* |
Printed by *R. E.* and are to be sold by | *John Whitlock* near *Stationers-Hall.*
| MDCXCV. |

Not in Wing; apparently considered only as part of No. 378 (Wing, M2163).
Copy owned by University of Western Ontario Library.

380   [double-ruled border] | POEMS | UPON | Several Occasions. | ———
| Compos'd at several times. | ——— | BY | Mr. *JOHN MILTON.* | ———
| The Third Edition. [black letter] | ——— | *LONDON:* | Printed for *Jacob
Tonson* at the *Judge's* Head, near the *Inner-* | *Temple-Gate* in *Fleet-street.* 1695. |

Folio. A–D + D E–Q^2; iv + 64 pp. [i], title page; [ii], blank; [iii–iv], Con-
tents; 1–34, texts of English poems; [35], title page for Latin poems; [36],
blank; 37–60, Latin poems and testimonies. Four pages unnumbered: 1–9,
x, x, 10–11, x, x, 12–60. Poems appear in different arrangement from that
of Edition 2 (No. 313):
"Lycidas," pp. 1–3
"L'Allegro," pp. 3–4
"Il Penseroso," pp. 4–6
"A Mask," pp. 6–12 (eleven pages)
"Arcades," pp. 12–13
"Ode on the Morning of Christ's Nativity," pp. 13–16
Psalm 114, p. 16
Psalm 136, pp. 16–17
"Fair Infant Elegy," pp. 17–18
"The Passion," pp. 18–19
"On Time," p. 19
"Upon the Circumcision," pp. 19–20
"At a Solemn Music," p. 20
"Epitaph on the Marchioness of Winchester," pp. 20–21
"Song: On May Morning," p. 21
"On Shakespear," p. 21
"On the University Carrier," p. 21
"Another on the same," pp. 21–22
"At a Vacation Exercise," pp. 22–23
"On the New Forcers of Conscience," p. 23
Sonnet 1, p. 23
Sonnet 2, p. 23
Sonnet 3, p. 23–24
Canzone, p. 24
Sonnet 4, p. 24
Sonnet 5, p. 24
Sonnet 6, p. 24

Omits "Philosophus ad regem" and "In Effigei Ejus Sculptorem."

Title page for Latin poems:
—— | Joannis Miltoni | *LONDINENSIS* | *POEMATA.* | Quorum plera-
que intra Annum Ætatis | Vigesimum Conscripsit. | —— |

Wing, M2162. Copy owned by Yale University Library.

381 [double-ruled border] | THE | POETICAL | WORKS | OF | Mr. John
Milton.| CONTAINING, | Paradise Lost, Paradise Regain'd, | *Sampson
Agonistes*, and his Poems | on several occasions. | —— | TOGETHER
WITH | Explanatory NOTES on each Book of the | *PARADISE LOST*,
and a *TABLE* | never before Printed. | ===== | *LONDON:* | Printed for
Jacob Tonson, at the *Judges-Head* near the *Inner-Temple-* | Gate in *Fleet-street*,
M DC XC V. |

Folio in twos and fours. π^1 A χ B^2 C–Z Aa–Xx^4 Yy–Zz Aa^2; [A]^1 B–Z
Aa–Zz Aaa–Zzz Aaaa–Mmmm^2 χ^1; A–R^2 A–H^4; A–D +D E–Q^2. x
+ 350, ii + 322, ii + 66, vi + 58, iv + 64 pp. π^1 at beginning and
χ^1 at end of *Annotations* are conjugate. Arrangement: Preliminary materi
al, *Table, Paradise Lost*, Subscribers, *Annotations, Paradise Regain'd, Samson
Agonistes, Poems.* Various copies have differing arrangements. For example,
a copy in the Princeton University Library places the subscribers and Table
after *Paradise Lost* and *Annotations* after *Samson Agonistes.* Wing, H3663,
M2163, M2151, M2162. Copy owned by New York Public Library, shelf
mark: 8-*NCF / + / 1695.

Title page for *Paradise Lost:*
[double-ruled border] | Paradise Lost. | A | POEM | In Twelve Books. |
—— | The AUTHOUR | *JOHN MILTON.* | —— | *The Sixth Edition,
with Sculptures.* | —— | To which is added, | Explanatory NOTES upon
each BOOK, and a TABLE | to the POEM, never before Printed. | ——
| *LONDON,* | Printed by *Tho. Hodgkin,* for *Jacob Tonson,* at the | Judge's-
Head near the *Inner-Temple Gate,* in *Fleet-street.* | M DC XCV. |

π^1 A χ B^2 C–Z Aa–Xx^4 Yy–Zz Aa^2; x + 350 pp. Reissue of 1688 fourth
edition of *Paradise Lost* (see Nos. 345–347). [i], title page for *Poetical Works;*
[ii], blank; [iii], title page for *Paradise Lost;* [iv], blank; [v], The Verse; [vi],
blank; [vii–ix], *Table;* [x], blank; 1–343, text of *Paradise Lost;* [344], blank;
[345–350], Subscribers. Frontispiece, Robert White's engraved portrait with
John Dryden's epigram, and illustrations from 1688 *Paradise Lost* tipped in.
No verse numbers given for the poem. First printing and issue of this edition of *Paradise Lost;* see Nos. 376 and 382 for second printing and issue.
Pp. 219–[220] in first section (*Paradise Lost*) repeated.

Heading for *Table:*
===== | A | TABLE | Of the most remarkable Parts of | MILTON's *Paradise
Lost.* | Under the Three Heads of | *Descriptions, Similies,* and *Speeches.* | [etc.] |

First printing of *Table*; see Nos. 376 and 382 for second printing.

Title page for *Annotations*:
====== | ANNOTATIONS | ON | MILTON's | Paradise Lost. | WHERE-
IN | The Texts of Sacred Writ, relating to the POEM, | are Quoted; The
Parallel Places and Imitations of | the most Excellent *Homer* and *Virgil*, Cited
and | Compared; All the Obscure Parts render'd in | Phrases more Familiar;
The Old and Obsolete | Words, with their Originals, Explain'd and made
| Easie to the *English* Reader. | ———— | By *P. H.* φιλοποιετες. | ———— |
Uni, cedit MILTONUS, *Homero* | *Propter Mille annos*   Juv. vii.38. | ————
| *LONDON,* | Printed for *Jacob Tonson,* at the *Judges Head* near the *Inner-
Temple-* | *Gate* in *Fleet-street,* MDCXCV. |

[A]¹ B–Z Aa–Zz Aaa–Zzz Aaaa–Mmmm² χ¹; ii + 322 pp. π¹ and χ¹ are
conjugate. [i], title page for *Annotations*; [ii], blank; 1–321, text of *Annotations*; [322], blank. P. H. is identified as Patrick Hume.

Text of *Paradise Regain'd* and *Samson Agonistes* is a reissue of No. 348 (1688
edition).

Text of *Poems* is a reissue of No. 380 (1695 edition).

382   [double-ruled border] | THE | POETICAL | WORKS | OF | Mr. John
Milton. | CONTAINING, | Paradise Lost, Paradise Regain'd, | *Sampson
Agonistes,* and his Poems | on several Occasions. | ———— | TOGETHER
WITH | Explanatory NOTES | on each Book of the | *PARADISE LOST,*
and a *TABLE* | never before Printed. | ====== | *LONDON:* | Printed for
Jacob Tonson, at the *Judges-Head* near the *Inner-Temple-* | *Gate* in *Fleet-street,*
M DC XC V. |

Different issue of No. 381. Folio in twos and fours. π² A–B² C–Z Aa–Yy⁴;
[A]¹ B–Z Aa–Zz Aaa–Zzz Aaaa–Mmmm² χ¹; A–H⁴ I²; A–H⁴; A–D + D
E–Q². 2 + iv + 348; ii + 322; ii + 66, vi + 58; iv + 64 pp. Pp. 219–[220]
in first section (*Paradise Lost*) repeated. Various copies have differing ar-
rangements. For example, *Annotations* may appear last as in a copy in the
Folger Shakespeare Library. Wing, H3663, M2163, M2151, M2154,
M2177, M2162. Copy owned by New York Public Library, shelf mark:
*NCF / + / 1695.

Texts of *Paradise Lost* and *Table* same as No. 376 with preliminary leaf: [1],
title page for *Poetical Works*; [2], blank. Second printing and issue of *Paradise
Lost*, and second printing of *Table*; compare No. 381.

Text of *Annotations* same as that in No. 381.

Text of *Paradise Regain'd* and *Samson Agonistes* is a reissue of No. 379 (1695
edition).

Text of *Poems* is a reissue of No. 380 (1695 edition).

383   [double-ruled border] | THE | POETICAL | WORKS | OF | Mr. John Milton. | CONTAINING, | Paradise Lost, Paradise Regain'd, | *Sampson Agonistes,* and his Poems | on several Occasions. | —— | TOGETHER WITH | Explanatory NOTES | on each Book of the | *PARADISE LOST,* and a *TABLE* | never before Printed. | === | *LONDON:* | Printed for *Jacob Tonson,* at the *Judges-Head* near the *Inner-Temple-* | *Gate* in *Fleet-street,* M DC XC V. |

Different issue of No. 382. Only the text of *Paradise Regain'd* and *Samson Agonistes* is different, being a reissue of No. 348 (1688 edition). See No. 381 for Wing numbers. Copy owned by University of Kentucky Library.

1696

384   [double-ruled border] | A | DETECTION | OF THE | Court and State [black letter] | OF | ENGLAND | DURING | The Four last Reigns, | AND THE | INTER-REGNUM. | Consisting of | Private Memoirs, &c. | With Observations and Reflections. | AND AN | *Appendix,* discovering the present State of the Nation. | —— | The Second Edition corrected. [black letter] | —— | To which are added | Many other Secrets, ["Secrets" in black letter] never before made publick | As also, a more impartial Account of the *CIVIL* | *WARS* in *England,* than has yet been given. | —— | In Two Volumes. | —— | By *ROGER COKE,* Esquire. | —— | *LON-DON,* | Printed in the Year, MDCXCVI. |

Author: Roger Coke. Edition 2. Octavo. A–L Aa–Mm^8 Nn^4 χ^1 Aaa–Eee^8 Fff^4 Aaaa–Nnnn Aaaaa–Eeeee^8(–Eeeee8); xlii + 134 + 200, ii + 88 + 208 + 78 pp. (752 pp. total). Eeeee8 used as χ1. [i], title page; [ii], blank; [iii–xi], An Apology to the Reader; [xii–xlii], Introduction; 1–134, Book I; 1–200, Book II; [i], title page for Vol. 2; [ii], blank; 1–88, Book III; 1–208, Book IV; 1–77, Appendix; [78], blank.

Vol. 2: same title page except "VOL. II." for "In Two Volumes." In Book III (first gathering, pp. 1–88, Aaa–Eee^8 Fff^4): Letter to the State of Holland, dated 1 April 1653, incomplete, given in English, p. 19 (Bbb2); Letter to States General, dated 1 April 1653, incomplete, given in English, p. 19 (Bbb2); Articles of Peace with the Dutch (Columbia No. 167E) cited and incompletely given in English, pp. 39–40 (Ccc4–Ccc4v). Dates may be in error; heading for p. 19 is "1652". Letters may not derive from Milton's copies. Wing, C4974. Copy owned by Newberry Library.

385   SAMUELIS LIBERI BARONIS de PUFENDORF | *De* | REBUS | A | CAROLO | GUSTAVO | SVECIÆ REGE | GESTIS | COMMEN-TARIORUM | LIBRI SEPTEM | ELEGANTISSIMUS TABULIS

ÆNEIS | EXORNATI | *Cum* | TRIPLICI INDICI. | [device] | *NORIMBERGÆ* | Sumptibus CHRISTOPHORI RIEGELII. | *Literis KNORZIANIS.* | ANNO M.DC. XCVI. |

Folio in fours. $\pi^2 \chi^2 \chi\chi^4$ $A^4(-A1)$ B-Z Aa-Zz Aaa-Zzz Aaaa-Iiii^4 Kkkk^2 a-h^4; x + 628 + 64 pp. Cancel stub between $\chi\chi4$ and A2. [i], half title; [ii], blank; [iii], title page; [iv], blank; [v-vi], dedication; [vi-viii], prose dedication; [ix-x], preface; [1], half title; [2], blank; [3-4], summary; [5]-626, work; [627-628], blank; [1], half title; [2], blank; 3-10, Swedish treaty and related material; 11-53, other treaties and documents; [54-56], Table 1; [57-62], Table 2; [63-64], Table 3. Extensive illustrations tipped in.

Attribution: Swedish treaty (Columbia No. 170), 17 July 1656, cited, pp. 221-222; published in Latin ("Foedus Anglicum") in Appendix (new signatures and pagination), pp. 3-10. Reference to Milton, p. 219. Copy owned by Trinity College Library, Dublin.

386   [double-ruled border] | A | SUPPLEMENT | To the First EDITION of the | DETECTION | OF THE | Court and State [black letter] | OF | ENGLAND | DURING THE | Four last Reigns, | AND THE | INTER-REGNUM. | Containing many *Secrets* never before | made publick: As also a more Impartial | Account of the *Civil Wars* in *England,* | than has yet been given. | ———— | By *Roger Coke,* Esq; | ———— | *LONDON,* | Printed for *Andrew Bell* at the Sign of the *Cross-keys* in the | *Poultrey* near *Stocks-market.* 1696. |

Author: Roger Coke. First edition of material included in No. 384, revision of the 1694 edition of *A Detection of the Court and State.* Octavo. π^1 A-N^8 O^4; ii + 216 pp. [i], title page; [ii], blank; 1-216, work. Letter to the State of Holland and letter to the States General, pp. 152-153. Articles of Peace with the Dutch (Columbia No. 167E), pp. 185-187. Wing, C4981. Copy owned by Folger Shakespeare Library.

387   LA VIE | D'OLIVIER | CROMWEL. | *Par* GREGOIRE LETI. | TOME PREMIER. | [device] | A AMSTERDAM, | Chez HENRI DESBORDES, dans | le Kalver-straat, près le Dam. | ———— | *M. DC. XCVI.* |

A reissue of No. 371. Vol. I: Duodecimo. ã^{12} ẽ^6 A-X^{12}; xxxvi + 476 + 28 pp. [i-ii], blank; [iii], title page; [iv], blank; [v-xiv], dedication; [xv-xxiv], translator's note; [xxv-xxxv], To the Reader; [xxxvi], "Avis"; 1-476, work; [477-504], index.

Vol 2: LA VIE | D'OLIVIER | CROMWEL. | TOME SECOND. | [different device] | A AMSTERDAM, | Chez HENRI DESBORDES, dans le | Kalver-straat, près le Dam. | ———— | *M. DC. XCVI.* |

Duodecimo. π^2 A-Z^{12} Aa^8 Bb^6; iv + 555 + 25 pp. Bb7-8 used for π^2.

[i–ii], blank; [iii], title page; [iv], blank; 1–555, work; [556–579], index; [580], blank. Contents as in No. 371. Copy owned by Cambridge University Library.

Johann Georg Theodor Graesse cites a French edition from Paris in 1700, in three volumes and duodecimo, in *Trésor de Livres Rares et Précieux* (Milano: Görlich, 1950). No such edition is otherwise known; see also Nati Krivatsy, compiler, *Bibliography of the Works of Gregorio Leti* (New Castle, Delaware: Oak Knoll Books 1982), p. 35.

1697

388   [double-ruled border] | A | DETECTION | OF THE | Court and State [black letter] | OF | ENGLAND | DURING | The Four Last REIGNS | And the INTER-REGNUM. | Consisting of | Private Memoirs, &c. | With Observations and Reflections. | AND AN | *APPENDIX*, discovering the present State of the Nation. | Wherein are many SECRETS never before made pub- | lick: As also, a more impartial Account of the CIVIL | WARS in *England*, than has yet been given. | ——— | In Two Volumes. | ——— | By *ROGER COKE*, Esquire. | ——— | The Third Edition very much corrected: [black letter] | With an Alphabetical Table. | ——— | *London*, Printed for Andr. Bell [name in black letter] at the Cross- | keys and Bible in *Cornhill*. MDCXCVII. |

Edition 3 of No. 384. Octavo. A–Z Aa–Xx^8; 704 pp. [1], title page; [2], blank; 3–682, work; [683–702], Index; [703–704], Advertisements. Letter to the State of Holland, dated 1 April 1653, incomplete, given in English, p. 357. Letter to States General, dated 1 April 1653, incomplete, given in English, p. 358. (Dates may be in error; letters may not have derived from Milton's.) Articles of Peace with the Dutch (Columbia No. 167E) cited and incompletely given in English, pp. 375–376. Wing, C4975. Copy owned by Folger Shakespeare Library.

389   Herrn | Samuel Freyherrns von Pufendorf | Sieben Bücher | Von denen | Thaten | Carl Gustaus | Königs in Schweden, | Mit | Vortrefflichen Kupffern ausgezieret und mit | nöthingen Registern versehen | aus dem Lateinischen ins Hoch-Teutsche übersetzet | Von | S. R. | [device] | Nürnberg, | In Verlegung Christoph Riegels. | Gedruckt mit Knorzischen Schrifften. | An. M. DC. XCVII. |

German translation of No. 385. Two volumes. Folio in fours. Vol. 1:)(-)( )(^{2} A–Z Aa–Zz Aaa–Ddd^4 Eee^1; viii + 402 pp. [i–ii], blank; [iii], title page; [iv], blank; [v–vi], dedication; [vi–viii], dedicatory preface; [1], half title; [2], blank; [3-4], summary; [5]-402, work. Vol. 2: Eee^4(-Eee1) Fff-Zzz Aaaa-Zzzz Azzzz-Hhhhh a-c^4; 420 pp. [403], half title; [404], blank; [405-406], summary; [407]-688, work; [689], half title; [690] blank; [691]-696, Swedish treaty (Columbia No. 170); 696-697, relative documents; 698-734, other documents; [735-751], Table 1; [752-798], Table 2; [1], half title; [2], blank; 3-24, Erklärungen. Illustrations tipped in. Discussion of Milton's work as Secretary, pp. 245-246. Listed in Table 2. Copy owned by Newberry Library.

390 HISTOIRE | DU REGNE | *DE* | CHARLES | GUSTAVE | ROY DE SVEDE | *COMPRISE* | EN SEPT | COMMENTAIRES | ENRICHIS DE TAILLES DOUCES | TRADUITE EN FRANCOIS SUR LE FATIN | *DE* | MONSIEUR LE BARON SAMUEL de PUFENDORF. | AVEC TROIS INDICES. | [device] | *IMPRIME à NUREMBERG AUX FRAIS* | DE CHRISTOPHLE RIEGEL | par KNORZ Imprimeur. | 1697. |

French translation of No. 385. Folio in fours. χ-$\chi\chi^2$ A-Z Aa-ZZ Aaa-Zzz Aaaa-Zzzz Aaaaa-Bbbbb a-d^4 e^6; viii + 752 + 44 pp. [i], half title; [ii], blank; [iii], title page; [iv], blank; [v], dedication; [vi-viii], dedicatory preface; [1], half title; [2], blank; [3-4], summary; [5]- 752, work; [1], half title; [2], blank; 3-7, Swedish Treaty (Columbia No. 170); 7-8, related documents; 8-35, other documents; [36-38], Table 1; [38-42], Table 2; [43-44], Table 3. Volume II contains the portraits, not tipped in as frontispieces in Volume I. Discussion of Milton's work as Secretary, Book III, Section 80, is on pp. 260-261. The Treaty is dated 15 June 1655. Copy owned by British Library.

390A HET LEVEN | VAN | OLIVIER | CROMWEL, | BEHELSENDE | *Des selfs Staatkundige en doorslepene handelingen,* | *onmatige heerssucht, overgroote schynheyligheyt,* | *en verlokkende welspreekenheyt;* | Waar door hy des selfs eygen Koning en Souve- | reyn CAREL de I. buyten eenigh exempel, sijn | proces heeft doen maken, ter dood laten | executeren, en sigh selfs tot een Pro- | tector van de vryheyt van Enge- | landt heeft doen verklaren. | *Alles door* GREGORIO LETI *naauwkeuriglyk* | *in 't Italiaans beschreven.* | Met Figuren. | *EERSTE DEEL.* | [device] | IN 'S GRAVENHAGE, | —— | By MEYNDERT UYTWERF, Boekverkooper | in de Hofstraat, MDCXCVII. |

Dutch translation of No. 361. Two volumes. Octavo. Volume 1: π^1 *8(-8) A-Z Aa-Ll^8 Mm-Oo^6; 2 + xiv + 586 pp. *8 used for π1. Cancel stubs between Nn7 and Oo1. [1], blank; [2], portrait; [i], title page; [ii], blank; [iii-xiv], Foreword; 1-562, work; [563-586], Index.

Volume 1 was given a second edition, with text and register totally reset, and cancels between *7 and A1, and between Nn6 and Oo1. The portrait is missing. Differences on title page: ... Koning en | Souvereyn CAREL de I. buyten eenigh exempel, syn | proces heeft doen maken, ter dood laten executeren, | en sigh selfs tote een Protector van de vryheyt | van Engelandt heeft doen verklaren. | ... *EERSTE DEEL.* | De tweed Druk, van nieuws oversien. | [different device] | IN 's GRAVENHAGE, | ——— | By MEYNDERT UYTWERF, Boekverkooper in de | Hoff-straat, MDCXCVII. |

Volume 2: title page same as first copy except: *TWEEDE DEEL.* | Den tweeden Druk van nieuws oversien en verbetert. | [same device as in first copy] |

A–Z Aa–Tt^8; 672 pp. [1], title page; [2], blank; 3–650, work; [651–671], Index; [672], blank. Illustrations tipped in.

State papers in Latin and Dutch with reference to Milton as translator (in Dutch) on p. 615:
Columbia No. 5, in Dutch, pp. 64–65
Columbia No. 6, in Dutch, pp. 67–68
Columbia No. 9, in Dutch, pp. 68–70
Columbia No. 1, in Dutch, pp. 76–78
Columbia No. 11, in Latin, pp. 105–106, and Dutch, pp. 106–107
Columbia No. 10, in Dutch, pp. 185–187
Columbia No. 13, in Dutch, pp. 188–190
Columbia No. 22, in Latin, pp. 281–283, and Dutch, pp. 283–284
Columbia No. 40, in Latin, pp. 351–354
Columbia No. 167E (in part), in Dutch, pp. [367–370]
Columbia No. 46, in Dutch, pp. 381–382
Columbia No. 47, in Dutch, p. 391
Columbia No. 50, in Latin, pp. 394–395, and Dutch, p. 396
Columbia No. 52, in Latin, pp. 427–430, and Dutch, pp. 430–432
Columbia No. 56, in Latin, pp. 432–435, and Dutch, pp. 435–437
Columbia No. 58, in Latin, pp. 437–439, and Dutch, pp. 439–440
Columbia No. 51, in Latin, pp. 441–444, and Dutch, pp. 444–448
Columbia No. 59, in Latin, pp. 454–456, and Dutch, pp. 456–458
Columbia No. 62, in Latin, pp. 458–460
Columbia No. 64, in Latin, pp. 461–463
Columbia No. 63, in Latin, pp. 463–465
Columbia No. 60, in Latin, pp. 465–466
Columbia No. 57, in Latin, pp. 488–489, and Dutch, pp. 488–489
Columbia No. 91, in Dutch, pp. 495–496
Columbia No. 116, in Dutch, p. 526
Columbia No. 115, in Dutch, p. 526
Columbia No. 118, in Dutch, pp. 532–533
Columbia No. 119, in Dutch, p. 533
Columbia No. 110, in Latin, pp. 538–542, and Dutch, pp. 542–546

Columbia No. 112, in Latin, pp. 546–547, and Dutch, pp. 547–548
Columbia No. 109, in Dutch, pp. 550–551
Columbia No. 120, in Dutch, pp. 557–559
Columbia No. 124, in Dutch, pp. 602–604
Columbia No. 125, in Dutch, pp. 604–605
Columbia No. 126, in Dutch, pp. 605–607
Columbia No. 128, in Dutch, pp. 607–609
Columbia No. 130, in Dutch, pp. 609–610
Columbia No. 131, in Dutch, pp. 610–611
Columbia No. 132, in Dutch, pp. 612–613
Columbia No. 133, in Dutch, pp. 613–614
Columbia No. 134, in Dutch, pp. 615–617
Columbia No. 135, in Dutch, pp. 631–632
Columbia No. 136, in Dutch, pp. 633–634

Copies owned by Universiteits-Bibliotheek, Amsterdam.

Wilbur C. Abbott, in *A Bibliography of Oliver Cromwell* (Cambridge, Mass.: Harvard University Press, 1929), lists as No. 1207, an edition in Dutch from Amsterdam in 1692. Apparently no such edition exists; see Nati Krivatsy, compiler, *Bibliography of the Works of Gregorio Leti* (New Castle, Delaware: Oak Knoll Books, 1982), p. 33.

391   [double-ruled border] | THE | Secrets of Government, [black letter] | AND | Misteries of State, | Plainly laid open, in all the several | Forms of Government | IN THE | CHRISTIAN WORLD. | ——— | Published by | *JOHN MILTON*, Esq; | ——— | Printed in the Year, 1697. |

Reprint of No. 256. Octavo. $A^4(\pm A1) B^8(\pm B1) C$-$Q^8$; viii + 240 pp. Cancel stub between A and B. [i], title page; [ii], blank; [iii]–iv, To the Reader (Milton's preface); v–viii, Contents; 1–238, work; [239–240], Advertisement. Wing, R187. Copy owned by Folger Shakespeare Library.

392   [double-ruled border] | THE | Secrets of Government, [black letter] | AND | Misteries of State, | Plainly laid open, in all the several | Forms of Government | IN THE | CHRISTIAN WORLD. | ——— | Published by | *JOHN MILTON*, Esq; | ——— | Printed in the Year, 1697. |

Reissue of No. 391. Octavo. $[A]^1 B$-Q^8; ii + 240 pp. New title page on different paper from rest of volume with sig. A of No. 391 discarded. [i], title page; [ii], blank; 1–238, work; [239–240], Advertisement. Not in Wing. Copy owned by Carl H. Pforzheimer Library, New York City.

393   [double-ruled border] | THE | WORKS | OF M.ʳ John Milton. | ——— | [device] | ===== | Printed in the Year M DC XC VII. |

Edition of most of the English prose. Folio in fours. π^2 A–Z Aa–Zz Aaa–Zzz

Aaaa–Cccc⁴; 4 + vi + 570 pp. [1], title page; [2], blank; [3], Contents; [4], blank; [i], title page for *Doctrine and Discipline of Divorce*; [ii], blank; [iii–vi], To the Parlament; 1–56, text of *Doctrine and Discipline of Divorce* (No. 62); [57], title page for *Tetrachordon*; [58], blank; [59–61], To the Parlament; 62–127, text of *Tetrachordon* (No. 72); 127–144, text of *Colasterion* (No. 66); [145], title page for *The Judgement of Martin Bucer*; [146], blank; [147–150], To the Parlament; [151–152], Testimonies; 153–169, text of *The Judgement of Martin Bucer* (No. 63); 170–202, text of *Of Reformation* (No. 56); [203], title page for *The Reason of Church-Government*; 204, Preface; 205–243, text of *The Reason of Church-Government* (No. 59); 243–260, text of *A Treatise of Civil Power* (No. 273); 260–284, text of *Considerations Touching the Likeliest Means to Remove Hirelings* (No. 268); 284–294, text of *Of Prelatical Episcopacy* (No. 54); 294–325, text of *Animadversions* (No. 47); 325–361, text of *An Apology for Smectymnuus* (No. 58); 361–371, text of *The Ready and Easy Way* (No. 275); 371–397, text of *Areopagitica* (No. 61); 397–422, text of *The Tenure of Kings and Magistrates* (No. 85); 422–427, text of *Brief Notes upon a Late Sermon* (No. 274); 428–434, text of *Of True Religion* (No. 312); [435], title page for *Eikonoklastes*; [436], blank; [437–439], Preface; 440–530, text of *Eikonoklastes* (No. 78); 530–556, text of *Articles of Peace* (No. 77); 556–568, text of *Observations upon the Articles of Peace* (No. 77); [569–570], blank.

Approximations of title pages given on separate pages; partial title pages introduce other texts. Gives Edition 2 of *Tenure* and Edition 1 of *Eikonoklastes* and *The Ready and Easy Way*. Omits *Of Education, Accedence Commenc't Grammar, History of Britain, Declaration, or Letters Patents, The Character of the Long Parliament*, and *A Brief History of Moscovia*. Wing, M2086. Copy owned by University of Kentucky Library.

1698

394 [double-ruled border] | COMOEDIA | Joannis Miltoni, | Viri clarissimi, | (Quæ agebatur in Arce *Ludensi*) | PARAPHRASTICE | REDDITA. | ——— | *A* GULIELMO HOGÆO. | ——— | [device] | ——— | ANNO DOMINI 1698. |

Translator: William Hog. Latin verse translation of *A Mask*. Quarto. A–G⁴; viii + 48 pp. [i], title page; [ii], blank; [iii–vi], dedicatory epistle; [vii–viii], dedicatory poem; 1–47, work; [48], blank. Wing, M2100. Copy owned by Henry E. Huntington Library.

395 [rubricated] | A | Complete Collection | OF THE | Historical, Political, and Miscellaneous | WORKS | OF | John Milton, | Both ENGLISH and LATIN. | With som PAPERS never before Publish'd. | ——— | In Three Volumes, [black letter] | ——— | To which is Prefix'd | the LIFE of the

AUTHOR, | Containing, | Besides the History of his Works, | Several Extraordinary Characters of Men and | Books, Sects, Parties, and Opinions. | ――― | *AMSTERDAM,* | Finish'd in the Year M. DC. XC. VIII. |

Published in London. Three volumes. Volumes appear separately or I and II may be combined. Volume III has separate signatures and pagination; sometimes it is catalogued as a separate volume. This printing is sometimes erroneously called "Toland's Edition." Some half titles for separate works are dated 1694.

Vol. 1: Folio in fours and sixes. π^2 $*^2$ a–e^4 [A]^2 B–R^4 S^6 T–V^4 X^4($\pm$ X2, X3) Y–Z^4 Aa–Ll^4 Mm^6 [Mm]^1 Nn–Zz^4 Aaa–Iii^4 Kkk^6; 48 + iv + 454 pp. Signature given as: "[Mm]". Erratic pagination. [1], half title; [2], White's version of the Faithorne portrait; [3], title page; [4], blank; 5–47, John Toland's *Life* (No. *1624*); 48, Francini's poem; [i], title page for Vol. 1; [ii], blank; [iii–iv], General Contents; [1], half title; [2], blank; 3–120, text of *History of Britain* (see No. 306); [121–139], Index for *History of Britain*; [140], blank; [137], half title; [138], blank; 139–167, text of *Animadversions* (No. 47); [168], blank; 169–200, text of *An Apology for Smectymnuus* (No. 58); 201–237, text of *The Reason of Church-Government* (No. 59); [238], blank; 239–247, text of *Of Prelatical Episcopacy* (No. 54); [248], blank; 249–[277], text of *Of Reformation* (No. 56); [278], blank; [273], half title; [274], blank; 275–326, text of *Doctrine and Discipline of Divorce* (No. 62); 327–383, text of *Tetrachordon* (No. 72); [384], blank; 385–408, text of *The Judgement of Martin Bucer* (No. 63); 409–422, text of *Colasterion* (No. 66); 423–[443], text of *Areopagitica* (No. 61); [444], blank. Copy in Newberry Library has an additional leaf preceding what is here called π1: [i], blank; [ii], portrait; [1], title page; [2], Contents; [3], half title; [4], blank; 5-same.

The History of Britain is a version allegedly revised and augmented by Milton. Cancel, ff. X2-3, in *Animadversions* occurs at same point as in Edition 1. Toland's *Life* also prints the testimonies from Dati, Manso, Salsilli, and Selvaggi.

Title page for Vol. 2:
[black only] | A | Complete Collection | OF THE | Historical, Political, and Miscellaneous | WORKS | OF | John Milton, | Both ENGLISH and LATIN. | With som PAPERS never before Publish'd. | ――― | The Second Volume. [black letter] | The Contents whereof follow in the next Leaf. | ――― | [device] | ――― | *AMSTERDAM,* | Finish'd in the Year M. DC. XC. VIII. | [Place this Title before the Signature Lll.] |

Signatures and pagination are continuous with Vol. 1. Folio in fours. π^2 Lll–Xxx^4 [3X]^2 Yyy–Zzz^4 [4A]–[4C]^4 Aaaa–Zzzz^4 5A–5K^4 5L^2 5M–5S^4; vi + 442 pp. Signatures given as here recorded. [i], title page; [ii], blank; [iii–iv], Contents; [v], half title; [vi], blank; 443–526, text of *Eikonoklastes* (No. 78); 527–528, 525–526, 527–528, advertisements concerning Pamela's prayer, Charles's duplicity, Charles II's proclamation, Anglesey's memorandum, etc.; 529–544, text of *The Tenure of Kings and Magistrates* (No. 84); 545–568, 545–555, *Observations on the Articles of Peace* (No. 77); [556], blank; 557–656, text of *Defensio prima* in Joseph Washington's English translation (No. 359); [657], half title; [658], blank; 659–740, text of *Letters of State* in Edward Phillips's English translation (No. 367); 741–755, text of *A Treatise of Civil Power* (No. 273); [756], blank; 757–778, text of *Considerations Touching the Likeliest Means to Remove Hirelings* (No. 268); 779–781, text of *Letter to a Friend*; [782], blank; 683–797, text of *A Ready and Easy Way* (No. 276); [798], blank; 799–800, text of *Present Means*; 801–805, text of *Brief Notes upon a Late Sermon* (No. 274); [806], blank; 807–812, text of *Of True Religion* (No. 312); [813], half title; [814], blank; 819–838, text of *A Brief History of Moscovia* (No. 332); 839–843, text of *Declaration, or Letters Patents* (No. 316); [844], blank; 845–850, text of *Of Education* (No. 64); 851–872, text of *Accedence Commenc't Grammar* (No. 300).

First printing of *Letter to a Friend* and *Present Means*. Omits *The Character of the Long Parliament*. Gives Edition 1 of *Tenure* and *Eikonklastes*; Edition 2 of *The Ready and Easy Way*.

Title page for Vol. 3:
[black only] | Joannis Miltoni | OPERA | OMNIA LATINA. | VIZ. | I. Defensio pro Populo Anglicano, contra Claudii | Salmasii Defensionem Regiam. | II. Defensio secunda pro Populo Anglicano, con- | tra Alexandrum Morum Ecclesiasten. | III. Defensio pro se, cui adjungitur Joannis Philippi | Responsio ad Apologiam Anonymi cujusdam | Tenebrionis pro Rege & Populo Anglicano In- | fantissimam. | IV. Literæ Senatus Anglicani, nec non Crom- | welli, &c nomine ad jussu conscriptæ. | V. Artis Logicæ Institutio ad Petri Rami metho- | dum concinnata. | VI. Epistolarum Familiarium liber unus, quibus ac- | cesserunt ejusdem, jam olim in Collegio adolescen- | tis, Prolusiones quædam oratoriæ. | Nunc primùm junctim edita. | —— | AMSTELODAMI, | Anno M. DC. XC. VIII. |

Folio in fours. π^2 *A-*Z *Aa-*Yy^4 *Zz^6; iv + 372 pp. [i-ii], blank; [iii], title page; [iv], blank; 1–77, text of *Defensio prima* (No. 98), without 1658 postscript; [78], blank; 79–105 [i. e., 113; error is continued], text of *Defensio secunda* (No. 185); [106], blank; 107–137, text of *Defensio pro se* (No. 209); 137–146, text of "Supplement" (No. 209); 147–166, text of John Phillips's *Responsio* (No. 139); 167–237, text of *Literae* (No. 321); [238], blank; 239–320, text of *Artis Logicae Plenior Institutio* (No. 310); 321–363, text of *Epistolarum Familiarium Liber Unus* with Prolusions (No. 317); [364], blank.

Wing, M2087. Copy owned by University of Kentucky Library.

396 [black only] | A | Complete Collection | OF THE | Historical, Political, and Miscellaneous | WORKS | OF | John Milton, | Both ENGLISH and

LATIN. | With some PAPERS never before Publish'd. | ———— | In Three
Volumes. [black letter] | Of which the Contents follow in the next Page.
| ———— | To which is Prefix'd | The LIFE of the AUTHOR, | Contain-
ing, | Besides the History of his Works, | Several Extraordinary Characters
of Men and | Books, Sects, Parties, and Opinions. | ———— | Printed in
the Year M. DC. XC. VIII. and sold by the Book- | sellers of *London* and
Westminster. | Price bound 40 *s.* |

Variant issue of No. 395. Vol. 1. Folio in fours and sixes. $\pi^1 \pi\pi^1 *2(\pm *1)$
a-e^4 [A]^2 B-R^4 S^6 T-V^4 X^4($\pm$X2, X3) Y-Z Aa-Ll^4 Mm^6 [Mm]^1 Nn-
Zz Aaa-Iii^4 Kkk^6; ii + 48 + iv + 454 pp. Signature given as: "[Mm]".
Cancel stub between *1 and *2. [1], half title; [2], portrait; [3], title page;
[4], Contents; [i], half title; [ii], blank; 5-as in No. 395. Coleridge, p. 98,
reports that some copies of No. 395 also include the additional half title and
blank verso [i–ii]; compare Newberry copy reported here under No. 395.
Not in Wing. Copy owned by University College Library, London.

397 [double-ruled border] | EXAMEN | Poeticum Duplex: | SIVE | *Musarum
Anglicanarum* | Delectus Alter; | Cui subjicitur | EPIGRAMMATUM | SEU
| Poematum Minorum | Specimen Novum. | ———— | *LONDINI:* | Impens-
sis Ric: Wellington, ad insigne chelyos in | Cœmeterio Divi Pauli.
MDCXCVIII. | [rubricated] |

Octavo. A^8 π^4(-π4) B-P^8, π^1 A-C^8 D^4; xvi + 2 + iv + 224, ii + 56
pp. π^4(-π4) and π^1 constitute a half signature; misbound. [i–ii], Advertisement; [iii], divider; [iv], blank; [v], title page; [vi], blank; [vii–ix], preface;
[x], blank; [xi–xv], Index; [xvi], blank; [1], preface; [2], blank; i–iii, Index; [iv], Advertisement; 1–219, text of Musarum Anglicanarum Delectus
Alter; [220–224], blank; [i], divider; [ii], blank; 1–56, text of Epigrammatum
... Specimen Novum.

Elegia septima, pp. 194–198 (authorship acknowledged); *Elegia prima*, pp.
199–203 (authorship acknowledged); *Elegia sexta*, pp. 204–208 (authorship
acknowledged), *Epitaphium Damonis* (called "Ecloga Damon"), pp. 209–219
(authorship not acknowledged). All four poems are listed and acknowledged
in Index, A8v (that is, p. [xv] of first section).

In inventorum Bombardae, p. 55; *Ad Leonoram Romae Canentem*, p. 55. Both poems
listed and unacknowledged in Index, π3 (that is, p. iii of preliminary material
bound into first section). None of the Epigrams are acknowledged.

Anonymous six-line Latin poem, "In Miltonum Poetam," on p. 9 of *Epigrams*,
a translation of Dryden's epigram.

Wing, E3708. Copy owned by Folger Shakespeare Library.

1699

398 *JOANNIS MILTONI* | Sententiæ Potestati REGIÆ | Adversantis Refutatio. | Cui Annexæ sunt, | ANIMADVERSIONES | IN | Execrabilem Libellum, | Cui Titulus est, | *"Joannis Miltoni* Angli Defensio Secunda. Con- | "tra infamem Libellum anonymum, cui ti- | "tulus, Regii Sanguinis Clamor ad Cœlum | "adversus Parricidas Anglicanos. | ————— | Authore | EDMUNDO ELISIO, *coll. Ball.* | apud OXONIENSES quondum Socio. | ————— | *LONDINI:* | Typis *J. M.* Impensis *R. Wilkin,* ad Insigne | Capitis Regis in Cœmeterio D. Pauli, 1699. |

Author: Edmund Elys. Octavo. A^8; 16 pp. [1], half title; [2], blank; [3], title page; [4], blank; 5-10, Sententiæ; 11-15, Animadversions; [16], blank. In Latin. Wing, E675B. Copy owned by Henry E. Huntington Library.

399 [double-ruled border] | *MILTON's* | Paradise Lost | Imitated in Rhyme. | In the *Fourth Sixth* and *Ninth* Books; | CONTAINING | The Primitive *LOVES.* | The *BATTEL* of the *Angels.* | The *FALL* of *MAN.* | ————— | By Mr. *John Hopkins.* | ————— | *In Magnis vel voluisse Sat est.* | ————— | *LONDON,* | Printed for *Ralph Smith,* at the *Bible* under the *Royal* | *Exchange* in *Cornhill,* 1699. |

Adaptations by John Hopkins. Quarto. A-B$^{4(+B3)}$ C-I^4; viii + 66 pp. Extra unsigned leaf between B2 and B3. Pages 9-10 repeated in pagination. [i], title page; [ii], blank; [iii-v], dedicatory poem; [vi-viii], preface; [viii], advertisements; [1], half title; [2], blank; 3-10, 9-15, "The Primitive Loves"; [16], blank; [17], half title; [18], blank; 19-39, "Battel of the Angels"; [40], blank; [41], half title; [42], blank; 43-56, "Fall of Man"; 57-63, "Bellona and Astrea," poem by Hopkins; [64], blank. Wing, H2747. Copy owned by Henry E. Huntington Library.

400 PARAPHRASIS | POETICA | IN TRIA | *JOHANNIS MILTONI,* | Viri Clarissimi, | POEMATA, | *VIZ* | PARADISUM AMISSUM, | PARADISUM RECUPERATUM, | ET | SAMSONEM AGONISTEN. | AUTORE | *GULIELMO HOGÆO.* | [device] | *ROTERDAMI,* | Apud ELIAM YVANS. | 1699. |

Reissue of No. 352. A$^{8(\pm A2, -A1, A8)}$ a^8 b^2 B-Z Aa-Kk^8; xxxvi [xxxii] + 512 pp. [i-ii], cancelled; [iii], title page; [iv], blank; v-xviii, dedication [xv-xvi, cancelled]; xix-xxi, prefatory poem; xxii-xxiii, To the Reader; [xxiv], To the Readers; [xxv], blank; [xxvi], half title for *Paradise Lost*; [etc. as in No. 352]. The cancelling of the title page A2 extended to the cancellation of A1 and A8, creating a lacuna in the text of the dedication. Copy owned by Magdalen College Library, Oxford.

1700

401 [double-ruled border] | *OLIVER CROMWELL*'s | LETTERS | TO |
FOREIGN PRINCES | AND | STATES, | For strengthning and preserv-
ing the | *Protestant Religion and Interest.* | WITH AN | APPENDIX. | ──────
| *LONDON,* | Printed for *John Nutt,* near *Stationers-* | *Hall.* 1700. |

Quarto. [A]^1 B–G^4; ii + 48 pp. [i], title page; [ii], blank; 1–39, texts of
state papers; 40–45, Appendix; 46–48, blank. Pp. 47–48 missing; perhaps
G4 was used for A1. Nineteen state papers in English translation by Edward Phillips (see No. 367): Columbia Nos. 50, 51, 52, 53, 54, 55, 56, 58,
59, 110, 112, 111, 48, 49, 62, 75, 79, 87, 88. Each headed by description
of contents. Anonymous appendix discusses Milton's function as Secretary
and the value of his work on the letters. Wing, C7116A. Copy owned by
Folger Shakespeare Library.

402 [rubricated] | RECUEIL | DES | TRAITEZ | DE PAIX, DE TRÊVE,
DE NEUTRALITÉ, | DE SUSPENSION D'ARMES, DE CONFÉDÉRA-
TION, | D'ALLIANCE, DE COMMERCE, DE GARANTIE, | ET
D'AUTRES | ACTES PUBLICS, | COMME | CONTRACTS DE MAR-
RIAGE, TESTAMENTS, | MANIFESTES, DECLARATIONS DE
GUERRE, &c. | Faits entre des Empereurs, lois, Republiques, Princes,
& autres | Puissances de l'Europe, & des autres Parties du Monde. | *Depuis
la Naissance de* JESUS-CHRIST *jusqu'à présent.* | SERVANT A ÉTABLIR.
| LES DROITS DES PRINCES | ET DE | FONDEMENT A
L'HISTOIRE. | Rassemblez avec soin d'un grand nombre d'Ouvrages im-
primez, où ils étoient dispersez, & de divers Recueils | publiez ci-devant,
ausquels on a ajouté plusieurs Pièces, qui n'avoient jamais été imprimées.
| *Le tout redigé par ordre Chronologique, & accompagné de* NOTES, *de* TABLES
| CHRONOLOGIQUES & ALPHABETIQUES, & *des Noms* | *des*
AUTEURS *dont on s'est servi.* | TOME PREMIER. | Contenant les Préfaces
& les Traitez depuis DXXXVI. jusqu'en MDI. | [device] | *A AMSTER-
DAM,* | Chez HENRY ET LA VEUVE DE T. BOOM. | A LA HAYE,
| Chez [bracket] ADRIAN MOETJENS, | HENRY VAN BULDEREN.
| ────── | MDCC. |

Four volumes. Quarto. Differences for Vol. 3: ... | TOME TROISIÉME
| Contenant les Traitez depuis MDCI. jusqu'en MDCLXI. | ... | M. DCC. |

State paper (attributed), pp. 620–622 (Iiii2v–Iiii3v): "No. CCCXVIII.
*Manifeste du Parlement d'*ANGLETERRE *contre les* PROVINCES-UNIS *des
Pays-bas, publié* le 31. *JUILLET,* 1652. Aitzema. Historia Pacis, page 804."
See No. 190. In Latin.

State paper, Columbia No. 170 (attributed), pp. 694–696 (Ssss3v–Ssss4v):
"No. CCCXLIII. *Traité entre* CHARLES GUSTAVE *Roi de Suède,* &

OLIVIER CROMWEL *Protecteur d'Angleterre; par lequel de Traité d'Alliance fuit entre les deux Etats, le* 11. *Avril,* 1654. *est confirmé & expliqué. Fait à Londres en* 1656. Manuscrit." In Latin.

Copy owned by New York Public Library.

1700 (?)

403   AN | ESSAY | Towards the | THEORY | OF THE | INTELLIGIBLE WORLD. | Intuitively Considered. | Designed for Forty-nine parts. | PART III. | Consisting of a Preface, a Postscript, and | a little something between. | ———— | *By* GABRIEL JOHN. | ———— | Enriched with a Faithful Account of his Ideal Voyage, | and Illustrated with Poems by several Hands, as | likewise with other strange things not insufferably | Clever, nor furiously to the Purpose. | ———— | The Archetypally Second Edition [black letter] | ———— | Θελας, θελον, μανιvας. *Why,* | *Should all Mankind be mad but I? You that are wisest tell me why.* | Tribues HIS temporis quantum poterîs, | Poteris autem quantum voles. *Tully's Offices.* | ———— | Printed in the Year One Thousand Seven | Hundred, &c. |

Author: Thomas D'Urfey. Apparently only this part was published in only this one edition; the date may likewise be satiric.

"De Idea Platonica," pp. 17–18, printed without acknowledgment.

Appropriations from Dryden's *State of Innocence* in poem on p. 160; allusion in note. Wing, D2721. Copy owned by Folger Shakespeare Library.

Before 1701

404   Copenhagen. Kongelige Bibliotek. MS. Gl. Kgl. S.3579 8º.

Scribal copy of *Defensio prima.* Date of MS: probably after 1666, the date of "The Second Advice," often assigned to Marvell. "Johañis Miltoni Angli, Pro Populo Anglicano Defensio contra Claudii Anonymi, alias Salmasii defensionem regiam." 196 pp. 1–11, Præfatio; 12, blank (a later hand has written in English that the manuscript is in Milton's own hand); 13–180, text; 181–182, blank; 183–188, "The Second Advice to a Painter"; 189–196, blank.

405   Edinburgh. Edinburgh University Library. Laing MS III 256/13.

Transcription of *Of Prelatical Episcopacy* from printed edition, with title page transcribed. 11 leaves, unpaged. Microfilm in University of Illinois Library.

406   London. British Library. Egerton MS 203.

Transcript of *Paradise Lost* from 1674 edition with poems by Barrow and Marvell, the Verse, and the Arguments. No title page. 187 leaves, the first of which is blank.

407 London. British Library. Sloane MS 1030.

Commonplace book with the section on the Severn from "Milton Cronicle of Engl." in French translation, f. 90v.

408 London. British Library. Sloane MS 1506.

"Notes taken out of Milton concerning ye History of England," in 38 folio pages with 3 additional folio pages of non-Miltonic notes.

409 London. British Library. Sloane MS 3324.

Paradise Lost I, 1, to I, 175, given in French prose translation, ff. 273–288v, with three additional blank leaves between f. 286 and f. 287. Ff. 287–288 are an earlier version of the last part of the translation, with deletions and corrections.

410 London. Lambeth Palace Library. MS 841. Item 8.

Holograph (?) copy of William Hog's Latin translation of *Lycidas* (see No. 370 in this bibliography), entitled "Lycidas Miltoni." 7 leaves, unpaged. Microfilm in University of Illinois Library.

411 Nürnberg. Germanisches Nationalmuseum. MS Hs 40 660.

Christopher Wegleiter, holograph, "Gedichte 1685-1693." Includes: Johann Miltons | Verlustigtes Paradies. | Das Erste Buch. | Ff. [116–121], unpaged. 190 German alexandrines in couplets (not 195 as previously recorded), rendering *PL* I, 1–196. Appears after material dated 1693.

412 Oxford. Bodleian Library. Rawlinson MS A.260.

State paper, Columbia No. 44, copy in Latin, p. 8.

State paper, Columbia No. 45, copy in Latin, p. 9.

State paper, Columbia No. 65, copy in Latin, p. 12.

State paper, Columbia No. 122, copy in Latin, pp. 21–22.

Possible attributions in parallel Latin letters to the Swiss cantons and to Geneva, pp. 45 and 46. See Columbia No. 170B for the latter. Another possible attribution in Latin, a letter to Mazarin, dated 29 June 1654, on p. 20. See No. 196 in this bibliography. Date of MS: uncertain.

413 Oxford. Bodleian Library. Rawlinson MS A.261.

State paper, Columbia No. 44, copy in Latin, f. 5.

State paper, Columbia No. 45, copy in Latin, ff. 5v–6.

State paper, Columbia No. 65, copy in Latin, f. 7.

State paper, Columbia No. 122, copy in Latin, ff. 11–12.

State paper, Columbia No. 46, copy in Latin, f. 19.

State paper, Columbia No. 48, copy in Latin, ff. 24–25.

State paper, Columbia No. 49, copy in Latin, f. 25v.

State paper, Columbia No. 122, copy in Latin, ff. 27–28.

State paper, Columbia No. 52, copy in Latin, ff. 46–47.

Columbia No. 122 appears twice with variations.

Possible attributions in Latin, parallel letters to Geneva (see Columbia No. 170B) and to Basel, ff. 3v and 4–4v.

Another possible attribution in Latin, a letter to Mazarin, dated 29 June 1654, on f. 11–11v. See No. 196 in this bibliography. Date of MS: uncertain.

414   Washington, D. C. Folger Shakespeare Library. MS V.b.93. Index Poeticus.

Citations from *Comus* and the minor poems, passim, as "M M" and "M P". Abbreviations noted in Index, p. [895]: "A Mask Milton M M" and "Mr Jo Miltons Poems   M P".

415   Washington, D. C. Folger Shakespeare Library. Henry Oxenden's MS, V.b.110.

Brief quotations and summaries of *Defensio secunda* (1654), pp. 421–423, and of Salmasius's *Defensio Regia* (1650), pp. [441–442]. Listed in Index, p. 536.

416   Wellington, New Zealand. Alexander Turnbull Library. MS G MIL 111,610.

IOHN MiLTON | An Englishman | HIS DEFENCE | For the People of England, | Against the | DEFENCE = ROYALL | of | CLAVDIVS ANONYMVS, | that is, a Namelesse Author, | otherwise | SALMASIVS. | London. | Printed for Du = Gard | In the yeare of our Lord | 1651. |

Anonymous English translation in manuscript, apparently predating 1692 and different from Joseph Washington's translation (see No. 359). Octavo. 368 pp.; pp. 1–345, but pagination is suspended between chapters and each chapter is begun on a recto, with 6 blank pages preceding and 3 blank pages following. Derives from Madan No. 1 (No. 98) or from an edition derived from it; does not derive from Madan No. 2 (No. 101) or Madan No. 14 (No. 259). The translation is more literal and closer than others (including those in the Columbia Edition and Yale Prose). Marginal and flyleaf notes.

Secondary Bibliography

Secondary Bibliography

1637

See No. 40 in Part I for Henry Lawes's letter.

1641

1   *A Compendious discourse, proving episcopacy to be of apostolicall, and consequently of divine institution.* London: Printed by E. G., for Richard Whitaker, 1641.

Author: Peloni Almoni, Cosmopolites (pseudonym). Printer: Edward Griffin. Allusion concerning episcopacy controversy, p. [3]. Dated: May. Wing, C5607. Copy owned by New York Public Library.

2   *A Defence of The Humble remonstrance, against the frivolous and false exceptions of Smectymnvvs* [etc.]. London: Printed for Nathaniel Butter, 1641.

Author: Joseph Hall. Edition 1. Quarto. A–L^4 M^2 N–Z^4 Aa–Bb^4; viii + 188 pp. Paged: 1–84 89–168 [2] 169–182 193–200. Errors in signatures and pagination. Discussion directed "To the Postscript" (attributed; see No. 48), pp. 163–168. See Wing, H378. Copy owned by University of Kentucky Library.

3   *A Defence of The Humble remonstrance, against the frivolous and false exceptions of Smectymnvvs* [etc.]. London: Printed for Nathaniel Butter, 1641.

Edition 2 of No. *2*. Quarto. A–Z Aa^4. Discussion of *A Postscript*, pp. 159–164. See Wing, H378. Copy owned by University of Kentucky Library.

4   *A Discovrse opening the natvre of that episcopacie, which is exercised in England* [etc.]. London: Printed by R. C., for Samuel Cartwright, 1641.

Author: Robert Greville, Lord Brooke. Edition 1. Possible influence (with paraphrasing) from *Of Prelatical Episcopacy*, passim. Dated: November (?). Wing, B4911. Copy owned by New York Public Library.

Stationers' register. See G. E. Briscoe Eyre, ed. *A Transcript of the Registers of the Worshipful Company of Stationers; from 1640–1708 A. D.* London: 1913–1914.

5   Entry for Smectymnuus' *An Answer to a Book*, under 20 March 1640 (i. e., 1641), I (1913), 16.

1642

6   *A Discovrse opening the natvre of that episcopacie, which is exercised in England* [etc.]. *The second edition, corrected and enlarged.* London: Printed by R. C., for Samuel Cartwright, 1642.

Edition 2 of No. *4.* Wing, B4912. Copy owned by New York Public Library.

7   *The Holy state. By Thomas Fuller, B. D. and Prebendarie of Sarum* [etc.]. Cambridge: Printed by Roger Daniel, for John Williams, 1642.

Author: Thomas Fuller. Edition 1. Allusion with quotation from *Of Reformation* in "Life of Bishop Ridley," Book IV, Chap. 11, pp. 291–292. Wing, F2443. Copy owned by New York Public Library.

8   *A Letter lately sent by a reverend bishop from the Tower, to a private friend: and by him thought fit to be published.* London: Printed in the Yeare, 1642.

Author: Joseph Hall. Dated: 24 January 1641/2. Allusion to episcopacy controversy, pp. 5–6. Wing, H390. Copy owned by Folger Shakespeare Library.

9   *A Letter lately sent by a reverend bishop from the Tower, to a private friend: and by him thought fit to be published.* London: Printed for Nath: Butter, 1642.

Another edition of No. *8.* Allusion, p. 5. Wing, H391. Copy owned by Folger Shakespeare Library.

10   *A Modest confutation of a slanderous and scurrilous libell, entituled, Animadversions upon the remonstrants defense against Smectymnuus.* 1642.

Author: anonymous; sometimes ascribed to Joseph Hall and his son Robert. Place: London. Dated: March. Wing, H393. Copy owned by University of Kentucky Library.

1643

11   Lord Delamere. Ephemerides. MS diary of Samuel Hartlib for 1643.

In Sheffield University Library. Allusion. Printed in G. H. Turnbull. *Hartlib, Dury and Comenius.* London: Hodder and Stoughton, 1947, p. 40.

12 *The Serpent salve, or, a remedie for the biting of an aspe*. Printed at York by Stephen Bulkley, 1643.

Author: John Bramhall. Allusion concerning episcopacy controversy, pp. 211-212. Not in Wing (1); Wing (2), B4236A. Copy owned by York Minster Library.

13 *The Serpent salve, or, a remedie for the biting of an aspe*. Printed in the year, 1643.

Another edition of No. *12*. Place: York (not Dublin as previously speculated). Text identical with No. *12*; ornaments indicate printer was Stephen Bulkley. Wing, B4236. Copy owned by New York Public Library.

1644

14 *An Answer to a book, intituled, The Doctrine and discipline of divorce, or, a plea for ladies and gentlewomen, and all other maried women against divorce* [etc.]. London: Printed by G. M., for William Lee, 1644.

Author: anonymous. Dated: November. Wing, M3304. Copy owned by New York Public Library.

15 *An Answer to Mr. William Prynn's Twelve questions concerning church government* [etc.].

Author: Henry Robinson. Place: London. Date: 1644. Allusion to divorce views, p. 18. Wing, R1665. Copy owned by New York Public Library.

16 *The Compassionate samaritane: vnbinding* [etc.]. Printed in the yeare, 1644.

Author: William Walwyn. Edition 1. Possible allusions concerning episcopacy controversy, A4–A4v and pp. 53–54. Wing, W681. Copy owned by Yale University Library.

17 *The Compassionate samaritane: vnbinding* [etc.]. Printed in the yeare 1644.

Another issue of No. *16*, with differing collation and conjugate blank leaves. Not in Wing. Copy owned by Henry E. Huntington Library.

18 *The Compassionate samaritane vnbinding* [etc.]. *The second edition, corrected, and enlarged*. Printed in the Yeare 1644.

Edition 2 of No. *16*. Wing, W681A. Copy owned by Folger Shakespeare Library.

19 *A Dialogue, arguing that arch-bishops, bishops, curates, neuters, are to be cut-off by the law of God* [etc.]. London: Printed by T. B. and M. S., 1644.

Author: Hezekiah Woodward. Influence from anti-episcopal tracts, especially *Of Reformation* and *Animadversions*; see, e. g., pp. 23, 29–30. Wing, W3486. Copy owned by Union Theological Seminary Library (McAlpin Collection).

20   *The Glasse of Gods providence towards his faithfull ones. Held forth in a sermon preached to the two houses of Parliament, at Margarets Westminster, Aug. 13. 1644* [etc.]. London: Printed by G. M., for Th. Underhill, 1644.

Author: Herbert Palmer. Allusion to divorce views, p. 57. Dated: November. Wing, P235. Copy owned by New York Public Library.

21   *Inquiries, into the causes of our miseries, whence they issue-forth upon us* [etc.]. Printed for Tho. Vnderhill, 1644.

Author: Hezekiah Woodward. Place: London. Influenced by *Areopagitica*; see, for example, p. 1. Dated: December. Wing, W3491. Copy owned by Henry E. Huntington Library.

22   *The Sentence from scriptvre and reason against arch-bishops and bishops with their curats* [etc.]. Printed in the yeare, Anno Dom. 1644.

Reissue of No. *19*. Wing, W3501. Copy owned by British Library.

Stationers' register. See G. E. Briscoe Eyre, ed. *A Transcript of the Registers of the Worshipful Company of Stationers; from 1640–1708 A. D.* London: 1913–1914.

23   Entry for *Of Education*, under 4 June 1644, I (1913), 117.
24   Entry for *The Judgement of Martin Bucer*, under 15 July 1644, I (1913), 122.
25   Entry for the anonymous *An Answer to a Book*, under 31 October 1644, I (1913), 135.

26   *Twelve considerable serious questions touching church government.* London: Printed by I. D., for Michael Sparke, Sr., 1644.

Author: William Prynne. Edition 1. Allusion concerning episcopacy controversy, p. 7. Wing, P4117. Copy owned by New York Public Library.

27   *Twelve considerable serious questions touching church government.* London: Printed by F. L., for Michael Sparke, Sr., 1644.

Edition 2 of No. *26*. Wing, P4116. Copy owned by New York Public Library.

28   *A Vindication of churches, commonly called Independent* [etc.]. London: Printed for Henry Overton, 1644.

Author: Henry Burton. Edition 1. Allusion to divorce views, p. 41. Wing, B6175. Copy owned by Union Theological Seminary Library (McAlpin Collection).

29   *A Vindication of churches, commonly called Independent* [etc.]. *The second edition* [etc.]. London: Printed for Henry Overton, 1644.

Edition 2 of No. *28*. Wing, B6176. Copy owned by Union Theological Seminary Library (McAlpin Collection).

30   *A Vindication of churches, commonly called Independent* [etc.]. *The third edition* [etc.]. London: Printed for Henry Overton, 1644.

Edition 3 of No. *28*. Not in Wing (1); Wing (2), B6176A. Copy owned by New York Public Library.

1645

SEE ALSO NOS. 70 AND 71 IN PART I FOR LETTER FROM HENRY WOTTON, AS WELL AS HENRY LAWES'S LETTER, HUMPHREY MOSELEY'S PREFACE, AND TESTIMONIES.

31   *A Dissvasive from the errours of the time: wherein the tenets of the principall sects, especially of the independents, are drawn together in one map, for the most part, in the words of their own authours* [etc.]. London: Printed for Samuel Gillibrand, 1645.

Author: Robert Baillie. Edition 1, Issue (or impression) 1: last page given as 242 (i. e., 252). Allusions concerning divorce controversy, pp. [xvii], 116, 144–145 (with quotation from *Doctrine and Discipline of Divorce*). Wing, B456. Copy owned by New York Public Library.

32   *Heresiography: or, a description of the heretickes and sectaries of these latter times* [etc.]. London: Printed by M. Okes, and are to be sold by Robert Trot, 1645.

Author: Ephraim Pagitt. Edition 1. Allusion and discussion concerning divorce controversy, A3v. Wing, P174. Copy owned by Union Theological Seminary Library (McAlpin Collection).

33   *Heresiography: or, a description of the hereticks and sectaries of these latter times* [etc.]. London: Printed by W. Wilson, for John Marshall and Robert Trot, 1645.

Edition 2 of No. *32*. Only one leaf of A signature in copy reported; copy in Princeton Theological Seminary Library has no A signature. Allusions concerning divorce controversy, [Av] and p. 142. Wing, P175. Copy owned by British Library.

34 Κατα-βαπτισται κατ'απτυστοι. *The dippers dipt. Or, the Anabaptists duck'd and plung'd over head and eares, at a disputation in Southwark* [etc.]. London: Printed for Nicholas Bourne and Richard Royston, 1644..

Author: Daniel Featley. Edition 1. Allusion concerning divorce controversy, pp. [xiii–xiv]. Dated: January 1645. Not in Wing. Copy owned by Union Theological Seminary Library (McAlpin Collection).

35 Κατα-βαπτισται κατ'απτυστοι. *The dippers dipt* [etc.]. London: Printed for Nicholas Bourne and Richard Royston, 1645.

Edition 2 of No. *34.* Printer: Thomas Pursley. Allusion, B2v. Wing, F585. Copy owned by New York Public Library. Second copy in Henry E. Huntington Library has a variant engraved frontispiece.

36 Κατα-βαπτισται κατ'απτυστοι. *The dippers dipt* [etc.]. London: Printed for Nicholas Bourne and Richard Royston, 1645.

Edition 3 of No. *34.* Allusion, B2v. Wing, F586. Copy owned by William Andrews Clark Library.

37 Lord Delamere. MS letter from Sir Cheney Culpepper to Samuel Hartlib, dated 12 November 1645.

In Sheffield University Library. Allusion concerning educational work. Printed in part in G. H. Turnbull. *Hartlib, Dury and Comenius.* London: Hodder and Stoughton, 1947, p. 9.

Stationers' register. See G. E. Briscoe Eyre, ed. *A Transcript of the Registers of the Worshipful Company of Stationers; from 1640–1708 A. D.* London: 1913–1914.

38 Entry for *Poems,* under 6 October 1645, I (1913), 196.

1646

39 Lord Delamere. MS letter from John Hall to Samuel Hartlib, dated 17 December 1646.

In Sheffield University Library. Allusion. Printed by G. H. Turnbull in *Review of English Studies,* N. S. 4 (1953) 227.

40 Lord Delamere. MS letter from John Hall to Samuel Hartlib, dated 21 December 1646 (?).

In Sheffield University Library. Allusion concerning *Of Education.* Printed by G. H. Turnbull. *Hartlib, Dury and Comenius*. London: Hodder and Stoughton, 1947, p. 39.

41   *A Dissvasive from the errours of the time* [etc.]. London: Printed for Samuel Gillibrand, 1645.

Second issue (or impression) of No. *31*; last page given as 252. Sometimes called Edition 2. Dated: 22 January 1646. Wing, B457. Copy owned by Union Theological Seminary Library (McAlpin Collection).

42   *The First and second part of Gangræna* [etc.]. *The third edition, corrected and much enlarged* [etc.]. London: Printed by T. R. and E. M., for Ralph Smith, 1646.

Author: Thomas Edwards. Printers: Thomas Ratcliffe and Edward Mottershead. Edition 3 of Nos. *43* and *49*. Allusions to divorce views in Part I, p. 29 and margin. Edition 3 of Part I is listed as Wing, E230.

Separate title page for Part II:
The Second part of Gangræna [etc.]. London: Printed by T. R. and E. M., for Ralph Smith, 1646.

Reissue of No. *50*. Allusion to divorce views in Part II, p. 9. Copy owned by Alexander Turnbull Library reissues No. *49* with allusion on pp. 10–11. Edition 3 of Part II is listed as Wing, E235.

Combined edition: Wing, E227. Copy owned by Princeton Theological Seminary Library.

43   *Gangræna: or a catalogue and discovery of many of the errours, heresies, blasphemies, and pernicious practices of the sectaries of this time* [etc.]. London: Printed for Ralph Smith, 1646.

Author: Thomas Edwards. Edition 1 of Part I. Allusion to divorce views, p. 34 and margin. Wing, E228. Copy owned by Princeton Theological Seminary Library.

44   *Gangræna: or a catalogue and discovery of many of the errours, heresies, blasphemies and pernicious practices of the sectaries of this time* [etc.]. *The second edition enlarged* [etc.]. London: Printed for Ralph Smith, 1646.

Edition 2 of No. *43*. Wing, E229. Copy owned by New York Public Library.

45   *THE HUMBLE ADVICE of the assembly of divines, now by authority of Parliament sitting at Westminster, concerning a confession of faith* [etc.]. London: Printed for the Company of Stationers.

Dated: 1646. First edition of what became known as the Confession of Faith.

Note capitalization of first three words. In 54 pp. Allusion to Milton's divorce views, Chapter XXIV, Section 6, p. 41. Wing, W1427. Copy owned by British Library.

Earlier, shorter version in 38 pp. (Wing, W1428) does not include Chapter XXIV. *Articles of Christian Religion* (London: Printed for Edmund Husband, June 27, 1648) is also an earlier version without the allusion to Milton.

46   *The humble ADVICE of the assembly of divines, now by authority of Parliament sitting at Westminster, concerning a confession of faith* [etc.]. London: Printed for the Company of Stationers.

Dated: 7 December 1646. In 54 pp. Allusion, p. 41. See Wing, W1427. Copy owned by Cambridge University Library.

47   Κατα-βαπτισται κατ'απτυστοι. *The dippers dipt* [etc.]. *The fourth edition.* London: Printed for Nicholas Bourne and Richard Royston, 1646.

Edition 4 of No. *34*. Allusion, p. [vii]. Wing, F587. Copy owned by Yale University Library.

48   *Little Non-such: or, certaine new questions moved out of ancient truths* [etc.]. London: Printed for H. P., 1646.

Author: anonymous. Satire on *Doctrine and Discipline of Divorce*; 16 pp. Wing, L2552. Copy owned by Union Theological Seminary Library (McAlpin Collection).

49   *The Second part of Gangræna: or a fresh and further discovery of the errors, heresies, blasphemies, and dangerous proceedings of the sectaries of this time* [etc.]. London: Printed by T. R. and E. M., for Ralph Smith, 1646.

Author: Thomas Edwards. Printers: Thomas Ratcliffe and Edward Mottershead. Edition 1 of Part II. Allusion concerning divorce controversy, pp. 10–11. Wing, E234. Copy owned by New York Public Library.

50   *The Second part of Gangræna: or a fresh and further discovery of the errors, heresies, blasphemies, and dangerous proceedings of the sectaries of this time* [etc.]. London: Printed by T. R. and E. M., for Ralph Smith, 1646.

Edition 2 of No. *49*. Allusion, p. 9. Not in Wing. Copy owned by Union Theological Seminary Library (McAlpin Collection).

51   *The Third part of Gangræna. Or, a new and higher discovery of the errors, heresies, blasphemies, and insolent proceedings of the sectaries of these times* [etc.]. London: Printed for Ralph Smith, 1646.

Author: Thomas Edwards. Only edition of Part III. Possible allusions concerning divorce controversy, pp. 26–27 [i. e., 42–43], 188 [i. e., 204]. French and Parker following him refer to pp. 113–116 [i. e., 129–132], but there is no allusion to Milton there. Wing, E237. Copy owned by New York Public Library.

52   *Twelve considerable serious cautions, very necessary to be observed, in, and about a reformation.* London: Printed by M. S., for Henry Overton, 1646.

Author: John Goodwin. Printer: Matthew Simmons. Allusion concerning divorce views in preface (facing title page), "To the 'Impartial Reader'," by John Bachiler. Dated: February. Wing, G1211. Copy owned by Union Theological Seminary Library (McAlpin Collection).

1647

53   *A Catalogue of the several sects and opinions in England and other nations. With a briefe rehearsall of their false and dangerous tenents.*

Broadside. Colophon: "Printed by R. A. 1647." Gives picture of divorcer and six-line verse, apparently alluding to Milton. Wing, C1411. Copy owned by British Library.

54   Lord Delamere. Ephemerides. MS diary of Samuel Hartlib for 1647 (?).

In Sheffield University Library. Allusions concerning educational work. Printed in G. H. Turnbull. *Hartlib, Dury and Comenius.* London: Hodder and Stoughton, 1947, p. 40.

55   Lord Delamere. MS letter from John Hall to Samuel Hartlib, dated 4 January 1646 [i. e., 1647].

In Sheffield University Library. Allusion. Printed by G. H. Turnbull in *Review of English Studies*, N. S. 4 (1953) 227.

56   Lord Delamere. MS letter from John Hall to Samuel Hartlib, dated 8 January 1646 [i. e., 1647].

In Sheffield University Library. Allusion. Printed by G. H. Turnbull in *Review of English Studies*, N. S. 4 (1953) 227.

57   Lord Delamere. MS letter from John Hall to Samuel Hartlib, dated 7 February 1646 [i. e., 1647].

In Sheffield University Library. Allusion. Printed by G. H. Turnbull in *Review of English Studies*, N. S. 4 (1953) 227.

58   Lord Delamere. MS letter from John Hall to Samuel Hartlib, dated March 1647 (?).

In Sheffield University Library. Allusion. Printed by G. H. Turnbull in *Review of English Studies*, N. S. 4 (1953) 228.

59   *Ecclesiastes, or, a discourse concerning the gift of preaching as it fals under the rules of art* [etc.]. *The second edition* [etc.]. London: Printed by M. F., for Samuel Gellibrand, 1647.

Author: John Wilkins. Allusion concerning divorce views, p. 87. Does not appear in Edition 1 (1646). Wing, W2189. Copy owned by Union Theological Seminary Library (McAlpin Collection).

60   Ερotοπαιγνιον *or the Cyprian Academy* [etc.]. London: Printed by W. W. and are to be sold by J. Hardesty, T. Huntington, and T. Jackson, 1647.

Author: Robert Baron. Written ca. April 1647. Edition 1. Numerous imitations and appropriations from the 1645 *Poems*; see, for example, pp. 44 and 55 of Part I, and pp. 3, 28, 34, 43, 45, 95 of Part II (separate signatures and pagination). Wing, B889. Copy owned by Folger Shakespeare Library.

61   *Heresiography: or, a description of the hereticks and sectaries of these latter times by E. Pagitt. The third edition with some additions* [etc.]. London: Printed for W: L:, 1647.

Edition 3 of No. *32*. Engraved title page with date inked over as "1645." Includes a drawing of a "Divorser." Allusions concerning divorce controversy, pp. A4v, 87, 150–151. Wing, P177. Copy owned by Columbia University Library. Copy in William Andrews Clark Library has date inked over as "1646."

62   *Heresiography: or, a discription of the heretickes and sectaries sprang up in these latter times* [etc.]. *The fourth edition* [etc.]. London: Printed by W. W., for William Lee, 1647.

Edition 4 of No. *32*. With engraved title page, including drawing of a "Divorser." Allusions, pp. B1v, 86–87, 145; Table (twice), Z2, Z3. Wing, P178. Copy owned by New York Public Library.

63   *THE HUMBLE ADVICE of the assembly of divines, now by authority of Parliament sitting at Westminster, concerning a confession of faith* [etc.]. London: Printed for the Company of Stationers.

Dated: 1647. Another edition of No. *45*. Note capitalization of first three words; cf. No. *46*. In 56 pp. Allusion, p. 44. See Wing, W1429. Copy owned by British Library.

64 [The humble] *ADVICE of the assembly of divines, now by authority of Parliament sitting at Westminster, concerning a confession of faith* [etc.]. London: Printed for the Company of Stationers.

Dated: 29 April 1647. Another edition of No. *45*, and cf. Nos. *46* and *63*. In 56 pp. Allusion, p. 44. See Wing, W1429. Copy owned by Cambridge University Library.

65 *The Humble Advice of the assembly of divines, now by authority of Parliament sitting at Westminster, concerning a confession of faith* [etc.]. Printed at London; And Re-printed at Edenburgh by Evan Tyler, 1647.

Another edition of No. *45*. Allusion, p. 44. See Wing, W1430. Copy owned by British Library.

66 *The Humble Advice of the assembly of divines, now by authority of Parliament sitting at Westminster, concerning a confession of faith* [etc.]. Printed at London; and Re-printed at Edenburgh by Evan Tyler, 1647.

Another edition of No. *45*. Typographic differences from No. *65*. Allusion, p. 44. See Wing, W1430. Copy owned by British Library.

67 *The Humble ADVICE of the assembly of divines, now by authority of Parliament sitting at Westminster, concerning a confession of faith* [etc.]. Printed at London; And Re-printed at Edinburgh by Evan Tyler. 1647.

Another edition of No. *45*. Note differences from No. *65*. Allusion, p. 44. See Wing, W1430. Copy owned by British Library.

68 *The Humble Advice of the assembly of divines, now by authority of Parliament sitting at Westminster; concerning a confession of faith* [etc.]. Printed at London: And Re-printed at Edinburgh by Evan Tyler. 1647.

Another edition of No. *45*. Note differences in punctuation and spelling from No. *65*. Cf. Nos. *69* and *70*: Nos. *68, 69*, and *70* are different issues; note typographical differences and compare the spellings on p. 2 of "Glatians" and "Pphilemon," "Glatians" and "Philemon," and "Galatians" and "Philemon." Allusion, p. 44. See Wing, W1430. Copy owned by Bodleian Library.

69 *The Humble Advice of the assembly of divines, now by authority of Parliament sitting at Westminster, concerning a confession of faith* [etc.]. Printed at London; and Re-printed at Edinburgh by Evan Tyler, 1647.

Another issue of No. *68*, which see. See Wing, W1430. Copy owned by Bodleian Library.

70　*The Humble advice of the assembly of divines, now by authority of Parliament sitting at Westminster; concerning a confession of faith* [etc.]. Printed at London; and Re-printed at Edinburgh by Evan Tyler, 1647.

Another issue of No. *68*, which see. See Wing, W1430. Copy owned by Bodleian Library.

71　Κατα-βαπτισται κατ'απτυστοι. *The dippers dipt* [etc.]. *The fifth edition, augmented* [etc.]. London: Printed for N. B. and Richard Royston, 1647.

Edition 5 of No. *34*. Allusion, A4r. Wing, F588. Copy owned by Dr. Williams's Library.

72　Oxford. Bodleian Library. Clarendon State Papers. MS 29.

Letter from Edward Hyde, Lord Clarendon, to Sir Edward Nicholas, dated 7 April 1647, f. 183. Copy by William Edgeman, endorsed by Clarendon. Allusion to *Doctrine and Discipline of Divorce.*

73　*These trades-men are preachers in and about the City of London. Or. A discovery of the most dangerous and damnable tenets that have been spread within this few yeares* [etc.].

Broadside. Colophon: "*Printed and Published according to Order. 1647.*" Dated: 26 April 1647. Item 20 alludes to Milton's position on divorce. Wing, T883. Copy owned by British Library.

The broadside is entered in the index to the Thomason collection by its sub-title: "A Discovery of the Most Dangerous and Damnable Tenets" (Vol. 2, p. 505), and microfilmed as Reel 669.f.11 (6). It is not listed in the University Microfilm cross-reference to Wing, *The Thomason Tracts 1640–1661. An Index to the Microfilm Edition of the Thomason Collection of the British Library* (1978).

1648

74　Lord Delamere. Ephemerides. MS diary of Samuel Hartlib for 1648.

In Sheffield University Library. Allusion concerning *History of Britain* and *Brief History of Moscovia*. Printed in G. H. Turnbull. *Hartlib, Dury and Comenius.* London: Hodder and Stoughton, 1947, pp. 40–41.

75　Lord Delamere. MS letter from John Sadler to Samuel Hartlib, dated 17 August 1648 (?).

In Sheffield University Library. Allusion. Printed in G. H. Turnbull. *Hartlib, Dury and Comenius*. London: Hodder and Stoughton, 1947, p. 41.

76   Ερoτoπαιγνιoν *or the Cyprian Academy* [etc.]. London: Printed by W. W. and are to be sold by J. Hardesty, T. Huntington, and T. Jackson, 1648.

Edition 2 of No. *60*. Wing, B890. Copy owned by Princeton University Library.

77   *A Glasse for the times by which according to the scriptures, you may clearly behold the true ministers of Christ, how farre differing from false teachers. With a briefe collection of the errors of our times, and their authors names.* London: Printed by Robert Ibbitson, 1648.

Author: T. C. Allusion concerning divorce views, p. 6. Wing, C132. Copy owned by Union Theological Seminary Library (McAlpin Collection).

78   *Heresiography, or a discription of the heretickes and sectaries sprang up in these latter times* [etc.]. *The fourth edition* [etc.]. London: Printed by W. W., for William Lee, 1648.

Reissue of No. *62*. With illustrated title page:
Heresiography or a description of the hereticks and sectaries of these latter times by E. Pagitt. The fourth edition with some additions [etc.]. London: Printed for W. L., 1647.

Wing, P179. Copy owned by Newberry Library.

79   *The Holy state. By Thomas Fuller bachelour of divinitie, & prebendary of Sarum* [etc.]. Cambridge: Printed by R. D., for John Williams, 1648.

Edition 2 of No. *7*. Printer: Roger Daniel. Reference on p. 291 and margin. Wing, F2444. Copy owned by Henry E. Huntington Library.

80   *The Humble Advice of the assembly of divines, now by authority of Parliament sitting at Westminster, concerning a confession of faith* [etc.]. Printed at London and reprinted at Edenbrough. MDCXLVIII.

Another edition of No. *45*. Octavo. Unpaged. Allusion, c4r. Wing, W1432. Copy owned by British Library.

81   *The Humble Advice of the assembly of divines, now by authority of Parliament sitting at Westminster; concerning a confession of faith* [etc.]. London: Printed for Robert Bostock, 1648.

Another edition of No. *45*. Quarto. Allusion, p. 44. Wing, W1431. Copy owned by Bodleian Library.

82   *A Testimony to the truth of Jesus Christ, and to our solemn league and covenant; as
      also against the errours, heresies and blasphemies of these times, and the toleration of
      them* [etc.]. London: Printed by A. M., for Tho. Underhill, 1648.

      Author: anonymous. Printer: Augustine Mathewes. Allusion concerning
      divorce controversy, p. 19 and margin. Wing, T823. Copy owned by New
      York Public Library.

83   *A true and perfect picture of our present reformation* [etc.]. Printed in the first yeare
      of King Charles His Imprisonment, 1648.

      Author: anonymous. Allusions to divorce views, A1v and p. 16. Wing,
      T2438. Copy owned by Folger Shakespeare Library.

1649

84   *Anarchia Anglicana: or, the history of independency. The second part. Being a con-
      tinuation of relations and observations historicall and politique upon this present Parlia-
      ment, begun anno 16. Caroli primi. By Theodorus Verax* [etc.]. Printed in the Year,
      1649.

      Author: Clement Walker. Place: London. Unhooked A's in the first line
      of title page; no Greek in preliminaries; no errata. 256 pp. Allusion con-
      cerning divorce controversy, pp. 196-197. Wing, W316. Copy owned by
      Union Theological Seminary Library (McAlpin Collection).

85   *Anarchia Anglicana: or, the history of independency. The second part. Being a con-
      tinuation of relations and observations historicall and politique upon this present Parlia-
      ment, begun anno 16. Caroli primi. By Theodorus Verax* [etc.]. Printed in the Yeare,
      M. DC. XL.IX.

      Different edition of No. *84*. Hooked A's in first line of title page; with Greek
      in preliminaries; with errata. 262 pp. Allusion, pp. 199-200 and margins.
      Wing, W317. Copy owned by Folger Shakespeare Library.

86   *A Brief relation of some affairs and transactions* [etc.]. No. 9. 13-20 November
      1649.

      Colophon: "London, Printed by Matthew Simmons, for J. D. 1649." Notice
      concerning publication of *Eikonoklastes*, p. 96. Copy owned by British
      Library.

87   *The Confession of faith, and the larger and shorter catechisme* [etc.]. Edinburgh:
      Printed by Gedeon Lithgovv, 1649.

Another edition of No. *45*. Allusion, p. 53. Not in Wing. Copy owned by the National Library of Scotland.

88   The Confession of faith and the larger and smaller catechisme [etc.]. Amsterdam: Printed by Luice Elsever, for Andrew Wilson and are to be sold at his shop in Edinburgh. 1649.

Another edition of No. *45*. Probably printed by Gideon Lithgow in Edinburgh. Allusion, p. 39. Copy owned by Henry E. Huntington Library.

89   The Confession of faith and catechisms [etc.]. London: Printed for Robert Bostock.

Another edition of No. *45*. Dated: 1649. Duodecimo. Allusion, p. 52. Wing, C5760. Copy owned by British Library.

90   A Declaration of the Parlament of England, concerning their late endeavors in a peaceable waie, to remove all misunderstandings, and differences between the Common-wealth of England, and the Kingdom of Scotland [etc.]. London: Printed for Matthew Simmons, 1649.

Partial translation of No. *109*. Printed on B3–4 C–D^4; pp. 11–28. See Wing, E1498. Copy owned by Folger Shakespeare Library.

91   A Declaration of the Parliament of England concerning their late endeavors, in a peaceable way [etc.]. London: Printed for Matthew Simmons, 1649.

Translation of No. *109*. A–D^4. See pp. 7–12 for influence from *Tenure of Kings and Magistrates*. See Wing, E1498. Copy owned by Folger Shakespeare Library.

92   The Devilish conspiracy, hellish treason, heathenish condemnation, and damnable murder [etc.]. London: Printed in the Yeare, 1648.

Author: John Warner. Dated: early 1649. Allusion to divorce controversy, pp. 18–19. Wing, W902. Copy owned by Folger Shakespeare Library.

93   The Discoverer. Being an answer to a book entituled, Englands new chain, the second part, discovered [etc.]. London: Printed by Matthew Simmons, 1649.

Author: John Canne (?). Allusion to *Tenure of Kings and Magistrates*, p. 44 margin. Wing, C437. Copy owned by Union Theological Seminary Library (McAlpin Collection).

94   ΕΙΚΩΝ ΒΑΣΙΛΙΚΗ. Vel imago regis Caroli. In illis suis ærumnis et solitudine [etc.]. Hagæ-Comitis: Ex Officina Samuelis Broun, 1649.

Translator: John Earle. First edition, first issue. Dedication to Charles II (sig. A1–4, pp. [iii–x]) apparently includes *Eikonoklastes* in its refutation of criticisms of *Eikon Basilike*. See especially A3r. Wing, E289. Copy owned by Union Theological Seminary Library (McAlpin Collection).

95 ΕΙΚΩΝ ΒΑΣΙΛΙΚΗ. *Vel imago regis Caroli. In illis suis ærumnis et solitudine* [etc.]. Hagæ-Comitis: Ex Officina Samuelis Broun, 1649.

Variant of No. *94*. I3r is reset, with a slightly different text. See Wing, E289. Copy owned by British Library.

96 ΕΙΚΩΝ ΒΑΣΙΛΙΚΗ. *Vel imago regis Caroli. In illis suis ærumni et solitudine* [etc.]. Hagæ-Comitis: Ex Officina Samuelis Broun, 1649.

First edition, second issue, of No. *94*. Dedication to Charles II (sig. A3–6, pp. [v–xii]); see especially A5r. See Wing, E294. Copy owned by University of Kentucky Library.

97 ΕΙΚΩΝ ΒΑΣΙΛΙΚΗ. *Vel imago regis Caroli, in illis suis ærumnis & solitudine* [etc.]. Hagæ-Comitis: Typis S. B. Impensis J. Williams, & F. Eglefield, 1649.

Duodecimo edition of No. *94*, printed by Roger Daniel in London. Double border of ornaments. Dedicatory letter on A2–5, with reference on A4r. See Wing, E294. Copy owned by British Library.

98 ΕΙΚΩΝ ΒΑΣΙΛΙΚΗ. *Vel imago regis Caroli, in illis suis ærumnis et solitudine* [etc.]. Hagæ-Comitis: Typis S. B. Impensis J. Williams & F. Eglesfield, 1649.

Another duodecimo edition of No. *94*, printed by W. Bentley, London. No border. Dedicatory letter on A3–6, with reference on A5r. See Wing, E294. Copy owned by British Library.

99 ΕΙΚΩΝ ΒΑΣΙΛΙΚΗ. *Oder Abbeldung des Königes Karl in seinem Drangfahlen und gefänglicher Vermahrung* [etc.]. Gedruckt im Jahr Christi 1649.

German translation of No. *94*, with Earle's letter to Charles II on (*)iiiv. Copy owned by Folger Shakespeare Library.

100 *Electra of Sophocles: presented to her highnesse the Lady Elizabeth; with an epilogue, shewing the parallel in two poems, The Return, and The Restauration*. The Hague: Printed for Sam. Brown, 1649.

Author: Christopher Wasse (or Wase). Allusion to divorce views, E8, in "The Return," new pagination, p. 3. Copy owned by Union Theological Seminary Library (McAlpin Collection).

101 *The Golden rule. Or, justice advanced* [etc.]. *The first part* [etc.]. London: Printed for Peter Cole, 1649.

Author: John Canne. Influence from *Tenure of Kings and Magistrates,* passim. Wing, C440. Copy owned by New York Public Library.

102 Ὑβριστοδίκαι. *The obstructours of justice. Or a defence of the honourable sentence passed upon the late king, by the high court of justice* [etc.]. London: Printed for Henry Cripps and Lodowick Lloyd, 1649.

Author: John Goodwin. Discussion of *Tenure of Kings and Magistrates* with quotations, pp. 47, 53, 71, 73, 78-80, 94-95, 123. Wing, G1170. Copy owned by Folger Shakespeare Library.

103 *An Humble motion to the Parliament of England concerning the advancement of learning: and reformation of the universities. By J. H.* London: Printed for John Walker, 1649.

Author: John Hall. Allusion to *Areopagitica*, pp. 28-29. See also pp. 25-26 for possible influence from *Of Education*. Wing, H350. Copy owned by New York Public Library.

104 *The Kingdomes faithfull and impartial scout.* No. 18. 25 May-1 June 1649. London: Printed for Robert Wood, 1649.

Phraseology in Gilbert Mabbott's reasons for arguing against licensing from *Areopagitica*, p. 143. Copy owned by Folger Shakespeare Library.

105 London. British Library. Egerton MS 2547.

Letter from John Earle to Charles II concerning his translation of *Eikon Basilike* into Latin (see No. *94*), ff. 1-4. Dated: 1649. Possible reference to Milton among others.

106 *The Metropolitan nuncio. Or, times only truth-teller* [etc.]. No. 2. 31 May-6 June 1649.

Author: John Hakluyt (?). Called No. 1 and dated May 30 to July 6, 1649, sig. B4, but No. 1 was called "Mercurius Militaris. Or Times only Truthteller" and dated May 22 to May 29, 1649, sig. A4. (See also remark, p. 2.) Former notations about Nos. *106* and *107* in this bibliography have confused numbers, dates, and titles.

There is a possible allusion to *Tenure of Kings and Magistrates* on pp. 6-7. Copy owned by British Library.

107 *The Metropolitan nuncio. Or times truth-teller* [etc.]. No. 3. 6-13 June 1649.

Author: John Hakluyt (?). Allusions to divorce views and to *Eikonoklastes*, p. [8]. Copy owned by British Library.

108 An Outcry of the youngmen and apprentices of London [etc.].

Author: John Lilburne. Place: London. Dated: 1649. Influence and language from *Tenure of Kings and Magistrates*, passim. Wing, L2152. Copy owned by Folger Shakespeare Library.

109 Parliamenti Angliæ declaratio: in quâ res nvpervm gestæ, et decretum de statu Angliæ regio in liberam rempublicam vertendo, asseruntur. Londini: Apud Franciscum Tytonium, Mensis Martii 22°. Anno 1648.

Author: Bulstrode Whitelocke. Dated: 1649. Apparently influenced by *Tenure of Kings and Magistrates*, passim; see, e. g., pp. 16–18. Allegedly uses state papers drawn up under Milton's inspection. Wing, E1290. Copy owned by Union Theological Seminary Library (McAlpin Collection).

110 A Perfect diurnall of some passages in Parliament. No. 304. 21–28 May 1649.

Possible allusion to *Areopagitica* in Gilbert Mabbott's deposition on licensing, p. 2531. Copy owned by British Library.

111 Resolutions and decisions of divers practicall cases of conscience [etc.]. London: Printed by M. F., for Nath. Butter and are to be sold by Humphrey Mosley, Abel Roper, and Iohn Sweeting, 1649.

Author: Joseph Hall. Discussion of divorce views, pp. 388–392. Wing, H406. Copy owned by Folger Shakespeare Library.

Stationers' register. See G. E. Briscoe Eyre, ed. *A Transcript of the Registers of the Worshipful Company of Stationers; from 1640–1708 A. D.* London: 1913–1914.

112   Entry as licenser, under 16 December 1649, I (1913), 333.

1650

113 The Academy of complements [etc.]. *The last edition* [etc.]. London: Printed for Humphrey Moseley, 1650.

Author: John Gough. Moseley's "Courteous Reader," dated 1650 or later, included on A4–A12v. Listing of 1645 *Poems* on A8, No. 92. Wing, G1402. Copy owned by Folger Shakespeare Library.

114 The Cid, a tragicomedy out of French made English [etc.]. *The second edition corrected and emended.* London: Printed by W. Wilson, for Humphrey Moseley, 1650.

Author: Pierre Corneille. Translator: Joseph Rutter. Included on D4–6 is Moseley's "Courteous Reader." Dated: 1650. Listing of *Poems* on D6 under "Choyce Poems," as No. 13. Wing, C6309. Copy owned by Folger Shakespeare Library, Copy 2.

115 *The Confession of faith, and the larger and shorter catechisme* [etc.]. Edinburgh: Printed by Evan Tyler, 1650.

Another edition of No. *45*. Allusion, p. 53. Apparently not in Wing. Copy owned by Cambridge University Library.

116 *The Confession of faith, and the larger and shorter catechisme* [etc.]. Edinburgh: Printed by Gideon Lithgow, 1650.

Another edition of No. *45*. Duodecimo. Allusion, p. 73. Wing, C5761. Copy owned by British Library.

117 *Courteous reader.* Catalogue of books by Humphrey Moseley.

Dated: 1650 or later. Quarto. A^4, but printed on three leaves only. Listing on A3, No. 42, of 1645 *Poems*. Found in the following, among other possible volumes, at end of volume:

Virgilio Malvezzi. *Considerations upon the lives of Alcibiades and Forlialanus* [etc.]. *Englished by Robert Gentilis, Gent.* London: Printed by William Wilson, for Humphrey Moseley, 1650. Bound between A6 and A7 of volume. Wing, M356. Copy owned by Folger Shakespeare Library.

James Howell. *Epistolæ ho-elianæ. Familiar letters domestic and forren* [etc.]. *The second edition* [etc.]. London: W.H., for Humphrey Moseley, 1650. Additional title page: *Additional letters of a fresher date. Never publish'd before, and composed by the same author* [etc.]. London: Printed by W. H., for Humphrey Moseley, 1650. Wing, H3072. Copy owned by New York Public Library.

Francisco de las Coveras [i. e., Francisco de Quintana]. *The History of Don Fenise. A new romance, written in Spanish by Francisco De las-Coveras. And now Englished by a person of honour.* London: Printed for Humphrey Moseley, 1651. Wing (1), C6632; (2) unlisted. Copy owned by Folger Shakespeare Library.

Sir Walter Ralegh. *Judicious and select essayes and observations. By that renowned and learned knight. Sir Walter Raleigh* [etc.]. London: Printed by T. W., for Humphrey Moseley, 1650. Added after p. [70] of "Sir Walter Rawleigh His Apologie." Wing, R170. Copy owned by Folger Shakespeare Library.

118 *Courteous reader.* Catalogue of books by Humphrey Moseley.

Dated: 1650 or later. Quarto. A^4, printed on four leaves. Listing on A3, No. 42, of 1645 *Poems*. Found in the following, among other possible volumes, at end of volume:

> James Howell. *Epistolæ ho-elianæ. Familiar letters domestic and forren* [etc.]. *The second edition* [etc.]. London: W. H., for Humphrey Moseley, 1650. Additional title page: *Additional letters of a fresher date. Never publish'd before, and composed by the same author* [etc.]. London: Printed by W. H., for Humphrey Moseley, 1650. P. 1 printed on sig. A. Wing, H3072. Copy owned by University of Kentucky Library.

> James Howell. *Epistolæ ho-elianæ. Familiar letters domestic and forren* [etc.]. *The second edition* [etc.]. London: W. H., for Humphrey Moseley, 1650. Additional title page: *Additional letters of a fresher date. Never publish'd before, and composed by the same author* [etc.]. London: Printed by W. H., for Humphrey Moseley, 1650. Variant: p. 1 printed on sig. Aa, with "Courteous Reader" inserted at beginning between (b)8 and Aa1. Wing, H3072. Copy owned by Medical Library, University of Kentucky.

> Edmund Waller. *Poems, &c. Written by Mr. Ed. Waller of Beckonsfield* [etc.]. London: Printed by T. W. for Humphrey Moseley, 1645. Wing, W511. Copy owned by Henry E. Huntington Library.

119 De bello Belgico. The history of the low-countrey warres. Written in Latine by Famianus Strada; in English by Sr. Rob. Stapylton Kt. London: Printed for Humphrey Moseley, 1650.

Listing in Moseley's catalogue, "Courteous Reader," included at end, L2v. Wing, S5777. Copy owned by New York Public Library.

120 Declaration of the Parlament of England, upon the marching of the armie into Scotland [etc.]. London: Printed by William Du-gard, 1650.

Added to this is a reissue of No. *90*:
A Declaration of the Parlament of England, concerning their late endeavors in a peaceable waie, to remove all misunderstandings, and differences between the Common-wealth of England, and the Kingdom of Scotland [etc.]. London: Printed for Matthew Simmons, 1649.

Wing, E1505. Copy owned by Union Theological Seminary Library (McAlpin Collection).

*121 Lord Delamere. Ephemerides. MS diary of Samuel Hartlib for 1650.

In Sheffield University Library. Allusion to *Areopagitica*. Printed in G. H. Turnbull. *Hartlib, Dury and Comenius*. London: Hodder and Stoughton, 1947, p. 41.

122 Lord Delamere. MS letter from Peter Smyth to John Beale (?), dated 11 April 1650.

In Sheffield University Library. Allusion with references to *Of Education* and *Eikonoklastes* (?). Printed in G. H. Turnbull. *Hartlib, Dury and Comenius*. London: Hodder and Stoughton, 1947, p. 41.

123 *A Discourse concerning the engagement: or, the northern subscribers plea* [etc.]. London: Printed for Francis Tyton, 1650.

Author: N. W. Allusion to *Tenure of Kings and Magistrates*, p. 5, margin. Wing, W85. Copy owned by Union Theological Seminary Library (McAlpin Collection).

124 *An Introduction to the Tevtonick philosophie* [etc.]. *Englished by D. F.* London: Printed by T. M. & A. C. for Nath. Brooks, 1650.

Author: Charles Hotham. Allusion by D. F. (Durant Hotham) in "To the Author," p. A3v. Wing, H2896. Copy owned by Yale University Library.

125 [Letter from Sir Edward Nicholas to Mr. Smith (Lord Hatton), dated 4 (14) December 1650.]

Allusion to Joseph Jane and *Eikonoklastes*. Printed in George F. Warner, ed. *The Nicholas Papers. Correspondence of Sir Edward Nicholas, Secretary of State.* Westminster: Nichols and Son, for the Camden Society, N. S., XL, 1886. I, 207.

126 [Letter from Gui Patin to Charles Spon, dated 24 May 1650.]

Allusion to *Defensio prima* (?). In French. Printed in *Lettres de Gui Patin Nouvelle Édition Augmentée de Lettres Inédites* [etc.]. Ed. Joseph-Henri Reveille-Parise. Paris: Chez J.-B. Baillière, 1846. II, 17–18. See also editions of Gui Patin, *Lettres Choisies*, in Indices III and IV to this bibliography.

127 London. British Library. Sloane MS 1325.

Letter "To ye Author" by Durant Hotham, brother of Charles Hotham (see No. *124*), with allusion, f. 13. Dated: 1650 (?).

128 *Mercurius pragmaticus*. Part 2, No. 39. 22–29 January 1650.

Allusion to divorce views and *Eikonoklastes*, p. [5]. Copy owned by British Library.

129 *Pocula Castalia.* [bracket] *The authors motto. Fortunes tennis-ball. Eliza. Poems. Epigrams, &c. By R. B. Gen.* [etc.]. London: Printed by W. H., for Thomas Dring, 1650.

Author: Robert Baron. Appropriations from the 1645 *Poems* in Thomas Moore's "To the Growing Branch of Virtue," a2v; Baron's "Pocula Castalia," A2v; and Baron's "Tuchesphaira: or, Fortunes Tennis Ball," in Song, Stanza 94, p. 27. Wing, B893. Copy owned by Columbia University Library.

130　*Resolutions and decisions of divers practicall cases of conscience* [etc.]. *The second edition, with some additionals*. London: Printed for N. B. and are to be sold by R. Royston, 1650.

Edition 2 of No. *111*. Publisher: Nathaniel Butter. Discussion of divorce views, pp. 296–299. Wing, H407. Copy owned by Folger Shakespeare Library.

131　*Respublica Anglicana or the historie of the Parliament in their late proceedings* [etc.]. London: Printed by F. Leach, for George Thompson, 1650.

Author: G. W.; sometimes assigned to George Wither. Allusion to *Tenure of Kings and Magistrates*, p. 41. Wing, W3187. Copy owned by New York Public Library.

Stationers' register. See G. E. Briscoe Eyre, ed. *A Transcript of the Registers of the Worshipful Company of Stationers; from 1640–1708 A. D.* London: 1913–1914.

132　Entry for *Defensio prima*, under 31 December 1650, I (1913), 357.

1651

133　Amsterdam. Universiteits-Bibliotheek. MS III.E.9.40.

Letter from Nicolas Heinsius to Isaac Vossius, dated 31 March (10 April) 1651. Allusion to *Defensio prima*. In Latin.

134　Amsterdam. Universiteits-Bibliotheek. MS III.E.9.45.

Letter from Nicolas Heinsius to Isaac Vossius, dated 14 (24) May 1651. Allusion to *Defensio prima*. In Latin.

135　Amsterdam. Universiteits-Bibliotheek. MS III.E.9.48.

Letter from Nicolas Heinsius to Isaac Vossius, dated 19 (29) May 1651. Allusion to Salmasius and notice of Milton's relationship. In Latin.

136　Amsterdam. Universiteits-Bibliotheek. MS III.E.9.50.

Letter from Nicolas Heinsius to Isaac Vossius, dated 7 (17) July 1651. Milton the man discussed. In Latin.

137   Amsterdam. Universiteits-Bibliotheek. MS III.E.9.51.

Letter from Nicolas Heinsius to Isaac Vossius, dated 3 (13) June 1651. Allusion to Salmasius. In Latin.

138   *Animadversions on a book, called A Plea for non-scribers* [etc.]. London: Printed by John Clowes, for Richard Wodnothe, 1651.

Author: Ephraim Elcock. References to *Eikonoklastes* and *Tenure of Kings and Magistrates*, pp. 5, 6–7, 60 and margin. Wing, E325. Copy owned by British Library.

139   *An Answer to the Marques of Worcester's last paper; to the late king* [etc.]. *To these is annext, Smectymnuo-Mastix: or, short animadversions upon Smectymnuus in the point of liturgie* [etc.]. London: Printed by Robert Wood, for Henry Seile, 1651.

Author: Sir Hamon L'Estrange. Separate title page, signatures, and pagination for *Smectymnuo-Mastix*, which does not specifically refer to Milton or the antiprelatical pamphlets. Wing, L1187 and L1191. Copy owned by University of Kentucky Library.

140   *Articles de foy de l'eglise d'Angleterre* [etc.]. Se vend à Charenton. Par Lovis Vendosme demeurant à Paris, 1651.

French translation of No. *45*. Allusion, pp. 90–91. Copy owned by Folger Shakespeare Library.

141   *Catalogus universalis librorum omnium in bibliotheca collegii Sionii.* London: Ex officina Rob. Leybourn, 1650.

Compiler: John Spencer. Apparently the date is in error and should be 1651. Listing of *Doctrine and Discipline of Divorce*, p. 97. Wing, S4959. Copy owned by Union Theological Seminary Library (McAlpin Collection).

141A *Catalogus universalis pro nundinis Francofurtensibus autumnalibus. de anno M. DC. LI* [etc.]. Francofurti, Impensis & typis Hæredum Sigismundi Latomi. 1651.

Listing: *Defensio prima.* Unchecked; copy not located.

142   *The Confession of faith, and the larger and shorter catechisme, first agreed upon by the assembly of divines at Westminster* [etc.]. First printed at Edenburg, and now reprinted at London for the Company of Stationers, 1651.

Duodecimo edition of No. *45*. Allusion, p. 53. Wing, C5762. Copy owned by Union Theological Seminary Library (McAlpin Collection).

143 Courteous reader. Catalogue of books by Humphrey Moseley.

Dated: 1651 or later. Folio. A–L². Listing on L2v, No. 44. Found in the following, among other possible volumes, at end of volume:

> Cardinal Bentivoglio. *Historicall relations of the United Provinces of Flanders, written originally in Italian by Cardinall Bentivoglio: and now rendred into English by the Right Honourable Henry earle of Monmouth.* London: Printed for Humphrey Moseley, 1652. Wing, B1911. Copy owned by Folger Shakespeare Library.

144 Courteous reader. Catalogue of books by Humphrey Moseley.

Dated: 1651 or later. Quarto. A⁴; unpaged. Listing of *Poems* on A3r, No. 59. Found in the following volume, among other possible volumes, at end of volume:

> Sir George Digby and Sir Kenelm Digby. *Letters between the Ld George Digby, and Sr Kenelm Digby K^t concerning religion.* London: Printed for Humphrey Moseley, 1651. Varying issue: this ends with last letter dated March 39, 1639. Wing, D4768. Copy owned by Trinity College Library, Cambridge.

145 I. N. D. N. J.C. Disputatio politica de potestate regia, quam consensu amplissimæ facultatis philosophicæ in illustri Rostochiensium academia præside clarissimo & consultissimo Dn. Christiano Woldenbergio [etc.]. Rostochi: Typis Johannis Richelii, 1651.

Author: Christian Woldenberg. Respondent: Christoph Turing. Place: Rostock, Germany. Dated: October. Dissertation discussing Salmasius' *Defensio regia* and *Defensio prima.* In Latin. Copy owned by PAN Library, Gdańsk, Poland.

146 Ecclesiastes, or, a discourse concerning the gift of preaching as it fals under the rules of art [etc.]. *The third edition* [etc.]. London: Printed by T. R. and E. M., for Samuel Gellibrand, 1651.

Edition 3 of No. *59*. Allusion, p. 119. Wing, W2190. Copy owned by Union Theological Seminary Library (McAlpin Collection).

147 ΕΙΚΩΝ ΑΚΛΑΣΤΟΣ. *The image unbroaken. A perspective of the impudence, falshood, vanitie, and prophannes, published in a libell entitled* ΕΙΚΩΝΟΚΛΑΣΤΗΣ *against* ΕΙΚΩΝ ΒΑΣΙΛΙΚΗ *or the pourtraicture of his sacred majestie in his solitudes and sufferings.* 1651.

Author: Joseph Jane. Place: London. Wing, J451. Copy owned by University of Kentucky Library.

148 Europaeische Sambstägige zeitung. No. 29. 1651.

Publisher: Martin Schumacher. Place: Hamburg. Report of confiscation and burning in Paris of *Defensio prima,* f. A2v. In German. Copy owned by PAN Library, Gdańsk, Poland.

149 Hollandse Mercurius. Vol. 2, February 1651.

Allusion to *Defensio prima,* p. 16. In Dutch. Copy owned by Henry E. Huntington Library.

150 Hollantse Mercurius. Vol. 2, July 1651.

Reference to burning of *Defensio prima,* p. 70. In Dutch. Copy owned by Henry E. Huntington Library.

151 Κατα-βαπτισται κατ'απτυστοι. The dippers dipt [etc.]. *The sixth edition* [etc.]. London: Printed by Richard Cotes, for N. B. and Richard Royston, 1651.

Edition 6 of No. *34.* Publisher: Nicholas Bourne. Allusion, p. [vii]. Wing, F589. Copy owned by Union Theological Seminary Library (McAlpin Collection).

152 Leipziger messrelation. Autumn 1651.

Report of confiscation and burning in Paris of *Defensio prima,* p. 45. In German. Copy owned by Stadtarchiv Stralsund, German Democratic Republic.

*153 [Letter from Johann Friedrich Gronovius to Nicolas Heinsius, dated 7 (17) October 1651.]

Allusion. In Latin. Printed in Pieter Burman, ed. *Sylloges Epistolarum a Viris Illustribus Scriptarum.* Leidæ: Apud Samuelem Luchtmans, 1727. III, 285-286. Copy owned by New York Public Library.

*154 [Letter from Nicolas Heinsius to Johann Friedrich Gronovius, dated 5 (15) May 1651.]

Allusion to Salmasian controversy. In Latin. Printed in Pieter Burman, ed. *Sylloges Epistolarum a Viris Illustribus Scriptarum.* Leidæ: Apud Samuelem Luchtmans, 1727. III, 257-259. Copy owned by New York Public Library.

*155 [Letter from Nicolas Heinsius to Johann Friedrich Gronovius, dated 10 (20) June 1651.]

Allusion to Salmasian controversy. In Latin. Printed in Pieter Burman, ed. *Sylloges Epistolarum a Viris Illustribus Scriptarum.* Leidæ: Apud Samuelem Luchtmans, 1727. III, 266-267. Copy owned by New York Public Library.

156 [Letter from Nicolas Heinsius to Johann Friedrich Gronovius, dated 18 (28) June 1651.]

Discussion of Salmasius. In Latin. Printed in Pieter Burman, ed. *Sylloges Epistolarum a Viris Illustribus Scriptarum*. Leidæ: Apud Samuelem Luchtmans, 1727. III, 269–272. Copy owned by New York Public Library.

157 [Letter from Nicolas Heinsius to Johann Friedrich Gronovius, dated 3 (13) July 1651.]

Allusion to Salmasian controversy. In Latin. Printed in Pieter Burman, ed. *Sylloges Epistolarum a Viris Illustribus Scriptarum*. Leidæ: Apud Samuelem Luchtmans, 1727. III, 273–274. Copy owned by New York Public Library.

158 [Letter from Nicolas Heinsius to Johann Friedrich Gronovius, dated 9 (19) July 1651.]

Biographical allusion. In Latin. Printed in Pieter Burman, ed. *Sylloges Epistolarum a Viris Illustribus Scriptarum*. Leidæ: Apud Samuelem Luchtmans, 1727. III, 275–277. Copy owned by New York Public Library.

159 [Letter from Nicolas Heinsius to Johann Friedrich Gronovius, dated 3 (13) October 1651.]

Allusion. In Latin. Printed in Pieter Burman, ed. *Sylloges Epistolarum a Viris Illustribus Scriptarum*. Leidæ: Apud Samuelem Luchtmans, 1727. III, 285. Copy owned by New York Public Library.

160 [Letter from Nicolas Heinsius to Isaac Vossius, dated 28 April (8 May) 1651.]

Allusion to *Defensio prima*. In Latin. Printed in Pieter Burman, ed. *Sylloges Epistolarum a Viris Illustribus Scriptarum*. Leidæ: Apud Samuelem Luchtmans, 1727. III, 599–601. Copy owned by New York Public Library.

161 [Letter from Nicolas Heinsius to Isaac Vossius, dated 8 (18) May 1651.]

On *Defensio prima* and the Elzeviers. In Latin. Printed in Pieter Burman, ed. *Sylloges Epistolarum a Viris Illustribus Scriptarum*. Leidæ: Apud Samuelem Luchtmans, 1727. III, 601–604. Copy owned by New York Public Library.

162 [Letter from Jacob Matthias to Thomas Bartholin, dated 26 June 1651.]

French dates 6 July 1651, as new style. Allusion concerning Salmasian controversy. In Latin. Printed in No. *573*.

163 [Letter from Gui Patin to M. Belin fils, dated 25 June (5 July) 1651.]

Allusion to Salmasian controversy. In French. Printed in *Lettres de Gui Patin*

Nouvelle Édition Augmentée de Lettres Inédites [etc.]. Ed. Joseph-Henri Reveille-Parise. Paris: J.-B. Baillière, 1846. I, 179.

164 [Letter from Georg Richter to Christopher Arnold, dated 19 (29) March 1651.]

Allusion to *Defensio prima* and the Salmasian controversy; printed in No. *546.*

165 [Letter from Georg Richter to Christopher Arnold, dated 26 July (5 August) 1651.]

Allusions to *Defensio prima* and *Areopagitica*; printed in No. *546.*

166 [Letter from Janus Vlitius to Nicolas Heinsius, dated 5 (10) December 1651.]

Allusion. In Latin. Printed in Pieter Burman, ed. *Sylloges Epistolarum a Viris Illustribus Scriptarum.* Leidæ: Apud Samuelem Luchtmans, 1727. III, 741-742. Copy owned by New York Public Library.

167 [Letter from Isaac Vossius to Nicolas Heinsius, dated 2 (12) April 1651.]

Allusion to *Defensio prima.* In Latin. Printed in Pieter Burman, ed. *Sylloges Epistolarum a Viris Illustribus Scriptarum.* Leidæ: Apud Samuelem Luchtmans, 1727. III, 594-595. Copy owned by New York Public Library.

168 [Letter from Isaac Vossius to Nicolas Heinsius, dated 9 (19) April 1651.]

Allusion to *Defensio prima.* In Latin. Printed in Pieter Burman, ed. *Sylloges Epistolarum a Viris Illustribus Scriptarum.* Leidæ: Apud Samuelem Luchtmans, 1727. III, 595-596. Copy owned by New York Public Library.

169 [Letter from Isaac Vossius to Nicolas Heinsius, dated 25 May (4 June) 1651.]

Allusion with citation of *Eikonoklastes.* In Latin. Printed in Pieter Burman, ed. *Sylloges Epistolarum a Viris Illustribus Scriptarum.* Leidæ: Apud Samuelem Luchtmans, 1727. III, 604-605. Copy owned by New York Public Library.

170 [Letter from Isaac Vossius to Nicolas Heinsius, dated 29 May (8 June) 1651.]

Biographical allusion. In Latin. Printed in Pieter Burman, ed. *Sylloges Epistolarum a Viris Illustribus Scriptarum.* Leidæ: Apud Samuelem Luchtmans, 1727. III, 616-618. Copy owned by New York Public Library.

171 [Letter from Isaac Vossius to Nicolas Heinsius, dated 1 (11) June 1651.]

Allusion to Salmasian controversy. In Latin. Printed in Pieter Burman, ed. *Sylloges Epistolarum a Viris Illustribus Scriptarum.* Leidæ: Apud Samuelem Luchtmans, 1727. III, 606. Copy owned by New York Public Library.

172 [Letter from Isaac Vossius to Nicolas Heinsius, dated 8 (18) June 1651.]

Allusion to Salmasian controversy. In Latin. Printed in Pieter Burman, ed. *Sylloges Epistolarum a Viris Illustribus Scriptarum*. Leidæ: Apud Samuelem Luchtmans, 1727. III, 607–608. Copy owned by New York Public Library.

173 [Letter from Isaac Vossius to Nicolas Heinsius, dated 26 July (5 August) 1651.]

Allusion to Salmasian controversy. In Latin. Printed in Pieter Burman, ed. *Sylloges Epistolarum a Viris Illustribus Scriptarum*. Leidæ: Apud Samuelem Luchtmans, 1727. III, 620–622. Copy owned by New York Public Library.

174 London. British Library. Egerton MS 2534.

Letter from Sir George Carteret to Sir Edward Nicholas, dated 9 (19) June 1651, signed "Milton," ff. 99–100r.

175 *Mercurius politicus*. No. 33, 16–23 January 1651.

Allusion to *Defensio prima*, pp. 545–546. Copy owned by Morgan Library.

176 *Mercurius politicus*. No. 37, 13–20 February 1651.

Allusion to *Defensio prima*, p. 604. Copy owned by Morgan Library.

177 *Mercurius politicus*. No. 39, 27 February–6 March 1651.

Allusion to *Defensio prima*, p. 638. Copy owned by Morgan Library.

178 *Mercurius politicus*. No. 43, 27 March–3 April 1651.

Allusion to Salmasian controversy, p. 697. Copy owned by Morgan Library.

179 *Mercurius politicus*. No. 45, 10–17 April 1651.

Allusion to *Defensio prima*, p. 722. Copy owned by Morgan Library.

180 *Mercurius politicus*. No. 48, 1–7 May 1651.

Allusion to *Eikonoklastes*, p. 776. Copy owned by Morgan Library.

181 *Mercurius politicus*. No. 56, 27 June–3 July 1651.

Allusion to burning of *Defensio prima*, p. 890 (error for 899). Copy owned by Morgan Library.

182 *Mercurius politicus*. No. 57, 3–10 July 1651.

Allusion to Salmasian controversy, pp. 914–915. Copy owned by Morgan Library.

183 *Mercurius politicus*. No. 58, 10–17 July 1651.

Allusion to burning of *Defensio prima*, p. [932]. Copy owned by Morgan Library.

184 *Mercurius politicus*. No. 66, 4–11 September 1651.

Allusion to Salmasius, p. 1056. Copy owned by Morgan Library.

185 *Mercurius politicus*. No. 82, 25 December 1651–1 January 1652.

Allusion to Salmasian controversy, pp. 1316–17. Copy owned by Morgan Library.

186 *Monarchy or no monarchy in England* [etc.]. London: Printed for Humfrey Blunden, 1651.

Author: William Lilly. Allusion to *Eikonoklastes*, pp. 80–81. Wing, L2228. Copy owned by Folger Shakespeare Library.

Allusion disappeared in Dutch translation: *Monarchy ofte geen monarchy in Engelant* [etc.]. Ghedruckt by Humpfrey Blunden, 1653. Reissued in 1665.

187 *Naamanis Bensenii Exercitatio politica de svmmae potestatis svbiecto vindicata a Ioannis Figlovii aliorumque ineptiis & calumniis, quas parturit liber de imperio absolute & relate considerato, oppositus V. Cl. Hermanno Conringio* [etc.]. Helmestadii: Cura Henningi Mvlleri, 1651.

Author: Naaman (Nahum) Bensen. References to and discussions of Milton's relationship to the regicides and *Defensio prima*; see K4v (Section XI), L1–L2v (Section XII), L3v (Section XIII), L4v (Section XIV), M4 (Section XV), O2–O2v (Section XVIII), P2 (Section XIX), Q4 (Section XXII), R4v (Section XXIII). Although not named, Milton seems to be included in remarks in the dedicatory letter from Hermann Conring and in a letter from Conring to Johann Figlow (Fichlau), which is included within the dedicatory letter. Copy owned by British Library.

188 *The Northern subscribers plea, vindicated* [etc.]. London: Printed by R. I. to be sold by John Wright, 1651.

Author: John Drew. Quotation from and reference to *Tenure of Kings and Magistrates*, pp. 40–41 and margin. Wing, D2165. Copy owned by Folger Shakespeare Library.

189 *Nouvelles ordinaires de Londres*. No. 30. 23 January (2 February)–30 January (9 February) 1651.

Colophon: "A Londres, par Guillaume Du-Gard." Allusion to Salmasius, p. 120. Copy owned by Bibliothèque Nationale.

190   *Nouvelles ordinaires de Londres.* No. 34. 20 February (2 March)–27 February
       (9 March) 1651.

       Colophon: "A Londres, par Guillaume Du-Gard." Discussion of *Defensio
       prima*, p. 136. Copy owned by Bibliothèque Nationale.

191   Oldenburg. Niedersächsische Staatsarchiv. Best. 20, Tit. 38, No. 73, Fasc.
       13.

       Two letters from Hermann Mylius to Herr Wolzogen, dated 17 October
       1651 and 31 October 1651, with allusions.

192   Oldenburg. Niedersächsische Staatsarchiv. Best. 20, Tit. 38, No. 73, Fasc.
       13.

       Letter from Hermann Mylius to Georg Wechkerlin, dated 20 October 1651.
       Reference to Oldenburg Safeguard, ff. 81v–82. Scribal copy. In Latin.
       Printed in Columbia XII, 338–344.

193   Oldenburg. Niedersächsische Staatsarchiv. Best. 20, Tit. 38, No. 73, Fasc.
       13.

       Hermann Mylius's "Diarium," dated 16 October 1651 through 17 December
       1651. The diary continues into 1652 (see No. *277*). Two versions: the
       "Konzept" is a rough draft; the "Reinschrift" is a fair copy. See ff. 75–82,
       88, 92v–93v, 95v, 96v, 97v, 104, 209v, 229, 242. Discussion of negotia-
       tions to bring Count of Oldenburg to England, with safeguard; friendship
       with Milton. Copies of letters to and from Milton are included; those from
       Milton are separately entered in this bibliography (Part I). In German with
       quoted documents in Latin.

194   Paris. Bibliothèque Nationale. MS F. L. 602.

       Order of French government, Toulouse, dated 7 (17) June 1651, ff. 21–22.
       Condemnation and burning order for *Defensio prima*. In French.

       Order of French government, Paris, dated 26 June (6 July) 1651, f. 23a.
       Condemnation order for *Defensio prima*. In French.

195   *A Perfect diurnall.* No. 70, 7–14 April 1651.

       Advertisement for *Defensio prima*, p. [962]. Copy owned by British Library.

196   *Pro rege et populo Anglicano apologia, contra Johannis polypragmatici, (alias Miltoni
       Angli) defensionem destructivam, regis & populi Anglicani.* Antverpiæ: Apud
       Hieronymum Verdussen, 1651.

       Author: John Rowland. Edition 1. Duodecimo. xxvi + 196 pp. In Latin.
       Copy owned by Folger Shakespeare Library.

197   *Pro rege & populo Anglicano apologia. Contra Johannis polypragmatici, (Alias Miltoni
      Angli) defensionem destructivam, regis & populi Anglicani.* Antverpiæ: Apud
      Hieronymum Verdussen, 1651.

      Edition 2 of No. *196.* Duodecimo. 156 pp. Copy owned by University of
      Kentucky Library.

198   *Reliquiæ Wottonianæ. Or, a collection of lives, letters, poems; with characters of sun-
      dry personages* [etc.]. London: Thomas Maxey, for R. Marriot, G. Bedel,
      and T. Garthwait, 1651.

      Author: Sir Henry Wotton. Edition 1. Letter to Milton, pp. 432–436. Wing,
      W3648. Copy owned by Columbia University Library.

      Stationers' register. See G. E. Briscoe Eyre, ed. *A Transcript of the Registers
      of the Worshipful Company of Stationers; from 1640–1708 A. D.* London:
      1913–1914.

199   Entry for licensing *Mercurius Politicus*, under 17 March 1651, I (1913), 362.
200   Entry for licensing *Mercurius Politicus*, under 17 April 1651, I (1913), 364.
201   Entry for licensing *Mercurius Politicus*, under 22 May 1651, I (1913), 368.
202   Entry for licensing *Mercurius Politicus*, under 29 May 1651, I (1913), 369.
203   Entry for licensing *Mercurius Politicus*, under 5 June 1651, I (1913), 370.
204   Entry for licensing *Mercurius Politicus*, under 12 June 1651, I (1913), 370.
205   Entry for licensing *Mercurius Politicus*, under 19 June 1651, I (1913), 371.
206   Entry for licensing *Mercurius Politicus*, under 26 June 1651, I (1913), 372.
207   Entry for licensing *Mercurius Politicus*, under 3 July 1651, I (1913), 372.
208   Entry for licensing *Mercurius Politicus*, under 10 July 1651, I (1913), 373.
209   Entry for licensing *Mercurius Politicus*, under 17 July 1651, I (1913), 374.
210   Entry for licensing *Mercurius Politicus*, under 24 July 1651, I (1913), 374.
211   Entry for licensing *Mercurius Politicus*, under 31 July 1651, I (1913), 375.
212   Entry for licensing *Mercurius Politicus*, under 7 August 1651, I (1913), 375.
213   Entry for licensing *Mercurius Politicus*, under 14 August 1651, I (1913), 376.
214   Entry for licensing *Mercurius Politicus*, under 21 August 1651, I (1913), 376.
215   Entry for licensing *Mercurius Politicus*, under 28 August 1651, I (1913), 377.
216   Entry for licensing *Mercurius Politicus*, under 4 September 1651, I (1913),
      377.
217   Entry for licensing *Mercurius Politicus*, under 11 September 1651, I (1913),
      378.
218   Entry for licensing *Mercurius Politicus*, under 18 September 1651, I (1913),
      378.
219   Entry for licensing *Mercurius Politicus*, under 25 September 1651, I (1913),
      379.
220   Entry for licensing *Mercurius Politicus*, under 2 October 1651, I (1913), 379.
221   Entry for licensing *A Perfect Diurnal*, under 6 October 1651, I (1913), 380.

222   Entry for licensing *Mercurius Politicus*, under 9 October 1651, I (1913), 380.

223   Entry for licensing *Mercurius Politicus*, under 16 October 1651, I (1913), 381.

224   Entry for licensing *Mercurius Politicus*, under 23 October 1651, I (1913), 381.

225   Entry for licensing *Mercurius Politicus*, under 30 October 1651, I (1913), 382.

226   Entry for licensing *Mercurius Politicus*, under 6 November 1651, I (1913), 382.

227   Entry for licensing *Mercurius Politicus*, under 13 November 1651, I (1913), 383.

228   Entry for licensing *Mercurius Politicus*, under 20 November 1651, I (1913), 383.

229   Entry for licensing *Mercurius Politicus*, under 27 November 1651, I (1913), 385.

230   Entry for licensing *Mercurius Politicus*, under 4 December 1651, I (1913), 385.

231   Entry for licensing *Mercurius Politicus*, under 11 December 1651, I (1913), 385.

232   Entry for licensing *Mercurius Politicus*, under 18 December 1651, I (1913), 386.

233   Entry for licensing *Mercurius Politicus*, under 25 December 1651, I (1913), 386.

234   *Verdediging voor den koning, ende het volck van Engeland, tegens Johannis Moey-al (alias Milton den Engelsman) sijn verderffelijcke bescherminghe, van den koning ende het volck van Engeland.* t'Hantwerpen, By Hieronymus Verdussen. 1651.

Dutch translation of No. *196*. Duodecimo in 251 pp. of text. Copy owned by British Library.

235   *Wochentliche Donnerstags zeitung.* No. 29. 1651.

Publisher: kaiserliches Postamt, Hamburg. Report of confiscation and burning in Paris of *Defensio prima*, f. A2–A2v. In German. Copy owned by PAN Library, Gdańsk, Poland.

1652

See also No. 131 in Part I for material in the *Eikon Basilike* controversy.

236   Amsterdam. Universiteits-Bibliotheek. MS III.E.9.111.

Letter from Nicolas Heinsius to Isaac Vossius, dated 22 August (1 September) 1652. Allusion to Salmasian controversy. In Latin.

237   Amsterdam. Universiteits-Bibliotheek. MS III.E.9.114.

Letter from Nicolas Heinsius to Isaac Vossius, dated 12 (22) September 1652. Allusion to blindness. In Latin.

238   Amsterdam. Universiteits-Bibliotheek. MS III.E.9.120.

Letter from Nicolas Heinsius to Isaac Vossius, dated 12 (22) October 1652. Allusion to Salmasius. In Latin.

239   Amsterdam. Universiteits-Bibliotheek. MS III.E.9.123.

Letter from Nicolas Heinsius to Isaac Vossius, dated 2 (12) November 1652. Allusion to Salmasian controversy. In Latin.

240   *As you were or the lord general Cromwel and the grand officers of the armie their remem-brancer* [etc.]. Printed May 1652.

Author: John Lilburne. Place: Amsterdam (?). Long quotation in English from *Defensio prima*, pp. 15–16. Wing, L2084. Copy owned by Union Theological Seminary Library (McAlpin Collection).

241   *Carolvs I., Britanniarvm Rex. A secvri et calamo Miltonii vindicatvs* [etc.]. Dvblini: Apud libervm correctorem, via regia, sub signo solutæ fascis, 1652.

Author: Claude Barthélemy Morisot. Published in Dijon. Defense of Charles I against Milton's charges. In Latin. Wing, M2774. Copy owned by Henry E. Huntington Library.

242   *Casparis Ziegleri Lipsiensis circa regicidium Anglorum exercitationes.* Lipsiæ: Apud Hæred. Henning. Grossi, Literis Lanckisianis Exscribebat Christoph. Cellarius, Anno 1652.

Examination of King Charles and the regicides. Milton and the Salmasian controversy are discussed in "Ad Lectorem," A6–A10. Copy owned by Henry E. Huntington Library.

There would seem to have been an edition from Jena also in 1652; unlocated.

243   *Catalogus universalis pro nundinis Francofurtensibus vernalibus, de anno M. DC. LII* [etc.]. Francofurti, Impensis & typis Hæredum Sigismundi Latomi, 1652.

Listing: D4v, *Defensio prima*. Copy owned by Bodleian Library.

244   *Catalogus universalis pro nundinis Francofurtensibus autumnalibus, de anno M. DC. LII* [etc.]. Francofurti, Impensis & typis Hæredum Sigismundi Latomi, 1652.

Listing: B1v, *Defensio prima*. Copy owned by Bodleian Library.

245 *The Confession of faith, and the larger and shorter catechism* [etc.]. First printed at Edenburgh, and now reprinted at London for the Company of Stationers, 1652.

Another edition of No. *45*; reissue of No. *142*. Allusion, p. 53. Wing, C5764. Copy owned by Princeton Theological Seminary Library.

Wing, C5765 lists an edition from Leith, the fourth, in 1653, at the National Library of Scotland, referring to Aldis 1473. This is an edition of the Confession of Faith of the Anabaptists. See Harry G. Aldis, *A List of Books Printed in Scotland Before 1700* (Edinburgh: National Library of Scotland, 1970), first published in 1904.

246 *The Confession of faith, and the larger and shorter catechisms* [etc.]. Edinburgh: Printed by the Heirs of George Anderson, 1652.

Another edition of No. *45*. Duodecimo. Allusion, p. 73. Wing, C5763. Copy owned by British Library.

247 Copenhagen. Kongelige Bibliotek. MS. Rostg. Saml. 39. 4°.

Wilhelmus [Olai] Worm, "Iter Anglicum anno MDCLII die ii. Maii inceptum et die xxx. Augusti absolutum" [etc.]. Allusion and epigram concerning the regicide, p. 11. Dated: 24 May 1652. In Latin.

248 Lord Delamere. MS letter from John Dury to Samuel Hartlib, dated 5 June 1652.

In Sheffield University Library. Allusion to Salmasian controversy. Printed in G. H. Turnbull. *Hartlib, Dury and Comenius.* London: Hodder and Stoughton, 1947, p. 41.

249 *Dissertationis ad quædam loca Miltoni pars prior; quam annuente Deo, præside, Dn. Iacobo Schallero, S. S. Theolog. Doct. et Philosoph. pract. professore. Solenniter defendere conabitur die mensis Septembris Erhardus Kieffer. Durlaco-Marchicus.* Argentorati: Typis Friderici Spoor, 1652.

Author: James (Jacob) Schaller. Respondent: Erhard Kieffer. Place: Strasbourg. German dissertation and defense on the Milton-Salmasius controversy (see No. *294*). In Latin. Copy owned by Sächsische Landesbibliothek, Dresden.

249A *Ecclesiastes, ofte een discoers | aengaende de gave van't prediken, soo als't volt onder de regulen des konsts* [etc.]. *De derde druck. In't Engelsch by een gestelt door Jo: Wilkins D. D. envertaete door J. G.* [etc.]. t'Amsteldam, By Jacob Benjamin, 1652.

Dutch translation of No. *59*. Translator: Johannis Grindal (?). Allusion, p. 163. Copy owned by Universiteits-Bibliotheek, Amsterdam.

250 The Hague. Algemeen Rijksarchief. Inventory of papers of Lieuw van Aitzema, No. 45.

Report, dated 5 March 1652, gives Milton's comment on the Racovian Catechism. In Dutch.

251 *The Holy state. By Thomas Fuller bachelour of divinitie, & prebendary of Sarum* [etc.]. *The third edition.* London: Printed by R. D., for John Williams, 1652.

Edition 3 of No. 7. Printer: Roger Daniel. Allusion, pp. 279–280. Wing, F2445. Copy owned by University of Kentucky Library.

252 *Irenodia gratulatoria, sive illustrissimi amplissimiq; viri Oliverii Cromwelli, &c. Epinicion. Dedicatum domino præsidi Bradshawo* [etc.]. Typis T. Newcomb, prostant à Johanne Holden.

Author: Payne Fisher. Place: London. Date: 1652. Allusion in Dedication, p. [vii] and margin. In Latin. Wing, F1027. Copy owned by Folger Shakespeare Library.

253 *Judiciall astrologie, judicially condemned. Upon a survey and examination of S^r· Christopher Heydons Apology for it, in answer to Mr. Chambers. And of Will. Ramsey's Morologie in his pretended reply (called lux veritatis) to Doctour Nathanael Homes his Demonologie. Together with the testimonies of M^r· W. Perkins Resolution to the countreyman; M^r· John Miltons Figure-caster; and Dr. Homes his Demonologie, all here exhibited against it* [etc.]. London: Printed by Roger Daniel, for Joseph Blaiklocke, 1652.

Author: William Rowland. Allusion?: implication of confusion with the well-known John Milton. Rowland calls him "Mr *J. Melton*" on p. 134 and "Master John Melton" on pp. 155–156, prints *Figure-Caster* on pp. 157–217, and notes "Thus farr *Milton*" on p. 217. Wing, R2174. Copy owned by Union Theological Seminary Library (McAlpin Collection).

254 Leipzig. Stadtarchiv. Bücherzensurakten I (1600–1690). Tit. XLVI.152.

Letter from Johann Georg, Elector of Saxony, to the Council of Leipzig, dated 3 May 1652, f. 9. Order to confiscate *Defensio prima*, printed by Hans Bauer and published by Tobias Riese. Scribal hand.

255 Leipzig. Stadtarchiv. Bücherzensurakten I (1600–1690). Tit. XLVI.152.

Draft of reply from Council of Leipzig to Johann Georg, Elector of Saxony, dated 22 May 1652, ff. 10–11v. Discussion of publication of *Defensio prima*. Bauer and Riese deny having printed or published book; no copies found. Scribal hand.

256 Leipzig. Stadtarchiv. Bücherzensurakten I (1600-1690). Tit. XLVI.152.

Letter from Johann Georg, Elector of Saxony, to the Council of Leipzig, dated 1 November 1652, f. 17. Answer to petition from Tobias Riese (12 October 1652, undiscovered), previously found guilty of publishing *Defensio prima* and fined; fine reduced. Scribal hand.

257 Leipzig. Stadtarchiv. Bücherzensurakten I (1600-1690). Tit. XLVI.152.

Petition from Tobias Riese (second) to Johann Georg, Elector of Saxony, dated 15 November 1652, f. 16. Requests waiving of remaining fine since others sold *Defensio prima* without penalty. Scribal hand.

258 Leipzig. Stadtarchiv. Bücherzensurakten I (1600-1690). Tit. XLVI.152.

Letter from Johann Georg, Elector of Saxony, to the Council of Leipzig, dated 28 November 1652, f. 15. Petition (see No. *257*) denied. Scribal hand.

259 Leipzig. Stadtarchiv. Bücherzensurakten I (1600-1690). Tit. XLVI.152.

Petition from Tobais Riese to Council of Leipzig, dated 14 December 1652, f. 18. Partial payment of fine; plea to waive remainder. Scribal hand.

260 Leipzig. Stadtarchiv. Bücherzensurakten I (1600-1690). Tit. XLVI.152.

Draft of letter from Council of Leipzig to Johann Georg, Elector of Saxony, dated 16 December 1652, ff. 19-20v. Action of Council following No. *258*, but request following No. *259*. Indicates Riese has admitted publication of *Defensio prima*. Scribal hand.

261 [Letter from Samuel Bochart to Claudius Salmasius, dated (September?) 1652.]

On the Salmasian controversy. Printed in No. *1318*.

262 [Letter from Johann Friedrich Gronovius to Nicolas Heinsius, dated 9 (19) November 1652.]

Allusion to Salmasius. In Latin. Printed in Pieter Burman, ed. *Sylloges Epistolarum a Viris Illustribus Scriptarum*. Leidæ: Apud Samuelem Luchtmans, 1727. III, 303-304. Copy owned by New York Public Library.

263 [Letter from Nicolas Heinsius to Petrus Bourdelotius, dated 1652.]

Allusion to Salmasian controversy. In Latin. Printed in Pieter Burman, ed. *Sylloges Epistolarum a Viris Illustribus Scriptarum*. Leidæ: Apud Samuelem Luchtmans, 1727. V, 711-714. Copy owned by New York Public Library.

264 [Letter from Nicolas Heinsius to Johann Friedrich Gronovius, dated 28 December 1652 (7 January 1653).]

Allusion to Salmasian controversy. In Latin. Printed in Pieter Burman, ed. *Sylloges Epistolarum a Viris Illustribus Scriptarum*. Leidæ: Apud Samuelem Luchtmans, 1727. III, 306–309. Copy owned by New York Public Library.

265 [Letter from Nicolas Heinsius to Isaac Vossius, dated 7 (17) December 1652.]

Allusion to Salmasian controversy. In Latin. Printed in Pieter Burman, ed. *Sylloges Epistolarum a Viris Illustribus Scriptarum*. Leidæ: Apud Samuelem Luchtmans, 1727. III, 652–657. Copy owned by New York Public Library.

266 [Letter from Janus Vlitius to Nicolas Heinsius, dated 12 (22) January 1652.]

Allusion. In Latin. Printed in Pieter Burman, ed. *Sylloges Epistolarum a Viris Illustribus Scriptarum*. Leidæ: Apud Samuelem Luchtmans, 1727. III, 742–743. Copy owned by New York Public Library.

267 [Letter from Rhodius to Nicolas Heinsius, dated 2 (12) January 1652.]

Allusion. In Latin. Printed in Pieter Burman, ed. *Sylloges Epistolarum a Viris Illustribus Scriptarum*. Leidæ: Apud Samuelem Luchtmans, 1727. V, 456–457. Copy owned by New York Public Library.

268 [Letter from Isaac Vossius to Nicolas Heinsius, dated 9 (19) July 1652.]

Biographical allusion concerning blindness. In Latin. Printed in Pieter Burman, ed. *Sylloges Epistolarum a Viris Illustribus Scriptarum*. Leidæ: Apud Samuelem Luchtmans, 1727. III, 637–640. Copy owned by New York Public Library.

269 [Letter from Isaac Vossius to Nicolas Heinsius, dated 22 August (1 September) 1652.]

Allusion to More scandal. In Latin. Printed in Pieter Burman, ed. *Sylloges Epistolarum a Viris Illustribus Scriptarum*. Leidæ: Apud Samuelem Luchtmans, 1727. III, 642–643. Copy owned by New York Public Library.

270 *The Life and reigne of King Charls, or, the pseudo-martyr discovered*. London: Printed for W. Reybold, 1651.

Author: Sir Hamon L'Estrange? Dated: 1652. Allusion, p. 179. Wing, M2127. Copy owned by University of Kentucky Library.

271 London. British Library. Additional MS 4180.

Letter from Sir Edward Nicholas to Sir Edward Hyde (Lord Clarendon), dated 21 (31) October 1652, f. 78. Transcribed by Thomas Birch. Allusion to *Regii Sanguinis Clamor.*

Letter from Sir Edward Nicholas to Mr. Smith (Lord Hatton), dated 4 (14) November 1652, f. 78v. Transcribed by Thomas Birch. Allusion to Salmasian controversy.

Letter from Sir Edward Nicholas to Sir Edward Hyde (Lord Clarendon), dated 4 (14) November 1652, f. 79. Transcribed by Thomas Birch. Allusion to Salmasian controversy.

272 *Mercurius politicus.* No. 84, 8-15 January 1652.

Allusion to Salmasius, p. 1344. Copy owned by Morgan Library.

273 *News from France. or, A description of the library of Cardinall Mazarini: before it was utterly ruined. Sent in a letter from Monsieur G. Nandaens, keeper of the republick library.* London: Printed for Timothy Garthwait, 1652.

A different edition of No. *281.* Allusions, A2v, A3r. On sig. B ff. appears: "Pauls Church-Yard Libri Theologici, Politici, Historici, Nundinis Paulinus [etc.]. Centuria Secunda." Not in Wing. Copy owned by British Library.

274 *Nouvelles ordinaires de Londres.* No. 125. 18 (28) November–25 November (5 December) 1652.

Colophon: "A Londres, par Guillaume Du-Gard." Notice of publication of Dury's translation of *Eikonoklastes*, p. 500. In French. Copy owned by Bibliothèque Nationale.

275 *Observations concerning the originall of government, upon Mr. Hobs Leviathan. Mr. Milton against Salmasius. H. Grotius De jure belli.* [etc.]. London: Printed for R. Royston, 1652.

Author: Sir Robert Filmer. Edition 1; remarks on Philip Hunton are not included. *Observations on Milton*, pp. 13–23. Wing, F918. Copy owned by New York Public Library.

276 *Observations concerning the originall of government, upon Mr. Hobs Leviathan. Mr. Milton against Salmasius. H. Grotius De jure belli. Mr. Huntons Treatise of monarchy.* [etc.]. London: Printed for R. Royston, 1652.

Edition 2 of No. *275. Observations on Milton*, pp. 12–22. Not in Wing. Copy owned by Folger Shakespeare Library.

277 Oldenburg. Niedersächsische Staatsarchiv. Best. 20, Tit. 38, No. 73, Fasc. 13.

Hermann Mylius's "Diarium," dated 1 January 1652 through 6 March 1652. Two versions: see No. *193* in this bibliography. Continuation of No. *193*: ff. 112, 114, 119, 120, 123v, 125–126, 128–128v, 134v, 136–136v, 144, 153–153v, 155v, 156, 157, 161, 162v, 163, 165v, 167v, 179–179v, 181v, 184, 189–189v, 198. In German with quoted documents in Latin.

278 Oldenburg. Niedersächsische Staatsarchiv. Best. 20, Tit. 38, No. 73, Fasc. 13.

Letter from Hermann Mylius to Herr Wolzogen, dated 9 January 1652, with allusion.

279 Marquis of Ormonde. MS Collections.

Letter from D. Vicqfort to Dr. Fraser, dated 12 (22) February 1652. Allusion to Salmasius. In French. See French III, 173.

280 Oxford. Bodleian Library. Clarendon State Papers. MS 43.

Letter from Edward Hyde, Lord Clarendon, to Mr. Taylor, dated 23 August [1652], f. 259. Allusion to arrival of *Defensio prima* in Germany.

281 *Pavl's Chvrch-Yard. Libri theologici, politici, historici, nundinis Paulnis (unà cum templo) prostant venales. Iuxta seriem alphabeti democratici. Done into English for the assembly of divines.*

Author: Sir John Birkenhead (?). Place: London. Date: 1652 (?); dated by Parker in 1659 (?). Apparently two listings in this mock, satiric catalogue: No. 43, *Defensio prima*, A2v, and No. 50, *Doctrine and Discipline of Divorce*, A3. Wing, B2970. Copy owned by Union Theological Seminary Library (McAlpin Collection). Copy owned by Columbia University Library has no title page, but seems to be this issue.

282 *Pro rege et populo Anglicano apologia, contra Johannis polypragmatici, (alias Miltoni Angli) defensionem destructivam, regis & populi Anglicani.* Antverpiæ: Apud Hieronymum Verdussen, 1652.

Edition 3 of No. *196*. Printer: Louis Elzevier. Duodecimo. xvi + 176 pp. In Latin. Copy owned by University of Kentucky Library.

Parker (*Milton's Contemporary Reputation* [1940], pp. 88, 90) states that this was printed twice in 1652 and implies by omission that it was printed only once in 1651; see also *Milton: A Biography*, pp. 1018–19. He specifies that the 1652 editions have 191 pp. and 122 pp. Perhaps he erred in the date of No. *196* (in xxvi + 196 pp.) for the first, but I have found no edition in 122 pp. No. *282*, copies of which are found in a number of libraries, was reissued (?) in 1653 (see No. *314*), unnoted by Parker.

283 *Regii sanguinis clamor ad cœlum adversus parricidas Anglicanos.* Hagæ-Comitum: Ex typographia Adriani Vlac, 1652.

Author: Peter du Moulin. Edition 1. Quarto. xvi + 172 pp. Dedication written by Alexander More. In Latin. Copy owned by Union Theological Seminary Library (McAlpin Collection).

284 *Regii sanguinis clamor ad cœlum adversus parricidas Anglicanos.* Hagæ-Comitvn: Ex typographia Adriani Vlacq, 1652.

Edition 2 of No *283.* Duodecimo. xvi + 148 pp. In Latin. Copy owned by William Andrews Clark Library.

285 *Regii sanguinis clamor ad cœlum adversus parricidas Anglicanos.* Hagæ-Comitum: Ex typographia Adriani Vlac, 1652.

Edition 3 of No. *283.* Duodecimo. xxiv + 190 pp. In Latin. Copy owned by University of Kentucky Library.

Stationers' register. See G. E. Briscoe Eyre, ed. *A Transcript of the Registers of the Worshipful Company of Stationers; from 1640–1708 A. D.* London: 1913–1914.

286 Entry for licensing *Mercurius Politicus,* under 1 January 1652, I (1913), 387.
287 Entry for licensing *Mercurius Politicus,* under 8 January 1652, I (1913), 388.
288 Entry for licensing *Mercurius Politicus,* under 15 January 1652, I (1913), 388.
289 Entry for licensing *Mercurius Politicus,* under 22 January 1652, I (1913), 389.

290 *Theophila, or loves sacrifice. A divine poem. Written by E. B. Esq; Several parts thereof set to fit aires by Mr. J. Jenkins* [etc.]. London: Printed by R. N., sold by Henry Seile and Humphrey Moseley, 1652.

Author: Edward Benlowes. Appropriations from minor poems ("Nativity Ode," "L'Allegro," "Il Penseroso," "Comus," "Lycidas"): Canto I, section 11, p. 2; Canto V, section 69, p. 76; Canto VII, section 65, p. 103; Canto XII, section 12, p. 221; Canto XII, section 54, p. 226; Canto XIII, section 95, p. 248. Wing, B1879. Copy owned by Arents Collection, New York Public Library.

291 *Veni; vidi; vici. The triumphs of the most excellent & illustrious, Oliver Cromwell ... done into English heroicall verse, by T: M: Jun. esq.* [etc.]. London: Printed for Iohn Tey, 1652.

Author: Payne Fisher. Translator: Thomas Manley. Allusion in The Epistle Dedicatory, B4v. Wing, F1044. Copy owned by Folger Shakespeare Library.

1653

292 *Abregé de l'histoire de ce siecle de fer* [etc.]. A Leyde, Chez Abraham à Geerevliet. cIɔ Iɔ C LIII.

Author: Jean-Nicholas Parival. Comment on Milton's secretarial role, Book VI, Chapter 8, p. 440. Copy owned by University of Illinois Library.

293 Cambridge. Trinity College Library. MS R.5.5.

Letter from Anne Sadleir to Roger Williams. Dated: 1653 (?). Allusion to antimonarchical works.

Letter from Roger Williams to Anne Sadleir. Dated: 1653 (?). Allusion to *Eikonoklastes*.

294 *Caspari Ziegleri Lipsienis circa regicidivm Anglorum exercitationes. Accedit Jacobi Schalleri. Dissertatio ad loca quædam Miltoni.* Lugd. Batavorum: Apud Johannem à Sambix, 1653.

Printer: Willem Christiaens. Publishers: Jean and Daniel Elzevier. Place: Leyden. Publication of two German dissertations, in Latin, on the English regicides and the Milton-Salmasius controversy: Nos. *242*, pp. 1–157, and *249*, pp. 159–262. Copy owned by Princeton University Library.

295 *Courteous reader.* Catalogue of books by Humphrey Moseley.

Dated: 1653 or later. Octavo. A^8; unpaged. Listing on A4, No. 66. Separate copy owned by the Bodleian Library; shelf mark: Wood 896 (2). Also found in the following, among other possible volumes, at end of volume:

Raphael Thorius. *Hymnus tabaci; a poem in honour of tabaco* [etc.]. London: Printed by T. N., for Humphrey Moseley, 1651. Translator: Peter Hausted. Wing, T1040. Copy owned by Folger Shakespeare Library.

Richard Brome. *Five new plays, (viz.) The* [bracket] *Madd couple well matcht. Novella. Court begger. City witt. Damoiselle.* London: Printed for Humphrey Moseley, Richard Marriot, and Thomas Dring, 1653. Wing, B4870. Copy owned by Folger Shakespeare Library.

Sir Francis Bacon. *The Naturall and experimentall history of winds* [etc.]. London: Printed for Humphrey Moseley and Tho. Dring, 1653. Translator: R. G. Wing, B305. Copy owned by Folger Shakespeare Library.

Gregorio Leti. *The Scarlet gown, or the history of all the present cardinals of Rome* [etc.]. London: Printed for Humphrey Moseley, 1653. Preface signed: N. N. Translator: Henry Cogan. Wing, N53. Copy owned by New York Public Library. Copy in Folger Shakespeare Library has Catalogue in uncropped condition.

James Shirley. *Six new plays* [etc.]. London: Printed for Humphrey Robinson and Humphrey Moseley, 1653. Wing, S3486. Copy owned by Folger Shakespeare Library.

296 *A Discourse concerning the gift of prayer* [etc.]. London: Printed by T. R. and E. M. for Samuel Gellibrand, 1653.

To which is added:
Ecclesiastes, or, a discourse concerning the gift of preaching [etc.]. *The fourth edition* [etc.]. London: Printed by T. R. and E. M. for Samuel Gellibrand, 1653.

Another edition of No. *59*. Reissue of No. *298*. Wing, W2180 and W2191. Copy owned by Henry E. Huntington Library.

297 *Dise Bücher seynd auss dem augspurger buechladen, vnd bey Johannes Weh buchhändlern, der zeit in Regenspurg, zufinden.* Anno 1653.

Listing of *Defensio prima*. Copy owned by Bayerischen Staatsbibliothek.

298 *Ecclesiastes, or, a discourse concerning the gift of preaching* [etc.]. *The fourth edition* [etc.]. London: Printed by T. R. and E. M. for Samuel Gellibrand, 1653.

Reissue of No. *146*. Issued also with No. *296*. Wing, W2191. Copy owned by Folger Shakespeare Library.

299 *The History of the warres of the Emperour Justinian in eight books* [etc.]. *Written in Greek by Procopius of Caesarea. English by Henry Holcroft, knight.* London: Printed for Humphrey Moseley, 1653.

Folio. L2 is a printing of "Courteous Reader." *Poems*, 1645, listed as No. 44 on L2v. Wing, P3640. Copy owned by British Library.

300 *Ein hundert dialogi, oder gespräch von unterschiedlichen sachen zu erbaulicher nachricht auch nutzlichem gebrauch vnd belustigung* [etc.]. In Verlegung Johann Görlius, 1653.

Author: Martin Zeiller. Discussions or allusions concerning the Salmasian controversy, Milton's contribution to the justification of the new government and Cromwell, and John Phillips's entry into the controversy. See "Vorrede," b2; Dialogue 77, pp. 524–525; Dialogue 81, pp. 580–581; Dialogue 83, p. 600; Dialogue 84, p. 606; Dialogue 85, p. 620; Dialogue 86, pp.

620–629; Dialogue 87, pp. 629–638; Dialogue 88, pp. 638–645; Summary of Dialogues, Nos. 86–88, pp. 809–811. Copy owned by Princeton University Library.

301 *A Letter of resolution to six quares, of present use in the Church of England.* London: Printed by J. Flesher, for R. Royston, 1653.

Author: Henry Hammond. Allusion to divorce views, pp. 122–127. Wing, H545. Copy owned by Union Theological Seminary Library (McAlpin Collection).

302 [Letter from Johann Friedrich Gronovius to Nicolas Heinsius, dated 21 (31) January 1653.]

Allusion to More. In Latin. Printed in Pieter Burman, ed. *Sylloges Epistolarum a Viris Illustribus Scriptarum.* Leidæ: Apud Samuelem Luchtmans, 1727. III, 662–663. Copy owned by New York Public Library.

303 [Letter from Nicolas Heinsius to Isaac Vossius, dated 18 (28) February 1653.]

Discussion of Salmasius and Latin poems. In Latin. Printed in Pieter Burman, ed. *Sylloges Epistolarum a Viris Illustribus Scriptarum.* Leidæ: Apud Samuelem Luchtmans, 1727. III, 667–671. Copy owned by New York Public Library.

304 [Letter from Ole Worm to his son Wilhelmus, dated 14 (24) September 1653.]

Allusion to Salmasius. In Latin. Printed in *Olai Wormii et ad eum doctorum virorum epistolæ* [etc.]. Havniæ, 1751. Copy owned by British Library.

305 London. British Library. Additional MS 37,346.

First volume of "The History of Whitelockes Ambassy from England to Sweden. With Notes Theruppon And touching the Government Publique Councells and Persons in those and in other Countries [etc.]." Author: Bulstrode Whitelocke. Allusion to *Defensio prima,* Book VI, Chapter 14, f. 74v (December 1653). Published by Henry Reeve as *A Journal of the Swedish Embassy* (London: Longman, Brown, Greene, and Longmans, 1855), I, 203.

305A München. Bayrisches Hauptstaatsarchiv. Bestand Kurbayern, Lit. 2636.

Reference to *Defensio prima* in recording of discussion and vote of Brunswick-Wolfenbüttel at Ratisbon diet, dated 6/16 July 1653, ff. 21v–22.

306 Oxford. Bodleian Library. Clarendon State Papers. MS 45.

Letter from Edward Hyde, Lord Clarendon, to Sir Edward Nicholas, dated

8 (18) January 1653, f. 18–18v. Remark that he knows nothing about Milton's book (*Defensio prima*) to be translated into French.

307 Oxford. Bodleian Library. Clarendon State Papers. MS 46.

Letter from Edward Hyde, Lord Clarendon, to Sir Edward Nicholas, dated 9 (19) September 1653, f. 262. Allusion to Salmasius and Milton.

308 Oxford. Bodleian Library. Rawlinson MS A.3.

Anonymous letter to John Thurloe, dated 3 (13) June 1653, p. 160. Allusion to Salmasian controversy. In French. Slightly different version printed in *A Collection of the State Papers of John Thurloe, Esq*; London: Printed for the Executors of the Late Mr. Fletcher Gyles, Thomas Woodward, and Charles Davis, 1742. Ed. Thomas Birch. I, 267. Copy owned by New York Public Library.

Anonymous letter to John Thurloe, dated 10 (20) June 1653, p. 220. Allusion to blindness. In French. Printed in *Thurloe*, above, I, 281.

309 Oxford. Bodleian Library. Rawlinson MS A.9.

Letter of intelligence, dated 18 December 1653, from Ratisbon, on the confiscation of Milton's books, p. 73. Printed in *A Collection of the State Papers of John Thurloe, Esq*; London: Printed for the Executors of the Late Mr. Fletcher Gyles, Thomas Woodward, and Charles Davis, 1742. Ed. Thomas Birch. III, 216. Copy owned by New York Public Library.

310 ΠΑΝΣΕΒΕΙΑ: *or, a view of all religions in the world* [etc.]. London: Printed for Iohn Saywell, 1653.

Author: Alexander Ross. Allusions to divorce views, pp. 400, 413. Wing, R1971. Copy owned by Union Theological Seminary Library (McAlpin Collection).

311 *Poems, by Francis Beaumont, gent.* [etc.]. London: Printed for William Hope, 1653.

Influence from and partial imitation of *A Maske* in "A Maske of the Gentlemen of Graies Inne, and the Inner Temple, by Mr Francis Beaumont," G6–H1v. The poem is apparently not by Beaumont. Wing, B1603. Copy owned by Folger Shakespeare Library.

312 *Poems: By Francis Beaumont, gent.* [etc.]. London: Printed for Laurence Blaiklock, and are to be sold at his Shop, 1653.

Another issue of No. *311*. Wing, B1602. Copy owned by Henry E. Huntington Library.

313 Polemica sive supplementum ad apologiam anonymam pro rege & populo Anglicano, adversus Jo: Miltoni defensionem populi Anglicani. Et Irænica sive cantus receptui ad Christianos omnes. Per Io: Rowlandum pastorem Anglicanum. 1653.

Author: John Rowland. Place: Amsterdam (?). Supplement to No. *196*, with admission of authorship. In Latin. Copy owned by Henry E. Huntington Library.

314 Pro rege et populo Anglicano apologia, contra Johannis polypragmatici, (alias Miltoni Angli) defensionem destructivam, regis & populi Anglicani. Antverpiæ: Apud Hieronymum Verdussen, 1653.

Edition 4 of No. *196*; reissue of No. *282* (?). Printer: Ludovic Elzevier (?). Duodecimo. xvi + 176 pp. Copy owned by University of Kentucky Library.

315 Two centvries of Pauls Church-yard [etc.]. *Done into English for the benefit of the assembly of divines, and the two universities.*

Another edition of No. *281*. Place: London. Date: 1653 (?). Octavo. A-H^4; 64 pp. Paged: [1] 2-8 7-62. Listings, pp. 10, 11. Wing, B2973. Copy owned by Folger Shakespeare Library.

Bibliotheca Parliamenti (1653) and *Classis Secunda* (1653) are not editions of this work.

316 Wraak-geschrev van het koninglyke bloed, tot den hemel, tegende Engelsche vader. Moorders. Tot Rotterdam, by Johan van Dalen, 1653.

Dutch translation of No. *283*, with dedication by van Dalen, and a poem on Charles and a foreword to the reader. Translator: Stermont (?). Copy owned by British Library.

317 Zürich. Staatsarchiv. Acta Anglicana, E II 457g.

Letter from Jean Baptiste Stouppe to M. Ulrich, dated 17 January 1653, p. 171, identifying Alexander More as author of *Regii Sanguinis Clamor*, and discussing the controversy with Milton. In French.

1654

See also No. 188 in Part I for More's *Fides Publica* (No. *319*) and discussion of Salmasian controversy.

318 Abregé de l'histoire de ce siecle de fer [etc.]. Sur l'imprimé à Leyde, 1654.

Another edition of No. *292*. Allusion, p. 547. Copy owned by Newberry Library.

319 *Alexandri Mori ecclesiastæ & sacrarum litterarum professoris Fides publica, contra calumnias Ioannis Miltoni.* Hagæ-Comitvm: Ex typographia Adriani Vlacq, 1654.

Author: Alexander More. Duodecimo. A–E^{12} F^6; 132 pp. [1], title page; [2], blank; 3–129, work; [130–131] Typographus Lectoris, by Vlacq; [132], blank. Copy owned by Newberry Library.

320 Cambridge. Trinity College Library. MS R.5.5.

Letter from Roger Williams to John Winthrop, dated 12 July 1654. Biographical allusion.

321 *Cases of conscience practically resolved* [etc.]. *The third edition much inlarged* [etc.]. London: Printed by R. H. and J. G. and are to be sold by Fr: Eglesfield, 1654.

Another edition of No. *111*; different issue of No. *346*. Wing, H371. Copy owned by British Library.

322 *Courteous reader.* Catalogue of books by Humphrey Moseley.

Dated 1654 or later. Octavo. A^8; unpaged. Listing of *Poems*, 1645, on A5, No. 89. Found in the following, among other possible volumes, at end of volume:

La Calprenide. *Cassandra. The fam'd romance* [etc.]. London: Printed for Humphrey Moseley, 1652. Anonymous translation. Wing (1), C106; not in Wing (2). Copy owned by Folger Shakespeare Library.

Giovanni Francisco Loredano. *Diania: an excellent new romance. Written in Italian by Gio. Francisco Loredano a noble Venetian. In foure books. Translated into English by Sir Aston Cokaine.* London: Printed for Humphrey Moseley, 1654. Wing, L3066. Copy owned by British Library.

Thomas Washbourne. *Divine poems, written by Thomas Washbourne* [etc.]. London: Printed for Humphrey Moseley, 1654. Wing, W1025. Copy (II) owned by Henry E. Huntington Library.

John Cotgrave. *The English treasury of wit and language* [etc.]. London: Printed for Humphrey Moseley, 1655. Wing, C6368. Copy owned by Princeton University Library.

Henry Vaughan. *Flores solitudinis* [etc.]. London: Printed for Humphrey Moseley, 1654. Wing, V121. Copy owned by Folger Shakespeare Library.

Jo. Raymond. *An Itinerary contayning a voyage, made through Italy, in the yeare*

1646, and 1647 [etc.]. London: Printed for Humphrey Moseley, 1648. Wing, R145. Copy owned by Folger Shakespeare Library.

Abraham Cowley. *The Mistress, or seuerall copies of love-verses* [etc.]. London: Printed for Humphrey Moseley, 1647. Wing, C6674. Copy owned by Folger Shakespeare Library.

Lodowick Carlell. *The Passionate lovers, a tragi-comedy* [etc.]. London: Printed for Humphrey Moseley, 1655. Wing, C581. Copy owned by Henry E. Huntington Library.

James Shirley. *Six new playes* [etc.]. London: Printed for Humphrey Robinson and Humphrey Moseley, 1653. Wing, S3486. Copy owned by Henry E. Huntington Library.

Philip Massinger. *Three new plays; viz. The* [bracket] *Bashful lover, Guardian, Very woman* [etc.]. London: Printed for Humphrey Moseley, 1655. Wing, M150. Copy owned by Folger Shakespeare Library.

323 Lord Delamere. MS letter from John Dury to Samuel Hartlib, dated 14 (24) April 1654.

In Sheffield University Library. Allusion concerning More. Printed in G. H. Turnbull. *Hartlib, Dury and Comenius*. London: Hodder and Stoughton, 1947, p. 42.

324 Lord Delamere. MS letter from John Dury to Samuel Hartlib, dated 19 (29) April 1654.

In Sheffield University Library. Allusion concerning More. Printed in G. H. Turnbull. *Hartlib, Dury and Comenius*. London: Hodder and Stoughton, 1947, p. 42.

325 Lord Delamere. MS letter from John Dury to Samuel Hartlib, dated 3 (13) October 1654.

In Sheffield University Library. Allusion concerning More. Printed in G. H. Turnbull. *Hartlib, Dury and Comenius*. London: Hodder and Stoughton, 1947, p. 43.

326 Lord Delamere. MS letter from John Dury to Samuel Hartlib, dated 18 (28) November 1654.

In Sheffield University Library. Allusion concerning blindness and More. Printed in G. H. Turnbull. *Hartlib, Dury and Comenius*. London: Hodder and Stoughton, 1947, p. 44.

327 Lord Delamere. MS letter from John Dury to Samuel Hartlib, dated 9 (19) December 1654.

In Sheffield University Library. Allusion concerning More. Printed in G.
H. Turnbull. *Hartlib, Dury and Comenius*. London: Hodder and Stoughton,
1947, p. 44.

328   *Exercitatio historico politica de republica antiqua veterum Germanorum* [etc.].
      Helmestadi: Typis Henningi Mülleri, 1654.

      Dissertation by N. Martini; Hermann Conring respondent. Corollarium
      IV by Conring refers to "Parricidium Anglicanum," G1v. Note in Conring's
      Opera (Brunsvigæ: Sumtibus Friderici Wilhelmi Meyeri, 1730), I, 25, cites
      Milton and Salmasius. Copies owned by Bodleian Library.

329   *Heresiography, or a description of the heretickes and sectaries* [etc.]. *The fift edition*
      [etc.]. London: Printed for William Lee, 1654.

      Edition 5 of No. *32*. Allusions, pp. B1v, 77, 129; listed in Table twice. Il-
      lustrated title page pictures a "Divorser" and the verso opposite lists con-
      tents, including "Divorsers." Wing, P180. Copy owned by Union Theological
      Seminary Library (McAlpin Collection).

330   [Letter from John Bramhall to his son, John Pierson, dated 9 (19) May 1654.]

      Reference to Salmasian controversy. Printed in Edward Berwick, ed. *The
      Rawdon Papers, consisting of letters on various subjects, literary, political, and ec-
      clesiastical, to and from Dr. John Bramhall* [etc.]. London: John Nichols and
      Son; sold also by R. Milliken, Dublin, 1819. Letter XLIII, p. 109.

331   [Letter from Medonius to Nicolas Heinsius, dated 30 October (9 November)
      1654.]

      Allusion to *Defensio secunda*. In Latin. Printed in Pieter Burman, ed. *Sylloges
      Epistolarum a Viris Illustribus Scriptarum*. Leidæ: Apud Samuelem Luchtmans,
      1727. V, 634. Copy owned by New York Public Library.

332   [Letter from John Pell to John Thurloe, dated 28 October 1654.]

      Allusion concerning More. Printed in Robert Vaughan. *The Protectorate of
      Oliver Cromwell* [etc.]. London: Henry Colburn, 1839. Two volumes. I, 73.
      Milton's name is printed as "Hulton."

333   [Letter from Princess Elizabeth Stuart to Carl Ludwig von der Pfalz, dated
      16 (26) October 1654.]

      Reference to Dury's translation of *Eikonoklastes*. Printed in *Briefe der Elisabeth
      Stuart, Königin von Böhmen, an ihren Sohn, den Kurfüsten Carl Ludwig von der Pfalz,
      1650–1662. Nach den im Königlichen Staatsarchiv zu Hannover Befindlichen
      Originalen. Herausgegeben von Anna Wendland*. Tübingen: 1902. Page 51.

334 [Letter from Isaac Vossius to Nicolas Heinsius, dated 20 (30) July 1654.]

Allusion to *Defensio secunda*. In Latin. Printed in Pieter Burman, ed. *Sylloges Epistolarum a Viris Illustribus Scriptarum*. Leidæ: Apud Samuelem Luchtmans, 1727. III, 675. Copy owned by New York Public Library.

335 London. British Library. Additional MS 4364.

Anonymous letter in "Extracts of Letters written to Mr Hartlib from Dantzigk, and sent to John Thurloe," dated 29 November 1654, f. 127v. Allusion concerning More. In Latin. French, III, 446, says the letter is dated "6. Januar: 1.6.54" (N. S.) or 27 December 1654 (O. S.).

336 London. British Library. Additional MS 37,346.

First volume of "The History of Whitelockes Ambassy from England to Sweden. With Notes therupon And touching the Government Publique Councells and Persons in those and in other Countries [etc.]." Author: Bulstrode Whitelocke. Allusion to *Defensio prima*, Book VI, Chapter 21, f. 262 (February 1653/4), and Book VI, Chapter 33, f. 270v (February 1653/4). Published by Henry Reeve as *A Journal of the Swedish Embassy* (London: Longman, Brown, Greene, and Longmans, 1855), I, 417 and 439–440.

337 London. British Library. Sloane MS 649.

Copy of No. *335*, f. 30v.

338 *Mercurius politicus*. No. 208, 1–8 June 1654.

Allusion to *Defensio secunda*, p. 3540. Copy owned by Morgan Library.

339 New York City. J. Pierpont Morgan Library. MS letter from John Durel to William Edgeman, dated 21 May 1654.

Allusion; purports to be writing answer to *Eikonoklastes*.

340 Oxford. Bodleian Library. Clarendon State Papers. MS 48.

Letter from John Nicholas to William Edgeman, dated 23 April 1654, f. 135–135v. Allusion to antimonarchical works, Joseph Jane, and his work's possible translation into French. Says Milton's book (*Defensio prima*) has been printed in French in England; no such translation is known.

341 Oxford. Bodleian Library. Rawlinson MS A.13.

Letter from Andrew Sandelands to John Thurloe, dated 11 April 1654, p. 119. Allusion. Printed in *A Collection of the State Papers of John Thurloe, Esq*;

London: Printed for the Executors of the Late Mr. Fletcher Gyles, Thomas Woodward, and Charles Davis, 1742. Ed. Thomas Birch. II, 226. copy owned by New York Public Library.

Letter from Mr. Augier's secretary to John Thurloe, dated 22 April (2 May) 1654, p. 301. Allusion. Printed in *Thurloe*, above, II, 246.

342   Oxford. Bodleian Library. Rawlinson MS A.15.

Anonymous letter to John Thurloe, dated 3 July 1654, pp. 462–464. Comment on *Defensio secunda* and Vlacq's reprinting. Printed in *A Collection of the State Papers of John Thurloe, Esq*; London: Printed for the Executors of the Late Mr. Fletcher Gyles, Thomas Woodward, and Charles Davis, 1742. Ed. Thomas Birch. II, 394. Copy owned by New York Public Library.

343   Oxford. Bodleian Library. Rawlinson MS A.16.

Anonymous letter apparently to John Thurloe, dated 24 July 1654, p. 146. Allusion. Printed in *A Collection of the State Papers of John Thurloe, Esq*; London: Printed for the Executors of the Late Mr. Fletcher Gyles, Thomas Woodward, and Charles Davis, 1742. Ed. Thomas Birch. II, 452. Copy owned by New York Public Library.

Letter apparently from John Thurloe to Alexander More, dated 7 August 1654, p. 455. Comment on *Defensio secunda*, its availability in Holland, and the appearance that More did indeed write *Regii Sanguinis Clamor*. Printed in *Thurloe*, above, II, 529.

344   Oxford. Bodleian Library. Rawlinson MS A.19.

Letter from the English agent to John Thurloe, dated 3 (13) November 1654, p. 504, having been begun on 10 November 1654. Discussion of More and Vlacq, pp. 510–512. French (III, 443–444, and altered in V, 443) says that the manuscript is erroneously paged 713–715 (reference to penciled pages of later date). He also dates it 3 November 1654 (as in the endorsement), saying the "1" is torn away, but that the printing in *Thurloe* gives "13." Actually the date "$\frac{13}{3}$" is visible although the manuscript is tightly bound at this point. Printed in *A Collection of the State Papers of John Thurloe, Esq*; London: Printed for the Executors of the Late Mr. Fletcher Gyles, Thomas Woodward, and Charles Davis, 1742. Ed. Thomas Birch. II, 708. Copy owned by New York Public Library.

345   *Reliquiæ Wottoniæ* [etc.]. *The second edition with large additions*. London: Printed by Thomas Maxey, for R. Marriot, G. Bedel, and T. Garthwait, 1654.

Edition 2 of No. *198*. Pagination is erratic. Letter to Milton, pp. 394–397. Wing, W3649. Copy owned by Union Theological Seminary Library (McAlpin Collection).

346 *Resolutions and decisions of divers practicall cases of conscience in continuall use amongst men* [etc.]. *The third edition, with some additionalls* [etc.]. London: Printed by R. Hodgkinson, and J. Grismond, 1654.

Edition 3 of No. *111*. Cancel title page. Discussion, pp. 296–299. Wing, H409. Copy owned by Princeton University Library.

Wing, H408, copy owned by Cambridge University Library, is listed as "another edition" dated 1654, but not the third edition; however, that copy is of the third edition.

347 *Tyrants and protectors set forth in their colours* [etc.]. London: Printed for H. Cripps and L. Lloyd, 1654.

Author: J. P. (John Price?). Paraphrased quotation from *Tenure of Kings and Magistrates*, p. 8. Wing, P3349. Copy owned by Union Theological Seminary Library (McAlpin Collection).

1655

See also No. 188 in Part I for More's *Fides Publica* (No. *319*), and Nos. 187 and 188 for discussion of Salmasian controversy.

348 *Abregé de l'histoire de ce siecle de fer* [etc.]. *Seconde edition reueüe, corrigée, augmentée, amplifiée en plusieurs endroits, & continuée jusques à l'an 1655. Par I. N. De Parival.* A Bruxelles: Chez François Vivien, 1655.

Another edition of No. *292*, but also published in 1654 (No. *318*). Comment, p. 477 and margin (Book VI, Chapter 8). In French. Copy owned by British Library.

349 *Alexandri Mori ecclesiastæ & sacrarum litterarum professoris Fides publica, contra calumnias Ioannis Miltoni.* Hagæ-Comitvm: Ex typographia Adriani Vlacq, 1654.

Duodecimo. A–E^{12} F^6 G–K^{12} L^6; 240 pp. Reissue of No. *319* to which is added *Supplementum*, No. *350*, with continuous signatures and pagination. [1], title page; [2], blank; 3–129, *Fides Publica*; [130–131], Typographus Lectori, by Vlacq; [132], blank; [133], title page for *Supplementum*; [134], Typographus Lectori, by Vlacq; 135–238, *Supplementum*; [239–240], blank. Date was not changed. Copy owned by Princeton University Library.

350 *Alexandri Mori ecclesiastæ & sacrarum litterarum professoris supplementum Fidei publicæ, contra calumnias Ioannis Miltoni.* Hagæ-Comitvm: Ex typographia Adriani Vlacq, 1655.

Duodecimo. Separate work and copy but with continuous signatures, G–K^{12} L^6; ii + 106 pp. Paged: x, x, 135–238, x, x. First edition; may have been issued separately from No. *349.* Copy owned by William Andrews Clark Library.

351 *A Catalogue of the most approved divinity-books, which have been printed or re-printed about twenty yeares past, and continued down to the present year, 1655. Mensis Martii 26.* London: Printed for John Rothwell, 1655.

Added on pp. 39 ff. is "Books Printed for, and sold by John Rothwell [etc.]"; listings: *Reason of Church-Government* and *Apology for Smectymnuus*, p. 43, and *Smectymnuus Redivivus*, p. 44. Wing, C1385A. Copy owned by British Library.

352 *The Confession of faith, and the larger and shorter catechism, agreed upon by the assembly of divines at Westminster, printed for the publick good.* 1655.

Another edition of No. *45.* Place: London. Allusion, p. 57. Wing, C5766. Copy owned by Union Theological Seminary Library (McAlpin Collection).

353 *A Discourse concerning the gift of prayer:* [etc.]. *Whereunto may be added, Ecclesiastes: or, a discourse concerning the gift of preaching, by the same authour.* London: Printed by T. M. for Samuel Gellibrand, 1655.

Another edition of No. *296.* Includes reissue of 1653 *Ecclesiastes* (No. *298*). Wing, W2181 and W2191. Copy owned by Princeton Theological Seminary Library.

354 *A Discourse concerning the gift of prayer:* [etc.]. *Whereunto may be added, Ecclesiastes: or, a discourse concerning the gift of preaching, by the same authour.* London: Printed by T. M. for Samuel Gellibrand, 1655.

Another issue of No. *353.* To this is added: *Ecclesiastes, or, a discourse concerning the gift of preaching* [etc.]. London: Printed for Samuel Gellibrand, 1659.

Another reissue of No. *146.* Allusion, p. 119. Wing, W2181 (*A Discourse*) and not in Wing (*Ecclesiastes*). Copy owned by Henry E. Huntington Library.

355 *Epistolæ ho-elianæ. Familiar letters domestic and forren* [etc.]. *The third edition* [etc.]. London: Printed for Humphrey Moseley, 1655.

Author: James Howell. In *A Fourth Volume of Familiar Letters* [etc.]. London: Printed for Humphrey Moseley, 1655. Allusion in letter VII to Sir Edward Spencer, p. 19. Entry in Index on K2. Wing, H3073; and citing *Fourth Volume* separately, Wing, H3078, although apparently not published separately. Copy owned by Medical Library, University of Kentucky.

356 *Epistolæ ho-elianæ. Familiar letters domestic and forren* [etc.]. *The third edition* [etc.]. London: Printed for Humphrey Moseley, 1655.

Variant of No. *355*. Title pages are different; e. g., "Councel" rather than "Councell" in No. *355*. See Wing, H3073. Copy owned by Medical Library, University of Kentucky.

357 *The First anniversary of the government under his highness the Lord Protector.* London: Printed by Thomas Newcomb, and are to be sold by Samuel Gellibrand, 1655.

Author: Andrew Marvell. Appropriations: ll. 151–152 ("Nativity Ode"), p. 9; l. 218 ("Lycidas"), p. 12; l. 358 ("Lycidas"), p. 19. Wing, M871. Copy owned by Henry E. Huntington Library.

358 London. British Library. Additional MS 33,509.

Thomas Stringer, "A Satyr ag$\overline{st}$ J. M.," f. 84v, entered with manuscript reversed. (Manuscript is a prose commonplace book on various subjects.) Dated: ca. 1655.

359 London. British Library. Egerton MS 2535.

Letter from Joseph Jane to Sir Edward Nicholas, dated 10 September 1655, ff. 391–392. Reference to Dury's translation of *Eikonoklastes.*

360 ΠΑΝΣΕΒΕΙΑ: *or, a view of all religions in the world* [etc.]. *The second edition, enlarged and perfected* [etc.]. London: Printed by T. C. for John Saywell, 1655.

Edition 2 of No. *310.* Allusions, pp. 376, 389, 395 (?), 425. Wing, R1972. Copy owned by Union Theological Seminary Library (McAlpin Collection).

361 ΠΑΝΣΕΒΕΙΑ: *or, a view of all religions in the world* [etc.]. *The second edition, enlarged and perfected* [etc.]. London: Printed by T. C. for John Saywell, 1655.

A different issue of No. *360.* See sig. Aaa6b, which is a book listing. See Wing, R1972. Copy owned by Bodleian Library.

362 *The Publick intelligencer.* No. 14. 31 December 1655–7 January 1656.

Discussion of More and Milton, p. 222. Copy owned by British Library.

363 Zürich. Staatsarchiv. E II 457c (Duraeana de Syncretismo, III, 363).

Letter from John Dury to J. Frays, dated 20 (30) May 1655. Allusion to antimonarchical works. In French.

364 Zürich. Staatsarchiv. E II 457c (Duraeana de Syncretismo, III, 271).

Letter from J. Frays to Ulrich, dated 19 (29) May 1655. Allusion to antimonarchical works. In French.

1656

365 *Claudii Salmasii, viri maximi, epistolarum liber primus. Accedunt, de laudibus et vita ejusdem, prolegomena* [etc.]. Ludguni Batavorum: Typis Adriani Wyngaerden, 1656.

Editor: Antonius Clementius. Place: Leyden. Allusions, pp. liii, lxix. In Latin. Copy owned by University of Kentucky Library.

365A [*Commentatio de bibliothecis, ad virum Cl. Davidem Schirmerum.* Freibergae, 1656.]

Author: Christianus Funccius. Allusion (?). Separate copy unlocated; see No. *576*.

366 *Comparatio inter Claudium Tiberium principem & Olivarium Cromwellium protectorem instituta à Petro Negeschio excusa typis anno MDCLVI.*

Author: Peter Negesch; real name, Peter Schultz. Place: Holland (?). Unpaged. π^1 A–D^4; 34 pp. Allusions with discussions, pp. [8], [17–20], [22], [32]. Copy owned by Dr. Williams's Library, London.

367 *Confessio fidei in conventu theologarum authoritate parliamenti Anglicani indicto elaborata* [etc.]. Cantabrigiæ: Excudebat Johannes Field, 1656.

First edition of Latin version of No. *45*, by G. D., i. e., William Dillingham. Allusion, p. 65. Wing, C5737. Copy owned by Princeton Theological Seminary Library.

368 *The Confession of faith, and the larger and shorter catechisms* [etc.]. Edinburgh: Printed by Gideon Lithgow, 1656.

Another edition of No. *45*. Allusion, p. 57. Not in Wing (1); Wing (2), C5766A. Copy owned by New York Public Library.

369 *The Confession of faith, and the larger & shorter catechism, first agreed upon by the assembly of divines at Westminster* [etc.]. First printed at Edinburgh, and now re-printed at London for the Company of Stationers. 1656.

Another edition of No. *45*. Duodecimo. Allusion, p. 53. Wing, C5767. Copy owned by Union Theological Seminary Library (McAlpin Collection).

370 *Courteous reader.* Catalogue of Humphrey Moseley.

Dated: 1656 or after. Quarto. a^4 b^2; 12 pp. Listing of *Poems*, 1645, No. 92, a4v. Added at end of the following volume:

Lodowick Carlell. *The Famous tragedy of Osmond the Great Turk* [etc.]. London: Printed for Humphrey Moseley, 1657. Wing, C579. Copy owned by Columbia University Library.

371 *Courteous reader.* Catalogue of Humphrey Moseley.

Dated: 1656 or after. Octavo. a^8; 16 pp. Listing of *Poems*, 1645, No. 92, a4r. Added at end of the following volume:

Robert Arnauld d'Andilly. *Manner of ordering fruit-trees. By the Sieur Le Gendre* [etc.]. London: Printed for Humphrey Moseley, 1660. Translator: John Evelyn (?). Wing, L943A. Copy owned by Henry E. Huntington Library.

372 *Courteous reader.* Catalogue of Humphrey Moseley.

Dated: 1656 or after. Octavo. a^8 b^2; 20 pp. Listing of *Poems*, 1645, No. 92, a4v. Added at end of the following volumes among others:

Thomas Barker. *Barker's delight: or, the art of angling* [etc.]. *The second edition much enlarged* [etc.]. London: Printed for Humphrey Moseley, 1659. Wing, B786. Copy owned by New York Public Library.

Thomas Washbourne. *Divine poems, written by Thomas Washbourne* [etc.]. London: Printed for Humphrey Moseley, 1654. Wing, W1025. Copy (I) owned by Henry E. Huntington Library.

Sir John Suckling. *The Last remains of Sr John Suckling* [etc.]. London: Printed for Humphrey Moseley, 1659. Wing, S6130. Copy owned by Newberry Library.

Sir George and Sir Kenelm Digby. *Letters between the Ld George Digby, and Sr Kenelm Digby Kt concerning religion.* London: Printed for Humphrey Moseley, 1651. Varying issue: this ends with last letter dated March 39, 1639. Wing, D4768. Copy owned by Cambridge University Library.

T. M. *The Life of a satyricall pvppy, called Nim* [etc.]. London: Printed for Humphrey Moseley, 1657. Author: Thomas May. Wing, M1411. Copy owned by Folger Shakespeare Library.

T. W. *A New catalogue of the dukes, marqueses, earls, viscounts, barons* [etc.]. London: Printed for Tho: Walkley, 1658. Author: apparently Thomas Walkley. Wing, W465. Copy owned by Folger Shakespeare Library.

Edmund Waller and Sidney Godolphin, translators. *The Passion of Dido for Aeneas* [etc.]. London: Printed for Humphrey Moseley, 1658. Wing, V633. Copy owned by Henry E. Huntington Library.

Edmund Waller. *Poems, &c. written by Mr. Ed. Waller* [etc.]. London: Printed by T. W. for Humphrey Mosley, 1645. Wing, W511. Copy owned by Newberry Library.

Gregorio Leti. *The Scarlet gown: or the history of all the present cardinals of Rome* [etc.]. London: Printed for Humphrey Moseley, 1660. Preface signed: N. N. Translator: Henry Cogan. Wing, N54. Copy owned by Folger Shakespeare Library.

Lodowick Carlell. *Two new playes* [etc.]. London: Printed for Humphrey Moseley, 1657. Uncropped issue of "Courteous Reader." Wing, C582. Copy owned by Henry E. Huntington Library.

Thomas Middleton. *Two new playes. viz.* [bracket] *More dissemblers besides women. Women beware women* [etc.]. London: Printed for Humphrey Moseley, 1657. Uncropped issue of "Courteous Reader" with wide margins. Wing, M1989. Copy owned by Folger Shakespeare Library.

Richard Flecknoe. *Miscellania or, poems of all sorts, with divers other pieces* [etc.]. London: Printed by T. R., for the Author, 1653. Wing, F1231. Copy owned by Folger Shakespeare Library.

373   *Ecclesiastes, or a discourse concerning the gift of preaching* [etc.]. *The fifth edition* [etc.]. London: Printed by T. R. and E. M. for Samuel Gellibrand, 1656.

Another edition of No. *59*. Reissue (?) of No. *298*. Copy owned by William Andrews Clark Library.

374   *Glossographia: or a dictionary, interpreting all such hard words* [etc.]. London: Printed by Tho. Newcomb, and are to be sold by Humphrey Moseley and George Sawbridge, 1656.

Author: Thomas Blount. Advertisement for *Poems*, a4v. Wing, B3334. Copy owned by Henry E. Huntington Library.

375   *The History of this iron age*: [etc.]. *Written originally by J. Parival, and now rendred into English, by B. Harris, gent.* London: Printed by E. Tyler, and are to be sold by J. Crook, S. Miller, and T. Davis, 1656.

Edition 1 of translation of No. *292*. Comment, p. 255 and margin (Part 2, Chapter VIII). Wing, P361. Copy owned by Columbia University Library.

376   *Nouvelles ordinaires de Londres*. No. 298. 7 (17) February–14 (24) February 1656.

Colophon: "A Londres, par Guillaume Du-Gard." Discussion of *Defensio pro se*, p. 1194. In French. Copy owned by Bibliothèque Nationale.

377 *Piscatoris poemata: vel panegyricum carmen in diem inaugurationis Olivari, &c. recitatum nuper in Aulâ Medii-Templi, Decemb. 17. MDCLV* [etc.]. Londini: Typis Thomæ Newcombii, 1656.

> Author: Payne Fisher. Separate title page and no pagination for: *Irenodia gratulatoria, sive ... Bradshawo, cæterisque Concilii-Statu-conseltis, &c. Editio secunda luculentior, & emendatior.* Edition 2 of No. *252.* Allusion: Dedication, p. [vi], margin. Wing, F1034. Copy owned by Folger Shakespeare Library.

378 *The Preacher, or the art and method of preaching* [etc.]. London: Printed for Edw. Farnham, 1656.

> Author: William Chappell. "A Catalogue of Books Printed and to be sold by Edw. Farnham [etc.]" lists "The Works of Mr. *John Milton,* concerning *Divorce,* digested into one Volume," A6v. No such collection is known. Wing, C1957. Copy owned by Union Theological Seminary Library (McAlpin Collection).

379 *The Publick intelligencer.* No. 19. 4 (11) February 1656.

> Discussion of More and Milton, pp. 299–300. Copy owned by British Library.

1657

380 *A Catalogue of approved divinity-books* [etc.]. London: Printed for John Rothwell, 1657.

> Second title page:
> *A Catalogue of the most approved divinity-books, which have been printed or reprinted about twenty years past, and continued down to this present year, 1657, Mensis Junii 12.* London: Printed for John Rothwell, 1657.

> In added section, "Books Printed for, and are to be sold by John Rothwell," after p. 95, are listed *Reason of Church-Government* and *Apology for Smectymnuus* in the 1654 reissue, p. 93 [*recte* 101], and *Smectymnuus Redivivus,* p. 92 [*recte* 102]. Wing, R2003. Copy owned by Bodleian Library.

381 *A Catalogue of the most vendible books in England* [etc.]. London: Printed in the Year, 1657.

> Bookseller: William London. Listings: *Reformation, Episcopacy, Reason, Apology, Defensio prima* (4° and 2°), *Eikonoklastes, Doctrine and Discipline of Divorce* (P1v); *Poems* (Ee4). Wing, L2849. Copy owned by Cambridge University Library.

382   *Catalogus librorum in omni genere insignium, quorum copia suppetit Octaviano Pulleyn,*
      bibliopolæ ad insigne rosæ in cæmiterio Paulino juxta Cochleam. Londini: 1657.

      Listings: p. 46, *Defensio prima*; p. 64, *Defensio prima, Defensio secunda,* More's
      Fides Publica, Defensio pro se. Wing, P4201. Copy owned by Bodleian Library.

383   *Clamor, rixa, joci, mendacia, furta, cachini, or, a severe enquiry into the late oneirocritica*
      published by John Wallis [etc.]. London: 1657.

      Author: Henry Stubbe (?). References, pp. 13, 16, 19 (echoing *Of Prelatical
      Episcopacy*), and 45. Wing, W563. Copy owned by British Library.

384   *Comparatio inter Clavdivm Tiberivm principem, et Olivarivm Cromwellivm protec-*
      torem. Instituta à Petro Negeschio. Excusa typis anno 1657.

      Another edition of No. *366.* Place: Uppsala (?). See pp. 9, 16–18, 20, 28.
      Copy owned by Yale University Library.

385   *Courteous reader.* Catalogue of Humphrey Moseley.

      Dated: later than 1656. Octavo. a B^8; 32 pp. Listing of Milton's *Poems,* 1645,
      No. 92, a4v. Added at end of the following volume:

          Edmund Waller. *Poems, &c. Written by Mr. Ed. Waller* [etc.]. London: T.
          W., for Humphrey Moseley, 1645. Edition 2. See Wing, W511. Copy
          owned by Bodleian Library.

386   *Dissertationis ad quædam loca Miltoni pars posterior, quam adspirante Deo præside*
      Dn. Iacobo Schallero, SS. Theol. Doct. & Philos. Pract. Prof. Ord. h. t. Facult.
      Phil. Decano. Solenniter defendet die 17 Mens. September. Christophorus Güntzer,
      Argentorat. Argentorati: Typis Friderici Spoor, 1657.

      Author: Christopher Güntzer. Separate publication of Güntzer's disserta-
      tion on the Milton-Salmasius controversy. In Latin. Copy owned by British
      Library.

387   *Dissertationis ad quædam loca Miltoni pars prior et posterior, quas adspirante Deo*
      præside Dn. Iacobo Schallero, SS. Theol. Doct. & Philos. Pract. Prof. Ord. h. t.
      Facult. Phil. Decano. Solenniter defenderunt Erhardus Kieffer, Durlaco-Marchicus,
      & Christophorus Güntzer, Argentoratensis. Argentorati: Typis Friderici Spoor,
      1657.

      Authors: Jacob Schaller, Erhard Kieffer and Christopher Güntzer. Reprints
      of Schaller's dissertation (No. *249*) and of Kieffer's (No. *249*) and Güntzer's
      (No. *386*) dissertations. Copy owned by Cambridge University Library.

388   The English | PARNASSUS: | OR, | A HELPE | TO | English Poesie.
      | Containing *A Collection* | [etc.]. | Together with | A short Institution to

English Poe- | sie, by way of PREFACE. | London: Printed for Tho. Johnson, 1657.

Author: Joshua Poole. Allusion, p. [42]. Appropriations, passim. Wing, P2814. Copy owned by Arents Collection, New York Public Library.

389 The English | PARNASSUS: | OR, | A HELPE | TO | English Poesie. | Containing | A short Institution of that Art; | A Collection | [etc.]. London: Printed for Tho. Johnson, 1657.

Different issue of No. 388. Not in Wing. Copy owned by Newberry Library.

390 Hollandsche mercurius, behelsende het gedenckweerdigste in Christenrijck voor-gevallen, brinnen 't gantsche jaer 1650 [emblem]. Tot Haerlem, gedruckt by Pieter Casteleyn.

Date: 1657 (?). Reprint with illustrated title page: Hollantse Mercvrivs, Historisch wÿs vervatende het voornaemste in Christenryck A. 1650 voorgevallen. Tot Haerlem, gedruckt by Pieter Casteleijn. Boeck-drucker opde Marckt. 1651.

Issue of February 1651 (No. 149): allusion to Defensio prima, Vol. 2, p. 18.

Issue of July 1651 (No. 150): allusion to Defensio prima, Vol. 2, p. 79.

In Dutch. Copy owned by New York Public Library.

391 Killing noe murder. Briefly discourst in three quaestions. By William Allen.

Author: Edward Sexby, but Silius Titus may also have contributed to it. Place: London? or Amsterdam? Date: 1657? Edition 1. Allusion, p. 11. Wing, T1310. Copy owned by Folger Shakespeare Library.

392 Vergelyckinge tusschen Claudius Tiberius, kayser van Romen, en Olivier Cromwel, protector of misschien toekomendem konick van Engelant [etc.]. Tot Brussel Anno 1657.

Dutch translation of No. 366. See pp. 8, 15, 17, 19, 27–28. Copy owned by British Library.

1658

393 Abregé de l'histoire de ce siecle de fer [etc.]. Troisiesme edition reveüe, corrigée, augmentée, amplifiée en plusieurs endroits, & continuée jusques à l'an 1655. Par I. N. De Parival. A Bruxelles: Chez François Vivien, 1658.

Edition 3 of No. 292; reissue of No. 348. Copy owned by British Library.

394   *The Academy of complements* [etc.]. London: Printed for Humphrey Moseley, 1658.

Another issue of No. *113*. Wing, G1404. Copy owned by Folger Shakespeare Library.

395   *A Catalogue of the most vendible books in England* [etc.]. London: Printed in the Year, 1658.

Reprint of No. *381*. Wing, L2850. Copy owned by Folger Shakespeare Library.

396   *A Compleat history of the life and raigne of King Charles from his cradle to his grave. Collected and written by William Sanderson esq.* London: Printed for Humphrey Moseley, Richard Tomlins, and George Sawbridge, 1658.

Possible allusion to *Eikonoklastes*, p. 324. Wing, S646. Copy owned by New York Public Library.

397   *The Confession of faith, together with the larger and lesser catechismes* [etc.]. London: Printed for the Company of Stationers, and are to be sold by J. Rothwell.

Another edition of No. *45*. Dated: 1658. "Edition 1" for Rothwell. Allusion, p. 85. Not in Wing. Copy owned by New York Public Library.

398   *The Confession of faith, together with the larger and lesser catechismes* [etc.]. London: Printed for the Company of Stationers, and are to be sold by J. Rothwell.

Different issue of No. *397*. Dated: 1658. Allusion, pp. 85–78 [86]. Paging and signatures erratic; e. g., pp. 85–78, sig. N4, are followed by p. 95, sig. P1. Not in Wing. Copy owned by Folger Shakespeare Library.

399   *The Confession of faith, together with the larger and lesser catechismes* [etc.]. London: Printed for the Company of Stationers, and are to be sold by J. Rothwel,

Different issue of Nos. *397* and *398*. Date apparently omitted in error; note comma. Dated: 1658. Allusion, pp. 85–86 (correct pagination). Not in Wing. Copy owned by Princeton Theological Seminary Library.

400   *The Confession of faith, together with the larger and lesser catechismes* [etc.]. London: Printed by E. M. for the Company of Stationers, and are to be sold by John Rothwell, 1658.

Different issue or edition of No. *397*. Allusion, pp. 85–86 (correct pagination). See Wing, C5768 and C5796. Copy owned by Newberry Library.

401   *The Confession of faith, together with the larger and lesser catechismes* [etc.]. *To which is annexed two sheets of church-government with the scriptures at large.* [*The second edition.*] [etc.]. London: Printed by E. M. for the Company of Stationers, and are to be sold by John Rothwel, 1658.

Another edition of No. *45*. "[The second edition.]" is printed in brackets in black letter. Allusion, pp. 85–86 (correct pagination). See Wing, C5768 and C5796. Copy owned by Bodleian Library.

402   *The Confession of faith, together with the larger and lesser catechismes* [etc.]. *To which is annexed two sheets of church-government with the scriptures at large.* [*The second edition.*] [etc.]. London: Printed by E. M. for the Company of Stationers, and are to be sold by John Rothwel, 1658.

Different issue of No. *401*. With second title page: *An Ordinance of the lords and commons assembled in parliament* [etc.]. London: Printed for J. Rothwel, 1658. (See No. *415*.) Allusion, pp. 85–86 (*recte* 95–96). See Wing, C5768 and C5796, the only entries for 1658, apparently to the same edition and same issue. Copy owned by William Andrews Clark Library.

403   *The Confession of faith, together with the larger and lesser catechismes* [etc.]. *To which is annexed two sheets of church-government with the scriptures at large.* [*The second edition.*] [etc.]. London: Printed by E. M. for the Company of Stationers, and are to be sold by John Rothwel, 1658.

Different issue of Nos. *401* and *402*. Allusion, pp. 85–86 (*recte* 95–96). See Wing, C5768 and C5796. Copy owned by Folger Shakespeare Library.

404   *The Confession of faith, together with the larger and lesser catechismes* [etc.]. *To which is annexed two sheets of church-government with the scriptures at large.* [*The second edition.*] [etc.]. London: Printed by E. M. for the Company of Stationers, and are to be sold by John Rothwel, 1658.

Different issue of Nos. *401, 402, 403*. Allusion, pp. 95–96 (correct pagination). See Wing, C5768 and C5796. Copy owned by University of Kentucky Library.

405   *The Confession of faith, together with the larger and lesser catechismes* [etc.]. *The second edition* [etc.]. London: Printed by E. M. for the Company of Stationers, and are to be sold by John Rothwel, 1658.

Another edition of No. *45*. Allusion, pp. 84–85. Mispaged at sig. P ff. With "A Table," Ff1v–Ff4v, made up for use with No. *404* (?); e. g., "In what cases *Marriage* may be dissolved. *Con.* 95" (rather than p. 84; p. 95 deals with Baptism). See Wing, C5768 and C5796. Copy owned by Folger Shakespeare Library.

406 *The Confession of faith, together with the larger and lesser catechismes* [etc.]. *The second edition* [etc.]. London: Printed by E. M. for the Company of Stationers, and are to be sold by John Rothwel, 1658.

Another edition of No. *45*. Revised edition (note in text), but mispaged with note at end of the Table (Ff4v) to correct. With second title page: *An Ordinance of the lords and commons assembled in parliament* [etc.]. London: Printed for J. Rothwel, 1658. (See No. *415* and cf. No. *402*.) Allusion, pp. 85–86 (*recte* 95–96). See Wing, C5768 and C5796. Copy owned by Henry E. Huntington Library.

407 *The Confession of faith, together with the larger and lesser catechismes* [etc.]. *The second edition* [etc.]. London: Printed by E. M. for the Company of Stationers, and are to be sold by John Rothwel, 1658.

Different issue of No. *406*. Allusion, pp. 85–86 (*recte* 95–96). See Wing, C5768 and C5796. Copy owned by Folger Shakespeare Library.

408 *The Confession of faith, together with the larger and lesser catechismes* [etc.]. *The second edition* [etc.]. London: Printed by E. M. for the Company of Stationers, and are to be sold by John Rothwel, 1658.

Another issue of Nos. *406* and *407*. Allusion, pp. 95–96. See Wing, C5768 and C5796. Copy owned by Princeton Theological Seminary Library.

409 *The Confession of faith, together with the larger and lesser catechismes* [etc.]. *The second edition* [etc.]. London: Printed by E. M. for the Company of Stationers, and are to be sold by John Rothwel, 1658.

Different issue of No. *408*. Typographical differences. See Wing, C5768 and C5796. Copy owned by Princeton Theological Seminary Library.

410 Copenhagen. Kongelige Bibliotek. MS. G.k.S. 2259. 4°.

Author: "Ambiorigis Ariovisti," whom a later hand identifies as "Henr. Erastii," but now established as Henrik Ernst. "Annotationes ad Joannis Miltoni Angli Præfationem Libri, quem scripsit pro Populi Anglicani Defensione Psal. XXXIII. Jehova gentium consilia dissolvit populatum conatus reddit irritos," an antagonistic set of comments on *Defensio prima*. 30 pp. [1], title page; [2], poem antagonistic to Milton; [3], half-title; [4], blank; [5–26], text; [27–30], blank. Preface dated: 1 January 1658. In Latin.

411 *The Humble Advice of the assembly of divines, by authority of parliament sitting at Westminster; concerning a confession of faith* [etc.]. London: Printed by S. Griffin for the Company of Stationers, and to be sold by J. Rothwell, 1658.

Another edition of No. *45*. Allusion, pp. 85–78 (*recte* 86); cf. No. *398*. Wing, W1433. Copy owned by Yale University Library.

412 *The Humble advice of the assembly of divines, now by authority of parliament sitting at Westminster, concerning a larger catechism* [etc.]. *The second edition.* London: Printed by S. Griffin for the Company of Stationers, and J. Rothwel.

Another edition of No. *411.* Title page should read "Concerning A Confession of Faith." Dated: 1658. Preface is signed by Thomas Manton. Allusion, pp. 85–86. Wing, W1434. Copy owned by British Library.

413 [Letter from Samuel Hartlib to Robert Boyle, dated 2 February 1658.]

Allusion. Printed in *The Works of the Honourable Robert Boyle.* London: Printed for A. Millar, 1744. Ed. Thomas Birch. V, 272. Copy owned by Columbia University Library.

414 *Mercurius politicus.* No. 443, 18–25 November 1658.

Advertisement for *Defensio prima,* p. 29 (index). Copy owned by Morgan Library.

415 *An Ordinance of the lords and commons assembled in parliament* [etc.]. London: Printed for J. Rothwel, 1658.

Another edition of No. *45.* Allusion, pp. 85–86 (correct pagination). Not in Wing. Copy owned by Henry E. Huntington Library.

416 ΠΑΝΣΕΒΕΙΑ: *or, a view of all religions in the world* [etc.]. *The third edition, enlarged and perfected* [etc.]. London: Printed for John Saywell, 1658.

Edition 3 of No. *310*; see No. *361.* Wing, R1973. Copy owned by University of Kentucky Library. Wing, R1973A, an edition of 1659 supposedly at Yale University, does not exist.

Stationers' register. See G. E. Briscoe Eyre, ed. *A Transcript of the Registers of the Worshipful Company of Stationers; from 1640–1708 A. D.* London: 1913–1914.

417 Entry for *Cabinet-Council,* under 4 May 1658, II (1913), 176.

418 *Traicté politique, composé par William Allen Anglois* [etc.]. Lugduni, Anno 1658.

French translation of No. *391.* Translator: J. Carpentier de Mariguy (?). Allusion, p. 72. Copy owned by Folger Shakespeare Library.

419 *Traicté politique composé par William Allen, Anglois, et traduit nouvellement en françois* [etc.]. Lugduni, Anno 1658.

Another translation of No. *391.* Allusion, p. 127. Copy owned by Newberry Library.

1659

420   *Abrégé de l'histoire de ce siècle de fer* [etc.]. *Derniere edition, reueuë & corrigée* [etc.].
      Sur l'Imprimé à Leyde, 1659.

      Another edition of No. *292*; reissue (?) of No. *318*. Allusion, p. 547. Copy
      owned by Folger Shakespeare Library.

421   *Aphorisms political.* London: Printed by J. C. for Henry Fletcher.

      Author: James Harrington. Dated: 1659. Edition 1. Possible influence from
      Considerations Touching the Likeliest Means to Remove Hirelings in aphorisms Nos.
      XV–XXXVIII, pp. 2–5. Wing, H804. Copy owned by Henry E. Hun-
      tington Library.

422   *Aphorisms political. The second edition enlarged* [etc.]. London: Printed by J. C.
      for Henry Fletcher, 1659.

      Edition 2 of No. *421*. Wing, H805. Copy owned by Folger Shakespeare
      Library.

423   *Catalogus librorum, omnium facultatum & variarum linguarum, qui in officina Ioan-
      nis Blaev, venales reperiunter.* Amstelaedami, apud Joannem Blaev, 1659.

      Listings in Appendix: *Defensio prima*, 4°, p. 70; *Defensio prima*, 12°, p. 70;
      Defensio secunda, 8°, p. 70; Phillips's *Responsio*, p. 72; Rowland's *Polemica*,
      p. 74. Copy owned by Columbia University Library.

424   *Comparatio inter Claudium Tiberium principem et Olivarium Cromwellium protec-
      torem* [etc.]. 1659.

      Another edition of No. *366*. Copy owned by Bibliothèque Nationale.

425   *Confessio fidei in conventu theologorum authoritate parliamenti Anglicani indicto elaborata*
      [etc.]. Cantabrigiæ: Excudebat Johannes Field, 1659.

      Reissue of No. *367*. Wing, C5738. Copy owned by Princeton Theological
      Seminary Library.

426   *The Confession of faith, first agreed upon by the assembly of divines at Westminster.*

      Another edition of No. *45*. No title page. Listed as Edinburgh, 1659, since
      it is continuous with "The Larger Catechism. Edinburgh, Printed by Ge-
      deon Lithgovv, 1659." and with "The Summe of Saving Knowledge. Edin-
      burgh, Printed by Gedeon Lithgovv, 1659." No title page for The Shorter
      Catechism. Allusion, pp. 57–58. Not in Wing. Copy owned by National
      Library of Scotland.

427 [*Ecclesiastes, or, a discourse concerning the gift of preaching* (etc.). London: Printed for Samuel Gellibrand, 1659.]

See No. *354*. No separate copy located.

428 *A Guild-Hall Elegie, Upon the Funerals of that Infernal Saint Iohn Bradshaw President of the High Court of Iustice.*

Broadside. Author: O. P. (?). Dated: 1659. Reference to *Eikonoklastes*. Wing, P90. Copy owned by Harvard University Library.

429 *The Historie of this iron age* [etc.]. *Written originally by J. Parival, and now rendred into English, by B. Harris, gent. The second edition corrected and much enlarged.* London: Printed for J. Crook, Simon Miller, and Thomas Davies, 1659.

Edition 2 of No. *375*. Reference, p. 262 and margin. Not in Wing. Copy owned by Folger Shakespeare Library.

430 *Killing, no murder: with some additions briefly discourst in three questions* [etc.]. London: 1659.

Edition 2 of No. *391*. Allusion, p. [11]. Wing, T1311. Copy owned by Union Theological Seminary Library (McAlpin Collection).

431 *A Light shining out of darkness: or occasional queries submitted to the judgment of such as would enquire into the true state of things in our times* [etc.]. London: Printed in the Year 1659.

Author: Henry Stubbe. Expanded edition of work with the same title and date. Reference to *Of Reformation* with quotation of translation from Dante, pp. 174–175 and margin. Wing, S6057. Copy owned by Union Theological Seminary Library (McAlpin Collection).

432 *Mercurius politicus*. No. 554, 10–17 February 1659.

Advertisement for *Treatise of Civil Power*, p. 237. Copy owned by Morgan Library.

433 *Mercurius politicus*. No. 585, 1–8 September 1659.

Advertisement for *Considerations Touching the Likeliest Means to Remove Hirelings*, p. 713. Copy owned by Morgan Library.

434 *Mercurius politicus*. No. 591, 13–20 October 1659.

Advertisement for *Considerations Touching the Likeliest Means to Remove Hirelings*, p. [809]. Copy owned by Morgan Library.

435 Oxford. Bodleian Library. Locke MS d.10. Lemmata Ethica Argumenta et Authores 1659.

Author: John Locke. Holograph. Quotation from *Of Reformation*, p. 93.

436 *The Panegyrike and the Storme two poëtike libels by Ed. Waller vassa'll to the vsvrper answered by more faythfvll svbiects to his sacred ma^{ty} King Charles ye second* [etc.]. 1659.

Author: Richard Watson. Place: London. Allusion in "To the Pvsillanimovs Authovr of the Panegyrike," A4 and marginal notes. Wing, W1092. Copy owned by Folger Shakespeare Library.

437 *The Publick intelligencer*. No. 163. 7–14 February 1659.

Advertisement for *Treatise of Civil Power*, p. 221. Copy owned by British Library.

438 *The Publick intelligencer*. No. 174. 25 April–2 May 1659.

Advertisement for *Treatise of Civil Power*, p. 397. Copy owned by Library of Congress.

439 *The Re-publicans and others spurious good old cause, briefly and truly anatomized*. 1659.

Author: William Prynne. Place: London. Allusion to *Defensio prima*, p. 10. Wing, P4052. Copy owned by Union Theological Seminary Library (McAlpin Collection).

440 *Resolutions and decisions of divers practical cases of conscience. In continual use amongst men* [etc.]. *The fourth edition, with some additionalls* [etc.]. London: Printed by R. Hodgkinson, and J. Grismond, 1659.

Edition 4 of No. *111*; reissue of No. *346*. Wing, H409A. Copy owned by Henry E. Huntington Library.

Stationers' register. See G. E. Briscoe Eyre, ed. *A Transcript of the Registers of the Worshipful Company of Stationers; from 1640–1708 A. D.* London: 1913–1914.

441 Entry for *Treatise of Civil Power*, under 16 February 1659, II (1913), 214.

442 *A True and perfect narrative of what was done, spoken by and between Mr. Prynne, the old and newly forcibly late secluded members, the army officers, and those now sitting* [etc.]. 1659.

Author: William Prynne. Place: London. Allusion to antimonarchical works,

p. 50. Wing, P4113. Copy owned by Union Theological Seminary Library (McAlpin Collection).

1660

443   *Abregé de l'histoire de ce siecle de fer* [etc.]. *Qvatriesme edition reveuë, corrigée, augmentée, amplifiée en plusieurs endroits, & continuée jusques à l'an 1655. Par I. N. De Parival.* A Bruxelles: Chez François Viviens, 1660.

Edition 4 of No. *292*; reissue of No. *393*. Copy owned by New York Public Library.

444   *Ad Ioannem Miltonum responsio, opus posthumum, Claudii Salmasii.* Divione: Typis Philiberti Chavance, 1660.

Author: Claudius Salmasius. Place: Dijon. Edition 1. Preface by Claudius Salmasius, Jr. Copy owned by Folger Shakespeare Library.

445   *Anarchia Anglicana: or the history of independency. The second part. Being a continuation of relations and observations historicall and politique upon this present parliament, begun anno 16. Caroli primi. By Theodorus Verax* [etc.]. Printed in the Yeare, M. DC. XL.IX.

Reissue of No. *85*. Dated: 1660. Unhooked A's in first line of title page. Wing, W318. Copy owned by Princeton Theological Seminary Library.

446   *Be merry and wise, or a seasonable word to the nation. Shewing the cause, the growth, the state, and the cure of our present distempers.* London: Printed March 13. in the Year, 1660.

Author: Sir Roger L'Estrange (?). Allusion to *Ready and Easy Way*, p. 6. Wing, B1555. Copy owned by British Library.

All previous citations have erred in following E. M. Clark's edition of *Ready and Easy Way* (1915), pp. 167, 172–173, although French IV, 304, says that his date comes from the Thomason copy: all report the allusion on p. 86, which is the reference in No. *476*.

447   *The Blazing star ... or, Nolls nose. Newly revised, and taken out of his tomb.* London: Printed for Theodorus Microcosmus, 1660.

Author: Collonel Baker. Publisher: anonymous (pseudonym). Allusions, pp. [i], 5. Wing (1), B477; Wing (2), B478. Copy owned by Henry E. Huntington Library.

448 *A Breife description or characters of the religion and manners of the phanatiques in generall* [etc.]. London: Printed, and are to be sold by most Stationers; 1660.

Author: anonymous. Reference to Milton's divorce views, p. 33. Wing, B4573. Copy owned by British Library.

449 *Britains triumph, for her imparallel'd deliverance.* London: Printed for W. Palmer, 1660.

Author: G. S. (George Starkey?). Allusion, p. 15. Wing, S25. Copy owned by Henry E. Huntington Library.

450 *By the King. A proclamation* [etc.]. London: John Bill, 1660.

Author: Charles II. Published form of No. *485*. Issue 1. Broadside, printed on rectos of two quarto sheets. Wing, C3323. Copy owned by Yale University Library.

451 *By the King. A proclamation* [etc.]. London: John Bill and Christopher Barker, 1660.

Issue 2 of No. *450*. Wing, C3322. Copy owned by Yale University Library.

452 *By the King. A proclamation* [etc.]. London: John Bill and Christopher Barker, 1660.

Issue 3 of No. *450*. Typographical differences from No. *451*. Not in Wing. Copy owned by Yale University Library.

453 *A Catalogue of new books, by way of supplement to the former being such as have been printed from that time, till Easter Term, 1660.* London: Printed by A. M., and are to be sold by Luke Fawn and Francis Tyton, 1660.

Bookseller: William London. Listing of *A Treatise of Civil Power* and *Considerations Touching the Likeliest Means to Remove Hirelings*, B2v, and of *The Cabinet-Council*, C2. Wing, L2848. Copy owned by Yale University Library.

454 *The Censure of the rota upon Mr Miltons book, entituled, The Ready and easie way to establish a free common-wealth* [etc.]. London: Paul Giddy, 1660.

Author: anonymous. Wing, H808. Copy owned by Union Theological Seminary Library (McAlpin Collection).

455 *The Character of the parliament commonly called the rump, &c.* [etc.]. London: Printed, and sold by the Booksellers of London.

Author: anonymous. Dated: 1660. Apparent allusion, pp. 2–3. Wing (1), C2026A; not in Wing (2). Copy owned by Union Theological Seminary Library (McAlpin Collection).

456 *The Character of the Rump*. London: Printed in the Year 1660.

Satiric anti-Interregnum description of the members of the Rump. Discussion of Milton's influence, pp. 2–3. Wing, C2027. Copy owned by British Library.

457 *Claudii Salmasii ad Johannem Miltonum responsio, opus posthumum*. Londini: Typis Tho. Roycroft, impensis Jo. Martin, Ja. Allestry, & Tho. Dicas, 1660.

Edition 2 of No. *444*. Wing, S736. Copy owned by University of Kentucky Library.

458 *Confessio fidei in conventu theologorum authoritate parliamenti Anglicani indicto, elaborata* [etc.]. Glasguæ: Excudebat Andreas Anderson, 1660.

Another edition of No. *367*. Allusion, pp. 88–89. Wing, C5739. Copy owned by Bodleian Library.

459 *Confessio fidei in conventu theologorum authoritate parliamenti Angelicani indicto, elaborata* [etc.]. Glasguæ: Excudebat Andreas Anderson, Impensis Societatis Stationatiorum. Anno Dom M DC LX.

Another issue of No. *458*. Note "Angelicani"; the third "t" in "Stationatiorum" should correctly be an "r." Wing, C5739A. Copy owned by British Library.

460 *Confessio fidei in conventu theologorum authoritate parliamenti Anglicani indicto elaborata* [etc.]. Edinburgi: Excudebat Gideon Lithgo, 1660.

Another edition of No. *367*. Allusion, pp. 51–52. Wing (2), C5739B. Copy owned by Henry E. Huntington Library.

461 *The Confession of faith, and the larger and shorter catechism* [etc.]. Edinburgh: Printed by Evan Tyler, 1660.

Another edition of No. *45*. Allusion, pp. 57–58. Wing, C5768B. Copy owned by Christ Church College Library, Oxford.

462 *The Confession of faith, and the larger & shorter catechism* [etc.]. First printed at Edinburgh, and now re-printed at London for the Company of Stationers, 1660.

Another edition of No. *45*. Duodecimo. Allusion, p. 53. Wing, C5768C. Copy owned by British Library.

463 *The Dignity of kingship asserted: in answer to Mr. Milton's Ready and easie way to establish a free common-wealth* [etc.]. London: E. C., for H. Seile and W. Palmer, 1660.

Author: G. S. (George Starkey? Gilbert Sheldon?). Wing, S3069. Copy owned by Henry E. Huntington Library.

464 [illustrated title page] | *The Discription of the severall sorts of Anabaptists with the*[ir] *manner of rebaptizing.* | [legend unreadable]

Another edition of No. *34*. Listed as 1660. Reissue of No. *151*. "The[ir]", last two letters written over in ink. Not in Wing. Copy owned by Princeton Theological Seminary Library.

465 *Discursus publicus de jure ac potestate parlamenti Britannici* [etc.]. Jenæ: Typis Georgi Sengenwaldi, 1660.

Author: Johannes Andreas Gerhard. Extensive discussion of the Salmasian controversy with quotation from *Defensio prima*, A3 (Section 3); A4–B1 (Section 5); B1 (Section 6); B3–B4 (Section 8: "Contra Miltonum Disputatur"); and C1v–C2 (Section 9). Copy owned by British Library.

466 *Double your guards; in answer to a bloody and seditious pamphlet* [etc.]. London: Printed in the year 1660.

Author: Sir Roger L'Estrange. Allusion apparently intending Milton, p. 3. Wing, D1956. Copy owned by Newberry Library.

467 ΕΙΚΩΝ ΒΑΣΙΛΙΚΗ. *Or, the true pourtraicture of his sacred majesty Charls the II. In three books ... By David Lloyd, M. A.* London: Printed for H. Brome, and H. Marsh, 1660.

Issue 1. Allusion to *Defensio prima*, II, 65. Wing, L2640. Copy owned by Folger Shakespeare Library.

468 ΕΙΚΩΝ ΒΑΣΙΛΙΚΗ. *Or, the true pourtraicture of his sacred majesty Charls the II. In three books ... By R. F. Esq; an Eye-witness* [etc.]. London: Printed by H. Brome, and H. Marsh, 1660.

Issue 2 of No. *467*. Not in Wing. Copy owned by Cambridge University Library.

469 *An Essay of a loyal brest* [etc.]. London: Printed by John Field, 1660.

Author: William Fairebrother. Allusion in poem, "To the Right Honorable, the Two Houses of Parliament," p. 5. Wing, F110. Copy owned by Yale University Library.

470 *An Exact accompt of the receipts, and disbursments expended by the committee of safety, upon the emergent occasion of the nation* [etc.]. London: Printed for Jer. Hanzen, 1660.

Author: M. R. Possible allusion to Sonnet 20, p. 6. Wing, R44. Copy owned by Columbia University Library.

471 *Faenestra in pectore. Or, familiar letters* [etc.]. London: Printed by R. and W. Leybourn, for William Grantham, 1660.

Author: Thomas Forde. "Letter to Mr. T. P.," dated ca. 15 October 1660, pp. 103–106; discussion of divorce views. Wing, F1548. Copy owned by Henry E. Huntington Library.

472 *A Free-Parliamentary-letany. To the tune of An Old souldier of the queenes.*

Broadside, printed on one side. Dated: 1660. Allusion in Stanza 4 to *Doctrine and Discipline of Divorce*. Wing, F2117. Copy owned by Folger Shakespeare Library.

473 *Hollantze Merkurius.* No. 249, December 1660.

Allusion to imprisonment, pp. 163–164. In Dutch. Copy owned by Henry E. Huntington Library.

474 *The Idea of the law charactered from Moses to King Charles* [etc.]. London: Printed for the author, and are to be sold in St. Dunstons-Church-yard in Fleetstreet, 1660.

Author: John Heydon. Remarks on *Eikonoklastes* in "Part III. The Idea of Tyranny" in "An Epilogue," which appears at the beginning, N4v–N5. Wing, H1671. Copy owned by Folger Shakespeare Library.

475 Κατα-βαπτισται χατ'απτυστοι. *The dippers dipt* [etc.]. *The seventh edition* [etc.]. London: Printed by E. C., for N. Bourne and R. Royston, 1660.

Edition 7 of No. *34*; reissue of No. *151*; may be the same as No. *464*. Wing, F590. Copy owned by Union Theological Seminary Library (McAlpin Collection).

476 *L'Estrange his apology: with a short view, of some late and remarkable transactions, leading to the happy settlement of these nations* [etc.]. London: Printed for Henry Brome, 1660.

Author: Sir Roger L'Estrange. Allusions in reprints of *Be Merry and Wise* (No. *446*), called "A Seasonable Word," p. 86; and *Treason Arraigned* (No. *518*), called "A Sober Answer to a Jugling Pamphlet," p. 113, and "Plain English," pp. 116, 118, 143, 157. To this are added reprints of No. *496* (note spelling of "Broome" on title page) and No. *505*. Wing, L1200. Copy owned by University of Kentucky Library. Copy owned by Henry E. Huntington Library does not include Nos. *496* or *505*.

477 [Letter from Jean Chapelain to Nicolas Heinsius, dated 25 October (4 November) 1660.]

Allusion to Salmasius. In French. Printed in *Lettres de Jean Chapelain, de l'Académie Française, publiées par Ph. Tamizey de Larroque* [etc.]. Paris: Imprimerie Nationale, 1883. II, 110.

478 [Letter from Jean Chapelain to Claudius Salmasius, Jr., dated 4 (14) October 1660.]

Allusion to Salmasius. In French. Printed in *Lettres de Jean Chapelain, de l'Académie Française, publiées par Ph. Tamizey de Larroque* [etc.]. Paris: Imprimerie Nationale, 1883. II, 102–104.

479 [Letter from Nicolas Heinsius to Johann Friedrich Gronovius, dated c. 1660.]

Allusion. In Latin. Printed in Pieter Burman, ed. *Sylloges Epistolarum a Viris Illustribus Scriptarum.* Leidæ: Apud Samuelem Luchtmans, 1727. III, 407–408. Copy owned by New York Public Library.

480 [Letter from Gui Patin to M. Belin, dated 12 October 1660.]

Allusion. In French. Printed in *Lettres de Gui Patin Nouvelle Édition Augmentée de Lettres Inédites* [etc.]. Ed. Joseph-Henri Reveille-Parise. Paris: Chez J.-B. Baillière, 1846. I, 255. See also editions of Gui Patin, *Lettres Choisies*, in Indices III or IV in this bibliography.

481 [Letter from Gui Patin to André Falcourt, dated 15 July 1660.]

Also dated 5 July and 13 July in other editions. Political allusion. In French. Printed in *Lettres de Gui Patin Nouvelle Édition Augmentée de Lettres Inédites* [etc.]. Ed. Joseph-Henri Reveille-Parise. Paris: Chez J.-B. Baillière, 1846. III, 238. See also editions of Gui Patin, *Lettres Choisies*, in Indices III or IV in this bibliography.

482 [Letter from Gui Patin to André Falcourt, dated 8 October 1660.]

Allusion. In French. Printed in *Lettres de Gui Patin Nouvelle Édition Augmentée de Lettres Inédites* [etc.]. Ed. Joseph-Henri Reveille-Parise. Paris: Chez J. - B. Baillière, 1846. III, 270. See also editions of Gui Patin, *Lettres Choisies*, in Indices III or IV in this bibliography.

483 [Letter from Ezekiel Spanheim to Nicolas Heinsius, dated 3 (13) December 1660.]

Allusion to Salmasius. In Latin. Printed in Pieter Burman, ed. *Sylloges Epistolarum a Viris Illustribus Scriptarum.* Leidæ: Apud Samuelem Luchtmans, 1727. III, 811–813. Copy owned by New York Public Library.

484 London. British Library. Sloane MS 649.

Anonymous letter, dated 10 August 1660, f. 42. Allusion to *Defensio secunda*. In Latin.

485 London. Public Record Office. SP 45/11.

By the King [Charles II]. A proclamation [etc.]., p. 14. Dated 13 August 1660. Suppression of *Defensio prima* and *Eikonoklastes*. The official copy.

486 *The London printers lamentation, or, the press oppresst, and overpresst.*

Dated: 3 September 1660 (Thomason). Allusion, p. 5. Wing, L2906. Copy owned by British Library.

487 *Mercurius politicus.* No. 610, 1–8 March 1660.

Advertisement for *The Ready and Easy Way*, p. 1151, with errata for Edition 1 (No. 275). Copy owned by Morgan Library.

488 *Mercurius publicus.* No. 20, 10–17 May 1660. London.

Advertisement for Starkey's *The Dignity of Kingship Asserted*, p. 31. Copy owned by Henry E. Huntington Library.

489 *Mercurius publicus.* No. 25, 14–21 June 1660. London.

Allusion to the proclamation of the king, p. 391. Copy owned by Henry E. Huntington Library.

490 *Mercurius publicus.* [No. 20], 13–20 June 1660. Edinburgh, Re-printed by Christopher Higgins, 1660.

Allusion to the proclamation of the king, p. 303. See No. *489*. Copy owned by Cambridge University Library.

491 *Mercurius publicus.* No. 28, 5–12 July 1660. London.

Advertisement for Starkey's *The Dignity of Kingship Asserted*, p. 457. Copy owned by Henry E. Huntington Library.

492 *Mercurius publicus.* No. 33, 9–16 August 1660. London: J. Macock and Thomas Newcomb.

Notice and proclamation (No. *450*), pp. 536–539. Various paging errors. Copy owned by Henry E. Huntington Library.

493 *Mercurius publicus.* [No. 29], 15–22 August 1660. Printed at London, and Re-printed at Edinburgh, by Christopher Higgins, 1660.

Notice of proclamation, p. 456, and printing of proclamation, pp. 458–459. See No. *492*. Copy owned by Cambridge University Library.

494 *Mercurius publicus.* No. 37, 6–13 September 1660. London.

Notice of burning of books, p. 578. Copy owned by Henry E. Huntington Library.

495 *Mercurius publicus.* No. 49, 29 November–6 December 1660. London.

Advertisement for Salmasius's *Responsio*, p. 785. Copy owned by Henry E. Huntington Library.

496 *No blinde guides, in answer to a seditious pamphlet of J. Milton's, intituled Brief notes upon a late sermon* [etc.]. London: Printed for Henry Brome, 1660.

Author: Sir Roger L'Estrange. Wing, L1289. Copy owned by New York Public Library.

497 *The Out-cry of the London prentices for justice to be executed upon John Lord Hewson* [etc.]. London: Printed for Gustavus Adolphus, 1659.

Author: anonymous. Dated: 1660. Unfavorable allusion to blindness, p. 6. Wing, O598. Copy owned by Folger Shakespeare Library.

498 Oxford. All Souls College Library. Codrington MS 259.

Copy of the King's proclamation (No. *485*), ff. 57v–59.

499 Oxford. Bodleian Library. Rawlinson MS C.366.

Copy of the king's proclamation (No. *485*), ff. 266v–267v. In hand of Erasmus Harby.

500 Oxford. Bodleian Library. Tanner MS 102.

Note by Anthony Wood, dated 1660, f. 71v. On the removal of Milton's books from the Bodleian Library.

501 *The Parliamentary intelligencer.* No. 26 [i. e., 25], 11–18 June 1660.

Allusion to proclamation of parliament, p. 399. Copy owned by Henry E. Huntington Library.

502 *The Parliamentary intelligencer.* No. 26, 18–25 June 1660.

Allusion to burning of books, pp. 401–402. Copy owned by Henry E. Huntington Library.

503 *The Parliamentary intelligencer.* No. 34, 13–20 August 1660.

Notice and reprint of king's proclamation (No. *450*), pp. 538–540. Copy owned by Henry E. Huntington Library.

504 *The Parliamentary intelligencer.* No. 37, 3–10 September 1660.

Notice of burning of books, p. 589. Copy owned by Henry E. Huntington Library.

505 *Physician cure thy self: or, an answer to a seditious pamphlet, entitled: Eye-salve* [etc.]. London: Printed for H. B., 1660.

Author: Sir Roger L'Estrange. Publisher: Henry Brome. Allusion, p. 2. Wing P2146. Copy owned by Princeton University Library.

506 *The Picture of the good old cause drawn to the life in the effigies of Master Prais-God Barebone. Several examples of Gods judgements on some eminent engagers against kingly government.* London: Printed, and are to be sold at divers Book-sellers shops, 1660.

Broadside. Dated: 14 July 1660. Item 3 is concerned with Milton's books against Salmasius. Copy owned by British Library.

507 *A Plea for limited monarchy, as it was established in this nation, before the late war* [etc.]. London: Printed by T. Mabb, for William Shears, 1660.

Author: Sir Roger L'Estrange. Probable allusion to *Ready and Easy Way*, p. 3. Wing, L1285. Copy owned by Princeton University Library.

508 *Poems. The golden remains of those so much admired dramatick poets, Francis Beaumont & John Fletcher* [bracket] *gent.* [etc.]. *The second edition enriched with the addition of other drolleries by several wits of these present times.* London: Printed for William Hope, 1660.

Dedication signed L. B. (i. e., Laurence Blaiklock); see No. *312*. Reissue of section with "A Maske of the Gentlemen of Graies Inne," G6–H1v. Wing, B1604. Copy owned by Folger Shakespeare Library.

509 *Royal and other innocent bloud crying aloud to heaven for due vengeance* [etc.]. London: Printed by A. Warren, for Daniel White, 1660.

Author: George Starkey. Allusion to *Defensio prima*, p. 18. Wing, S5287. Copy owned by New York Public Library.

510 *Salmasius his dissection and confutation of the diabolical rebel Milton in his impious doctrine of falshood* [etc.]. London: Printed for J. G. B. Anno 1660. and are to be sold in Westminster-Hall, St. Pauls Church-yard, and the Royal Exchange.

Reprint of No. *147*. Bookseller: John Garfield. Dedication (added), pp. [1–2]; Introduction (added), pp. 3–4; The Preface Examined (added), pp. 5–56; *Eikon Aklastos*, pp. 57–267; Errata, p. [268]. Cancel between inserted "A2" and A2. Wing, J452A. Copy owned by Folger Shakespeare Library.

511   *Several treatises of worship & ceremonies, by the reverend Mr. William Bradshaw* [etc.]. Printed for Cambridge and Oxford, and to be sold in Westminster Hall, and Pauls Church-Yard, 1660.

Added on p. [123] is: "August 1660. Books lately printed to acquaint those that are studious what are extant, divers of them being Printed this Month," with the legend, "Printed for J. Rothwel, 1660." Listed is *Smectymnuus Redivivus*. Wing, B4161. Copy owned by British Library.

512   *The Shaking of the olive-tree. The remaining works of that incomparable prelate Joseph Hall, D. D.* [etc.]. London: J. Cadwel, for J. Crooke, 1660.

Author: Joseph Hall. Allusion to divorce views, p. 161, in "The Mourner in Sion." Wing, H416. Copy owned by Columbia University Library.

There was no edition in 1659 (Wing, H415). The titlepage of the copy in the Library of Trinity College, Dublin, has been mutilated; the date and part of the legend, being torn away, a later hand has inaccurately added the date 1659.

513   *A Short view of some remarkable transactions* [etc.]. London: Printed for Henry Brome, 1660.

Author: Sir Roger L'Estrange. Reissue of No. *476*, including *L'Estrange his Apology, A Seasonable Word, A Sober Answer to a Jugling Pamphlet*, and *Plain English*, but excluding Nos. *496* and *505*. Wing, L1308. Copy owned by Yale University Library.

514   *The Spirit of the phanatiques dissected. And the solemne league and covenant solemnly discussed in 30 queries.* For W. Wallis, 1660.

Author: William Collinne. Place: London. Allusion to *Ready and Easy Way*, pp. [7–8]. Wing, C5354. Copy owned by Henry E. Huntington Library.

Stationers' register. See G. E. Briscoe Eyre, ed. *A Transcript of the Registers of the Worshipful Company of Stationers; from 1640–1708 A. D.* London: 1913–1914.

515   Entry for Starkey's *Dignity of Kingship Asserted*, under 31 March 1660, II (1913), 255.

516   Entry for Salmasius' *Responsio*, under 19 September 1660, II (1913), 278.

517   *A Third conference between O. Cromwell and Hugh Peters in Saint James's Park.* London: Printed by Tho. Rubb, 1660.

    Author: anonymous. Allusion, p. 8. Wing, T905. Copy owned by Folger Shakespeare Library.

518   *Treason arraigned. In answer to Plain English* [etc.]. London: Printed in the year, 1660.

    Author: Sir Roger L'Estrange. Publisher: Henry Brome. Allusions, pp. 2–3, 5, 22 (error for 30). Wing, T2073. Copy owned by Henry E. Huntington Library.

519   ["Upon *John Milton*'s not suffering for his Traiterous Book when the Tryers were Executed   1660."]

    Anonymous poem said to have been written in a copy of *Eikonoklastes*. See Jonathan Richardson (citing his son) in *Explanatory Notes and remarks on Milton's Paradise Lost*. London: Printed for James, John, and Paul Knapton, 1734. P. xcv. Copy owned by New York Public Library.

520   *Vera historia unionis non veræ inter Græcos et Latinos, sive concilii Florentini exactissima narratio Græce scripta per Sylvesterium Sguropulum. Transtulit in sermonem. Latinum notasque adjecit Robertus Creyghton.* Hagæ-Comitis: Ex Typographia A. Vlacq, 1660.

    Author: Sylvester Sgouropolos. Allusions to antimonarchical views and works, written by Robert Creighton in the notes, sig. c. Copy owned by British Library.

521   *Virtus rediviva a panegyrick on our late King Charles the I. &c. of ever blessed memory* [etc.]. Printed by R. & W. Leybourn, for William Grantham, 1660.

    Author: T. F. (Thomas Forde). Second title page intact with legend: "London: Printed by R. & W. Leybourn, for William Grantham, 1660." Included with its own title page is No. *471*. Wing, F1549. Copy owned by British Library.

522   Wolfenbüttel. Herzog-August-Bibliothek. Folio 649. 84.12 Extrav.

    "Commercium literarium Joh. Christiani de Boineburg et Hermanni Conringii a. 1660–1664" is a (generally scribal) manuscript collection of letters largely from and to Baron Boineburg and Conring. Those items printed in Gruber (see below) and French are sometimes different in accidentals.

Allusion to Salmasius and Milton in letter from Joannes Christianus, Baron Boineburg, to Hermann Conring, dated 13 December 1660, f. 3. In Latin. Printed in Io. Daniel Gruber. *Commercii Epistolici Leibnitiani* [etc.]. I, 431. Copy owned by New York Public Library.

Allusion to Salmasius's two defenses in letter from Ezekiel Spanheim to Baron Boineburg (?), dated 8 December 1660, f. 5v. In Latin.

1661

523 *Abrege' de l'histoire de ce siecle de fer. Premiere partie* [etc.]. *Qvatriesme edition. Reveue, corrigée, augmentée, amplifiée en pleusieurs endroits, & continuée jusque à l'an 1655* [etc.]. Sur l'Imprimé, A Bruxelles, Chez François Vivien, 1661.

Another edition of No. *292*, in three volumes. Allusion, I, 577. Copy owned by Bibliothèque Nationale. Copy in Yale University Library has part of legend and date cropped, thus dated 1660? in error.

524 *Joh. Lassenii. Adeliche tisch-reden in sich begreiffende zwölff lehrreiche | nietzliche und anmuhtige gespräch* [etc.]. Nürnberg: In verlegung Johann Andreas Endters | und Wolffgang | des Jüngern | seel. Erben. 1661.

Author: Johannes Lasenius. Comment, pp. 264–265. Copy owned by British Library.

525 *The Compleat history of independency. Upon the parliament begun 1640. By Clem. Walker, esq; Continued till this present year 1660. which fourth part was never before published.* London: Printed for Ric. Royston and Ric. Lownds, 1661.

Separate title page and pagination:
Anarchia Anglicana: or the history of independency. The second part. Being a continuation of relations and observations historical and politick upon this present parliament, begun anno 16. Caroli primi. By Theodorus Verax [etc.]. London: Printed for R. Royston, 1661.

Reprint of No. *85*. Wing, W324. Copy owned by Yale University Library.

526 *A Discourse opening the nature of that episcopacy which is exercised in England* [etc.]. London: Printed in the year 1661.

Another edition of No. *4*. Wing, B4912A (incorrectly dated). Copy owned by William Andrews Clark Library.

527 *Disputatio inauguralis exhibens diversa juris themata quæ opitulante Christo opt. max. sine præside* [etc.]. Heidelbergæ: Typis Algidii Walteri, 1659.

Second title page:
Johannes Friderici Böckelmanni J. U. D. in Acad. Heidelb. Professoris Ordinarii &
p. t. rectoris Disputatio inauguralis cum epistola apologetica ejusdem. Duisburgi: Typis
Adriani Wyngærden, 1661.

Allusion to divorce tracts, p. 123 and margin, in "Epistola Ad Lectorem,"
which was added in 1661. Copy owned by Bodleian Library.

528 *Elenchi motuum nuperorum in Anglia pars prima* [etc.]. Londini: Typis J. Flesher
& prostant apud R. Royston in Ivy Lane   1661.

Author: George Bate. Allusion to antimonarchical works, pp. 237–238; listed
in Index, p. [261]. Wing (1), B1078; Wing (2), B1080. Copy owned by
University of Kentucky Library.

529 *Heresiography, or a description of the hereticks and sectaries* [etc.]. *The sixt edition,*
whereunto is added this year 1661 [etc.]. London: Printed for William Lee, 1661.

Edition 6 of No. *32*. Allusions concerning divorce views, pp. [A3–A3v], 100,
233–234; listed in Index, twice: under Divorcers and Milton. A3 bound
before title page. Wing, P181. Copy owned by New York Public Library.

530 *Hollandtse Mercurius* [etc.]. *Elfde Deel.* Haerlem: Pieter Casteleyn, 1661.

Reprint of No. *473*. Biographical allusion, pp. 163–164. In Dutch. Copy
owned by New York Public Library.

531 *Konincklijcke Beeltenis, ofte waerachtige historie van Karel de II* [etc.]. Te Dordrecht,
voor Abraham Andriesz, 1661.

Dutch translation of No. *528*. Allusion in second book, pp. 208–209. Copy
owned by Folger Shakespeare Library.

532 [Letter from Robert Baillie to William Spang, dated 31 January 1661.]

Allusion in Letter 199. Printed in *Letters and journals* [etc.]. *Now first pub-*
lished from the MSS of Robert Baillie, D. D. [etc.]. Edinburgh: Printed for
William Creech and William Gray. Sold, in London, by J. Buchland, G.
Keith, and Mess. Dillies, 1775. Two volumes. II, 442. Copy owned by Folger
Shakespeare Library.

533 [Letter from Joannes Christanus, Baron Boineburg, to Hermann Conring,
dated 27 May (6 June) 1661.]

Allusion to Salmasian controversy. Printed in Io. Daniel Gruber. *Commercii*
Epistolici Leibnitiani [etc.]. Hanoveræ et Gottingæ, Apud Schmidios Fratres,
1745. I, 538. In Latin. Copy owned by New York Public Library.

534   *The Life of the most learned, reverend and pious Dr H. Hammond* [etc.]. London: Printed by J. Flesher, for Jo. Martin, Ja. Allestry and Tho. Dicas, 1661.

Author: John Fell. Allusion concerning divorce views, pp. 67–68. Wing, F617. Copy owned by Yale University Library.

535   *Monarchy triumphing over traiterous republications* [etc.]. London: Printed, by T. R. for William Palmer, 1661.

Reissue of No. *463*. Wing, S3069A. Copy owned by Henry E. Huntington Library.

536   Note, dated 7 January 1660 (i. e., 1661).

Author: anonymous. Remarks Milton's release from prison. Found on end flyleaf of copy of 1652 *Defensio prima* (No. 138) in Rutgers University Library (shelf mark: XDA/396/A3S32/1652). In German. See French IV, 360.

537   Philadelphia, Pennsylvania. University of Pennsylvania Library. Thomas Flatman MS. ENG 28 (formerly 821 / F61.1).

Composite manuscript written from both directions, containing sententiae from Tertullian and "Miscellanies by | Tho: Flatman." Dated 9 November 1661 through 1670. No foliation. Verbal appropriations throughout poems; first edition, 1674 (see No. *686*).

538   *Regii sanguinis clamor ad cœlum adversus parricidas Anglicanos. Editio secunda.* Hagæ-Comitum: Ex Typographia Adriani Ulac, 1661.

Reissue of Edition 3, No. *285*. Copy owned by University of Kentucky Library.

539   *Tom Tyler and his wife. An excellent old play* [etc.]. *The second impression.* London: 1661.

Author: anonymous. Bookseller: Francis Kirkman. Catalogue of books appended; listing of "John Milton   Miltons Mask," p. 10. Wing, T1792A. Copy owned by Yale University Library.

540   *Virtus rediviva a panegyrick on our late King Charles the I. &c. of ever blessed memory* [etc.]. Printed by R. and W. Leybourn, for William Grantham and Thomas Basset, 1661.

A different issue of No. *521*. Place: London. Wing, F1550. Copy owned by Henry E. Huntington Library.

541   *Virtus rediviva a panegyrick on our late King Charles the I. &c. of ever blessed memory* [etc.]. London: Printed by R. and W. Leybourn, for William Grantham and Thomas Basset, 1661.

Different issue of No. *540*. Portraits are different also. See Wing, F1550. Copy owned by Henry E. Huntington Library.

542 Wolfenbüttel. Herzog-August-Bibliothek. Folio 649. 84.12 Extrav.

See No. *522*. Allusion to Salmasian controversy in letter from Hermann Conring to Joannes Christianus, Baron Boineburg, dated perhaps 16 (26) June 1661, f. 82v. In Latin. Printed in Io. Daniel Gruber. *Commercii Epistolici Leibnitiani* [etc.]. Hanoveræ et Gottingæ, Apud Schmidios Fratres, 1745. I, 550. Copy owned by New York Public Library. Also printed in *Conringiana Epistolica. Sive Animadversiones Variæ Ervditionis Ex B. Hermanni Conringii Epistolis Miscellaneis Nondvm Editis Libatæ*. Cvra Christophori Henrici Ritmeieri, P. P. Helmstadii 1708. Typis et Svmpt. G. W. Hammii. Allusion, p. 94; listed in Index. Copy owned by British Library.

Allusion to Salmasian controversy in letter from Joannes Christanus, Baron Boineburg, to Hermann Conring, dated 1 July 1661, f. 96–96v. In Latin. Printed in Gruber, above, I, 572–573. Copy owned by New York Public Library.

1662

See No. 281 in Part I for allusion.

543 ΒΑΣΙΛΙΚΑ. *The Workes of King Charles the martyr* [etc.]. London: Printed by James Flesher, for R. Royston, 1662.

Editor: Richard Perrinchief. Allusion concerning *Eikonoklastes* and *Defensio prima* in "The Life of Charles I," pp. 94–95. Wing, C2075. Copy owned by Ted-Larry Pebworth and Claude J. Summers, University of Michigan — Dearborn. Variant issue: Q1v cancel has variant text; see Copy 2 owned by Alexander Turnbull Library.

544 *The Confession of faith, and the larger & shorter catechism* [etc.]. London: Printed by J. H., for the Company of Stationers, 1662.

Another edition of No. *45*. Allusion, p. 53. Not in Wing. Copy owned by Princeton Theological Seminary Library.

545 ["Democracy Rampant."]

Anonymous poem satirizing Milton. Dated: 1662 (?) In unlocated manuscript (p. 343) formerly owned by J. H. Gurney, Keswick Hall. Printed in *Twelfth Report of the Commission of Historical Manuscripts*, Appendix, Part 9 (1891), p. 140, in "Miscellanea," Section XXIII.

546   *Georgii Richteri J. C. Ejusque familiarium, epistolæ selectiores, ad viros nobilissimos clarissimosq*; [etc.]. Norimbergæ, Typis & Sumtibus Michaelis Endteri, 1662.

Allusion to *Defensio prima* and the Salmasian controversy in letter to Christopher Arnold, dated 19 (29) March 1651, p. 481; allusions to *Defensio prima* and *Areopagitica* in letter to Arnold, dated 26 July (5 August) 1651, pp. 483, 491. In Latin. Copy owned by Newberry Library.

547   *Heresiography, or a description and history of the hereticks and sectaries* [etc.]. *The sixth edition* [etc.]. London: Printed for William Lee, 1662.

Edition 6 of No. *32*. Illustration of "Divorser" on reissued illustrated title page (see No. *61*): *Heresiography*. London: Printed for W. L., 1647. References to divorcers or views on divorce: pp. A3v (misbound), 100, 133, [233–234]. Listings in Index under Divorcers and Milton. Wing, P182. Copy owned by Princeton Theological Seminary Library.

548   *Historie of Verhael van Saken van Staet en Oorlogh* [etc.]. In's Graven-Hage, by Johan Vely, 1662.

Author: Lieuwe van Aitzema. Volume VII, Book 31, p. 205, discussion of Salmasian controversy. In Dutch. Copy owned by Henry E. Huntington Library.

549   *The History of the wicked plots and conspiracies of our pretended saints* [etc.]. London: Printed by E. Cotes, for A. Seile, 1662.

Author: Henry Foulis. Allusions to antimonarchical works, pp. 4, 24. Wing, F1642. Copy owned by Yale University Library.

550   [Letter from Joannes Christianus, Baron Boineburg, to Hermann Conring, dated 27 July (6 August) 1662.]

Allusion to Salmasian controversy. Printed in Io. Daniel Gruber. *Commercii Epistolici Leibnitiani* [etc.]. Hanoveræ et Gottingæ, Apud Schmidios Fratres, 1745. II, 882–883. In Latin. Copy owned by New York Public Library.

551   [Letter from Joannes Christianus, Baron Boineburg, to Hermann Conring, dated 6 (16) October 1662.]

Discussion of Salmasian controversy. Printed in Io. Daniel Gruber. *Commercii Epistolici Leibnitiani* [etc.]. Hanoveræ et Gottingæ, Apud Schmidios Fratres, 1745. II, 946–948. In Latin. Copy owned by New York Public Library.

552   [Letter from Edward Hyde, Earl of Clarendon, to John Gauden, dated 13 March 1661 (1662?).]

On the authorship of *Eikon Basilike*: version printed in No. *1377*, p. 37; reference with some quotation given in No. *1378*, p. 18; different version printed in Christopher Wordsworth's *Who Wrote Eikon Basilike?* (London: John Murray, 1824), in "Documentary Supplement," p. 22. Has also been dated 1661.

553 *The Life of the most learned, reverend, and pious Dr H. Hammond* [etc.]. *The second edition.* London: J. Flesher, for Jo. Martin, Ja. Allestry and Tho. Dicas, 1662.

Edition 2 (reissue) of No. *534*. Wing, F618. Copy owned by Union Theological Seminary Library (McAlpin Collection).

554 *The Traytors perspective-glass. Or sundry examples of Gods just judgments executed upon many eminent regicides, who were either fomenters of the late bloody wars against the king, or had a hand in his death.* London: 1662.

Author: I. T. (John Taylor?). Allusion concerning antimonarchical works, pp. 21–22. Wing, T521. Copy owned by Union Theological Seminary Library (McAlpin Collection).

555 *Die Verschmähete doch wieder erhöhete majestäht | das ist kurtzer entwurf | der begäbnüsse Karls des zweiten | königs von Engelland |* [etc.]. Amsterdam: Joachim Noschen, 1662.

Author: Filip von Zesen. Illustrated title page dated 1661. Allusion to antimonarchical works, pp. 185–186. In German. Copy owned by Folger Shakespeare Library.

556 Wolfenbüttel. Herzog-August-Bibliothek. Folio 649. 84.12 Extrav.

See No. *522*. Discussion and biographical comments on Salmasius, as well as his *Epistolæ* and Alexander More, in letter from Johann Henricus Hottinger to Baron Boineburg, dated 18 January 1662, ff. 194–197v. Milton is not specifically cited. In Latin.

Allusion to writings in letter from Hermann Conring to Joannes Christianus, Baron Boineburg, dated 4 (14) October 1662, f. 282v. In Latin. Printed in Io. Daniel Gruber. *Commercii Epistolici Leibnitiani* [etc.]. Hanoveræ et Gottingæ, Apud Schmidios Fratres, 1745. II, 951. Copy owned by New York Public Library.

Allusion to writings in letter from Joannes Christianus, Baron Boineburg, to Hermann Conring, dated 24 October (3 November) 1662, f. 284. In Latin. Printed in Gruber, above, II, 963–964. Copy owned by New York Public Library.

1663

557   A Brief chronicle of the late intestine warr in the three kingdoms of England, Scotland
      & Ireland with the intervening affairs of treaties, and of the occurrences relating thereunto.
      London: Printed by J. Best, for William Lee, 1663.

      Author: James Heath. Edition 2, Issue 1. Allusion to antimonarchical works
      in Second Part, p. 435. Wing, H1320. Copy owned by Yale University
      Library.

558   A Brief chronicle of the late intestine warr in the three kingdoms of England, Scotland
      & Ireland [etc.]. The second impression, greatly enlarged. London: Printed by J.
      Best for William Lee, 1663.

      Edition 2, Issue 2, of No. 557. A second title page for second part has legend:
      "London, Printed by J. B. for W. Lee   1663." See Wing, H1320. Copy
      owned by Henry E. Huntington Library.

559   Cabala, or an impartial account of the non-conformists private designs, actings and
      wayes. From August 24. 1662. to December 25. in the same year. London: Printed
      in the year, 1663.

      Author: Sir John Birkenhead (?). Allusion, p. 12. Not in Wing. Copy owned
      by Folger Shakespeare Library.

560   Cabala, or an impartial account of the non-conformists private designs, actings and
      ways. From August 24. 1662. to December 25. in the same year. The second edition
      corrected. London: Printed in the Year, 1663.

      Edition 2 of No. 559. Wing, B2965. Copy owned by Union Theological
      Seminary Library (McAlpin Collection).

561   Considerations and proposals in order to the regulation of the press together with diverse
      instances of treasonous, and seditious pamphlets, proving the necessity thereof. Lon-
      don: Printed by A. C., 1663.

      Author: Sir Roger L'Estrange. Allusion to Tenure of Kings and Magistrates,
      p. 19. Wing, L1229. Copy owned by Yale University Library.

562   Elenchi motuum nuperorum in Anglia pars prima [etc.]. Londini: Typis J. Flesher.
      Prostat venalis apud R. Royston S. Regiæ Majestatis Bibliopolam, 1663.

      Another edition of No. 528. Allusion, p. 133, and listed in Index, p. [155].
      Wing, B1081. Copy owned by University of Kentucky Library.

563   Elenchi motuum nuperorum in Anglia pars prima [etc.]. Londini: Typis J. Flesher,
      & prostat apud R. Royston in Ivy Lane, 1663.

Another issue of No. *562.* Not in Wing. Copy owned by Folger Shakespeare Library.

564 *Elenchi motuum nuperorum in Anglia. Pars prima* [etc.]. Amstelodami: 1663.

Another edition of No. *528.* Allusion, p. 161. No index. Copy owned by Princeton University Library.

565 John Evelyn of Wotton. MS Diary of John Evelyn. Under date of 24 October 1663.

Allusion. See E. S. de Beer. *The Diary of John Evelyn.* Oxford: Clarendon Press, 1955. III, 365.

566 *The Holy state* [etc.]. *The fourth edition.* London: Printed by John Redmayne for John Williams, 1663.

Edition 4 of No. *7.* Allusion, pp. 279–280 and margin. Wing, F2446. Copy owned by Ted-Larry Pebworth and Claude J. Summers, University of Michigan — Dearborn.

567 *Jo. Henrici Boecleri Museum ad amicum.* Argentorati Apud Simonem Paulli Bibliop. 1663.

Author: Johann Heinrich Boecler. Place: Strasbourg. Discussion of Salmasius and Milton, pp. 27–41. In Latin. Copy owned by British Library.

568 *Juris regii* ανιπειθινοι *et solutissimi, cum potestate summa nulli, nisi deo soli* [etc.]. Hauniæ: Literis Henrici Gödiani, 1663.

Author: Johannes Wandalinus [Hans Wandal]. Discussion of *Defensio prima*, Book I, Chapter 3, p. 15; Book I, Chapter 4, pp. 23–24. Copy owned by Bodleian Library.

569 [Letter from the Comte de Cominges to Charles II, dated 23 March (2 April) 1663.]

Allusion to antimonarchical works. In French. Printed in *Diary and Correspondence of Samuel Pepys, F. R. S.* [etc.]. Ed. Richard, Lord Braybrooke. Philadelphia: David McKay, N. D. Edition 4. IV, 342.

570 [Letter from the Comte de Cominges to King Louis XIV of France, dated 2 April 1663.]

Allusion to antimonarchical works. In French. Printed in J. J. Jusserand. *A French Ambassador at the Court of Charles the Second.* London: T. Fisher Unwin, 1892. Page 205.

571 *Practical rhetorick. Or, certain little sentences varied according to the rules prescribed by Erasmus* [etc.]. London: Printed for T. Johnson, 1663.

Author: Joshua Poole. Listing of *The Cabinet-Council* in "Books lately printed, and sold by Thomas Johnson," O8. Wing, P2817. Copy owned by Dr. Williams's Library, London.

572 ["Pretense of Conscience No Excuse for Rebellion," Sermon Preached Before King Charles II, 30 January 1663.]

Author: Robert South. On Judges xix.30. Printed in *Sermons Preached Upon Several Occasions* (Oxford: Clarendon Press, 1823). III, 415–449. See p. 439 for discussion of Milton and quotation in Latin from *Defensio prima*. Not the same sermon as: *A Sermon Preach'd before King Charles II, on the Fast (Appointed Jan. 30.) For the Execrable Murder of His Royal Father. By Robert South. D. D. Now first Printed.* London: Printed for Eliz. Sawbridge, and sold by Arthur Betsworth. [1705?]. However, see p. 21 for the phrase and discussion of "Pretense of Conscience." Copy owned by British Library.

573 *Thomæ Bartholini epistolarum medicinalium à doctis vel ad doctos scriptarum, centuria I. & II. Cum indicibus necessariis.* Hafniæ: Typis Matthiæ Godicchenii, impensis Petri Haubold, 1663.

Author: Thomas Bartholin. Discussion of Salmasian controversy. Letter 10 (of second hundred) from Jacob Matthias to Bartholin, dated 26 June 1651, pp. 436–437. French dates 6 July 1651 (new style). Listed in Index. In Latin. Copy owned by Princeton University Library.

574 *Toleration discuss'd* [etc.]. London: Printed for Henry Brome, 1663.

Author: Sir Roger L'Estrange. Allusions to *Tenure of Kings and Magistrates*, pp. 34, 45 and margin, 71 and twice in margin, 84, 85 and margin, 105 margin. Wing, L1315. Copy owned by Columbia University Library.

575 *A Treatise of the execution of justice, wherein is clearly proved, that the execution of judgement and justice, is as well the peoples as the magistrates duty; and that if magistrates pervert judgement, the people are bound by the law of God to execute judgment without them, and upon them.*

Author: John Twyn (?). Place: London. Dated: 1663. A–B^4 C^6 D^4; 32 pp. Influenced throughout by *Tenure of Kings and Magistrates*. Wing, T2095. Copy owned by William Andrews Clark Library.

576 *Virorum illustri fama decantatorum ad Davidem Schirmerum … constitutum noviter bibliothecarium schediasmata. Liber adoptivus.* Dresdæ: Typis Melchioris Bergen, 1663.

Author: David Schirmer. Reprints No. *365A* without allusion. Copy owned by British Library.

1664

577 *A Brief chronicle of the late intestine warr in the three kingdoms of England, Scotland & Ireland* [etc.]. *The second impression greatly enlarged* [etc.]. London: Printed by J. B. for W. Lee, 1663.

Edition 2, Issue 3, of No. *557*. Dated: 1664. A second title page for second part has legend: "London: Printed for W. Lee, 1664"; title page between pp. 410 and 411. Part Three also has separate title page, dated 1664, appearing between pp. 624 and 625. Wing, H1319. Copy owned by Library of Congress.

578 *Discursus exoterici de supremis curiis seu Parlamentis Galliae et Angliæ* [etc.]. Jenæ: Typis Joh. Jac. Bauhoferi, 1664.

Author: Johannes Andreas Gerhard. Extensive discussion of Milton and *Defensio prima* with quotations: "Discursus prior ac Parlamentis Galliæ, præprimis Parisiano," section 5 ("Discrepantia Parlamentarium Galliæ a Parlamentis Britanniæ"), B4v–C1; "Discursus posterior de Jure ac Potentate Parlamenti Britannici," section 6 ("Parlamenti Convocatio Antiqva ac Freqvens"), E4–E4v; section 7 ("Parlamenti Convocatio Penes Regis Arbitrium"), F1; section 8 ("Parlamentum universum Inferus Ipso Rege"), F1v–F2; section 9 ("Contra Miltonum Disputatur"), F2–F2v; section 10 ("Parlamenti Jus Ac Potestas In statu Reip. Turbato"), F2v–F3v. Copy owned by Folger Shakespeare Library.

579 London. British Library. Stowe MS 76.

Gesta Britannica, by Roger Ley (?). Allusion, f. 301v. Dated: ca. April 1664. See French IV, 397–398.

580 ΠΑΝΣΕΒΕΙΑ: *or, a view of all religions in the world* [etc.]. *The fourth edition, enlarged and perfected* [etc.]. London: Sarah Griffin, for J. S. and are to be sold by John Williams, 1664.

Edition 4 (reissue?) of No. *310*. Allusions concerning divorce views, pp. 376, 389, 395 (?), 425. Wing, R1974. Copy owned by Columbia University Library.

581 *Poor robin. 1664. An almanack after a new fashion.*

Colophon: "London, Printed for the Company of Stationers." "Blinde Milton" noted under 3 November. Wing, A2183. Copy owned by British Library.

582   *Resolvtions de divers cas de conscience* [etc.]. A Geneve pour Pierre Chouët, 1664.

French translation of No. *111*. Discussion, pp. 316–318. Copy owned by Dr. Williams's Library, London.

1665

583   *Abbrege' de l'histoire de ce siecle de fer* [etc.]. *Sixiesme edition. Nouuellement reueuë, corrigée & augmentée de plusieurs notes à la marge & du nombre des années pour la commoditié du lecteur. Premiere partie.* Imprimé à Lyon & se vend A Paris, Par la Compagnie de Libraire Dv Palais. M.DC.LXV.

Volume 2 reads: "DEVXIÉME PARTIE. A Bruxelles, Chez François Vivien, M.DC.LXV." Another edition of No. *292*. Allusion in Vol. 2, in Book I, Chapter 8, pp. 66–67 and margin. Copy owned by University of Illinois Library.

584   Hannover. Bibliotheca Regia Hannoverana. MS IV.352.

Hermann Conring, "De Rebus-Publicus Per Totum Terrarum Orbem Præcipuis et celebrioribus [etc.], Helmstadij MDCLXV," holograph. Discussion of Salmasius and Milton on Eee6v–Eee7 in section entitled, "De Republica Anglicana." See also No. *1708*.

585   *Historia ecclesiastica et politica.* Lugd. Batav. et Roterod. Ex officina Hackiana, 1665.

Author: Georg Horn. Reference to divorce views, pp. 278–279. Reference to Cromwell's letters to various governments about the Piedmont massacre, pp. 351–352. Listed in Index. Copy owned by Princeton Theological Seminary Library.

586   *Poor robin. 1665. An almanack after a new fashion.*

Colophon: "London: Printed for the Company of Stationers." Allusion ("Blinde Milton") under 3 November. Wing, A2184. Copy owned by New York Public Library.

587   *A Sermon preached the 30th of January at White-Hall, 1664. Being the anniversary commemoration of K. Charls the I, martyr'd on that day* [etc.]. London: Printed by Henry Herringman, 1665.

Author: Henry King. Allusion to *Eikonoklastes*, p. 34. Wing, K507. Copy owned by New York Public Library.

1666

588 *Abregé de l'histoire de ce siecle de fer premiere partie* [etc.]. *Sixième edition.* A Brux-elles: Chez Balthazar Vivien, 1666.

Another edition of No. *292.* Allusion, p. 477 and margin. Copy owned by Cambridge University Library.

589 *Abregé de l'histoire de ce siecle de fer* [etc.]. A Lyon: Chez B. Rivière, 1666.

Another edition of No. *292.* Reprint of No. *583.* Copy owned by Bibliothè-que Nationale.

590 [illustrated title page] *Georgii Hornii Historia ecclesiastica et politica. Editio nova auctior & emendatior.* Lugd. Batav. et Roterod. Ex officina Hackiana, 1666.

Another edition of No. *585.* Discussions, pp. 280–281, 353–354. Listed in Index, V2. Copy owned by New York Public Library.

591 *The Pernicious consequences of the new heresie of the Jesuits against the king and the state* [etc.]. London: Printed by J. Flesher, for Richard Royston, 1666.

Author: Pierre Nicole (?). Allusion in "Dedicatory Preface," A4v. Wing, N1138. Copy owned by Folger Shakespeare Library.

592 *Poor robin. 1666. An almanack after a new fashion.*

Colophon: "London, Printed for the Company of Stationers." Listed under 29 November is "Blind *Milton.*" Wing, A2185. Copy owned by Bodleian Library.

1667

593 *A Discourse concerning the gift of prayer* [etc.]. *Whereunto may be added, Ecclesiastes; or, a discourse concerning the gift of preaching, by the same author.* London: Printed by A. M., for Sa. Gellibrand, 1667.

Another edition of No. *296,* to which is added No. *608.* Wing, W2182 and W2193. Copy owned by Union Theological Seminary Library (McAlpin Collection).

594 London. Public Record Office. MS 30/24.

A book list by John Locke, found in the Earl of Shaftesbury's Papers, dated 1667?, includes *Of Reformation, Doctrine and Discipline of Divorce,* and *Areopagitica.*

595 New Haven, Connecticut. James Osborn Collection, Yale University Library. MS PB VII/15.

Copy of Andrew Marvell's "Last Instructions to a Painter," dated "September 1667." Echoes from *Paradise Lost*, passim.

596 *A Paraphrase upon the psalms of David.* London: Printed by R. White, for Octavian Pullein, 1667.

Author: Samuel Woodford. Possible allusion to shorter poetry in preface, b1v–b2. Wing, B2491. Copy owned by New York Public Library.

597 *Poor robin. 1667. An almanack after a new fashion.*

Colophon: "London, Printed for the Company of Stationers." Allusion under 2 November. Wing, A2186. Copy owned by Folger Shakespeare Library.

Stationers' register. See G. E. Briscoe Eyre, ed. *A Transcript of the Registers of the Worshipful Company of Stationers; from 1640–1708 A. D.* London: 1913–1914.

598 Entry for *Paradise Lost*, under 20 August 1667, II (1913), 381.

1668

599 *Memoires of the lives, actions, sufferings, & deaths of those noble, reverend, and excellent personages, that suffered by death, sequestration, decimation, or otherwise, for the Protestant religion ... with the Life and martyrdom of King Charles I.* London: Printed for Samuel Speed, and sold by him, by John Wright, John Symmes, and James Collins, 1668.

Author: David Lloyd. Includes edition of No. *543.* Allusion to *Eikonoklastes* and *Defensio prima*, p. 221 and margin. Wing, L2642. Copy owned by Yale University Library.

600 *Orbis illustratus seu nova historico-politico-geographica, imperiorum rerumqve publicarum per totum terrarum orbem, descriptio* [etc.]. Imp. Johannis Naumanni, Bibliopolæ Hamburgensis. Razeburgi, Typis Nicolai Nissen, 1668.

Author: Johann Friedrich Pöpping. Book 2 is devoted to Britain; reference to *Defensio prima*, pp. 300–301 and margin. Copy owned by Yale University Library.

601 Oxford. Bodleian Library. Tanner MS 45.

Letter from Sir John Hobart to John Hobart, dated 22 January 1667/8, f. 258. Favorable comment on *Paradise Lost*.

602   Oxford. Bodleian Library. Tanner MS 45*.

Letter from Sir John Hobart to John Hobart, dated [30 January 1667/8], f. 271. Favorable comment on *Paradise Lost*.

603   *A Paraphrase upon the psalms of David*. London: Printed for R. W. for Jo. Dunmore, and Octavian Pulleyn Jun., 1668.

Reissue of No. *596* with 1667 title page intact. Wing, B2492. Copy owned by Henry E. Huntington Library.

604   *Poor robin. 1668. An almanack after a new fashion*.

Colophon: "London, Printed for the Company of Stationers." Allusion noted under 2 November. Wing, A2187. Copy owned by British Library.

1669

605   *A Catalogue of books printed for John Starkey book-seller, at the Miter in Fleet-street near Temple-Bar*.

Disbound. Folio. *2. Dated: 1669 (?). Listing of *Accedence Commenc't Grammar*, *2. Not in Wing. Copy owned by Henry E. Huntington Library.

606   *A Confession of faith, and the larger and shorter catechisms* [etc.]. Glasgow, By Robert Sanders, 1669.

Another edition of No. *45*. Allusion, pp. 54–55. Copy owned by New College, Edinburgh.

607   *A Continuation of the friendly debate* [etc.]. London: Printed for R. Royston, 1669.

Author: Simon Patrick. Octavo; xvi + 456 pp. Appropriations from 1650 *Eikonoklastes*, pp. 127–129. See Wing, P779. Another 1669 (later?) edition in xvi + 248 pp. does not include this section. Copy owned by Princeton Theological Seminary Library.

608   *Ecclesiastes: or, a discourse concerning the gift of preaching, as it falls under the rules of art. The fifth impression, corrected and enlarged* [etc.]. London: Printed by A. Maxwell, for SA. Gellibrand, 1669.

Another edition of No. *59*. Imprint has: "St. Paul's." Allusion, p. 181. See also No. *593*. See Wing, W2193. Copy owned by Union Theological Seminary Library (McAlpin Collection).

609 *Ecclesiastes: or, a discourse concerning the gift of preaching, as it falls under the rules of art. The fifth impression, corrected and enlarged* [etc.]. London: Printed by A. Maxwell, for SA. Gellibrand, 1669.

Another issue of No. *608*. Imprint has: "St. Pauls." See Wing, W2193. Copy owned by Henry E. Huntington Library.

610 *Francisci Vavassoris societ. Jesu de epigrammate liber et epigrammatum libri tres.* Parisiis: E typographia Edmundi Martini, 1669.

Author: Francis Vavassor. Discussion of Milton and Salmasius, Chapter 22, pp. 301-302. In Latin. Copy owned by William Andrews Clark Library.

611 *History natural and experimental of life & death* [etc.]. London: Printed for William Lee, 1669.

Author: Sir Francis Bacon. Added on Hhhh1-2 but not in signature sequence is: "A Catalogue of Books Printed for John Starkey [etc.]." Listings: No. 5, *Tetrachordon*, Hhhh1; No. 61, *Paradise Regain'd* and *Samson Agonistes*, Hhhh2v; No. 69, *Accedence Commenc't Grammar*, Hhhh2v. Date of catalogue is apparently 1671 or later. Not in Wing. Copy owned by Folger Shakespeare Library.

612 *Mercurius librarius: or, a catalogue of books printed and published at London in Trinity-Term, 1669.* No. 4.

Dated: 28 June 1669. Colophon: "Collected by *John Starkey* and *Robert Clavel*, and are to be sold by *John Starkey* at the *Miter* in *Fleetstreet* near *Temple-Bar*." Listing of *Accedence Commenc't Grammar*. Copy owned by Henry E. Huntington Library.

613 *Poor robin. 1669. An almanack after a new fashion.*

Colophon: "London, Printed for the Company of Stationers." Allusion under 1 November. Wing, A2188. Copy owned by New York Public Library.

614 *The Present state of the United Provinces of the low-countries* [etc.]. London: Printed for John Starkey, 1669.

Author: William Aglionby. Added on T7-12 is "Books Printed for, and Sold by John Starkey [etc.]." Listing of *Accedence Commenc't Grammar* as No. 42, T12. Wing, A766. Copy owned by Newberry Library.

1670

615 *Il Cardinalismo di Santa Chiesa; or the history of the cardinals* [etc.]. London: Printed for John Starkey, 1670.

Author: Gregorio Leti. Folio. Printed on A4v is: "A Catalogue of Some Books lately Printed for John Starkey [etc.]," with listing of *Accedence Commenc't Grammar*. Additional and separately printed catalogue included at end of volume; see No. *605*. Wing, L1330. Copy owned by Union Theological Seminary Library (McAlpin Collection).

616 *A Catalogue of books printed and published at London in Michaelmas-term, 1670.* No. 3.

Dated: 22 November 1670. Colophon: "*Collected by* Robert Clavel *in Cross-keys Court in* Little Britain." Listing of *History of Britain, Paradise Regain'd* and *Samson Agonistes*. Copy owned by Henry E. Huntington Library.

617 *A Catalogue of books printed for John Starkey* [etc.].

Folio. Printed on *^{2} with listing of *Accedence Commenc't Grammar*, *2. See also No. *605*. Found in:

Nicholas Perrault. *The Jesuits morals* [etc.]. London: Printed for John Starkey, 1670. Folio in fours. Bound: π^2 A^4 a–b^4 c^1 *^{2} B^4-etc. Wing, P1590. Copy owned by Union Theological Seminary Library (McAlpin Collection).

618 *Confessio fidei, in conventu theologorum authoritate parliamenti Anglicani indicto elaborata* [etc.]. Edinburgi, Excudebat ex Officina Societatis Stationariorum, 1670.

Another edition of No. *367*. Allusion, pp. 51–52. Wing, C5740. Copy owned by National Library of Scotland.

619 *Confessio fidei in conventu theologorum authoritate parliamenti Anglicani indicto elaborata* [etc.]. Glasguæ: Excudebat Robertus Sanders, 1670.

Another edition of No. *367*. Allusion, p. 50. Wing, C5741. Copy owned by Bodleian Library.

620 *The Grounds & occasions of the contempt of the clergy and religion enquired into. In a letter written to R. L.* London, Printed by W. Godbid for N. Brooke at the Angel in Cornhill. 1670.

Author: John Eachard. Edition 1: no comma after "Brooke" in legend; the last word in l. 26, p. 49, reads "ungovern-". Allusion to divorce views in Preface, A4v–A5. See Wing, E50. Copy owned by Cambridge University Library.

621   *The Grounds & occasions of the contempt of the clergy and religion enquired into. In
      a letter written to R. L.* London, Printed by W. Godbid for N. Brooke at the
      Angel in Cornhill. 1670.

      Another issue of No. *620*: no comma after "Brooke"; last word, l. 26, p.
      49: "ungoverna-". See Wing, E50. Copy owned by Cambridge University
      Library.

622   *The Grounds & occasions of the contempt of the clergy and religion enquired into. In
      a letter written to R. L.* London, Printed by W. Godbid for N. Brooke, at
      the Angel in Cornhill. 1670.

      Another issue of No. *620*: comma after "Brooke,"; last word, l. 26, p. 49:
      "ungo-". See Wing, E50. Copy owned by Cambridge University Library.

623   *The Grounds & occasions of the contempt of the clergy and religion enquired into. In
      a letter written to R. L.* London, Printed by W. Godbid for N. Brooke, at
      the Angel in Cornhill. 1670.

      Another issue of No. *620*: comma after "Brooke,"; last word, l. 26, p. 49:
      "trouble-". See Wing, E50. Copy owned by Cambridge University Library.

624   *The Grounds & occasions of the contempt of the clergy and religion enquired into. In
      a letter written to R. L.* London, Printed by W. Godbid for N. Brooke, at
      the Angel in Cornhill. 1670.

      Another issue of No. *620*: comma after "Brooke,"; last word, l. 26, p. 49:
      "and". See Wing, E50. Copy owned by Cambridge University Library.

625   *The Natural history of Wiltshire; by John Aubrey, F. R. S. (Written between 1656
      and 1691.) Edited, and elucidated by notes, by John Britton, F. S. A.* [etc.]. Lon-
      don: J. B. Nichols and Son, 1847.

      Author: John Aubrey. Allusion to *History of Britain*, p. 50, written ca. 1670.

626   *Petri Molinæi P. F. Παρεργα. Poematum libelli tres* [etc.]. Cantabrigiæ: Typis
      Joann. Hayes, Impensis Joannis Creed, 1670.

      Author: Peter Du Moulin. Allusions to the controversy between du Moulin
      and Milton: Book II, sig. F8; II, 36–42 (with poem originally in *Regii
      Sanguinis Clamor* [No. *283*], entitled "In impurissimum nebulonem Joannem
      Miltonum [etc.]"); III, 141–142 (section entitled, "Epistolam quam iambo
      in Miltonum author subjunxerat [etc.]"). Each book has separate title page
      and pagination; books II and III are given publication dates of 1669. In
      Latin. Wing, D2561. Copy owned by University of Kentucky Library.

627   *Poor robin. 1670. An almanack after a new fashion.*

Colophon: "London, Printed for the Company of Stationers." Allusion in Observations, under 2 November. Wing, A2189. Copy owned by Folger Shakespeare Library.

628 *Sacrarum profanarumque phrasium poeticarum thesaurus* [etc.]. Londini: Impensis Georgium Sawbridge, 1669.

Author: Johann Buchler. Edition of 1670, to which is added in continuous pagination Edward Phillips's *Tractatulus de Carmine Dramatico Poetarum Veterum* [etc.]. Londini: Typis T. Newcomb, 1670. Notice and discussion in *Tractatulus*, in section entitled, "Compendiosa Enumeratio Poetarum &c.," p. 399. In Latin. Wing lists only the 1669 edition of Buchler as B5303. Copy owned by Princeton Theological Seminary Library.

Parker (*Milton: A Biography*, II, 1128) cites p. 270 in error.

Stationers' register. See G. E. Briscoe Eyre, ed. *A Transcript of the Registers of the Worshipful Company of Stationers; from 1640–1708 A. D.* London: 1913–1914.

629   Entry for *Paradise Regain'd* and *Samson Agonistes*; under 10 September 1670, II (1913), 415.

630 *Toleration discuss'd; in two dialogues* [etc.]. London: Printed by E. C. and A. C., for Henry Brome, 1670.

Author: Sir Roger L'Estrange. Revised version of No. *574*. Quotations from *Tenure of Kings and Magistrates*, pp. 64–65 and margins; allusion, p. 63. Wing, L1316. Copy owned by University of Kentucky Library.

631 *Wiltshire. The topographical collections of John Aubrey* [etc.]. Devizes: Henry Bull, for the Wiltshire Archaelogical and Natural History Society, 1862.

Author: John Aubrey. Ed. John Edward Jackson. Preface dated 28 April 1670. Quotations from *History of Britain* and allusion, pp. 66, 74, 258.

1671

SEE ALSO NO. 308 IN PART I FOR DISCUSSION INVOLVING GOVERNMENTAL WORK.

632 *A Catalogue of books. Printed for John Starkey* [etc.].

Quarto. A^4; 8 pp. Catalogue made up in part in May 1670. Listings: *Tetrachordon*, A2v; *Paradise Regain'd* and *Samson Agonistes*, A3v; *Accedence Commenc't Grammar*, A4. Added at end to:

Benjamin Priolo. *The History of France under the ministry of Cardinal Mazarine* [etc.]. London: Printed for J. Starkey, 1671. Translator: Christopher Wasse. Wing, P3506A. Copy owned by Folger Shakespeare Library.

John Milton. *Paradise Regain'd. A Poem. In IV Books. To which is added Samson Agonistes* [etc.]. London: Printed by J. M., for John Starkey, 1671. Wing, M2152. Copy owned by University of Michigan Library.

633   *A Catalogue of books. Printed for John Starkey* [etc.].

Quarto. A^4; 8 pp. Listings: *Paradise Regain'd* and *Samson Agonistes*, A4; *Accedence Commenc't Grammar*, A4v. Added at end to:

Jean Gailhard. *The Present state of the princes and republicks of Italy, with observations on them. The second edition corrected and enlarged* [etc.]. London: Printed for John Starkey, 1671. Wing, G126. Copy owned by Folger Shakespeare Library.

634   *A Catalogue of books. Printed for John Starkey* [etc.].

Quarto. A^4; 8 pp. Listings: *Accedence Commenc't Grammar*, A3v; *Paradise Regain'd* and *Samson Agonistes*, A4v. Added at end to:

The Novels of Dom Francisco de Quevedo Villegas [etc.]. London: Printed for John Starkey, 1671. Wing, Q192. Copy owned by Newberry Library.

635   *Confessio fidei, in conventu theologorum, authoritate parliamenti Anglicani indicto, elaborata* [etc.]. Edinburgi: Excudebat ex Officinâ Societas Stationariorum, Anno Dom. 1671.

Another edition of No. *367.* Allusion, pp. 51–52. Wing, C5742. Copy owned by British Library.

636   *The Confession of faith and the larger and shorter catechism* [etc.]. Edinbourg: Printed by George Swintoun and Thomas Brown, and are to be sold by James Glen and David Trench, 1671.

Another edition of No. *45.* Duodecimo. Allusion, pp. 57–58. Wing, C5769. Copy owned by British Library.

637   *The Grounds & occasions of the contempt of the clergy and religion enquired into. In a letter written to R. L.* London: Printed by W. G. for N. B., 1671.

Edition 2 of No. *620.* Comment, A2v–A3. Wing, E51. Copy owned by British Library.

638   *Iconoclastes: or a hammer to break down all invented images, image-makers and image-worshippers. Shewing how contrary they are both to the law and gospel.* 1671.

Author: George Fox. Place: London. Possible allusion in title. Wing, F1846. Copy owned by Yale University Library.

639 *Nicomède. A tragi-comedy, translated out of the French of Monsieur Corneille, by John Dancer* [etc.]. London: Printed for Francis Kirkman, 1671.

Added is Kirkman's catalogue, "A True, perfect, and exact Catalogue of all the Comedies, Tragedies, Tragi-Comedies, Pastorals, Masques, and Interludes [etc.]," with "A Mask" but not Milton's name listed on p. 10. Cf. No. *539*. Wing, C6315. Copy owned by Folger Shakespeare Library.

640 *Petri Molinæi P. F. Παρεργα. Poematum libelli tres* [etc.]. Cantabrigiæ: Typis Joann. Hayes, Impensis Joannis Creed, 1671.

Reissue of No. *626*. Wing, D2562. Copy owned by British Library.

641 *The Present interest of England stated. By a lover of his king and country.* London: Printed for D. B., 1671.

Author: Sir T. Osborn (?) or Slingsby Bethel (?). Reference, p. 28 and margin, to "Sir *Walter Rawleighs Cabinet Counsellor.*" Wing, B2072. Copy owned by New York Public Library.

642 *The Present state of the United Provinces of the low-countries* [etc.]. *Collected by W. A. Fellow of the Royal Society. The second edition corrected.* London: Printed for John Starkey, 1671.

Edition 2 of No. *614*. Added on T7–12 is "Catalogue of Books Printed for John Starkey Book-seller." Listings: *Paradise Regain'd* and *Samson Agonistes*, No. 26, T10; *Accedence Commenc't Grammar*, No. 43, T11v. Wing, A767. Copy owned by British Library.

1672

643 *Animadversions upon Sr Richard Baker's Chronicle, and it's continuation. Wherein many errors are discover'd, and some truths advanced* [etc.]. Oxon: Printed by H. H., for Ric. Davis, 1672.

Author: Thomas Blount. Printer: Henry Hall. Allusions with quotations from *History of Britain*, pp. 20 and margin, 58, 98–99 and margin. Wing, B3327. Copy owned by Columbia University Library.

644 *The Annals of love, containing select histories of the amours of divers princes courts, pleasantly related.* London: Printed for John Starkey, 1672.

Printed on Dd7v–Dd8 Ee⁴ is: "A Catalogue of Books Printed for John Starkey [etc.]." Listings: *Tetrachordon*, Dd7v–Dd8; *Paradise Regain'd* and *Samson*

Agonistes, Ee4; *Accedence Commenc't Grammar*, Ee4v. Wing, A3215. Copy owned by Folger Shakespeare Library.

645 *A Catalogue of books continued, printed, and published in London in Easter term, 1672.* No. 9. 13 May 1672.

Colophon: "*Collected by* Robert Clavel *in Cross-keys Court in* Little Britain." Listing of *Artis Logicæ*. Copy owned by Henry E. Huntington Library.

646 *Catalogus variorum & raressimorium quavis facultate, materia & lingua, librorum tam compactorum, quam incompactorum, Frederici Leonard, Bibliopolæ Parisiensis, & Regis Typographi.* M. DC. LXXII.

Place: Paris. Listings: p. 98, *Eikonoklastes* (Dury's French translation) and *Defensio prima.* Copy owned by British Library.

647 Dublin. Marsh's Library. MS.

Letter from Elie Bouhereau to Marquis Turon de Beyrie, dated 22 November 1672. Discussion of Milton's controversy with Alexander More with the quotation of one sentence from *Defensio secunda.* In French.

648 *Francisci Vavassoris societ. Jesu de epigrammate liber et epigrammatum libri tres. Editio auctior.* Parisiis. Ex officina Edmundi Martini, M.DC.LXXII.

Another edition of No. *610.* Copy owned by Yale University Library.

649 *The Grounds and occasions of the contempt of the clergy and religion enquired into* [etc.]. London: Printed by E. T. and R. H. for Nath. Brooke, 1672.

Second title page: *The Grounds and occasions of the contempt of the clergy and religion enquired into* [etc.]. *The eighth edition.* London: Printed by E. Tyler and R. Holt, for Nathaniel Brooke, 1672.

Edition 8 (?) of No. *620*; Editions 3-7 are unknown. Wing, E52. Copy owned by Henry E. Huntington Library.

650 *The History of the twelve Caesars* [etc.]. London: Printed for John Starkey, 1672.

Author: Caius Tranquillus Suetonius. "A Catalogue of Books Printed for John Starkey [etc.]" is included on Kk3-8 (pp. [501-512]). Listed are: *Tetrachordon*, pp. [501-502]; *Paradise Regain'd* and *Samson Agonistes*, p. [511]; and *Accedence Commenc't Grammar*, p. [512]. A note informs that "This Catalogue was Printed in February, 1672." Wing, S6147. Copy owned by Henry E. Huntington Library.

651 *Jo. Henrici Boecleri Museum ad amicum. Editio secunda.* Argentorati, Apud Simonem Paulli Bibliop. 1672.

Edition 2 of No. *567.* Discussion, pp. 31-46. Copy owned by British Library.

652   *Montelions predictions, or the hogen mogen fortuneteller* [etc.]. London: Printed by
      S. and B. Griffin, for Thomas Palmer, 1672.

      Author: John Phillips. Appropriation from *Paradise Lost*, p. 8. Wing, P2094.
      Copy owned by Henry E. Huntington Library.

653   ΠΑΝΣΕΒΕΙΑ: *or, a view of all religions in the world* [etc.]. *The fourth edition,
      enlarged and perfected* [etc.]. Printed for John Williams, 1672.

      Place: London. Reissue of No. *580*. Wing, R1975. Copy owned by Co-
      lumbia University Library.

654   *Reliquiæ Wottonianæ: or, a collection of lives, letters, poems; with characters of sun-
      dry personages* [etc.]. *The third edition, with large additions.* London: Printed by
      T. Roycroft, for R. Marriott, F. Tyton, T. Collins, and J. Ford, 1672.

      Edition 3 of No. *198*. Letter, pp. 342–344. Wing, W3650. Copy owned by
      New York Public Library.

655   *Samuelis Pufendorfii de jure naturæ et gentium libri octo* [etc.]. Londini Scanorum
      Sumtibus Adami Junghaus imprimebat vitus Haberegger | Acad. Typog.
      Anno M DC LXXII.

      Reference, p. 749. Discussion of divorce views and quotations from *Doc-
      trine and Discipline of Divorce*, Book VI, Chapter 1, Section 24, on pp. 791–795.
      Copy owned by Folger Shakespeare Library.

      Stationers' register. See G. E. Briscoe Eyre, ed. *A Transcript of the Registers
      of the Worshipful Company of Stationers; from 1640–1708 A. D.* London:
      1913–1914.

656   Entry for *History of Britain*, under 29 December 1672, II (1913), 451.
657   Entry for *History of Britain*, under 29 December 1672, II (1913), 452.

1673

See also No. 313 in Part I for letter from Henry Wotton as well as Henry
Lawes's letter and testimonies.

658   *A Catalogue of all the books printed in England since the dreadful fire of London, in
      1666. To the end of Michaelmas term, 1672.* London: Printed by S. Simmons,
      for R. Clavel, 1673.

      Second pagination, p. 13, two advertisements; p. 31, advertisement; p. 47,
      two advertisements. Wing, C4598. Copy owned by Henry E. Huntington
      Library.

659 *A Catalogue of books continued, printed, and published in London in Hilary term, 1673.* No. 12. 7 February 1673.

Colophon: "*Collected by* Robert Clavel *in Cross-keys Court in* Little Britain." Listing of *Artis Logicæ.* Copy owned by Henry E. Huntington Library.

660 *A Catalogue of books continued, printed and published in London in Easter term, 1673.* No. 13. 6 May 1673.

Colophon: "*Collected by* Robert Clavel *in Cross-keys Court in* Little Britain." Listing of *Of True Religion.* Copy owned by Henry E. Huntington Library.

661 *A Catalogue of books continued, printed and published in London in Michaelmas term, 1673.* No. 15. 24 November 1673.

Colophon: "*Collected by* Robert Clavel *in Cross-keys Court in* Little Britain." Listing of *Poems*, 1673. Copy owned by Henry E. Huntington Library.

662 *A Common-place-book out of The Rehearsal transpros'd* [etc.]. London: Printed for Henry Brome, 1673.

Author: Sir Roger L'Estrange (?). Allusion to *Accedence Commenc't Grammar*, pp. 35–36. Wing, M869. Copy owned by Henry E. Huntington Library.

663 Dublin. Marsh's Library. MS.

Letter from Elie Bouhereau to Marquis Turon de Beyrie, dated 22 August 1673. Allusion to No. *647* and Milton. In French.

664 *Epistolæ ho-elianæ. Familiar letters domestic and forren* [etc.]. *The fourth edition* [etc.]. London: Printed for Thomas Guy, 1673.

Edition 4 of No. *355*. Allusion concerning divorce views, pp. 442–443. Wing, H3074. Copy owned by Medical Library, University of Kentucky.

665 *Epistolæ ho-elianæ. Familiar letters domestic and forren* [etc.]. *The fourth edition* [etc.]. London: Printed for Thomas Guy, 1673.

Variant issue of No. *664*. See, for example, "Editi on" on title page. Copy owned by Medical Library, University of Kentucky.

666 ΠΑΝΣΕΒΕΙΑ: *or, a view of all religions in the world* [etc.]. *The fifth edition, enlarged and perfected by Alexander Ross* [etc.]. London: Printed for John Williams, 1673.

Edition 5 of No. *310*; reissue of No. *653*. Wing, R1975A. Copy owned by British Library.

667   *Chr. Funcci Quadripartitum historico-politicum orbis hodie-imperantis breviarum* [etc.].
      Gorlicii Impensis Joh. Ad. Kaestneri, Bibliop. Typis Christophori Zipperi.
      An. 1673.

      Author: Christian Funck (Christianus Funccius). Discussion with quota-
      tion of Milton's writing of *Defensio prima*, p. 552 (under "Regnum Britan-
      nicum," Item LVII, Section LIIX). Copy owned by University of Göttingen
      Library.

668   *The Rehearsall transpros'd: the second part* [etc.]. London: Printed for Nathaniel
      Ponder, 1673.

      Author: Andrew Marvell. Discussion of friendship and rebuttal of Leigh
      (see No. *672*), pp. 377–389. Wing, M882. Copy owned by University of
      Kentucky Library.

669   *A Reproof to The Rehearsal transprosed, in a discourse to its author.* London: Printed
      for James Collins, 1673.

      Author: Samuel Parker. Allusions to biography and writings, pp. 125, 191,
      212, 340 (?). Wing, P473. Copy owned by Yale University Library.

670   *S'too him Bayes: or some observations upon the humour of writing rehearsal's transpros'd*
      [etc.]. Oxon: Printed in the year of 1673.

      Author: Anthony Hodges (?). Allusion to Salmasian controversy, p. 130.
      Wing, M890. Copy owned by Yale University Library.

671   *Toleration discuss'd; in two dialogues* [etc.]. London: Printed by A. C., for Henry
      Brome, 1673.

      Another edition of No. *630*. Wing, L1317. Copy owned by Fordham Univer-
      sity Library.

672   *The Transproser rehears'd: of the fifth act of Mr. Bayes's play* [etc.]. Oxford: Printed
      for Thomas Sawbridge, 1673.

      Author: Richard Leigh (?). Allusions and criticism concerning the Salma-
      sian controversy, the antimonarchical works, *Accedence Commenc't Grammar,
      Paradise Lost*, the antiprelatical tracts, and biography: pp. 9, 30, 32, 41–43,
      55, 72, 98, 110, 113, 126–128, 131–133, 135–137, 146–147. Wing, L1020.
      Copy owned by Yale University Library.

1674

See also No. 318 in Part I for John Dryden's epigram and commendatory poems by Samuel Barrow and Andrew Marvell.

673   *A Catalogue of books continued, printed and published in London in Easter term, 1674.* No. 17. 26 May 1674.

Colophon: "*Collected by* Robert Clavel *in Cross-keys Court in* Little Britain." Listing of *Epistolarum Familiarium Liber Unus.* Copy owned by Henry E. Huntington Library.

674   *A Catalogue of books continued, printed and published in London in Trinity term, 1674.* No. 18. 6 July 1674.

Colophon: "*Collected by* Robert Clavel *in Cross-keys Court in* Little Britain." Listing of *Paradise Lost.* Copy owned by Henry E. Huntington Library.

675   *Catalogus impressorum librorum bibliothecæ Bodlejanæ in academia Oxoniensis. Cura & opera Thomæ Hyde è Coll. Reginæ Oxon. protobibliothecarii.* Oxonii: E Theatro Sheldoniano, 1674.

Listings: pp. 210 (under Divorce), 252 (under Sr Rob. Filmer), 457 (eight listings under Milton, including *Paradise Regain'd* dated 1670), 471 (under Alexander Morus, both *Regii Sanguinis Clamor* and *Fides Publica*). Wing, O864. Copy owned by University of Kentucky Library.

676   *Catalogus librorum ex variis Europæ partibus advectorum. Per Robertvm Scott bibliopolam Londinensem.* Londini, Venales Prostant, apud dictum Robertum Scott, 1674.

Listings of *Defensio prima* and Salmasius's *Defensio Regia,* p. 129. Wing (1), C1437; Wing (2), entry cancelled. Copy owned by Yale University Library.

677   *Catalogus librorum qui in bibliopolio Danielis Elsevirii venales extant.* Amstelodami: Ex officina Elseviriana, 1674.

Advertisements for *Poems, Defensio prima* (2° and 4°), *Defensio pro Se, Defensio secunda* (8° and 12°), p. 121. Copy owned by Folger Shakespeare Library.

678   *De scriptis et scriptoribus anonymis atque pseudonymus syntagma* [etc.]. Hamburgi: Sumptibus Christiani Guthii, 1674.

Author: Vincent Placcius. Second gathering, with separate signatures and pagination: *De scriptoribus occultis detectis tractatus duo* [etc.]. Hamburgi: Sumptibus Christiani Guthii, 1674.

Reference to Milton's response to Salmasius, Chap. III, Item CXXV, p. 35. Copy owned by New York Public Library.

679 *A Discourse concerning the gift of prayer* [etc.]. *Whereunto may be added, Ecclesiastes* [etc.]. London: Printed by A. M. for Sa. Gellibrand, 1674.

Another edition of No. *296*, to which is added a reissue of No. *608*. Wing, W2182A and W2193. Copy owned by William Andrews Clark Library.

680 *A Discourse concerning the gift of prayer* [etc.]. *Whereunto may be added, Ecclesiastes* [etc.]. London: Printed by A. M. for Sa. Gellibrand, 1674.

Another issue of No. *679*. Added is the 1675 sixth impression of *Ecclesiastes*, No. *694*. Wing, W2182A and W2193A. Copy owned by Princeton University Library.

681 *Historia et antiquitates universitatis Oxoniensis* [etc.]. Oxonii: E Theatro Sheldoniano, 1674.

Author: Anthony Wood. Allusion in "Editor Lectori" by John Fell, in Book II, Pppppp1. In Latin. Wing, W3385. Copy owned by Folger Shakespeare Library.

Earlier issue owned by Bodleian Library, with notes and alterations in Wood's hand, does not include "Editor Lectori."

Wing, W3384, an alleged edition of 1673 in the Union Theological Seminary Library, does not exist, nor does Wing, W3386, an alleged edition of 1684 in the Bodleian Library and Magdalen College Library, Oxford.

682 *The History of the wicked plots and conspiracies of our pretended saints* [etc.]. *The second edition* [etc.]. Oxford: Printed by Hen. Hall, for Ric. Davis, 1674.

Edition 2 of No. *549*. Wing, F1643. Copy owned by Yale University Library.

683 London. British Library. Additional MS 28954.

List of works compiled by Mr. Ellis, f. 9 (in modern foliation since many leaves are blank; pp. 28–29 counting blank pages). Dated: 1674–76.

684 *The Memoires of Philip de Comines* [etc.]. London: Printed for John Starkey, 1674.

Printed on Qq6v–Qq8 (four sides only) is: "A Catalogue of Books Printed for John Starkey [etc.]." Listing: No. 21, *Paradise Regain'd* and *Samson Agonistes*, Qq7v. Wing, C5543. Copy owned by University of Kentucky Library.

685 Oxford. Bodleian Library. Wood MS F.40.

Letter from Thomas Blount to Anthony Wood, dated 19 November 1674,

f. 192. Reference to Milton's being dead. Published in *The Life and Times of Anthony Wood, Antiquary, of Oxford. 1632–1695, described by himself* [etc.]. Oxford: Printed for the Oxford Historical Society at the Clarendon Press, 1892. Ed., Andrew Clark. Vol. 21 of Oxford Historical Society Publications. II, 297.

686 *Poems and songs. By Thomas Flatman.* London: Printed by S. and B. G., for Benjamin Took and Jonathan Edwin, 1674.

Edition 1. Verbal appropriations throughout. Wing, F1151. Copy owned by Henry E. Huntington Library.

687 *Poor robin. 1674. An almanack after a new fashion.*

Colophon: "London, Printed for the Company of Stationers." Allusion, under 2 November. Wing, A2193. Copy owned by Folger Shakespeare Library.

688 *The Rehearsall transpros'd: the second part* [etc.]. London: Printed for Nathaniel Ponder, 1674.

Edition 2 of No. *668*. See pp. 339–342. Wing, M883. Copy owned by University of Kentucky Library.

689 *A Sermon preached before the Right Honourable the Lord Major and Aldermen, &c. At Guild-Hall Chappel, January the 30th 1673/4* [etc.]. London: Printed for Nathaniel Brooke.

Author: Richard Meggott. Date: 1674. Possible allusions to antimonarchical works, pp. 33, 45–46. Wing, M1621. Copy owned by Yale University Library.

Stationers' register. See G. E. Briscoe Eyre, ed. *A Transcript of the Registers of the Worshipful Company of Stationers; from 1640–1708 A. D.* London: 1913–1914.

690   Entry for *State of Innocence*, under 17 April 1674, II (1913), 479.
691   Entry for *Epistolarum Familiarium Liber Unus*, under 1 July 1674, II (1913), 481.

692 *The Workes of the reverend and learned Henry Hammond, D. D. The first volume* [etc.]. London: Printed by Elizabeth Flesher, for Richard Royston and Richard Davis, 1674.

Collected edition including No. *301*. Discussion of divorce views in reprint of *A Letter of Resolution to Six Quaeres*, pp. 457–458. Wing, H506. Copy owned by Union Theological Seminary Library (McAlpin Collection).

Wing lists as H524, *A Collection of Such Discourses* (1657), copy supposedly only in the Bodleian Library, but it does not exist. There has apparently been conflation with *A Collection of Such Replies* (1657), copy only in the Bodleian Library (Wing, H523).

1675

693 *The Confession of faith, together with the larger and lesser catechismes* [etc.]. *To which is annexed two sheets of church-government with the scriptures at large. The fourth edition* [etc.]. Printed at London, for the Company of Stationers, Anno 1658. And re-printed at Glasgow, by Robert Sanders, 1675.

Another edition of No. *45*. Allusion, p. 82. Wing, C5770 and C5797; entered twice. Copy owned by Union Theological Seminary Library (McAlpin Collection).

694 *Ecclesiastes: or, a discourse concerning the gift of preaching* [etc.]. *The sixth impression, corrected and enlarged* [etc.]. London: A. Maxwell, for Sa: Gellibrand, 1675.

Another issue of No. *608*. Allusion, p. 181. Wing, W2193A. Copy owned by Princeton University Library.

695 *The General catalogue of books printed in England since the dreadful fire of London, 1666. To the end of Trinity Term, 1674* [etc.]. *Collected by Robert Clavel.* London: Printed by Andrew Clark, for Robert Clavel, 1675.

Listings, pp. 34, 47, 76, 82, 83 (2), 104 (2), 113 (2), 118, 119. Wing, C4600. Copy owned by Princeton University Library.

696 London. Friends' Library. Holograph MS of Thomas Ellwood's *Rhapsodia*.

Dated: 1675 or after. "Epitaph on Milton," pp. 145–146. Facsimile printed in *Milton Newsletter*, Vol. 1, No. 2 (May 1967) 20–22.

697 London. Public Record Office. SP Car. II.370/38.

Anonymous letter, dated April 1675, allusion. Printed in *Calendar of State Papers, Domestic Series, March 1st 1675, to February 19th, 1676 Preserved in the Public Record Office*. Ed. F. H. Blackburne Daniell. London: Mackie and Co., 1907. XVII, 89.

698 Oxford. Bodleian Library. Wood MS F.39.

Letter from John Aubrey to Anthony Wood, dated 12 January 1674/5, on place of Milton's burial, f. 288. A note from Wood appears on f. 289v.

Letter from John Aubrey to Anthony Wood, dated 23 January 1674/5, on his visit to see Milton's grave, f. 284.

Letter from John Aubrey to Anthony Wood, dated Shrove Tuesday, 1674/5, note, f. 286.

Letter from John Aubrey to Anthony Wood, dated 18 May 1675, on burial, f. 296. Note by Wood appears on f. 297v.

699   ΠΑΝΣΕΒΕΙΑ: *or, a view of all religions in the world* [etc.]. *The fifth edition* [etc.]. London: Printed for John Williams, and sold by Ben. Billingsley and Tho. Cockeril, 1675.

Edition 5 of No. *310*. Allusions, pp. 376, 389, 395 (?), 425. Wing, R1976. Copy owned by Princeton Theological Seminary Library.

700   *Politischer discursus, zwischen monogamo und polygamum von der polygamia* [etc.]. Gedruckt zu Freyburch, Im Jare Anno 1675. dem 1. Januarius.

Author: Johan Leyser (Lyser). Allusion, E4v. Copy owned by British Library.

701   *A Replie to a person of honour* [etc.]. London: Printed for Henry Brome, 1675.

Author: Peter Du Moulin. Reference to *Eikonoklastes* or *Defensio prima* and Du Moulin's *Regii Sanguinis Clamor*, p. 40. Parker (II, 1201) erroneously lists pp. 10 and 45 as well; p. 10 has a reference to *Regii Sanguinis Clamor*, and p. 45 (given as 37) is a reprint of a 1642 Proclamation. Wing, D2564. Copy owned by Union Theological Seminary Library (McAlpin Collection).

702   *Theatrum poetarum, or a compleat collection of the poets, especially the most eminent, of all ages* [etc.]. *Together with a prefatory discourse of the poets and poetry in generall* [etc.]. London: Printed for Charles Smith, 1675.

Author: Edward Phillips. Comment and entry, pp. 18–28 (Preface), 113–114 (second pagination, under Milton), 114–115 (second pagination, under John Phillips). Wing, P2075. Copy owned by Yale University Library.

A copy in the Bodleian Library has Anthony Wood's holograph notes; he remarks alongside the entry to Phillips citing but not naming Milton that the reference is to Milton, "a rogue," and that John is the author's brother.

703   *The Works of the famous Nicolas Machiavel* [etc.]. London: Printed for John Starkey, 1675.

Issue one. Listings of "A Catalogue of Books Printed for John Starkey [etc.]." Folio in fours, Zzz2–Zzz4, unpaged. *Tetrachordon* (item 4, Zzz2), *Paradise Regain'd* and *Samson Agonistes* (item 67, Zzz4), *Accedence Commenc't Grammar* (item 73, Zzz4). See Wing, M128. Copy owned by Princeton University Library.

704   *The Works of the famous Nicholas Machiavelli* [etc.]. London, Printed for J. S. and are to be sold by Robert Boulter, 1675.

Different issue of No. *703*. "A Catalogue of Books Printed for John Starkey [etc.]," Lll2–Lll4, unpaged. Listings of *Tetrachordon* (item 4, Lll2); *Paradise Regain'd* and *Samson Agonistes* (item 67, Lll4); and *Accedence Commenc't Grammar* (item 73, Lll4). See Wing, M128. Copy owned by Newberry Library.

1676

705 *Aureng-Zebe: a tragedy. Acted at the Royal Theatre* [etc.]. London: Printed by T. N., for Henry Herringman, 1676.

Author: John Dryden. Imitation of *Samson Agonistes*, Act I (four lines; Emperor: "Unmov'd she stood, and deaf to all my prayers [etc.]"), p. 8. Wing, D2245. Copy owned by Folger Shakespeare Library.

706 *Bibliotheca curiosa in qua plurimi rarissimi atque paucis cogniti scriptores, interq́; eos antiquorium ecclesiæ doctorum* [etc.]. Regiomonti et Francofurti sumptibus Martini Hallervordii Typis Johannis Nisii, Anno 1676.

Author: Johannes Hallervordius. Allusion in listing of 1660 Salmasius work, p. 51. Copy owned by Columbia University Library.

707 *Britannia antiqua illustrata or, the antiquities of ancient Britain* [etc.]. London: Printed by Tho. Roycroft, for the author, 1676.

Author: Aylett Sammes. Allusions, pp. 48, 50, 83, 387, 476–477 (on translation from Gildas in *History of Britain* with quotation), 559 (with quotation from *History of Britain*). Wing, S535. Copy owned by Yale University Library.

708 *Catalogus cujuscumque facultatis & linguæ librorum, abhinc 2 a 3 annorum spatio in Germania, Gallia, & Belgi, &c. Novissime impressorum. Singulis semestribus continuandus*, Amstelædami: Apud Jansenio-Waesbergius.

Dated: 1676. Listing: p. 17, *Artis Logicæ*. Copy owned by Bodleian Library.

709 *Catalogus variorum & insignium librorum instructissimae Bibliothecae clarissimi doctissimiq' viri Lazari Seaman, S. T. D.* [etc.]. Cura Gulielmi Cooper bibliopolae. Londini: Apud Ed. Brewster & Guil. Cooper, 1676.

Listings: *Areopagitica*, p. 60; *Tenure of Kings and Magistrates*, p. 63; *Reason of Church-Government, Of Prelatical Episcopacy, Apology for Smectymnuus*, p. 64. Wing, S2173. Copy owned by Henry E. Huntington Library.

710 *A Chronicle of the late intestine war in the three kingdoms of England, Scotland and Ireland* [etc.]. *To which is added a continuation to this present year 1675* [etc.]. *by J. P.* London: Printed by J. C., for Thomas Basset, 1676.

Another edition of No. *557*. Continuation written by John Phillips. Allusion, p. 236 and margin. Wing, H1321. Copy owned by University of Kentucky Library.

711 *Elenchi motuum nuperorum in Anglia, Pars III. Sive, motus compositi* [etc.]. Londini: Typis Guil. Godbid, prostant autem venales apud Mosem Pitt, 1676.

Author: Thomas Skinner. Discussion of antimonarchical position, p. 90. Wing, S3948. Copy owned by University of Kentucky Library.

712 *Elenchus motuum nuperorum in Anglia* [etc.]. Londini: Typis R. W. pro R. Royston; & Prostat venalis apud J. Martyn, R. Chiswell, & B. Tooke, 1676.

Another edition of No. *528*. Allusion, p. 120; included in Index, A8. Wing, B1082. Copy owned by University of Kentucky Library.

713 The Hague. Algemeen Rijksarchief. Holland 203; Foreign Entry Books, London, No. 66.

Letter from Daniel Elsevier to Sir Joseph Williamson, dated 20 November 1676. On publication of *Literae*. In French.

714 *Das Königliche marck aller länder | das ist: Politischer discurs zwischen polygamo und monogamo von der polygamia* [etc.]. Freburgi: Apud Henricum Cunrath, 1676.

Another edition of No. *700*. Allusion, F4. Copy owned by British Library.

715 [Letter from Christopher Arnold to Theophilus Spizelius, dated 5 May 1676.]

Discussion concerning Salmasian and More controversies. Printed in Johan G. Schelhorn, *Amœnitatis Literariæ* [etc.]. Francofurti & Lipsiæ, Apud Daniel Bartholomæi & Filium, 1731. XIV, 571–573. Copy owned by Newberry Library.

716 London. Public Record Office. SP 29/386/65.

Statement by Daniel Skinner, dated 18 October 1676, concerning publication of state papers.

717 London. Public Record Office. SP 84/202.

Letter from John Ellis to Sir Joseph Williamson, dated 23 October 1676, ff. 389–390. Discussion of letters of state recently published (i. e., *Literae*).

718 London. Public Record Office. SP 84/203.

Letter from Sir Leoline Jenkins to Sir Joseph Williamson, dated 6 November 1676, ff. 24–25. Discussion of *Literae*, Daniel Skinner, his manuscript of the state papers, and negative appraisal of Milton.

Letter from Daniel Elsevier to Sir Joseph Williamson, dated 20 November 1676, ff. 106–107. Original of No. *713*.

719 *The London Gazette*. No. 1172. Thursday, February 8 to Monday, February 12. 1676. Printed by Tho: Newcomb in the Savoy, 1676.

Advertisement for *The State of Innocence, and Fall of Man*. Copy owned by New York Public Library.

720 Oxford. Bodleian Library. Rawlinson MS A.185.

Samuel Pepys papers. Letter from Sir Leoline Jenkins to Pepys, dated 9 August 1676, recommending Daniel Skinner as secretary, f. 204.

Letter from Daniel Skinner to Pepys, dated 19 November 1676, on difficulties in publishing Milton's work, f. 271–271v. Additional note requests Sir Joseph Williamson's feelings in the matter, f. 273. Notation on envelope, f. 274, in different hand.

Letter from Daniel Skinner to Pepys, dated 5 July 1676, concerning recommendation, ff. 396–397v. In Latin.

721 Oxford. Bodleian Library. Rawlinson MS A.352.

Letter from Sir Joseph Williamson to Sir Leoline Jenkins, dated 31 October 1676, f. 277, concerning Daniel Skinner's becoming Chudleigh's secretary. Williamson says Skinner was party to publishing Milton's works, which are to be printed by the Elzeviers in Holland, including *Literae*. Admonition of Skinner for friendship with Milton.

Letter from Sir Joseph Williamson to Mr. Chudleigh, dated 28 November 1676, f. 295, discussion of Daniel Skinner's friendship with Milton.

722 *Poems and songs. By Thomas Flatman. The second edition with additions and amendments* [etc.]. London: Printed by S. and B. G., for Benjamin Took and Jonathan Edwin, 1676.

Edition 2 of No. *686*. Wing, F1152. Copy owned by Robert H. Taylor, Princeton, New Jersey.

723 *Politischer discurs zwischen polygamo und monogamo von der polygamia oder vielweiberey auffgesetzt und mit mehr als 100*. Argumenten erklärct. von J. L. Friburgi, Apud Henricum Cunrath. Anno. 1676.

Another edition of No. *700*. Page numbers and signatures cropped. See [F4] for allusion. Copy owned by Andover-Harvard Law Library, Harvard University.

724   *Poor robin. 1676. An almanack after a new fashion.*

Colophon: "London, Printed for the Company of Stationers." Allusion, under
2 November. Wing, A2195. Copy owned by Folger Shakespeare Library.

725   *Chr. Funcci Quadripartitum historico-politicum orbis hodie-imperantis breviarum* [etc.].
Lipsiæ, Impensis J. A. Kæstneri, 1676.

Edition 2 of No. *667.* Copy owned by Bibliothèque Nationale.

726   *The Royal martyr: or, the life and death of King Charles I* [etc.]. London: Printed
by J. M., for R. Royston, 1676.

Author: Richard Perrinchief. First published in No. *543.* Milton as author
of *Eikonoklastes* and *Defensio prima*, pp. 209–210. Wing, P1601. Copy owned
by Union Theological Seminary Library (McAlpin Collection).

727   *The Works of the most reverend father in God, John Bramhall, D. D.* [etc.]. Dublin:
Printed at His Majesties Printing-House, Anno. Dom. 1676.

Editor: John Vesey. Collected edition including No. *12.* Reprint of *The
Serpent-Salve*, Dublin, 1675, Vol. II (continuous pagination): allusion to an-
tiepiscopal tracts, p. 598 and margin. Wing, B4210. Copy owned by University of Kentucky Library. No copy of *The Serpent-Salve* from 1675 is known.

728   *The Works of the most reverend father in God, John Bramhall D. D.* [etc.]. Dublin:
Printed by Benjamin Tooke, 1676.

Another issue of No. *727.* See Wing, B4210. Copy owned by Newberry
Library.

729   *The Works of the most reverend father in God, John Bramhall D. D.* [etc.]. Dublin:
Printed by Benjamin Tooke, 1676.

Another issue of No. *727.* See, e. g., pp. c2; different signatures in *Life.*
See Wing, B4210. Copy owned by Newberry Library.

1677

730   *An Account of the growth of popery, and arbitrary government in England* [etc.].
Amsterdam, Printed in the Year 1677.

Author: Andrew Marvell. Place: London. Title page in this issue has double-
ruled border and no comma before date. Possible influence from *Areopagitica*;
see especially pp. 60–61 and 72–73, and compare *Areopagitica*, pp. 36 and

34–35. Possible reference to divorce views, pp. 48–49. Wing, M860. Copy owned by New York Public Library.

731 *An Account of the growth of popery and arbitrary government in England* [etc.]. Amsterdam, Printed in the Year, 1677.

Different edition of No. *730*. Title page has no border and comma before date. References cited in No. *730* will be found on pp. 44, 55, 66. See Wing, M860. Copy owned by Newberry Library.

732 *Bibliographia historico-politico-philologica curiosa* [etc.]. Germanopoli, 1677.

Author: Johann Heinrich Boecler. Listing of *Defensio prima*, p. [143] (i. e., I8). Copy owned by Columbia University Library.

733 *A Catalogue of books continued, printed and published at London in Hilary-term, 1676.* No. 10. 12 February 1676.

Dated: 1677. Colophon: "*Collected by* Robert Clavel *in Cross-keys Court in* Little Britain." Listing of *The State of Innocence.* Copy owned by Henry E. Huntington Library.

734 *A Catalogue of books continued, printed, and published at London in Easter-term, 1677.* No. 11. 28 May 1677.

Listing of *The History of Britain.* Copy owned by Henry E. Huntington Library.

735 *Catalogus variorum & insignium librorum selectissimæ bibliothecæ Reverendi viri D. Thomæ Kidner, A. M.* [etc.]. Per Guilielmum Cooper, bibliopolam [etc.].

Dated: 6 February 1677. Listings: *Doctrine and Discipline of Divorce, Paradise Lost, Tetrachordon*, p. 19; *Paradise Lost* (twice), *Poems* (1673 ["1633"]), p. 40. Wing, K422. Copy owned by Henry E. Huntington Library.

736 *Charismatum sacrorum trias, sive bibliotheca Anglorum theologica* [etc.]. Impensis Martini Hallervordii bibliopolæ, ex officina Reichiana, 1677.

Author: Martin von Kempen. Place: Königsberg. Reference to divorce position on pp. 337, 461 (*Tetrachordon*), and 484 (comment: "Jesuitis felicior, ipso diabolo audacior"). Listing in second index, (d1)v. Copy owned by Newberry Library.

737 *The Diary and autobiography of Edmund Bohun esq.* [etc.]. Privately printed at Beccles, by Read Crisp, 1853.

Editor: S. Wilton Rix. Reference to *Literae* as "dry and useless," p. 4, under date of 31 March 1677. Favorable comment on *History of Britain*, p. 33, under date of 4 August 1677. In Latin; translations given. Copy owned by New York Public Library.

738   An Elegie upon the death of the Reverend Mr. Thomas Shepard, late teacher of the church at Charlstown in New-England [etc.]. Cambridge, Mass.: Printed by Samuel Green, 1677.

Author: Urian Oakes. Influence, passim, from Samson Agonistes in imagery and diction. Evans 240. Copy owned by New York Public Library.

739   The English parnassus: or a help to English poesie [etc.]. London: Printed for Henry Brome, Thomas Bassett, and John Wright, 1677.

Another edition of No. 388. Allusion, p. 34, and appropriations from Poems (1645) throughout. Wing, P2815. Copy owned by University of Kentucky Library.

740   A Fresh suit against Independency: or the national church-way vindicated, the independent church-way condemned [etc.]. London: Printed for Walter Kettilby, 1677.

Author: Thomas Lamb. Allusion to Hirelings, p. 94 and margin. Wing, L120. Copy owned by Union Theological Seminary Library (McAlpin Collection).

741   Georgii Hornii historia ecclesiastica. cum annotationibus Daniels Hartnaccii, Pomerani. Lipsiæ: Prostant apud Jo. Ad. Kästnerum, Bibliop. Görliceus. Literis Wittigavianis, 1677.

Another edition of No. 585. Reference to divorce views, p. 580; discussion of letters, pp. 654–655. Listed in Index. Copy owned by Cambridge University Library.

742   Gerhardi Feltmanni J Cti & in Academ. Gromvig. antecessorus primarii tractatus de polygamia [etc.]. Leipzig: In verlegung Matthäuss Birckners | Druckts Johann Köhler | 1677.

Allusion, p. 214. Copy owned by British Library.

743   The Hague. Algemeen Rijkarchief. Holland 203; Foreign Entry Books, London, No. 66.

Letter from Sir Joseph Williamson to R. Meredith, dated 19 (29) January 1677. On the publication of Literae.

744   The Hague. Algemeen Rijkarchief. Holland 204; Foreign Entry Books, London, No. 66.

Letter from R. Meredith to Sir Joseph Williamson, dated 5 February 1677. On the publication of Literae.

Letter from R. Meredith to Sir Joseph Williamson, dated 9 February 1677. See No. *746*.

Letter from R. Meredith to Sir Joseph Williamson, dated 12 February 1677. See No. *746*.

Letter from Daniel Elzevier to Daniel Skinner, Sr., dated 19 February 1677. On the publication of *Literae*. In French.

Letter from R. Meredith to Sir Joseph Williamson, dated 26 February 1677. On the publication of *Literae*.

Letter from Daniel Elzevier to Daniel Skinner, Sr., dated 16 March 1677. On the publication of *Literae*. In French.

745 [Letter from William Perwich to William Bridgeman, dated 15 March 1677.]

On the publication of *Literae*. Printed in Charles R. Sumner's translation and edition of *A Treatise of Christian Doctrine* [etc.]. Cambridge: Cambridge University Press, 1825. Pp. xi–xii.

746 London. Public Record Office. MS SP 82/204.

Letter from Roger Meredith to Sir Joseph Williamson, dated 9 February 1677, ff. 101v–102. Reference to "Milton's book" (i. e., *Literae*).

Letter from Roger Meredith to Sir Joseph Williamson, dated 2/12 February 1677, f. 108v. Reference to "Milton's book" (i. e., *Literae*).

Printed denunciation in Latin of the publication of *Literae*, 1676, f. 120. Apparently a printer's flyer. Columbia Edition (XVIII, 648) prints the advertisement and assigns it to the Elzeviers "when they planned to print Skinner's MS."

747 London. Public Record Office. SP Car. II. 390/159 (1).

Letter from Dr. Isaac Barrow to Daniel Skinner, dated 13 February 1677, f. 372. Allusion to publishing "any writing mischievous to the Church or State."

748 *Memoires of the lives, actions, sufferings & deaths of those noble, reverend, and excellent personages* [etc.]. *With the life and martyrdom of King Charles I* [etc.]. London: Printed for Dorman Newman, 1677.

Another edition of No. *467*. Wing, L2643. Copy owned by British Library.

749 Oxford. Bodleian Library. Rawlinson MS A.185.

Samuel Pepys papers. Letters from Daniel Skinner to Pepys, dated 28 January 1677, ff. 133–134v. Discussion of attempts to publish Milton's works.

750   *Poems. By N. Tate.* London: Printed by T. M., for Benj. Tooke, 1677.

Author: Nahum Tate. Opposition to *Paradise Lost*'s substance and verse in "On the Present Corrupted State of Poetry," pp. 14–19. Reference to "a meer Fools Paradise," in "The Match," p. 70; appropriation from "Nativity Ode" in "On Snow Fall'n in Autumn, and Dissolv'd by the Sun," pp. 88–89. Wing, T208. Copy owned by Folger Shakespeare Library.

751   *Poor robin. 1677. An almanack after a new fashion.*

Colophon: "London, Printed for the Company of Stationers." Allusion, under 3 November. Copy owned by Henry E. Huntington Library.

752   *The Reasoning apostate: or modern latitude-man consider'd, as he opposeth the authority of the king and church* [etc.]. London: Printed for T. Basset, 1677.

Author: John Warly [Warley]. Allusion to *Treatise of Civil Power*, pp. 24–25; use of the tract is noted on *4v. Wing, W877. Copy owned by Union Theological Seminary Library (McAlpin Collection).

753   *The Rival queens, or the death of Alexander the Great* [etc.]. London: Printed for James Magnes and Richard Bentley, 1677.

Author: Nathaniel Lee. Imitation, Act IV, p. 44. Wing, L865. Copy owned by University of Kentucky Library.

754   THE | State of Innocence, | AND | FALL of MAN: | AN | OPERA. | Written in Heroique Verse, | And Dedicated to her *Royal Highness*, | THE | DUTCHESS. | ——— | by *John Dryden*, Servant to His Majesty. | ——— | [two lines in Latin from Ovid's *Metamorphoses*] | ——— | *LONDON:* Printed by *T. N.* for *Henry Herringman*, at the | Anchor in the Lower Walk of the *New Exchange*. 1677. |

Quarto. π^1 A b^4 c^2 B–G^4(–G4); xxii + 46 pp. G4 used as π1. [i], title page; [ii], blank; [iii–viii], dedication; [ix–x], Lee's poem; [xi–xxii], preface; 1–45, work; [46], blank. Based on *Paradise Lost*, with discussion in preface and allusion in Nathaniel Lee's congratulatory poem. Wing, D2372. Copy owned by Folger Shakespeare Library. Another copy is misbound: A4 bound before A1.

755   THE | State of Innocence, | AND | FALL of MAN: | AN | OPERA. | Written in Heroique Verse, | And Dedicated to Her *Royal Highness*, | THE | DUTCHESS. | ——— | By *John Dryden*, Servant to His Majesty. | ——— | [two-line epigraph] | ——— | *LONDON:* Printed by *T. N.* for *Henry Herringman*, at the | Anchor in the Lower Walk of the *New Exchange*. 1677. |

Edition 2 of No. *754.* Typographical differences. Quarto. π^1 A b^4 c^2

B-G^4(-G4); xxii + 46 pp. G4 used for π1. Wing, B2373. Copy owned by
Henry E. Huntington Library.

756 *The Works of the most reverend father in God, John Bramhall D. D.* [etc.]. Dublin:
Printed by Benjamin Tooke, 1677.

Another edition of No. *727*, but with reprint of *The Serpent-Salve*, 1674 (edition otherwise unknown). Wing, B4211. Copy owned by Columbia University Library.

757 *The Works of the most reverend father in God, John Bramhall D. D.* [etc.]. Dublin:
Printed by Benjamin Tooke, 1677.

Another edition (reissue?) of No. *727*. The recto of the sixth leaf of the collection has rules in the heading, and the seventh leaf is correctly positioned after the Life. Cf. No. *758*. Copy owned by Newberry Library.

758 *The Works of the most reverend father in God, John Bramhall D. D.* [etc.]. Dublin:
Printed by Benjamin Tooke, 1677.

Another issue of No. *757*. The recto of the sixth leaf of the collection has no rules in the heading, and the seventh sheet is incorrectly positioned before the Life. Cf. No. *757*. Copy owned by Newberry Library.

1678

759 *An Account of the growth of popery, and arbitrary government* [etc.]. Printed at *Amsterdam*, and recommended to the reading of all *English* Protestants.

Another edition of No. *730*. Dated: 1678. Folio. Imitations, pp. 20, 24; influence, p. 16. Wing, M861. Copy owned by Folger Shakespeare Library.
Apparently Wing, M862, is another copy of this edition.

760 *Bibliotheca vetus et nova* [etc.]. Altdorfi: Henrici Meyeri, apud Wolffgangi
Mauritii et Johannis Andreæ, 1678.

Author: Georg Matthias König. Entry concerned with Salmasian controversy, p. 541. Copy owned by British Library.

761 *Catalogus librorum ex bibliotheca nobilis cujusdam Angli* [etc.]. Per Nathanielem
Ranew, bibliopolam The catalogues will be distributed gratis, by Nathaniel
Ranew — bookseller, 1678.

Owner: Gabriel Sanger. Listings: p. 48, item 130, *Smectymnuus Redivivus*
(1660); p. 89, No. 16, item 11, *Tenure of Kings and Magistrates*. Wing, S681.
Copy owned by British Library.

762   *Catalogus librorum in quavis lingua & facultate insignium instructissimarum*
      bibliothecarum tum clarissimi doctissimique viri D. Doctoris Benjaminis Worsley [etc.].
      Per Joan. Dunmore & Ric. Chiswell, Bibliopolas [etc.]. 1678.

      Listings: *Epistolarum Familiarium Liber Unus*, p. 31; *Artis Logicae*, p. 46; a group
      consisting of works by Salmasius, Du Moulin, and More, and the three
      Defenses, p. 47 (second pagination). *Eikon Aklastos*, p. 14; *History of Britain*,
      p. 17; *Doctrine and Discipline of Divorce*, p. 18; Salmasius's 1660 volume, p.
      21; *Poems* (1673), p. 38; and *Civil Power, Hirelings, Accedence Commenc't Gram-*
      mar, p. 55 (third pagination). *Areopagitica, Doctrine and Discipline of Divorce*,
      p. 16; "Unlawfulness and danger of limited Prelaty," assigned to Milton,
      and *Prelatical Episcopacy*, p. 26 (new pagination). Wing, W3612. Copy owned
      by British Library.

763   *Catalogus variorum & insignium librorum instructissimæ bibliothecæ clarissimi doc-*
      tissimiq; viri Thomæ Manton, S. T. D. [etc.]. Per Guilielmum Cooper,
      Bibliopolam [etc.]. 1678.

      Listings: *History of Britain* and *Paradise Lost*, p. 38; *Tenure of Kings and*
      Magistrates, p. 43; "Milton's good English, or Reason pointing out the safest
      way of Settlement in this kingdom 1648" and *Areopagitica*, p. 47 (i. e., 45).
      Wing M519. Copy owned by British Library.

764   *Catalogus variorum & insignium librorum instructissimarum bibliothecarum doctiss.*
      clarissimorumq; virorum D. Johannis Godolphin, J. U. D. et D. Oweni Phillips,
      A. M. [etc.]. Per Gulielmum Cooper Bibliopolam [etc.]. 1678.

      Dated: 11 November 1678. Listing: *Paradise Lost*, p. 5 (second pagination).
      Wing, G942. Copy owned by Henry E. Huntington Library.

765   *Catalogus variorum librorum instructissimæ bibliothecæ* [etc.]. *Ex bibliotheca clarissimi*
      Gisberti Voetii [etc.].

      Dated: 25 November 1678. Listings: *Defensio secunda*, p. 83; *Defensio prima*
      and *Artis Logicae* (twice), p. 100; group of works including Salmasius, *Defen-*
      sio prima, More, *Defensio pro Se*, Du Moulin, *Defensio secunda*, p. 104. *Paradise*
      Lost, p. 10 (new pagination). Wing, V675. Copy owned by British Library.

766   *A Discourse concerning the gift of prayer* [etc.]. *Whereunto may be added, Ecclesiastes*
      [etc.]. London: Printed by A. M. and R. R., for Edw. Gellibrand, 1678.

      Another edition of No. *296*, to which is added a copy of No. *783*. Wing,
      W2183 and W2194. Copy owned by Union Theological Seminary Library
      (McAlpin Collection).

767   *The English parnassus: or a help to English poesie* [etc.]. London: Printed for
      H. Brome, T. Bassett, J. Wright, and sold by Joseph Hindmarsh, 1678.

Reissue of No. *739*. Wing, P2816. Copy owned by Princeton University Library.

768 *Epistolæ ho-elianæ. Familiar letters, domestic and forren* [etc.]. *The fifth edition* [etc.]. London: Printed for Thomas Guy, 1678.

Edition 5 of No. *355*, reissue of No. *664*. Wing, H3075. Copy owned by University of Kentucky Library.

769 *Francisci Vavassoris societ. Jesu de epigrammate liber et epigrammatvm libri quatuor. Aucto libro editio.* Parisiis: Ex officina Edmundi Martini, 1678.

Another edition of No. *610*. Comment on Milton and Salmasius, pp. 301–302. Copy owned by British Library.

770 *Henry the Third of France, stabb'd by a fryer. With the fall of the Guise* [etc.]. London: Printed by B. G., for Sam. Heyrick, 1678.

Author: Thomas Shipman. Preface, "To Roger L'Estrange, Esq;": disavowal of Milton's blank verse and reference to Thomas Rymer's promised discussion (see No. *778*), A4v–*1. Wing, S3441. Copy owned by Columbia University Library.

771 [Letter from John Wilmot, Earl of Rochester, to George Savile, Marquis of Halifax, dated July 1678.]

Allusion to *Paradise Lost* I. Printed in No. *1528*.

772 *Linguæ Latinæ liber dictionarius quadripartitus. A Latine dictionary, in four parts* [etc.]. London: Printed for T. Basset, J. Wright, and R. Chiswell, 1678.

Author: Adam Littleton. No indication of the use of Milton's lost Latin thesaurus, but see No. *1363*. In Latin and English. Wing, L2563. Copy owned by New York Public Library.

773 *M. Johannis Diecmanni vindiciæ legis monogamicæ, primùm brevi examine in Johannis Lyseri discursum politicum Germanicum de polygamia* [etc.]. Stadæ: Typis Casparis Holvveinii, A. 1678.

Discussion in "Iteratæ Vindiciæ legis monogamicæ, seu Responsio Apologetica, Lyseriano Examini Examinis opposita," Section XXX, pp. 173–174. Listed in indices under Divortium and under name. Copy owned by Bibliothèque Nationale.

774 New Haven, Connecticut. James Osborn Collection, Yale University Library. MS b54.

Copy of John Ayloffe's "Andrew Marvell's Ghost. Aug: 1678," pp. 1089–90. See No. *1210.*

775 Oxford. Bodleian Library. Wood MS F.39.

Letter from John Aubrey to Anthony Wood, dated 17 August 1678, f. 311, on Milton's burial. Note by Wood, f. 387v.

776 *A Paraphrase upon the psalms of David. The second edition corrected by the author.* London: J. M., for John Martyn, John Baker, and Henry Brome, 1678.

Edition 2 of No. *596.* Possible allusion, a4v. Wing, B2529. Copy owned by New York Public Library.

777 THE | State of Innocence, | AND | FALL of MAN: | AN | OPERA. | Written in Heroick Verse; | And Dedicated to Her Royal *Highness* | THE | DUTCHESS. | ──── | By *John Dryden*, Servant to His Majesty. | ──── | [two lines in Latin from Ovid's *Metamorphoses*] | ──── | *LONDON:* Printed by *H. H.* for *Henry Herringman*, at the | Anchor in the Lower Walk of the *New Exchange.* 1678. |

Edition 3 of No. *754.* Quarto. A–H^4; xx + 44 pp. [i], title page; [ii], blank; [iii–iv], Dedication; [vii–viii], Lee's poem; [ix–xx], Preface; 1–44, text. Wing, D2374. Copy owned by Folger Shakespeare Library.

778 *The Tragedies of the last age consider'd and examin'd* [etc.]. London: Printed for Richard Tonson, 1678.

Author: Thomas Rymer. Allusion to blank verse, p. 143. Wing, R2430. Copy owned by Folger Shakespeare Library.

1679

779 *Behemoth: or, an epitome of the civil wars of England from 1640, to 1660* [etc.]. London: Printed Anno Dom. 1679.

Author: Thomas Hobbes. Edition 3 of No. *788.* Allusion to Salmasian controversy, p. 172. Wing, H2213. Copy owned by Columbia University Library.

780 *Catalogus librorum in plurimis linguis maxime insignium bibliothecarum viri eruditi Stephani Watkins, D. Doctoris Thomæ Sherley* [etc.]. Per Gulielmo Cooperum, bibliopolam [etc.]. 1679.

Listings: *Eikonoklastes*, p. 24; *Artis Logicae*, p. 32; *Literae*, p. 33. Further listings in "Appendix" by Richard Chiswell: *History of Britain*, M2v; *Epistolarum Familiarium Liber Unus*, N2; *Paradise Lost*, P2; *Smectymnuus Answer*, p. 9, and *Doctrine and Discipline of Divorce* (1645), p. 26, in new pagination. Wing, W1077. Copy owned by British Library.

781 *The Confession of faith and the larger & shorter catechism* [etc.]. Printed in the Year 1679.

Another edition of No. *45*. Place: Leyden (?). Allusion, p. 83. Copy owned by Cambridge University Library.

782 *Dagon's Fall: or the knight turn'd out of commission.*

Author: anonymous. Date: 1679? or 1680?. No title page. A^1; 2 pp. Possible influence from *Samson Agonistes* in language and image. Wing, D111. Copy owned by Bodleian Library.

783 *Ecclesiastes: or, a discourse concerning the gift of preaching, as it falls under the rules of art. The sixth impression, corrected and enlarged* [etc.]. London: Printed by A. M. and R. R., for Edw. Gellibrand, 1679.

See No. *766*. Allusion, p. 181. Wing, W2194. Copy owned by Union Theological Seminary Library (McAlpin Collection).

784 *Female excellence: or, woman display'd, in several satyrick poems. By a person of quality* [etc.]. London: Printed for Norman Nelson, 1679.

Author: anonymous. Wing assigns to Rochester. Four poems, two of which may show some influence from *Paradise Lost*; see, e. g., the second, "A Satyr upon Woman's Usurpation." Wing, R1749. Copy owned by Bodleian Library.

785 *The Free-holders grand inquest, touching our sovereign lord the king and his parliament. To which are added Observations upon forms of government* [etc.]. London: Printed in the year 1679.

Another issue of No. *276*. Continuous signatures, separate paging for *Observations upon Aristotle* and *Observations concerning the original of government*, but the remainder continues pagination as if it were continuous throughout. *Observations concerning the original of government* reprinted on N1–R8v; allusion on half-title, N1, and *Observations on Milton* on O5–P4v, pp. 17–32. See Wing, F913 and F914. Copy owned by New York Public Library.

786 *The Free-holders grand inquest, touching our sovereign lord the king and his parliament. To which are added Observations upon forms of government* [etc.]. London: Printed in the year 1679.

Different issue of No. *785*. Signatures and pagination are continuous. Reissue of 1679 title page for *Reflections concerning the original of government* (No. *800*) on A7 (no pagination). *Observations concerning the original of government* reprinted on N1–R8v (omitting the discussion of Phillip Hunton, which follows), pp. [i–viii], 165–236, with half-title on N1. *Observations on Milton* given on O5–P4v, pp. 181–196. See Wing, F913 and F914. Copy owned by Princeton University Library.

787   *Gewissenhaffte gedancken vom ehstande zusammen getragen von Gottlieb Warmund.* Friburg. Gedruckt durch Henricum Kunrad, 1679.

Another edition of No. *700*. Allusion, Section XI, p. [7]. Copy owned by University of Chicago Library.

788   *The History of the civil wars of England. From the year 1640, to 1660* [etc.]. Printed in the year 1679.

Author: Thomas Hobbes. Place: London. Edition 1 of *Behemoth*. Octavo. A^1 B–T^8 V^4. Allusion to Salmasian controversy, p. 229. Wing, H2239. Copy owned by Columbia University Library.

789   *The History of the civil wars of England. From the year 1640, to 1660* [etc.]. Printed in the year, 1679.

Edition 2 of No. *788*. Place: London. Octavo in twelves. A^1 B–N^{12}. Allusion, p. 229. Wing, H2240. Copy owned by Union Theological Seminary Library (McAlpin Collection).

790   *A Just vindication of learning: or, an humble address to the high court of Parliament in behalf of the liberty of the press. By Philopatris* [etc.]. London: 1679.

Author: Charles Blount. Adapted from *Areopagitica*, 18 pp. Milton discussed in Proem. Wing, B3307. Copy owned by Yale University Library.

791   *Naboth's vinyard: or, the innocent traytor* [etc.]. London: Printed for C. R., 1679.

Author: John Caryll. Folio. Imitation drawn from *Paradise Lost* in ll. 205–214, p. 10. Wing, C745A. Copy owned by New York Public Library.

792   *Naboth's vinyard: or, the innocent traytor* [etc.]. London: Printed for C. R., 1679.

Another edition of No. 791. Quarto. Imitation, pp. 10–11. Wing, C745B. Copy owned by Folger Shakespeare Library.

793   *Narration veritable de l'execrable conspiration du parti papiste* [etc.]. Suivant la copie de Londres   1679.

Author: Titus Oates. Anonymous French translation of No. *806*. Dated:

1679 (?). Reference to Milton as a papist, p. 10. Copy owned by Princeton University Library.

Another French translation does not include section with allusion; see *Relation veritable de l'Horrible Conspiration des Papistes* [etc.]. A Londres. Chez Thomas Newcomb, & se vendent chés Richard Bentley, & chez André Forrester, 1679. Copy in Bibliothèque Nationale.

794   *Noah's flood, or, the destruction of the world. An opera* [etc.]. London: Printed by M. Clark, and sold by B. Tooke, 1679.

Author: Edward Ecclestone. Words only. Allusions: Richard Saunders, "To My Worthy and Ingenious Freind, Mr. Edward Ecclestone, Upon His Publishing his Opera," p. [vii]; John Learned, "To his Worthy and Ingenious Friend, Mr. Edward Ecclestone, upon his Publishing Noah's Flood, or the Destruction of the World," p. [viii]; John Norton, "To His Ingenious Friend, Mr. Ecclestone, on his Opera," p. [x]; "Epistle to the Reader," pp. [xii–xiv]. Cited in the "Epistle" are *Paradise Lost* and *The State of Innocence*, with quotations from both. Influences from both works are found throughout the opera, although only that from *The State of Innocence* has sometimes been cited. Wing, E140. Copy owned by Henry E. Huntington Library.

795   *Order and disorder: or, the world made and undone. Being meditations upon the creation and the fall; as it is recorded in the beginning of Genesis.* London: Printed by Margaret White, for Henry Mortlack, 1679.

Author: Sir Allen Apsley. Influence from *Paradise Lost*, passim. Wing, A3594. Copy owned by Folger Shakespeare Library.

796   Oxford. All Souls College Library. Codrington MS 116.

Copy of John Ayloffe's "Marvell's Ghost. 1679," ff. 11v–12. See No. *1210*.

797   Oxford. Bodleian Library. Wood MS F.39.

Letter from John Aubrey to Anthony Wood, dated St. John's Day, 1679, f. 327v. Allusion.

798   *A Paraphrase upon the canticles* [etc.]. London: Printed by J. D. for John Baker and Henry Brome, 1679.

Author: Samuel Woodford. See No. *596*. Revised preface. Paraphrase of lines in *Paradise Lost* and discussion of blank verse, b6v–c3. Not in Wing. Copy owned by Princeton University Library.

799   *Poems in two parts* [etc.]. London: Printed for Tho. Cockeril, 1679.

Author: Samuel Slater. Possible influence from *Paradise Lost* in first poem,

"A Discourse Concerning the Creation, Fall, and Recovery of Man." There is an allusion in "To the Reader," A2v. Wing, S3967. Copy owned by Newberry Library.

800   *Reflections concerning the original of government, upon ... III. Mr. Milton against Salmasius* [etc.]. London: Printed in the Year 1679.

Author: Sir Robert Filmer. Reprint of No. *276*; separate pagination. Discussion on pp. 17–32. Wing, F928. Copy owned by Union Theological Seminary Library (McAlpin Collection).

801   *The Reformed Catholique: or, the true Protestant* [etc.]. London: Printed for Henry Brome, 1679.

Author: Sir Roger L'Estrange. Allusion, pp. 16–17. Wing, L1289. Copy owned by New York Public Library.

802   *The Reformed Catholique: or, the true Protestant* [etc.]. *The second edition corrected.* London: Printed for Henry Brome, 1679.

Edition 2 of No. *801*. Allusion, p. 17. Wing, L1290. Copy owned by Columbia University Library.

803   *The Reformed Catholique: or the true Protestant* [etc.]. Dublin, Reprinted, M.DC,LXXIX.

Another edition of No. *801*. Allusion, pp. 8–9. Wing, L1291. Copy owned by Trinity College Library, Dublin.

804   *Sacrarum profanarúmque phrasium poeticarum thesaurus* [etc.]. Londini: Typis Thomæ Newcombe, 1679.

Reissue of No. *628*, including Phillips's appendix with title page dated 1679. Wing, B5305. (Wing, B5304, is also a copy of this edition.) Copy owned by Princeton Theological Seminary Library.

805   *A Sermon preached on the thirtieth of January, 1678/9. Being the anniversary of the martyrdom of King Charles the first* [etc.]. London: Printed for Jonathan Edwin, 1679.

Author: Edward Pelling. Allusion to *Tenure of Kings and Magistrates*, p. 4. Wing, P1091. Copy owned by New York Public Library.

806   *A True narrative of the horrid plot and conspiracy of the Popish party* [etc.]. *With a list of such noblemen, gentlemen, and others, as were the conspirators* [etc.]. *By Titus Otes, D. D.* London: Printed for Thomas Parkhurst, and Thomas Cockerill, 1679.

Collation: π^2 B^2 a^2 B–S^2. Allusion to Milton as a papist, first B2. See Wing, O59. Copy owned by New York Public Library.

807 *A True narrative of the horrid plot and conspiracy of the Popish party* [etc.]. *With a list of such noblemen, gentlemen, and others, as were the conspirators* [etc.]. *By Titus Oates, D. D.* London: Printed for Thomas Parkhurst, and Thomas Cockerill, 1679.

Another edition of No. *806.* Collation: π^2 a–b^2 B–S^2. Allusion, (a)2. Not in Wing. Copy owned by Princeton University Library.

808 *A True narrative of the horrid plot and conspiracy of the Popish party* [etc.]. *By Titus Otes, D. D. With a list of such noblemen, gentlemen, and others, as were the conspirators* [etc.]. London: Printed for Thomas Parkhurst, and Thomas Cockerill, 1679.

Another issue of No. *807.* Collation: π^2 a–b^2 B–S^2. Without portrait as frontispiece. Allusion, (a)2. Wing, O59. Copy owned by New York Public Library.

809 *A True narrative of the horrid plot and conspiracy of the Popish party* [etc.] *By Titus Oates, D. D. With a list of such noblemen, gentlemen, and others, as were the conspirators* [etc.]. London: Printed for Thomas Parkhurst, and Thomas Cockerill, 1679.

Another issue of No. *807.* Collation: π^2 a–b^2 B–S^2. With portrait as frontispiece. Allusion, (a)2. Wing, O60. Copy owned by New York Public Library.

810 *A True narrative of the horrid plot and conspiracy of the Popish party* [etc.]. *By Titus Oates, D. D. With a list of such noblemen, gentlemen, and others, as were the conspirators* [etc.]. London: Printed for Thomas Parkhurst, and Thomas Cockerill, 1679.

Another edition of No. *806.* Collation: π^2 (a)^2 (a)^2 B–S^2. Allusion, first (a)2. See Wing, O59. Copy owned by Henry E. Huntington Library.

811 *A True narrative of the horrid plot and conspiracy of the Popish party* [etc.]. *By Titus Oates, D. D. With a list of such noblemen, gentlemen, and others that were the conspirators* [etc.]. London: Printed for Thomas Parkhurst, and Thomas Cockerill, 1679.

Another edition of No. *806.* Collation π^2 B^2 (a)^2 B–S^2. Allusion, first B2. See Wing, O59. Copy owned by Henry E. Huntington Library.

812 *A True narrative of the horrid plot and conspiracy of the Popish party* [etc.]. Edinburgh: Re-printed by the Heir of Andrew Anderson, 1679.

Another edition of No. *806*. Allusion, A2. Not in Wing. Copy owned by Folger Shakespeare Library.

813 *A True narrative of the horrid plot and conspiracy of the Popish party* [etc.]. Reprinted at Dublin, by Benjamin Took and John Crook; And are to be sold by Mary Crook, MDCLXXIX.

Quarto edition of No. *806*. Allusion, A3. Wing, O61 (incorrectly calling it a folio). Copy owned by Trinity College Library, Dublin.

814 *Vornehmer leute gedancken vom ehestande. Zusammen getragen von Gottlieb Warmund.* Gedruckt zu Friburg durch Henricum Kunrad | 1679.

Another edition of No. *700*. Allusion, Section XI, p. [7]. Copy owned by British Library.

815 *Waerachtig verhael, van het schrickelijck verraet, en samensweering van de Paepsche partye* [etc.] t'Amsterdam | by de Wedeuw Bruynings, en Jan Bouman, 1679.

Dutch translation of No. *806*. Allusion, p. 5. Copy owned by New York Public Library.

816 *Waerachtig verhael, van het schrickelyck verraet, en samensweeringh van de Paepsche partye* [etc.]. Tot Groningen, by Rembertus Huysman, 1679.

Another edition of No. *815*. Copy owned by Bibliothèque Nationale.

817 *Warhaffte erzehlung von der schröcklichen verrätheren der papisten | wider das leben sr. königl maytt. Die regiérung in Engeland | und die protestinende religion. Aussdem Frantzösischen in Teutsche übersetzet.* Anno 1679.

German translation of No. *806*. Allusion, Aiiv. Copy owned by British Library.

1680

818 *An Additional discovery of Mr. Roger L'Estrange his further discovery of the popish plot: wherein Dr. Titus Oates, and the rest of the king's evidences are vindicated* [etc.]. London: Printed in the Year, 1680.

Author: B. W. Quotation from Oates concerning Milton as papist, p. 15. Wing, W3. Copy owned by Princeton University Library.

819 *Behemoth. The history of the civil wars of England, from the year 1640, to 1660* [etc.]. Printed in the Year 1680.

Another edition of No. *788*. Place: London. Allusion, p. 229. Wing, H2214. Copy owned by Princeton University Library.

820   *Bibliographia juridica & politica novissima perpetuo continuanda* [etc.]. Amstelædami: Apud Janssonio-Waesbergios, 1680.

Compiler: Cornelius à Beughem. Listings: pp. 156 (*Defensio prima*, twice, one of which is given as published in Amsteldam, 1652, in duodecimo; *Defensio secunda*; and *Literae*); 159 (More's *Fides Publica*, Hagæ-Comitus, 1654, in octavo, and "More's" *Regii Sanguinis Clamor*, 1652); 179 (Phillips' *Responsio*); 200 (Rowland's *Polemica*); 205 (1660 Salmasius); 206 (Schaller's dissertation); 244 (Dutch translation of *Defensio prima*, 1651); 256 (Ziegler's dissertation); 377 (Index); 380 (Index, Phillips). Others also listed in Index. Copy owned by Columbia University Library.

821   *Bibliotheca Bissæana: sive catalogus librorum* [etc.].

Date: 1680 (?). Bookseller: Benjamin Tooke. Listings: p. 22, *Defensio prima*, *Literae*; p. 67, *Paradise Lost, History of Britain, Tetrachordon*; p. 69, *Paradise Regain'd*. Not in Wing. Copy owned by Newberry Library.

822   *Bibliotheca Charnockiana sive catalogus librorum selectissimæ bibliothecæ clarissimi, doctissimiq; viri Domini Steph. Charnock, S. T. B. nuperrime defuncti* [etc.]. 1680.

Dated: 4 October 1680. Place: London. Listing: p. 28, *Reason of Church-Government*. Wing, C3707. Copy owned by British Library.

823   *Bibliotheca Digbeiana, sive catalogus librorum in variis linguis editorum* [etc.].

Collectors: Sir Kenelm and Sir George Digby. Booksellers: Henry Brome and Benjamin Tooke. Dated: 19 April 1680. Listings: pp. 30 (*Epistolarum Familiarium Liber Unus*); 35 (*Artis Logicae*); 89 and 98 (*Paradise Lost*); 107 (*Of Prelatical Episcopacy*); 109 (*Of Education*); 113 (*Of True Religion*); and 116 (*Brief Notes*). Wing, D1421. Copy owned by Henry E. Huntington Library.

824   *Caesar Borgia; son of Pope Alexander the sixth: a tragedy* [etc.]. London: Printed by R. E., for R. Bentley and M. Magnes, 1680.

Author: Nathaniel Lee. Printer: R. Everingham (?). Allusion to Paradise of Fools (*PL* III, 487–496) and imitation: Act V, Scene 2, p. 69. Wing, L846. Copy owned by University of Kentucky Library.

825   *Catalogus variorum librorum in selectissimus bibliothecis doctissimarum virorum; viz. D. Hen. Stubb nuperrime Londinensis D. Dillinghami de Oundle Northamptoniensis D. Thomæ Vincent Londinensis D. Cantoni Westmonasteriensis* [etc.].

Dated: 29 November 1680. Place: London. Bookseller: John Dunton.

Listings: p. 27, *Defensio prima*; p. 44, *Epistolarum Familiarium Liber Unus, Artis Logicae, Defensio prima*; (second pagination), p. 33, *Paradise Lost*; p. 59, *Paradise Lost*; p. 149, "Miltons Paradrae lost." Wing, S6031. Copy owned by British Library.

826   *Confessio fidei, in conventu theologorum authoritate parliamenti Anglicani indicto elaborata* [etc.]. Edinburgi, Excudebat Hæres Andreæ Anderson, 1680.

Another edition of No. *367*. Allusion, pp. 51–52. Wing, C5743. Copy owned by New College Library, Edinburgh.

827   *Les Conspirations d'Angleterre, ou l'histoire des troubles suscités dans ce royaume, de puis l'an 1600. Jusques a l'an 1679, inclusivement.* Cologne: Chez Jean le Blanc, 1680.

Includes anonymous French translation of No. *806*, as "Recit veritable de l'execrable conspiration du parti papiste [etc.]." Allusion to Milton as papist, p. 428. Copy owned by New York Public Library.

828   *An Exact catalogue of all the comedies* [etc.]. Oxon: Printed by L. Lichfield, for Nicholas Cox, 1680.

Compiler: Gerard Langbaine. Listing of "Milton's Masque," p. 10. Wing, L373A. Copy owned by Bodleian Library.

829   *The Free-holders grand inquest, touching our sovereign lord the king and his parliament. To which are added Observations upon forms of government* [etc.]. London: Printed in the Year 1680.

Author: Sir Robert Filmer. Reissue of No. *785*. Title page of reprint, A7: "Reflections concerning the original of government, upon ... III. Mr. Milton against Salmasius [etc.]. London: Printed in the Year 1679." See No. *800*. *Observations*, No. *276*, given on pp. 181–196. Wing, F915. Copy owned by University of Kentucky Library.

830   *A Further discovery of the plot: dedicated to Dr. Titus Oates, by Roger L'Estrange.* London: Printed for Henry Brome, 1680.

Edition 1. Folio. Quotation from Titus Oates concerning Milton as papist, p. 3. Wing, L1251. Copy owned by Newberry Library.

831   *A Further discovery of the plot: dedicated to Dr. Titus Oates, by Roger L'Estrange.* London: Printed for Henry Brome, 1680.

Edition 2 of No. *830*. Quarto. Quotation from Oates, p. 17. Wing, L1252. Copy owned by Princeton University Library.

832   *A Further discovery of the plot: dedicated to Dr. Titus Oates, by Roger L'Estrange.*
      The third edition. London: Printed for Henry Brome, 1680.

      Edition 3 of No. *830*; reissue of No. *831*. Wing, L1254. Copy owned by
      Columbia University Library.

833   *A General catalogue of all the stich'd books and single sheets &c. Printed the two last*
      years, commencing from the first discovery of the Popish plot, (September 1678.) and
      continued to Michaelmas term 1680. London: Printed by J. R., 1680.

      Listing of Charles Blount's *A Just Vindication* (No. *790*), p. 18. Wing, G496.
      Copy owned by Union Theological Seminary Library (McAlpin Collection).

834   *The General catalogue of books, printed in England since the dreadful fire of London*
      MDCLXVI. To the end of Trinity-term MDCLXXX [etc.]. *Collected by R. Clavell.*
      London: Printed by S. Roycroft, for Robert Clavell, 1680.

      Listings: pp. 45, 55, 74 (3), 88 (*The State of Innocence*), 95. Wing, C4601.
      Copy owned by Columbia University Library.

835   *The Good old way or, a discourse offer'd to all true-hearted protestants concerning the*
      ancient way of the church, and the conformity of the Church of England thereunto: as
      to its government, manner of worship, rites and customes [etc.]. London: Printed
      for Jonathan Edwin, 1680.

      Author: Edward Pelling. Allusion with quotation from *Tenure of Kings and*
      Magistrates and of Oates's statement, pp. 114–115 and margin. Wing, P1082.
      Copy owned by Yale University Library.

836   *The History of the Turkish empire from the year 1623. To the year 1677* [etc.]. Lon-
      don: Printed by J. M., for John Starkey, 1680.

      Author: Sir Paul Rycaut. Included on sigs. Aaaa1-2 is "A Catalogue of Books
      Printed for John Starkey, Bookseller [etc.]." Listed are: *Tetrachordon*, No.
      4, Aaaaa1v; *Paradise Regain'd* and *Samson Agonistes*, No. 61, Aaaa2v; and *Ac-*
      cedence Commenc't Grammar, No. 69, Aaaa2v. Wing, R2406. Copy owned by
      Folger Shakespeare Library.

837   *Horace's art of poetry. Made English by the Right Honorable the Earl of Roscommon.*
      London: Printed for Henry Herringman, 1680.

      Possible influence from *Paradise Lost* and "The Verse." In blank verse. Preface
      remarks "the constraint of Rhyme" in Ben Jonson's version. Wing, H2768.
      Copy owned by Bodleian Library.

838   *LEstrange's narrative of the plot* [etc.]. London: Printed by J. B., for Hen.
      Brome, 1680.

Author: Sir Roger L'Estrange. Edition 1. Allusion concerning Milton as papist, pp. 6-7. Wing, L1275. Copy owned by Columbia University Library.

839 *LEstrange's narrative of the plot* [etc.]. *The second edition.* London: Printed by J. B., for Hen. Brome, 1680.

Edition 2 of No. *838* (reissue). Wing, L1276. Copy owned by Princeton University Library.

840 *LEstrange's narrative of the plot* [etc.]. *The third edition.* London: Printed by J. B., for Hen. Brome, 1680.

Edition 3 of No. *838* (reissue). Wing, L1277. Copy owned by British Library.

841 *The Loyal intelligence; or, news both from city and country.* No. 1. 16 March 1679/80.

Notes on *L'Estrange's Narrative of the Plot* (No. *838*) quote allusion. Copy owned by Henry E. Huntington Library.

842 *Patriarcha: or, the natural power of kings* [etc.]. London: Printed and are to be sold by Walter Davis, 1680.

Author: Sir Robert Filmer. Allusion in letter from Peter Heylyn to Sir Edward Filmer, A4v. Wing, F922. Copy owned by Yale University Library.

843 *Patriarcha; or the natural power of kings* [etc.]. London: Printed for Ric. Chiswell, Matthew Gillyflower and William Henchman, 1680.

Reissue of No. *842*. Wing, F923. Copy owned by Yale University Library.

844 *Political discourses of Sir Robert Filmer, Baronet, viz. Patriarcha, or the natural power of kings. The Free-holders grand-inquest. Observations upon Aristotles Politicks. Directions for obedience to government. Also Observations upon Mr. Hobbs's Leviathan. Mr. Milton against Salmatius* [etc.]. London: Printed in the year 1680.

Reprints of Nos. *842* and *785*, but with separate title page for *Reflections* (No. *800*). *Observations on Milton* therefore appear on pp. 17-32, separately paged. Wing, F925. Copy owned by William Andrews Clark Library.

845 *The Power of kings; and in particular, of the king of England* [etc.]. London: Printed for W. H. and T. F. and are to be sold by Walter Davis, 1680.

Author: Sir Robert Filmer. Publisher: William Henchman. Allusion to antimonarchical work, in preface, A2. Wing, F926. Copy owned by Yale University Library.

846   *The Power of parliaments in the case of succession; or, a seasonable address to the high court of parliament, touching the present grievances of the nation* [etc.]. London: Printed for M. R., 1680.

> Author: Matthew Rider. Allusion to antimonarchical views (as in *Tenure of Kings and Magistrates*), p. 2 and passim; allusion to Salmasian controversy with quotation from *Defensio prima*, pp. 39–40. Wing, R1444. Copy owned by Union Theological Seminary Library (McAlpin Collection).

847   *Self-conflict: or, the powerful motions between the flesh & spirit* [etc.]. London: Printed for Robert Sollers, 1680.

> Author: Jacob Cats. Allusion in "To the Reader," A3v. Wing, C1524. Copy owned by Folger Shakespeare Library.

848   *The True protestants litany.* Printed in the year, 1680.

> Broadside. Place: London. Possible allusion. Wing, T2867. Copy owned by Henry E. Huntington Library.

849   *The Vision of purgatory, anno 1680* [etc.]. London: Printed by T. N., for Henry Brome, 1680.

> Author: Edward Pettit. Fictional view of Milton as a papist agent, pp. 99–101. Wing, P1891A. Copy owned by Union Theological Seminary Library (McAlpin Collection).

1681

850   *Absalom and Achitophel. A poem.* [epigraph]. London, Printed for *J. T.* and are to be Sold by *W. Davis* in *Amen-Corner*, 1681.

> Author: John Dryden. Publisher: Jacob Tonson. Edition 1, Issue 1. iv + 32 pp. Page 6 uncorrected; catchword, "Not". Imitative poem with appropriations from *Paradise Lost* throughout. See Wing, D2212. Copy owned by Berg Collection, New York Public Library.

851   *Absalom and Achitophel. A poem.* [epigraph]. London, Printed for *J. T.* and are to be Sold by *W. Davis* in *Amen-Corner*, 1681.

> Edition 1, Issue 2, of No. *850.* Page 6 partially corrected: "Patron" in line 134 and catchword, "Not". See Wing, D2212. Copy owned by Folger Shakespeare Library.

852   *Absalom and Achitophel. A poem.* [epigraph]. London, Printed for *J. T.* and are to be Sold by *W. Davis* in *Amen-Corner*, 1681.

Edition 1, Issue 3, of No. *850*. Page 6 corrected; catchword, "Oh". See Wing, D2212. Copy owned by Princeton University Library.

853 *Absalom and Achitophel. A poem.* [epigraph]. London, Printed for *J. T.* and are to be Sold by *W. Davis* in *Amen-Corner*, 1681.

Edition 2, Issue 1, of No. *850*. Line 9 reads "To Wives". Poems by Nathaniel Lee and Richard Duke laid in, and twelve lines added on p. 7 (as added in Edition 2) with note at bottom of p. 6 and catchword changed to "So". Allusion in Lee's poem. Wing, D2215. Copy owned by Henry E. Huntington Library.

854 *Absalom and Achitophel. A poem.* [epigraph]. *The second edition; augmented and revised.* London: Printed for J. T., and are to be sold by W. Davis, 1681.

Edition 2, Issue 2, of No. *850*. A-D^4 E^2. Line 9 reads "To Wives", and l. 530, p. 14, correctly printed with "old". Includes Lee's "To the Unknown Author of This Excellent Poem," allusion, A4. See Wing, D2217. Copy owned by William Andrews Clark Library.

855 *Absalom and Achitophel. A poem.* [epigraph]. *The second edition; augmented and revised.* London: Printed for J. T., and are to be sold by W. Davis, 1681.

Edition 2, Issue 3, of No. *850*. A-D^4 E^2. Line 9 reads "Two Wives", and l. 40 [530], p. 14, incorrectly printed without "old". See Wing, D2217. Copy owned by William Andrews Clark Library.

856 *Absalom and Achitophel. A poem. With all the additions.* [epigraph].

Date: 1681?. Place: Dublin? Bound: A1-2 π1 A3-4 B-E^4(-E4). E4 may have been used for π1. [1], title page; [2], blank; [3-4], To the Reader; [two uncounted pages], commendatory poems; [5; but numbered 1]-38, work. Page 6, *recte*, follows p. 5 which is numbered p. 1. Lee's poem, π1v. Wing, D2213. Copy owned by Folger Shakespeare Library.

857 *Absalom and Achitophel. A poem.* [epigraph]. *The second edition; augmented and revised.*

Date: 1681. Place: Dublin. A second edition of No. *850*. Quarto. A-D^4; pages, [6] 7-32. Line 9: "To Wives". Lee's poem, A4, pp. [5-6]. Wing, D2214. Copy owned by Henry E. Huntington Library.

858 *Bibliotheca medici viri clarissimi Nathanis Paget, M. D.* [etc.].

Dated: 24 October 1681. Place: London. Bookseller: William Cooper. Listings: p. 28, *Epistolarum Familiarium Liber Unus* (twice), *Artis Logicae*;

p. 34, *Eikonoklastes*; p. 36, *Paradise Lost* (twice), *Apology*; p. 38, *Areopagitica*; p. 39, *Tetrachordon* (twice), *Paradise Regain'd*; p. 40, *Paradise Lost*; p. 43, *Civil Power*. Wing, P167. Copy owned by British Library.

859 *Bibliotheca Norfolciana: sive catalogus libb. manuscriptorum & impressorum in omni arte & lingua, quos illustriss. princeps Henricus dux Norfolciæ, &c. Regiæ Societati Londinensi pro scientia naturali promovenda donavit.* Londini: Ric. Chiswel, 1681.

Listings, pp. 157 (*History of Britain*), 161 (*Literae*). Wing, N1230. Copy owned by New York Public Library.

860 *A Catalogue of books continued, printed, and published at London, in Easter-term, 1681.* No. 3.

Listing of *Character of the Long Parliament*. Copy owned by Henry E. Huntington Library.

861 *A Catalogue of books continued, printed and published at London, in Trinity term, 1681.* No. 4.

Colophon: "Printed for the Book-sellers of London." Listing of *Paradise Regain'd* and *Samson Agonistes*. Copy owned by Henry E. Huntington Library.

862 *Catalogus librorum bibliothecæ reverend. & eruditi viri D. Samuelis Brooke* [etc.].

Dated: 21 March 1680/81. Place: London. Bookseller: William Cooper. Listing: p. 37, *Reason of Church-Government*. Wing, B4916. Copy owned by British Library.

863 *Catalogus librorum in bibliothecis selectissimus doctissimorum virorum; viz. D. Georgii Lawsoni Salopiensis. D. Georgii Fawleri Londiniensis. D. Oweni Stockdoni Colcestriensis. D. Thomæ Brooks Londinensis* [etc.]. 1681.

Dated: 30 May 1681. Place: London. Bookseller: Edward Millington. Listing: p. 19 (second pagination), *Paradise Lost*. Wing, L705. Copy owned by British Library.

864 *Catalogus librorum, in quavis lingua & facultate insignium instructissimarum bibliothecarum reverendi doctissimiq; domini D. Doctoris Gulielmi Outrami, nuper ecclesiæ Westmonasteriensis canonica: nec non eruditi clarissimique viri D. Thomæ Gatakeri* [etc.].

Dated: 12 December 1681. Place: London. Bookseller: William Cooper. Listings: p. 31, *Artis Logicae* (twice), *Defensio prima* (?), *Literae*; p. 41, *History of Britain*; p. 62, Filmer's *Observations*. Wing, O600. Copy owned by British Library.

865 *Catalogus librorum Latinorum in diversis Europæ partibus impressorum ab anno 1670. usque ad annum 1680* [etc.]. Londini: Impensis Roberti Clavel, 1681.

Listings, pp. 182, 189 (2; name misspelled). Not in Wing. Copy owned by Columbia University Library.

866 *Catalogus librorum officinæ Danielis Elsevirii; designans libros, qui ejus typis & impensis prodierunt, aut quorum aliàs copia ipsi suppetit, & quorum auctio habebitur* Amstelodami: 1681.

Unpaged. Listing, A2v (Phillips's *Responsio*). Copy owned by New York Public Library.

867 *Catalogus librorum qui in bibliopolio Danielis Elsevirii venales extant, & quorum auctio habebitur inædibus defuncti* Amstelodami: 1681.

Listings, pp. 19 (Phillips's *Responsio*), 302 (six titles), 349 (Phillips's *Responsio*), 221 (that is, 421; Salmasius's 1660 *Responsio*), 442 (Schaller's dissertation), 491 (Ziegler's dissertation). Copy owned by New York Public Library.

868 *A Collection of several tracts in quarto, written most since the discovery of the Popish plot 1678* [etc.]. London: Printed for Henry Brome, 1681.

Author: Sir Roger L'Estrange. Reissues of Nos. *802*, *832*, and *839*. Omitted from gathering is *Toleration Discussed*, although listed on title page. See Wing, L1225. Copy owned by Princeton University Library.

869 *A Collection of several tracts in quarto, written most since the discovery of the Popish plot 1678* [etc.]. London: Printed by T. B. for Henry Brome, 1681.

Different edition of No. *868*. Reissues of Nos. *894*, *802*, *832*, *839*, and *875*. See Wing, L1225. Copy owned by Henry E. Huntington Library.

870 *A Collection of several tracts in quarto, written most since the discovery of the Popish plot 1678* [etc.]. London: Printed by T. B. for Henry Broome, 1681.

Different issue from No. *869*. Includes Nos. *894* and *802*, *A Seasonable Memorial*, *The Third Edition* (1681), and Nos. *876* and *840*. See Wing, L1225. Wing, L1225A appears to be a ghost. Copy owned by Trinity College Library, Dublin.

871 *The Dissenters sayings. The second part* [etc.]. London: Printed for Joanna Brome, 1681.

Author: Sir Roger L'Estrange. Edition 1. Quotations from *Eikonoklastes*, pp. 32, 47 (2), 74–75 (4). Wing, L1245. Copy owned by New York Public Library.

872 *The Dissenters sayings. The second part* [etc.]. *The second edition.* London: Printed for Joanna Brome, 1681.

Edition 2 of No. *871*. Wing, L1246. Copy owned by Princeton Theological Seminary Library.

873 *The Dissenters sayings, in requital for L'Estrange's sayings* [etc.]. London: Printed for Henry Brome, 1681.

Author: Sir Roger L'Estrange. Different book from No. *871*. Quotation from *Tenure of Kings and Magistrates*, p. 31. Wing, L1240. Copy owned by Columbia University Library.

874 *The Dissenters sayings, in requital for L'Estrange's sayings* [etc.]. *The second edition.* London: Printed for Henry Brome, 1681.

Edition 2 of No. *873*. Wing, L1241. Copy owned by New York Public Library.

875 *The Dissenters sayings, in requital for L'Estrange's sayings* [etc.]. *The third edition.* London: Printed for Joanna Brome, 1681.

Edition 3 of No. *873*. Wing, L1242. Copy owned by Columbia University Library.

876 *A Further discovery of the plot: dedicated to Titus Oates, by Roger L'Estrange. The fourth edition.* London: Printed for Henry Brome, 1681.

Edition 4 of No. *830*. Allusion, p. 19. Wing, L1255. Copy owned by Princeton University Library.

877 *Heraclitus ridens: or, a discourse between jest and earnest* [etc.]. No. 10, 4 April 1681.

Editor: Thomas Flatman. Publisher: Benjamin Tooke. Milton's position on censorship, parliament, and the assembly of divines, pp. 62–64. Copy owned by Yale University Library.

878 *Jus Cæsaris et ecclesiæ vere dictæ. Or a treatise wherein independency, presbytery, the power of kings, and of the church* [etc.]. London: Printed for the author, and are to be sold by John Kersey and Henry Faythorn, 1681.

Author: William Denton. "The Summe of Mr. J. M. His Treatise" [*Treatise of Civil Power*], pp.1–3, with further allusions on pp. 3, 4. Reference to *Tenure of Kings and Magistrates*, p. 67.

"An Apology for the Liberty of the Press," added with new signatures (A^6) and pagination, but linking catchword. No title page; pp. 1–9 + [3]. Argument adapted from *Areopagitica*. Wing, D1066. Copy owned by Henry E. Huntington Library.

879   *Miscellaneous poems.* London: Printed by Robert Boulter, 1681.

Author: Andrew Marvell. Appropriations and reference: "The Garden," ll. 53–56 ("Il Penseroso"), p. 50. "Fleckno, an English Priest at Rome," l. 28 ("Lycidas"), p. 55. "On Mr. Milton's Paradise Lost," pp. 61–62. "Upon Appleton House, to my Lord Fairfax," pp. 76–103 (various poems and possibly *Apology*), passim. "The First Anniversary of the Government under O. C.," ll. 151–152, 218, 358 ("Nativity Ode," "Lycidas"), pp. 123, 125, 128. "A Poem upon the Death of O. C.," ll. 227–246, 299–304 ("Lycidas"). Wing, M872. Copy owned by Yale University Library.

Copy omits "The First Anniversary" (in British Library copy c.59.i.8), and "A Poem Upon th Death of O. C." (partially in British Library copy, pp. 140–144). Full text of latter poem given in *The Works of Andrew Marvell, esq.* [etc.]. London: Printed for the editor by Henry Baldwin, and sold by Dodsley [et al.], 1776. Vol. 3. Edited by Colonel Edward Thompson. Copy owned by New York Public Library.

880   Oxford. Bodleian Library. Aubrey MS 8.

"Auctarium Vitarum à JA Collectarum A^O D$^{\overline{m}}$ 1681," ff. 63–66, 68–68v. Minutes for Milton's Life by John Aubrey. Name is listed on f. 5v.

881   Oxford. Bodleian Library. Ballard MS 14.

Letter from J. Gregorius (i. e., John Aubrey) to Anthony Wood, dated 20 December 1681, f. 134. Allusion.

882   Oxford. Bodleian Library. Tanner MS 456a.

Letter from John Aubrey to Anthony Wood, dated 22 October 1681, f. 27. On Milton's life.

883   *A Paradox against life. Written by the lords in the Tower. An heroick poem* [etc.]. London: Printed for James Vade, 1681.

Author: anonymous. Probable influence in language and image from *Paradise Lost.* Wing, P331. Copy owned by Bodleian Library.

884   *Patriarcha non monarcha. The patriarch unmonarch'd: being observations on a late treatise and divers other miscellanies, published under the name of Sir Robert Filmer baronet* [etc.]. *By a lover of truth and of his country.* London: Printed for Richard Janeway, 1681.

Author: Sir James Tyrrell. Allusion to antimonarchical works, pp. A3 (preface), 96–97, [137] (following p. 136 but given as 97; new pagination). Wing, T3591. Copy owned by Union Theological Seminary Library (McAlpin Collection).

885   *Satyrs upon the Jesuits: written in the year 1679* [etc.]. London: Printed for Joseph Hindmarsh, 1681.

Author: John Oldham. Includes reissue of No. *891*; separate title page, signatures, and pagination. Wing, O244. Copy owned by Princeton University Library.

886   *A Sermon preached before the aldermen of the City of London, at St. Lawrence-Church, Jan 30. 1680/1. Being the day of the martyrdome of K. Charles I* [etc.]. London: Printed for Richard Chiswel, 1681.

Author: Gilbert Burnet. Allusion to *Eikonoklastes*, p. 7. Wing, B5875. Copy owned by Yale University Library.

887   *A Sermon preached before the aldermen of the City of London, at St. Lawrence-Church, Jan 30. 1680/1 being the day of the martyrdome of K. Charles I. The second edition.* London: Printed for Richard Chiswel, 1681.

Edition 2 of No. *886*. Wing, B5876. Copy owned by Folger Shakespeare Library.

888   *A Sermon preached before the king on the 30/1 of January 1680/1* [etc.]. London: Printed by J. Macock, for R. Royston, 1681.

Author: Francis Turner. Allusion to *Eikonoklastes*, pp. 40–41. Wing, T3280. Copy owned by Princeton Theological Seminary Library.

889   *A Short view of the late troubles in England* [etc.]. Oxford: Printed at the Theater for Moses Pitt, 1681.

Author: Sir William Dugdale. Folio. $A^4(-A4)$ B–F^2 G–V^4 X^2 Aa–Nn^4 Oo^2 Pp^1 Aaa–Kkk^4 Mmm–Qqq^4 Aaaa–$Mmmm^4$ $Nnnn^1$ Aàaaa^2 Bbbbb–$Zzzzz^4$ Aaaaaa–$Fffff^4$ Ggggg–$Iiiiii^2$. Paged: [6] 1–136 185–294 361–439 [1] 449–488 553–650 [4] 737–959 [13]. Last six pages are a book catalogue. Allusion to *Eikonoklastes*, p. 380. Wing, D2492. Copy owned by Union Theological Seminary Library (McAlpin Collection).

890   *A Short view of the late troubles in England* [etc.]. *By Sir William Dugdale* [etc.]. Oxford: Printed at the Theater for Moses Pitt, 1681.

A different issue of No. *889*. Collation: π^1 [χ]^1 $A^4(-A4)$ B–F^2 etc. Title page is a cancel, using A4. π1 is a portrait, tipped in. See Wing, D2492. Copy owned by British Library.

891   *Some new pieces never before publisht* [etc.]. London: Printed by M. C. for Jo. Hindmarsh, 1681.

Author: John Oldham. Allusion in "Bion," p. 82. Wing, O248. Copy owned by Henry E. Huntington Library.

892 Robert H. Taylor, Princeton, New Jersey. MS, entitled "A Collection of Choyce Poems. Lampoons, and Satyrs from 1673 to 1689," bound as "Restoration Poems."

Anonymous poem, "An Essay of Scandal"; allusion, p. 96. Dated: 1681.

893 *Thomæ Hobbes Angli Malmesburiensis philosophi vita* [etc.]. Carolopoli: Apud Eleutherium Anglicanum, sub Signo Veritatis, 1681.

Edited and completed by R. B. (Richard Blackburne). Colophon: Londini: Apud Guil. Crooke. Allusions by the editor, pp. 70 and 100 (in reference to Filmer's *Observations*). Wing, H2268. Copy owned by Union Theological Seminary Library (McAlpin Collection).

894 *Toleration discuss'd; in two dialogues* [etc.]. *The third edition.* London: Printed for H. Brome, 1681.

Edition 3 of No. *630.* Quotations from *Tenure of Kings and Magistrates*, pp. 32–33 and margins. Wing, L1318. Copy owned by Princeton University Library.

895 *Tracts of Thomas Hobb's of Malmsbury* [etc.]. London: Printed for William Crooke, 1681.

Allusions in Hobbes's autobiography finished by R. B. (No. *893*): pp. 141 (second part), 197 (in reference to Filmer's *Observations*). Wing, H2264. Copy owned by Union Theological Seminary Library (McAlpin Collection).

896 *A True and exact history of the succession of the crown of England* [etc.]. London: Printed for Cave Pulleyn, 1681.

Author: Robert Brady. Edition 1. Reference to *Defensio prima*, p. 2. Wing, B4195. Copy owned by Folger Shakespeare Library.

1682

897 *Absalom and Achitophel. A poem* [epigraph]. *The third edition; augmented and revised.* London: Printed for J. T., and are to be sold by W. Davis, 1682.

Edition 3 of No. *850.* Includes Lee's "To the Unknown Author of This Excellent Poem," A3. Wing, D2218. Copy owned by Folger Shakespeare Library.

898 *Absalom and Achitophel. A poem.* [epigraph]. *The fourth edition; augmented and revised.* London: Printed for J. T., and are to be sold by W. Davis, 1682.

Edition 4 of No. *850.* Includes Lee's "To the Unknown Author of This Excellent Poem," A3. Wing, D2219. Copy owned by Princeton University Library.

899 *Absalom and Achitophel. A poem.* [epigraph]. *The fifth edition, augmented and revised.* London: Printed for Jacob Tonson, 1682.

Edition 5 of No. *850* Includes Lee's poem, A2v. Wing, D2220. Copy owned by Folger Shakespeare Library.

900 *Absalom senior: or, Achitophel transpros'd. A poem.* [etc.]. London: Printed for S. E. and sold by Langley Curtis, 1682.

Author: Elkanah Settle. Folio. Allusion to and imitation of *Paradise Lost*, pp. 2–3. Wing, S2652. Copy owned by Princeton University Library.

901 *Absalom senior: or, Achitophel transpros'd. A poem. Revis'd with additions.* [epigraph]. London: Printed for S. E. and sold by Langley Curtis, 1682.

Another edition of No. *900.* Quarto. Allusion and imitation, pp. 2–3. Wing, S2653. Copy owned by Folger Shakespeare Library.

902 *Absalon et Achitophel. Carmine Latino heroico.* Oxon: Typis Lichfieldianis prostant apud Ricardum Davis, 1682.

Latin translation of No. *850* by William Coward. Wing, D2221. Copy owned by Columbia University Library.

903 *Absalon et Achitophel. Poema Latino carmine donatum* [etc.]. Oxon: Typis Lichfieldianis, prostant apud Johannem Crosley, 1682.

Latin translation of No. *850* by Francis Atterbury and Francis Hickman. Wing, D2222. Copy owned by Princeton University Library.

904 *Acta eruditorum anno MDCLXXXII* [etc.]. Lipsiæ: Prostant apud J. Grossium & J. F. Gleditschium. Typis Christophori Günteri, 1682.

No. 9 (September). Allusion in review of Morhof's *Unterricht von der Teutschen Sprache und Poesie*, p. 274. In Latin. Copy owned by New York Public Library.

905 *Arcana dominationis in rebus gestis Olivirii Cromwelli loco dissertationis historico-politicæ sub præsidio Dn. M. Joh. Andreæ Schmidts* [etc.]. Jenæ, Literis Krebsianis.

Author: Johannes Frischmuth. Dated: 1682. Reference to *Defensio secunda*, pp. 4–5 and margin (Section 7) and p. 36 with quotation (Section 60). Discussion of Salmasius's *Responsio*, pp. 10, 15, 36 and margins, without mention of Milton; and Ziegler cited, p. 22 and margin. Copy owned by British Library.

906 *Behemoth. The history of the causes of the civil-wars of England* [etc.]. London: Printed for W. Crooke, 1682.

Another edition of No. *788*. Allusion to Salmasian controversy, p. 269. Wing, H2215. Copy owned by University of Kentucky Library.

907 *Bibliotheca Heinsiana, sive catalogus librorum quos magno studio & sumptu, dum viveret, collegit vir illustris Nicolaus Heinsius, Dan. Fil., in duas partes divisus.* Lugduni in Batavis, apud Joannem de Vivii, 1682.

Listing under "Catalogi Bibliothecæ Heinsianæ Pars Posterior," item 360 (i. e., 460), p. 47. Copy owned by Columbia University Library.

908 *Bibliotheca Smithiana: sive catalogus librorum* [etc.]. Per Richardum Chiswel, bibliopolam. [etc.].

Owner: Richard Smith. Dated: 15 May 1682. Listings on p. 114, Ziegler, three works by Salmasius, *Defensio prima*, More, *Pro se defensio*, Du Moulin, *Defensio secunda*; p. 124, *Epistolarum Familiarium Liber Unus*; p. 186, *Eikon Aklastos*; p. 190, *History of Britain, Paradise Lost*; p. 206, *Paradise Regain'd* and *Samson Agonistes, History of Britain*; p. 221, *Hirelings, Ready and Easy Way*; p. 385, Filmer's *Observations, Tenure of Kings and Magistrates*; p. 388, *Eikonoklastes, Tenure, Areopagitica, Doctrine and Discipline of Divorce, An Answer to Doctrine and Discipline of Divorce, Colasterion, Judgement of Martin Bucer, Of Education, Brief Notes*, L'Estrange's *No Blind Guides*, "Kingship maintained against J. Milton, 1660." The last item, otherwise unrecorded, is apparently by a William Lincoln. Wing, S4151. Copy owned by Newberry Library.

909 *Bibliothèque choisie de M. Colomiés.* La Rochelle: Pierre Savouret, 1682.

Author: Paul Colomiès. Discussion of Du Moulin's "Clamor Regii Sanguinis," pp. 19–20. Copy owned by Folger Shakespeare Library.

910 *A Catalogue of books continued, printed, and published at London in Hilary term, 1681/2.* No. 6.

Listing of *A Brief History of Moscovia.* Copy owned by Henry E. Huntington Library.

911 *Catalogus librorum in omni facultate & linguæ, ex variis partibus Europæ allatorum, per Johannem Gellibrand, bibliopolam Londinensem.* Londini: In Cœmeterio Paulino. 1682.

Listings: p. 15, *Defensio prima*; p. 21, Salmasius's *Responsio*. Wing, G481. Copy owned by Bodleian Library.

912 *A Collection of several tracts in quarto* [etc.]. London: Printed for Joanna Brome, 1682.

Another edition of No. *868*. Reissues of Nos. *894* and *802*. Wing, L1225A. Copy owned by Union Theological Seminary Library (McAlpin Collection).

913 *The Daniel Catcher. The life of the prophet Daniel: in a poem* [etc.]. Printed in the Year 1713.

Revised edition of No. *917A*. Printer: William Bradford. Place: New York City. Pp. 1–53. See also "Earths Felicities, Heavens Allowances. A Blank Poem"; influence from blank verse of *Paradise Lost*, pp. 55–73. Written in 1680s. Evans 1650. Copy owned by American Antiquarian Society, Worcester, Massachusetts.

914 *An Essay upon poetry*. London: Printed for Joseph Hindmarsh, 1682.

Author: John Sheffield, Lord Buckingham. Allusion, p. 21. Wing, B5339. Copy owned by Princeton University Library. Wing, B5340, reported with date 1683, does not exist.

915 *Heraclitus ridens: or, a discourse between jest and earnest* [etc.]. No. 64, 18 April 1682.

Editor: Thomas Flatman. Publisher: Benjamin Tooke. Allusion, p. 149. Copy owned by Yale University Library.

916 *Heraclitus ridens: or, a discourse between jest and earnest* [etc.]. No. 67, 9 May 1682.

Editor: Thomas Flatman. Publisher: Benjamin Tooke. Allusion to divorce tracts, p. 165. Copy owned by Yale University Library.

917 *Heraclitus ridens: or, a discourse between jest and earnest* [etc.]. No. 80, 8 August 1682.

Editor: Thomas Flatman. Publisher: Benjamin Tooke. Allusion to *Areopagitica* and Charles Blount's *A Just Vindication*, p. 240. Copy owned by Yale University Library.

917A *The History of the Babylonish cabal; or the intrigues, progression, opposition, defeat, and destruction of the Daniel catchers; in a poem.* London: Printed for Richard Baldwin, 1682.

Author: Richard Steere. 36 pp. Influence from *Paradise Lost*, passim. Wing, S5397. Copy owned by Henry E. Huntington Library.

918   *The Journals of all the parliaments during the reign of Queen Elizabeth, both of the House of Lords and House of Commons* [etc.]. London: Printed for John Starkey, 1682.

Collected by Sir Simonds D'Ewes. Revised and published by Paul Bowes. No signatures. Added on 4X1v–4X2 is "A Catalogue of Books Printed for John Starkey [etc.]." Folio. Listings: No. 51, *Paradise Regain'd* and *Samson Agonistes*, 4X2v; No. 57, *Accedence Commenc't Grammar*, 4X2v. Wing, D1250. Copy owned by Folger Shakespeare Library.

919   *Julian the apostate: being a short account of his life* [etc.]. London: Printed for Langley Curtis, 1682.

Author: Samuel Johnson. Edition 1. Octavo. 172 pp. Partially adapted from *Defensio prima*; see particularly "The Preface to the Reader," pp. iii–xxix. Wing, J830. Copy owned by New York Public Library.

920   *Julian the apostate: being a short account of his life* [etc.]. London: Printed for Langley Curtis, 1682.

Another edition of No. *919*. Duodecimo. xxiv + 94 pp. Wing, J829. Copy owned by British Library.

921   *The Lancashire witches and Tegue o Divelly the Irish priest*. London: Printed for John Starkey, 1682.

Author: Thomas Shadwell. Printed on A3v is: "Books of Poetry and Plays Printed for John Starkey." Listing: *Paradise Regain'd* and *Samson Agonistes*. Wing, S2853. Copy owned by Folger Shakespeare Library.

922   *Love given o're: or, a satyr against the pride, lust, and inconstancy, &c. of woman*. London: Printed for Andrew Green, 1682.

Author: Robert Gould. Imitation of *Paradise Lost*, p. 2. Wing, G1422. Copy owned by William Andrews Clark Library. Wing, G1423, erroneously cites this copy (along with others) as an edition of 1683; no such edition exists.

923   *The Loyalty of popish principles examin'd. In answer to a late book entituled Stafford's Memoirs* [etc.]. London: Printed by S. Roycroft, for Thomas Flesher, 1682.

Author: Robert Hancock. Discussion of Milton and Roman Catholicism, with references to *Eikonoklastes* and *Defensio prima*, pp. 32–37, 50. Wing, H643. Copy owned by Union Theological Seminary Library (McAlpin Collection).

924   *Mac Flecknoe, or a satyr upon the true-blew-Protestant poet, T. S. By the author of Absalom & Achitophel*. London: Printed for D. Green.

Author: John Dryden. Imitations of *Paradise Lost* with parody of *PL* VI, 719–722, in ll. 135–138, p. 10. Wing, D2303. Copy owned by Folger Shakespeare Library.

925   *The Medall. A satyre against sedition* [etc.]. London: Printed for Jacob Tonson, 1682.

Author: John Dryden. Edition 1, Issue 1. No Latin lines at end, D2v. Allusion in "Epistle to the Whigs," p. [vi]. See Wing, D2311. Copy owned by Princeton University Library.

926   *The Medall. A satyre against sedition* [etc.]. London: Printed for Jacob Tonson, 1682.

Edition 1, Issue 2, of No. *925*. Two Latin lines at end, D2v. See Wing, D2311. Copy owned by Columbia University Library.

927   *The Medall: a satyre against sedition* [etc.]. Edinburgh: Re-printed anno dom. 1682.

Another edition of No. *925*. Allusion, p. [v]. Wing, D2312. Copy owned by Henry E. Huntington Library.

928   *The Medall. A satyre against sedition* [etc.]. Dublin: Reprinted for Robert Thornton, 1682.

Another edition of No. *925*. Allusion, p. 5. Wing, D2313. Copy owned by Henry E. Huntington Library.

929   *Memorials of the English affairs* [etc.]. London: Printed for Nathaniel Ponder, 1682.

Author: Sir Bulstrode Whitelocke. Edited by Arthur Annesley, Earl of Anglesey. Reference to Milton's work as secretary, p. 633 (under May 1656). Wing, W1986. Copy owned by University of Wisconsin Library.

930   *Mr. Hunt's argument for the bishops right: with the Postscript* [etc.]. London: Printed for the Author, and are to be sold by the Booksellers, 1682.

Author: Thomas Hunt. "Postscript" adapted from *Defensio prima*, lvi + 111 pp. (new pagination). Wing, H3749A. Copy owned by Yale University Library.

931   *The Observator.* No. 133, 6 May 1682. London: Printed for Joanna Brome.

Author: Sir Roger L'Estrange. Allusion. Copy owned by Columbia University Library.

932   *The Observator*. No. 157, 19 June 1682. London: Printed for Joanna Brome.

Author: Sir Roger L'Estrange. Allusion. Copy owned by Columbia University Library.

933   *The Observator*. No. 190, 16 August 1682. London: Printed for Joanna Brome.

Author: Sir Roger L'Estrange. Allusions. Copy owned by Columbia University Library.

934   *The Observator*. No. 208, 20 September 1682. London: Printed for Joanna Brome.

Author: Sir Roger L'Estrange. Allusion. Copy owned by Columbia University Library.

935   Marquess of Ormonde. MS letter.

Letter from Earl of Longford to Marquess of Ormonde, dated 4 March 1681 [1682]. Allusion. Published in Historical MSS Commission. *Calendar of the MSS of the Marquess of Ormonde, K. P.* London: Hereford Times Limited, 1911. VI, 335.

936   *A Pleasant conference upon the Observator, and Heraclitus: together with a brief relation of the present posture of the French affairs.* London: Printed for H. Jones, 1682.

Author: John Phillips. Reference to *Paradise Lost*, p. 3. Wing, P2540. Copy owned by Folger Shakespeare Library.

937   *Poems and songs. By Thomas Flatman. The third edition with additions and amendments* [etc.]. London: Printed for Benjamin Tooke, 1682.

Edition 3 of No. *686*. Wing, F1153. Copy owned by Henry E. Huntington Library.

938   *A Sermon on the martyrdom of King Charles I. Preached January 30. 1681* [etc.]. London: Printed by Miles Flesher, for Richard Davis, 1682.

Author: Thomas Wilson. Allusions and quotations, pp. 16 and margin and note (from *Tenure of Kings and Magistrates*), 21 and margin (from *Tenure of Kings and Magistrates*), 32 (from *Tenure of Kings and Magistrates* and *Defensio prima*). Wing, W2937A. Copy owned by New York Public Library.

939   *A Sermon on the martyrdom of King Charles I. Preached January 30. 1681* [etc.]. London: Printed, and are to be sold by Walter Davis, 1682.

Another edition of No. *938*. Wing, W2937. Copy owned by Folger Shakespeare Library.

940 *A Sermon preached before the Lord Mayor, aldermen, and citizens of London, at Bow-Church, on the 30th. of January, 1681/2* [etc.]. London: Printed for Walter Kettilby, 1682.

Author: George Hickes. Allusions, pp. 17–18 and margin (*Tenure of Kings and Magistrates*), 19 and margin (*Tenure of Kings and Magistrates* with some paraphrasing), 23 and margin (*Eikonoklastes*). Wing, H1864. Copy owned by New York Public Library.

941 *A Sermon preached on the anniversary of that most execrable murder of K. Charles the first royal martyr* [etc.]. London: Printed for J. Williams and Joanna Brome, 1682.

Author: Edward Pelling. References to *Tenure of Kings and Magistrates*, pp. 12–13. Wing, P1090. Copy owned by New York Public Library.

942 *A Summons from a true-protestant conjurer, to Cethegus's ghost, to appear Septemb. 19. 1682.*

Author: Caleb Colle (?). Colophon: "London, Printed for S. B. 1682." A^2; 2 pp. Allusion in poem, ll. 36–37. Wing, S6176. Copy owned by Henry E. Huntington Library.

943 *Thomæ Hobbes Angli Malmesburiensis philosophi vita.* Carolopoli, Apud Eleutherium Angliarum, sub Signo Ventatis, 1682.

Another edition of No. *893*. References, pp. 33–34, 47. Wing, H2269. Copy owned by Newberry Library.

944 *Tracts of Mr. Thomas Hobb's of Malmsbury* [etc.]. London: Printed for W. Crooke, 1682.

Reissue of No. *895*. Wing, H2265. Copy owned by Columbia University Library.

945 *Unterricht von der teutschen sprache und poesie* [etc.]. Kiel: Joachim Neumann, 1682.

Author: Daniel Georg Morhof. Comment on Latin poems, p. 252; biographical notice, pp. 568–569 (Chapter VII). In German. Copy owned by Princeton University Library.

946 *The Visions of Dom Francisco D'e Quevedo Vellegass. The second part* [etc.]. London: Printed by T. Haly, and are to be sold by the Booksellers of London and Westminster, 1682.

Author: J. S. Gent. Prose work with some poetry. "The First Vision of the

Counsells of Hell," pp. 1–41, echoes *Paradise Lost* frequently in language; e. g., see p. 11. Wing, Q200A. Copy owned by University of Illinois Library.

1683

947 *Abregé de l'histoire de ce siècle de fer* [etc.]. Lyon: J. Girin et B. Rivière, 1683.

Another edition of No. *292*. See No. *589*. Copy owned by Bibliothèque Nationale.

948 *Annotations upon the Holy Bible* [etc.]. London, Printed by John Richardson, for Thomas Parkhurst, Dorman Newman, Jonathan Robinson, Brabazon Ailmer, Thomas Cockeril, and Benjamin Alsop, 1683.

Author: Matthew Poole. Two volumes. Influence and language from *Paradise Lost* in annotations to Genesis, without acknowledgment; see, e. g., Chapter III, verse 1. Cf. Poole's *Synopsis Criticorum Aliorumque Sacræ Scripturæ Interpretum et Commentatorium, Summa Studia et fide adornata* [etc.]. Francofurti ad Moenum: Typis & Impensis Balthasari Christophori Wustii, 1678. Wing, P2820. Copy owned by Newberry Library.

949 *The Art of poetry written in French by the Sieur de Boileau, made English.* London: Printed for R. Bentley, and S. Magnes, 1683.

Translated by Sir William Soame, altered by John Dryden. Apparent reference to *Paradise Lost* in Canto 3, pp. 40–41. Wing, B3464. Copy owned by Cambridge University Library.

950 *Beaufrons; or, a new-discovery of treason* [etc.]. London: Printed for Charles Morden, 1683.

Author: David Jenner. Allusion to *Eikonoklastes*, p. 24 and margin. Wing, J657. Copy owned by Princeton Theological Seminary Library. Apparently Wing, J656 (supposedly dated 1682) does not exist.

951 *Bibliotheca Lloydiana, sive catalogus variorum librorum selectissime bibliothecæ Rev. Doct. viri D. Joan. Lloydii, B. D.* [etc.]. Per Edvardum Millingtonum, bibliopolam. [etc.]. 1683.

Dated: 3 December 1683. Listings: *Defensio prima*, p. 22 (first pagination); *Of True Religion*, p. 27, and Filmer's *Observations*, p. 28 (last pagination). Wing, L2654. Copy owned by British Library.

952 *Catalogi cujuscumq; facultatis & linguæ librorum, in Germaniâ, Galliâ, Italiâ & Belgi, &c. novissimè impressorum. Semestre decimum quintum, a mense Iulio 1682. usque ad mensem Ianuarii 1683.* Amstelodami: Apud Janssonio-Wæsbergios, 1683.

Listing: p. 15 (*Literae*, 1682). Copy owned by Bodleian Library.

953 *Colonel Sidney's speech, delivered to the sheriff on the scaffold December 7th 1683.* Anno 1683.

Another edition of No. *988.* Quarto. See p. 4. Wing, S3765. Copy owned by British Library.

954 *The Complete courtier: or, Cupid's academy* [etc.]. London: Printed for W. T. and are to be sold by Joshua Conyers, 1683.

Author: J. Shurley, Gent.; i. e., John Shirley. Reprint of "Sweet Echo" from *A Mask*, p. 63, called "The Invocation"; echoes of *L'Allegro*, pp. 20, 35. Wing, S3503. Copy owned by Bodleian Library.

955 *The Confession of faith and the larger and shorter catechism* [etc.]. Edinbourg: Printed by George Swintoun and Thomas Brown, and are to be sold by Thomas Malthus, 1683.

Another edition of No. *45.* Allusion, pp. 57–58. Wing, C5770B. Copy owned by British Library.

956 *The Dissenters sayings, in requital for L'Estrange's sayings* [etc.]. *The fourth edition.* London: Printed for Joanna Brome, 1683.

Edition 4 of No. *873.* Wing, L1243. Copy owned by Princeton Theological Seminary Library.

957 *The Duke of Guise. A tragedy* [etc.]. London: Printed by T. H., for R. Bentley and J. Tonson, 1683.

Authors: John Dryden and Nathaniel Lee. Printer: Thomas Hodgkin (?). General influence from *Paradise Lost* throughout, but see especially Act IV, Scene [i], pp. 43–44. Probable allusion to *Paradise Lost* in Epistle Dedicatory, p. [v]. Wing, D2264. Copy owned by University of Kentucky Library.

958 *Gazette de France.* No. 46. 9 October 1683.

Notice of condemnation of books at Oxford University, pp. 585–586. In French. Microfilm owned by Princeton University Library.

959 *Georgii Hornii historia ecclesiastica et politica Editio nova, auctior emendatior.* Gorinchemi. Ex officina Corñ. Lever 1683.

Another edition of No. *585*; see No. *590.* Discussed, pp. 280–281, 353–354. Listed in Index. Copy owned by Princeton University Library.

960 *Joujan. Or, an answer to Julian the apostate. The second edition more correct, than*

the former. By a minister of London. London: Printed by Samuel Roycroft, for Walter Kettilby, 1683.

That is, "Jovian." Edition 2 of No. *962.* Wing, H1853. Copy owned by Columbia University Library.

961 *Journal des Sçavans, de l'an M. DC. LXXVII. Tome Cinqvième. Par le Sieur G. P. A. D. C.* Amsterdam: Chez Pierre le Grand, 1683.

Catalogue of works not reviewed: listing of *Epistolarum Familiarium Liber Unus* and *Artis Logicae* in appended catalogue, T10v. In French. Copy owned by New York Public Library.

962 *Jovian. Or, an answer to Julian the apostate. By a minister of London.* London: Printed by Sam. Roycroft, for Walter Kettilby, 1683.

Author: George Hickes. Edition 1. Reference to *Apology*, p. 238. Wing, H1852. Copy owned by Princeton University Library.

963 *The Judgment and decree of the University of Oxford past in their convocation July 21. 1683, against certain pernicious books and damnable doctrines destructive to the sacred persons of princes, their state and government, and of all humane society. Rendred into English, and published by command.* Printed at the Theater, 1683.

Place: Oxford. See especially Propositions 3 (p. 3) and 26 (p. 7) for condemnation of *Eikonoklastes* and *Defensio prima.* Wing, O891. Copy owned by Yale University Library.

964 *Korchelycke historie, van de scheppinge des werelts, tot 't jaer des heeren 1666* [etc.]. t'Amsterdam, By Balthus Brockholt, 1683.

Dutch translation of No. *585.* Reference concerning divorce, p. 305. Listed in Index. Copy owned by Harvard University Library.

965 *Lettres choisies de feu Monsieur Guy Patin* [etc.]. A Francfort, pour J. L. DuFour, 1683.

Letter XXIV. Au Meme [Charles Spon], dated 24 May 1650 (see No. *126*), allusion, p. 87. In French. Copy owned by Henry E. Huntington Library.

966 *Matchievel junior: or the secret-arts of the Jesuites* [etc.]. London: Printed for John Kidgell, 1683.

Author: W. S. Allusion, p. 23. Wing, S197. Copy owned by Yale University Library.

967 *A Narrative. Written by E. Settle* [etc.]. London: Printed, and are to be sold by Thomas Graves, 1683.

Author: Elkanah Settle. Allusion, p. [vi]. Wing, S2700. Copy owned by Columbia University Library.

968   *A New collection of songs and poems. By Thomas D'Urfey, Gent.* London: Printed for Joseph Hindmarsh, 1683.

"A Panegyrick on their Royal Highnesses, and Congratulating his Return from Scotland," pp. 25–30, employs some language perhaps deriving from *Paradise Lost*; see, for example, the last ten lines, p. 30. Wing, D2751. Copy owned by Library of Congress.

969   *Le Non-Conformiste Anglois dans ses ecris, dans ses sentiments, & dans sa pratique* [etc.]. Londres: Imprimé pour la Veuve du Sr Henry Broome, 1683.

Author: Sir Roger L'Estrange. Discussions of *Tenure of Kings and Magistrates*, p. 44 and margin, and *Eikonoklastes*, pp. 45, 74 and margins. Wing, L1280. Copy owned by Henry E. Huntington Library.

970   *The Observator.* No. 274, 18 January 1682 [1683]. London. Printed for Joanna Brome.

Author: Sir Roger L'Estrange. Allusion. Copy owned by Columbia University Library.

971   *The Observator.* No. 275, 20 January 1682 [1683]. London: Printed for Joanna Brome.

Author: Sir Roger L'Estrange. Allusion. Copy owned by Columbia University Library.

972   *The Observator.* No. 276, 22 January 1682 [1683]. London: Printed for Joanna Brome.

Author: Sir Roger L'Estrange. Allusion. Copy owned by Columbia University Library.

973   *The Observator.* No. 277, 24 January 1682 [1683]. London: Printed for Joanna Brome.

Author: Sir Roger L'Estrange. Allusion. Copy owned by Columbia University Library.

974   *The Observator.* No. 283, 3 February 1682 [1683]. London: Printed for Joanna Brome.

Author: Sir Roger L'Estrange. Allusion. Copy owned by Columbia University Library.

975   *The Observator*. No. 292, 19 February 1682 [1683]. London: Printed for Joanna Brome.

Author: Sir Roger L'Estrange. Allusion. Copy owned by Columbia University Library.

976   *The Observator*. No. 317, 11 April 1683. London: Printed for Joanna Brome.

Author: Sir Roger L'Estrange. Allusion. Copy owned by Columbia University Library.

977   *The Observator*. No. 382, 1 August 1683. London: Printed for Joanna Brome.

Author: Sir Roger L'Estrange. Allusion. Copy owned by Columbia University Library.

978   *The Observator*. No. 457, 17 December 1683. London: Printed for Joanna Brome.

Author: Sir Roger L'Estrange. Allusion. Copy owned by Columbia University Library.

979   ΠΑΝΣΕΒΕΙΑ: *or, a view of all religions in the world:* [etc.]. *The sixth edition, enlarged and perfected* [etc.]. London: Printed for John Williams, 1683.

Edition 6 of No. *310*. Allusions to divorce views, pp. 376, 389, 395 (?), 425. Wing, R1977. Copy owned by Columbia University Library.

980   *Remarks on Algernon Sidney's paper, delivered to the sheriffs at his execution.*

Author: Elkanah Settle. Colophon: "London, Printed for W. C. and are to be sold by W. Davis, 1683." Four pp. Sentences from *The Very Copy* (No. *988*), drawn from *Tenure of Kings and Magistrates*, quoted and commented on. Wing, S2715. Copy owned by Columbia University Library.

981   *Remarks on Algernoon Sidney's paper, delivered to the sheriffs at his execution.*

Another issue of No. *980*. Dated: 1683 (?). Not in Wing. Copy owned by Princeton University Library.

982   *A Sermon preached before the Lord Mayor, aldermen, and citizens of London, at Bow-Church, on the 30th. of January, 1681/2* [etc.]. London: Printed for Walter Kettilby, 1683.

Reissue of No. *940*. Wing, H1865. Copy owned by Union Theological Seminary Library (McAlpin Collection).

983   *The Situation of Paradise found out: being an history of a late pilgrimage into the Holy*

Land [etc.]. London: Printed by J. C. and F. C., for S. Lowndes and H. Faithorne, and J. Kersey, 1683.

Author: Henry Hare, Baron Coleraine. Printer: Freeman Collins. Allusion and quotations of *Paradise Lost* IV, 214–223; V, 291–297; IV, 236–241; IV, 543–545, on pp. 8–9. Wing, C5064. Copy owned by Princeton University Library.

984   Some animadversions on the paper delivered to the sheriffs, on Friday December, the 7th 1683. By Algernon Sidney, esq; before he was executed.

Colophon: "London: Printed by G. C. for John Cox [etc.]. 1683." Repetition of some of Sidney's language which he drew from *Tenure of Kings and Magistrates*, p. 3; see No. *988*. Wing, S4473. Copy owned by Henry E. Huntington Library.

Stationers' register. See G. E. Briscoe Eyre, ed. *A Transcript of the Registers of the Worshipful Company of Stationers; from 1640–1708 A. D.* London: 1913–1914.

985   Entry for *Paradise Lost*, under 24 July 1683, III (1914), 176.

986   Entry for *History of Britain* and of Salmasius's response, under 21 August 1683, III (1914), 184.

987   Entry for Salmasius' response, under August 1683, III (1914), 185.

988   The Very copy of a paper delivered to the sheriffs, upon the scaffold on Tower-hill, on Friday, Decemb. 7. 1683. By Algernoon Sidney, esq; before his execution there.

Colophon: "London: Printed for R. H. J. B. and J. R. and are to be sold by Walter Davis, 1683." Printers: Robert Horn, John Baker, and John Redmayne. Three pp. Sentences drawn from *Tenure of Kings and Magistrates*; see p. 2. Wing, S3766. Copy owned by Columbia University Library.

989   The Very copy of a paper delivered to the sheriffs, upon the scaffold on Tower-hill, on Friday Decemb. 7. 1683. By Algernon Sidney, esq; before his execution there.

Another issue of No. *988*. Not in Wing. Copy owned by University of Kentucky Library.

990   The very Copy of a paper delivered to the sheriffs upon the scaffold on Tower-hill on Friday December the 7th 1683. by Algernon Sidney esq; before his execution there.

Another edition of No. *988*. Colophon: "Dublin Reprinted by Mary Crooke on Ormond Key." Citations from *Tenure*, p. 2. Wing, S3767. Copy owned by Trinity College Library, Dublin.

991   A Vindication of the primitive Christians, in point of obedience to their prince, against the calumnies of a book intituled The Life of Julian [etc.]. London: Printed by J. C. and Freeman Collins, and are to be sold by Robert Kettlewell, 1683.

Author: Thomas Long. Detects Johnson's (No. *919*) and Hunt's (No. *930*) indebtedness to *Defensio prima*. See "The Epistle Dedicatory," pp. [xv–xix]; "To the Reader," p. [xxvi]; "An Appendix, containing a more full and particular Answer to Mr. Hunt's Preface and Postscript," pp. 291–347; "Reflections on the Behaviour of those Christians," pp. 180–186, 191–194, 196–197 (with quotations from *Defensio prima*). Wing, L2985. Copy owned by Union Theological Seminary Library (McAlpin Collection).

992 *The Vision of the reformation: or, a discovery of the follies and villanies* [etc.]. London: Printed for Joanna Brome, 1683.

Author: Edward Pettit. Allusion, p. 57; other possible but uncertain allusions, e.g., on pp. 123–124. Wing, P1895. Copy owned by Columbia University Library.

1684

See also Nos. *1470* and *1471*.

993 *Acta eruditorum anno MDCLXXXIV* [etc.]. Lipsiæ: Prostant apud J. Grossium & J. F. Gleditschium. Typis Christophori Güntheri, 1684.

No. 12 (December). Review of John Nalson's *An Impartial Collection of the Great Affairs of State*, p. 553, notes omission of mention of Milton. In Latin. Copy owned by New York Public Library.

994 *The Arraignment, tryal & condemnation of Algernon Sidney, esq; for high-treason* [etc.]. London: Printed for Benj. Tooke, 1684.

Reference to ideas and material drawn from *Tenure of Kings and Magistrates* in Sidney's *The Very Copy* (No. *988*), p. 60. Wing, A3754. Copy owned by University of Kentucky Library.

995 *Bibliotheca mathematica optimis libris diversarum linguarum refertissima* [etc.]. Per Edvardum Millingtonum, bibliopolam [etc.]. 1684.

Dated: 3 November 1684. Place: London. Owner: Sir Jonas Moore. Listings: p. 34, *History of Britain*; p. 37, *Poems* (1645). Wing, M2567. Copy owned by Newberry Library.

996 *Bibliotheca Oweniana, sive catalogus librorum plurimis facultatibus insignium, instructissimæ bibliothecæ Rev. Doct. Vir. D. Joan. Oweni* [etc.]. Per Edvardum Millingtonum, bibliopolam [etc.]. 1684.

Listings: *Defensio prima*, p. 23; *Epistolarum Familiarium Liber Unus* and *Artis Logicae*, p. 31; new pagination: *Paradise Lost*, p. 28; *History of Britain*, p. 30; *Animadversions* and Smectymnuus' *Answer*, p. 32. Wing, O714. Copy owned by British Library.

997 *Bibliotheca Sturbitchiana, sive catalogus variorum librorum antiquorum, & recentiorum* [etc.]. 1684.

Dated: 8 September 1684. Place: Cambridge. Bookseller: Edward Millington. Listings: p. 18, *Artis Logicae*; p. 40, *Poems* (1673). Wing, B2857. Copy owned by British Library.

998 *The Case of resistance of the supreme powers stated and resolved, according to the doctrine of the holy scriptures* [etc.]. London: Printed for Fincham Gardiner, 1684.

Author: William Sherlock. Edition 1. Discussion of *Defensio prima*, pp. 117–119 and margin. Wing, S3267. Copy owned by Princeton Theological Seminary Library.

999 *A Catalogue of books continued, printed and published at London in Trinity-term.* 1684. No. 16.

Colophon: "Printed for the Booksellers of London. 1684." Allusion in listing of MacKenzie's *Jus Regium*. Copy owned by Henry E. Huntington Library.

1000 *A Catalogue of books continued, printed and published at London in Michaelmas-term.* 1684. No. 17.

Colophon: "Printed for the Booksellers of London. 1684." Listing of Richard Bovet's *Pandemonium* and of *The State of Innocence*. Copy owned by Henry E. Huntington Library.

1001 *A Catalogue of the libraries of two eminent persons deceased* [etc.]. 1684.

Bookseller: Edward Millington. Listings in a later pagination: *History of Britain* and *Poems* (1673), p. 18. Wing, C1379. Copy owned by British Library.

1002 *Catalogus eximiæ & instructissimæ bibliothecæ clarissimi doctissimique viri D. Adriani vander Walle, J. U. D.* [etc.]. Lugduni-Batavorum: Apud Petrum vander Meersche, 1684.

Dated: 23 October 1684. Listing: p. 58, Salmasius's *Defensio Regia* and *Defensio prima*. Copy owned by British Library.

1003 *Catalogus librorum reverendi doctiq; viri Matth. Smallwood, S. T. P. & decani de Lychfield nuper defuncti* [etc.]. Londini, 1684.

Dated: 2 May 1684. Listings: p. 27, *Paradise Lost*; p. 35, *Doctrine and Disci-*

pline of Divorce, Tetrachordon, Of Reformation; p. 23, Du Moulin's *Regii Sanguinis Clamor*, More's *Fides Publicae, Defensio secunda*. Wing, S4010. Copy owned by British Library.

1004 *Catalogus librorum theologicorum, juridicorum, philologicorum, medicorum, &c. bibliothecæ D. D. Benj. Broeckhuysen* [etc.]. 1684.

Dated: 1 December 1684. Place: London. Bookseller: William Cooper. Listings: p. 13, *Defensio prima*; Appendix, p. 4, *Defensio prima*; p. 10, *Defensio prima*. Wing, B4840. Copy owned by British Library.

1005 *Catalogus variorum & insignium librorum* [etc.]. *Officinæ Joannis Janssonii à Waesberge, P. M.* [etc.]. Amstelodami: Apud Guilielmum Goeree, 1684.

Listings (second pagination), pp. 160 (3), 167 (Phillips' *Responsio*), 175 (Schaller's dissertation), 190 (Ziegler's dissertation). Copy owned by New York Public Library.

1006 *Catalogus variorum librorum bibliothecæ selectissimæ rev. doct. viri. D. Tho. Lye* [etc.]. 1684.

Dated: 17 November 1684. Place: London. Listings: p. 22, *Artis Logicae*; p. 43, *Moscovia*. Wing, L3529. Copy owned by British Library.

1007 *A Compendious history of all the popish & fanatical plots and conspiracies against the established government in church & state, in England, Scotland, and Ireland:* [etc.]. London: Printed for D. Brown and T. Goodwin, 1684.

Author: Thomas Long. Allusion, p. 93. Wing, L2963. Copy owned by Columbia University Library.

1008 *A Defence of Sir Robert Filmer, against the mistakes and misrepresentations of Alger-non Sidney, esq; in a paper delivered by him to the sheriffs* [etc.]. London: Printed for W. Kettilby, 1684.

Author: Edmund Bohun. Quotations from Sidney's *The Very Copy* (No. *988*), drawn from *Tenure of Kings and Magistrates*, given on pp. 10–11 with comment on pp. 11–12. Wing, B3450. Copy owned by New York Public Library.

1009 *The Free-holders grand inquest, touching our sovereign Lord the King and his parliament. To which are added Observations upon forms of government* [etc.]. *The fourth impression*. London: Printed for Rich. Royston, 1684.

Another edition of No. *785*. Allusions or discussion: Contents, p. [xiv]; *Observations concerning the original of government*, pp. [165], 181–196; *Patriarcha*, Letter, A4v (reissue of No. *842*). Wing, F916. Copy owned by Columbia University Library.

1010 Horace's art of poetry. Made English by the right honorable the earl of Roscommon. London: Printed for Henry Herringman, and sold by Joseph Knight and Thomas Saunders, 1684.

Another editon of No. *837*. Probable allusion in Preface, A2. Wing, H2769. Copy owned by British Library.

1011 An Introduction to the old English history, comprehended in three several tracts [etc.]. London: Printed by Tho. Newcomb, for Samuel Lowndes, 1684.

Author: Robert Brady. Allusion in *A True and Exact History of the Succession of the Crown of England*, p. 355. Wing, B4194. Copy owned by University of Kentucky Library.

1012 Jus regium: or, the just and solid foundations of monarchy in general; and more especially of the monarchy of Scotland: maintain'd against Buchanan, Naphtali, Dolman, Milton, &c. [etc.]. London: Printed for R. Chiswel, 1684.

Author: Sir George MacKenzie. Allusions, A4v (To the Reader), p. 116. Wing, M164. Copy owned by University of Kentucky Library.

1013 Jus regium: or, the just and solid foundations of monarchy in general; and more especially of the monarchy of Scotland: maintain'd against Buchanan, Naphtali, Dolman, Milton, &c. [etc.]. London: Printed for Richard Chiswel, 1684.

Another issue of No. *1012*. Wing, M163. Copy owned by Henry E. Huntington Library.

1014 Jus regium: or, the just, and solid foundations of monarchy [etc.]. Edinburgh: Printed by the Heir of Andrew Anderson, 1684.

Another edition of No. *1012*. Two sets of signatures and three sets of pages: [A]^2 B-G^4 H^2 F-O^4; π^2 A-C$^{8(-C8)}$ D-G^4. Allusion, A1v ("To the Reader"). Second allusion in "What follows is immediatly to be subjoyn'd ... ," p. 10 (G1v) of third pagination, added to "That the Lawful Successor Cannot be Debarr'd from succeeding to the Crown: [etc.]." Edinburgh: Printed by the Heir of Andrew Anderson, 1684. Wing, M162. Copy owned by Folger Shakespeare Library.

1015 Jus regium: or, the just, and solid foundations of monarchy [etc.]. Edinburgh: Printed by the Heir of Andrew Anderson, 1684.

Another issue of No. *1014*. [A]^2 B-G^4 H^2 F-O^4; π^2 A-C$^{8(-C7, C8)}$ D-G^4. Unpaged to p. 33; paged from second F1. Apparently unfinished; see p. 102 with catchword "The", which perhaps is supposed to be "That". See Wing, M162. Copy owned by William Andrews Clark Library.

1016 Linguæ Latinæ liber dictionarius quadripartitus [etc.]. London: Printed for T. Basset, J. Wright, and R. Chiswell, 1684.

Edition 4 (?) of No. *772*. Wing, L2564. Copy owned by Newberry Library.

1017 Miscellany poems. Containing a new translation of Virgills Eclogues, Ovid's Love elegies, Odes of Horace, and other authors; with several original poems [etc.]. London: Printed for Jacob Tonson, 1684.

Editor: John Dryden. Vol. 1 of six vols. with individual title pages. Appropriations or imitations: John Dryden, "Mac Flecknoe," pp. 1–11; "Absalom and Achitophel," pp. 25–73. Allusions: "The Medall," p. 80; Nathaniel Lee, "To the Unknown Authour of this Excellent Poem" (that is Dryden and "Absalom and Achitophel"), p. 20. Wing, D2314. Copy owned by Folger Shakespeare Library.

1018 Mr. Sidney his self-conviction: or, his dying-paper condemn'd to live, for a conviction to the present faction, and a caution to posterity. London: Printed by H. Hills Jun. for Robert Clavell, 1684.

Author: anonymous. Quotations from Sidney's speech (see No. *988*), some of which are drawn from *Tenure of Kings and Magistrates*, are commented upon extensively, pp. 8–16. Wing, S3762. Copy owned by Folger Shakespeare Library.

1019 Nouvelles de la republique des lettres. Mois de Mars 1684 [etc.]. Amsterdam: Chez Henry Desbordes, 1684.

Author: Pierre Bayle. Edition 1. Allusion to *Areopagitica* in Preface, *2v. In French. Copy owned by University of Michigan Library.

1020 Nouvelles de la republique des lettres. Mois d'Avril 1684 [etc.]. Amsterdam: Chez Henry Desbordes, 1684.

Author: Pierre Bayle. Edition 1. Discussion of *Tenure of Kings and Magistrates, Defensio prima*, and the Oxford proclamation (No. *963*), in Article III, pp. 141–142. In French. Copy owned by University of Michigan Library.

1021 The Observator, in dialogue. The first volume. By Roger L'Estrange, esq. [etc.]. London: Printed by J. Bennet, for William Abington, 1684.

Reissue of *The Observator*; see Nos. *931–34, 970–78*. Copy owned by Columbia University Library.

1022 Of patience and submission to authority, a sermon preach'd before the Lord Mayor and the court of aldermen, at Guild-hall Chapel, on the 27th of January, 1683/4. By John

Moore, D. D. London: Printed for R. Royston; and Walter Kettilby, 1684.

On Hebrews x.36. Allusion, p. 40. Wing, L2545. Copy owned by Princeton University Library.

1023 *The Original of war: or, the causes of rebellion. A sermon preached in the Castle of Exon, on the 15th of January 1683* [etc.]. London: Printed by J. C. and F. Collins, for Daniel Brown; and are to be sold by Walter Davies, 1684.

Author: Thomas Long. Quotation from *Tenure of Kings and Magistrates*, p. 22. Wing, L2978. Copy owned by British Library.

1024 Oxford. Bodleian Library. Wood MS F.39.

Letter from John Aubrey to Anthony Wood; receipt dated 25 May 1684. On Sonnets 15 and 16, f. 372. Note by Wood, f. 372v.

1025 Oxford. Bodleian Library. Wood MS F.42.

Letter from William Joyner to Anthony Wood, dated 27 May 1684, ff. 322–323. Allusion.

1026 *Pandaemonium, or the devil's cloyster being a further blow to modern Sadduceism* [etc.]. London: Printed for J. Walthoe, 1684.

Author: Richard Bovet. Allusion, p. 9, and title. Wing, B3864. Copy owned by Henry E. Huntington Library.

1027 *Pandaemonium, or the devil's cloyster being a further blow to modern Sadduceism* [etc.]. London: Printed for Tho. Malthus, 1684.

Another edition of No. *1026*. Allusion, p. 15, and title. Wing, B3864A. Copy owned by Folger Shakespeare Library.

1028 *Poems and translations by John Oldham.* London: Printed for Joseph Hindmarsh, 1684.

Allusion in "Bion," p. 82. Wing, O238. Copy owned by Columbia University Library.

1029 *Poems written on several occasions, by N. Tate. The second edition enlarged.* London: Printed for B. Tooke, 1684.

Edition 2 of No. *750*. Includes "On the Present Corrupted State of Poetry," pp. 16–21; "The Match," p. 67; "On Snow fall'n in Autumn, and Dissolv'd by the Sun," p. 80. Adds "Hor. Ode 5th, lib. 3," pp. 155–156, which seems to owe something to Milton's version. Wing, T211 (and T209 in error). Copy owned by Folger Shakespeare Library.

1030 *Prerogative and privilege represented in a sermon in the cathedral church of Rochester in Kent, March 18. 1683/4* [etc.]. London: Printed for B. Tooke and W. Kettilby, 1684.

Author: Richard Forster. Allusion, p. 32. Wing, F1606. Copy owned by Yale University Library.

1031 *Reflections upon Coll. Sidney's Arcadia; the old cause, being some observations upon his last paper, given to the sheriffs at his execution.* London: Printed for Thomas Dring, 1684.

Author: John Nalson. Probable allusion to *Paradise Lost*, p. 16. Wing, N114. Copy owned by Yale University Library.

1032 *Remains of Mr. John Oldham in verse and prose.* London: Printed for Jo. Hindmarsh, 1684.

Variant issue of No. *1043*. Title page of *Remains* and preface used to introduce collection, with remainder of volume bound at end. Gives 1685 *Satyrs* and 1684 *Some New Pieces* (No. *1037*). Not in Wing. Copy owned by Princeton University Library.

1033 *The Rival queens, or the death of Alexander the Great* [etc.]. London: Printed by J. Gain, for Richard Bentley, 1684.

Another edition of No. *753*. Imitation, p. 38. Wing, L866. Copy owned by University of Kentucky Library.

1034 *The Royal martyr: or, the life and death of King Charles I* [etc.]. *The third edition.* London: Printed by J. M. for R. Royston, 1684.

Another edition of Nos. *543* and *726*. Discussion, pp. 226–227. Wing, P1602. Copy owned by Henry E. Huntington Library.

1035 *The Royal martyr: or, the life and death of King Charles I* [etc.]. *The third edition.* London: Printed by J. M. for R. Royston, 1684.

Another issue of No. *1034*, to which are added the 1685 *Eikon Basilike* and the 1697 *Vindication*, Edition 2 (No. *1552*). Not in Wing. Copy owned by British Library.

1036 *Samuelis Pufendorfii de jure naturæ et gentium libri octo. Editio secunda, auctior multo, et emendatior.* Francofurti ad Moenum, sumptibus Friderici Knochii. Charactere Joannis Philippi Andreæ 1684.

Another edition of No. *655*. Reference, p. 831; discussion, pp. 875–880. Copy owned by Folger Shakespeare Library.

1037 *Some new pieces never before publish'd* [etc.]. London: Printed by M. C. for Jo. Hindmarsh, 1684.

Author: John Oldham. Printer: Mary Clark. A^8 + $a^4(-a4)$ B–H^8 I^6 with I5 signed I3 and I3–4 added later. Allusion in "Bion," p. 82. Wing, O249. Copy owned by New York Public Library.

1038 *Some new pieces never before publish'd* [etc.]. London: Printed by M. C. for Jo. Hindmarsh, 1684.

Different issue of No. *1037*. A^8 + $a^4(-a4)$ added after A^1 B–F^8 G^2 H–L^8. a4 cancelled (?); L8, blank and missing. Not in Wing. Copy owned by Folger Shakespeare Library.

1039 THE | State of Innocence, | AND | FALL of MAN: | AN | OPERA. | Written in Heroick Verse; | And Dedicated to Her Royal *Highness* | THE | DUTCHESS. | ———— | By *John Dryden*, Servant to His Majesty. | ———— | [two lines in Latin from Ovid's *Metamorphoses*] | ———— | *LONDON:* Printed by *H. H.* for *Henry Herringman*, and are | to be sold by *Joseph Knight*, and *Francis Saunders*, at the An- | chor in the Lower Walk of the *New Exchange*. 1684. |

Quarto. A–G^4; xvi + 40 pp. [i], title page; [ii], blank; [iii–vi], Dedication; [vii–viii], Lee's poem; [ix–xvi], Preface; 1–38, work; [39–40], Plays Printed. See Wing, D2375. Copy owned by University of Kentucky Library.

1040 To the Reader. It is not customary with me to make long harangues [etc.].

Title page missing. Dated: 24 March 1683/4. Listings: p. 45, *Paradise Lost*; p. 46, *Accedence Commenc't Grammar*. Copy owned by British Library.

1041 *Triumphant chastity: or, Josephs self-conflict* [etc.]. London: Printed for Benjamin Crayle, 1684.

Another edition of No. *847*. Wing, C1525. Copy owned by Princeton University Library.

1042 *The Visions of government, wherein the antimonarchical principles and practices of all fanatical commonwealths-men, and Jesuitical politicians are discovered, confuted, and exposed* [etc.]. London: Printed by B. W., for Edward Vize, 1684.

Author: Edward Pettit. Milton as Papist, "The Third Vision," pp. 148–149. Wing, P1892. Copy owned by Union Theological Seminary Library (McAlpin Collection).

1043 *The Works of Mr. John Oldham, together with his Remains.* London: Printed for Jo. Hindmarsh, 1684.

Begins with *Satyrs upon the Jesuits* [etc.]. *The third edition corrected*. London: Printed for Joseph Hindmarsh, 1685.

Allusion in reissue of No. *1037*. Wing, O225. Copy owned by Princeton University Library.

1044 [*The Works of Mr. John Oldham, together with his Remains*. London: Printed for Jo. Hindmarsh, 1684.]

Different issue of No. *1043*. No title page; contents page, A1v, lists Part I (*Satyrs upon the Jesuits* and *The Passion of Byblis*) and Part II (*Some new pieces, Poems and translations*, and *Remains*). Begins with *Satyrs ... The second edition more corrected* (1682); includes *Some new pieces* (1681), reissue of No. *891; Poems and translations* (1683); and *Remains* (1684). Allusion in "Bion" in reissue of No. *891*. See Wing, O224. Copy owned by University of Kentucky Library.

1045 [*The Works of Mr. John Oldham*. London: Printed by M. C. for Jo. Hindmarsh, 1684.]

Another issue of No. *1043*. No title page. Includes *Satyrs* (1682), *Some new pieces* (1684), *Poems and translations* (1684), and *Remains* (1684). Edition of *Some new pieces* seems to be the variant of No. *1037*, that is, No. *1038*. Allusion in "Bion," p. 82. See Wing, O225 and O249. Copy owned by Bodleian Library.

1046 *The Works of the reverend and learned Henry Hammond, D. D.* [etc.]. *The second edition* [etc.]. London: Printed for R. Royston and R. Davis, 1684.

Collected edition including No. *301*. Four vols. Discussion of divorce views in *A Letter of Resolution*, I, 598–599. Wing, H508. Copy owned by Princeton University Library.

1685

1047 *Aureng-Zebe, a tragedy. Acted at the Royal Theatre* [etc.]. London: Printed by J. M., for Henry Herringman, and are to be sold by Jos. Knight and F. Saunders, 1685.

Author: John Dryden. Imitation of *Samson Agonistes*, Act I, pp. 7–8. Wing, D2246. Copy owned by Columbia University Library.

1048 *Beaufrons; or, a new discovery of treason, under the fair-face and mask of religion* [etc.]. London: Printed for Charles Morden, and are to be sold by Joseph Hindmarsh, 1685.

Another edition of No. *950*. Wing, J658. Copy owned by Henry E. Huntington Library.

1049 *Bibliographia historia chronologica et geographica, novissima, perpetuo continuanda* [etc.]. Amstelædami: Apud Janssonio-Waesbergios, 1685.

Compiler: Cornelius à Beughem. Listings: pp. 176 (*History of Britain*, noted in Latin, published in quarto, dated "1668"); 449 (*History of Britain*, noted in English, published in octavo, dated "166."); 666 (Index). Copy owned by Columbia University Library.

1050 *Bibliotheca Sturbrigiensis sive catalogus variorum librorum antiquorum, & recentiorum* [etc.]. 1685.

Dated: 8 September 1685. Place: London. Bookseller: Edward Millington. Listings: p. 14, *Artis Logicae*; p. 15, *Artis Logicae*; p. 16, *Literae, Defensio prima*; p. 18, *Defensio prima, Regii Sanguinis Clamor* (assigned to More). Wing, B2858. Copy owned by British Library.

1051 *The Cataclysm: or general deluge of the world: an opera, adorned with various sculptures* [etc.]. London: Printed for T. M. and sold by Iohn Holford, 1685.

Another edition of No. *794*. Allusions: pp. [vii], comment by Saunders; [viii], comment by Leanerd; [x], comment by Norton; [xii–xiv], Preface. Wing, E138. Copy owned by Henry E. Huntington Library.

1052 *A Catalogue containing variety of ancient, and modern English books* [etc.]. 1685.

Dated: 30 November 1685. Place: London. Bookseller: Edward Millington. Listing: p. 32, *History of Britain*. Wing, C1255. Copy owned by British Library.

1053 *A Catalogue of the library of books French and English, of Mr. Peter Hushar, merchant of London, deceased* [etc.]. 1685.

Dated: 18 November 1685. Place: London. Bookseller: Edward Millington. Listings: p. 20, *Paradise Lost, Paradise Regain'd*. Wing, H3810. Copy owned by British Library.

1054 *A Catalogue of the library of choice books Latin and English of the reverend and learned Dr. Richard Lee* [etc.]. 1685.

Dated: 28 April 1685. Place: London. Listings: p. 25, *Doctrine and Discipline of Divorce*; p. 26, *Tetrachordon*; p. 28, *Answer to Doctrine and Discipline of Divorce*. Wing, L886. Copy owned by British Library.

1055 *Catalogus librorum omnium qui reperiuntur Parisiis in bibliopolio viduæ Edmundi Martini & Joannis Boudot*, 1685.

Listings: p. 150, *Defensio prima, Epistolarum Familiarium Liber Unus, Literae, Artis Logicae.* Copy owned by Bodleian Library.

1056 Catalogus librorum theologicorum, philologicorum, mathematicorum, &c. Dris Stokes & aliorum [etc.]. 1685.

Dated: 1 December 1685. Place: London. Owner: Richard Stokes. Bookseller: William Cooper. Listing: p. 59, *Poems* (1673). Wing, S5726. Copy owned by British Library.

1057 Catalogus variorum librorum ex bibliothecis selectissimis doctissim. virorum nuperrime defunctorum [etc.]. 1685.

Dated: 19 October 1685. Place: London. Bookseller: Thomas Parkhurst. Listings: p. 61, *History of Britain*; p.76, *Poems* and Latin Poems. Wing, P491. Copy owned by British Library.

1058 Catalogus variorum librorum quavis facultate insigniorum bibliotecharum instructissimarum Rev. Doct. Amb. Atfield S. T. D. nuperrime Londinensis [etc.].

Dated: 25 May 1685. Place: London. Bookseller: Edward Millington. Listings: p. 26, *Defensio prima*, Rowland's *Pro Rege Apologia*; p. 28, Salmasius's *Defensio Regia* "contra Miltonum" and *Defensio prima*; p. 30, *Defensio prima*, Rowland's *Pro Rege Apologia*; p. 31, Smectymnuus' *Answer*; p. 32, *Censure of the Rota*; p. 51, *Moscovia*; p. 53, *Paradise Regain'd, Moscovia, History of Britain.* Wing, A4106. Copy owned by British Library.

1059 A Collection of 86 songs [etc.]. Printed by N. T., 1685.

Author: Nathaniel Thompson. Different edition (second?) of No. *1060.* Wing, T1005. Copy owned by Folger Shakespeare Library.

1060 A Collection of loyal poems, all of them written upon the two late plots [etc.]. Printed by N. T., 1685.

Author: Nathaniel Thompson. Place: London. So-called third edition. Influence and appropriated phrases: "The Ghost of the late Paliament [sic] to the New one to meet at Oxford," opening from "Comus," pp. 27-29; "The Recovery," from "Lycidas" and *Paradise Lost*, pp. 31-34; "A Poem on the Coronation," l. 1 from "On Time," p. 388. Wing, T1003. Copy owned by Princeton University Library.

A Choice Collection of 180 Loyal Songs. All of them written since the Two late Plots ... The Third Edition with many Additions (London: Printed by N. T., 1685) does not print these poems; see copy in Henry E. Huntington Library. Nor does *A Collection, Of One Hundred and Eighty Loyal Songs, All Written since 1678. The Fourth Edition with many Additions* (London: Printed, and are to be Sold by Richard Butt, 1694); see copy in William Andrews Clark Library.

1061 *A Collection of several tracts and dsicourses, written in the years 1678, 1679, 1680,*
1681, 1682, 1683, 1684, 1685 [etc.]. London: Printed for Ric. Chiswell,
1685.

Note "dsicourses." Author: Gilbert Burnet. Includes reissue of No. *886.* See
Wing, B5770. Copy owned by Union Theological Seminary Library
(McAlpin Collection).

1062 *A Collection of several tracts and discourses, written in the years 1678, 1679, 1680,*
1681, 1682, 1683, 1684, 1685 [etc.]. London: Printed for Ric. Chiswell,
1685.

Different issue of No. *1061.* See Wing, B5770. Copy owned by New York
Public Library.

1063 *A Compendious view of the late tumults & troubles in this kingdom* [etc.]. London:
Printed by Edw. Jones, for S. Lownds, 1685.

Author: James Wright. Allusion to Milton as papist and burning of books
at Oxford, p. 178. Wing, W3692. Copy owned by Columbia University
Library.

1064 *The Confession of faith, and the larger and shorter catechisms* [etc.]. Edinburgh:
Printed by the Heir of Andrew Anderson, 1685.

Another edition of No. *45.* Allusion, p. 55. Wing, C5771. Copy owned by
National Library of Scotland.

1065 *The Dissenters sayings. Two parts in one. Published in their own words* [etc.]. London: Printed for Charles Brome, 1685.

Author: Sir Roger L'Estrange. Quotations from *Eikonoklastes*, pp. 25, 35,
53 (apparently twice); quotation from *Tenure of Kings and Magistrates*, p. 38.
Wing, L1244. Copy owned by Columbia University Library.

1066 *Elenchus motuum nuperorum in Anglia: Or, a short historical account of the rise and*
progress of the late troubles in England. In two parts [etc.]. *Motus compositi: or,*
the history of the composing the affairs of England [etc.]. London: Printed for Abel
Swalle, and are to be sold by Samuel Eddowes, 1685.

Authors: George Bate and Thomas Skinner. Translator: Thomas Skinner
(or A. Lovell). Allusion to antimonarchical works, in Part I, p. 159. No
Index to this part. Discussion, pp. 59–60 and margin, in Part III, written
by Thomas Skinner. See Wing, B1083. Copy owned by Columbia University Library.

1067 *Elencus motuum nuperorum in Anglia: Or, a short historical account of the rise and*
progress of the late troubles in England. In two parts [etc.]. *Motus compositi: or,*

the history of the composing the affairs of England [etc.]. London: Printed for Abel Swalle, 1685.

Different edition of No. *1066* with new signatures and pagination. Allusions and discussions as in No. *1066*. See Wing, B1083. Copy owned by University of Kentucky Library.

1068 An Essay on translated verse. By the Earl of Roscommon [etc.]. *The second edition corrected and enlarg'd.* London: Printed for Jacob Tonson, 1685.

Author: Wentworth Dillon, Earl of Roscommon. Allusion and imitation, ll. 377–403, pp. 24–[25] and margin. Wing, R1931. Copy owned by Columbia University Library.

1069 An Essay upon poetry [etc.]. London: Printed for Jo. Hindmarsh, 1685.

Author: John Sheffield, Lord Buckingham. Allusion, p. 21. Wing, B5341. Copy owned by Folger Shakespeare Library.

1070 The Grounds and occasions of the contempt of the clergy and religion enquired into in a letter written to R. L. The ninth edition. London: Printed by R. Holt, for Obadiah Blagrave, 1685.

Another edition of No. *620*. Allusion, A4–A4v. Wing, E53. Copy owned by Union Theological Seminary Library (McAlpin Collection).

1071 Jugemens des scavans sur les principaux ouvrages des auteurs. Paris: Chez Antoine De Zalier, 1685.

Author: Adrian Baillet. Vol. 2, Part 2. In "Critiques Grammairiens," allusion to Salmasian controversy, p. 427. Copy owned by Princeton University Library.

1072 Lettres choisies de feu Monsieur Gvy Patin [etc.]. A Paris: Chez Jean Petit, 1685.

See No. *126*. Lettre XXIV, pp. 86–87. Copy owned by British Library.

1073 London. British Library. Additional MS 4239.

"The Life of Adam Martindale ... written by himself." Dated: 1685. No title page. Allusion, f. 43 (Chapter IV, Section XXIV). Published by Richard Parkinson, editor (Manchester: Printed for the Chetham Society, 1845), allusion, p. 99.

1074 Love given o're: or, a satyr against the pride, lust, and inconstancy, &c. of woman. London: Printed for R. Bentley, and J. Tonson, 1685.

Another edition of No. *922*. See p. 2. Wing, G1424. Copy owned by Bodleian Library.

1075 *Maggots: or, poems on several subjects, never before handled. By a schollar.* London: Printed for John Dunton, 1685.

Author: Samuel Wesley (?). Quarto. Imitative line (see "Nativity Ode," 68) in "Out of Lucian's true History, Part the First," p. 119 and note on p. 122. Wing, W1374. Copy owned by Columbia University Library.

1076 *Maggots: or, poems on several subjects, never before handled. By a scholar.* London: Printed for John Dunton, 1685.

Edition 2 of No. *1075*. Octavo. Wing, W1375. Copy owned by Bodleian Library.

1077 *The Method and order of reading both civil and ecclesiastical histories* [etc.]. London: Printed by M. Flesher, for Charles Brome, 1685.

Author: Degory Wheare. Translator and editor: Edmund Bohun. Notice of *History of Britain* in additon by Bohun, pp. 170-171; allusion, p. 177. Listed in Index. Wing, W1592. Copy owned by New York Public Library.

1078 *Miscellany poems. In two parts.* [etc.]. London: Printed for Jacob Tonson, 1685.

Reissue of No. *1017* with 1684 title page included, to which is added No. *1090*. Not in Wing. Copy owned by Folger Shakespeare Library.

1079 *Nouvelles de la republique des lettres. Mois d'Avril 1685.* Amsterdam: Chez Henry Desbordes, 1685.

Author: Pierre Bayle. Milton's championing of Cromwell and divorce, Article I, p. 352. Copy owned by University of Chicago Library.

1080 *Nouvelles de la republique des lettres. Mois d'Aout 1685.* Amsterdam: Chez Henry Desbordes, 1685.

Author: Pierre Bayle. References to *Eikonoklastes*, Article IX, pp. 904-905. Copy owned by Folger Shakespeare Library.

1081 *On Thursday the 26. of this instant November 1685* [etc.] *will be exposed to sale to booksellers part of the stock of Mr. Richard Davis, bookseller of Oxford* [etc.].

Place: Oxford. Folio. A^2; 4 pp. Listing: p. 1, *History of Britain*. Wing, D431. Copy owned by British Library.

1082 *Patriarcha: or the natural power of kings* [etc.]. *The second edition* [etc.]. *To which is added, A Preface to the reader in which this piece is vindicated from the cavils and misconstructions of the author of a book stiled Patriarcha non monarcha. And also a conclusion or postscript. By Edmund Bohun, esq*; London: Printed for R. Chiswel, W. Hensman, M. Gilliflower, and G. Wells, 1685.

Author: Sir Robert Filmer. Discussion of Filmer's *Observations* in Preface, by Bohun, f3v-f4. Allusion in letter from Peter Heylyn to Sir Edward Filmer, p. [182] (i. e., N3v), given at end. See No. *842*. Wing, F924. Copy owned by Columbia University Library.

1083 *Poems by several hands, and on several occasions*[.] *Collected by N. Tate.* London: Printed for J. Hindmarsh, 1685.

Allusion in John Evelyn, "To Envy," p. 91. Wing, T210. Copy owned by Yale University Library.

Also published as "The Immortality of Poesie. To Envy," pp. 250–253, in *Tixall Poetry; with Notes and Illustrations by Arthur Clifford, Esq.* [etc.]. Edinburgh: James Ballantyne and Co., 1813, with a note on the authorship. See also No. *1752*.

1084 *Reliquiæ Wottonianæ: or, a collection* [etc.]. *The fourth edition, with additions of several letters to the Lord Zouch, never publish'd till now.* London: Printed for B. Tooke and T. Sawbridge, 1685.

Edition 4 of No. *198*. Letter to Milton, pp. 342–344. Wing, W3651. Copy owned by Ted-Larry Pebworth and Claude J. Summers, University of Michigan — Dearborn.

1085 *Salus Britannica: or, the safety of the protestant religion, against all the present apprehensions of popery fully discust and proved* [etc.]. London: Printed for Tho. Graves, 1685.

Author: anonymous. Allusion, p. 22. Wing, S511. Copy owned by Folger Shakespeare Library.

1086 *A Sermon preached before the king on the 30th of January, 1684/5. Being the fast for the martyrdom of King Charles the first of blessed memory* [etc.]. London: Printed for Robert Clavell, 1685.

Author: Francis Turner. Allusion, p. 16. Wing, T3287. Copy owned by New York Public Library.

1087 *A Sermon preached in the King's chappel at White-Hall, upon the 29th of May, 1685* [etc.]. London: Printed for Walter Kettilby, 1685.

Author: Thomas Turner. Allusion and quotation, p. 8 and margin. Wing, T3340. Copy owned by New York Public Library.

1088 *A Sermon preached on the 30th. of January, 1684. The day of martyrdom of King Charles I. of blessed memory* [etc.]. London: Printed by T. M., and are to be sold by Randal Taylor, 1685.

Author: Edward Pelling. Probable allusion to *Tenure of Kings and Magistrates*, pp. 31–32. Wing, P1097. Copy owned by New York Public Library.

1089 *Spiegel der sibyllen, van vierderley vertooningen* [etc.]. Amsterdam: Timotheus ten Hoorn, 1685.

Author: Joannes Aysma. Milton cited in preliminary material as one of the authors consulted. Copy owned by New York Public Library.

1090 *Sylvæ: or, the second part of Poetical miscellanies* [etc.]. London: Printed for Jacob Tonson, 1685.

Editor: John Dryden. Discussion in Preface, a7v–a8. See also No. *1078*. Wing, D2379. Copy owned by Berg Collection, New York Public Library.

1091 *The Visions of purgatory, anno 1680. In which the errors and practices of the church and court of Rome are discover'd* [etc.]. *The second edition corrected*. London: Printed by M. Flesher for Charles Brome, 1685.

Edition 2 of No. *849*. Wing, P1894. Copy owned by Henry E. Huntington Library.

1686

1092 *Acta eruditorum   anno MDCLXXXVI* [etc.]. Lipsiæ: Prostant apud J. Grossium & J. F. Gleditschium. Typis Christophori Guntheri, 1686.

No. 6 (June). Review of MacKenzie's *Jus Regium*, p. 315. In Latin. Copy owned by New York Public Library.

1093 *Bibliotheca Angleseiana, sive catalogus variorum librorum in quavis linguâ & facultate insignium* [etc.]. Per Thomam Phillippum [etc.]. 1686.

Dated: 25 October 1686. Place: London. Owner: Arthur Annesley, Earl of Anglesey. Listings: p. 49, *Defensio secunda, Defensio pro se*; p. 50, *Literae*; p. 84, *Eikonoklastes* (French translation); new pagination: p. 46, Smectymnuus, *Answer*; p. 47, *Of True Religion*; p. 48, *Doctrine and Discipline of Divorce*, Smectymnuus, *Answer*; p. 49, *Doctrine and Discipline of Divorce*; p. 65, *Of Reformation* "with about 12 other Tracts"; p. 67, *Complete Collection, Ready and Easy Way, Tenure* and *Ready and Easy Way* (together); p. 68, *Areopagitica*; p. 70, *Doctrine and Discipline of Divorce, Of Reformation*; p. 71, *Doctrine and Discipline of Divorce, Eikonoklastes*, Filmer's *Observations*. Wing, A3166. Copy owned by Newberry Library.

1094 *Catalogi variorum in quavis lingua & facultate insignium tam antiquorum quam recentium librorum Richardi Davis bibliopolæ. Pars secunda* [etc.]. 1686.

Dated: 4 October 1686. Place: Oxford. Booksellers: William Cooper and Edward Millington. Listings: p. 59, *Literae, Artis Logicae*; p. 62, *Artis Logicae*; p. 147, *Poems* (1673), *Paradise Regain'd*; p. 150, *Paradise Regain'd*; p. 155, *Poems* (1673); p. 159, *Poems* (1673). Wing, D427. Copy owned by British Library.

1095 A Collection of choice books in divinity, history, philosophy [etc.]. 1686.

Dated: 8 February 1686. Place: London. Booksellers: Richard Chiswell, Edward Millington. Listing: p. 5 (in error), *Moscovia*. Wing, C5119. Copy owned by British Library.

1096 Commentariorum de rebellione Anglicana ab anno 1640. Usque ad annum 1685. Pars prima. Autore R. M. eq. aur. [etc.]. Londini: Impensis L. Meredith and T. Newborough, 1686.

Author: Sir Roger Manley. Milton's denigration of Charles, p. 226. Listed in Index. Wing, M437. Copy owned by Yale University Library.

1097 Commentariorum de rebellione Anglicana ab anno 1640. Usque ad annum 1685. Pars prima. Autore R. M. eq. aur. [etc.]. Londini: Typis E. Horton & R. Holt, 1686.

Another edition of No. *1096*. Wing, M438. Copy owned by British Library.

1098 John Evelyn of Wotton. Diary of John Evelyn, under 9 June 1686.

Allusion. See E. S. deBeer. *The Diary of John Evelyn*. Oxford: Clarendon Press, 1955. IV, 514.

1099 The Female advocate: or, an answer to a late satyr against the pride, lust and inconstancy, &c. of woman [etc.]. London: Printed by H. C., for John Taylor, 1686.

Author: S. F. Probable influence from *Paradise Lost* in first part; possible reference to divorce views, p. 3. Wing, F56. Copy owned by Henry E. Huntington Library.

1100 The Great birth of man: or, the excellency of man's creation and endowments above the original of woman. A poem. London: Printed for J. M. and sold by John Taylor, 1686.

Author: M. S. (Matthew Stevens?). Imitation of *Paradise Lost*, particularly in narrative elements dealing with Adam and Eve. Pp. 1–24. Wing, S114. Copy owned by New York Public Library.

1101 I. N. J. Usum divortiorum ex divino et humano. hocque civili æque ac canonico jure, præside Dn. Henrico Fincken [etc]. Literis Henrici Meyeri, Univ. typographia.

Author: Johannes Eccard. Place: Altdorf. Date: 1686 (?). Reference in heading, p. 38; discussion of divorce views as Section IV, Part V, pp. 46–47. Microfilm owned by New York Public Library.

1102 *Jugemens des Scavans sur les principaux ouvrages des auteurs tome quatrième contenant les poetes cinquième partie.* A Paris: Chez Antoine Dezallier, 1686.

Author: Adrien Baillet. Volume 9 in series. Under "Modernes," section 4, "Des Poëtes Anglois," is listed "Jean Milton," p. 458. Copy owned by Folger Shakespeare Library.

1103 *Kerkelycke historie, van de scheppinge des werelts, tot 't jaer des heeren 1666* [etc.]. *Den tweeden Druck.* t'Amsterdam, By Baltes Boeckholt, 1686.

Edition 2 of No. *964.* Copy owned by British Library.

1104 *Love given over: or, a satyr against the pride, lust, and inconstancy, &c. of woman. Amended by the author.* London: Printed for R. Bentley and J. Tonson, 1686.

Another edition of No. *922.* Imitation, p. 2. Wing, G1425. Copy owned by Princeton University Library.

1105 *The Loyalty of popish principles examin'd. In answer to Stafford's Memoirs* [etc.]. London: Printed for Thomas Flesher, 1686.

Another edition of No. *923.* Wing, H644. Copy owned by Bodleian Library.

1106 *Nouvelles de la republique des lettres. Mois de Mars 1684. Seconde edition revûë & corrigée par l'auteur.* Amsterdam: Chez Henry Desbordes, 1686.

Edition 2 of No. *1019.* Allusion, A2v. Copy owned by Columbia University Library.

1107 *Nouvelles de la republique des lettres. Mois d'Avril 1684. Seconde edition revûë & corrigée par l'auteur.* Amsterdam: Chez Henry Desbordes, 1686.

Edition 2 of No. *1020.* Copy owned by Folger Shakespeare Library.

1108 *Nouvelles de la republique des lettres. Mois d'Avril 1685. Seconde edition revûë & corrigée par l'auteur.* Amsterdam: Chez Henry Desbordes, 1686.

Edition 2 of No. *1079.* Discussion, p. 364. Copy owned by Newberry Library.

1109 *Nouvelles de la republique des lettres. Mois d'Août 1685. Par le Sieur B .... Professeur en philosophie & en historie à Rotterdam. Seconde edition revûë & corrigée par l'auteur.* Amsterdam: Chez Henry Desbordes, 1686.

Edition 2 of No. *1080.* Allusions in Article VII, p. 908. Copy owned by Columbia University Library.

1110 *The Observator.* No. 137, 30 January 1686. London: Printed for Charles Brome.

Advertisement for *Paradisus Amissa.* Copy owned by Folger Shakespeare Library.

1111 *Poems and songs, by Thomas Flatman. The fourth edition, with many additions and amendments.* London: Printed for Benjamin Tooke, 1686.

Edition 4 of No. *686.* Wing, F1154. Copy owned by Henry E. Huntington Library.

1112 *Tyrannick love; or, the royal martyr. A tragedy* [etc.]. London: Printed for H. Herringman, and are to be sold by Joseph Knight and Francis Saunders, 1686.

Author: John Dryden. Advertisement for *State of Innocence,* I4. Wing, D2396. Copy owned by University of Chicago Library.

1113 *The Visions of government, &c. Wherein the antimonarchical principles and practices of all phanatical commonwealths-men, and Jesuistical politicians are discovered, confuted, and exposed* [etc.]. *The second edition.* London: Printed by B. W., for Edward Vize, 1686.

Edition 2 of No. *1042.* Wing, P1893. Copy owned by Columbia University Library.

1114 *The Works of Mr. John Oldham, together with his remains.* London: Printed for Jo. Hindmarsh, 1686.

Collected edition including No. *1037;* see No. *1043.* Issue with catchwords for *Satyrs* on pp. 34–37, "can," "our," "tax," "where," and with 1684 *Remains.* Allusion in "Bion," in *Some New Pieces,* 1684, p. 82. Wing, O226. Copy owned by Union Theological Seminary Library (McAlpin Collection).

1115 *The Works of Mr. John Oldham, together with his remains.* London: Printed for Jo. Hindmarsh, 1686.

Different issue of No. *1114,* and including No. *1028.* Issue with catchwords for *Satyrs* on pp. 34–37, "Brave," "Are," "or," "your," and with 1687 *Remains.* Allusion in "Bion," in *Poems and Translations,* 1684, p. 82. Wing, O228. Copy owned by Columbia University Library.

1687

1116 *Acta eruditorum   anno MDCLXXXVII* [etc.]. Lipsiæ: Prostant apud J. Grossium & J. F. Gleditschium. Typis Christophori Guntheri, 1687.

No. 10 (October). Allusion in review of Langbaine's *Lives of the Most Famous English Poets*, p. 579. In Latin. Copy owned by New York Public Library.

1117 ΒΑΣΙΛΙΚΑ. *The Works of King Charles the martyr:* [etc.]. *The second edition.* London: Printed for Ric. Chiswell, 1687.

> Edition 2 of No. *543.* Allusion, p. 59. Wing, C2076. Copy owned by Henry E. Huntington Library.

1118 *Bibliotheca Goesiana sive catalogus librorum* [etc.]. Lugdvni Batavorum, apud Johannem de Vivie, 1687.

> Collector: William Goes. "Catalogi Goesiani Pars Altera, Continens Libros, Historicos, Literatores, Poëtas, & Antiquarios," with new signatures and pagination: listings, p. 30, item 210 (*Defensio prima*); p. 51, item 32 (Rowland's *Apologia pro rege & populo*) and item 33 (*Defensio secunda*). Copy owned by Columbia University Library.

1119 *Bibliotheca Jacombiana, sive catalogus variorum librorum plurimis facultatibus insignium instructissimæ bibliothecæ Rev. Doct. Thomas Jacomb, S. T. D.* [etc.]. 1687.

> Dated: 31 October 1687. Place: London. Bookseller: Edward Millington. Listings: p. 39, *Defensio prima*, Salmasius' *Responsio*; p. 45, *Literae*; p. 46, *Accedence*; p. 60, "*Smectymnuus* with the Answers and Replies Collected into one Volume *Lond.* 1640"; p. 77, *Civil Power, Hirelings*; p. 81, *History of Britain*; p. 84, *Paradise Regain'd* and *Samson Agonistes*; p. 88, *Areopagitica*. Wing, J113. Copy owned by British Library.

1120 *Bibliotheca Massoviana: sive catalogus variorum librorum* [etc.]. Per Edvardum Milingtonum, bibliopolam [etc.]. 1687.

> Listings: p. 30, *Defensio secunda* and *Pro se defensio, Literae, Defensio Prima* and Rowland's *Pro Rege Apologia*; p. 61, *History of Britain*. Wing, M1029. Copy owned by Newberry Library.

1121 *Bibliotheca Maynardiana: sive catalogus variorum librorum bibliothecæ selectissimæ Rev. viri D. Maynard* [etc.]. 1687.

> Dated: 13 June 1687; Wing gives 20 June. Place: London. Bookseller: Edward Millington. Listings: p. 18, *Paradise Regain'd*; p. 67, *Doctrine and Discipline of Divorce*. Wing, M1449. Copy owned by British Library.

1122 *Bibliotheca selectissima, diversorum librorum, viz. theologicarum* [etc.]. Per Edvardum Millingtonum bibliopol. Lond. [etc.]. 1687.

> Dated: 18 April 1687. Owner: John Maitland, Duke of Lauderdale. Listings: p. 18, Salmasius' *Apologia*; p. 33, *Artis Logicae, Defensio secunda*, More's *Fides*

Publica and *Supplement*; p. 35, *Defensio prima*, Rowland's *Pro Rege Apologia*. Wing, L606 (and M2071A). Copy owned by Henry E. Huntington Library.

1123 *A Catalogue of books, of the several libraries of the honourable Sir William Coventry, and the honourable Mr. Henry Coventry, sometime secretary of State to King Charles II* [etc.]. 1687.

Dated: 9 May 1687. Place: London. Listings: p. 30, *Defensio prima*, *Literae*; p. 39, *Paradise Lost*. Wing, C6626. Copy owned by Bodleian Library.

1124 *A Catalogue of Latin, French, and English books, consisting of divinity* [etc.]. 1687.

Dated: 17 October 1687. Listings: p. 7, *Artis Logicae*; p. 20, *Areopagitica*; p. 23, *History of Britain*; p. 37, *History of Britain*. Wing, C1352. Copy owned by British Library.

1125 *A Catalogue of the libraries of Mr. Jer. Copping, late of Sion College, gent. and Anscel Beaumont, late of the Middle Temple, esq; with others* [etc.].

Dated: 21 March 1686/7. Listings: second pagination, p. 16, *Paradise Regain'd*; third pagination, p. 3, *Doctrine and Discipline of Divorce*; p. 13, *Cabinet-Council*; p. 14, *History of Britain*. Wing, C6107. Copy owned by British Library.

1126 *Catalogus librorum bibliothecæ instructissimæ Eduardi Wray* [etc.].

Dated: 20 June 1687. Place: London. Bookseller: William Cooper. Listings: p. 37, *Paradise Lost*; p. 46, *Civil Power*. Wing, W3666. Copy owned by British Library.

1127 *Catalogus librorum tam antiquorum quam recentium in omni facultate insignium* [etc.].

Dated: 28 February 1686/7. Place: Oxford. Bookseller: Thomas Bowman. Listings: G1v, *Defensio prima*; L*2v, *Poems* (1673), *Paradise Lost, Paradise Regain'd*. Wing, C1448. Copy owned by British Library.

1128 *The Confession of faith, and the larger and shorter catechisms* [etc.]. Glasgow: Printed by, Robert Sanders, 1687.

Another edition of No. 45. Allusion, p. 47. Wing, C5772. Copy owned by British Library.

1129 *The Duke of Guise. A tragedy. Acted by their majesties servants* [etc.]. London: Printed by R. E., for R. Bentley and J. Tonson, 1687.

Another edition of No. 957. Printer: R. Everingham (?). Possible allusion, p. [v]. Influence from *Paradise Lost*, see especially p. 36. Wing, D2265. Copy owned by University of Kentucky Library.

1130 *The Female advocate: or, an answer to a late satyr against the pride, lust and inconstancy of woman* [etc.]. London: Printed by H. C., for John Taylor, 1687.

Edition 2 of No. *1099*. See p. 4. Wing, F56A. Copy owned by Henry E. Huntington Library.

1131 [illustrated title page]. *Georgii Hornii historia ecclesiastica et politica cum notis et continuatione*. Apud Lugd Bat, Iohannim Verbesser, Iordanum Luchtmans, 1687.

[title page]. *Georgii Hornii historia ecclesiastica, illustrata notis & observationibus* [etc.]. Lugd. Batavorum. Apud Johannem Verbesser Jordanum Luchtmans 1687.

Another edition of No. *585*. Editor: M. Leydecker. Reference to divorce views, p. 446; discussion of letters, pp. 513–515. Not listed in Index. Copy owned by Cambridge University Library.

1132 *The Hind and the panther transvers'd to the story of the country-mouse and the city-mouse*. [etc.]. London: Printed for W. Davis, 1687.

Author: Matthew Prior. Allusions, pp. 12, 16. Wing, P3511. Copy owned by Berg Collection, New York Public Library.

1133 *The Hind and the panther. Transvers'd to the story of the country-mouse and the city-mouse*. [etc.]. Printed in the year, 1687.

Apparently printed in Dublin by Andrew Crook and Samuel Helsham. Another edition of No. *1132*. Allusions, pp. 15, 18. Wing, P3512. Copy owned by Folger Shakespeare Library.

1134 *The History of the most renowned Don Quixote of Mancha* [etc.]. London: Printed by Tho. Hodgkin, and are to be sold by John Newton, 1687.

Translator: J. P. (John Phillips). Possible influence in translation of Quixote's discussion of poetry from *Of Education* (and perhaps *Apology*), pp. 362–363 (Part II, Book I, Chapter XVI). Wing, C1774A. Copy owned by Folger Shakespeare Library.

1135 *The History of the most renowned Don Quixote of Mancha* [etc.]. London: Printed by Thomas Hodgkin, and sold by William Whitwood, 1687.

Another issue of No. *1134*. Wing, C1774. Copy owned by William Andrews Clark Library.

1136 *The Lives of the most famous English poets, or the honour of Parnassus; in a brief essay of the works and writings of above two hundred of them* [etc.]. London: Printed by H. Clark, for Samuel Manship, 1687.

Author: William Winstanley. Listing in contents, p. [xxvi]; biographical notice, p. 195; allusion, p. 210 (under John Phillips). Wing, W3065. Copy owned by University of Kentucky Library.

Copy owned by the University of Iowa listed in the National Union Catalogue as 1686 is a copy of this edition.

1137 The London Gazette. Number 2300. 1 December–5 December 1687.

Colophon: "Printed by *Tho: Newcomb* in the *Savoy.* 1687." Advertisement for *Paradise Lost*, Edition 4. Copy owned by Henry E. Huntington Library.

1138 Lyric poems, made in imitation of the Italians [etc.]. London: Printed by J. M. for Jos. Knight and F. Saunders, 1687.

Author: Philip Ayres. Allusion, p. [viii]. Wing, A4312. Copy owned by Yale University Library.

1139 Momus triumphans: or, the plagiaries of the English stage [etc.]. London: Printed for Nicholas Coxe, and are to be sold by him in Oxford, 1687.

Author: Gerard Langbaine. *A Masque* is listed under ascriptions with the note "Ascrib'd to J. Milton," p. 31; Index, p. [37], refers to p. 3. Wing, L377A. Copy owned by Folger Shakespeare Library.

1140 Notes upon Mr. Dryden's poems in four letters. By M. Clifford, late master of the Charter House, London. To which are annexed some reflections upon The Hind and panther. By another hand [etc.]. London: Printed in the Year, 1687.

Author of "Reflections on the Hind & Panther": Thomas Brown. Allusion, p. 36. Wing, C4706. Copy owned by Columbia University Library.

1141 Oxford. Bodleian Library. Wood MS D.4.

"Julij Mazarini Cardinalis Epitaphium," poem erroneously alleged to be by Milton, ff. 129–130. The so-called Anonymous Life of Mr. John Milton, but written by Cyriack Skinner. Holograph. Ff. 140–144. Dated: c. 1687. First published by Edward S. Parsons in *English Historical Review* 17 (1902) 95–100.

1142 The State of church-affairs in this island of Great Britain under the government of the Romans, and British kings. London: Printed by Nat. Thompson, for the Author, and are to be sold by the Booksellers of London, 1687.

Author: anonymous, but often assigned to Sir Christopher Milton. Influence from *History of Britain*, passim. Wing, M2085. Copy owned by Union Theological Seminary Library (McAlpin Collection).

1143 Robert H. Taylor, Princeton, New Jersey. MS Poetical Miscellany.

Dated: 1687?. Ayloffe's "Marviles Ghost," pp. 105–107; see No. *1210.* "Lord Lucas His Ghost," pp. 189–192; see No. *1210.*

1144 Tyranny no magistracy, or a modest and compendious enquirie into the nature, and boundaries of that ordinance of magistracy [etc.]. Printed in the Year 1687.

Author: anonymous. Influence from *Tenure of Kings and Magistrates,* passim. Wing, T3571. Copy owned by Bodleian Library.

1145 Washington, D. C. Folger Shakespeare Library. MS C.c.1 (3).

Letter from Francis Atterbury to Jacob Tonson, dated 15 November 1687, from Christ Church, Oxford. Lists thirty-one subscribers to *Paradise Lost,* Edition 4 (1688). Printed in Edmond Malone, ed. *The Critical and Miscellaneous Prose Works of John Dryden.* London: H. Baldwin and Son, for T. Cadell, Jun., and W. Davies, 1800. I, i, 203–204.

1688

SEE ALSO NOS. 345, 346, AND 347 IN PART I FOR DRYDEN'S POEM ON MILTON. SEE ALSO No. *1253.*

1146 Annotations upon the Holy Bible [etc.]. London: Printed by Robert Roberts, for Thomas Parkhurst, Dorman Newman, Jonathan Robinson, Brabazon Ailmer, Thomas Cockerill, and Benjamin Alsop, 1688.

Another edition of No. *948.* Volume 1: see annotations to Genesis iii, B3v–C1. Wing, P2821. Copy owned by British Library.

1147 Anti-Baillet ou critique du livre de Mr. Baillet, intitulé Jugemens des savans [etc.]. La Haye: Chez Estienne Foulque et Louis van Dole, 1688.

Author: Gilles Menage. Two vols. Allusion from Baillet (see No. *1071*), concerning Salmasius, I, 7. Copy owned by New York Public Library.

1148 Bibliotheca Gulstoniana, sive catalogus variorum librorum [etc.].

Dated: 11 June 1688. Place: London. Owner: William Gulston. Bookseller: Edward Millington. Listings: p. 26, *Defensio prima;* p. 43, Salmasius' *Responsio.* Wing, G2227. Copy owned by British Library.

1149 A Catalogue of choice and valuable books English and Latin, &c. [etc.]. 1688.

Dated: 30 April 1688. Bookseller: Edward Millington. Listings: Dryden's

The State of Innocence, p. 23; Salmasius' Responsio, p. 64. Wing, C1295. Copy owned by Bodleian Library.

1150 Catalogus librorum instructissimæ bibliothecæ nobilis cujusdam Scoto-Britanni [etc.].

Dated: 30 October 1688. Place: London. Owner: John Maitland, Duke of Lauderdale. Bookseller: Benjamin Walford. Listings: p. 65, Salmasius' Responsio; p. 136, History of Britain; p. 139, Paradise Regain'd and Samson Agonistes. Wing, L608. Copy owned by British Library.

1151 [Christiani Thomasii, institutionum jurisprudentiæ divinæ libri tres. (etc.). Halæ Magdeburgicæ, Literis Salfeldianis, 1688.]

Reference in Book III, Chapter III, Section 67. Copy unlocated.

1152 Christiani Thomasii Institutiones jurisprudentiæ divinæ [etc.]. Francofurti et Lipsæ, Sumptib. Mauritii Georgii Weidmanni, 1688.

Volume 3: Book III only. Reference, Book III, Chapter III, Section 67, p. 134. Copy owned by Bibliothèque Nationale.

1153 The Confession of faith. And the larger & shorter catechism [etc.]. The former editions being very full of faults in every page, are now faithfully corrected for the benefit of the reader. Printed in the Year 1688.

Another edition of No. 45. Place: Edinburgh. Allusion, p. 83. Wing, C5773. Copy owned by Folger Shakespeare Library.

1154 The Confession of faith: together with the larger and lesser catechisms [etc.]. The third edition [etc.]. London: Printed for the Company of Stationers, and are to be sold by Tho. Parkhurst and Dorman Newman, 1688.

Another edition of No. 45. Allusion, pp. 98–99 [recte 122–123]. Wing, C5772A and C5798. Copy owned by New York Public Library.

1155 Danielis Georgi Morhofi Polyhistor sive de notitia auctorum et rerum commentarii [etc.]. Lubecæ: Sumptibus Petri Böckmanni, 1688.

Biographical synopsis, pp. 304–305 (Book I, Chapter 24). Copy owned by British Library.

1156 Epistolæ ho-elianæ. Familiar letters, domestic and forren [etc.]. The sixth edition [etc.]. London: Printed for Thomas Guy, 1688.

Edition 6 of No. 355. Allusion, p. 442. Wing, H3076. Copy owned by University of Kentucky Library.

1157 The Great birth of man: or, the excellency of man's creation and endowments above *the original of woman. A poem. The second edition. By M. S.* [etc.]. London: Printed for J. M. and sold by John Taylor, 1688.

Edition 2 of No. *1100*; reissue with cancel title page. Wing, S114A. Copy owned by Henry E. Huntington Library.

1158 Julianus den apostaat, of kort begrijp van zijn leven [etc.]. Tot Vrystaad, Ao. 1688.

Dutch translation of No. *919*. Partially adapted from *Defensio prima*; see particularly "Bericht Aan den Leezer," pp. 110–130. Copy owned by Henry E. Huntington Library.

1159 Lettres choisies de feu Mr. Guy Patin [etc.]. *Seconde edition.* A Paris: Chez Jean Petit, 1688.

See No. *126*. Lettre XXIV, p. 75. Copy owned by British Library.

1160 Lustiger und ernsthaffter monats-gespräche anderer theil | in sich begreiffend die sechs ersten monate des 1688. Jahres mit einem zweyfachen register. Halle, Gedruckt und verlegt von Christoph Salfelden, Churfürstlichen Brandenburgischen Hof- und Regierungs-Buch-drucker, 1688.

Author: Christian Thomas (Thomasius). In issue for June: allusion to Salmasian controversy, p. 737. Listed in Register I. Copy owned by Yale University Library.

1161 Lustiger und ernsthaffter monats-gespräche anderer theil | in sich begreiffend die sechs letzen monate des 1688. Jahres mit einem zweyfachen register. Halle, Gedruckt und verlegt von Christoph Salfelden, Churfürstlichen Brandenburgischen Hof- und Regierungs-Buch-drucker, 1688.

Author: Christian Thomas (Thomasius). In issue for December: allusions, pp. 760–761, 774, 775. Listed in Register I. Copy owned by Yale University Library.

1162 The Man of honour.

Author: Charles Montagu, Earl of Halifax. No title page; apparently the first edition published in London in 1688. Quarto. *2; 4 pp. Imitation of *Paradise Lost*, ll. 51–54, 66–69, on p. 2. Not in Wing. Copy owned by Princeton University Library.

1163 Miscellany poems. Containing a new translation of Virgills Eclogues [etc.]. London: Printed for Thomas Chapman, 1688.

Author: John Dryden. "MacFlecknoe," pp. 1–11 (no title page); "Absalom and Achitophel," pp. [13]–73 (Sixth Edition: Printed for Jacob Tonson, 1683), with Lee's poem; "The Medall," pp. [75]–104 (Second Edition: Printed for Jacob Tonson, 1683). Wing, D2315. Copy owned by Folger Shakespeare Library.

1164 Momus triumphans: or, the plagiaries of the English stage [etc.]. London: Printed for N. C., and are to be sold by Sam. Holford, 1688.

Another edition of No. *1139*. Publisher: Nicholas Cox. Listings of *Comus* and *Samson Agonistes*: pp. 17, 31 and note, 37 (Index), 39 (Index). Wing, L377. Copy owned by Columbia University Library.

1165 A New catalogue of English plays [etc.]. London: Printed for Nicholas Cox, and are to be sold by him in Oxford, 1688.

Another issue of No. *1164*. Wing, L377B. Copy owned by Folger Shakespeare Library.

1166 Poems to the memory of that incomparable poet Edmond Waller esquire. By several hands. London: Printed for Joseph Knight and Francis Saunders, 1688.

Allusion in anonymous poem, "On the Death of Mr. Waller," p. 22. Wing, P2724. Copy owned by Columbia University Library.

1167 Plutarch's lives. Translated from the Greek by several hands. In five volumes [etc.]. London: Printed by T. Hodgkin for Jacob Tonson, 1688.

Dryden's Plutarch. Volume 1 includes "Books Printed for Jacob Tonson," with advertisement for *Paradise Lost*, p. [653]. Not in Wing. Copy owned by Henry E. Huntington Library.

1168 Poor Robin. 1688. An almanack after a new fashion.

Colophon: "London, Printed for the Company of Stationers, 1688." Under November 8 is listed Smectymnus [sic]. Copy owned by Henry E. Huntington Library.

1169 The Princess of Cleve. The most famed romance [etc.]. *Rendred into English by a person of quality, at the request of some friends.* London: Printed for R. Bentley and S. Magnes, 1688.

Author: Marie Madeleine (Pioche de la Vergne), Comtesse de la Fayette. Two advertisements in "Some Books Printed for R. Bentley," S3. Wing, L170. Copy owned by Yale University Library.

1170 The Reasons of Mr. Bays changing his religion. Considered in a dialogue between Crites, Eugenius, and Mr. Bays [etc.]. London: Printed for S. T., and are to be sold by the Booksellers of London and Westminster, 1688.

Author: Thomas Brown. Catchword, p. 1: "Chri-"; catchword, p. 19:

"Freewill,". Jibe against Dryden's "tagging" of *Paradise Lost* in *The State of Innocence*, pp. 18–19, 21. Wing, B5069. Copy owned by University of Kentucky Library.

1171 *The Reasons of Mr. Bays changing his religion. Considered in a dialogue between Crites, Eugenius, and Mr. Bays* [etc.]. London: Printed for S. T. and are to be sold by the Booksellers of London and Westminster, 1688.

Another issue of No. *1170*. Catchword, p. 1: "Man"; catchword, p. 19: "Freewill,". See Wing, B5069. Copy owned by Newberry Library.

1172 *Samuelis Pufendorfii de jure naturæ et gentium libri octo. Editio ultima, auctior multo, et emendatior.* Amstelodami: Apud Andream ab Hoogenhuysen, 1688.

Different edition of No. *655*. Reference, p. 570. Discussion of divorce views and quotations from *Doctrine and Discipline of Divorce*, Book VI, Chapter i, Section 24, on pp. 601–604. Copy owned by Folger Shakespeare Library.

1173 *Some reflexions upon a treatise call'd Pietas Romana & Parisiensis lately printed at Oxford* [etc.]. Oxford: Printed at the Theater, 1688.

Author: James Harrington, the younger. Allusion to *Of Education*, p. 26. Wing, H834. Copy owned by New York Public Library.

1174 *A Third collection of papers relating to the present juncture of affairs in England* [etc.]. London: Printed, and are to be sold by Rich. Janeway, 1688.

Allusion in "Popish Treaties not to be rely'd on: In a letter from a Gentleman at York, to his Friend in the Prince of Orange's Camp," p. 35. Wing, T900. Copy owned by New York Public Library.

1689

1175 *Bibliotheca curiosa, sive catalogus variorum ac in quavis facultate insignium, librorum* [etc.]. 1689.

Dated: 3 April 1689. Bookseller: Samuel Ravenshaw. Listings: p. 15, *Artis Logicae*, Salmasius' *Responsio*. Wing, B2822. Copy owned by Bodleian Library.

1176 *A Catalogue of the libraries of books of Mr. Matthews Mr. Vanam Mr. Crow late of London Merch. 1688/9.*

Dated: 28 January 1688/9. Bookseller: Edward Millington. Listing: p. 22, *Paradise Regain'd*. Wing, M1323. Copy owned by Bodleian Library.

1177 A Catalogue of valuable books, viz. in divinity, humanity [etc.].

Dated: 16 December 1689. Place: London. Bookseller: Edward Millington. Listings: p. 6, *Civil Power, Hirelings*. Wing, C1416. Copy owned by British Library.

1178 Catalogus librorum instructissimæ bibliothecæ doctissimi cujusdam equitis in plurimis linguis & facultatibus insignium [etc.]. *Collectio secunda* [etc.].

Dated: 28 October 1689. Owner: John Maitland, Duke of Lauderdale. Bookseller: Benjamin Walford. Listings: p. 37, *Defensio prima*; p. 43, *Epistolarum Familiarium Liber Unus, Literae*; p. 48, *Defensio prima, Defensio pro se*, Salmasius' *Responsio*; p. 83, *Paradise Lost*; p. 88, *Paradise Regain'd*; p. 89, *Hirelings*; p. 100, *Hirelings*; p. 113, *Tenure*; p. 117, *Eikonoklastes*; p. 125, *Tenure* (twice). Wing, L609 (?). Copy owned by Bodleian Library.

1179 Christiani Funcci Qvadripartitum historico-polit. orbis hodie-imperantis breviarium [etc.]. Wratislaviæ, Impensis Joh. Ad. Kaestneri, Bibliopol. Litteris Joh. Rudolphi Leonis. 1689.

Author: Christian Funck (Christianus Funccius). Discussion with quotation of Milton's writing of *Defensio prima*, p. 368 (under "Regnum Britannicum," Item LVII, Section LIIX). Listed in Index. Copy owned by Cambridge University Library.

1180 A Collection of the newest and most ingenious poems, songs, catches, &c. against popery [etc.]. London: Printed in the year 1689.

Imitation from *Paradise Lost* in Charles Montagu's "The Man of Honour," ll. 51–54, 66–69, on p. ii. There is no catchword on p. ii in this edition (cf. No. *1181*). Wing, C5205. Copy owned by Newberry Library.

1181 A Collection of the newest and most ingenious poems, songs, catches, &c. against popery [etc.]. London: Printed in the year 1689.

Different edition of No. *1180*. Contents pages have been reset, and catchword on p. ii is "A New". Wing, C5206. Copy owned by Newberry Library.

1182 Confessio fidei in conventu theologorum authoritate parliamenti Anglicani indicto elaborata [etc.]. Edinburgi: Ex Officina Societatis Bibliopolarum Anno Dom. 1689.

Another edition of No. *367*. Allusion, p. 67. Wing, C5743A. Copy owned by National Library of Scotland.

1183 The Confession of faith, and the larger and shorter catechism [etc.]. Edinburgh: Printed by John Reid, 1689.

Another edition of No. *45.* Allusion, pp. 57–58. Wing, C5774. Copy owned by National Library of Scotland.

1184 Decas decadem dive plagiariorum & pseudonymorum centuria, accessit exercitatio de lexicis Græcis, eodem auctore [etc.]. Lipsiæ: Frid. Lanckischii, 1689.

Author: Johann Albert Fabricius. Discussion under LII. Claudius Salmasius, H4 (i. e., pp. [63–64]). Copy owned by British Library.

1185 The Dying speeches of several excellent persons, who suffered for their zeal against popery, and arbitrary government [etc.]. London: Printed in the Year, 1689.

The third item on pp. 18–22 is:
The very Copy of a Paper delivered to the Sheriffs, upon the scaffold on Tower-Hill, on Friday December 7. 1683. By Algernon Sidney, Esq; before his execution there.

See No. *988*; sentences drawn from *Tenure*, p. 19. Wing, D2957. Copy owned by British Library.

1186 Eleventh collection of papers relating to the present juncture of affairs in England and Scotland, viz. An Answer to the desertion discuss'd [etc.]. London printed, and are to be sold by Richard Janeway, 1689.

Verbal adaptation of a sentence from *Pro Populo Adversus Tyrannos* [*The Tenure of Kings and Magistrates*], 1689, p. 1, in *An Answer to the Desertion Discuss'd*, p. 2; author: Edmund Bohun. Wing, E498. Copy owned by Henry E. Huntington Library.

Work is separately listed by Wing, C3446, and erroneously assigned to Jeremy Collier.

1187 Freymüthige jedoch vernunfft- und gesetzmässiger gedancken über allerhand | fürnelich aber neue Bücher, Julius des 1689. Jahrs. Entworffen van Christian Thomas. Halle | Gedruckt und verlegt von Christoph Salfelden | Chur-Fürstl. Brandenb. Hoff- und Regierungs-Buchdrucker. 1689.

In issue for November: discussion of Salmasian controversy, pp. 945–946. Copy owned by Bibliothèque Nationale.

1188 The Great birth of man. Or, the excellency of man's creation and endowment above the original of woman. A poem. The third edition. By M. S. [etc.]. London: Printed and are to be sold by most Book-sellers in Westminster and London.

Edition 3 of No. *1100*. Dated: 1689. Wing, S115. Copy owned by William Andrews Clark Library.

1189 The Historian unmask'd: or, some reflections on the late history of passive-obedience. [etc.]. London: Printed, and are to be sold by Richard Baldwin, 1689.

Author: Thomas Long. Allusion, p. 29. Wing, L2969. Copy owned by Princeton University Library.

1190 *The History of passive obedience since the Reformation.* Amsterdam: Printed for Theodore Johnson, 1689.

Author: Abednego Seller. Allusions, pp. A3-A4, 18 (quotation from Oxford proclamation, No. *963*), 99 (quotation from Moore's sermon, No. *1022*). Wing, S2453. Copy owned by New York Public Library. Copy in Trinity College Library, Dublin, is this edition; Wing, S2454 apparently does not exist.

1191 *Julian the apostate: being a short account of his life* [etc.]. *The fourth edition* [etc.]. London: Printed for Richard Chiswell, 1689.

Edition 4 of No. *919*. Wing, J831. Copy owned by British Library.

1192 *Killing no murder: briefly discoursed in three questions. By Col. Titus, alias William Allen* [etc.]. Re-printed in the Year M.DC.LXXXIX.

Place: London. Another edition of No. *391*; see p. 19. Duodecimo in fours. See Wing, K474. Copy owned by Yale University Library.

1193 *Killing no murder: briefly discoursed in three questions. By Col. Titus, alias William Allen* [etc.]. London: Re-printed in the Year M.DC.LXXXIX.

Another issue of No. *1192*. Quarto. A-D^4; [iv] 27 [1] pp. See Wing, K474. Copy owned by University of Kentucky Library.

1194 *Killing no murder: briefly discoursed in three questions. By Col. Titus, alias William Allen* [etc.]. London: Reprinted in the Year 1689.

Another edition of No. *391*. Octavo in fours. Allusion, p. 31. See Wing, K474 and T1312. Copy owned by Folger Shakespeare Library.

1195 *Killing no murder: briefly discoursed in three questions. By William Allen.* Reprinted in the Year 1689.

Another edition of No. *391*. Quarto. [A]^1 B-E^4(-E4); [ii] 1-27 [3] pp. E4 used for [A]1. Allusion, p. 19. See Wing, K474. Copy owned by Newberry Library.

1196 *Killing no murder: briefly discoursed in three questions. By Willian Allen.* Reprinted in the Year 1689.

Another issue of No. *1195*. Octavo in fours. See Wing, K474. Copy owned by New York Public Library.

1197 A Letter to the author of a late paper, entituled, A Vindication of the divines of the Church of England, &c. In defence of The History of passive obedience. Printed in the year, 1689.

Author: George Hickes. Allusion, p. 5. Wing, H1856. Copy owned by Henry E. Huntington Library.

1198 Lettres choisies de feu Mr Guy Patin [etc.]. A Rotterdam, Chez Reinier Leers, 1689.

See No. *126.* Lettre XXIV, p. 77. Copy owned by Yale Medical School Library.

1199 The Muses farewel to popery and slavery, or, a collection of miscellany poems, satyrs, songs, &c. [etc.]. London: Printed for N. R. H. F. and J. K. and are to be sold by the Book-Sellers of London and Westminster, 1689.

Edition 1. Imitation from *Paradise Lost* in Charles Montagu's "The Man of Honour," pp. 3–4; see No. *1162.* Wing, M3140. Copy owned by University of Kentucky Library.

1200 New Haven, Connecticut. James Osborn Collection, Yale University Library. MS b111.

"A Collection of Loyal Poems": anonymous, "On Dr G. Burnet," p. 152, allusion in l. 88. Dated: 1689.

1201 New Haven, Connecticut. James Osborn Collection, Yale University Library. MS PB VII/15.

Copy of Andrew Marvell's "Last Instructions to the Painter," dated 1689. See No. *1212.*

1202 Observations upon Mr. Johnson's remarks, upon Dr. Sherlock's book of non-resistance [etc.]. London: Printed in the Year 1689.

Author: William Sherlock. Allusion, p. 16. Wing, S3305. Copy owned by Union Theological Seminary Library (McAlpin Collection).

1203 Oxford. Bodleian Library. Locke MS c.44.

"Adversaria Physica," unpaged. Dated: 1689–91. Notices: "Miltons sovereigne right of the people 4° Lond: *89*," f. 63v; "Paradise Lost," f. 64.

1204 Oxford. Bodleian Library. Wood MS F.39.

Letter from John Aubrey to Anthony Wood, dated St. Peter's Day [29 June] 1689. Biographical allusion from Phillips; Milton was at Cambridge, never at Oxford, f. 386v. Note by Wood, f. 387v.

1205 *Poems and translations, written upon several occasions, and to several persons. By a late scholar of Eaton* [etc.]. London: Printed for Henry Bonwicke, 1689.

Author: Charles Goodall. "A Propitiatory Sacrifice, To the Ghost of J_____ M_____ by way of Pastoral, in a Dialogue between Thyrsis and Corydon," pp. 110–117. Listed in Contents, pp. [xi]–xii. Wing, G1092. Copy owned by Yale University Library.

1206 *Poems chiefly consisting of satyrs and satyrical epistles. Licensed Jan. 8th 1688/9.* London: Printed, and are to be sold by most Booksellers in London and Westminster, 1689.

Author: Robert Gould. Possible allusion and imitation: "A Satyr Against Woman" ("Love Given Over"), p. 142; "Jack Pavy, alias, Jack Adams," p. 257. Wing, G1431. Copy owned by Henry E. Huntington Library.

1207 *Sidney redivivus: or the opinions of the late honourable Collonel Sidney, as to civil government* [etc.]. London: Printed for H. Smith, and sold by most book-sellers, 1689.

Includes a summary of *The Very Copy* (No. *988*), with influence from *Tenure of Kings and Magistrates*, p. 6. Wing, S3764. Copy owned by Union Theological Seminary Library (McAlpin Collection). Wing, S3763, dated 1688, does not exist.

1208 *State tracts: being a collection of several treatises relating to the government. Privately printed in the reign of K. Charles II.* London: Printed in the Year, 1689.

Includes Marvell's *An Account of Popery* (No. *730*) on pp. 69–135; see pp. 85, 92, 99–100 for Miltonic passages. Wing, S5329. Copy owned by British Library.

Stationers' register. See G. E. Briscoe Eyre, ed. *A Transcript of the Registers of the Worshipful Company of Stationers, from 1640–1708 A. D.* London: 1913–1914.

1209   Entry for prose works, under 30 January 1689, III (1914), 345.

1210 *A Third collection of the newest and most ingenious poems, satyrs, songs, &c. against popery and tyranny, relating to the times. Most of which never before printed.* London: Printed in the Year 1689.

Quotations from "Comus" as ll. 1 and 11 in John Ayloffe's "Marvell's Ghost," p. 5. Imitation of Attendant Spirit's opening and final speeches from "Comus" in "The E. of Essex's Ghost. 1687," p. 22 (i.e., "Lord Lucas's Ghost"). Wing, T902. Copy owned by Columbia University Library.

1211 *A Third collection of papers relating to the present juncture of affairs in England* [etc.]. *The second edition* [etc.]. London: Printed, and are to be sold by Rich. Janeway, 1689.

Edition 2 of No. *1174*. Wing, T901. Copy owned by New York Public Library.

1212 *The Third part of the collection of poems on affairs of state* [etc.]. London: Printed in the year 1689.

Appropriations and influence in Marvell's "The Last Instructions to a Painter," pp. 1–24; see pp. 5 (*Paradise Lost*), 22 [*recte* 15] ("Comus"). Wing, T913. Copy owned by Princeton University Library.

1690

SEE ALSO NO. 350 IN PART I FOR MATERIAL ON THE *Eikon Basilike* CONTROVERSY AND NO. 351 FOR DISCUSSION OF MILTON'S GOVERNMENTAL WORK.

1213 *An Answer to a late pamphlet, entituled obedience and submission to the present government, demonstrated from Bp. Overall's convocation-book. With a postscript in answer to Dr. Sherlock's Case of allegeiance.*

No title page. Colophon, p. 48: "London: Printed for Jos. Hindmarsh, 1690." Author: Thomas Wagstaffe. Allusion, p. 23. Wing, W202. Copy owned by New York Public Library.

1214 *Anti-Baillet ou critique du livre de Mr. Baillet, intitule' Jugemens des savans* [etc.]. La Haye: Chez Louis & Henry van Dole, 1690.

Another edition of No. *1147*. Copy owned by New York Public Library.

1215 *Aurenge-Zebe: a tragedy. Acted at the Royal Theatre* [etc.]. London: Printed for Henry Herringman, 1690.

Another edition of No. *1047*. Imitation of *Samson Agonistes*, pp. 7–8. Wing, D2247. Copy owned by Newberry Library.

1216 *Auteurs deguisez sous des noms etrangers*; [etc.]. Paris: Chez Antoine Dezallier, 1690.

Author: Adrian Baillet. Allusion concerning Alexander More and *Regii Sanguinis Clamor*, pp. 517–518. Copy owned by New York Public Library.

1217 *Avis important aux refugiez* [etc.]. Amsterdam: Chez Jaques le Censeur, 1690.

Author: Pierre Bayle. Reference to Milton's commendation of Cromwell in *Defensio secunda*, pp. 97–98. Discussion of Salmasian controversy, without mention of Milton, pp. 144–147. Discussion and quotation of the Oxford proclamation (No. *963*), with remarks from the *Gazette* (No. *958*), pp. 224–229. Copy owned by Folger Shakespeare Library.

1218 Bibliotheca locupletissima ex bibliothecis duorum virorum doctissimorum quorum unus theologus alter mediciis, nuper defunctorum conflata [etc.].

Dated: 2 April 1690. Place: London. Bookseller: John Bullord. Listings: p. 19, *Artis Logicae*; p. 20, *Artis Logicae*; p. 39, *History of England*. Wing, B2838. Copy owned by British Library.

1219 Bibliotheca realis & instructissima, sive catalogus variorum librorum, in quavis linguae & facultate insignium reverend. Doctoris petri Scott vindesorii pubend nuper defuncti [etc.].

Dated: 28 April 1690. Place: London. Listing: p. 23, *Paradise Lost*. Wing, S2077. Copy owned by British Library.

1220 Bibliotheca selecta seu catalogus librorum cujusdam generosi nuper defuncti, in quâvis linguæ & facultate insignium [etc.].

Dated: 7 April 1690. Place: London. Listing: p. 3, *Defensio prima*. Wing, B2851. Copy owned by British Library.

1221 The Case of resistance of the supreme powers stated and resolved, according to the doctrine of the Holy Scriptures. The second edition. London: Printed for T. Basset, and W. Crooke, and are to be sold by Randal Taylor, 1690.

Author: William Sherlock. Discussion of *Defensio prima*, pp. 117–119 and margin. Wing, S3268. Copy owned by Union Theological Seminary Library (McAlpin Collection).

1222 Censura celebriorium authorum: sive tractatus [etc.]. Londini: Impensis Richardi Chiswel, 1690.

Author: Sir Thomas Pope Blount. Quotation from Hermann Conring's "De Regno Angliae," concerning Salmasius, p. 720. See No. *1708*. Wing, B3346. Copy owned by Columbia University Library.

1223 Certain passages which happened at Newport [etc.]. London: Printed for Richard Chiswell, 1690.

Author: Edward Cooke. Allusion, A3v–A4. Wing, C5997. Copy owned by Folger Shakespeare Library.

1224 The Confession of faith, and the larger and shorter catechisms [etc.]. Glasgow: Printed by Robert Sanders, 1690.

Another edition of No. *45*. Allusion, p. 47. Wing, C5775. Copy owned by Christ Church College Library, Oxford.

1225 *A Continuation of the history of passive obedience since the reformation.* Amsterdam: Printed for Theodore Johnson, 1690.

Author: Abednego Seller. Discussion of *Eikonoklastes* and Joseph Jane's answer, pp. 131–132; quotation from Hancock concerning Milton as alleged papist, pp. 187–188 (see No. *923*). Wing, S2449. Copy owned by Princeton Theological Seminary Library.

1226 *The Deluge: or, the destruction of the world, an opera* [etc.]. London: Printed for James Knapton, 1690.

Reissue of No. *794*, with cancel title page. Wing, E139. Copy owned by British Library.

1227 *A Discourse concerning the gift of prayer* [etc.]. *Whereunto may be added, Ecclesiastes* [etc.]. London: Printed for J. Lawrence; and A. Churchil, 1690.

Another edition of No. *296*, to which is added a copy of No. *783*. Wing, W2184 and W2194. Copy owned by Henry E. Huntington Library.

1228 *A Discourse concerning the gift of prayer* [etc.]. *Whereunto may be added, Ecclesiastes* [etc.]. London: Printed for J. Lawrence; and A. Churchil, 1690.

Another issue of No. *1227*, but to which is added a copy of No. *1353*. Wing, W2184 and W2195. Copy owned by Princeton University Library.

1229 *Don Sebastian, King of Portugal* [etc.]. London: Printed for Jo. Hindmarsh, 1690.

Author: John Dryden. Allusion, in Preface, a1v. Wing, D2262. Copy owned by Folger Shakespeare Library.

1230 *The English part of the library of the late Duke of Lauderdale, being a catalogue of choice books* [etc.].

Date: 27 May 1690. Listing: p. 8, *History of Britain.* Wing, L611. Copy owned by Newberry Library.

1231 *Freymüthige lustige und ernsthaffte iedoch vernunfft- und gesetz-mässige gedancken oder monats-gespräche, über allerhand | fürnehmlich aber neue bücher durch alle zwölff monate des 1688. und 1689. Jahrs durchgeführet von Christian Thomas.* Halle, Gedruckt und verlegt von Christoph Salfelden, Chur-Fürstl. Brandenb. Hoff- und Regierungs-Buchdrucker. 1690.

Two volumes. Listing of Salmasian controversy in issue for June 1688, I,

737; listed in Index, Lll8v. Various references in issue for December 1688, II, 760–761, 774–775; in Index (incorrect), Ddd4. Copy owned by Newberry Library.

1232 *Freymüthige jedoch vernunfft- und geretz-mätzige gedancken über allerhand | fürnemlich aber neue bücher durch alle zwölff monat des 1689 Jahrs. Durchgeführet und allen seinen. Feinden | insonderheit aber Herrn Hector Gottfried Masio zugleignet von Christian Thomas.* Halle | Gedruckt und verlegt von Christoph Salfelden | Chur-Fürstl. Brandenb. Hoff- und Regierungs-Buchdrucker. 1690.

Discussion of Salmasian controversy in issue for November 1689, pp. 945–946. Copy owned by Yale University Library.

1233 *The Fundamental constitution of the English government* [etc.]. London: Printed by J. D., for the author, 1690.

Author: William Atwood. Allusion in quotation of letter from Peter Heylyn to Sir Edward Filmer, p. 4 (see No. *842*). Wing, A4171. Copy owned by New York Public Library.

1234 *The Late converts exposed: or the reasons of Mr. Bayes's changing his religion. Considered in a dialogue. Part the second* [etc.]. London: Printed for Thomas Bennet, 1690.

Author: Thomas Brown. Allusion, p. 25. Wing, B5061. Copy owned by University of Kentucky Library.

1235 [Letter from Vincent Minutoli to Pierre Bayle, dated 5/15 December 1690.]

Discussion of *Paradise Lost*. In French. Published in Emile Gigas. *Choix de la Correspondance Inédite de Pierre Bayle 1670–1706* [etc.]. Copenhague: G. E. C. Gad, 1890. Page 579.

1236 *Love given over: or, a satyr against the pride, lust, and inconstancy, &c. of woman. Amended by the author.* London: Printed for R. Bentley and J. Tonson, 1690.

Another edition of No. *922*. See p. 2. Wing, G1426. Copy owned by Henry E. Huntington Library.

1237 *The Muses farewel to popery & slavery, or, a collection of miscellany poems, satyrs, songs, &c.* [etc.]. *The second edition, with large additions* [etc.]. London: Printed for S. Burgess, and are to be sold by the Booksellers of London and Westminster, 1690.

Edition 2 of No. *1199*. Charles Montagu's "The Man of Honour," pp. 2–3 (see No. *1162*). "The E. of Essex's Ghost, 1687" (i.e., "Lord Lucas's Ghost"), pp. 178–180 (see No. *1210*). Wing, M3141. Copy owned by Princeton University Library.

1238 *New poems, consisting of satyrs, elegies, and odes* [etc.]. London: Printed for J. Bullord, and A. Roper, 1690.

Author: Thomas D'Urfey. Imitation of *Paradise Lost* in "An Ode to the Queen," pp. 19–21. Wing, D2754. Copy owned by Folger Shakespeare Library.

1239 *A Pastoral dialogue. A poem* [etc.]. London: Printed for Richard Baldwin, 1690.

Author: Nahum Tate. Allusion in poem, p. 27. Influence from *Comus*, passim. Wing, T202A. Copy owned by Yale University Library.

1240 *Plain English: humbly offered to the consideration of his majesty, and his great council, the lords and commons in Parliament assembled.* London: Printed in the Year, 1690.

Author: anonymous. Possible allusion to Milton in discussing Whigs, pp. 25–26. Wing, P2356. Copy owned by Columbia University Library.

1241 *The Rival queens, or, the death of Alexander the Great* [etc.]. London: Printed for Richard Bentley, 1690.

Another edition of No. *753*. Imitation: Act IV, p. 38. Wing, L867. Copy owned by University of Kentucky Library.

1242 *Seasonable reflections, on a late pamphlet, entituled, A History of passive obedience since the Reformation* [etc.]. London: Printed for Robert Clavell, 1690.

Author: Thomas Bainbrigg. Allusions, pp. 54, 66. Wing, B474. Copy owned by New York Public Library.

1243 *The Second part of Mr. Waller's poems* [etc.]. London: Printed for Tho. Bennet, 1690.

Author: Edmund Waller. Francis Atterbury's Preface: discussion of rhyme, A8v. Wing, W521. Copy owned by Yale University Library.

1244 THE | State of Innocence, | AND | FALL of MAN: | AN | OPERA. | Written in Heroick Verse; | And dedicated to Her Royal *Highness* | THE | DUTCHESS. | ——— | By Mr *John Dryden.* | ——— | [two-line quotation from Ovid's *Metamorphoses*] | $\equiv$ | *LONDON*, | Printed by *J. M.* for *Henry Herringman*, and are to be sold by | *Abel Roper*, near *Temple-Barr*, in *Fleetstreet*, 1690. |

Edition 5 of No. *754*. Quarto. A–G^4; xvi + 40 pp. [1], title page; [ii], blank; [iii–vi], dedication; [vii–viii], Lee's poem; [ix–xvi], Preface; 1–38, work; [39], advertisement including *The State of Innocence*; [40], blank. Wing, D2376. Copy owned by University of Wisconsin.

1245 Two treatises of government: in the former, the false principles, and foundation of Sir Robert Filmer, and his followers, are detected and overthrown [etc.]. London: Printed for Awnsham Churchill, 1690.

Author: John Locke. Dated: December 1689. Edition 1, Issue 1: pp. 235–237 set in larger type and p. 240 omits Section 21 (sig. Q).

Allusion in preface, A5v. See Wing, L2766. Copy owned by Union Theological Seminary Library (McAlpin Collection).

The allusion is not translated in *Du Gouvernement Civil. Où l'on traitte de l'origine, des Fondemens, de la Nature, du Pouvoir, & des Fins des Sociétez politiques* (Amsterdam, 1691), David Mazel, translator (?). Copy owned by Cambridge University Library.

1246 Two treatises of government: in the former, the false principles, and foundation of Sir Robert Filmer, and his followers, are detected and overthrown [etc.]. London: Printed for Awnsham Churchill, 1690.

Edition 1, Issue 2, of No. *1245*: pp. 235–237 in regular type and Section 21 included on pp. 239–240 (sig. Q8). Allusion in preface, A5. Wing, L2766. Copy owned by Henry E. Huntington Library.

1691

See also Nos. 354 and 355 in Part I for advertisements, and No. 357 for Dryden's epigram on Milton.

1247 An Account of the English dramatick poets [etc.]. Oxford: Printed by L. L., for George West and Henry Clements, 1691.

Author: Gerard Langbaine. Printer: Leon Lichfield. Allusions and discussions: listed in contents, a8; reference to Dryden's borrowing from *Samson Agonistes* in *Aureng-Zebe*, p. 157 and note; allusion, p. 168; discussion of *The State of Innocence*, p. 172; allusion under Ecclestone, pp. 185–186; allusion under Fletcher, p. 207; biographical notice, pp. 375–377; allusions under Shakespeare, pp. 456, 458, 459; allusion under R. A., Gent., p. 517. Listed in Index, Nn4, Nn6, Nn6v. Wing, L373. Copy owned by University of Kentucky Library.

1248 Advice to a young lord, written by his father [etc.]. London: Printed for, and are to be sold by R. Baldwin, 1691.

Author: Thomas Fairfax. To this is added "Catalogue of Books Worth the Perusing. Sold by the Booksellers of London and Westminster," which lists as item 5, *State of Innocence*, pp. [138-139], and item 7 "Milton's Paradise Lost, in Twelve Books, Fol. with Cutts," p. [139]. Wing, F255A. Copy owned by British Library.

1249 *Athenæ Oxonienses. An exact history of all the writers and bishops who have had their education in the most ancient and famous university of Oxford* [etc.]. *The first volume* [etc.]. London: Printed for Tho. Bennet, 1691.

Author: Anthony Wood. Life, in *Fasti*, pp. 880-884. Allusions, p. 373 (2), under Ralegh; in *Fasti*, p. 888, under Edmund Ludlow. Listed in Index. Wing, W3382. Copy owned by University of Kentucky Library.

Wood's own copy in the Bodleian Library (shelf mark: MS Wood 431.a) has three holograph notes attached to pp. 881-883 concerning associated publications.

1250 *The Athenian Mercury.* Vol. 2, No. 14, dated 11 July 1691. London: Printed for P. Smart, 1691.

Allusions. Copy owned by New York Public Library.

1251 *Bibliotheca Cudworthiana, sive catalogus variorum librorum plurimis facultatibus insignium bibliothecæ instructissimæ rev. doct. Dr. Cudworth, S. T. P.* [etc.]. 1690/1.

Dated: 2 February 1690/1; Wing gives 9 February. Owner: Ralph Cudworth. Bookseller: Edward Millington. Listings: p. 18, *Defensio prima*, Salmasius' *Responsio*; p. 37, *Colasterion*. Wing, C7464. Copy owned by British Library.

1252 *Bibliotheca selectissima librorum omnigenorum, viz. theologicarum* [etc.]. 1691.

Dated: 9 November 1691. Listings: p. 47, *Defensio prima*, Rowland's *Pro Rege Apologia*; p. 81, *Tetrachordon*; p. 105, *History of Britain*; p. 110, *Eikonoklastes*. Wing, B2854. Copy owned by British Library.

1253 *Britannia rediviva: a poem on the birth of the prince* [etc.]. London: Printed for J. Tonson, 1688.

Reissue of 1688 edition. Page [21] prints an advertisement for works by Dryden, including *The State of Innocence*; its colophon reads: "*LONDON* Printed, and are to be Sold by *Jacob Tonson* at the Sign of the *Judge's Head* in *Chancery-Lane* near *Fleet-street*, 1691." Wing, D2253. Copy owned by Henry E. Huntington Library.

1254 *A Catalogue of books continued, printed and published in London in Trinity-term, 1691.* No. 41.

Advertisement. Copy owned by British Library.

1255 A Catalogue of English & Latin books, viz. divinity [etc.].

Dated: 16 March 1690/1. Place: London. Bookseller: William Miller. Listings: p. 33, *Poems*; p. 34, *Artis Logicae*. Wing, C1316. Copy owned by British Library.

1256 A Catalogue of Mr. T. Bromley's library, consisting of excellent, Latin and English books [etc.].

Dated: 26 August 1691. Place: London (?). Bookseller: Thomas Bennet (?). Listing: p. 12, *Civil Power*. Wing, B4888. Copy owned by British Library.

1257 The Design of part of the book of Ecclesiastes [etc.]. London: Printed for James Knapton, 1691.

Author: William Wollaston. Allusion with quotation from the note on Verse in *Paradise Lost*, in "To the Reader," p. 22 and margin. Wing, W3253. Copy owned by Union Theological Seminary Library (McAlpin Collection).

1258 An Essay on poetry: by the Right Honourable, the Earl of Mulgrave[.] *The second edition.* London: Printed for Jo. Hindmarsh, 1691.

Edition 2 of No. *914.* Poems given in Latin and English, facing; Latin translated by J. N. and titled "Tentamen de Arte Poetica." Allusion, p. 30 and margin (Latin), p. 31 (English). Wing, B5357. Copy owned by Folger Shakespeare Library.

1259 The History of the rebellions in England, Scotland and Ireland [etc.]. London: Printed for L. Meredith and T. Newborough, 1691.

English translation of No. *1096*; see Part I, Book V, p. 206. Wing, M440. Copy owned by Yale University Library.

1260 A Letter from Major General Ludlow to Sir E. S. [etc.]. Amsterdam: 1691.

Author: anonymous. Addressed to Edward Seymour. Postscript, pp. 29–30, gives Pamela's prayer from Sidney's *Arcadia* and from *Eikon Basilike*, in parallel columns. Wing, L1489. Copy owned by New York Public Library.

1261 Lettres choisies de feu Mr. Guy Patin [etc.]. A Cologne: Chez Pierre Du Laurens, 1691.

See Nos. *126, 481, 482, 480.* Three volumes. Vol. 1: Lettre XXXIX, p. 168. Vol. 2: Lettre CLXXXVII, p. 135; Lettre CCVI, p. 209; Lettre CCVII, pp. 219–220. Copy owned by British Library.

1262 Novus reformator vapulans: or, the Welch Levite tossed in a blanket [etc.]. London: Printed for the Affigns of Will. Pryn, next Door to the Devil, 1691.

Author: Thomas Brown. Reference to Latin translation of *Paradise Lost*, A1 (preface). Wing, B5067. Copy owned by New York Public Library.

1263 Novus reformatus vapellans: or, the Welch Levite tossed in a blanket. [etc.]. London: Printed for the Assigns of Will. Pryn, next Door to the Devil, 1691.

Different edition of No. *1262*. Reference on A2. Wing, B5066. Copy owned by Arents Collection, New York Public Library.

1264 Our modern demagogue's modesty and honesty in its true light. Being a vindication of the royal martyr's sacred memory, from the antiquated calumnies and fictions, of the villain Milton [etc.]. *In a letter to a friend.*

Author: anonymous. Place: London. Dated: 1691. A^4; 8 pp. Wing, O592. Copy owned by William Andrews Clark Library.

1265 Oxford. Bodleian Library. Wood MS F.42.

Letter from William Joyner to Anthony Wood, dated 16 September 1691, f. 326. Allusion.

1266 A Pastoral dialogue. A poem [etc.]. London: Printed for Richard Baldwin, 1691.

Another edition of No. *1239*. Wing, T202B. Copy owned by Folger Shakespeare Library.

1267 The Plagiary exposed: or an old answer to a newly revived calumny against the memory of King Charles I. Being a reply to a book intitled King Charles's case [etc.]. London: Printed for Tho. Bennet, 1691.

Author: Samuel Butler. Allusion in anonymous preface, A2v. Wing, B6327. Copy owned by Princeton University Library.

1268 A Poem, occasioned by his majesty's voyage to Holland, the congress at the Hague, and present siege of Mons [etc.]. London: Printed for Richard Baldwin, 1691.

Author: Nahum Tate. Allusion in poem, p. 5. Wing, T205. Copy owned by Henry E. Huntington Library.

1269 A Poem, occasioned by the late discontents & disturbances in the state [etc.]. London: Printed for Richard Baldwin, 1691.

Another edition of No. *1239*. Wing, T206. Copy owned by Folger Shakespeare Library.

1270 The Reasons of Mr. Bays changing his religion [etc.]. *The second edition with additions.* London: Printed for T. B. and A. Roper, 1691.

Edition 2 of No. *1170*. Allusion, p. 19. Wing, B5070 (?). Copy owned by Union Theological Seminary Library (McAlpin Collection).

1271 Restitution to the royal author or a vindication of King Charls the Martyr's most excellent book; intituled 'ΕΙΚΩΝ ΒΑΣΙΛΙΚΗ *from the false, scandalous, and malicious reflections lately published against it. Licensed, May 10. 1691: Z. Isham.* London: Printed for Samuel Keble, 1691.

Author: anonymous; sometimes assigned to Keble. Earl of Anglesey's memorandum on Gauden's authorship reprinted and discussed, pp. 3 ff. Pamela's prayer reprinted, pp. 7-8. Authorship of *Eikon Basilike* discussed, pp. 3-8. Wing, R1175. Copy owned by Henry E. Huntington Library.

1272 A Satyrical epistle to the female author of a poem, call'd Silvia's revenge, &c. By the author of the Satyr against woman [two-line epigraph from *Paradise Lost*]. London: Printed for R. Bentley, 1691.

Author: Robert Gould. Wing, F1436. Copy owned by Henry E. Huntington Library.

1273 The Works of Mr. John Dryden [etc.]. London: Printed and are to be sold by Jacob Tonson, 1691.

Four volumes. Includes reprints of *The State of Innocence*, No. *1244; Aureng-Zebe*, No. *1282; Duke of Guise*, No. *1129; Don Sebastian*, No. *1229; Britannia Rediviva*, No. *1253; Absalom and Achitophel*, No. *898*; and *The Medall*, No. *926*. Vol. 1: listing of *State of Innocence*, I4, in 1686 *Tyrannick Love*, No. *1112*. Wing, D2207. Copy owned by Worcester College Library, Oxford.

1692

SEE ALSO NOS. 360 AND 362 IN PART I FOR AN ADVERTISEMENT AND FOR DRYDEN'S POEM ON MILTON, RESPECTIVELY.

1274 Appendix librorum quorum auctio habenda est propre Templum Beatæ Mariæ, Nov. 28. 1692.

Place: Oxford. Listing: p. [ii], Salmasius' *Responsio*. Wing, A3570. Copy owned by British Library.

1275 An Argument proving, that the abrogation of King James by the people of England from the regal throne [etc.]. London: Printed for the Author, 1692.

Author: Samuel Johnson. Edition 1 (?). Allusion to *Paradise Lost*, p. 11. See Wing, J821. Copy owned by New York Public Library.

1276 An Argument proving, that the abrogation of King James by the people of England from the regal throne [etc.]. London: Printed for the Author, 1692.

Edition 2 (?) of No. *1275.* Allusion, p. 16. See Wing, J821. Copy owned by Columbia University Library.

1277 An Argument proving, that the abrogation of King James by the people of England from the regal throne [etc.]. London: Printed for the Author: And are to be sold by Richard Baldwin, 1692.

Edition 3 (?) of No. *1275.* Allusion, p. 16. Wing, J821A. Copy owned by New York Public Library.

1278 An Argument proving, that the abrogation of King James by the people of England from the regal throne [etc.]. *The fourth edition.* London: Printed for the Author, 1692.

Edition 4 of No. *1275.* Allusion, p. 16. Wing, J822. Copy owned by New York Public Library.

1279 Athenæ Oxonienses. An exact history of all the writers and bishops who have had their education in the most ancient and famous university of Oxford [etc.]. *The second volume* [etc.]. London: Printed for Tho. Bennet, 1692.

Author: Anthony Wood. Allusions, pp. 196 under Henry Jeanes; 226 under James Heath; 249 under Matthew Griffith; 293 under William Davenant; 439 and 441 under James Harrington; 548 under Thomas Hunt; 572 under Thomas Gawen; 582 under George Morley; 619 (2) and 621 under Samuel Parker; 643 under Theodore Haak; 893, in *Fasti,* under Roscommon; 906, in *Fasti,* under Sir George MacKenzie. Listed in Index. Wing, W3383A. Copy owned by University of Kentucky Library.

1280 The Athenian mercury. Vol. 5, No. 14, dated 16 January 1692. London: Printed for John Dunton.

Question 3: "Whether Milton and Waller were not the best English Poets? and which the better of the two?" Copy owned by New York Public Library.

1281 The Athenian mercury. Vol. 8, No. 6, dated 17 September 1692. London: Printed for P. Smart, 1692.

Allusion and imitation of *Paradise Lost* in anonymous poem; note also citation of "Pandemonium." Copy owned by New York Public Library.

1282 Aureng-Zebe, a tragedy. Acted at the Royal Theatre [etc.]. London: Printed for Henry Herringman; and are to be sold by R. Bentley, J. Tonson, F. Saunders, and T. Bennet, 1692.

Another edition of No. *1047*. Imitation of *Samson Agonistes*, p. 7. Wing, D2248. Copy owned by Princeton University Library.

1283 *Avis important aux refugiez sur leur prochain retour en France* [etc.]. Paris: Chez la Veuve de Gabriel Martin, 1692.

Another edition of No. *1217*. Reference, p. 87. Discussion, pp. 119–121. Discussion and quotations, pp. 195–198. Copy owned by Princeton University Library.

1284 *Bibliotheca Barhamiana: or a catalogue of Mr. Barhams books, (lately deceased)* [etc.].

Dated: 7 June 1692. Listing: p. 22, *Civil Power*. Wing, B765. Copy owned by British Library.

1285 *Bibliotheca Hoyleana: sive catalogus variorum librorum diversis facultatibus insignium, bibliothecæ selectissimæ Johannis Hoyle* [etc.]. 1692.

Dated: 14 Novembris 1692. Place: London. Bookseller: Edward Millington. Listings: p. 1, *Defensio prima*; p. 2, *Defensio prima, Eikonoklastes*; p. 4, *Defensio secunda*; p. 12, *History of Britain, Paradise Lost*; p. 20, *Poems* (1690 [?]), *Epistolarum Familiarium Liber Unus*; p. 24, *Paradise Regain'd*. Wing, H3201. Copy owned by British Library.

1286 *Bibliotheca instructissima ex bibliothecis duorum doctissionorum theologorum Londinen. nuper defunctorum, composita* [etc.].

Dated: 25 January 1691/2. Place: London. Owner: John Maitland, Duke of Lauderdale. Bookseller: John Bullord. Listings: p. 16, *Defensio prima*; p. 20, *Defensio secunda*; p. 23, *Literae*; p. 4 (another pagination), *Paradise Lost*. Wing, L605. Copy owned by British Library.

1287 *Bibliotheca lectissima: or, a catalogue of Greek, Latin and English books in most faculties* [etc.].

Dated: 20 May 1692. Place: London. Bookseller: Nathaniel Rolls. Listings: p. 7, *Artis Logicae, Defensio prima*. Wing, B2836. Copy owned by British Library.

1288 *Bibliotheca ornatissima: or, a catalogue of excellent books as well Greek, Latin, &c. as English, in all faculties* [etc.].

Dated: 18 April 1692. Place: London. Bookseller: Nathaniel Rolls. Listings: p. 20, *Defensio prima*; p. 27, Salmasius' *Responsio*; p. 30, *Defensio secunda*; p. 32, *Artis Logicae, Literae, Defensio prima*, Rowland's *Pro Rege Apologia*; p. 33, *Literae, Defensio prima*, Rowland's *Pro Rege Apologia, Artis Logicae*; p. 102 [*recte* 58], *Paradise Lost*; p. 65, *Paradise Regain'd* and *Samson Agonistes*; p. 68, *Paradise Lost*. Wing, B2845. Copy owned by British Library.

1289 Bibliotheca selectissima: or, a catalogue of books [etc.].

Dated: 9 February 1692. Place: London. Bookseller: John Bullord. Listings: p. 3, "*Salmasius* against *Milton's Iconoklaste*"; p. 10, *Poems, Eikonoklastes*. Wing, B2855. Copy owned by British Library.

1290 Catalogi, librorum theologicarum, historicarum, ac miscellanearum, Lat. Gr. &c. qui vendes prostant Westmonasterii apud Sam. Ravenshaw, bibliop. Lond. à Die Mensis Februarii 5. 1691/2 [etc.]. *Pars Prior* [etc.]. Londini: 1691/2.

Listings: p. 23, *Defensio secunda*; p. 26, Salmasius' *Responsio*; p. 28, *Artis Logicae*. Wing, C1254. Copy owned by British Library.

1291 Catalogi variorum librorum in quavis lingua & facultate insignium, tam antiquorium quam recentium, Richardi Davis bibliopolæ pars quarta [etc.]. 1692.

Dated: 11 April 1692. Owner: Dr. Pocock. Booksellers: Richard Davis and Edward Millington. Listings: p. 40, *Epistolarum Familiarium Liber Unus*; p. 42, *Artis Logicae*; p. 43, *Artis Logicae*. Wing, D429. Copy owned by Bodleian Library.

1292 A Catalogue of ancient and modern English books: especially of the writings of the most famous divines of our own nation's [etc.]. 1692.

Dated: 9 May 1692. Place: London. Bookseller: Edward Millington. Listing: p. 32, *Paradise Regain'd* and *Samson Agonistes*. Wing, C1276. Copy owned by British Library.

1293 A Catalogue of books continued, printed and published in London in Hilary-term, 1691. No. 43.

Dated: 1691/2. Allusion in advertisement for *Vindiciæ Carolinæ*. Copy owned by Henry E. Huntington Library.

1294 A Catalogue of books continued, printed and published in London in Easter term, 1692. No. 44.

Allusion in advertisement for *The Arts of Empire*. Copy owned by British Library.

1295 A Catalogue of books continued, printed and published in London in Trinity-term, 1692. No. 45.

Listing of Ralegh's *The Arts of Empire*. Copy owned by Henry E. Huntington Library.

1296 A Catalogue of books continued, printed and published in London in Michaelmas-term, 1692. No. 46.

Reference in announcement of publication of *Vindiciae Carolinae* and of *The Arts of Empire*. Copy owned by Henry E. Huntington Library.

1297 A Catalogue of extraordinary Greek and Latin books, published by Stephens, Aldus, and other curious editors. Also a choice collection of medicinal and chymical books, being the library of Mr. Andrew Clench [etc.].

Dated: 1 June 1692. Place: London. Bookseller: John Bullord. Listings: p. 15, *Paradise Lost, Paradise Regain'd*. Wing, C1331. Copy owned by British Library.

1298 Catalogus librorum bibliothecæ juris utriusque, tam civilis quam canonici, publici quam privati, feudalis quam variorum regnorum [etc.]. Edinburgi: Georgii Mosman, 1692.

Preface by Sir George MacKenzie. Listing of *Defensio prima*, p. 140. Wing (1), C1432; Wing (2), cancelled. Copy owned by Yale University Library.

1299 Catalogus librorum tam antiquorum quam recentium in omni facultate insignium [etc.].

Dated: 9 November 1692. Place: Oxford. Listings: D2v, Salmasius' *Responsio*; F2v, Hog's *Paradisus Amissa*. Wing, C1449. Copy owned by British Library.

1300 The Character of King Charles I [etc.]. London: Printed, and are to be sold by R. Tayler, 1692.

Author: Richard Hollingworth. Discussion of Pamela's prayer with possible allusion to Milton's alleged insertion of it in *Eikon Basilike*, pp. 11–12. Wing, H2500. Copy owned by Union Theological Seminary Library (McAlpin Collection).

1301 The Compleat library: or news for the ingenious [etc.]. *July, 1692* [etc.]. London: Printed for John Dunton.

Vol. 2: listing on p. 211 indicates rarity of Milton's works. Microfilm owned by New York Public Library.

1302 The Defence of the Parliament of England in the case of James the II. Or, a treatise of regal power and of the right of the people [etc.]. *Written in Latin by P. Georgeson Kt. Translated by S. Rand*. London: Printed for Timothy Goodwin, 1692.

Discussion and use of Milton's argument against Salmasius, pp. 21–24 and margin. Wing, G533. Copy owned by Yale University Library.

1303 Don Sebastian. King of Portugal: a tragedy acted at the Theatre Royal [etc.]. London: Printed for Jo. Hindmarsh, 1692.

Author: John Dryden. Allusion in Preface, a1–a1v. Wing, D2263. Copy owned by Folger Shakespeare Library.

1304 *The Gentleman's journal: or the monthly miscellany* [etc.]. Vol. 1 (March), 1692. London: Printed for Rich. Parker, and are to be sold by Rich. Baldwin.

Editor: Peter Motteux. Notice of new edition of *Paradise Lost* (that of 1695), p. 9. Copy owned by New York Public Library.

1305 *The History of Oliver Cromwell: being an impartial account* [etc.]. By R. B. Licensed and Entred. London: Printed for Nath. Crouch, 1692.

Author: R. B. (Richard Burton, pseudonym of Nathaniel Crouch). Apparent reference to Milton as learned author discussing Cromwell's achievements, pp. 174–175. See pp. 146–147 of *Defensio secunda*. Wing, C7331. Copy owned by British Library.

1306 *Lebens-lauff des berühmten theologi Herrn D. Johannis Lassenii* [etc.].

Dated: 1692 (?). Editor: Ernst Christian Baldichius (?). Allusion, p. 26. Copy owned by Royal Library, Copenhagen.

1307 *A Letter from General Ludlow to Dr. Hollingworth, their majesties chaplain at St. Botolph-Aldgate* [etc.]. Amsterdam: 1692.

Author: Edmund Ludlow (?). Probably printed in London. Allusion, p. viii. Adapts parts of *Eikonoklastes*, pp. 31–49. Wing, L1469. Copy owned by University of Kentucky Library.

1308 *Lettres choisies de feu Mr. Guy Patin* [etc.]. A Paris: Chez Jean Petit, 1692.

Two volumes. Vol. 1: Lettre XXXIX, p. 101 (see No. *126*); Lettre CLXXXVIII, dated 13 July 1660, p. 451 (see No. *481*); Lettre CCVII, p. 496 (see No. *482*); Lettre CCVIII, p. 502 (see No. *480*). Copy owned by Newberry Library.

1309 *Lettres choisies de feu Mr. Guy Patin* [etc.]. A Paris: Chez Jean Petit, 1692.

Another edition of No. *1308*. Three volumes. Vol. 1: Lettre XXIV, p. 75 (see No. *126*). Vol. 2: Lettre CCXCVII, p. 268 (see No. *481*); Lettre CCXIII, p. 308 (see No. *482*); Lettre CCCXIV, pp. 314–315 (see No. *480*). Copy owned by British Library.

1310 *Lettres choisies de feu Mr. Guy Patin* [etc.]. A Cologne: Chez Pierre Du Laurens, 1692.

Another edition of No. *1308*. Three volumes. Vol. 1: Lettre XXXIX, p. 89 (see No. *126*). Vol. 2: Lettre CLXXXVII, p. 74 (see No. *481*); Lettre

CCVI, p. 114 (see No. *482*); Lettre CCVII, p. 120 (see No. *480*). Copy owned by University of Illinois Library.

1311 *Ludlow no lyar, or a detection of Dr. Hollingworth's disingenuity in his second defence of King Charles I* [etc.]. Amsterdam: 1692.

Author: anonymous; attributed to Joseph Wilson (pseudonym?), signer of prefatory letter, or to Slingsby Bethell. Probably printed in London. Argues for Gauden's authorship of *Eikon Basilike* by repeating Walker's arguments (see No. *1325*) and by reference to Pamela's prayer. Adapted in part from *Eikonklastes*, especially the Preface, pp. iii–xx. Wing, B2068. Copy owned by Yale University Library.

1312 *Miscellany poems: in two parts* [etc.]. *The second edition.* London: Printed for Jacob Tonson, 1692.

Author: John Dryden. Volume 1 includes *MacFlecknoe*, pp. 1–11, without title page (see No. *924*); *Absalom and Achitophel*, pp. [13]–72, "The Seventh Edition; augmented and revised" (see No. *854*); and *The Medall*, pp. [73]–102, "The Third Edition" (see No. *925*). To this is added the 1685 *Sylvae* (No. *1090*). Wing, D2316. Copy owned by Folger Shakespeare Library.

1313 *Miscellany poems: in two parts* [etc.]. *The second edition.* London: Printed for Jacob Tonson, and are to be sold by Joseph Hindmarsh, 1692.

Another issue of No. *1312*, with 1685 *Sylvae*. Wing, D2317. Copy owned by William Andrews Clark Library.

1314 *Miscellany poems: in two parts* [etc.]. *The second edition.* London: Printed for Jacob Tonson, and are to be sold by Joseph Hindmarsh, 1692.

Another issue of No. *1312*, with 1693 *Sylvae* (No. *1376*). Apparently Wing, D2380; no 1692 edition of *Sylvae* has been located. Copy owned by Yale University Library.

1315 *Miscellany poems upon several occasions: consisting of original poems, by the late Duke of Buckingham, Mr. Cowly, Mr. Milton* [etc.]. London: Printed for Peter Buck, 1692.

Editor: Charles Gildon. Ascriptions of "Julii Mazarini, Cardenalis, Epitaphium," pp. 29–33; and "In Urbanum VIII. P. M.," p. 33. Listed in Contents, B8. Wing, G733A. Copy owned by Yale University Library.

1316 *The Passion of Byblis, made English. From Ovid. Metam. Lib. 9. By Mr. Dennis.* London: Printed for Rich. Parker, 1692.

Author: John Dennis. Edition 1. Discussion of Milton, C1. Wing, O690. Copy owned by William Andrews Clark Library.

1317 A Present for the ladies: being an historical vindication of the female sex [etc.]. London: Printed for Francis Saunders, 1692.

Author: Nahum Tate. Probable reference to Adam and Eve in *Paradise Lost*, pp. 2-3. Wing, T212. Copy owned by Folger Shakespeare Library.

1318 Samuelis Bocharti opera omnia, hoc est Phaleg, Canaan, et Hierozoicon [etc.]. *Editio tertia* [etc.]. Lugduni Batavaroum, Apud Cornelium Boutesteyn, & Jordanum Luchtmans. Trajecti ad Rhenum, Apud Gulielmum vande Water, 1692.

Two volumes. Vol. 1 consists of *Samuelis Bocharti geographia sacra, seu Phaleg et Canaan, cui accedunt variæ dissertationes philologicæ, geographicæ, theologicæ &c. Antehac ineditæ* [etc.]. *Editio tertia prioribus multo correctior, & splendidior. Procuravit Petrus de Villemandy.* Lugduni Batavorum: Apud Cornelium Boutesteyn, & Jordanum Luchtmans: Trajecti ad Rhenum: Apud Gulielmum vande Water, 1692. Included is letter from Bochart to Salmasius, concerning Salmasian controversy, dated [September?] 1652, pp. 1253-54 (see No. *261*). Copy owned by Princeton University Library. New York Public Library has copy of Vol. 1 that seems to have been a separate issue.

1319 A Second defence of King Charles I [etc.]. London: Printed for S. Eddowes and are to be sold by Randal Taylor, 1692.

Author: Richard Hollingworth. Allusion in Postscript, p. [54]. Wing, H2504. Copy owned by New York Public Library.

1320 THE *State of INNOCENCE,* | AND | Fall of MAN: | AN | OPERA. | Written in Heroick VERSE; and Dedicated to Her Royal HIGHNESS | THE | DUTCHESS. | —— | By Mr. JOHN DRYDEN. | —— | [two lines in Latin from Ovid's *Metamorphoses*] | —— | *LONDON,* | Printed for *Henry Herringman,* and are to be Sold by *Abel* | *Roper,* at the *Mitre* near *Temple-Barr,* in *Fleet-street.* 1692.|

Quarto. A-G^4; xvi + 40 pp. [i], title page; [ii], blank; [iii–vi], Dedication; [vii–viii], Lee's poem; [ix–xvi], Preface; 1-38, work; [39] Books, including *The State of Innocence*; [40], blank. Wing, D2377. Copy owned by Folger Shakespeare Library.

1321 State tracts: being a farther collection of several choice treatises relating to the government. From the year 1660. to 1689 [etc.]. London: Printed, and are to be sold by Richard Baldwin, 1692.

Includes *The Judgement and Decree of the University of Oxford* (No. *963*), pp. 153-156 (see especially pp. 153, 155), and Sidney's *The very Copy of a Paper* (No. *988*), pp. 267-269 (see especially p. 268). Wing, S5331. Copy owned by Newberry Library.

Stationers' register. See G. E. Briscoe Eyre, ed. *A Transcript of the Registers of the Worshipful Company of Stationers; from 1640-1708 A. D.* London: 1913-1914.

1322 Entry for *Linguae Romanae Dictionarium*, under 26 November 1692, III (1914), 411.

1323 Entry for *Linguae Romanae Dictionarium*, under 28 November 1692, III (1914), 412.

1324 *The Tragedies of the last age, consider'd and examin'd* [etc.]. *The second edition.* [etc.]. London: Richard Baldwin, 1692.

Edition 2 of No. *778*. Allusion, p. 143. Wing, R2431. Copy owned by Rutgers University Library.

1325 *A True account of the author of a book entituled* ΕΙΚΩΝ ΕΑΣΙΛΙΚΑ [sic], [etc.]. London: Printed for Nathanael Ranew, 1692.

Author: Anthony Walker. Prints memorandum by Anglesey, p. 23, but there is no specific citation of Milton in the volume. Wing, W310. Copy owned by University of Kentucky Library.

1326 *A Vindication of some among our selves against the false principles of Dr. Sherlock* [etc.]. London: Printed in the year 1692.

Author: George Hickes. Allusion, p. 45. Wing, H1878. Copy owned by Union Theological Seminary Library (McAlpin Collection).

1327 *Vindiciæ Carolinæ: or, a defence of* 'ΕΙΚΩ'Ν ΒΑΣΙΛΙΚΗ, *the portraicture of his sacred majesty in his solitudes and sufferings. In reply to a book intituled* 'ΕΙΚΟΝΟΚΛΑΣΤΗ'Ε, *written by Mr. Milton, and lately re-printed at Amsterdam.* London: Printed by J. L., for Luke Meredith, 1692.

Author: Richard Hollingworth (?). John Wilson also possible author. References, discussion, some quotation, passim. Wing, H2505. Copy owned by Yale University Library.

1328 [*The Works of Mr. John Dryden.* London: Printed for Jacob Tonson, 1692.]

No title page. Includes "MacFlecknoe," B⁴; "Absalom and Achitophel," C-H⁴ I1; and "The Medal," I2-4 K-L⁴ M². Pp. 1-84. Separate title pages for "Absalom and Achitophel" and "The Medal"; none for "MacFlecknoe." "MacFlecknoe," pp. 1-8; "Absalom and Achitophel," pp. [20]-57, with allusions in "To the Reader," p. 12, and Lee's poem, p. 14; and "The Medal," allusion in "Epistle to the Whigs," p. 63. Wing, D2304. Copy owned by Columbia University Library.

1329 *The Works of Mr. John Oldham, together with his Remains*. London: Printed for Jo. Hindmarsh, 1692.

Another reissue containing *Satyrs* (1685), *The Passion of Byblis* (1685), *Poems and Translations* (1684), *Poems and Translations* (1683), and *Remains* (1693). Date of *Works* is thus questionable. "Bion," with allusion on p. 82, is included in the first *Poems and Translations* (1684); see No. *1028*. Wing, O229. Copy owned by Folger Shakespeare Library.

1330 *The Young-students-library, containing extracts and abridgments of the most valuable books* [etc.]. *By the Athenian Society*. London: Printed for John Dunton, 1692.

Author: John Dunton. Article from *The Athenian Gazette*, No. *1280*, listed in Table. Wing, D2635. Copy owned by Folger Shakespeare Library.

1693

See also No. 363 in Part I for Dryden's epigram on Milton. See also No. *1314*.

1331 *An Argument proving, that the abrogation of King James by the people of England from the regal throne* [etc.]. *The fifth edition*. London: Printed by J. D. for the Author, and are to be sold by Richard Baldwin. 1693.

Edition 5 of No. *1275*. Allusion, p. 16. Wing, J823. Copy owned by British Library.

1332 *An Argument proving, that the abrogation of King James by the people of England from the regal throne* [etc.]. *The fifth edition*. London: Printed for the Author, 1693.

Another issue of No. *1331*. Wing, J823A. Copy owned by Henry E. Huntington Library.

1333 *The Athenian mercury*. Vol. 12, No. 1. 24 October 1693. London: Printed for John Dunton, 1693.

Allusion. Copy owned by New York Public Library.

1334 *Bibliotheca Blewitiana, being an excellent collection of books* [etc.].

Dated: 31 January 1693. Place: London (?). Owner: Matthew Blewit (Wing gives Martin). Bookseller: John Bullord. Listing: p. 18, "Milton agst. K. Charles, & other Tracts." Wing, B3189. Copy owned by British Library.

1335 *Bibliotheca Cropperiana, sive catalogus bibliothecæ incomparabilis Doct. V. D. Johan. Cropperi, Londinens. defuncti* [etc.]. 1693.

Dated: 19 June 1693. Place: London. Bookseller: Edward Millington. Listings: p. 6, *Literae*; p. 10, *Eikonoklastes, History of Britain*. Wing, C7238. Copy owned by British Library.

1336 Bibliotheca Meggottiana, sive catalogus variorum librorum bibliothecæ instructissimæ R. D. V. Dr. Meggot nuperimé Dean. Wintoniens. defuncti [etc.]. *1693.*

Dated: 6 November 1693. Owner: Richard Meggott. Place: London. Bookseller: Edward Millington. Listing: p. 8, *Defensio prima*. Apparently Wing, M1617. Copy owned by British Library.

1337 Bibliotheca Morganiana: or a catalogue of the library of Mr. Silvanus Morgan [etc.].

Dated: 5 April 1693 (Wing gives 4 April). Listing: p. 10, *Paradise Lost* and *Paradise Regain'd*. Apparently Wing, M2739. Copy owned by British Library.

1338 Bibliotheca Sparkiana, or, a catalogue of the library of the Reverend Dr. Tho. Sparkes, Prebend. of Lichfield lately deceased [etc.].

Dated: 3 July 1693. Listings: p. 8, *Defensio prima*; p. 19, *History of Britain*; p. 20, *Poems*. Wing, S4821. Copy owned by British Library.

1339 A Catalogue of ancient and modern books, viz. divinity [etc.].

Dated: 10 July 1693. Place: Norwich. Bookseller: Edward Millington. Listings: p. 34, *A Defense of the English People* (twice). Wing, C1273. Copy owned by Bodleian Library.

1340 A Catalogue of books continued, printed and published in London in Hilary-term, 1692. No. 47.

Dated: 1692/3. Allusion in advertisement for *Vindiciae Carolinae*. Copy owned by Henry E. Huntington Library.

1341 A Catalogue of books continued, printed and published in London in Easter term, 1693. No. 48.

Allusion in advertisement for *Linguae Romanae Dictionarium*. Copy owned by British Library.

1342 A Catalogue of excellent English books [etc.].

Dated: 27 June 1693. Listings: p. 9, *Tetrachordon, History of Britain*. Wing, C1329. Copy owned by British Library.

1343 A Catalogue of Greek, Latin and English books both ancient and modern, on most subjects [etc.].

Dated: 26 April 1693. Bookseller: Joseph Shelton. Listing: p. 10, *Paradise Regain'd*. Wing, C1337. Copy owned by British Library.

1344 A Catalogue of valuable books, viz., divinity [etc.].

Dated: 18 October 1693. Bookseller: Joseph Shelton. Listing: p. 6, Rowland's *Pro Rege Apologia*. Wing, C1418. Copy owned by British Library.

1345 Catalogus librorum, beati domini Johannis Lassenii [etc.]. Copenhagen: Impensis Johan Jacob Bornheinrich, 1693.

Dated: 28 August 1693. Unpaged. Listing: *Scriptum Parlamenti Reipublicae Angliae*. Copy owned by Royal Library, Copenhagen.

1346 Catalogue variorum librorum in omnigena literatura [etc.].

Dated: 20 November 1693. Bookseller: Edward Millington. Listings: p. 25, *Epistolarum Familiarium Liber Unus*; p. 27, *Paraphrasis Poetica*; p. 28, Salmasius' *Responsio*; p. 29, *Epistolarum Familiarium Liber Unus*; p. 31, *Literae, Defensio prima*, Salmasius' *Responsio*; p. 32, *Artis Logicae*. Wing, C1459. Copy owned by British Library.

1347 A Collection of poems by several hands. Most of them written by persons of eminent quality [etc.]. London: T. Warren, for Francis Saunders, 1693.

"A Catalogue of Books Printed for, and Sold by Francis Saunders," listing of *Paradise Lost* and *Paradise Regain'd* (in folio), T3v. Apparently reference is to the editions of 1688 although Saunders is not listed as an associated bookseller of these or other editions of the epics. Wing, C5174. Copy owned by New York Public Library.

1348 A Compleat journal of the votes, speeches and debates both of the House of Lords and House of Commons [etc.]. London: Printed for Jonathan Robinson, Jacob Tonson, A. & J. Churchil, and John Wyat, 1693.

Edition 2 of No. *918*. Reissue of Starkey's catalogue. Wing, D1248. Copy owned by Folger Shakespeare Library.

A different issue printed for Jonathan Robinson alone (Wing, D1247) was owned by Cambridge University Library, but is now lost. No other copy has been located.

1349 The Confession of faith, and the larger and shorter catechisms [etc.]. Glasgow: Printed by Robert Sanders, 1693.

Another edition of No. *45*. Allusion, p. 41 (*recte* 48). Wing, C5776. Copy owned by Bodleian Library.

1350 *A Confutation of atheism from the origin and frame of the world. The third and last part. A sermon preached at St. Mary-le-Bow, December the 5th. 1692* [etc.]. London: Printed for H. Mortlack, 1693.

Author: Richard Bentley. Two quotations from *Paradise Lost*, p. 40. Wing, B1918. Copy owned by University of Wisconsin Library.

1351 *The Death of King Charles I. Proved a down-right murder, with the aggravations of it. In a sermon at St. Botolph Aldgate, London, January 30. 1692/3* [etc.]. London: R. Norton, for Walter Kettilby, 1693.

Author: Richard Hollingworth. Allusion in "The Epistle Dedicatory," a2. Denies claim that John Gauden wrote *Eikon Basilike*. Wing, H2501. Copy owned by Yale University Library.

1352 *Dr. Walker's true, modest, and faithful account of the author of* ΕΙΚΩΝ ΒΑΣΙΛΙΚΗ, [etc.]. London: R. Taylor, 1693.

Author: Thomas Long. Allusions, pp. i (political pun on *Paradise Lost* and *Paradise Regain'd*), 1-2, 5. Anglesey's memorandum is given on p. 26. Discussion of Charles I's alleged plagiarism of prayers, pp. 59-60, 55-56 (i. e., 61-62). Wing, L2965. Copy owned by New York Public Library.

1353 *Ecclesiastes: or, a discourse concerning the gift of preaching* [etc.]. *The seventh edition, corrected and much enlarg'd*. London: Printed for J. Lawrence, and A. and J. Churchill, 1693.

Another edition of No. *59*. Allusion to divorce views, p. 301. Advertisement also for A. and S. Churchill's "*Milton*'s Paradice Regain'd." Wing, W2195. Copy owned by New York Public Library.

1354 *Examen poeticum: being the third part of miscellany poems* [etc.]. London: R. E., for Jacob Tonson, 1693.

Editor: John Dryden. Printer: R. Everingham (?). Issue 1: A-B^8 b^4 B-Z Aa-Gg^8 Hh^3 Aaa^8 B-F^8 G^2. Influence from and imitations of *Paradise Lost* in Thomas Yalden's "A Hymn to the Morning. In Praise of Light. An Ode," pp. 127-131, and "A Hymn to Darkness," pp. 132-137. The contrastive poems may also owe something to Milton's companion poems. Influence from "L'Allegro" in "Against Sloth, When the King was at Oxford," pp. 175-177. Wing, D2277. Copy owned by Berg Collection, New York Public Library.

1355 *Examen poeticum: being the third part of miscellany poems* [etc.]. London: R. E., for Jacob Tonson, 1693.

Issue 2 of No. *1354*: A-B^8 b^4 B-Z Aa-Gg^8 Hh^3 X^1 Aaa-Fff^8. X2 signature paged: 305-306; Aaa signature, unpaged; Bbb-Fff signatures, reset and paged. Not in Wing. Copy owned by Princeton University Library. Copy in Henry E. Huntington Library omits additional X^1 signature.

1356 The Folly and unreasonableness of atheism [etc.]. London: J. H., for H. Mortlock, 1693.

Reissue of No. *1350*. Wing, B1930. Copy owned by Union Theological Seminary Library (McAlpin Collection).

1357 The Fourth volume of Plutarch's lives [etc.]. London: Printed for Jacob Tonson, 1693.

Printed on Ggg4: "Books Printed for Jacob Tonson [etc.]." Listings: *Poems* with *Of Education, Paradise Lost* with cuts, *Paradise Regain'd* and *Samson Agonistes*. Not in Wing. Copy owned by Folger Shakespeare Library.

1358 Gentleman's Journal, or the monthly miscellany [etc.]. Vol. II (February 1693). London: R. Parker, and are to be sold by Rich. Baldwin.

Editor: Peter Motteux. Anonymous poem, "On Rebellious Spirits," pp. 44-45, imitation of *Paradise Lost*. Copy owned by New York Public Library.

1359 The History of Oliver Cromwell; being an impartial account [etc.]. London: Printed for Nath Crouch, 1603.

Dated: 1693. Another edition of No. *1305*. Wing, C7332. Copy owned by Folger Shakespeare Library.

1360 Leben und todt des weyland hoch-ehrwürdigen, hoch-edlen, und hochgelahrten herrn | herrn Johannis Lassenii [etc.]. Copenhagen: 1693.

Discussion of Lassenius's contact with Milton, pp. 6-7. Copy owned by Royal Library, Copenhagen.

1361 The Life and death of King Charles the First, written by Dr. R. Perinchief: together with 'ΕΙΚΩ'Ν ΒΑΣΙΛΙΚΗ *representing his sacred majesty in his solitudes and sufferings. And a vindication of the same King Charles the martyr. Proving him to be the author of the said* 'ΕΙΚΩ'Ν ΒΑΣΙΛΙΚΗ, *against a memorandum of the late Earl of Anglesey, and against the groundless exceptions of Dr. Walker and others.* London: Printed for Joseph Hindmarsh, 1693.

Another edition of No. *1035*, including *Eikon Basilike* (1685) and Wagstaffe's 1693 *Vindication* (No. *1378*). Discussion of Milton on pp. 226-227. Wing, P1595. Copy owned by British Library.

1362 The Life of our blessed lord & saviour Jesus Christ. An heroic poem: [etc.]. London: Printed for Charles Harper, and Benj. Motte, 1693.

Author: Samuel Wesley. Influence and appropriations (some of which are noted) from *Paradise Lost, Paradise Regain'd*, and *Il Penseroso*; see, for example, Book III, lines 639 ff.

Citations and allusions: Preface, a1v, a3, b1; within poem, p. 345 and margin (note use of "Pandemonium," Book X, line 163); in notes, pp. 25 (for l. 19), 27 (for l. 124), 107 (for l. 4), 108 (three: for ll. 321, 350, 639), 109 (two: for ll. 646, 755), 112 (for l. 1200), 317 (for l. 781), 325, 345 (for l. 167).

Allusions also in prefatory poems: Nahum Tate's "To Mr Samuel Wesley on his Divine Poem of the Life of Christ," in poem and in margin (twice), b2v; Thomas Taylor's "To My Ingenious Friend Mr. Samuel Wesley, on his Poem the Life of Christ," b4. Tate sees Wesley as completing Milton's *Paradise Regain'd*.

Wing, W1371. Copy owned by Folger Shakespeare Library.

1363 *Linguæ Romanæ dictionarium luculentum novum. A new dictionary* [etc.]. *The whole completed and improved from the several works of Stephens, Cooper, Gouldman, Holyoke, Dr. Littleton, a large manuscript, in three volumes, of Mr. John Milton, &c.* [etc.]. Cambridge: Printed for W. Rawlins, T. Dring, R. Chiswell, C. Harper, W. Crook, J. Place, and the Executors of S. Leigh, 1693.

Further allusion in preface, A2v. Wing, L2354. Copy owned by Princeton University Library.

1364 *Miscellanies in verse & prose* [etc.]. London: Printed for James Knapton, 1693.

Author: John Dennis. Allusion in preface, a8v–b1. Wing, D1034. Copy owned by New York Public Library.

1365 *The Oracles of reason* [etc.]. London: 1693.

Author: Charles Blount. Influence in recounting the temptation of Adam and Eve; see Chapter VII: "The 7th and 8th. Chapters of Dr. Burnet's Archiologize Philosophicae ... All written originally in Latin, and now rendred into English by Mr. H. B.," pp. 25–28. Wing, B3312. Copy owned by Yale University Library.

1366 *A Present for the ladies: being an historical account of several illustrious persons of the female sex* [etc.]. *The second edition corrected, with additions.* London: Printed for Francis Saunders, 1693.

Edition 2 of No. *1317*. Wing, T213. Copy owned by Folger Shakespeare Library.

1367 *Plutarch's lives. Translated from the Greek, by several hands. In five volumes. Vol. 1* [etc.]. London: R. E., for Jacob Tonson, 1693.

Printed on Bbb4: "Books Printed for Jacob Tonson [etc.]." Listing: *Paradise Lost* with cuts. Not in Wing. Copy owned by Folger Shakespeare Library.

1368 *Reasons humbly offered for the liberty of unlicens'd printing. To which is subjoin'd, the just and true character of Edmund Bohun, the licenser of the press. In a letter from a gentleman in the country, to a member of Parliament.* London: Printed in the Year 1693.

Author: Charles Blount. Adaptation of *Areopagitica*, pp. 3–9 (called "Reasons etc."), signed J. M. Wing, B3313. Copy owned by Columbia University Library.

1369 *The Royal martyr: or, the history of the life and death of K. Charles I. Together with Eikon Basilike or the pourtraiture of his sacred majesty in his solitudes and sufferings.* London: Printed for M. R. and sold by J. Hindmarsh, 1693.

Another edition of No. *1035*. Discussion appears on pp. 226–227. Compare No. *1361*. Wing, P1603. Copy owned by Henry E. Huntington Library.

1370 *The Satires of Decimus Junius Juvenalis. Translated into English verse* [etc.]. London: Printed for Jacob Tonson, 1693.

Author: John Dryden. Discussion of epic and satire in Dedication ("Original and Progress of Satire"), pp. viii–ix, xii–xiii, xvii, l–li. Wing, J1288. Copy owned by Princeton University Library.

1371 *Scrina reserata: a memorial offer'd to the great deservings of John Williams, D. D.* [etc.]. Edw. Jones, for Samuel Lowndes, 1693.

Author: John Hacket. Place: London. Written in the 1650's. Second part was separately published with the following title page: *A Memorial offer'd to the great deservings of John Williams, D. D.* [etc.]. *Part II* [etc.]. London: Printed for Samuel Lowndes, 1693.

Antagonistic discussion of *Eikonoklastes* and Salmasian controversy, pp. 161–162. Wing, H171. Copy owned by New York Public Library.

1372 *The Second volume of Plutarch's lives. Translated from the Greek, by several hands. The third edition.* London: Printed for Jacob Tonson, 1693.

Printed on Tt2v: "Books Printed for Jacob Tonson [etc.]." Listings: *Poems* with *Of Education, Paradise Lost* with cuts, *Paradise Regain'd* and *Samson Agonistes*. Wing, D2367. Copy owned by Folger Shakespeare Library.

1373 *State tracts: being a collection of several treatises relating to the government. Privately printed in the reign of K. Charles II.* London: Printed in the Year 1693.

Another issue of No. *1208*. Wing, S5330. Copy owned by British Library.

1374 State tracts: being a collection of several treatises relating to the government. Privately printed in the reign of K. Charles II. London: Printed in the Year 1693.

Second title page:
State-tracts. In two parts. The first part being a collection of several treatises relating to the government, privately printed in the reign of King Charles II. The second part consisting of a farther collection of several choice treatises relating to the government, from the year 1660. to 1689 [etc.]. London: Printed, and are to be sold by Richard Baldwin, 1693.

Reissues of Nos. *1208* (and *1373*) and *1321*. Separate title page for Part II as given in No. *1321*. Wing, S5332. Copy owned by British Library. Copies exist without the second title page.

Stationers' register. See G. E. Briscoe Eyre, ed. *A Transcript of the Registers of the Worshipful Company of Stationers; from 1640-1708 A. D.* London: 1913-1914.

1375 Entries, under 21 August 1693, III (1914), 428. Six entries for *Linguae Romanae Dictionarium*, although Milton is not named.

1376 Sylvæ: or, the second part of the poetical miscellanies [etc.]. *The second edition.* London: Printed for Jacob Tonson, 1693.

Edition 2 of No. *1090*. Allusion, a3v-a4 [signed a5]. Wing, D2381. Copy owned by Yale University Library.

1377 Truth brought to light: or, the gross forgeries of Dr. Hollingworth [etc.]. London: 1693.

Author: Edward Ludlow (?). Controversy over Pamela's prayer in *Eikon Basilike*, p. 31. Version of letter from Clarendon, dated 13 March 1661/2, p. 37. Wing, T3153. Copy owned by University of Kentucky Library.

1378 A Vindication of King Charles the martyr, proving that his majesty was the author of ʼΕΙΚΩΝ ΒΑΣΙΛΙΚῊ *against a memorandum* [etc.]. London: Printed for Joseph Hindmarsh, 1693.

Author: Thomas Wagstaffe. Part of Clarendon's letter of 13 March 1661/2 (with allusion to Milton), p. 18, with accompanying discussion. Anglesey's memorandum given on p. 3. Wing, W218. Copy owned by Union Theological Seminary Library (McAlpin Collection).

1379 The Works of Mr. John Dryden, in four volumes [etc.]. London: Printed for Jacob Tonson, 1693.

Appropriately varying title pages for each volume. Reissues. Vol 2: 1692 *State of Innocence* (No. *1320*); 1692 *Aureng-Zebe* (No. *1282*) with imitation on

p. 7. Vol. 3: 1687 *Duke of Guise* (No. *1129*); 1692 *Don Sebastian* (No. *1303*). Vol. 4: *MacFlecknoe*, no title page, dated, 1692 (?), B⁴, 1-8 pp.; *Absalom and Achitophel*, dated 1692, "Seventh Edition," pp. 10–57; *The Medall*, dated 1692, "Third Edition," pp. 59–83; 1691 *Britannia Rediviva* (No. *1253*), with 1688 title page and advertisement intact on p. [21]. Cf. No. *1312* for *MacFlecknoe, Absalom and Achitophel*, and *The Medall*. Wing, D2208. Copy owned by William Andrews Clark Library.

1694

SEE ALSO NOS. 367 AND 368 IN PART I FOR EDWARD PHILLIPS' "LIFE OF MR. JOHN MILTON."

1380 The Annual miscellany: for the year 1694. Being the fourth part of miscellany poems [etc.]. London: R. E., for Jacob Tonson, 1694.

Compiler: John Dryden. Printer: R. Everingham (?). See Contents, p. [v]. Matthew Prior, "To My Lady Dursley, On Her Reading *Milton's Paradise Lost*," pp. 110–111; Charles Dryden, "On the Happyness of a Retir'd Life," p. 200 (allusion); Joseph Addison, "An Account of the Greatest English Poets," pp. 321–323 (poetic discussion). Wing, D2237. Copy owned by Folger Shakespeare Library.

1381 The Athenian mercury. Vol. 13, No. 28. 12 May 1694. London: Printed for John Dunton, 1694.

Advertisement. Copy owned by New York Public Library.

1382 The Athenian mercury. Vol. 16, No. 3. 26 December 1694. London: Printed for John Dunton, 1694.

Discussion in Question 1, on rhyme. Copy owned by New York Public Library.

1383 Aureng-Zebe, a tragedy. Acted at the Royal Theatre [etc.]. London: Printed for Henry Herringman; and sold by R. Bentley, J. Tonson, F. Saunders, and T. Bennet, 1694.

Another edition of No. *1049*. Imitation of *Samson Agonistes*, p. 7. Wing, D2249. Copy owned by New York Public Library.

1384 Bibliotheca Ashmoliana a catalogue of the library of the learned and famous Elias Ashmole, esq; [etc.].

Dated: 22 February 1693/4. Bookseller: Edward Millington. Listing: p. 19, *Moscovia*. Wing, A3981. Copy owned by British Library.

1385 *Bibliotheca Cogiana: sive catalogus diversorum librorum bibliothecæ ornatissimæ R. D. D. Nath. Cogæ* [etc.]. 1694.

Dated: 17 November 1694. Place: Cambridge. Owner: Nathaniel Coga. Bookseller: Edward Millington. Listings: p. 23, *Artis Logicae* (twice); p. 40, *Artis Logicae*; p. 41, *Literae*. Wing, C4890. Copy owned by British Library.

1386 *Bibliotheca excellentissima: composed of the libraries of two persons of great quality containing an extraordinary collection of books* [etc.].

Dated: 1694. Bookseller: John Bullord. Listings: p. 5, *Defensio prima*; p. 11, *Literae*. Wing, B2824. Copy owned by British Library.

1387 *Bibliotheca luculenta sive catalogus librorum in omni ferè lingua & facultate* [etc.].

Dated: 31 January 1693/4. Bookseller: Edward Millington. Listings: p. 19, *Defensio prima*; p. 28, *Literae, Defensio prima*; p. 29, Rowland's *Pro Rege Apologia*. Wing, B2839. Copy owned by British Library.

1388 *A Catalogue of ancient and modern books especially of the writings of the most eminent divines of our own nation* [etc.]. London: Printed by Tho. James, 1694.

Dated: 24 September 1694. Listing: p. 20, *Moscovia*. Wing, C1277. Copy owned by British Library.

1389 *A Catalogue of choice Latin and English books, on most subjects* [etc.].

Dated: 28 November 1694. Listing: p. 8, *Paradise Lost* and *Paradise Regain'd*. Wing, C1304. Copy owned by British Library.

1390 *A Catalogue of Latin and English books in folio and quarto* [etc.].

Dated: 15 March 1694. Listing: p. 4, *Tetrachordon*. Wing, C1317 (title incorrect). Copy owned by British Library.

1391 *A Catalogue of very good Latin and English books, on most subjects: being the library of the late worthy divine, Mr. John Starkey* [etc.].

Dated: 11 October 1694. Listing: p. [ii], *Paradise Lost*. Wing, S5291. Copy owned by British Library.

1392 *Catalogvs bibliothecæ Conringianæ* [etc.]. Helmestadi, Typis & Sumptibus Georgii-Wolfg. Hammii, 1694.

Catalogue of Hermann Conring. Listings: pp. 198–199, item 137, Du Moulin; p. 199, item 143, Rowland's *Pro Rege Apologia* (1651) and Phillips' *Responsio* (1652); and item 150, *Defensio prima* (1651) and *Defensio secunda*. Copy owned by Columbia University Library.

1393 *Censura celebriorum authorum: sive tractatvs* [etc.]. Genevæ, Apud Samvelem De Tovrnes, 1694.

> Another edition of No. *1222*. Listing with quotation, p. 1027. Copy owned by Newberry Library.

1394 *Chorus poetarum: or, poems on several occasions* [etc.]. London: Printed for Benjamin Bragg, 1694.

> Editor: Charles Gildon. Date given as: "MDCLXIXIV." "To Christina, Queen of Sweden," p. 19, in Latin. Ascribed in the eighteenth century to Milton; here ascribed to Andrew Marvell, but probably by Fleetwood Shepherd. Not in Wing. Copy owned by Folger Shakespeare Library.

1395 *Christiani Thomasii* [etc.]. *Institutionum jurisprudentiæ divinæ libri tres* [etc.]. *Editio secunda priori multo auctior* [etc.]. Halæ, Sumtibus Christophori Salfeldii, 1694.

> Edition 2 of No. *1152*. Reference in Book III, Chapter III, Section 67, p. 134. Further reference in "Eröffnet Der Studierenden Jugend in Halle | ein Collegium Privatum Uber seine Institutiones Jurisprudentiæ Divinæ," p. 73 (separate pagination). Copy owned by University of Marburg Library.

1396 *The Common-wealths-man unmasqu'd* [etc.]. London: Printed, and sold by Randal Taylor, 1694.

> Author: Thomas Rogers. Discussion, pp. 67–68. Wing, R1829. Copy owned by Folger Shakespeare Library.

1397 *The Compleat French-master, for ladies and gentlemen* [etc.]. London: Printed for Tho. Salusbury, 1694.

> Author: Abel Boyer. Discussion of *Accedence Commenc't Grammar* in "The Preface to the Reader," A6. Omitted in Edition 2 (1699). Wing, B3913. Copy owned by Folger Shakespeare Library.

1398 *The Compleat Library.* Vol. III [etc.]. April, 1694. London: Printed for John Dunton, 1694.

> Book intended for review, "Mr. Milton's Letters," p. 140. Microfilm owned by New York Public Library.

1399 *Confessio fidei in conventu theologorum authoritate parliamenti Anglicani indicto, elaborata* [etc.]. Edinburgi: Apud Andreæ Anderson Hæredes & Successores, 1694.

> Another edition of No. *367*. Allusion, p. 48. Wing, C5743B. Copy owned by Dr. Williams's Library, London.

1400 Confessio fidei in conventu theologorum authoritate parliamenti Anglicani indicto, elaborata [etc.]. Edinburgi: Ex officinâ typographicâ Georgii Mosman, 1694.

Another edition of No. *367.* Reference, pp. 53–54. Wing, C5744. Copy owned by Folger Shakespeare Library.

1401 The Confession of faith. And the larger & shorter catechism [etc.]. *The former editions being very full of faults in every page, are now faithfully corrected for the benefit of the reader.* Printed in the Year 1694.

Another edition of No. *45.* Place: London (?). Allusion, p. 80. Wing, C5776A. Copy owned by Christ Church College Library, Oxford.

1402 De re poetica: or, remarks upon poetry. With characters and censures of the most considerable poets, whether ancient or modern. Extracted out of the best and choicest criticks [etc.]. London: Ric. Everingham, for R. Bently, 1694.

Author: Sir Thomas Pope Blount. Cited in Contents, second A1v. Allusions, pp. 1, 105, 215. Discussion (lengthy quotations from Dryden, No. *1370,* and *The Athenian Mercury,* No. *1280*), pp. 135–138. Wing, B3347. Copy owned by New York Public Library.

1403 A Discourse of government, as examined by reason, scripture, and law of the land [etc.]. London: Printed for Samuel Lowndes, 1694.

Author: Sir Philip Warwick. Written: 1678. Allusion, A4. Wing, W991. Copy owned by Columbia University Library.

1404 The Gentleman's journal: or the monthly magazine [etc.]. Vol. III (April). London: Printed for Henry Rhodes, 1694.

Editor: Peter Motteux. Notice of Thomas Power's Latin verse translation of *Paradise Lost,* p. 97. Copy owned by New York Public Library.

1405 Henrich Ludolff Benthems P. C. und S. Engländischer kirch- und schulen-staat. Lüneburg: Verlegts Johann Georg Lipper, 1694.

Discussion of Theodor Haak, Ernst von Berge, and Milton, and various works including the state papers, *Defensio prima,* and *Paradise Lost,* pp. 57–59. Copy owned by British Library.

1406 In memory of Joseph Washington, esq; late of the Middle Temple, an elegy [etc.]. Licens'd November 7. 1694. Edward Cooke.

No title page. Author: Nahum Tate. Colophon: "London, Printed for Richard Baldwin, near the Oxford-Arms in Warwick-Lane, 1694." Folio. A^2; 4 pp. Allusion. Wing, T189. Copy owned by Folger Shakespeare Library.

1407 Innocui sales. A Collection of new epigrams [etc.]. London: Printed by T. Hodgkin; and are to be sold by Matth. Gillyflower, 1694.

Author: Henry Killigrew. Epigram No. 17, "On Milton and Marvel," p. 15. Wing, I209A. Copy owned by Folger Shakespeare Library.

1408 [Letter from John Dryden to John Dennis, dated ca. March 1694.]

Allusion. Printed in No. *1499.*

1409 [Letter from Thomas Gill to Charles Hatton, dated 1 May 1694.]

On authorship of *Eikon Basilike.* Printed in No. *1552.*

1410 A Letter out of Suffolk to a friend in London [etc.]. London: 1694.

Author: Thomas Wagstaffe. Allusion, p. 18. Wing, W209. Copy owned by New York Public Library.

1411 The Library of Mr. Tho. Britton, smallcoal-man. Being a curious collection of books in divinity [etc.].

Dated: 1 November 1694. Place: London. Bookseller: John Bullord. Listings: p. 12, *Hirelings, Civil Power*; p. 13, *Eikon Aklastos*; p. 15, *Doctrine and Discipline of Divorce*; p. 18, *Moscovia*; p. 28, "Miltons Reply to the Answer to the Observations on his Majesties Answers and Expresses." Wing, B4828. Copy owned by British Library.

1412 The Life of our blessed lord and saviour Jesus Christ. An heroic poem [etc.]. London: Printed for C. Harper and B. Motte; to be sold by Roger Clavel, 1694.

Reissue of No. *1362.* Wing, W1372. Copy owned by Princeton University Library.

1413 The Method and order of reading both civil and ecclesiastical histories [etc.]. *The second edition* [etc.]. London: Printed for Charles Brome, 1694.

Edition 2 of No. *1077.* References, pp. 172, 178, and Index. Wing, W1593. Copy owned by Newberry Library.

1414 Miscellaneous letters and essays, on several subjects [etc.]. *By several gentlemen and ladies.* London: Printed for Benjamin Bragg, 1694.

Editor: Charles Gildon. "To Mr. T. S. in Vindication of Mr. Milton's Paradise Lost," pp. 41–44: discussion of language, style, subject. Erratum (p. 132 [232]) adds signature: "I. I."; but also attributed to Gildon.

Two allusions in "Some Reflections on Mr. Rymer's Short View of Tragedy, and an Attempt at a Vindication of Shakespear, in an Essay directed to John Dryden Esq;", p. 81: on blank verse.

Wing, G732. Copy owned by Yale University Library.

1415 *Miscellanies: in five essays* [etc.]. London: Printed for Sam. Keeble and Jo. Hindmarsh, 1694.

Author: Jeremy Collier. Part One of *Essays*. Allusion in "To the Reader," A2. Wing, C5256. Copy owned by New York Public Library.

1416 *Monatliche unterredungen einiger guten freunde von allerhand büchern und andern* [etc.]. Verlegt von J. Thomas Fritschen, 1694.

Author: Wilhelm Ernst Tentzel. Place: Leipzig. Issue for October 1694, Chapter V, pp. 830–832, discussion of Theodore Haak, Ernst von Berge, and *Paradise Lost.* Copy owned by Yale University Library.

1417 *A Poem on the late promotion of several eminent persons in church and state* [etc.]. London: Printed for Richard Baldwin, 1694.

Author: Nahum Tate. Allusion, p. 11. Wing, T207. Copy owned by Folger Shakespeare Library.

1418 *The Present state of Europe, or, the historical and political monthly mercury* [etc.]. London: Printed for Henry Rhodes and John Harris, 1694.

Vol. V, No. 11, for November. Allusion to *Literae*, p. 378. Copy owned by New York Public Library.

1419 *Reflections upon ancient and modern learning* [etc.]. London: J. Leake, for Peter Buck, 1694.

Author: William Wotton. Allusions, pp. 8–10 (to *Paradise Lost*), 29. Wing, W3658. Copy owned by New York Public Library.

1420 *The Rival queens, or, the death of Alexander the Great* [etc.]. *The second edition.* London: Printed for Richard Bentley, 1694.

Another edition of No. *753.* Imitation, p. 38. Wing, L868. Copy owned by University of Kentucky Library.

1421 *Samuelis Pufendorfii de jure naturæ et gentium libri octo. Editio nova, auctior multo, et emendatior* [etc.]. Francofurti ad Moenum, Sumtibus Friderici Knochii. Typis Joannis Wustii. 1694.

Another edition of No. *655.* Allusion, p. 831; discussion, pp. 875–880. Copy owned by Bibliothèque Nationale.

1422 *Some observations upon the keeping the thirtieth of January, and twenty ninth of May.*
London: Printed, and are to be sold by Ric. Baldwin, 1694.

Author: J. G. G. (John [Jean] Gailhard). Reference to *Eikonoklastes*, p. 10.
Wing, G129. Copy owned by Union Theological Seminary Library
(McAlpin Collection).

1423 [Testimonial statement by Francis Bernard, dated 10 May 1694.]

On the authorship of *Eikon Basilike.* Printed in No. *1552.*

1424 *A Treatise of the situation of paradise, written by P. D. Huet Bishop of Soissons.*
To which is prefixed a map of the adjacent countries. Translated from the French original.
London: Printed for James Knapton, 1694.

Author: Pierre Daniel Huet. Advertisement for "Miltons Paradise Lost, with
Cuts." on I10. Wing, H3302. Copy owned by Union Theological Seminary
Library (McAlpin Collection).

1425 *A True protestant bridle: or some cursory remarks upon a sermon preached before the*
Lord Mayor at St. Mary-Le-Bow, Jan. 30th 1693/4 [etc.]. London: Printed and
are to be sold by most of the Booksellers of London and Westminster, 1694.

Author: Thomas Rogers. Allusions, pp. 7–8, 24. Wing, R1843. Copy owned
by Folger Shakespeare Library.

1426 *Twelve sermons preached upon several occasions. By Robert South, D. D. The second*
volume. Never before printed. London: J. H., for Thomas Bennett, 1694.

Reference to "Fools Paradise," amidst discussion of Roman Catholics, pp.
545–546, in "An Account of the Natures and Measures of Conscience: In
Two Sermons on 1 John III.21. Preached Before the University at Christ-
church, Oxon. The *First* Preached on the 1st. of Nov. 1691." See Wing,
S4746. Copy owned by Union Theological Seminary Library (McAlpin
Collection).

1427 *Two treatises of government* [etc.]. *The second edition corrected.* London: Printed
for Awnsham and John Churchill, 1694.

Edition 2 of No. *1245.* Allusion in Preface, A3v. Reference to *Paradise Regain'd*
in advertisement of books sold by A. and J. Churchill, p. [359]. Wing,
L2767. Copy owned by Yale University Library.

1428 *The Works of Mr. John Dryden. In four volumes* [etc.]. London: Printed for Jacob
Tonson, 1694.

Similar to No. *1379.* Included are: Vol. 2, 1695 *State of Innocence* (No. *1471*);

1694 *Aureng-Zebe* (No. *1383*). Vol. 3, 1687 *Duke of Guise* (No. *1129*); 1692 *Don Sebastian* (No. *1303*). Vol. 4, *MacFlecknoe, Absalom and Achitophel, The Medall*, and *Britannia Rediviva*, all as in No. *1379*. Wing, D2209. Copy owned by William Andrews Clark Library.

1429 The Works of Mr. Nathaniel Lee, in one volume [etc.]. London: Printed for R. Bentley, 1694.

Reissue of *The Rival Queens*, 1677 (see p. 44 for imitation; No. *753*). To this are added copies of later printings of *Caesar Borgia* (No. *1485*; see pp. 68-69) and *The Duke of Guise* (No. *1611*; see p. 36). Wing, L845A. Copy owned by Columbia University Library.

A William Andrews Clark copy of bound plays of Lee (apparently separate and original issues, with no composite title page) is listed as Wing, L845, dated 1687. Fourteen other various title pages for *Works* have been cited with varying dates and printing legends; none of these have been discovered and none are listed in Wing.

1695

See also Nos. 380, 381, 382, and 383 in Part I for Lawes's letter, Wotton's letter, and testimonies, and Nos. 376, 377, 378, 381, 382, and 383 for Dryden's epigram on Milton.

1430 The Athenian mercury. Vol. 18, No. 20. 21 September 1695. London: Printed for John Dunton, 1695.

Allusion in Question 2, on learning Latin. Copy owned by New York Public Library.

1431 Bibliotheca Belwoodiana: or, a catalogue of the library of Roger Belwood [etc.].

Dated: 4 February 1695. Place: London. Bookseller: John Bullard [sic]. Listings: p. 1, *Defensio prima*; p. 6, *Defensio pro se, Defensio secunda, Artis Logicae*; p. 8, *Defensio pro se*, More's *Fides Publica, Literae*; p. 15, *Eikonoklastes, Doctrine and Discipline of Divorce, Tetrachordon, Bucer*, Salmasius' *Responsio, Tenure*; p. 18, *Defense of the English People*; p. 21, *Paradise Lost, Paradise Regain'd, Poems* (1673); p. 24, *Civil Power*; p. 41, *True Religion*. Wing, B1863. Copy owned by British Library.

1432 Bibliotheca eximia the library of a learned person of quality [etc.].

Dated: 22 August 1695. Booksellers: Fra. Mills and W. Turner. Listing: p. 25, *Defensio prima* "cum aliis Tract." Wing, B2825. Copy owned by British Library.

1433 *Bibliotheca Harringtoniana, being an excellent collection of books* [etc.].

Dated: 13 February 1695. Owner: James Harrington, the younger. Bookseller: John Nicholson. Listings: p. [ii], *Literae*; p. 15, *Defensio secunda*. Wing, H829 (title incorrect). Copy owned by British Library.

1434 *Bibliotheca Littletoniana. The Library of the reverend and learned Adam Littleton, D. D. Prebendary of Westminster* [etc.].

Dated: 15 April 1695. Bookseller: John Bullord. Listing: p. 10, *Accedence Commenc't Grammar*. Wing, L2559 (title incorrect). Copy owned by British Library.

1435 *Bibliotheca mathematica & medica Scarburghiana; or, the mathematical and physical parts of the famous library of Sir Charles Scarburgh, Kn, M. D.* [etc.].

Dated: 18 February 1695. Bookseller: Christopher Bateman. Listings: p. 22, *History of Britain, Eikonoklastes*; p. 24, *Poems* (1673), *Paradise Regain'd*. Wing, S819. Copy owned by British Library.

1436 *Bibliotheca Scarburghiana; or, a catalogue of the incomparable library of Sir Charles Scarburgh, Kn^t, M. D.* [etc.].

Dated: 8 February 1694/5. Bookseller: Christopher Bateman. Listings: p. 26, *Defensio prima*; p. 27, *Defensio prima*. Wing, S820. Copy owned by British Library.

1437 *Bibliotheca Tillotsoniana: or a catalogue of the curious library of Dr. John Tillotson late lord archbishop of Canterbury* [etc.]. *Together with the library of Mr. Seth-Mountley Buncle* [etc.]. 1695.

Dated: 9 April 1695. Listings: p. 28, *Defensio prima;* p. 44, *Defensio prima*; p. 62, *Defensio prima*, Du Moulin's *Regii Sanguinis Clamor*. Wing, T1187 (incorrect title). Copy owned by British Library.

1438 *Bibliothecæ noblissimæ pars tertia & ultima, sive collectio multifaria diversorum librorum plurimis facultatibus, præ-cæteris eximiorum ex celeberrimis Europæ, typographiis prodeuntium* [etc.]. 1695.

Dated: 20 June 1695. Place: London. Bookseller: Edward Millington. Listings: p. 26, *Defensio prima*; p. 38, *Smectymnuus Redivivus, Apology*; p. 40, *Poems*, Latin (1645). Wing, B2863. Copy owned by British Library.

1439 *Bibliothecæ nobilissimæ pars tertia & ultima, sive collectio multifaria diversiorum librorum plurimis facultatibus, præ-cæteris eximiorum ex celeberrimis Europæ, typographiis prodeuntium* [etc.]. 1695.

Partially different catalogue from No. *1438*. Listings: p. 26, *Defensio prima*; p. 38, *Paradise Lost, History of Britain*; p. 96, *Poems*, Latin (1645). See Wing, B2863. Copy owned by British Library.

1440 Bibliothecæ nobilissimæ: sive collectio multifaria diversorum librorum plurimis facultatibus, præ-cæteris eximiorum ex celeberrimis Europæ typographiis prodeuntium. Pars posterior [etc.]. *Una cum bibliotheca selectissima Rev. Doct. V. D. Jo. Scott Londinens. defuncti.* [etc.]. *1695.*

Dated: 23 May 1695. Place: London. Bookseller: Edward Millington. Listing: p. 28, *Doctrine and Discipline of Divorce*. Wing, S2038. Copy owned by British Library.

1441 Bibliothecæ nobilissimæ: sive collectio multifaria diversorum librorum plurimis facultatibus, præ-cæteris eximiorum ex celeberrimis Europæ typographiis prodeuntium. Pars prior [etc.]. *1694/5.*

Dated: 21 February 1694/5. Place: London. Bookseller: Edward Millington. Listing: p. 43, *Defensio prima*. Wing, B2862. Copy owned by British Library.

1442 Bibliothecæ Stawellianæ pars prima; or, a catalogue of curious books [etc.].

Dated: 3 December 1695. Owner: John late Lord Stawel, Baron of Somerton. Bookseller: John Bullord. Listings: p. 10, *Defensio prima*; p. 22, *Defensio prima*. Wing, S5348 (incorrect title). Copy owned by British Library.

1443 A Catalogue of books continued, printed and published in London in Hilary-term, 1694. No. 55.

Dated: 1694/5. Two advertisements; one for Hog's translation of "Lycidas," the other for *History of Britain*. Copy owned by British Library.

1444 A Catalogue of books continued, printed and published in London in Michaelmas-term, 1695. No. 58.

Allusion in advertisement for Filmer's *Observations*. Copy owned by Henry E. Huntington Library.

1445 A Catalogue of Latin and English books to be sold at auction [etc.].

Dated: 2 January 1695. Listings: p. [iii], *History of Britain, Artis Logicae*; p. 5, *Tenure*; p. 7, *Poems*. Wing, C1342. Copy owned by British Library.

1446 A Collection of excellent English books, consisting of divinity [etc.].

Dated: 23 April 1695. Owner: John Tillotson. Bookseller: John Nicholson. Listings: p. 14, *Paradise Lost*; p. 15, *Tenure, Doctrine and Discipline of Divorce,*

Areopagitica, Answer to Doctrine and Discipline of Divorce. Wing, T1188 (incorrect title). Copy owned by British Library.

1447 *The Court of death. A Pindarique poem, dedicated to the memory of her most sacred majesty, Queen Mary* [etc.]. London: Printed for James Knapton, 1695.

Author: John Dennis. Allusion in preface, a2, indicating Milton's influence on the poem. Wing, D1028. Copy owned by Princeton University Library.

1448 *The Court of death. A Pindarique poem, dedicated to the memory of her most sacred majesty, Queen Mary* [etc.]. *The second edition*. London: Printed for James Knapton, 1695.

Edition 2 of No. *1447*. Wing, D1029. Copy owned by Yale University Library.

1449 *Danielis Georgi Morhofi polyhistor. Sive de notitia auctorum et rerum commentarii* [etc.]. *Editio secunda auctior*. Lubecæ: Sumptibus Petri Böckmanni, 1695.

Edition 2 of No. *1155*. Copy owned by Henry E. Huntington Library.

1450 *De arte graphica. The art of painting, by C. A. Du Fresnoy. With remarks. Translated into English. Together with an original preface containing a parallel betwixt painting and poetry. By Mr. Dryden* [etc.]. London: J. Heptinstall, for W. Rogers, 1695.

Author: John Dryden. Allusion in "Observations on the Art of Painting," p. 108. Wing, D2458. Copy owned by Yale University Library.

1451 *De boekzaal van Europe, gesticht door P. Rabus* [etc.]. Rotterdam: Pieter vander Slaart, 1695.

Vol. VI, May–June 1695, pp. 419, 433: allusions in review of Sir Thomas Pope Blount's *De Re Publica*. In Dutch. Copy owned by New York Public Library.

1452 *De boekzaal van Europe, gesticht door P. Rabus* [etc.]. Rotterdam: Pieter vander Slaart, 1695.

Vol. VII, July–August 1695, p. 36: allusion in review of Leti's life of Cromwell. In Dutch. Copy owned by New York Public Library.

1453 *A Discourse concerning the gift of prayer* [etc.]. *Whereunto may be added, Ecclesiastes* [etc.]. London: Printed for J. Lawrence; and A. and J. Churchil, 1695.

Another edition of No. *296*, to which is added No. *1353*. Wing, W2185 and W2195. Copy owned by Henry E. Huntington Library.

1454 *The Dramatick works of Mr. John Dryden. In three volumes. Vol. I.* [etc.]. London: Printed for R. Bentley, 1695.

Vol. II:

The Dramatick works of Mr. John Dryden. In three volumes. Vol. II. Containing, ... State of Innocence. Aurenzebe [etc.]. London: Printed for R. Bentley, 1695.

Reissue of 1692 *State of Innocence* (No. *1320*) and 1694 *Aureng-Zebe* (No. *1383*).

Vol. III:

The Dramatick works of Mr. John Dryden. In three volumes. Vol. III. Containing, Duke of Guise ... Don Sebastian [etc.]. London: Printed for R. Bentley, 1695.

Reissue of 1687 *Duke of Guise* (No. *1129*) and 1692 *Don Sebastian* (No. *1303*).

Wing, D2211. Copy owned by Princeton University Library.

1455 Elegies on the Queen and Archbishop. London: B. Motte, for C. Harper, 1695.

Author: Samuel Wesley. Imitation in "On the Death of Her Late Sacred Majesty Mary, Queen of England," p. 11 (Stanza XV); see *PL* X, 831–834. Wing, W1368. Copy owned by University of Kentucky Library.

1456 Elegies on the Queen and Archbishop [etc.]. *The second edition, with additions and alterations.* London: Printed by B. Motte, for C. Harper, 1695.

Edition 2 of No. *1455.* Some of the Miltonic echoes are altered or disappear, but see Stanzas XIII, p. 9, and XV, pp. 10–11. Wing, W1369. Copy owned by Bodleian Library.

1457 The First volume of the works of Mr. John Dryden [etc.]. London: Printed for Jacob Tonson, 1695.

Two volumes. Second volume (appropriately changed title page) includes 1692 *State of Innocence* (No. *1320*) and 1694 *Aureng-Zebe* (No. *1383*). Not in Wing. Copy owned by William Andrews Clark Library.

1458 The First volume of the works of Mr. John Dryden [etc.]. London: Printed for Jacob Tonson, 1695.

Four volumes with appropriately changed title pages. Vol. 2 includes 1695 *State of Innocence* (No. *1472*) and 1699 *Aureng-Zebe* (No. *1593*). Vol. 3 includes 1699 *Duke of Guise* (variant issue, No. *1612*) and 1692 *Don Sebastian* (No. *1303*). Vol. 4 includes *MacFlecknoe*, 1692 *Absalom and Achitophel*, 1692 *The Medall*, and 1691 *Britannia Redivivus*, all as in Nos. *1379* and *1428.* Wing, D2210. Copy owned by William Andrews Clark Library.

1459 Gloriana. A funeral Pindarique poem: sacred to the blessed memory of that ever-admir'd and most excellent princess, our late gracious soveraign lady Queen Mary [etc.]. London: Printed for Samuel Briscoe, 1695.

Author: Thomas D'Urfey. Imitations of *Paradise Lost* throughout; see, for example, Stanza VII and compare III, 645-653. Wing, D2730. Copy owned by New York Public Library.

1460 *Mausolaeum: a funeral poem on our late gracious sovereign queen Mary, of blessed memory.* London: Printed for B. Aylmer, and W. Rogers, and R. Baldwin, 1695.

Author: Nahum Tate. Allusion, p. 10. Wing, T194. Copy owned by Folger Shakespeare Library.

1461 *The Miscellaneous works of Charles Blount, esq; containing ... V. A just vindication of learning, and of the liberty of the press* [etc.]. Printed in the Year 1695.

Place: London. "Account of the Life and Death of the Author," A^{12}, followed by two sets of signatures. First set is a reissue of *Oracles of Reason*, 1693, with citation of "An Apology for the Liberty of the Press" on a6v and influence from *Paradise Lost*, pp. 25-28 (see No. *1365*). Second set includes 1679 *Anima Mundi*, 1695 *Great is Diana*, 1695 *An Appeal from the Country to the City*, and 1695 *A Just Vindication*. Each has a separate title page and pagination.

A Just Vindication of Learning, and the Liberty of the Press. London, Printed in the Year 1695. Sigs. K^{12} L^6; viii + 28 pp. [1], title page; [ii], blank; [iii-vii], Poem; [viii], blank; 1-23, work; 24, Postscript; 25-27, "A Dialogue"; [28], blank. See No. *790*. Wing, B3296. Copy owned by University of Kentucky Library. Copy owned by Union Theological Seminary Library (McAlpin Collection) binds *A Just Vindication* before *An Appeal from the Country*.

It is possible that *A Just Vindication* was issued separately, for it appears separately from *The Miscellaneous Works* in various libraries. However, Wing B3308, citing a different quarto edition, does not exist; all copies listed are duodecimo, K^{12} L^6.

1462 *Monsieur Bossu's treatise of the epick poem: containing many curious reflexions, very useful and necessary for the right understanding and judging of the excellencies of Homer and Virgil. Done into English from the French, with a new original preface upon the same subject, by W. J. To which are added, An Essay upon satyr, by Monsieur D'Acier; and A Treatise upon pastorals, by Monsieur Fontanelle.* London: Printed for Tho. Bennet, 1695.

Translator: W. J. Reference to Rymer's remarks and quotations of Dryden's statement in his preface to Juvenal: Preface, a2v-a3. See Nos. *778* and *1370*. Not in Wing. Copy owned by University of Kentucky Library.

1463 *The Mourning muse of Alexis. A pastoral. Lamenting the death of our late gracious Queen Mary of ever blessed memory* [etc.]. London: Printed for Jacob Tonson, 1695.

Author: William Congreve. Edition 1. Influence from *Comus* and *Lycidas*. Wing, C5859. Copy owned by Princeton University Library.

1464 *The Mourning muse of Alexis. A pastoral. Lamenting the death of our late gracious Queen Mary of ever blessed memory* [etc.]. *The second edition.* London: Printed for Jacob Tonson, 1695.

Edition 2 of No. *1463*. Wing, C5860. Copy owned by Folger Shakespeare Library.

1465 *The Mourning muse of Alexis. A pastoral. Lamenting the death of our late gracious Queen Mary of ever blessed memory* [etc.]. *The third edition.* London: Printed for Jacob Tonson, 1695.

Edition 3 of No. *1463*. Wing, C5861. Copy owned by Bodleian Library.

1466 *The Mourning muse of Alexis. A pastoral. Lamenting the death of our late gracious Queen Mary of ever blessed memory* [etc.]. *The third edition.* Dublin: Reprinted for William Norman, and Jacob Milner, 1695.

Another edition of No. *1463*. Wing, C5862. Copy owned by British Library.

1467 *A Pindarique ode, humbly offer'd to the king on his taking Namure* [etc.]. London: Printed for Jacob Tonson, 1695.

Author: William Congreve. Folio. "Books Printed for Jacob Tonson," C2v, lists *The Poetical Works*, 1695. Wing, C5871. Copy owned by William Andrews Clark Library.

1468 *Prince Arthur, an heroick poem. In ten books* [etc.]. London: Printed for Awnsham and John Churchil, 1695.

Author: Sir Richard Blackmore. Edition 1. Imitations, passim. Wing, B3080. Copy owned by University of Kentucky Library.

1469 *Prince Arthur, an heroick poem. In ten books* [etc.]. *The second edition corrected.* London: Printed for Awnsham and John Churchil, 1695.

Edition 2 of No. *1468*. Wing, B3081. Copy owned by Yale University Library.

1470 THE | State of Innocence, | AND | FALL of MAN: | AN | OPERA. | Written in Heroick Verse; | And Dedicated to Her Royal *Highness* | THE | DUTCHESS. | ——— | By *John Dryden*, Servant to His *Majesty*. | ——— | [two lines in Latin from Ovid's *Metamorphoses*] | ——— | *LONDON:* Printed by *H. H.* for *Henry Herringman*, and are | to be sold by *Joseph Knight*, and *Francis Saunders*, at the An- | chor in the Lower Walk of the *New Exchange.* 1684. |

Reprint in 1695 (?); see No. *1039*. Quarto. A–E^4 F^2 G^4; xvi + 36 pp. [i], title page; [ii], blank; [iii–vi], Dedication; [vii–viii], Lee's poem; [ix–xvi], Preface; 1–36, work. See Wing, D2375. Copy owned by Folger Shakespeare Library.

1471 THE | State of Innocence, | AND | FALL of MAN: | AN | OPERA. | Written in Heroick Verse; | And Dedicated to Her Royal *Highness* | THE | DUTCHESS. | —————— | By *John Dryden*, Servant to His *Majesty*. | —————— | [two lines in Latin from Ovid's *Metamorphoses*] | —————— | *LONDON:* Printed by *H. H.* for *Henry Herringman*, and are | to be sold by *Joseph Knight*, and *Francis Saunders* at the An- | chor in the Lower Walk of the *New Exchange*. 1684. |

See No. *1470*; typographical differences on title page. Quarto. A–E^4 F^2 G^4; xvi + 36 pp. Sig. G marked F. [i], title page; [ii], blank; [iii–vi], Dedication; [vii–viii], Lee's poem; [ix–xvi], Preface; 1–36, work. See Wing, D2375. Copy owned by Folger Shakespeare Library.

1472 THE | State of Innocence, [black letter] | AND | Fall of MAN: | AN | OPERA. | Written in Heroick VERSE; and | Dedicated to Her Royal HIGHNESS | THE | DUTCHESS. | —————— | By Mr. JOHN DRYDEN. | —————— | [two-line quotation from Ovid's *Metamorphoses*] | —————— | *LON-DON:* | Printed for *Hen. Herringman*, and are to be Sold by *J. Tonson*, | *F. Saunders*, and *T. Bennet*. 1695. |

Edition 7. Quarto. A–F^4 G^2; xvi + 36 pp. [i], title page; [ii], blank; [iii–vi], Dedication; [vii–viii], Lee's poem; [ix–xvi], Preface; 1–36, work. Wing, D2378. Copy owned by University of Wisconsin Library.

1473 THE | State of Innocence, [black letter] | AND | Fall of MAN: | AN | OPERA. | Written in Heroick VERSE: and | Dedicated to Her Royal HIGHNESS | THE | DUTCHES. | —————— | By Mr. JOHN DRYDEN. | —————— | [two-line quotation from Ovid's *Metamorphoses*] | —————— | *LON-DON:* | Printed for *Hen. Herringman*, and are to be Sold by *J. Tonson*, | *F. Saunders*, and *T. Bennet*. 1695. |

Title page has typographical differences from No. *1472*. Sigs. A–B have been reset. Not in Wing. Copy owned by Folger Shakespeare Library.

1474 *The Temple of death, a poem; written by the Marquis of Normanby. Horace of the Art of Poetry, made English by the Earl of Roscommon* [etc.]. *The second edition corrected.* London: Printed by Tho. Warren for Francis Saunders, 1695.

No Edition 1 is recorded. Reference in preface, B1v; translation, pp. 5–32, with metric influence from *Paradise Lost*. Given on p. [274] is "A Catalogue of Books Printed for, and Sold by Francis Saunders," which lists "Mr *Milton*'s

Paradice Lost and Regain'd." Wing, T663. Copy owned by British Library.

1475 *Thomæ Crenii Animadversiones philologicæ et historicæ* [etc.]. Roterdami: Sumptibus Isaaci van Ruynen, 1695.

Author: Thomas Crusius. Reference to Vavassor's epigram on Salmasius and Milton (see No. *610*), Vol. 1, Chapter 4, p. 73. Copy owned by British Library.

1476 *The Urim of conscience* [etc.]. London: J. M. and B. B., for A. Roper, E. Wilkinson and R. Clavel, 1695.

Author: Sir Samuel Morland. Allusions to *Paradise Lost*, pp. 13–14, 135. Possible influence from the epic, passim. Wing, M2785. Copy owned by Union Theological Seminary Library (McAlpin Collection).

1477 [*The Works of Mr. John Dryden. In four volumes.* London: 1695.]

No general title page. Vol. I: *The First volume of the Works of Mr. John Dryden* [etc.]. London: Printed for Jacob Tonson, 1695. Vol. II: *The Second volume of the Works of Mr. John Dryden* [etc.]. London: Printed for Jacob Tonson, 1695. Includes reissues of 1695 *State of Innocence* (No. *1472*) and 1694 *Aureng-Zebe* (No. *1383*). Vol. III: *The Third Volume of the Works of Mr. John Dryden* [etc.]. London: Printed for Jacob Tonson, 1695. Includes reissues of 1687 *Duke of Guise* (No. *1129*) and 1692 *Don Sebastian* (No. *1303*). Vol. IV: *The Fourth volume of the Works of Mr. John Dryden* [etc.]. London: Printed for Jacob Tonson, 1695. Includes reissues of *MacFlecknoe, Absalom and Achitophel, the Medall,* and *Britannia Rediviva* as in Nos. *1379, 1428,* and *1458.* Wing, D2210. Copy owned by Princeton University Library.

1478 *The Works of Mr. John Oldham. Together with his Remains.* London: Printed for Nathaniel Rolls, 1695.

Reissues of *Satyrs upon the Jesuits* (1685), *The Passion of Byblis* (1685), *Poems and Translations* (1684), *Poems and Translations* (1694), and *Remains* (1693). "Bion," with allusion on p. 82, appears in *Poems and Translations* (1684), No. *1028.* Wing, O230. Copy owned by Henry E. Huntington Library. British Library copy, without title page, is Alexander Pope's autographed copy.

1696

SEE ALSO NO. 385 IN PART I FOR AN ALLUSION.

1479 *Acta ervditorvm anno M DC XCVI publicata* [etc.]. Lipsiæ: Prostant apud Joh. Grossii hæredes & Joh. Thom. Fritschium. Typis Iohannis Georgii, 1696.

No. 1 (January). 1695 *Poetical Works* noted under Libri Novi, p. 51. In Latin. Copy owned by University of Kentucky Library.

1480 Acta ervditorvm anno M DC XCVI publicata [etc.]. Lipsiæ: Prostant apud Joh. Grossii hæredes & Joh. Thom. Fritschium. Typis Iohannis Georgii, 1696.

No. 5 (May). Review of 1695 *Poetical Works*, pp. 226–227. In Latin. Copy owned by University of Kentucky Library.

1481 Acta ervditorvm anno M DC XCVI publicata [etc.]. Lipsiæ: Prostant apud Joh. Grossii hæredes & Joh. Thom. Fritschium. Typis Iohannis Georgii, 1696.

Listings in Index, pp. 568, 592. Copy owned by University of Kentucky Library.

1482 Annotations upon the Holy Bible [etc.]. *The third edition. With the addition of a new concordance and tables, by Mr. Sam. Clark. The whole corrected and amended by the said Mr. Sam. Clark, and Mr. Edward Veale. With large contents to each chapter* [etc.]. London: Printed for Thomas Parkhurst, Jonathan Robinson, Thomas Cockerill Senr & Junr, Brabazon Aylmer, John Lawrence, and John Taylor, 1696.

Edition 3 of No. *948*. Discussion on Genesis iii on B3–B4v. Wing, P2822 and P2824. Copy owned by Folger Shakespeare Library.

1483 The Athenian mercury. Vol. 19, No. 24. 18 January 1696. London: Printed for John Dunton, 1696.

Allusion. Copy owned by New York Public Library.

1484 Bibliotheca Stawellianæ pars secunda; or, a catalogue of curious books [etc.].

Dated: 4 February 1696. Owner: John, late Lord Stawel, Baron of Somerton. Bookseller: John Bullord. Listings: p. 13, *Paradise Lost*; p. 14, "An Answer to Milton's Iconoclastes 1681"; p. 19, Ralegh's *Arts of Empire*; p. 22, *History of Britain, Eikonoklastes*; p. 24, *Poems* (1673), *Paradise Regain'd*. Wing, S5348 (incorrect title). Copy owned by British Library.

1485 Caesar Borgia [etc.]. London: Printed for R. Bentley, 1696.

Another edition of No. *824*. Imitation, Act V, Scene ii, pp. 68–69. Wing, L847. Copy owned by University of Kentucky Library.

1486 A Catalogue of books printed in England since the dreadful fire of London in 1666. To the end of Michaelmas term, 1696 [etc.]. *The fourth edition.* London: Printed for R. Clavel and Benj. Tooke, 1696.

Listings: pp. 49, 51 (2), 74 (3), 77, 79, 89, 105 (4) [one a listing of *Paradise*

Lost in ten books, erroneously supposed to be for Jacob Tonson], 110 (*The State of Innocence*), 120 (2). Wing, C4599. Copy owned by Princeton University Library.

1487 A Catalogue of English books in divinity [etc.].

Dated: 3 December 1696. Bookseller: Thomas Axe. Listings: p. 7, *Defensio prima, Eikonoklastes*. Wing, C1320. Copy owned by British Library.

1488 Catalogus librorum tam antiquorum quam recentium in omni facultate insignium [etc.].

Dated: 5 May 1696. Place: Oxford. Owner: George Ashwell. Auctioneer: D. Michaelis. Listings: G2v, *Artis Logicae, Defensio prima*; H1v, *Defensio prima, Artis Logicae*; Q1, *Paradise Regain'd*; K1, Filmer's *Observations* (in section called "Bound Volumes"). Wing, A3993. Copy owned by British Library.

1489 Catalogus præstantissimorum & exquisitissimorum raroque occurrentium librorum [etc.]. Lugduni Batavorum, apud Petrum Venderaa, 1696.

Catalogue of Rippertia Groenendijck. Listings: p. 192, item 263, *Artis Logicae*; p. 205, item 559, *Defensio prima*; p. 207, item 622, Dutch translation of *Defensio prima*. Copy owned by Columbia University Library.

1490 A Curious collection of books and pamphlets: being the stock of Mr. William Miller, late of London, bookseller [etc.].

Dated: 1696 (?). Listings: p. 42, *Civil Power*, "Milton on Parliament power"; p. 67, *Tetrachordon, Bucer*; p. 78, *State of Innocence*; p. 87, *Accedence Commenc't Grammar*. Wing, M2067 (incorrect title). Copy owned by British Library.

1491 Disquisitio de enthusiasmo poëtico, quam in academicâ Holsatorum inclytâ Christian-Albertina, præside [etc.]. *die XIIX. Julii A. C. M,DC XCVI. publicè tuebitur Sebastianus Kortholt, auctor*. Kiloni, Imprimebat Joach. Reumann, Acad. Typogr.

Entry for Milton, Section 9, p. 19. Copy owned by British Library.

1492 An Essay in defence of the female sex [etc.]. London: Printed for A. Roper and E. Wilkinson, and R. Clavel, 1696.

Author: Mary Astell (?). Edition 1, Issue 1. $A^8 B^4 B^8$ etc. Allusion, p. 50. Wing, A4058. Copy owned by University of Kentucky Library.

1493 An Essay in defence of the female sex [etc.]. London: Printed for A. Roper and E. Wilkinson, and R. Clavel, 1696.

Different issue of No. *1492*. $A^8 B^4 B^8$ etc., but first B^4 reset with different text on B4v (same as B4 and text of B4v in Edition 2, No. *1494*). Errata of Issue 1 omitted but none made in Issue 2. Not in Wing. Copy owned by Folger Shakespeare Library.

1494 An Essay in defence of the female sex [etc.]. *The second edition* [etc.]. London: Printed for A. Roper and E. Wilkinson, and R. Clavel, 1696.

Edition 2 of No. *1492.* Wing, A4059. Copy owned by Folger Shakespeare Library.

1495 The General history of England as well ecclesiastical as civil [etc.]. London: Printed for Henry Rhodes, John Dunton, John Salusbury, and John Harris, 1696.

Author: Sir James Tyrrell. Vol. 1: allusions and quotations, pp. vi and viii (Preface), 17 (with quotation from *History of Britain*), 20, 136. Listed in An Alphabetical Table, p. lxiii. Quotation of last paragraph of Book VI of *History of Britain*, p. 116 (second pagination). Wing, T3585. Copy owned by British Library.

1496 The Grounds and occasions of the contempt of the clergy and religion enquired into. In a letter written to R. L. The tenth edition. London: Printed for E. Blagrave, and are to be sold by the Booksellers of London and Westminster, 1696.

Another edition of No. *620.* Allusion to divorce views, a1v. Wing, E55. Copy owned by Columbia University Library.

1497 Histoire de ce siecle contenant les miseres & calamités des derniers temps [etc.]. *Nouvelle edition. Reveuë, corrigée de plusieurs fautes, & augmentée de quantité de notes* [etc.]. Lyon: Chez Jean-Bapt. & Nicolas de Ville, 1696.

Another edition of No. *292.* Three volumes. Allusion, II, 66–67 and margin (running title: "Abbrege de l'Histo. De Ce Siecle"; Book I, Chapter 8). Copy owned by University of Southern California Library.

1498 Letters and essays, on several subjects: philosophical, moral, historical, critical, amorous, &c. In prose and verse [etc.]. *By several gentlemen and ladies.* London: Printed, and are to be sold by Daniel Browne and Tho. Axe, 1696.

Reissue of No. *1414.* Apparently Wing, G733. Copy owned by Columbia University Library.

1499 Letters upon several occasions: written by and between Mr. Dryden, Mr. Wycherly, Mr. -- Mr. Congreve, and Mr. Dennis [etc.]. London: Printed for Sam. Briscoe, 1696.

Published by John Dennis. Allusion in letter from Dryden to Dennis, un-dated (ca. March 1694), pp. 56–57. Wing, D1033. Copy owned by New York Public Library.

1500 London. St. Paul's Cathedral Library. MS 52.D.14.

Transcriptions of John Donne's Sermons by Knightley Chetwoode, to which is added a Commonplace Book of poetic transcriptions by Katherine Butler, dated 1696. "In imitation of Milton" ["The Splendid Shilling"], by Mr. [John] Philips, pp. 1–6. First published in *A Collection of Poems ... With Several Original Poems, Never Before Printed* (London, 1701), pp. 393–400, and reprinted in Charles Gildon, ed., *A New Miscellany of Original Poems, on Several Occasions* (London, 1701), pp. 212–221. Copies owned by Yale University Library.

1501 *Observations concerning the original and various forms of government, as described, viz. ... 3d. Mr. Milton against Salmatius* [etc.]. London: Printed for R. R. C., and are to be sold by Samuel Keble, and Daniel Brown, 1696.

Another edition of No. *275*. *Observations* on Milton listed in contents ("A Collection of the several tracts written by Sir Robert Filmer Knight") as No. II, on A7. Half-title for *Observations* given on N1, unpaged; *Observations* reissued on N1–R8 (omitting the discussion of Philip Hunton, which follows), pp. [i–viii] 165–236. *Observations* on Milton given on O5–P4v, pp. 181–196. A reissue of *Patriarcha* with separate signatures and pagination completed the volume but without half-title; instead there are two blank pages. Allusion in letter appears on A4v. Title page of collection does not include *Patriarcha* but Contents does. Wing, F919. Copy owned by Princeton University Library.

Wing, F908, *Works*, supposedly owned by St. John's College Library, Cambridge, does not exist.

1502 *Observations concerning the original and various forms of government, as described, viz. ... 3d. Mr. Milton against Salmatius* [etc.]. London: Printed for R. R. C., and are to be sold by Tho. Axe, 1696.

Another issue of No. *1501* with *Patriarcha* appearing first. Wing, F920. Copy owned by Library of Congress. Copy in University of Kentucky Library does not include *Patriarcha* although it is listed on Contents page.

1503 ΠΑΝΣΕΒΕΙΑ: *or, a view of all religions in the world*: [etc.]. *The sixth edition* [etc.]. London: Printed for M. Gillyflower, and W. Freeman, 1696.

Another edition of No. *310*. Allusions, pp. 274 and 300 (note that this edition is not revised as in No. *360*). Wing, R1978. Copy owned by Princeton University Library.

1504 *Poems, (&c.) on several occasions: with Valentinian; a tragedy* [etc.]. London: Printed for Jacob Tonson, 1696.

Author: John Wilmot, Lord Rochester. Allusion in John Oldham's "Bion," called "A Pastoral, in Imitation of the Greek of Moschus; Bewailing the Death of the Earl of Rochester," p. x. Wing, R1757. Copy owned by Berg Collection, New York Public Library.

1505 *Poems on several occasions* [etc.]. London: Printed for R. Parker, 1696.

Author: John Oldmixon. Allusion in letter "To Mr. Walter at Rome," pp. 103–104. Wing, O261. Copy owned by Columbia University Library.

1506 *Prince Arthur* [etc.]. *The third edition corrected.* London: Printed for Awnsham and John Churchil, 1696.

Edition 3 of No. *1468.* Wing, B3082. Copy owned by Princeton University Library.

1507 *Remarks on a book entitluled, Prince Arthur, an heroick poem* [etc.]. London: Printed for S. Heyrick and R. Sare, 1696.

Author: John Dennis. Quotation of *Paradise Lost*, A3; allusion, A4. Discussion with long quotations from *Paradise Lost*, on fallen angels, pp. 129–132. Quotations from *Prince Arthur* (No. *1468*) throughout. Wing, D1040. Copy owned by New York Public Library.

1508 *The Revengeful mistress; being an amorous adventure of an English gentleman in Spain* [etc.]. London: Printed for R. Bentley and R. Wellington, 1696.

Author: Philip Ayres. Allusion to "Fools Paradise," p. [viii]. Wing, A4313. Copy owned by Yale University Library.

1509 *Ten sermons upon several occasions* [etc.]. London: Printed for Tho. Bennet, 1696.

Author: Richard Meggott. Allusions in "A Sermon Preached Before the Lord Major and Aldermen of London, at Guild-Hall Chapel, January the 30th," pp. 224, 235–236. See No. *689.* Wing, M1633. Copy owned by Folger Shakespeare Library.

1697

See also Nos. 389 and 390 in Part I for allusions.

1510 *Ad Augustissimum, invictissimumque magnæ Britanniæ, &c. legem, Gulielmum III* [etc.]. Londini: Typis F. Collins, 1697.

Author: William Hog. Influence from *Paradise Lost* throughout. Wing, H2350. Copy owned by British Library.

1511 *Augustus Britannicus: a poem upon the conclusion of the peace of Europe, at Rijswick in Holland, upon the 20th. of September, 1697* [etc.]. London: Printed; and sold by E. Whitlock, 1697.

Author: John Phillips. Influence from *Paradise Lost* in language. Wing, P2079. Copy owned by William Andrews Clark Library.

1512 *Bibliopolii Littleburiani pars quarta: continens philologos, poetas, oratores* [etc.].

Dated: 15 March 1697. Owner: Robert Littlebury. Bookseller: John Bullord. Listings: p. 16, *Defensio prima*, Salmasius' *Responsio*, Phillips' *Responsio*. Wing, L2557. Copy owned by British Library.

1513 *Bibliotheca Annesleiana: or a catalogue of choice Greek, Latin and English books, both ancient and modern* [etc.].

Dated: 18 March 1696/7. Owner: Samuel Annesley. Bookseller: Edward Millington. Listings: p. 9, *Defensio secunda, Artis Logicae*; p. 17, *History of Britain*; p. 18, *Civil Power*. Wing, A3226 (incorrect title). Copy owned by British Library.

1514 *Bibliotheca Bernardina: sive Catalogus virorum librorum* [etc.]. 1697.

Dated: 25 October 1697. Owner: Edward Bernard. Bookseller: Edward Millington. Listing: p. 11, *Civil Power*. Wing, B1985. Copy owned by British Library.

1515 *Bibliotheca selectissima: sive, catalogus variorum librorum antiquorum & recentiorum variis facultatibus clarissimorum. R. D. V. D. Michael Harding* [etc.]. 1697.

Dated: 8 November 1697. Place: Oxford. Bookseller: Edward Millington. Listings: E1v, *Literae, Artis Logicae*; L1v, *History of Britian*. Wing, H700. Copy owned by British Library.

1516 *Bibliothecæ Prestonianæ pars II: or, a curious collection of books* [etc.].

Dated: 24 November 1697. Owner: Lord Viscount Preston. Bookseller: Abel Swall. Listings (pagination is erratic): B2v, Du Moulin's *Regii Sanguinis Clamor*; p. 11, *Defenso pro se*; p. 14, *Artis Logicae*, Rowland's *Pro Rege, Defensio prima*; *** 4, *History of Britain*. Wing, P3312 (incorrect title). Copy owned by British Library.

1517 *Catalogi librorum manuscriptorum Angliæ et Hiberniæ in unum collecti, cum indice alphabetico*. Oxoniæ: E Theatro Sheldoniano, 1697.

Compiler: Edward Bernard. Listing of Life in Wood MSS (that is, No. *1144*), No. 8492, item 4, p. 363. Listed also in Index. Wing, C1253. Copy owned by New York Public Library.

1518 *A Catalogue of books, continued, printed and published in London in Michaelmas-term, 1697.* No. 8.

Reference in listing of *Vindiciae Carolinae.* Copy owned by Henry E. Huntington Library.

1519 *A Catalogue of English, Greek, and Latin books, both antient and modern* [etc.].

Dated: 13 October 1697. Bookseller: Thomas Axe. Listings: p. 7, *Eikonoklastes, Defensio prima, Paradise Lost*; p. 9, *History of Britain.* Wing, C1323. Copy owned by British Library.

1520 *A Catalogue of Latin and English books, both antient and modern* [etc.].

Dated: 12 July 1697. Listings: p. 4, *History of Britain, Poems*; p. 8, *Poems.* Wing, C1343. Copy owned by British Library.

1521 *A Catalogue of theological, philosophical, historical, philological, medicinal & chymical books* [etc.].

Dated: 1697 (?). Owner: Dr. Luke Rugeley. Bookseller: John Bullord. Listings: p. 10, *Epistolarum Familiarium Liber Unus*; p. 38, *Paradise Lost*; p. 40, *Paradise Regain'd*; p. 48, *Eikon Aklastos.* Wing, R2210 (incorrect title). Copy owned by British Library.

1522 *The Challenge, sent by a young lady to Sir Thomas -- &c. or, the female war* [etc.]. London: Printed, and sold by E. Whitlock, 1697.

Author: John Dunton. Letter XIX, p. 210, discussion of quoted lines from *Samson Agonistes*, ll. 1053-60; letter signed "Thomas." Letter XXI, pp. 233-234, quotation of lines from *Samson Agonistes*, ll. 748-758; letter signed "Mr. Ralph Axtel." Wing, C1796. Copy owned by Folger Shakespeare Library.

1523 *The Confession of faith, and the larger and shorter catechisms* [etc.]. Edinburgh: Printed by the Heirs and Successors of Andrew Anderson, 1697.

Another edition of No. *45.* Allusion, p. 49. Wing, C5776B. Copy owned by National Library of Scotland.

1524 *Dictionaire historique et critique: par Monsieur Bayle* [etc.]. Rotterdam: Chez Reiner Leers, 1697.

Author: Pierre Bayle. Two volumes in four. Biographical and critical notice: under Milton, Vol. 2, Part 1, pp. 587–590 and notes. Additions and Corrections, under Milton, Vol. 2, Part 1, p. 1327, including letter from Gui Patin, dated 13 July 1660 (No. *481*). Discussion, under Alexander Morus, Vol. 2, Part 1, pp. 616–617 and notes, 620–621 and notes. Copy owned by Columbia University Library.

1525 *An Essay in defence of the female sex* [etc.]. *The third edition with additions* [etc.]. London: Printed for A. Roper, and R. Clavel, 1697.

Edition 3 of No. *1492*. Wing, A4060. Copy owned by Folger Shakespeare Library.

1526 *An Essay on poetry; written by the Marquis of Normanby, and the same render'd into Latin by another hand. With several other poems, viz. ... A Poem on the promotion of several eminent persons in church and state, by Mr. Tate* [etc.]. London: Printed for F. Saunders, 1697.

Reprints of Nos. *1258* and *1417*. Same paging, but here signatures in No. *1258* are I1v, I2. Wing, B5338. Copy owned by Folger Shakespeare Library.

1527 *Essays upon several moral subjects* [etc.]. *The second edition corrected and much enlarged* [etc.]. London: Printed for R. Sare and H. Hindmarsh, 1697.

Edition 2 of No. *1415*. Allusion in "A Preface to The Office of a Chaplain," Part I of volume, p. 161. Wing, C5253. Copy owned by Princeton University Library.

1528 *Familiar letters: written by the right honourable John late Earl of Rochester, and several other persons of honour and quality.* [etc.]. London: Printed by W. Onley, for Sam Briscoe, 1697.

Two volumes. Volume 1 prints a letter from Rochester to Henry [i. e., George] Savile [Marquis of Halifax], on p. 12, with an allusion to *Paradise Lost* I. The letter is dated July 1678 in Jeremy Treglow's edition of *The Letters of John Wilmot, Earl of Rochester* (Chicago: University of Chicago Press, 1980). Wing, R1743. Copy owned by British Library.

1529 *The General history of England, both ecclesiastical and civil* [etc.]. London: Printed, and are to be sold by W. Rogers, J. Harris, R. Knaplock, A. Bell, and T. Cockerill, 1697.

Another issue of No. *1495*. Three volume edition in five volumes, 1697–1704. Wing, T3586. Copy owned by New York Public Library.

1530 *King Arthur. An heroick poem. In twelve books* [etc.]. London: Printed for Awnsham and John Churchil, and Jacob Tonson, 1697.

Author: Sir Richard Blackmore. Allusion, p. xiii (preface); imitations, passim. Wing, B3077. Copy owned by University of Kentucky Library.

1531 [Letter from Huet Evêque d'Avranches (Pierre Daniel Huet) to Philippe de la Mare, dated 29 April 1697.]

Allusion. In French. Printed in Gilles Menage. *Menagiana ou les bon mots* [etc.]. A Paris: Florentin Delaulne, 1715. Two volumes. Edition 3. II, 28. Copy owned by Library of Congress.

1532 [Letter from Michel le Vassor to Pierre Bayle, dated 23 April (3 May) 1697.]

Allusion. In French. Published in Emile Gigas. *Choix de la Correspondance Inédite de Pierre Bayle 1670-1706* [etc.]. Copenhague: G. E. C. Gad, 1890. Page 508.

1533 The Library of the right honourable William late Lord Bereton [etc.]. *By John Bullard.* [etc.].

Date: 1697. Listing of *Paradise Lost*, No. 27, p. 20. Not in Wing. Copy owned by Newberry Library.

1534 The Life and death of King Charles the first [etc.]. London: Printed for H. Hindmarsh, 1697.

Another edition of No. *1034*, with Wagstaff's *Vindication* (No. *1552*). Discussion, pp. 226–227. Wing, P1596. Copy owned by Yale University Library.

1535 The Life of our blessed lord and saviour Jesus Christ. An heroic poem: [etc.]. *The second edition* [etc.]. London: Printed for Charles Harper, and are to be sold by him and Roger Clavel, 1697.

Edition 2 of No. *1362*. Allusions: in prefatory poems and Preface, a1v, a3, b1; within poem, p. 331 and margin; in notes, pp. 25, 27, 107, 108, 109, 112, 323, 331, 351. Wing, W1373. Copy owned by New York Public Library.

1536 The Life of our blessed lord & saviour Jesus Christ. An heroic poem: [etc.]. *The second edition* [etc.]. London: Benj. Motte, for Charles Harper, 1697.

Different issue of No. *1535*. Wing, W1373A. Copy owned by Princeton University Library.

1537 Miscellany poems, by Mr. Dennis [etc.]. *The second edition with large additions.* London: Printed for James Knapton, 1697.

Edition 2 of No. *1364*. Allusion in preface, a8v–b1; and discussion of Milton's poetry in preface to *The Passion of Byblis*, d2–d3v (reissue of No. *1539*). Not in Wing. Copy owned by Folger Shakespeare Library.

1538 Miscellany poems, by Mr. Dennis [etc.]. *The second edition with large additions.* London: Printed for Sam. Briscoe, 1697.

Different issue of No. *1537*. Wing, D1035. Copy owned by Henry E. Huntington Library.

1539 The Passion of Byblis, made English [etc.]. *The second edition.* London: Printed for Sam. Briscoe, 1697.

Edition 2 of No. *1316*. Preface with discussion of Milton's poetry, d2–d3v. Wing, O691. Copy owned by Folger Shakespeare Library.

1540 [Poems and translations by John Oldham. London: Printed for H. Hindmarsh, 1697.]

Allusion in "Bion," p. 82. See No. *1586*. No separate issue or copy recorded.

1541 Poems chiefly consisting of satyrs, viz. Upon woman, upon the playhouse, upon man. A scourge for ill wives. A panegyrick on folly. Together with some satyrical epistles, and other occasional pieces [etc.]. *The second edition.* London: Printed for J. K. and sold by R. Baldwin, 1697.

Edition 2 of No. *1206*. Wing, G1432. Copy owned by British Library.

1542 Poems on affairs of state: from the time of Oliver Cromwell, to the abdication of K. James the second. Written by the greatest wits of the age. Viz.... Mr. Milton [etc.]. Printed in the year 1697.

Allusions: Preface, A3v–A4; Contents, A6, which erroneously lists "Directions to a Painter said to be written by Sir John Denham, but believed to be writ by Mr. Milton." Imitations: Andrew Marvell's "The Last Instructions to a Painter," pp. 58–82, see especially pp. 62 (*Paradise Lost*) and 73 (*Comus*); John Ayloffe's "Marvil's Ghost," pp. 169–170, ll. 1, 11 from *Comus*; "The Lord Lucas's Ghost, 1687" (anonymous), pp. 183–185, drawn from *Comus*. Wing, P2719. Copy owned by University of Kentucky Library.

1543 Poetischer versuch, in einem helden-gedicht und etlichen schäffer-gedichten [etc.]. Hamburg | In Verlegung Zacharias Hertel, 1704.

Author: Christian Wernicke. Prints "Auf die Schlesischen Poeten," pp. 170–177, with allusion and discursive note on p. 172, and written 1697 (?); and "Milton mit Blindheit gestrafft," pp. 352–353, on *Paradise Lost* and the Salmasian controversy, with discursive note, written before 1701. Listed in Index. Copy owned by Yale University Library.

1544 The Post Boy. No. 319. 20–22 May 1697.

> Colophon: "London, Printed by and for B. Beardwell." Advertisement for *Complete History of England.* Copy owned by William Andrews Clark Library.

1545 Reflections upon ancient and modern learning [etc.]. *The second edition, with large additions* [etc.]. London: J. Leake, for Peter Buck, 1697.

> Edition 2 of No. *1419.* Wing, W3659. Copy owned by New York Public Library.

1546 A Review of Mr. Richard Baxter's life [etc.]. London: F. C. and are to be sold by E. Whitlock, 1697.

> Author: Thomas Long. Allusion, p. 68. Wing, L2981. Copy owned by New York Public Library.

1547 The Satires of Decimus Junius Juvenalis. Translated into English verse [etc.]. *The second edition, adorn'd with sculptures.* London: Printed for Jacob Tonson, 1697.

> Edition 2, Issue 1, of No. *1370.* See pp. xii–xiv, xx–xxi, xxviii, lxxxiv–lxxxv. Wing, J1289. Copy owned by William Andrews Clark Library.

1548 The Satires of Decimus Junius Juvenalis. Translated into English verse. By Mr. Dryden, and several other eminent hands [etc.]. London: Printed for Jacob Tonson; and are to be sold by Robert Knaplock, 1697.

> Edition 2, Issue 2 (called Edition 3 in Wing), of No. *1370;* see No. *1547.* Wing, J1290. Copy owned by Columbia University Library.

1549 A Sermon preach'd before the House of Lords, in the Abbey-Church at Westminster, upon Monday, January 31. 1697. London: R. R., for W. Rogers, 1697.

> Author: John Moore. Two quotations from *Character of the Long Parliament,* p. 27; one from *Eikonoklastes,* p. 33. Wing, M2555. Copy owned by Folger Shakespeare Library.

1550 State-poems; continued from the time of O. Cromwel, to this present year 1697. Written by the greatest wits of the age, viz.... Mr. Milton [etc.]. Printed in the year 1697.

> Allusions: Preface, A2. "The Giants Wars," 1682, p. 25 (Pandemonium). Matthew Prior's "The Hind and the Panther Transvers'd," pp. 87, 92. Nahum Tate's "In Memory of Joseph Washington," 223–225 (alluding to the translation of *Defensio prima*). Poem often ascribed to Milton reprinted: "Julii Mazarini, Cardinalis, Epitaphium," pp. 58–60. Imitation: Charles Montagu's "The Man of Honour," ll. 51–54, 66–69, pp. 112–113. There is no allusion in l. 42, p. 20, of "A Charge to the Grand Inquest of England. 1674." Wing, P2720. Copy owned by University of Kentucky Library.

1551 *Twelve sermons preached upon several occasions. By Robert South, D. D. The second volume. The second edition corrected.* London: Tho. Warren, for Thomas Benet, 1697.

> Edition 2 of No. *1426.* Allusion to Fool's Paradise, p. 481. Wing, S4748. Copy owned by Folger Shakespeare Library.

1552 *A Vindication of King Charles the martyr, proving that his majesty was the author of* 'ΕΙΚΩΝ ΒΑΣΙΛΙΚΗ [etc.]. *The second edition, with additions.* London: Printed for H. Hindmarsh, 1697.

> Edition 2 of No. *1378.* Gives Anglesey's memorandum, p. 3; Clarendon's letter and Gauden's letter to Clarendon, pp. 20–22; and further information from Henry Hills, the printer, with a letter to Charles Hatton from Thomas Gill, dated 1 May 1694, and the testimony of Francis Bernard, dated 10 May 1694, pp. 50–51. Wing, W219. Copy owned by University of Kentucky Library.

1553 *The Works of Virgil: containing his pastorals, georgics, and Aeneis.* [etc.]. London: Printed for Jacob Tonson, 1697.

> Author: John Dryden. Edition 1, Issue 1: π^1 A^2 *-**4 ***-***** $+^2$ $+ +^{4(- + + 4)}$ B–Z Aa–Zz Aaa–Zzz Aaaa–Ffff^4 Gggg^2 Hhhh–Iiii^4 Kkkk^2. Allusions in dedication, "To the Most Honourable John, Lord Marquess of Normanby, Earl of Mulgrave," pp. 154, 180, 186. Large paper issue. Illustrations tipped in. Wing, V616. Copy owned by New York Public Library.
>
> Copy in Columbia University Library bound: π^1 A^2 $+^2$ $+ +^{4(- + + 4)}$ *-**4 ***-*****^{2} B–Z^4 etc. Copy in variant state of page numbers owned by William Andrews Clark Library.

1554 *The Works of Virgil: containing his pastorals, georgics, and Aeneis.* [etc.]. London: Printed for Jacob Tonson, 1697.

> Edition 1, Issue 2, of No. *1553.* π^1 A–Hh^4 Ii^2 Kk–ZZ Aaa–Zzz Aaaa–Ssss^4. Same pagination. See Wing, V616. Copy owned by Trinity College Library, Dublin.

1698

SEE ALSO NOS. 395, 396 IN PART I FOR JOHN TOLAND'S *Life of Milton* (NO. *1624*), INCLUDING TESTIMONIES PRINTED IN *Poems*, 1645, AS WELL AS MATERIALS CONCERNING THE *Eikon Basilike* CONTROVERSY. SEE NO. 397 FOR DRYDEN'S POEM ON MILTON.

1555 *The Ancient and present state of Muscovy, containing a geographical, historical and political account of all those nations and territories under the jurisdiction of the present czar* [etc.]. London: Printed for A. Roper, and A. Bosvile, 1698.

Author: Jodocus Crull. Allusion, p. [xii]. Chapter IV of *A Brief History of Moscovia* adapted as Chapter XII. Wing, C7424. Copy owned by New York Public Library.

1556 *Bibliotheca Levinziana sive catalogus diversorum librorum plurimis facultatibus, linguisq;* [etc.]. 1698.

Dated: 29 June 1698. Owner: William Levinz. Bookseller: Edward Millington. Listing: (later pagination), p. 13, *Paradise Lost.* Wing, L1826. Copy owned by British Library.

1557 *Bibliotheca librorum novorum collecta a L. Neocoro & Henrico Sikio. Tomus III. Mensis Julius & Augustus. Anno 1698.* Trajecti ad Rhenum. Apud Francisium Halman, Guilielmum vande Water. Bibl. 1698.

Notice of publication of Hog's *Paraphrasis Poetica in Tria ... Poemata* (Roterodami, 1698), p. 596. Copy owned by New York Public Library.

1558 *A Catalogue of the library of the late learned Dr. Francis Bernard* [etc.]. *The sale to begin on Tuesday, Octob. 4. 1698* [etc.].

Listings in Part II, pp. 95, 97 (separate pagination). Listings in Part III, pp. 55, 83, 88 (separate pagination). Wing, B1992. Copy owned by Yale University Library.

1559 *A Defence of dramatick poetry: being a review of Mr. Collier's view of the immorality and profaneness of the stage.* London: Printed for Eliz. Whitlock, 1698.

Author: Edward Filmer. Allusions and quotations: pp. 99 (*Paradise Lost* II, 575–581) and 106 (*Paradise Lost* I, 263). Wing, F905. Copy owned by Columbia University Library.

1560 *A Defence of the parliament of 1640. And the people of England, against King Charles I. And his adherents* [etc.]. London: Printed 1698.

Author: anonymous. Discussion of Pamela's prayer with parallel citations and of Anglesey's memorandum, quoted, pp. 15–17. Review of controversy over authorship of *Eikon Basilike*, pp. 18 ff.; various documents referenced and quotation from Clarendon's letter mentioning Milton, p. 20. Wing, D818. Copy owned by Henry E. Huntington Library.

1561 *Discourses concerning government, by Algernon Sidney* [etc.]. *Published from an original manuscript of the author.* London: Printed, and are to be sold by the Booksellers of London and Westminster, 1698.

Quotation from *Paradise Lost* IX, p. 53 (Chapter 1, Section 19). Influenced by *Defensio prima* and *Tenure of Kings and Magistrates*. Wing, S3761. Copy owned by Yale University Library.

1562 *Essays upon several moral subjects* [etc.]. *The third edition.* London: Printed for R. Sare and H. Hindmarsh, 1698.

Edition 3 of No. *1415.* Allusion, p. 179. Wing, C5254. Copy owned by University of Chicago Library.

1563 *A Farther defence of dramatick poetry: being the second part of the review of Mr. Collier's view of the immorality and profaneness of the stage. Done by the same hand.* London: Printed for Eliz. Whitlock, 1698.

Author: Edward Filmer. Allusion to Pandaemonium in quotation from Collier, and note spelling of "Dalilah," p. 48. Wing, F906. Copy owned by Columbia University Library.

1564 *The General history of England, both ecclesiastical and civil* [etc.]. London: W. Rogers, J. Harris, R. Knaplock, A. Bell, and T. Cockerill, 1698.

Reissue of Volume 1 of No. *1495,* with reset title page. Wing, T3587. Copy owned by New York Public Library.

1565 *The Grounds and occasions of the contempt of the clergy and religion* [etc.]. London: Printed for J. Philips, H. Rhodes, J. Taylor, and R. Bently, 1698.

Another edition of No. *620.* Allusion to divorce views, A1v. Either not in Wing or Wing, E56. Copy owned by Columbia University Library.

1566 *The History of Oliver Cromwel, lord protector of the Commonwealth of England, Scotland, and Ireland* [etc.]. *The third edition enlarged.* London: Printed for Nath. Crouch, 1698.

Edition 3 of No. *1305.* Allusion, pp. 174–175. Wing, C7332A. Copy owned by British Library.

1567 *The History of sin and heresy attempted* [etc.]. London: H. Hindmarsh, 1698.

Author: Charles Leslie. Discussion of *Paradise Lost* in Preface, A2v–A3. The work itself is in refutation, among other aims, of Milton's treatment of the fallen angels in *Paradise Lost.* Wing, L1135. Copy owned by Union Theological Seminary Library (McAlpin Collection).

1568 *A Letter to a member of parliament, shewing, that a restraint on the press is inconsistent with the protestant religion, and dangerous to the liberties of the nation.* London: Printed by J. Darby, and sold by Andr. Bell, 1698.

Author: Matthew Tindal. Influence from *Areopagitica* throughout. Wing, L1680. Copy owned by Rutgers University Library.

1569 [*The Lives and characters of the English dramatick poets* (etc.). London: Printed for Tho. Leigh.]

Title page missing. Authors: Gerard Langbaine and Charles Gildon. Dated: 1698?, but catalogued as 1699. Variant and earlier edition of No. *1626*. Leaf signed *L4 not included and various typographical differences throughout. References as in No. *1626* except for omission of allusion under R. A. Gent., p. *151. Not in Wing. Copy owned by New York Public Library.

1570 *The Method and order of reading both civil and ecclesiastical histories* [etc.]. *By Degory Wheare, Camden reader of history in Oxford. To which is added, An Appendix concerning the historians of particular nations, as well ancient as modern. By Nicholas Horseman. The third edition, with amendments. With Mr. Dodwell's invitation to gentlemen to acquaint themselves with antient history. Made English, and enlarged, by Edmund Bohun, esq*; London: Printed for Charles Brome, 1698.

Edition 3 of No. *1077*. Discussion of *History of Britain*, p. 172; allusion, p. 178; listing in Index. Wing, W1594. Copy owned by Folger Shakespeare Library.

1571 *Miscellanea sacra: or poems on divine & moral subjects. Collected by N. Tate, servant to His Majesty. The second edition, with additions of several poems and meditations in prose.* London: Printed for Hen. Playford, 1698.

Author: Nahum Tate, "Upon the Present Corrupted State of Poetry," a2–a2v, opposed to *Paradise Lost*'s substance and verse. Wing, T196. Copy owned by Columbia University Library.

1572 Oxford. Bodleian Library. Rawlinson MS D.1120.

Diary of Zachary Merrill (?), dated 1698. Mentions various works and secretaryship, and comments that Milton died a papist, f. 67v.

1573 *The Poetical remains of the Duke of Buckingham, Sir George Etheridge, Mr. Milton, Mr. Andrew Marvel, Madam Behn, Lord Rochester, Sir John Denham, Mr. Walker, Mr. Shadwell, Madam Philips* [etc.]. London: Printed, and are to be sold by Thomas Minton, 1698.

Editor: Charles Gildon. The Duke of Buckingham was George Villiers. No poems by Milton appear and none are ascribed to him. "To Christina, Queen of Sweden, By Mr. Marvel" (in Latin) and "English'd by Sir F. S." (that is, Fleetwood Shepard), ascribed to Milton in the eighteenth century, is given on pp. 19-20. Wing, B5321. Copy owned by British Library.

1574 The Post Man. No. 552. 17–20 December 1698.

Printed for A. Baldwin. Advertisements for *A Complete Collection* and Toland's *Life.* Copy owned by Henry E. Huntington Library.

1575 The Post Man. No. 553. 20–22 December 1698.

Printed for A. Baldwin. Advertisements for *A Complete Collection* and Toland's *Life.* Copy owned by Henry E. Huntington Library.

1576 Samuelis Puffendorfii analecta politica, quibus multæ, raræ, gravissimæque hujus disciplinæ quæstiones variis dissertationibus explicantur et enodantur. Amstelædami: Apud Janssonio-Waesbergiss. 1698.

Discussion of King Charles and the Commonwealth's justification of action, as justified, for example, in *Defensio prima*, Section 29, particularly pp. 68–70. Milton not directly cited. Copy owned by Trinity College Library, Dublin.

1577 Samuelis Pufendorfii de jure naturæ et gentium. Libri octo. Editio ultima, auctior multo, & emendatior. Amstelædami: Apud Joannem Pauli, 1698.

Another edition of No. *655.* See pp. 570, 601–604. Copy owned by Trinity College Library, Dublin.

1578 A Short view of the immorality, and profaneness of the English stage [etc.]. London: Printed for S. Keble, R. Sare, and H. Hindmarsh, 1698.

Author: Jeremy Collier. Edition 1. Allusion to "Pandemonium," p. 84. Wing, C5263. Copy owned by New York Public Library.

1579 A Short view of the immorality and profaneness of the English stage [etc.]. *The second edition.* London: Printed for S. Keble, R. Sare, and H. Hindmarsh, 1698.

Edition 2 of No. *1578.* Wing, C5264. Copy owned by Princeton University Library.

1580 A Short view of the immorality and profaneness of the English stage [etc.]. *The third edition.* London: Printed for S. Keble, R. Sare, and H. Hindmarsh, 1698.

Edition 3 of No. *1578.* Wing, C5265. Copy owned by New York Public Library.

1581 The Stage condemn'd [etc.]. London: Printed for John Salusbury, 1698.

Author: George Ridpath. Allusion, p. 196. Wing, R1468. Copy owned by Folger Shakespeare Library.

Stationers' register. See G. E. Briscoe Eyre, ed. *A Transcript of the Registers* of the Worshipful Company of Stationers; from 1640–1708 A. D. London: 1913–1914.

1582   Entry for John Toland's *Life of Milton*, under 15 December 1698, III (1914), 485.

1583 *The Triumph of peace. A poem* [etc.]. London: Printed for Jacob Tonson, 1698.

Author: John Hughes. Influence from *Paradise Lost* in language (e. g., p. 3) and possibly from *Lycidas* (e. g., p. 4). Wing, H3313. Copy owned by William Andrews Clark Library.

1584 *Two treatises of government* [etc.]. London: Printed for Awnsham and John Churchill, 1698.

Another edition of No. *1245*. Reference, A3. Wing, L2768. Copy owned by University of Kentucky Library. Copy in Christ's College Library, Cambridge, has Locke's holograph notes and alterations; a gift of Thomas Hollis (1764), it remains in his binding.

1585 *A Vindication of the stage* [etc.]. London: Printed for Joseph Wild, 1698.

Author: anonymous. Possible influence from "Of a Dramatic Poem," *Samson Agonistes*, p. 27. Wing, V532. Copy owned by Folger Shakespeare Library.

1586 *The Works of Mr. John Oldham. Together with his Remains*. London: Printed for H. Hindmarsh, 1698.

Reprint of No. *1478*, with separate title pages and pagination, plus contents leaf: 1697 *Satyrs upon the Jesuits*; 1697 *Poems and Translations*; 1698 *Poems and Translations*; 1697 *Remains*. Allusion in "Bion," p. 82, of 1697 *Poems and Translations* (No. *1540*). Wing, O231. Copy owned by New York Public Library.

1587 *The Works of Virgil: containing his pastorals, georgics, and Aeneis* [etc.]. *The second edition*. London: Printed for Jacob Tonson, 1698.

Edition 2 of No. *1553*. Large paper issue. Discussions in Dedication, pp. 208–209, 234, 240. Wing, V617. Copy owned by Princeton University Library.

1699

1588 *Acta eruditorum anno M DC IC publicata* [etc.]. Lipsiæ: Prostant apud Joh. Grossii hæredes & Joh. Thom. Fritschium. Typis Johannis Georgii, 1699.

No. 5 (May). Listings of Toland's *Life* and *Remarks* on Toland under Libri Nova, p. 240. In Latin. Copy owned by New York Public Library.

1589 Acetaria. A discourse of sallets [etc.]. London: Printed for B. Tooke, 1699.

Author: John Evelyn. References, pp. 93 and note (with quotation from *Paradise Lost*), 188–189 and note (with quotations from *Paradise Lost*); listed in Table, under Paradisian Entertainment. Compare also pp. 146–148. Wing, E3480. Copy owned by Folger Shakespeare Library.

1590 Alter amyntor: or the case fairly stated between King Charles I. and Dr. Gauden Mr. Wagstaff and Mr. Toland, touching Icon Basilike. With short notes.

Broadside. Dated: 1699. Colophon: "*London*, Printed and are to be Sold by *J. Nutt*, near *Stationers*-Hall." Reference to *Eikonoklastes* and Clarendon's letter, and discussion of Anglesey's memorandum with reference to Milton. Wing, A2929. Copy owned by Harvard University Library.

1591 Amyntor: or, a defence of Milton's Life [etc.]. Sold by the Booksellers.

Author: John Toland. Place: London. Dated: 1699. Primarily concerned with own religious concepts and the controversy over *Eikon Basilike*. [A]^2 B-L^8 M^4 N^2; iv + 172 pp. See Wing, T1760. Copy owned by New York Public Library.

1592 Amyntor: or a defence of Milton's Life [etc.]. London: Printed, and are to be sold by the Book- | sellers of *London* and *Westminster*, 1699.

Different issue of No. *1591*. [A]^2 B-L^8 M^4 N^2; iv + 172 pp. See Wing, T1760. Copy owned by Princeton University Library. See also Samuel Richardson's copy bound with copy of No. *1624*, dated August 1725, in University of Kentucky Library.

1593 Aureng-zebe: or, the great mogul. A tragedy. As it is acted by his majesty's servants [etc.]. London: Tho. Warren, for Henry Herringman; and sold by J. Tonson, F. Saunders, and T. Bennet, 1699.

Another edition of No. *1047*. Imitation, p. 7. Wing, D2250. Copy owned by Princeton University Library.

1594 Bibliotheca Andertoniana, sive catalogus variorum librorum antiquorum & recentiorum variis facultatibus clarissimorum [etc.]. 1699.

Dated: 1 March 1698/9. Place: Oxford. Owner: William Anderton. Bookseller: John Bullord. Listing: p. 14, *Artis Logicæ*. Wing, A3111. Copy owned by British Library.

1595 Bibliotheca Skinneriana, & Hampdeniana, quarum illa complectitur libros omnes [etc.]. 1698/9.

Dated: 13 February 1698/9. Bookseller: Edward Millington. Listings: p. 23, *Literae*; p. 26, *Paradise Lost*; p. 30, *History of Britain*; p. 32, *Civil Power*; p. 51, *Eikonoklastes*. Wing, S3942. Copy owned by British Library.

1596 A Catalogue of books continued, printed and published in London in Hilary-term, 1698/9. No. 13.

Advertisement for *A True account with Life of Milton*, and allusion in advertisement for *Vindiciae Carolinae*. Copy owned by British Library.

1597 A Catalogue of books continued, printed and published in London in Easter term, 1699. No. 14.

Allusions in advertisements for *Amyntor* and *Some Reflections on … Amyntor*. Copy owned by British Library.

1598 A Catalogue of books, Latin and English, ancient and modern [etc.]. 1699.

Dated: 17 August 1699. Place: Worcester (?). Owner: J. Jones. Bookseller: Edward Millington. Listings: p. 50, *Defense of the People of England*; p. 53, *Paradise Regain'd*. Wing, J956 (incorrect title). Copy owned by British Library.

1599 A Catalogue of the library of Ralph Hough, esq; [etc.].

Dated: 1699 or later (?). Bookseller: John Bullord. Listings: p. 25, Salmasius's *Responsio, Defensio pro se*; p. 26, *Defensio prima*; p. 48, *Eikonoklastes, Tetrachordon, Doctrine and Discipline of Divorce, Of Reformation*. Wing, H2911. Copy owned by British Library.

1600 A Catalogue of valuable and choice books [etc.].

Dated: 1699 (?). Listings: p. 18, Salmasius' *Responsio*; p. 19, *Artis Logicae*; p. 22, *Epistolarum Familiarium Liber Unus*, "Epistola ad Amicum"; p. 29, *Defensio secunda, Defensio pro se, Defensio prima*, Phillips' *Responsio*, Salmasius' *Responsio*; p. 31, *Eikonoklastes* (1649); p. 35, *Eikonklastes* (1690); p. 39, Toland's *Life*; p. 43, *Works* (1698). Wing, C1413. Copy owned by British Library.

1601 Catalogus universalis librorum, in omni facultate, linguaque insignium, & rarissimorum; non solum ex catalogis bibliothecarum [etc.]. Londini: Apud Joannem Hartley, 1699.

Two volumes. Volume 1: Index, one listing, p. 82; one listing, p. 103. Section B: five listings, p. 89; one listing, p. 134. Volume 2: Section E, nine listings, p. 38; one listing, p. 158. Section Ff, one listing, p. 65; one listing, p. 88. Section G, two listings, p. 26 (*Paradise Lost* in twelve books dated 1699 and in three vols.; both unknown); four listings, p. 53; three listings, p. 77; one listing, p. 78; three listings, p. 93. Wing, H973. Copy owned by Folger Shakespeare Library.

1602 *Catalogus variorum librorum antiquorum & recentiorum variis facultatibus clarissimorum* [etc.]. 1699.

Dated: 15 March 1698/9. Place: Oxford. Bookseller: Benjamin Shirley. Listing: p. 57, *Accedence Commenc't Grammar*. Wing, C1456. Copy owned by British Library.

1603 *Copiosissima ac lectissima bibliotheca* [etc.]. *D. Conr. Joan. a Berghe, de Leeuw, P. M.* [etc.]. Hi libri publica auctione distrahentur in officina Joan. du Vivie et Isaci Severini bibliopol. Leidensium. 1699.

Listing on p. 249, *Defensio prima* (No. 838) and *Literae* (No. 839). Copy owned by Columbia University Library.

1604 *Cursory remarks upon some late disloyal proceedings, in several cabals: composed of an intermixture of interests*. London: Printed in the Year, 1699.

Author: anonymous. Allusion, pp. 6–7. Wing, C7687. Copy owned by New York Public Library.

1605 *A Defence of the vindication of K. Charles the martyr ... in answer to a late pamphlet intituled Amyntor. By the author of The Vindication*. London: W. Bowyer, and sold by most booksellers in London and Westminster, 1699.

Author: Thomas Wagstaffe. Controversy over *Eikon Basilike*, the insertion of Pamela's prayer, etc., pp. 31–33, 35, 87, 93–96. Wing, W206. Copy owned by University of Kentucky Library.

1606 *The Dispensary; a poem*. London: Printed, and sold by John Nutt, 1699.

Author: Samuel Garth. Edition 1. Imitations and appropriations from *Paradise Lost*: I, 85–96, pp. 5–6 (Pandemonium); III, 125–238, pp. 34–38 (from *PL* II); V, 113 ff., pp. 59 ff. (Querpo drawn from Satan and *PL* I, 283–287, IV, 987). Wing, G273. Copy owned by Princeton University Library.

1607 *The Dispensary: a poem. In six canto's* [etc.]. *The second edition, corrected by the author*. London: Printed: and sold by John Nutt, 1699.

Edition 2 of No. *1606*. Imitations and appropriations: pp. 6–7, 35–42, 66 ff. Wing, G274. Copy owned by New York Public Library.

1608 *The Dispensary: a poem. In six canto's* [etc.]. *The third edition, corrected by the author*. London: Printed: and sold by John Nutt, 1699.

Edition 3 of No. *1606*. Imitations and appropriations: pp. 6-7, 35-42, 66 ff. Wing, G275. Copy owned by Princeton University Library.

1609 A Dissertation upon the epistles of Phalaris. With an answer to the objections of the Honourable Charles Boyle, esquire [etc.]. London: J. H., for Henry Mortlock and John Hartley, 1699.

Author: Richard Bentley. Allusion, preface, p. ci. Wing, B1929. Copy owned by Union Theological Seminary Library (McAlpin Collection).

1610 The Dublin scuffle: being a challenge sent by John Dunton, citizen of London, to Patrick Campbell, bookseller in Dublin. London, (Printed for the Author) and are to be Sold by A. Baldwin, and by the Booksellers in Dublin, 1699.

Author: John Dunton. Included on pp. 19-32 is:
An Account of my Third Auction in Dublin, to be held at Patt's Coffee-House, over against St. Michael's Church in High-street, on Monday November 7th, 1698, with my Reasons for removing thither. In a second letter to those Gentlemen, who have bought Books at my two former Auctions.
Dated: 5 November 1698. Allusions: pp. 27 (to *Paradise Lost*), 29 (parody of lines in *Paradise Lost*), and 30. Wing, D2622. Copy owned by Yale University Library.

1611 The Duke of Guise. A tragedy [etc.]. London: Printed for R. Wellington and E. Rumball, 1699.

Another edition of No. *957*. Allusion: Epistle Dedicatory, A3. Imitation: Act IV, Scene ii, p. 36. Wing, D2267. Copy owned by Columbia University Library.

1612 The Duke of Guise. A Tragedy [etc.]. *To which is added, A Vindication of the play* [etc.]. London: Printed for Jacob Tonson, 1699.

Another edition of No. *957*. Allusion, A3. Without *The Vindication*. Wing, D2266. Copy owned by University of Kentucky Library.

1613 Elegies [etc.]. London: Printed for J. Wild, 1699.

Author: Nahum Tate. Allusions in "Mausoleum," p. 8, and "A Poem on the Late Promotion of Several Eminent Persons in Church and State," p. 124. Wing, T683. Copy owned by Folger Shakespeare Library.

1614 Excellentissima in quovis studiorum genere bibliotheca [etc.]. *Quam collegit Vir Illustressimus Arnoldus a Citters* [etc.]. *Publica auctione distrahenda in officina Joannis du Vivié, & Isaci Severini.* Bibliopolarum Leyd. Batavor. 1699.

Listings: p. 49, item 282, Salmasius' *Responsio*; p. 50, item 283, *Defensio prima*; p. 68, item 550, *Defensio prima*. Copy owned by Columbia University Library.

1615 The Folly and unreasonableness of atheism [etc.]. *The fourth edition corrected.* London: J. H., for H. Mortlock, 1699.

Author: Richard Bentley. Two quotations from *Paradise Lost* in "A Confutation of Atheism from the Origin and Frame of the World. The Third and Last Part. The Eighth Sermon preached December 5. 1692," p. 276. See No. *1350*. Wing, B1931. Copy owned by Union Theological Seminary Library (McAlpin Collection).

1616 Histoire des ouvrages de Savans [etc.]. Rotterdam: Reinier Leers, 1699.

Author: Henri Basnage de Beauval. Issue for February 1699. Article VIII, discussion of John Toland's *The Life of John Milton*, pp. 78–88. In French. Copy owned by Folger Shakespeare Library.

1617 Historische remarques der neuesten sachen in Europa des M. D. C. I. C. Jahres [etc.]. Hamburg in Verlegung Joachim Reumanus.

Description of contents of Toland's *Amyntor* in notice of publication, pp. 287–288. Copy owned by Princeton University Library.

1618 A Just defence of the royal martyr, K. Charles I [etc.]. London: Printed for A. Roper and R. Basset, and for W. Turner, 1699.

Author: William Baron. Allusions, pp. A3v–A4 (on Toland and Harrington), 10 (*Eikonoklastes*), 13 (*Defensio prima*). Discussions in *A Just Defence of the Royal Martyr, Charles I. Part II.* London: Printed for Abel Roper, 1699. Separate title page, signatures and pagination. See pp. 209–210 (work as Secretary), 216 (masculine style in poetry and prose). Wing, B897. Copy owned by University of Kentucky Library.

1619 A Just rebuke of a late unmannerly libel, in defence of the court: entituled, Cursory remarks upon some late disloyal proceedings, &c. London: Printed in the Year, 1699.

Author: anonymous. Allusions to Milton's antimonarchical works and the Salmasian controversy, p. 4. Not in Wing. Copy owned by Folger Shakespeare Library.

1620 A Letter to a member of parliament, shewing the necessity of regulating the press [etc.]. Oxford: Printed for George West and Henry Clements, 1699.

Author: John Gilbert (?). Often assigned to Daniel Defoe. Allusion, p. 37. Wing, D837. Copy owned by Folger Shakespeare Library.

1621 A Letter to the author of Milton's life. By a divine of the church of England. London: J. H. and are to be sold by John Nutt, 1699.

Author: J. C. Wing, C60. Copy owned by Princeton University Library.

1622 The Library of Mr Du Prat, being a collection of philological [etc.].

Dated: 2 May 1699. Bookseller: John Bullord. Listings: p. 33, *Eikonoklastes, Poems* (1671 [sic]); p. 40, *Defensio prima*. Wing, D2668. Copy owned by British Library.

1623 The Library of the Right Reverend Father in God, John Lloyd, D. D. [etc.]. 1699.

Dated: 6 February 1699. Place: London. Bookseller: John Bullord. Listings: p. 48, *Poems* (1645); p. 54, "Milton's Secrets of Government, and Mysteries of State," *Defensio prima*; p. 57, *Defensio prima*. Wing, L2656. Copy owned by British Library.

1624 The Life of John Milton, containing, besides the history of his works, several extraordinary characters of men and books, sects, parties, and opinions [etc.]. London: John Darby, 1699.

Author: John Toland. Includes Dati's letter and poems by Salsilli, Selvaggi, Manso, Dryden, and Barrow; Francini's is added on pp. 156–160. Catalogue of works, pp. 161–165 (from 1698 edition of prose, with advertisement for that edition). Errata, p. [166]. Wing, T1766. Copy owned by University of Kentucky Library. See also Samuel Richardson's copy bound with copy of No. *1592*, dated August 1725, owned by University of Kentucky Library.

1625 A Light shining out of darkness [etc.]. *The third edition.* London: Printed and sold by T. Sowle, 1699.

Author: Henry Stubbe. Discussion of antimonarchical views, pp. 241–242 and margins. Wing, S6058. Copy owned by Henry E. Huntington Library.

1626 The Lives and characters of the English dramatick poets [etc.]. *First begun by Mr. Langbain, improv'd and continued down to this time, by a careful hand.* London: Printed for Tho. Leigh and William Turner.

See No. *1569*. Dated: 1699 (?). Includes leaf signed *L4 and paged *151–*152, preceding L4 (pp. 151–152). Listed in Contents, p. [xiv]; biographical incident, p. 33 (under Davenant); use of *Samson Agonistes* in *Aureng-Zebe*, with quotation, pp. 42–43 (under Dryden); notice of *The State of Innocence*, p. 47 (under Dryden); reference to *The State of Innocence*, p. 53 (under Ecclestone); allusion, p. 57 (under John Fletcher); allusion, p. 74 (under Charles Hopkins); biographical notice, p. 100 (under Milton); two allusions, p. 128 (under Shakespeare); allusion, p. *151 (under R. A. Gent.); listed in Index (under *Masque at Ludlow Castle, Samson Agonistes,* and *The State of Innocence*). Wing, L375. Copy owned by University of Kentucky Library.

1627 The Lives and characters of the English dramatick poets [etc.]. *First begun by Mr. Langbain, improv'd and continued down to this time, by a careful hand.* London: Printed for Nich. Cox and William Turner, 1699.

Different issue of No. *1626.* Not in Wing. Copy owned by Columbia University Library.

1628 The Lives and characters of the English dramatick poets [etc.]. *First begun by Mr. Langbain, improv'd and continued down to this time, by a careful hand.* London: Printed for William Turner, 1699.

Another issue of No. *1626.* Wing, L376. Copy owned by Henry E. Huntington Library.

1629 Mr. Blackall's reasons for not replying to a book lately published, entituled, Amyntor. In a letter to a friend. London: Printed for Walter Kettilby, 1699.

Author: Offspring Blackall. Edition 1. Octavo. Wing, B3048. Copy owned by University of Kentucky Library.

1630 Mr. Blackall's reasons for not replying to a book lately published, entituled, Amyntor. In a letter to a friend. Printed for Walter Kettilby, 1699.

Edition 2 of No. *1629.* Place: London. Quarto: A–C^4. Wing, B3049. Copy owned by Bodleian Library.

1631 Musarum Anglicanarum analecta [etc.]. *Volume II* [etc.]. Oxon: E Theatro Sheldoniano, Impensis Joh. Crosley, 1699.

Volume I dated 1692. Reference to burning of books at Oxford and opposition to Charles in anonymous "Decreteum Oxonienæ, Anno 1683," pp. 170–171. Wing, M3137. Copy owned by Folger Shakespeare Library.

1632 Nouvelles de la republique des lettres. Mois d'Août 1699 [etc.]. Amsterdam: Chez Henry Desbordes, 1699.

Editor: Jaques Bernard. Article VII, discussion of John Toland's *Amyntor,* pp. 223–225. In French. Copy owned by Princeton University Library.

1633 Poems on affairs of state: from the time of Oliver Cromwell, to the abdication of K. James the second. Written by the greatest wits of the age. Viz.... Mr. Milton [etc.]. *The third edition, corrected and much enlarged.* Printed in the Year 1699.

Allusions: Preface, A2v, and advertisement listed on p. [268]; Index, A4. Imitations: Andrew Marvell's "Last Instructions to the Painter," ll. 147–150, p. 58, and pp. 68–69; John Ayloffe's "Marvell's Ghost," pp. 160–161; "Lord Lucas's Ghost," pp. 173–175. Wing, P2721. Copy owned by Princeton University Library.

1634 Poems on several occasions [etc.]. *By the author.* London: Printed for William Chandler, and William Davis, 1699.

Author: H. Walwyn. "On Mr. John Milton. To a Friend, who flatteringly desired me to send him some Verses on a propos'd Subject," pp. 22–24. Listed in Contents. Wing, W677. Copy owned by British Library.

1635 The Post Boy. No. 584. 3–5 January 1699.

Colophon: "London, Printed by and for B. Beardwell." Advertisement for Toland's *Life.* Copy owned by Henry E. Huntington Library.

1636 The Post Boy. No. 590. 17–19 January 1699.

Colophon: "London, Printed by and for B. Beardwell." Advertisement for *A Complete Collection.* Copy owned by Henry E. Huntington Library.

1637 The Post Boy. No. 656. 20–22 June 1699.

Colophon: "London, Printed by and for B. Beardwell." Advertisement for *A Complete Collection.* Copy owned by Henry E. Huntington Library.

1638 The Post Man. No. 559. 5–7 January 1699.

Printed for A. Baldwin. Advertisements for *A Complete Collection* and Toland's *Life.* Copy owned by Henry E. Huntington Library.

1639 The Post Man. No. 610. 4–6 May 1699.

Colophon: "Printed by F. Leach, for the Author, 1699." Advertisement for *A Complete Collection.* Copy owned by Henry E. Huntington Library.

1640 The Post Man. No. 628. 15–17 June 1699.

Colophon: "Printed for F. Leach, for the Author, 1699." Advertisement for *A Complete Collection.* Copy owned by Henry E. Huntington Library.

1641 The Post Man. No. 631. 22–24 June 1699.

Colophon: "Printed by F. Leach, for the Author, 1699." Listing of *Works* for sale in advertisement for Algernon Sidney's *Discourses.* Copy owned by Henry E. Huntington Library.

1642 Reflections on the stage, and Mr Collyer's Defence of the short view. In four dialogues. London: Printed for R. Parker and P. Buck, 1699.

Author: John Oldmixon. Discussion of *Paradise Lost*, pp. 11–12, with quotation of *Paradise Lost* I, 124, and p. 16. Allusions, pp. 97, 104. Wing, O262. Copy owned by Folger Shakespeare Library.

1643 *Remarks on the life of Mr. Milton, as publish'd by J. T. with a characters of the* *author and his party* [etc.]. London: Printed, and sold by J. Nutt, 1699.

Author: anonymous. Wing, R933. Copy owned by Princeton University Library.

1644 *A Sermon preached at St. Andrew's Plymouth, January 30th, 1698/9.* [etc.]. London: Sam. Darker, for Tho. Bennet, 1699.

Author: John Gilbert. Allusions in Preface, B2 and margin (*Literae*); B2v, C2v, D1 and margin (*Eikonoklastes*), D1v. Wing, G711. Copy owned by Union Theological Seminary Library (McAlpin Collection).

1645 *A Sermon preached before the honourable House of Commons, at St. Margaret's* *Westminster, January 30th. 1698/9* [etc.]. London: J. Leake, for Walter Kettilby, 1699.

Author: Offspring Blackall. On authorship of *Eikon Basilike*, p. 16 and margin. Wing, B3053. Copy owned by New York Public Library.

1646 *A Short view of the immorality and profaneness of the English stage:* [etc.]. *The fourth* *edition.* London: Printed for S. Keble and R. Sare, 1699.

Author: Jeremy Collier. Edition 4 of No. *1578.* See Wing, C5266. Copy owned by University of Kentucky Library.

1647 *A Short view of the immorality and profaneness of the English stage:* [etc.]. *The fourth* *edition.* London: Printed for S. Keble, R. Sare, and H. Hindmarsh, 1699.

Reissue of No. *1646.* See Wing, C5266. Copy owned by New York Public Library.

1648 *Some reflections on that part of a book called Amyntor, or the defence of Milton's life,* *which relates to the writings of the primitive fathers and the canon of the New Testa-* *ment. In a letter to a friend.* London: Printed for James Knapton, 1699.

Author: Samuel Clarke. Wing (1), C4498A; Wing (2), C4498. Copy owned by Princeton University Library.

1649 *The Stage acquitted. Being a full answer to Mr Collier, and the other enemies of the* *drama* [etc.]. London: Printed for John Barnes, and sold by M. Gilliflower, D. Brown, and R. Parker, 1699.

Author: A. D. Allusions, pp. 146, 175–177. Quotation of Milton's remarks on the dramatic poem, prefacing *Samson Agonistes*, pp. 175–177. Wing, S5160. Copy owned by New York Public Library.

1650 *State-poems; continued from the time of O. Cromwel, to the year 1697. Written by* *the greatest wits of the age, viz.... Mr. Milton* [etc.]. Printed in the year 1699.

Allusion in Contents, A2. Attribution: "Julii Mazarini Cardinalis Epitaphium," pp. 58-60. Allusions: "The Giants War," p. 25; Matthew Prior's "The Hind and Panther Transvers'd," pp. 87, 92; Nahum Tate's "In Memory of Jos. Washington," pp. 223-225. "A Charge to the Grand Inquest of England. 1674," l. 42, p. 20, does not allude to Milton. Imitation: Charles Montagu's "The Man of Honour," ll. 51-54, 66-69, pp. 112-113 (see No. *1162*). See Wing, P2721. Copy owned by Princeton University Library.

1651 Thomæ Crenii animadversiones philologicæ et historicæ [etc.]. Oxonii: E Theatro Sheldoniano, A. D. 1699 Excudebat Johannes Owens.

Another edition of No. *1475*. Allusion, pp. 76-77; noted in Index. Not in Wing. Copy owned by British Library.

1652 A True account of land forces in England; and provisions for them, from before the reputed conquest downwards: and of the regard had to foreigners. In a letter to A. V. C. T. T. T. &c. with ... Life of Milton [etc.]. London: Printed and are to be sold by J. Nutt, 1699.

Author: anonymous. References to Toland's *Life* and the Socinian controversy, pp. 51-52 and margin, 62 and margin, 68 and margin, 72 and margin. See also passim for Toland. Wing, T2337. Copy owned by Folger Shakespeare Library.

1700

SEE ALSO NO. 401 IN PART I FOR DISCUSSION OF GOVERNMENTAL WORK AND NO. 403 FOR AN ALLUSION.

1653 Acta eruditorum. Anno M D CC publicata [etc.]. Lipsiæ: Johannis Georgii, apud Joh. Grossii et Joh. Thom. Fritschium, 1700.

Review of Toland's *Life of Milton*, pp. 371-379, basically a summary with quotation of poems by Salsilli, Selvaggi, Manso, p. 373. References in Index V, p. 560, and Index Rerum, p. 575. In Latin. Copy owned by University of Wisconsin Library.

1654 [Annotations upon the Holy Bible (etc.). *Vol. I. Being a continuation of Mr. Poole's work by certain judicious and learned divines. The fourth edition. The whole corrected and amended by Mr. Sam. Clark, and Mr. Edward Veale* (etc.). London: Printed for Thomas Parkhurst, Jonathan Robinson, Brabazon Aylmer, John Lawrence, John Taylor, and Thomas Cockerill, 1700.]

Title page missing; supplied from Volume 2. Edition 4 of No. *948*. Wing, P2824A. Copy owned by Rutgers University Library.

1655 *Bibliotheca annua: or, the annual catalogue for the year, 1699. Being an exact catalogue of all English and Latin books, printed in England from January 1698/9, to March 25. 1700* [etc.]. A. Roper and W. Turner, sold by J. Nutt, 1700.

Place: London. No. 1. Listings, pp. 7, 42, 46 (5), 48. Not in Wing. Facsimile owned by New York Public Library.

1656 *Bibliotheca Carpzoviana sive catalogus librorum quos magno studio & sumtu, dum viveret, collegit Vir Nobilissimus Frider. Benedictus Carpzovius. Pars Prior* [etc.]. Lipsiæ: Typis ac sumtibus Andreæ Zeidleri, 1700.

In Volume 2, new signatures and pagination, with divider but no title page: "Bibliothecæ Carpzovianæ Pars Posterior." Listings: p. 92, *Defensio Regia, Defensio prima* (London, 1651), Ziegler's *Exercitationes* (Lipsiæ, 1653), *Literae* (1690), Ziegler's *Regicidio Anglorum* (Jena, 1652); p. 181, item 913 includes *Epistolae familiares*; p. 233, item 30 includes *Salmasii Responsio*; p. 425, Ziegler's *Exercitationes* (1652); p. 479, *Defensio prima* (4°, 1657 [sic]), Schaller's *Diss. adquædam* (1657), *Regii Sanguinis*, Peter Negesch's *Comparatio* (1659), *Defensio prima* (12°, 1651), [item 240 continuing to p. 480], Phillips' *Responsio*, Rowland's *Polemica*, *Defensio secunda*, More's *Fides Publica*, Ziegler's *Exercitationes* (Lipsiæ, 1652); p. 504, *Literae* (Lipsiæ, 1690). Copy owned by Columbia University Library.

1657 Boston. Massachusetts Historical Society. Diary of Samuel Sewall.

Reference to Toland's *Amyntor* in Diary, under date of 29 April 1700; II, 13. See *Collections of the Massachusetts Historical Society*, Fifth Series, Vol. 6 (Boston: Published by the Society, 1879).

1658 *The Canon of the New Testament vindicated; in answer to the objections of J. T. in his Amyntor.* London: Printed for Richard Sare, 1700.

Author: John Richardson. Allusions, pp. 1, 5. Wing, R1384. Copy owned by Union Theological Seminary Library (McAlpin Collection).

1659 *Carmen sæculare, for the year 1700. To the king* [etc.]. London: Printed for Jacob Tonson, 1700.

Author: Matthew Prior. Advertisement for *Poetical Works* in "Books Printed for Jacob Tonson," F2v. Wing, P3507. Copy owned by Princeton University Library.

1660 *A Catalogue of ancient and modern books. Viz. Divinity* [etc.].

Dated: December 2, 1700. Bookseller: Edward Millington. Place: Norwich. Listing: *Moscovia*, p. 29. Wing, C1275. Copy owned by Bodleian Library.

1661 *A Catalogue of books continued, printed and published in London in Easter term, 1700.* No. 18.

Advertisement. Copy owned by British Library.

1662 *A Catalogue of books continued, printed and published in London in Trinity-term, 1700.* No. 19.

Advertisement. Copy owned by British Library.

1663 *A Catalogue of the libraries of Sr Andrew Henley, Kt & Bart, and an eminent clergyman, both deceased* [etc.]. 1700.

Bookseller: John Bullord. Listings: p. 35, *Paradise Lost*; p. 43, *Eikon Aklastos* (Milton not mentioned); p. 48, *History of Britain*; p. 53, *Paradise Regain'd*. Wing, H1449. Copy owned by British Library.

1664 *A Catalogue of the library of a person of honour* [etc.].

Dated: 1700. Bookseller: Christopher Bateman. Listings: p. 17, *History of Britain*; p. 18, "Milton, of Divorce, (with other Tracts)" and "Answer to Eikon Basilike"; p. 24, *Letters of State*. Wing, C1380. Copy owned by British Library.

1665 *A Catalogue of the library of Mr. Henry Cook, painter, deceased* [etc.].

Dated: 1700 (?); Wing gives 1699 (?). Owner: Henry Cooke. Bookseller: John Bullord. Listings: p. 4, *Poetical Works*; p. 5, *History of Britain, Defensio prima*. Wing, C6011. Copy owned by British Library.

1666 *The Choice. A poem. By a person of quality.* London: Printed, and are to be sold by J. Nutt, 1700.

Author: John Pomfret. Imitative of "L'Allegro" and "Il Penseroso." Wing, P2794. Copy owned by Robert H. Taylor, Princeton, New Jersey.

1667 *The Choice. A poem. By a person of quality.* London: Printed, and are to be sold by J. Nutt, 1700.

Edition 2 of No. *1666*. Wing, P2795. Copy owned by Henry E. Huntington Library.

1668 *The Choice. A poem* [etc.]. *The third edition corrected.* London: Printed, and are to be sold by J. Nutt, 1700.

Edition 3 of No. *1666*. No preface. Wing, P2796. Copy owned by Bodleian Library.

1669 *The Confession of faith, and the larger and shorter catechism* [etc.]. Printed in the Year 1700.

Another edition of No. *45*. Reference, p. 74. Not in Wing. Copy owned by Folger Shakespeare Library.

1670 The Court of Neptune. A poem [etc.]. London: Printed for Jacob Tonson, 1700.

Author: John Hughes. Influence from *Lycidas* in language, p. 1. Wing, H3311. Copy owned by William Andrews Clark Library.

1671 Daniel Georg Morhofens Unterricht von der teutschen sprache und poesie [etc.]. Lubeck und Franckfurt: Johann Wiedemeyers, 1700.

Another edition of No. *945*. Allusions, pp. 183, 212, 231, 515, 672. Copy owned by Newberry Library.

1672 The Dispensary. A poem. In six canto's [etc.]. *The fourth edition, with additions.* London: Printed: and sold by John Nutt, 1700.

Edition 4 of No. *1606*. Imitations and appropriations: pp. 6-7, 35-43, 67ff. Wing, G276. Copy owned by University of Kentucky Library. Copy owned by Princeton University Library includes manuscript insertions, e. g., for p. 68, on sheets preceding and following the printed poem, made in early eighteenth century.

1673 An Epistle to a friend concerning poetry [etc.]. London: Printed for Charles Harper, 1700.

Author: Samuel Wesley. Allusions, ll. 119 (p. 4), 813–816 (p. 22). Wing, W1370. Copy owned by Yale University Library.

1674 An Epistle to Sr. Richard Blackmore, occasion'd by The New sessions of the poets. London: Printed for A. Baldwin, 1700.

Author: anonymous. The language of the poem derives in part from *Paradise Lost* in its imitation of Blackmore's work. Wing, E3167. Copy owned by Harvard University Library.

1675 An Essay concerning the divine right of tythes. By the author of The Snake in the grass. London: Printed for C. Brome, W. Keble White, E. Pool, and G. Strahan, 1700.

Author: Charles Leslie. Discussion of Milton's views in *Hirelings* in Preface, pp. iv–viii; allusions, pp. xi, xii. Cited in Contents, p. [xix]. Wing, L1132. Copy owned by Union Theological Seminary Library (McAlpin Collection).

1676 Essays upon several moral subjects. In two parts [etc.]. *The fourth edition.* London: Printed for Richard Sare and H. Hindmarsh, 1700.

Edition 4 of No. *1415*. Allusion, p. 179. Wing, C5255. Copy owned by Princeton University Library.

1677 Fables ancient and modern [etc.]. London: Printed for Jacob Tonson, 1700.

Author: John Dryden. Milton's relation with Spenser: Preface, *A1. Wing, D2278. Copy owned by University of Kentucky Library.

1678 Familiar and courtly letters, written by Monsieur Voiture [etc.]. London: Printed for Sam. Briscoe, and sold by J. Nutt, 1700.

Author: Vincent Voiture. Editor: Thomas Brown. Added is: *Letters of friendship and several other occasions: the second part* [etc.]. London: Printed for Sam. Briscoe, 1700. Reprint of No. *1499*. S6-8 T^4(-T2) Aa-Gg^8 Hh^1. Letter from Dryden to Dennis, with allusion, p. 50. Wing, V682. Copy owned by Folger Shakespeare Library.

1679 Funeral poems [etc.]. London: J. Gardyner, and sold by J. Nutt, 1700.

Another edition of No. *1613*. Wing, T188. Copy owned by Folger Shakespeare Library.

1680 The General history of England, both ecclesiastical and civil [etc.]. London: Printed, and are to be sold by W. Rogers, R. Knaplock, A. Bell, and T. Cockerill, 1700.

Another issue of No. *1495*. Wing, T3588. Copy owned by Library of Congress.

1681 An Historical account, and defence, of the canon of the New Testament. In answer to Amyntor. London: J. Darby, for Jonathan Robinson and Andrew Bell, 1700.

Author: Stephen Nye. Allusion, p. 42. Wing, N1507. Copy owned by Union Theological Seminary Library (McAlpin Collection).

1682 Homer and Virgil not to be compar'd with the two Arthurs. London: Printed by W. B. for Luke Meredith, 1700.

Author: Sir Richard Blackmore. "A Table of a small Number of the Observable Passages in Prince Arthur, King Arthur, the Paraphrase on Job," pp. 1-45, has numerous Miltonic borrowings in quotations from the first two poems. "A Letter to a Friend, Concerning the Late Poems, the Prince and King Arthur, and the Paraphrase on Job," pp. 65-165, cites images, lines, etc., discusses the verse, the hero, and epic poems, and language of epic poems, but assiduously avoids citing Milton, although *Paradise Lost* appears to be in the background. Wing, B3076. Copy owned by Bodleian Library.

1683 Iphigenia. A tragedy, acted at the Theatre in Little Lincoln-Inn-Fields [etc.]. London: Printed for Richard Parker, 1700.

Author: John Dennis. Allusion and quotation from *Of Education*: Preface, p. [vi]. Wing, D1031. Copy owned by Folger Shakespeare Library.

1684 Joannis Nicolai Hertii ... commentationum atque opusculorum et selectis et rarioribus ex purisprudentia universali [etc.]. *Argumentis, tomi tres*. Francofurti ad Moenvm, sumptibus Joannis Davidis Zunneri, 1700.

Author: Johann Nikolaus Hertius. Volume 1: in Philippis Christianus Pistorius, *Dissertatio. An summa rerum sit penes populum?*, allusions with quotation from Nahum Bensen (No. *187*), pp. 442–444, 458. Copy owned by Princeton University Library.

1685 Johann Hübners | Rector. Gymn. Martisb. jurtze fragen aus der politischen historia biss zum ausgange des siebenzehenden seculi continuiret [etc.]. *Anderer theil. Mit Kön. Poln und churfe. Sächf sonderbaren privilegio*. Im Jahr 1700. Verlegts Johann Friedrich Gleditsch.

Place: Leipzig. Notice concerning Milton and Salmasius, p. 982. Listed in Index. Copy owned by Cambridge University Library.

1686 [Killing no murder. 1700.]

Another alleged edition of No. *391*, listed in British Library catalogue but now destroyed. No copy has been located.

1687 [Leben und todt des weyland ... Johannis Lassenii. 1700.]

Another edition of No. *1360*. Copy unlocated.

1688 A Letter to a member of parliament, shewing, that a restraint on the press is inconsistent with the protestant religion, and dangerous to the liberties of the nation. The second impression. London: J. Darby, and sold by A. B., 1700.

Edition 2 of No. *1568*. See Wing, L1681. Wing lists the publisher as "A. Baldwin" in the copy owned by Edinburgh University Library, which copy gives "A. B." Copy owned by Folger Shakespeare Library.

1689 Liber primus principes Arcturi [etc.]. *Latine redditus. A Gulielmo Hogœo*. Londini, Anno. Dom. 1700.

William Hog's Latin translation of Sir Richard Blackmore's *Prince Arthur* (see No. *1468*). Hog's "Epistola Dedicatoria" discusses *Paradise Lost*, A3v. Wing, B3078. Copy owned by William Andrews Clark Library.

1690 Die Listige Juno. Wie solche von dem grossen Homer [etc.]. Hamburg: Gedruckt und verlegt durch Nicolaus Spieringk, 1700.

Author: Christian Heinrich Postel. Allusion in "Vorrede," a5v–a6. Copy owned by British Library.

1691 *Luctus Britannici: or the tears of the British muses; for the death of John Dryden, esq*; [etc.]. London: Printed for Henry Playford and Abel Roper, and sold by John Nutt, 1700.

Anonymous poem, "Gallus," allusion, p. 6 of new pagination. In Latin. Wing, L3451. Copy owned by Princeton University Library.

1692 *The Oceana of James Harrington, and his other works; som wherof are now first published from his own manuscripts. The whole collected, methodiz'd, and review'd, with an exact account of his life prefix'd, by John Toland* [etc.]. London: Printed for the Booksellers of London and Westminster, 1700.

Allusions by Toland on pp. vii, xxvi, xxviii. Wing, H816. Copy owned by Union Theological Seminary Library (McAlpin Collection).

1693 *An Ode by way of elegy, on the universally lamented death of the incomparable Mr. Dryden* [etc.]. London: Printed and sold by most Booksellers, 1700.

Author: Alexander Oldys. Allusions to verse, *Paradise Lost*, and *Paradise Regain'd*, in Stanza V, pp. 4–5. Wing, O267. Copy owned by Folger Shakespeare Library.

1694 *The Pacificator. A poem.* London: Printed, and are to be sold by J. Nutt, 1700.

Author: Daniel Defoe. Allusion in l. 130, p. 5. Wing, D839. Copy owned by Yale University Library.

1695 *Pauli Colomesii opuscula, in quibus multa critica, philologica, & ad historiam virorum doctorum XVI & XVII sæsulorum pertinentia.* Amstelodami: Apud Henricum & Viduam Theodori Boom, 1700.

Compiler: Paul Colomes. Listing of Salmasius' *Responsio*, p. 178. Copy owned by Columbia University Library.

1696 *Plutarch's lives. Translated from the Greek, by several hands. In five volumes. Vol. 1* [etc.]. London: R. E., for Jacob Tonson, 1700.

Printed on Bbb4 is: "Books Printed for Jacob Tonson [etc.]." Listing on Bbb4 of *Paradise Lost* with cuts. Not in Wing. Copy owned by Folger Shakespeare Library.

1697 *Regicides no saints nor martyrs: freely expostulated with the publishers of Ludlow's third volume, as to the truth of things and characters, with a touch at Amyntor's cavils against our king's curing the evil, and the thirtieth of January Fast* [etc.]. London: Printed for W. Keblewhite, 1700.

Author: William Baron. Allusion in refutation of Toland in *Life of Milton* and *Amyntor*, pp. 119 ff. Allusion to Marvell as friend of Milton and discussion of Milton's antimonarchical views, pp. 132–138. Wing, B898. Copy owned by Union Theological Seminary Library (McAlpin Collection).

1698 The Second volume of Plutarch's lives. Translated from the Greek, by several hands. London: Printed for Jacob Tonson, 1700.

Printed on Tt1v–Tt2v is: "Books Printed for Jacob Tonson [etc.]." Listed on Tt2v are *Poems* with *Of Education, Paradise Lost* with cuts, *Paradise Regain'd* and *Samson Agonistes*. Not in Wing. Copy owned by Folger Shakespeare Library.

1699 Some reflections upon marriage, occasion'd by the Duke & Dutchess of Mazarine's case; which is also consider'd. London: Printed for John Nutt, 1700.

Author: Mary Astell. Allusion, p. 29. Wing, A4067. Copy owned by Folger Shakespeare Library.

1700 The Way of the world [etc.]. London: Printed for Jacob Tonson, 1700.

Author: William Congreve. Printed on N2v is: "Books Printed for Jacob Tonson [etc.]." Listing: *Poetical Works* (1695). Wing, C5878. Copy owned by Folger Shakespeare Library.

1701 The Works of Mr. Abraham Cowley [etc.]. *The ninth edition* [etc.]. London: Printed for Henry Herringman; and are to be sold by Jacob Tonson and Thomas Bennet, 1700.

Listing of 1695, *Poetical Works*, in "Books Printed for Jacob Tonson," **2v, added at end. Wing, C6660. Copy owned by Princeton University Library.

Before 1701

*1701A*Aberystwyth, Wales. National Library of Wales. Powis MSS. Series II, Bundle XXI, No. 3.

Dryden's "The State of Innocence," called "The fall of Angells & Man by Drayden." Folio. 44 pp. + 4 blank pp. Scribal hand; title in different hand. MS discovered during research for *Index of English Literary Manuscripts*, Vol. II (1625–1700), by Peter Beal, to whom I am indebted for this information.

1702 An Appendix of some books omitted in transcribing the preceding catalogue for the press, and of some few others since come to hand.

Listing: p. 2, Eikon Aklastos. Wing, A3571. Copy owned by Bodleian Library; shelf mark: Wood 658.

1703 Cambridge, Massachusetts. Harvard University. Pusey Library, Harvard
Theatre Collection. MS Thr 9.

Dryden's "The State of Innocence," called "The Fall of Angels & Man in
Innocence   An Opera." Quarto. 50 pp.; 49–50, blank. Autograph corrections; see pp. 6, [35], 37, 39, 40, 43.

1704 *Catalogus impressorum librorum bibliothecæ Bodlejanæ in academia Oxoniensis. Cura*
& opera Thomae Hyde è Coll. Reginæ Oxon. protobibliothecarii. Oxonii: E Theatro
Sheldoniano, 1674.

John Locke's annotated, interleaved copy, in Locke Room, Clarendon
House, Oxford; shelf mark: 17/16. Formerly in Paul Mellon's Library, Old
Spring, Virginia. Listing of *Paradise Lost* (1669) and *Complete Collection* (1698).
See John Harrison and Peter Laslett, *The Library of John Locke.* Published
for the Oxford Bibliographical Society of Oxford University Press, 1965.
No. 1993, p. 189. *Pro Populo Adversus Tyrannus* listed here in Harrison and
Laslett is recorded elsewhere.

1705 Chicago. Newberry Library. MS / Y / 1845.7. Phillipps MS 12399. "Poems,
Songs, Epitaphs, Epigrams of the Seventeenth Century."

Vellum MS associated with the Chamberlaine family. Possible reference
to *Paradise Lost* in poem with illegible title, p. [1]. Influence from *Paradise
Lost* in poem entitled "The Creation," p. [19].

1706 *Choice pamphlets.*

Folio. A–B^2; 8 pp. Listings: p. 3, *Of True Religion,* "Bishop Halls Humble
Remonstrance, and the several Answers of Smectymnuus and the Defence
of it"; p. 6, *Of Reformation, Tetrachordon, Reason of Church-Government.* Copy
owned by British Library; shelf mark: 821.i.15/28.

1707 ["Discursus ad Lampadium Posterior ex Manuscripto Editus. Tractus de
Republica Romano-Germania."]

Author: Hermann Conring. Published in Volume 2 of Conring's *Opera,*
Brunsvigæ: Friderici Wilhelmi Meyeri, 1730. Allusion to Salmasian controversy, p. 261. Copy owned by Cambridge University Library. Early
Discursus in three parts, in which reference does not occur, appears as "Discursus ex Animadversiones ad Lampadij de Republ. Romano-Germanicâ
libellúm. Helmstadi," holograph manuscript, begun 1 September 1656 and
finished 14 March 1657, MS XIII.784, in the Bibliotheca Regia
Hannoverana.

"Privatæ Politicæ Prælectiones Excellentissimi Viri Hermanni Conringij Ad
Tractatum Jacobi Lampadij de Rep: Romano-Germanica," undated manu-

script in the Bibliotheca Regia Hannoverana. *De Repvblica Romano-Germanica Liber Vnvs Auctore Jacobo Lampadio J. C. Cum Annotatis Hermanni Conringii Ad Partes Priores duas ac Tertiæ Capita VII.* Helmestadi, Typis ac sumptibus Henningi Mulleri, 1671. Copy owned by British Library.

1708 [*Hermanni Conringii Examen rervmpvblicarvm potiorvm totivs orbis* (etc.).]

First announced in: *Hermanni Conringii Admonitio De Thesavro Rervm-pvblicarvm Totivs Orbis Qvadripartito Genevæ Hoc Anno Pvblicato.* Helmestadii, Excudebat Henric. David Müllervs, 1675 (copy owned by Herzog-August-Bibliothek). No edition found of *Examen* cited before that in Conring's *Opera* (Brunsvigæ: Sumtibus Friderici Wilhelmi Meyeri, 1730), Volume IV. However, Sir Thomas Pope Blount quoted from Conring's "De Regno Angliæ" in 1690 (see Nos. *1222* and *1393*), which is Chapter XXII of *Examen.*

For notices and discussions see Chapters XXII ("De Regno Angliae") and XXIII ("De Regno Scotiae") in *Opera*, IV, 193, 194, 221, 231: p. 193, note; p. 193, listing of *History of Britain*; p. 194, listing and discussion of *Eikonoklastes*, Perrinchief, *Defensio prima*, Salmasius' *Responsio*, Morisot's *Carolus I*, Phillips' *Responsio*, and *Defensio pro se*; p. 221 and note, discussion of Milton, Salmasius, Du Moulin (actually named), and More; p. 231, note, discussion of Milton's fabrications about Charles with reference to *Pro Rege Apologia* assigned to Bishop Bramhall. Copy owned by Cambridge University Library.

See No. *584* for first holograph version; "De Republica Scotica" precedes "De Republica Anglicana," which includes a discussion of Salmasius and Milton.

1709 London. British Library. Additional MS 4816.

Note by Arthur Annesley, Earl of Anglesey, discussing *Eikon Basilike*, f. 35; Milton is not specifically mentioned.

1710 London. British Library. Additional MS 23722.

Poetical miscellany: John Ayloffe's "Marveils Ghost," ff. 22v–23; "My Ld Lucas his Ghost" (expanded), ff. 32v–34. See No. *1210*.

1711 London. British Library. Additional MS 29497.

Poetical miscellany: Charles Montagu's "The Man of Honour," ff. 24v–26. See No. *1162*.

1712 London. British Library. Additional MS 34362.

Poetical miscellany: "Translated out of a Greeke fragment. 1680," reference to "Pandemonium" in poem, f. 101.

1713 London. British Library. Additional MS 37158.

Transcription of John Dryden's "The fall of Angells and man in innocence. An Opera," 16 folio pages; title page, f. 1.

1714 London. British Library. Burney MS 406.

Peter Du Moulin's verse is transcribed and dated after 1698, but other verses published in *Parerga* (1670) are entered in reverse apparently much earlier. "Iambus In impurissimum nebulonem Johannem Miltonum Parricidarum et Parricidii advocatum" appears with extensive rewritings on ff. 66v–71v in reverse (91–86 forward, but upside down).

1715 London. British Library. Harleian MS 7315.

Poetical miscellany: "A Charge to the Grand Inquest of England," called "Vpon the Parliament," allusion, f. 57; John Ayloffe's "Marveils Ghost," f. 119 (see No. *1210*).

1716 London. British Library. Sloane MS 836.

Transcription of passage from Dryden's preface to Juvenal (see No. *1370*), f. 83.

1717 London. British Library. Sloane MS 886.

Richard Smyth, "A Catalogue of all such Persons deceased Whome I knew in their Life time [etc.]. from M. DC. XXVIII," entry, f. 73v. Smyth died in 1675.

1718 London. British Library. Sloane MS 2332.

Poetical miscellany: Charles Montagu's "The Man of Honour," f. 6v (see No. *1162*).

1719 New Haven, Connecticut. James Osborn Collection, Yale University Library. MS b52/1.

Copies of "Julij Mazarini Cardinalis Epitaphium," pp. 109 and 141, which has been printed as Milton's.

1720 New Haven, Connecticut. James Osborn Collection, Yale University Library. MS b52/2.

Copy of "Lord Lucas his Ghost," f. 242–242v. See No. *1210*.

1721 New Haven, Connecticut. James Osborn Collection, Yale University Library. MS b115.

Copy of Charles Montagu's "The Man of Honour," ff. 10v–14v. See No. *1162*.

1722 New Haven, Connecticut. James Osborn Collection, Yale University Library. MS b135.

Copy of Sir Thomas Blount's *De Re Poetica*, with index; see No. *1402*. References, ff. 51–51v, 52.

1723 New Haven, Connecticut. James Osborn Collection, Yale University Library. MS f b108.

Copy of Charles Montagu's "The Man of Honour," pp. 291–298. See No. *1162*.

1724 New Haven, Connecticut. James Osborn Collection, Yale University Library. MS PB IV/54.

Copy of Dryden's "MacFlecknoe."

1725 New Haven, Connecticut. James Osborn Collection, Yale University Library. MS PB VI/62.

Copy of Charles Montagu's "The Man of Honour." See No. *1162*.

1726 New Haven, Connecticut. James Osborn Collection, Yale University Library. MS PB VII/42.

Selections "Out of Marvels Poems" includes "Agn̄st Rhime. To Milton," which is two lines from Marvell's poem on *Paradise Lost*.

1727 New Haven, Connecticut. James Osborn Collection, Yale University Library. MS PB XI/146.

Copy of Charles Montagu's "The Man of Honour." See No. *1162*.

1728 New Haven, Connecticut. James Osborn Collection, Yale University Library. MS PB XIII/93.

Copy of Charles Montagu's "The Man of Honour." See No. *1162*.

1729 Oxford. Bodleian Library. Additional MS A.48.

Copy of "The Lord Lucas His Ghost," ff. 45–46v. See No. *1210*.

1730 Oxford. Bodleian Library. Ashmole MS 436. Part I.

Milton's horoscope by John Gadbury, f. 119.

1731 Oxford. Bodleian Library. Don. MS b.8.

Copies of "Lord Lucas's Ghost" (see No. *1210*), called "A destestable Libell," pp. 554–555; and John Ayloffe's "Marvills Ghost" (see No. *1210*), pp. 572–573.

1732 Oxford. Bodleian Library. Don. MS e.23.

Copies of "Rawleigh's Ghost," ff. 44–45v, which employs the beginning of *Comus*, and Charles Montagu's "The Man of Honour" (see No. *1162*), ff. 49–51.

1733 Oxford. Bodleian Library. Don. MS e.24.

Copy of Charles Montagu's "The Man of Honour" (see No. *1162*), pp. 41–46.

1734 Oxford. Bodleian Library. Douce MS 357.

Copy of Charles Montagu's "The Man of Honour" (see No. *1162*), ff. 148v–149v.

1735 Oxford. Bodleian Library. Firth MS c.16.

Copy of Charles Montagu's "The Man of Honour" (see No. *1162*), pp. 147–152. Date of manuscript is uncertain; may be eighteenth century.

1736 Oxford. Bodleian Library. Locke MS b.2.

Book lists and sales; listings: *Paradise Lost*, f. 40; *Eikonoklastes*, f. 66. Most entries, like these, were made by John Locke before 1701.

1737 Oxford. Bodleian Library. Locke MS f.14. Lovelace Collection.

John Locke's notes, with some quotation, on *Areopagitica, Defensio prima, Doctrine and Discipline of Divorce*, and *Of Reformation*, pp. 5, 6 (2), 7 (2), 40. Holograph.

1738 Oxford. Bodleian Library. Locke MS f.16.

Listing of *Paradise Lost*, p. 155. John Locke's autograph.

1739 Oxford. Bodleian Library. Rawlinson MS c.146. (No. xxvi.)

Copy of Dryden's "The State of Innocence," called "The Fall of Angels, and Man. In Innocence," pp. 103–122. Folio. Date is uncertain; may be eighteenth century.

1740 Oxford. Bodleian Library. Rawlinson MS d.924.

"Lord Lucas his Ghostt," ff. 315–316; see No. *1210*. "Verses Made on the House of Com̄ons att Their Last Prorogas Being the 22th, novemb^r 1675," allusion in poem, f. 309.

1741 Oxford. Bodleian Library. Rawlinson Poetical MS 123.

John Oldham's holograph copy of Dryden's "MacFlecknoe" (incomplete), pp. 232-235.

1742 Oxford. Bodleian Library. Tanner MS 102.

Note on the 1660 proclamation against Milton (see No. *450*) in Anthony Wood's holograph, f. 71v.

1743 Oxford. Bodleian Library. Wood MS E.2 (69).

Listings: *Of Reformation*, p. 144; *Eikonoklastes*, p. 251; Ralegh's *Maxims* and *Aphorisms of State*, p. 257; *Hirelings*, p. 300; *Treatise of Civil Power*, p. 301; Index, p. 314. Anthony Wood's holograph.

1744 Oxford. Bodleian Library. Wood MS E.2 (72).

Notice of *Areopagitica*, p. 51, taken from John Aubrey's pamphlets, November 1688. Listings: *Epistolarum Familiarium Liber Unus* (?), p. 39; *Treatise of Civil Power*, p. 57; *Of True Religion*, p. 67; Latin poems, p. 218 and margin; and Index, p. 246. Milton's father is listed on p. 82 and in Index. Anthony Wood's holograph.

1745 Oxford. Bodleian Library. Wood MS E.10.

Catalogue of names and works: listing of *Eikonoklastes* and marginal citation of name, p. 314. Anthony Wood's holograph.

1746 Oxford. Bodleian Library. MS F.7.

Pedigree of Milton family and arms noted, p. 168.

1747 ΠΑΝΣΕΒΕΙΑ: *or, a view of all religions in the world* [etc.]. *The second edition, enlarged and perfected* [etc.]. London: Printed by T. C. for John Saywell.

Another edition of No. *310*. No date. Title page is similar to that of No. *361* without date, but the book is different from that edition. Allusions to divorce views, pp. 376, 389 only. Apparently not in Wing. Copy owned by Columbia University Library.

1748 Princeton, New Jersey. Collection of Robert Taylor. Restoration Poems. MS I.

Copy of John Ayloffe's "Marveils Ghost," pp. 148-149; see No. *1210*.

1749 San Marino, California. Henry E. Huntington Library. MS HM 973.

Anonymous play entituled, "Anna Bullen," which shows influence from the language of *Paradise Lost*.

1750 San Marino, California. Henry E. Huntington Library. MS EL. 11640.

Contemporary copy of Dryden's "The State of Innocence," called, "The fall of Angells or Man in Innocency." Folio. 21 unpaged leaves (last leaf blank).

1751 San Marino, California. Henry E. Huntington Library. RB 134219-29.

Item 8 of bound volume, largely printed works, is a contemporary manuscript copy of Dryden's "The State of Innocence," called, "The Fall of Angells or Man in Innocency." Folio. 22 unpaged leaves (last leaf blank).

1752 *Tixall letters or the correspondence of the Ashton family and their friends.* London: Printed for Longman, Hurst, Rees, Orme, and Brown, and for Archibald and John Ballantyne, 1815.

Editor: Arthur Clifford. Poem by Herbert Ashton, "Aspirations," and note of indebtedness to "Hail, wedded Love" (*PL* IV, 750), I, 202. Copy owned by Folger Shakespeare Library.

1753 Washington, D. C. Folger Shakespeare Library. MS V.b.94. Formerly MS 473.1.

Charles Montagu's "The Man of Honour," pp. 205-213. See No. *1162*.

Indices

Index I
Milton: His Works and Related Subjects

Index II

State Papers

state papers: 79, 81-83, 90, 94, 97, 113, 115, 117, 119-30, 132-35, 143-49, 151, 153-60, 162-65, 168-84, 189-97, 199, 201-8, 212, 213, 215-40, 242-55, 257, 258, 260, 262-64, 266, 267, 269-72, 296, 304, 308, 319, 321, 322, 329-31, 333, 343, 344, 351, 353-55, 360, 361, 367, 368, 371, 384-90, 395 (2), 401, 402, 412, 413; *90, 91, 109, 120, 192, 193, 585, 590, 713, 716-18, 720, 721, 737, 741, 743-47, 749, 780, 820, 821, 859, 864, 952, 959, 964, 1050, 1093, 1094, 1103, 1119, 1123, 1131, 1178, 1286, 1288, 1335, 1346, 1385-87, 1405, 1431, 1433, 1515, 1595, 1603, 1656, 1664*

Columbia Number

1: 82, 83, 271, 319, 321, 322, 333, 351, 361, 367, 368, 371, 387, 390A, 395 (2); Yale No. 5

2: 271, 319, 321, 322, 333, 351, 367, 368, 395 (2); Yale No. 6

3: 271, 319, 321, 322, 333, 351, 361, 367, 368, 390A, 395 (2); Yale No. 12

4: 271, 319, 321, 322, 333, 351, 361, 367, 368, 390A, 395 (2); Yale No. 11

5: 271, 319, 321, 322, 333, 351, 361, 367, 368, 371, 387, 390A, 395 (2); Yale No. 10

6: 271, 319, 321, 322, 333, 351, 361, 367, 368, 371, 387, 390A, 395 (2); Yale No. 7

7: 94, 271, 319, 321, 322, 330, 333, 351, 367, 368, 395 (2); Yale No. 24

8: 158, 271, 319, 321, 322, 333, 351, 367, 368, 395 (2); Yale No. 33

9: 271, 319, 321, 322, 333, 351, 361, 367, 368, 371, 387, 390A, 395 (2); Yale No. 13

10: 271, 319, 321, 322, 333, 351, 361, 367, 368, 371, 387, 390A, 395 (2); Yale No. 15

11: 271, 319, 321, 322, 333, 351, 361, 367, 368, 371, 387, 390A, 395 (2); Yale No. 14

12: 271, 319, 321, 322, 333, 351, 367, 368, 395 (2); Yale No. 16

13: 271, 319, 321, 322, 333, 351, 361, 367, 368, 371, 387, 390A, 395 (2); Yale No. 17

14: 271, 319, 321, 322, 333, 351, 361, 367, 368, 390A, 395 (2); Yale No. 19

15: 97, 271, 319, 321, 322, 333, 351, 361, 367, 368, 390A, 395 (2); Yale No. 25

16: 144 (2), 271, 319, 321, 322, 330, 333, 351, 367, 368, 395 (2); Yale No. 20

17: 271, 319, 321, 322, 333, 351, 361, 367, 368, 371, 387, 395 (2); Yale No. 29

18: 144 (2), 271, 321, 322, 333, 351, 367, 368, 395 (2); Yale No. 37

19: 153, 159, 271, 321, 322, 331, 333, 351, 367, 368, 395 (2); Yale No. 36

20: 321, 322, 333, 351, 395 (duplicate of No. 17)

21: 113, 271, 319, 321, 322, 330, 333, 351, 367, 368, 395 (2); Yale No. 28

22: 271, 321, 322, 333, 351, 361, 367, 368, 371, 387, 390A, 395 (2); Yale No. 61

23: 115, 271, 321, 322, 333, 351, 361, 367, 368, 390A, 395 (2); Yale No. 40

24: 120, 153, 271, 321, 322, 331, 333, 351, 367, 368, 395 (2); Yale No. 41

25: 144 (2), 271, 319, 321, 322, 331 (2), 333, 351, 367, 368, 395 (2); Yale No. 43

26: 271, 321, 322, 329, 331, 333, 351, 367, 368, 395 (2); Yale No. 42

27: 153, 271, 319, 321, 322, 331, 333, 351, 367, 368, 395 (2); Yale No. 46

28: 271, 321, 322, 333, 351, 367, 368, 395 (2); Yale No. 48

29: 120 (2), 145, 271, 321, 322, 333, 351, 367, 368, 395 (2); Yale No. 50

30: 120 (2), 145, 271, 321, 322, 333, 351, 367, 368, 395 (2); Yale No. 51

31: 153, 271, 319, 321, 322, 331, 333, 351, 367, 368, 395 (2); Yale No. 49

32: 158, 271, 321, 322, 333, 351, 367, 368, 395 (2); Yale No. 54

33: 271, 319, 321, 322, 333, 351, 367, 368, 395 (2); Yale No. 53

34: 271, 319, 321, 322, 333, 351, 367, 368, 395 (2); Yale No. 55

35: 120, 271, 319, 321, 322, 333, 351, 367, 368, 395 (2); Yale No. 52

36: 163, 164, 271, 319, 321, 322, 331, 333, 351, 367, 368, 395 (2); Yale No. 58

37: 163, 271, 319, 321, 322, 333, 351, 367, 368, 395 (2); Yale No. 60

38: 271, 319, 321, 322, 333, 351, 367, 368, 395 (2); Yale No. 62

39: 151 (2), 154, 271, 319, 321, 322, 333, 351, 367, 368, 395 (2); Yale No. 34

40: 165, 271, 319, 321, 322, 331 (2), 333, 351, 361, 367, 368, 371, 387, 390A, 395 (2); Yale No. 63

41: 271, 319, 321, 322, 333, 351, 367, 368, 395 (2); Yale No. 57

42: 271, 319, 321, 322, 333, 351, 367, 368, 395 (2); Yale No. 56

43: 271, 319, 321, 322, 333, 351, 367, 368, 395 (2); Yale No. 59

43a: 321, 322, 333, 351, 367, 368, 395 (2); not in Yale (see pp. 599-600)

44: 192, 271, 319, 321, 322, 333, 351, 361, 367, 368, 371, 387, 395 (2), 412, 413; Yale No. 64

45: 192 (2), 271, 319, 321, 322, 333, 351, 367, 368, 395 (2), 412, 413; Yale No. 65

46: 191, 199, 271, 319, 321, 322, 333, 351, 361, 367, 368, 371, 387, 390A, 395 (2), 413; Yale No. 68

47: 271, 319, 321, 322, 333, 351, 361, 367, 368, 371, 387, 390A, 395 (2); Yale No. 69

48: 180, 199, 271, 319, 321, 322, 333, 351, 367, 368, 395 (2), 401, 413; Yale No. 70

49: 180, 191, 271 (2), 319, 321, 322, 333, 351, 367, 368, 395 (2), 401, 413; Yale No. 71

50: 271, 319, 321, 322, 333, 351, 361, 367, 368, 371, 387, 390A, 395 (2), 401; Yale No. 72

51: 206, 215, 222, 258, 271, 319, 321, 322, 333, 351, 361, 367, 368, 371, 387, 390A, 395 (2), 401; Yale No. 73

52: 271, 319, 321, 322, 333, 351, 361, 367, 368, 371, 387, 390A, 395 (2), 401, 413; Yale No. 80

53: 215, 258, 271, 319, 321, 322, 333, 351, 367, 368, 395 (2), 401; Yale No. 74

54: 207, 212, 215, 258, 271, 319, 321, 322, 333, 351, 367, 368, 395 (2), 401; Yale No. 75

55: 215, 223, 258, 271, 319, 321, 322, 333, 351, 367, 368, 395 (2), 401; Yale No. 76

56: 213, 220, 258, 271, 319, 321, 322, 333, 351, 361, 367, 368, 371, 387, 390A, 395 (2), 401; Yale No. 82

57: 213, 220, 271, 319, 321, 322, 333, 344, 351, 361, 367, 368, 371, 387, 390A, 395 (2); Yale No. 83

58: 258, 271, 319, 321, 322, 333, 351, 361, 367, 368, 371, 387, 390A, 395 (2), 401; Yale No. 77

59: 206, 216, 222, 271, 319, 321, 322, 333, 343, 351, 361, 367, 368, 371, 387, 390A, 395 (2), 401; Yale No. 81

60: 271, 319, 321, 322, 333, 351, 361, 367, 368, 371, 387, 390A, 395 (2); Yale No. 86

61: 271, 319, 321, 322, 333, 351, 367, 368, 395 (2); Yale No. 85

62: 271, 319, 321, 322, 333, 351, 361, 367, 371, 387, 390A, 395 (2), 401; Yale No. 87

63: 229, 239, 271, 319, 321, 322, 333, 351, 361, 367, 368, 371, 387, 390A, 395 (2); Yale No. 89

64: 271, 319, 321, 322, 333, 351, 361, 367, 368, 371, 387, 390A, 395 (2); Yale No. 122

65: 271, 319, 321, 322, 333, 351, 367, 368, 395 (2), 412, 413; Yale No. 67

66: 271, 319, 321, 322, 333, 351, 367, 368, 395 (2); Yale No. 92

67: 239, 271, 319, 321, 322, 333, 351, 367, 368, 395 (2); Yale No. 95

68: 271, 319, 321, 322, 333, 351, 367, 368, 395 (2); Yale No. 97

69: 228, 271, 319, 321, 322, 333, 351, 367, 368, 395 (2); Yale No. 99

70: 228, 271, 319, 321, 322, 333, 351, 367, 368, 395 (2); Yale No. 98

71: 271, 319, 321, 322, 333, 351, 367, 368, 395 (2); Yale No. 103

72: 239, 271, 319, 321, 322, 333, 351, 367, 368, 395 (2); Yale No. 104

73: 271, 319, 321, 322, 333, 351, 367, 368, 395 (2); Yale No. 111

74: 231, 238, 271, 319, 321, 322, 333, 351, 367, 368, 395 (2); Yale No. 113

75: 225, 228, 233, 236, 239, 240, 271, 319, 321, 322, 333, 351, 367, 368, 395 (2), 401; Yale No. 109

76: 271, 319, 321, 322, 333, 351, 367, 368, 395 (2); Yale No. 105

77: 271, 319, 321, 322, 333, 351, 367, 368, 395 (2); Yale No. 106

78: 271, 319, 321, 322, 333, 351, 367, 368, 395 (2); Yale No. 107

79: 271, 319, 321, 322, 333, 351, 367, 368, 395 (2), 401; Yale No. 108

80: 228, 271, 319, 321, 322, 333, 351, 367, 368, 395 (2); Yale No. 110

81: 271, 319, 321, 322, 333, 351, 367, 368, 395 (2); Yale No. 112

82: 271, 319, 321, 322, 333, 351, 367, 368, 395 (2); Yale No. 114

83: 239, 271, 319, 321, 322, 333, 351, 367, 368, 395 (2); Yale No. 117

84: 271, 319, 321, 322, 333, 351, 367, 368, 395 (2); Yale No. 115

85: 271, 319, 321, 322, 333, 351, 367, 368, 395 (2); Yale No. 116

86: 271, 319, 321, 322, 333, 351, 367, 368, 395 (2); Yale No. 120

87: 227, 271, 319, 321, 322, 333, 351, 367, 368, 395 (2), 401; Yale No. 119

88: 271, 319, 321, 322, 333, 351, 367, 368, 395 (2), 401; Yale No. 121

89: 271, 319, 321, 322, 333, 351, 367, 368, 395 (2); Yale No. 142

90: 245, 271, 319, 321, 322, 333, 351, 367, 368, 395 (2); Yale No. 125

91: 251, 271, 319, 321, 322, 333, 351, 361, 367, 368, 371, 387, 390A, 395 (2); Yale No. 124

92: 252, 254, 271, 319, 321, 322, 333, 351, 367, 368, 395 (2); Yale No. 127

93: 271, 319, 321, 322, 333, 351, 395; Yale No. 126

94: 271, 319, 321, 322, 333, 351, 367, 368, 395 (2); Yale No. 128

95: 271, 319, 321, 322, 333, 351, 367, 368, 395 (2); Yale No. 129

96: 271, 319, 321, 322, 333, 351, 367, 368, 395 (2); Yale No. 130

97: 250, 271, 319, 321, 322, 333, 351, 367, 368, 395 (2); Yale No. 131

98: 271, 319, 321, 322, 333, 351, 367, 368, 395 (2); Yale No. 133

99: 248, 271, 319, 321, 322, 333, 351, 367, 368, 395 (2); Yale No. 132

100: 271, 319, 321, 322, 333, 351, 367, 368, 395 (2); Yale No. 134

101: 271, 319, 321, 322, 333, 351, 367, 368, 395 (2); Yale No. 135

102: 271, 319, 321, 322, 333, 351, 367, 368, 395 (2); Yale No. 136

103: 249, 255, 271, 319, 321, 322, 333, 351, 367, 368, 395 (2); Yale No. 137

104: 246 (2), 271, 319, 321, 322, 333, 351, 367, 368, 395 (2); Yale No. 138

105: 246 (2), 247, 271, 319, 321, 322, 333, 351, 367, 368, 395 (2); Yale No. 141

106: 271, 319, 321, 322, 333, 351, 367, 368, 395 (2); Yale No. 140

107: 271, 319, 321, 322, 333, 351, 367, 368, 395 (2); Yale No. 139

108: 264, 271, 319, 321, 322, 333, 351, 367, 368, 395 (2); Yale No. 143

109: 271, 319, 321, 322, 333, 351, 361, 367, 368, 371, 387, 390A, 395 (2); Yale No. 144

110: 258, 271, 319, 321, 322, 333, 351, 361, 367, 368, 371, 387, 390A, 395 (2), 401; Yale No. 151

111: 258, 266, 271, 319, 321, 322, 333, 351, 367, 368, 395 (2), 401; Yale No. 152

112: 213, 220, 271, 319, 321, 322, 333, 351, 361, 367, 368, 371, 387, 390A, 395 (2), 401; Yale No. 79

113: 271, 319, 321, 322, 333, 351, 367, 368, 395 (2); Yale No. 146

114: 271, 319, 321, 322, 333, 351, 367, 368, 395 (2); Yale No. 147

115: 271, 319, 321, 322, 333, 351, 361, 367, 368, 371, 387, 390A, 395 (2); Yale No. 149 (see also No. 150)

116: 271, 319, 321, 322, 333, 351, 361, 367, 368, 371, 387, 390A, 395 (2); Yale No. 148

117: 257, 271, 319, 321, 322, 333, 351, 367, 368, 395 (2); Yale No. 145

118: 263, 271, 319, 321, 322, 333, 351, 361, 367, 368, 371, 387, 390A, 395 (2); Yale No. 154

119: 271, 319, 321, 322, 333, 351, 361, 367, 368, 371, 387, 390A, 395 (2); Yale No. 155

120: 264, 271, 319, 321, 322, 333, 351, 361, 367, 368, 371, 387, 390A, 395 (2); Yale No. 153

121: 271, 319, 321, 322, 333, 351, 367, 368, 395 (2); Yale No. 158

122: 271, 319, 321, 322, 333, 351, 367, 368,

395 (2), 412, 413 (2); Yale No. 66
123: 271, 319, 321, 322, 333, 351, 395; Yale
Misc. 1
124: 271, 319, 321, 322, 333, 351, 361, 367,
368, 371, 387, 390A, 395 (2); Yale No.
159
125: 263, 271, 319, 321, 322, 333, 351, 361,
367, 368, 371, 387, 390A, 395 (2); Yale
No. 160
126: 271, 319, 321, 322, 333, 351, 361, 367,
368, 371, 387, 390A, 395 (2); Yale No.
161
127: 264, 271, 319, 321, 322, 333, 351, 367,
368, 395 (2); Yale No. 163
128: 271, 319, 321, 322, 333, 351, 361, 367,
368, 371, 387, 390A, 395 (2); Yale No.
162
129: 271, 272, 319, 321, 322, 333, 351, 367,
368, 395 (2); Yale No. 165
130: 271, 319, 321, 322, 333, 351, 361, 367,
368, 371, 387, 390A, 395 (2); Yale No.
164
131: 271, 319, 321, 322, 333, 351, 361, 367,
368, 371, 387, 390A, 395 (2); Yale No.
166
132: 271, 319, 321, 322, 333, 351, 361, 367,
368, 371, 387, 390A, 395 (2); Yale No.
167
133: 271, 319, 321, 322, 333, 351, 361, 367,
368, 371, 387, 390A, 395 (2); Yale No.
169
134: 271, 319, 321, 322, 333, 351, 361, 367,
368, 371, 387, 390A, 395 (2); Yale No.
168
135: 271, 319, 321, 322, 333, 351, 361, 367,
368, 371, 387, 390A, 395 (2); Yale No.
174
135 bis: 272 (2). *See note to* Yale No. 174
136: 271, 319, 321, 322, 333, 351, 361, 367,
368, 371, 387, 390A, 395 (2); Yale No.
175
137: 271, 319; Yale No. 8
138: 271, 319; Yale No. 45
139: 213, 215, 220, 258, 319; Yale No. 78
140: 235, 319; Yale No. 88
141: 228, 319; Yale No. 101
142: 224, 226, 228, 319; Yale No. 102
143: 271, 319; Yale No. 156

144: 263, 271, 319; Yale No. 157
145: 271, 319; Yale No. 93
146: 230, 238, 271, 319; Yale No. 94
147: 271, 319; Yale No. 171
148: 271, 319; Yale No. 172
149: 271, 319; Yale No. 170
150: 271, 272, 319; Yale No. 173
151: 79, 83; Yale No. 1
152: 143, 146 (3), 151 (3), 160, 308, 331 (2);
192, 193 (Oldenburg Safeguard); Yale
No. 35
154: 271 (duplicate of Columbia No. 49;
deleted)
155: 271, 330 (3); Yale No. 23
156: 271, 330 (3); Yale No. 22
157: 90, 271, 329, 330 (3); Yale No. 21
158: 271; Yale No. 18
159: 271; Yale No. 118
160: 271; Yale Misc. 3
161: 234, 271; Yale No. 90
162: 271; Yale No. 91
163: 271; Yale No. 100
164: 253, 271; Yale No. 123
165: 81; Yale No. 3
167C: 135
167D: 135
167E: *See* Articles of Peace (Dutch), *below*
169: 202-5, 217-19, 221, 304 (Spanish
Treaty); Yale No. 84
170: 228 (3), 232, 237, 242, 304, 385, 389,
390, 402 (Swedish Treaty); Yale No. 96
170A: 117, 330 (5). *See* Patrick, pp. 539-540
170B: 179, 183, 206, 412, 413; Yale Misc. 2
170C: 206

Dutch Manifesto: 121-30, 132, 133, 147,
148, 155-57, 190, 304, 331, 353-55, 360
402; Yale No. 47. *See* Columbia Edition
XVIII, 14 ff.

Articles of Peace (Dutch): 134, 148, 149,
168-78, 181, 182, 184, 189, 190,
193-195, 197, 201, 208, 267, 270, 296,
304, 353-55, 360, 361, 384, 386, 388,
390A; Yale No. 38

Safeguard for Duke of Holstein: 145, 146,
160, 162 (2), 331

Yale Number

Not numbered in Columbia

2: 79
3: 81. *See* Columbia Edition XVIII, 653
26: 329, 330
27: 113. *See* Columbia Edition XIII, 637–638
38: 134
150: 260, 262

Entries in this Bibliography of Possible Attributions

Not numbered in Columbia or Yale

115: *See* Patrick, p. 553
119
196: *See* French III, 402–3
224: *See* Columbia No. 142
243 (2): *See* French IV, 132, and 157–58
244 (2): *See* Patrick, p. 800, *for first item*
269 (6): *See* French V, 454, *for first four items*
331
384 (2)
386 (2)
388 (2)
412 (2): *See* French III, 402–3
413 (2): *See* French III, 402–3

References to State Papers

Columbia Number

1 Quàm diù
2 Perspecta nobis
3 Antonium Ascamum virum probum
4 Quis rerum nostrarum
5 Multa nos
6 Quotidiani ferè
7 Quàm gravitèr
8 Concilium status, quam primùm
9 Ut primum ad nos
10 Quod oratorem
11 De controversiis mercatorum
12 Studia vestra
13 Antonium Ascamum a nobis
14 Accipimus ab ornatissimis

15 Frequentes ad nos
16 Literas tuas hujus mensis
17 Literas Celsitudinis vestrae
18 Parlamentum Reipub. Angliae, cum antiquam amicitiam
19 Majestatis vestrae literas
21 Permagnas nobis
22 Mercatores quidam nostri
23 Concilium status cum ex mandato
24 Literas vestrae majestatis undevigesimo
25 Parlamentum Reipubl. Angliae literas vestras sexto
26 Parlamentum Reipubl. Angliae literas vestras quinto
27 Concilium status cum à Carolo
28 Concilium status, deliberatione habitâ
29 Praedictis dominis
30 Concilium, inspectis
31 Concilium status, cognito
32 Literae excellentiae vestrae 5/15 Novemb.
33 Allatum nuper
34 Parlamentum Reipub. Angliae literae vestrae Celsitudinis Augusti
35 Parlamentum Reipub. Angliae postquam
36 Parlamentum Reipub. Angliae literas Celsitudinis
37 Cum Parlamentum
38 Quanquam sapientissimo
39 Parlamentum Reipub. Angliae plurimam salutem
40 Literas vestras, Illustres
41 Cum graves
42 Graves ad nos
43 Parlamentum Reipub. Angliae cum intelligat
43a Damna illa
44 Per literas vestras Januarii
45 Literas vestras Maii secundo
46 Cum Suecorum
47 Quod accepi ex literis
48 Cum de voluntate
49 Ex literis vestris per oratorem
50 Perspectus ex literis tuis
51 Redditae sunt nobis
52 Ex literis vestris sexto
53 Pervenisse nuper
54 Edictum Ducis Sabandiae
55 Non dubitamus quin
56 Ex literis majestatis vestrae
57 Cum nobilem hunc
58 Quam severo nuper

59 Sumnum dolorem
60 Cum rebus vestris
61 Mercatores aliquot
62 Ex vestris ad nos
63 Cum amicorum
64 Questi sunt per libellum
65 Quam pacem et amicitiam
66 Ostendunt nobis
67 Perfunctus Legatione
68 Adierunt ad nos
69 Demonstrarunt nobis
70 Conqueruntur apud nos
71 Cum mercatoribus quibusdam
72 Cum amicitiam Majestatis
73 Detulerunt ad nos
74 Cum dandae
75 Non dubitamus nos
76 Die undecimo Julii proximi
77 Perlatum ad nos
78 Singulare tuum erga
79 Cum eundem nobiscum
80 Demonstratum est nobis
81 Inviti facimus
82 Transactâ jam feliciter
83 Tametsi ea est
84 Exhibuit nobis libellum
85 Gravem detulerunt
86 Pervenisse ad Majestatem
87 Literas Majestatis Vestrae sexto
88 Ad literas Celsitudinis vestrae
89 De benevolentia
90 Urbem vestram industriâ
91 Anglorum Genti
92 Vir nobilissimus
93 Mercatores quidam Londino-derrienses
94 Cum ea sit Celsitudinis
95 Cum Vir ornatissimum
96 Qui noster animus
97 Gulielmus Jepsonus
98 Qui hasce ad vos
99 Missus à nobis Vir
100 Ostendit nobis per libellum supplicem
Societas Mercatorum
101 Alteris ad Celsitudinem
102 Postulavit à Serenissimo
103 Nuntii rerum vestrarum
104 Redit ad vos
105 Georgius Duningus
106 Cum ea nostrae Reip.
107 Permagnam nobis

108 Multa simul
109 Quod satisfacturum
110 Meminisse potest
111 De Convallensibus
112 Illatae nuper
113 Thomam Vice Comitem
114 Cum Thomam
115 Cum illustrissimum virum
116 Ut nuntiatum est venisse
117 Cum Celsitudo vestra in omnibus
118 Quòd tam celeriter
119 Cum Regi Serenissimo
120 Quoties communium
121 Ostendit nobis per libellum supplicem
Joannes Buffield
122 Carolus Harbordus
123 Nos Commissarii
124 Cum Serenissimus Pater
125 Quanquam nihil mihi
126 Cum videar mihi
127 Binas accepi [Duas accepi; *see* Patrick,
p. 855]
128 Mitto ad Majestatem
129 Detulit ad nos
130 Gravem ad me detulit
131 Accepimus, idque non sine dolore
132 Proficiscitur in Galliam
133 Tametsi multa sunt
134 Per literas ad Eminentiam vestram
135 Cum visum sit
136 Cum voluntate
137 Cum non ita pridem
138 Navis cujusdam
139 Perlati ad nos
140 Cum ea jam eluceat
141 Cum de Religione
142 Tametsi patentes
143 Dunkirkam dedidisse
144 Redditae nobis unà cum
145 Gulielmus Lockartus
146 Cum videam vestris
147 Ostendunt nobis per supplicem
148 Queritur apud nos
149 Edidit nobis
150 Defert ad me
151 Quantis bellorum
152 Universis & singulis
170A Per Excellentem Virum
170B Cum ultro vir
170C Misso a Nobis, Occasione

Index III
Non-Miltonic Titles

Index IV

Authors of Non-Miltonic Works, Editors, Translators, Booksellers (Cataloguers)

Index V

Designers and Engravers

Index VI

Printers, Publishers, and Booksellers

Index VII
Owners of Printed Copies Cited

Index VIII

Manuscript Holdings of Cited Items